THE CAMBRIDGE COMPANION TO
COUNTER-REFORMATION SANCTITY

This groundbreaking Companion explores how Counter-Reformation sanctity reshaped religious identities, sacred traditions, and devotional practices that transformed Catholicism into the first global religion. Offering a fresh perspective on early modern Catholicism, it moves beyond traditional debates about Reformation and Reform and presents sanctity as the defining lens through which to view the period's transformative changes. By examining the lives, representations, and global impact of saints, this book demonstrates how sanctity countered the Protestant challenge and also transformed the very fabric of Catholicism between 1500 and 1750. Organized into four thematic sections – models of sanctity, the creation and contestation of sanctity, the representation of saints, and everyday interactions with saints – the volume also establishes the importance of the role of holiness during this pivotal period in Church history. Connecting history, theology, art history, and material culture, this interdisciplinary Companion serves as an indispensable resource for scholars and students seeking a comprehensive understanding of early modern Catholicism's influence on European and global history.

Jan Machielsen is a historian at Cardiff University. His previous publications include *The Basque Witch-Hunt*, *The War on Witchcraft* and *The Science of Demons*.

Emily Michelson is Professor of History at the University of St Andrews. She is the author of *The Pulpit and the Press in Reformation Italy* and *Catholic Spectacle and Rome's Jews: Early Modern Conversion and Resistance*.

Katrina B. Olds is Professor of History at the University of San Francisco and the author of *Forging the Past: Invented Histories in Counter-Reformation Spain*.

CAMBRIDGE COMPANIONS TO RELIGION
This is a series of companions to major topics and key figures in theology and religious studies. Each volume contains specially commissioned chapters by international scholars, which provide an accessible and stimulating introduction to the subject for new readers and nonspecialists.

Other Titles in the Series

AMERICAN CATHOLICISM Edited by Margaret M. McGuinness and Thomas F. Rzeznik

AMERICAN ISLAM Edited by Juliane Hammer and Omid Safi

AMERICAN JUDAISM Edited by Dana Evan Kaplan

AMERICAN METHODISM Edited by Jason E. Vickers

AMERICAN PROTESTANTISM Edited by Jason E. Vickers and Jennifer Woodruff Tait

ANCIENT MEDITERRANEAN RELIGIONS Edited by Barbette Stanley Spaeth

APOCALYPTIC LITERATURE Edited by Colin McAllister

APOSTOLIC FATHERS Edited by Michael F. Bird and Scott Harrower

AUGUSTINE'S CITY OF GOD Edited by David Vincent Meconi

AUGUSTINE'S "CONFESSIONS" Edited by Tarmo Toom

AUGUSTINE'S SERMONS Edited by Andrew Hofer

KARL BARTH Edited by John Webster

THE BIBLE, 2nd edition Edited by Bruce Chilton

THE BIBLE AND LITERATURE Edited by Calum Carmichael

BIBLICAL INTERPRETATION Edited by John Barton

BIBLICAL NARRATIVE Edited by Keith Bodner

BIBLICAL WISDOM LITERATURE Edited by Katharine J. Dell, Suzanna R. Millar, and Arthur Jan Keefer

BLACK THEOLOGY Edited by Dwight N. Hopkins and Edward P. Antonio

DIETRICH BONHOEFFER Edited by John de Gruchy

THE BOOK OF ISAIAH Edited by Christopher B. Hays

JOHN CALVIN Edited by Donald K. McKim

CHRISTIAN DOCTRINE Edited by Colin Gunton

CHRISTIAN ETHICS Edited by Robin Gill

CHRISTIAN HERESY Edited by Richard Flower

CHRISTIAN LITURGY Edited by Joris Geldhof

CHRISTIAN MYSTICISM Edited by Amy Hollywood and Patricia Z. Beckman

CHRISTIAN PHILOSOPHICAL THEOLOGY Edited by Charles Taliaferro and Chad V. Meister

CHRISTIAN POLITICAL THEOLOGY Edited by Craig Hovey and Elizabeth Phillips

CHRISTIANITY AND THE ENVIRONMENT Edited by Alexander J. B. Hampton and Douglas Hedley

(*continued after index*)

THE CAMBRIDGE COMPANION TO
COUNTER-REFORMATION SANCTITY

Edited by

Jan Machielsen
Cardiff University

Emily Michelson
University of St. Andrews

Katrina B. Olds
University of San Francisco

Shaftesbury Road, Cambridge CB2 8EA, United Kingdom

One Liberty Plaza, 20th Floor, New York, NY 10006, USA

477 Williamstown Road, Port Melbourne, VIC 3207, Australia

314–321, 3rd Floor, Plot 3, Splendor Forum, Jasola District Centre, New Delhi – 110025, India

103 Penang Road, #05–06/07, Visioncrest Commercial, Singapore 238467

Cambridge University Press is part of Cambridge University Press & Assessment, a department of the University of Cambridge.

We share the University's mission to contribute to society through the pursuit of education, learning and research at the highest international levels of excellence.

www.cambridge.org
Information on this title: www.cambridge.org/9781009199605

DOI: 10.1017/9781009199599

© Cambridge University Press & Assessment 2026

This publication is in copyright. Subject to statutory exception and to the provisions of relevant collective licensing agreements, no reproduction of any part may take place without the written permission of Cambridge University Press & Assessment.

When citing this work, please include a reference to the DOI 10.1017/9781009199599

First published 2026

A catalogue record for this publication is available from the British Library

A Cataloging-in-Publication data record for this book is available from the Library of Congress

ISBN 978-1-009-19960-5 Hardback
ISBN 978-1-009-19957-5 Paperback

Cambridge University Press & Assessment has no responsibility for the persistence or accuracy of URLs for external or third-party internet websites referred to in this publication and does not guarantee that any content on such websites is, or will remain, accurate or appropriate.

For EU product safety concerns, contact us at Calle de José Abascal, 56, 1°, 28003 Madrid, Spain, or email eugpsr@cambridge.org

In Memoriam A. Katie Harris (1969–2025)
Scholar, colleague, and friend

Contents

List of Contributors page ix

Introduction 1
JAN MACHIELSEN, EMILY MICHELSON,
AND KATRINA B. OLDS

Part I: *Models of Sanctity* 15

1   Bishops 17
    MADELINE MCMAHON

2   Martyrs 35
    ALEJANDRO CAÑEQUE

3   Female Saints 54
    REBECA SANMARTÍN BASTIDA

4   The Virgin Mary 72
    CHRISTINA H. LEE

5   Black Saints 90
    ERIN KATHLEEN ROWE

6   Catacomb Saints 107
    NORIA K. LITAKER

Part II: *Creating and Contesting Sanctity* 131

7   Canonization 133
    JAN MACHIELSEN

8   Regulating Relics 155
    A. KATIE HARRIS

9   Mysticism and the Discernment
    of Spirits 172
    ELEONORA CAPPUCCILLI

10 Miracles and Holy Bodies 193
    BRADFORD BOULEY

Part III: ***Representing Saints*** 211

  11 Liturgy 213
      ANTOINE MAZUREK

  12 Hagiography 235
      SIMON DITCHFIELD

  13 Images 257
      CLOE CAVERO DE CARONDELET

  14 Literature 279
      SUSANNAH BRIETZ MONTA

Part IV: ***Living with Saints*** 301

  15 Material Culture 303
      ANNE MARISS

  16 Confraternities 328
      MIGUEL A. VALERIO

  17 Pilgrimage 348
      ELIZABETH TINGLE

      Further Reading 373
      Index 384

Contributors

Bradford Bouley is Associate Professor of History at the University of California, Santa Barbara.

Alejandro Cañeque is Professor of History at the University of Maryland.

Eleonora Cappuccilli is a Marie Skłodowska-Curie Global Fellow at the University of Toronto and the University of Oslo.

Cloe Cavero de Carondelet is Visiting Lecturer in Spanish and Portuguese at Princeton University.

Simon Ditchfield is Professor of Early Modern History at the University of York.

A. Katie Harris was Professor of History at the University of California, Davis. She passed away just before this volume went to press.

Christina H. Lee is Professor of Spanish and Portuguese at Princeton University.

Noria K. Litaker is Associate Professor of History at the University of Nevada, Las Vegas.

Jan Machielsen is Reader in Early Modern History at Cardiff University.

Anne Mariss is Assistant Professor in Early Modern History at the University of Regensburg.

Antoine Mazurek is an independent scholar based in Lyon, France.

Madeline McMahon is Assistant Professor of History at the University of Texas at Austin.

Emily Michelson is Professor of History at the University of St Andrews.

Susannah Brietz Monta is Associate Professor of English at the University of Notre Dame.

Katrina B. Olds is Professor of History at the University of San Francisco.

Erin Kathleen Rowe is Professor of History at Johns Hopkins University.

Rebeca Sanmartín Bastida is Professor of Medieval and Early Modern Spanish Literature at the Universidad Complutense, Madrid.

Elizabeth Tingle is Professor Emerita in History at De Montfort University, Leicester.

Miguel A. Valerio is Associate Professor of Spanish and Portuguese at the University of Maryland.

Introduction

JAN MACHIELSEN, EMILY MICHELSON,
AND KATRINA B. OLDS

Whatever happened to Pedro Bautista Blázquez's toe? Church officials in Rome really wanted to know. In life, the toe had belonged to a Spanish Franciscan friar who became, in death, a potential saint. But finding the toe meant searching the globe. Pedro Bautista had met his end in Shogunate Japan, which had become, for a brief but frenetic time, his vineyard of the Lord. There, in Nagasaki, he founded a church and hospitals for the poor, and it was there that he lost his life – and his toe. On February 5, 1597, Pedro Bautista was martyred alongside twenty-five others, crucified in a neatly aligned row of crosses on a hill outside the city.[1]

News of pilgrims flocking to the execution site quickly reached Rome. As part of the martyrs' beatification process in the early 1620s, the Congregation of Rites, which oversaw saint-making, asked witnesses to comment on the location, which had been transformed from a "vile" place into one of "honor." The cardinals also knew that blood miraculously continued to flow from Pedro Bautista's wounds for days after his death, "which was witnessed and regarded as a miracle by all." The martyrs' blood and clothing were collected while their supposedly uncorrupted bodies were left on the cross. The blood-stained soil was itself gathered and treasured as a relic. At a secret beatification inquest in Nagasaki in 1622, the Japanese convert Michael Inoue recalled that devotees not only soaked "cloths and paper" in the blood of the martyrs, "but even scraped that which stuck to the crosses; and they took away

---

[1] On Pedro Bautista, see Elena Sainz Magaña, "San Pedro Bautista," in Real Academia de la Historia, *Diccionario Biográfico electrónico*. https://dbe.rah.es/biografias/8223/san-pedro-bautista. Long considered the leader of the martyrs of Nagasaki, the Franciscan was beatified along with his companions in 1627. In later writings, he was gradually eclipsed by the Japanese-born Jesuit Paul Miki. For the cult of the martyrs of Japan, see Hitomi Omata Rappo, *Des Indes lointaines aux scènes des collèges: Les reflets des martyrs de la mission japonaise en Europe, XVIe–XVIIIe siècles* (Münster: Aschendorff, 2020).

their clothing as relics until [the dead] were left stark naked."[2] One Christian had apparently gone further to engage in what one historian has called "sacred theft" by making off with Pedro Bautista's toe.[3]

Yet even with so many people milling about, and so much attention given to the martyrs' blood and bodies, nobody could unravel the mystery of the missing digit. Rumors of its fate, it seems, spread far and wide, along the same transoceanic itinerary taken by the friar himself: Just as Bautista had first traveled to Mexico in 1580 before making the daunting Pacific crossing to the newly colonized Philippines, and thence to Japan, so, too, did rumors about his toe's fate travel along colonial and missionary routes. On December 3, 1620, Pedro de Montoya testified in Mexico City that he had been in Manila as events unfolded in Nagasaki. This meant that he had not personally observed the supposed moment when one of the Japanese guards bit off the toe and made off with it between his teeth. But he did know the guard in question. Some time later, Montoya had even seen the toe "wrapped in linen full of blood" and had unsuccessfully offered the guard a sizable sum for it.[4] Another witness, the surgeon Juan Bautista de Aguirre, had lived in Nagasaki and could specify that the toe came from the right foot. He, too, had made an offer, but the guard refused to part with it, "for he kept it as a great relic."[5] A third witness, a Spaniard testifying in Macau, had arrived in Nagasaki a month after the crucifixion. He had also seen the lost body part and was able to identify it as a big toe.[6] None of the observers, however, could remember the guard's name. Some claimed to know him by sight, but he might in any case have been easy to recognize for, as a middle-aged Japanese Christian named Kobayashi Sōdai testified, the guard had worn the digit around his neck "as a great relic."[7] Despite these global efforts, neither the guard nor the treasured toe were ever found. Yet even without the actual object, the tale burnished the holiness of the Nagasaki Martyrs, not only in Japan, but around the globe.

As this anecdote suggests, when Catholicism went global during the early modern period, it did so through the practices, idioms, and

---

[2] Vatican City, Archivio Apostolico Vaticano [AAV], Cong. di Riti, MS 1222, fol. 29r–v.

[3] Patrick J. Geary, *Furta Sacra: Thefts of Relics in the Central Middle Ages* (Princeton, NJ, 1990).

[4] AAV, Cong. di Riti, MS 1220, fol. 39v.

[5] Ibid., fol. 54r.

[6] AAV, Cong. di Riti, MS 1224, fol. 45v. The witness, Cristóbal Sánchez, testified on November 14, 1622.

[7] AAV, Cong. di Riti, MS 1222, fol. 37v.

procedures of sanctity, in an uneven, messy, embodied process that often escaped control. Officially, the question of an individual's sanctity was adjudicated by the papacy through the formal processes of beatification and canonization (which from 1588 onward were overseen by the Congregation of Rites). Yet in the early modern period, as in the Middle Ages, "sanctity" always meant more than just canonization. Some of those venerated for their holiness, like Pedro Bautista, pursued sanctity in their own lives (and even deaths) to such a "heroic" degree that they received official recognition: The martyrs of Nagasaki were beatified in 1627 and canonized in 1862.[8] There were, however, many paths to holiness and they were rarely smooth. The pursuit of sanctity manifested itself in different ways and to different degrees, and neither aspirants to sanctity nor their (sometimes overexcited) followers always conformed to official expectations. What united the diverse and disparate members of the worldwide early modern Catholic community was, generally, a belief in the continued immanence of the sacred and the supernatural in everyday life, especially through the cult of saints. This devotion to palpable signs and symbols of the holy in this world not only bound early modern Catholics to their medieval forebears but also separated them from their Protestant rivals.

Crucially, sanctity did not adhere only to people and reputations. It was also, as the quest for Pedro Bautista's toe suggests, tangible. Its materiality allowed it to permeate every aspect of early modern Catholicism. Through images and relics, sanctity could be preserved, shared, consumed, and even stolen. Texts and narratives also mattered. Confessors and other advocates promoted specific holy men and women by documenting their deeds and virtues in written biographies (known as Lives) to wider communities. Sanctity shaped practices of devotion, from daily prayers to long-distance pilgrimage. In the newly connected global Catholicism of the early modern period, saints and the models they provided shaped religious identities in individual and often surprising ways, which authorities could attempt to guide and nurture – but all too often struggled to control, as suggested again by the fate of Pedro Bautista's errant toe. The quest for and defense of sanctity thus defined every facet of early modern Catholicism. Every aspect of its pursuit refuted the new Protestant dogmas of *sola fide*, *sola Scriptura*, and *sola gratia*. Indeed, we would argue that sanctity possesses a similar conceptual cogency to that Protestant triad, to the point that we might even

---

[8] *Index ac status causarum* (Vatican City, 1999), 561.

consider it a core organizational principle of early modern Catholicism – and we have used it as such to structure this volume.⁹

WHY "SANCTITY" INSTEAD OF "REFORM"?

Early modern Catholics proclaimed their Church to be *semper eadem*, ever the same, from the time of the apostles to the present day.¹⁰ Attempts to capture the ways in which the Catholic Church nevertheless *did* change have traditionally been dominated by the concept of "reform," suggesting a form of parity with the Protestant Reformation, which engulfed and then captured much of northern Europe. For much of the twentieth century, the historiography of early modern Catholicism was shaped by this contested concept. Debate raged as to whether such reform was an authoritarian, top-down response to counter the Protestant threat or an independent impulse emerging out of the reform movements of the later Middle Ages, with historians' positions all too often dictated by their own confessional allegiances. An extensive debate about nomenclature followed, in which historians enacted what Simon Ditchfield called a "hackneyed Punch-and-Judy show," fighting about whether "Counter-" or "Catholic" Reformation best encapsulated changes whose origins, extent, and impact were all contested. While the debate has moved on, alternative labels, even John O'Malley's compelling "early modern Catholicism," have not gained much traction. "Counter-Reformation" remains a convenient shorthand, which most historians now use, albeit divorced from its original context and confessional baggage.¹¹ In her introduction to the 2013 *Ashgate Research Companion to the Counter-Reformation* – a major source of inspiration for our project – Mary Laven, for instance, set out a "broaden[ed]," "stretched," and "reshaped" Counter-Reformation that promised both a "chronological extension" and "geographical expansion," as well as "new approaches," "new questions," and "new themes."¹²

---

⁹ Simon Ditchfield, "Thinking with Saints: Sanctity and Society in the Early Modern World," *Critical Inquiry* 35, no. 3 (2009): 552–84.

¹⁰ See, in particular, Giuseppe Antonio Guazzelli, "Cesare Baronio and the Roman Catholic Vision of the Early Church," in *Sacred History: Uses of the Christian Past in the Renaissance World*, ed. Katherine Van Liere et al. (Oxford, 2012), 52–71.

¹¹ Simon Ditchfield, "Of Dancing Cardinals and Mestizo Madonnas: Reconfiguring the History of Roman Catholicism in the Early Modern Period," *Journal of Early Modern History* 8, no. 3 (2004), 386–408, at 386; John W. O'Malley, *Trent and All That: Renaming Catholicism in the Early Modern Era* (Cambridge, MA, 2000).

¹² Mary Laven, "Introduction," in *The Ashgate Research Companion to the Counter-Reformation*, ed. Alexandra Bamji et al. (Farnham, 2013), 5.

As Laven's words already indicate, early modern Catholicism is a vibrant field of study, one that intersects with many wider historiographical trends, including the turn toward global history, increasing interest in lived experience and material culture, and questions of gender and race. Yet they also suggest that early modern Catholicism, as a field of study, is in urgent need of a new hermeneutical key. This Companion offers sanctity – that is, the pursuit and possession of holiness – as an alternative interpretive paradigm, and as a new prism through which to envision the Catholic Church in the early modern era, a period that not coincidentally also witnessed a wholesale revision of the process of saint making. This volume, then, moves beyond false parallels and equivalences – the understandable urge to furnish both Protestants and Catholics with a Reformation – to study Catholicism on its own terms and at a key moment in its history, a period of both unprecedented challenges and opportunities. We argue that sanctity provides this new prism, and that the function, diffusion, and appreciation of holiness became the single most defining characteristic of early modern Catholicism. Sanctity, more than Protestantism, determined how early modern Catholicism defined itself, how its adherents understood their religion, how it shaped their daily lives, and how we as historians should now study it.

We are, indeed, aware of two possible criticisms of our proposed framework. The first is that our pitch may seem confessional, perhaps even pious. As a cardinal in charge of saint-making recently put it, "sanctity is part of the Church's DNA."[13] And yet, as historians, we are not obliged to follow the Catholic Church's judgments, nor do we take its conclusions about the sanctity of particular individuals as preordained. Even – or perhaps especially – a towering Counter-Reformation figure like Carlo Borromeo, the archbishop of Milan, was the subject of scathing criticisms within the Catholic Church. As Chapter 1, by Madeleine McMahon, shows, Borromeo's eventual canonization had plenty of internal critics. Philip Neri, another future saint, denounced Borromeo as an "audacious robber of holy and learned men," who plundered from other dioceses to decorate his own.[14] The title of saint is both seductive and authoritative. It conveys an air of certainty and finality, removing any messiness and ambiguity from view. Historians should never treat the label as a

---

[13] Vincenzo Criscuolo et al., *Le cause dei santi: Sussidio per lo stadium*, 4th ed. (Vatican City, 2018), 10. The preface by Cardinal Angelo Amato is dated November 1, 2017.

[14] Cited in James Brodrick, *Robert Bellarmine: Saint and Scholar* (London, 1961), 49.

given, but study how it came to be applied. As the chapters in this Companion demonstrate, the history of early modern Catholicism looks very different when we approach saint-making as a contingent process, whose outcome only seems inevitable in hindsight.

This brings us to a second possible objection, namely, that the hermeneutic of "sanctity" merely returns us to earlier modes of Counter-Reformation historiography dominated by "great men."[15] We would be the first to concede that Catholic saints were the original celebrities and superheroes.[16] The popularity of individual saints or particular types of sainthood can reveal much about the priorities and preoccupations of early modern Catholicism. But ultimately saints – like modern celebrities – were also creations, and the creation process was often bound to overstate the star's own agency, power, and influence. This pattern is to some extent inevitable: To be declared a saint, one needed to demonstrate truly heroic levels of virtue, often accompanied by miraculous deeds. Yet there were many seemingly-deserving candidates for sainthood whose causes faltered or failed, and their stories challenge those narratives which place too great an emphasis on the agency of the saints themselves. Indeed, the fact that only the dead could become candidates for canonization points to the substantial role played by others in a saint's elevation.[17] This volume therefore highlights the agency of the many humans who helped to create saints – both official and unofficial ones – as a way of broadening the social and cultural history of early modern Catholicism to include, for example, the physicians who examined dead holy bodies for signs of divine favor, the hagiographers who celebrated their lives in writing, and the ordinary pilgrims who added their medallions to rosaries or who visited their shrines in search of a miracle cure. As the contributions collected in this Companion will suggest, the quest for sanctity was the single most defining characteristic of early modern Catholicism.

---

[15] For iterations of "great men" Counter-Reformation history, see Michael Mullett, *The Catholic Reformation* (London, 1999), x; Massimo Firpo, "Rethinking 'Catholic Reform' and 'Counter-Reformation': What Happened in Early Modern Catholicism – A View from Italy," *Journal of Early Modern History* 20 (2016): 293–312.

[16] Aviad Kleinberg, "Are Saints Celebrities?," *Cultural and Social History* 8, no. 3 (2011): 393–97; Simon Yarrow, *The Saints: A Short History* (Oxford, 2016), 1–2.

[17] For a good reflection on this process, see Gillian T. W. Ahlgren, *Teresa of Avila and the Politics of Sanctity* (Ithaca, NY, 1998).

A NEW PARADIGM FOR COUNTER-REFORMATION SCHOLARSHIP

The present collection illustrates the importance of sanctity as an interpretive paradigm in four ways. First, the pursuit of sanctity, or true holiness, was the consummate concern underlying early modern confessional conflicts, and lay at the heart of Catholic self-definition. Indeed, devotion to the saints deeply informed the original historiographical "Counter- vs. Catholic Reformation" debate. The saints formed the great dividing line between Protestants and Catholics.[18] Unsurprisingly, a sixty-five-year hiatus in official saint-making (between 1523 and 1588) has therefore often been depicted as "a failure of [papal] nerve."[19] As we have already seen, however, the saints never went away. In the face of Protestant attacks, saints – and the miracles they continued to work – proved to Catholics that their Church was possessed by the Holy Spirit, and not by a diabolical one. These Reformation polemics were dressed up in the contested language of true versus false sanctity. Christians had not forgotten that Saint Paul had warned about false apostles, or that Satan could appear as an "angel of light."[20] The early seventeenth century also saw extensive concerted Catholic efforts to both boost and regulate the numbers of the holy through the establishment of the Congregation of Rites and an active return to saint-making.

Second, sanctity also animated the lives of the Catholic faithful. Saints, to quote Pierre Delooz's famous dictum, were only ever saints for "other people," and it was only through the arduous efforts of others that any cause eventually succeeded.[21] Devotion to the saints and belief in the holiness of certain spaces and objects bound together all Catholics, whatever their status or background, even as the sacred also provided the ingredients that enabled them to individualize their faith. Saints shaped every aspect of individual Catholic lives: from their birth names to the preambles of their wills, from the daily liturgy to their roles as intercessors at times of illness or personal crisis. Saints

---

[18] For a history of this long debate, see O'Malley, *Trent and All That*.
[19] Peter Burke, "How to Become a Counter-Reformation Saint," in *The Counter-Reformation: The Essential Readings*, ed. David Luebke (Oxford, 1999 [original ed. 1984]), 129–42, at 131.
[20] Clare Copeland and Jan Machielsen, eds., *Angels of Light? Sanctity and the Discernment of Spirits in the Early Modern Period* (Leiden, 2013).
[21] Pierre Delooz, "Towards a Sociological Study of Canonized Sainthood," in *Saints and Their Cults: Studies in Religious Sociology, Folklore, and History*, ed. Stephen Wilson (Cambridge, 1983), 189–216, at 194.

inspired – and in cases such as Ignatius of Loyola and Teresa of Ávila literally created – new modes of interiorized prayer and offered new models of holiness for the faithful to pursue. The very personal and often self-conscious striving to be "like" a saint brought the devotions of both the Catholic faithful and their clergy to new heights of intensity. On the communal level, saints served as patrons and organizers. In life, they founded religious orders, led dioceses, or converted regions; in death, they were venerated as protectors of churches, regions, families, confraternities, exile communities, and more. Depending on the circumstances, their cults could inspire obedience to (secular or religious) authorities, or legitimate or encourage resistance, for example as patrons to a minority religion in Elizabethan England or to ethnic minorities in the Spanish empire. Whatever their precise role, the saints collectively were the hallmarks of Catholic identity writ large.

This brings us, third, to the usefulness of sanctity for historians. As models of holiness – as the chosen intercessors of ordinary Catholics – the community of saints represents the diversity of early modern Catholicism much better than did the Church's institutions, which were dominated by European clergymen. The cult of St. Benedict of Palermo, for instance, thrived among Black diasporic communities across the Spanish Habsburg empire because the saint was, as one devotee put it, "black like me."[22] The fate of Pedro Bautista shows that Catholicism spread beyond the borders of European empires as well. The presence, relics, activities, and memory of future saints enabled Catholicism to take root in new regions and sanctify them. Indeed, saints included women and men of all races and many nations, even though they were by no means a perfect representation of the faithful.

This last point – that saint-making was an unequal process – urges historians of sanctity to move beyond the small number of saints officially canonized during the period to examine the broader number of unofficial and aspiring saints, and hence to the study of sanctity more broadly. These "failed" saints – holy figures who did not receive official recognition from Rome – are as important as the success stories. Their lives remind us that claims to sanctity were invariably deeply contested, even among Catholics. Unsurprisingly, the adjudication of sanctity was a highly gendered process – female visionaries often fell victim

---

[22] Erin Rowe, *Black Saints in Early Modern Global Catholicism* (Cambridge, 2019), 87–124.

to charges of demonic possession – and a racialized one as well.[23] Not only institutional factors were at work, however. Collective memory and devotions mattered too. Some aspirant saints were demonized in life, others swiftly forgotten after death. Still other causes – for instance, those of the English Catholic martyrs – remained vibrant. Sustained by communities of followers, they finally received official recognition centuries later.

Fourth and finally, historians also need to revisit sanctity not only because it provided the Church's lifeblood, but also because it defined many of the key conflicts *within* Catholicism. The beatification proceedings of the martyrs of Nagasaki also bear witness to vicious infighting between Franciscans and Jesuits, for example. Sanctity by its very nature was controversial. Saints could inspire loyalty from adherents and suspicion from institutions in equal measure. Even those saints most strongly associated with the Counter-Reformation – such as Ignatius and Teresa – had run-ins with religious authorities. Widespread fears about fake saints, demonic possession, or unlicensed devotions all made canonization procedures contentious, lengthy, and expensive. Popular devotions may have sustained early modern Catholicism, but they also gave rise to institutional attempts to contain, regulate, or prevent them. In turn, the fact that successful canonizations were costly and rare also encouraged rivalry and competition between the adherents of different causes.

Sanctity thus reveals the innermost tensions within Catholic Reform, because it provided a language through which the faithful could give meaning to their faith. It sits at the intersection between individual communities and the universal Catholic Church, as a source of perpetual dialogue – and, often, opposition – between local religious practice and universal institutions and regulations. Its study helps us to understand the nested and contested nature of early modern Catholic identities and the equally complex issue of where agency within the Church really resided. In other words, because sanctity, in all its forms, mattered so much to so many early moderns, it offers scholars a uniquely powerful vision of Catholicism, one that both closely suits the period and encapsulates recent historiographical trends.[24] The study of sanctity, then, demands a bold and broad inquiry, which ranges from

---

[23] The historiography on female visionaries is extensive; for a survey, see Chapter 3 in this volume.
[24] See, e.g., Birgit Emich et al., eds., *Making Saints in a "Glocal" Religion: Practices of Holiness in Early Modern Catholicism* (Cologne, 2024).

popular beliefs to theological doctrines, from lived experiences to formal regulations, and from local customs to Roman institutions. By definition, then, its story is inherently global; it cannot be authentically written as a European history with a "world" section pasted in. Sanctity shows a Church that is decentered, driven less by its institutions than by a worldwide community of the faithful. The study of sanctity thus reflects and builds on the most recent scholarly developments in religious history – including the move away from concepts of reform. "Sanctity" also opens a window onto topics that are harder to define by other rubrics, but which very much defined people's lives in the early modern period, such as "holy bodies," "collections," "memory," and "sacred space."

As all the above suggests, it is impossible to understand any aspect of early modern Catholicism without touching on the subject of sanctity and how it was lived, contested, represented, and consumed. And yet Counter-Reformation sanctity has received remarkably little systematic treatment since Peter Burke's memorable but tentative 1984 essay, "How to Be a Counter-Reformation Saint" – with the notable exception of Gabriella Zarri's work on female sanctity.[25] Most key studies on sanctity as a whole have been produced by scholars of late antiquity or the later Middle Ages.[26] Scholarship from the last decade or so has increasingly emphasized – in works that include studies of the causes of individual saints,[27] groups or types of saints,[28] and the

---

[25] Burke, "How to Become a Counter-Reformation Saint"; for an English-language introduction to Zarri's work, see Gabriella Zarri, "Female Sanctity, 1500–1660," in *The Cambridge History of Christianity*, vol. 6: *Reform and Expansion 1500–1660*, ed. Ronnie Po-chia Hsia (Cambridge, 2007), 180–200.

[26] For late antiquity, see Peter Brown's classic *The Cult of the Saints: Its Rise and Function in Latin Christianity* (enlarged ed., Chicago, 2014). Key studies in the field of medieval sanctity are Robert Bartlett, *Why Can the Dead Do Such Great Things? Saints and Worshippers from the Martyrs to the Reformation* (Princeton, NJ, 2013); Caroline Walker Bynum, *Holy Feast and Holy Fast: The Religious Significance of Food to Medieval Women* (Berkeley, 1987); Aviad Kleinberg, *Prophets in Their Own Country: Living Saints and the Making of Sainthood in the Later Middle Ages* (Chicago, 1992); and André Vauchez, *Sainthood in the Later Middle Ages* (Cambridge, 1997).

[27] See, e.g., Clare Copeland, *Maria Maddalena de' Pazzi: The Making of a Counter-Reformation Saint* (Oxford, 2016); Matthias Emil Ilg, *Constantia et Fortitudo: Der Kult des kapuzinischen Blutzeugen Fidelis von Sigmaringen zwischen "Pietas Austriaca" und "Ecclesia Triumphans*," 2 vols. (Münster, 2016).

[28] Examples include Rappo, *Des Indes lointaines aux scènes des collèges*; Rowe, *Black Saints*; Ruth Noyes, *Peter Paul Rubens and the Counter-Reformation Crisis of the Beati moderni* (London, 2017); and the special issue "How to Be a Jesuit Saint," *Journal of Jesuit Studies* 9, no. 3 (2022).

movement of holy images, objects, and narratives locally and globally[29] – that sanctity was central to the early modern world. Through these valuable case studies, the field has moved definitively away from an earlier, more reductive vision of saints that depicted them instrumentally, as objects of confessional polemic, as papal bargaining chips, or as symbols that stood for something else more "real," such as political, civic, or religious identity. Thus, rather than looking *through* saints toward something else, more recent scholarship has asked how various facets of early modern culture could be understood by looking *with* saints. Our volume advances this approach, drawing on emerging work to create an authoritative synthesis that will be a key resource for the future study of early modern Catholicism in all its diversity.

The framework laid out above necessarily entails an interdisciplinary approach. Reflecting what Simon Ditchfield has called the "dynamic nature and range of the cultural work performed by sanctity and the cult of saints," contributors speak to the role of sanctity in relation not merely to ecclesiastical history but also to art history and material culture, the history of scholarship, popular culture, science and medicine, high politics, sacred space, memory, judicial proof, empire and colonialism, and more.[30] Our volume brings together these various threads into a cohesive overview of this growing and vibrant field. It provides a valuable road map to this area of inquiry and to the many fields with which it intersects. We hope it will shape scholarly conversations for many years to come.

SECTION OBJECTIVES AND OUTLINES

Through four parts, this book charts how sanctity was conceptualized, represented, and experienced – activities that both mutually reinforced and challenged one another. The holiness of saints was celebrated, defended, and imitated by others and – formally speaking – recognized only after their death. In a wide range of contexts, from hagiographies to canonization proceedings, saints did not speak but were talked *about*. Part I, "Models of Sanctity," therefore looks two ways. On the one hand, the chapters, proceeding from the fundamentally imitative nature of sanctity, examine both standard (confessor, martyr, and virgin) and

---

[29] See, e.g., Karin Vélez, *The Miraculous Flying House of Loreto: Spreading Catholicism in the Early Modern World* (Princeton, NJ, 2019); A. Katie Harris, *The Stolen Bones of St. John of Matha* (Philadelphia, 2023).

[30] Ditchfield, "Thinking with Saints," 584.

emerging categories of official sainthood to ask how they mattered in the Counter-Reformation era. On the other hand, they also remind the reader that saints, for all their alleged supernatural virtues, were humans with agency too. These two elements are linked. Following on from Paul's exhortation in 1 Corinthians 11 to "be imitators of me, as I am of Christ," some of the towering figures of early modern Catholicism molded themselves according to classical or medieval models. Chapter 1, by Madeline McMahon, examines how the traditional typology of confessor-bishop saints fared in an era when bishops themselves dramatically altered and expanded their roles in the wake of the Council of Trent (1545–1563). Chapter 2, by Alejandro Cañeque, explores how the ancient martyrs, the first and original category of saint, became newly relevant in the early modern period, as Catholics pushed or defended their faith across various frontiers in Asia and the Americas. Using Spain as her case study, in Chapter 3 Rebeca Sanmartín Bastida analyzes the fate of competing models of female sanctity, rooted in models provided by Catherine of Siena and Teresa of Ávila, in the face of changing interests and shifting institutional concerns. Chapter 4, on devotion to the Virgin Mary, by Christina Lee, recognizes the unique and growing importance of the Marian cult in the early modern period, as its different iterations traversed the globe while also taking root in new local contexts, in areas as diverse as Mexico and the Philippines. In Chapter 5, Erin Rowe details how images of ancient Black Christians began to proliferate throughout early modern Catholic churches, in response to the rapid acceleration of the transatlantic slave trade and increasing diplomatic relations with the rulers of Ethiopia. Finally, in Chapter 6, Noria Litaker discusses the growing popularity of new "old" saints, discovered in Rome's Catacombs and transported both to Catholicism's confessional frontiers beyond the Alps and to the New World.

Part II, "Creating and Contesting Sanctity," shows how sanctity (and holy sites) were discerned, debated, studied, and authenticated. The stakes were high – the holiness of saints also extended to the movements they founded, the theological ideas they propagated, the visions they received, the places they had lived, the locations of their bodies and relics, and, implicitly, to the followers who had promoted their causes. Such power also sparked fears of heresy and false prophecy, particularly from female visionaries. Were their visions gifts from God? Or were these women frauds or, worse, demonically possessed? In Chapter 7, Jan Machielsen reexamines the evolution of the troubled state of the very process of canonization after the interruption of the sixteenth century, demonstrating the difficulties that Roman institutions faced in containing popular enthusiasm once the proceedings resumed. In Chapter 8, A. Katie Harris shows how the theory and practice of authenticating holy relics reveals broader concerns about the exuberant and vibrant devotional cultures of Counter-Reformation sanctity. The failure of these efforts demonstrates, once again, Catholicism's long and messy history, as local traditions could be deeply rooted while piety could inspire forgery. In Chapter 9, Eleonora Cappuccilli explores the practice of discernment of spirits – identifying the (demonic or divine) origins of visions – using two famous but very different female mystics as her guides. She shows how their distinct visions and spiritual gifts had unsettling social, gendered, and political ramifications that caused them to articulate different approaches to this vexing problem. In Chapter 10, Bradford Bouley reconstructs the connections between the rise of professional medicine and the increasing reliance on autopsy as a standard to establish a potential saint's bona fides, as their ascetic or uncorrupted bodies provided evidence of divine grace and intercession.

Part III, "Representing Saints," considers how the cults of (potential) saints were expressed in the arts: through the liturgy during church services, in saints' Lives, in literature, and in the visual arts. It considers how hagiographers and visual artists represented and thus promoted candidates for sainthood, while navigating or circumventing the constraints imposed by the Inquisition and other ecclesiastical institutions. In Chapter 11, Antoine Mazurek highlights how the text and placement of a saint's liturgy in printed prayer books allowed communities to celebrate local heroes without falling foul of ever-shifting universal standards. In Chapter 12, Simon Ditchfield charts the many attempts to set the genre of hagiography on a more secure footing, reminding us that while saints' official Lives could foster devotion and promote a cult, they were also vulnerable to Protestant attack. In Chapter 13, Cloe Cavero de Carondelet reveals the high stakes involved in depicting potential saints as holy people in art, without causing tension or undermining their chances at official canonization. Using examples from England's persecuted Catholic minority, Susannah Brietz Monta in Chapter 14 demonstrates the broad scope of literature generated by the cult of the saints in drama, poetry, and prose across the ever-expanding Catholic world, encouraging a sense of community and shared Catholic identity.

Part IV, "Living with Saints," reveals how saints and sanctity saturated ordinary Catholic lives through objects, spaces, rituals, and collections. Attention to the role of saints in the household, and their intercession in everyday life, lets us understand the shape of early modern communities. In Chapter 15, Anne Mariss uses rosaries to examine the way material objects could be used to express deeply personal affection for saints, and highlights the objects' critical role in moments of crisis. Using Black confraternities as a case study, Miguel Valerio in Chapter 16 shows the vital role of such organizations in organizing mutual aid, fostering saintly devotions, and maintaining communal bonds. Black confraternities also enabled Afrodescendants to navigate social hierarchies and visibly assert their presence in the Catholic world. Finally, in Chapter 17 Elizabeth Tingle traces the practice of pilgrimage, local or distant, in everyday life, showing the range of benefits to individual pilgrims and their communities. She follows pilgrims on their quests for healing, penitence, and spiritual growth and demonstrates that shrines and saints continued to act as focal points for devotion.

In concluding, the editors would like to record their thanks. First of all, we wish to acknowledge the support of Beatrice Rehl and her team at Cambridge University Press for recognizing this volume's potential at an early stage. From the outset, this Companion has also been a truly collaborative effort. We would like to thank our expert group of contributors, whose invaluable work we have all too briefly summarized. We remain grateful for their support and enthusiasm – and for their patience with us as editors. We owe a particular debt to Simon Ditchfield for his comments on draft chapters and for stepping in to fill a last-minute gap in our roster.

As the volume entered production, we received the sad news of A. Katie Harris's passing. Katie's prodigious scholarship and generosity of spirit contributed immeasurably to this volume. We therefore dedicate it to her memory. May it be a worthy tribute to a much-missed colleague and friend.

Part I

Models of Sanctity

1 Bishops

MADELINE MCMAHON

It was a grand occasion. The bishop transferred the newly rediscovered remains of the martyred dead into a new setting with a solemn procession. He invited bishops of neighboring dioceses to attend; the group, dressed in their miters and copes, led the procession as it wound its way through the decorated streets, lit by torches and accompanied by music. The event celebrating the saints ended with a banquet for the poor in the bishop's home, where twenty-four impoverished men from different parishes across town each received a ceramic plate and some money at the end of the meal.

This scene mirrors the actions described by Peter Brown in his classic book *The Cult of the Saints*, where the late antique bishop used relic translations, feast days, and charity "like an electrician who rewires an antiquated wiring system: more power could pass through stronger, better-insulated wires towards the bishop as leader of the community."[1] As Brown argued, this rewiring of the sanctity also helped the Church in the Latin West redirect its growing resources in ways that seemed appropriate to both Roman mores and Christian doctrine. The saints became outlets for the wealth of bishops and generated social energy in the community.

Processions reworked the conduits of sanctity's unseen energy in the early centuries of institutional Christianity. Yet the events described above took place in 1578. The procession and banquet were organized by bishop Gabriele Paleotti (1522–1597), not the

---

I would like to thank Simon Ditchfield, Jan Machielsen, and Katrina Olds for their insightful comments on this essay. For helpful conversations that directed me to different sources, I am grateful to Jorge Cañizares-Esguerra, Grace Harpster, and Jan Machielsen.

[1] Peter Brown, *The Cult of the Saints: Its Rise and Function in Latin Christianity* (Chicago, 1981), 37.

bishop saint Ambrose (d. 397), whom Brown credits with setting an example in the late antique western Church for how bishops could interact with and promote the cult of the saints. This was no accident: Paleotti was purposefully trying to imitate Ambrose, going so far as to translate the bodies of martyrs that the old Milanese archbishop had once moved on a visit to Bologna. In his every action, as described in a booklet printed to recount the occasion, he did "as the ancients did," and more specifically as Ambrose had done. The new stone placed to mark the martyrs' resting place recalled past episcopal translations of these bones.[2] Paleotti intended his procession of Saints Vitalis and Agricola as a historical reenactment, which connected not only his people to these martyrs, but himself as bishop to St. Ambrose. As a result, he was in fact doing something different from what Ambrose had done when he famously moved the bodies of Gervasius and Protasius in Milan or those of Vitalis and Agricola in Bologna. Paleotti participated in a mode of episcopal holiness that was crucially important in the early modern Catholic Church: imitation of past bishop saints.

Paleotti's effort to fashion himself into Ambrose's avatar took place during what Peter Burke has called a "crisis of canonizations," the period between 1523 and 1588 when no saints were formally canonized in Rome and "the very idea of a saint was under fire."[3] Burke points out that in the period after this crisis, from 1588 through 1767, being a "pastor" or "good shepherd" – that is, a good bishop – was one of the few proven paths to sainthood. Chief among these new "good shepherds" was Carlo Borromeo (1538–1584, can. 1610), the first bishop saint to be canonized after Burke's "crisis," and also the first contemporary saint in the new wave of canonizations. Beginning with his entrance into Milan as archbishop, Borromeo (much like his friend Paleotti) styled himself as a second Ambrose.[4] Saintly models were a crucial guide to Borromeo as a modern "living" saint and, indeed, for many bishops seeking to find ways toward sainthood as the "crisis of canonizations" drew to a close.

---

[2] Bologna, Archiginnasio 17-ECCL.BOLOGN.H 13; *Ordine et cerimonia servatasi in Bologna nella processione della translatione delle sante reliquie de' santi Vitale, & Agricola* ([Bologna], 1578).

[3] Peter Burke, "How to Be a Counter-Reformation Saint," in *The Historical Anthropology of Early Modern Italy: Essays on Perception and Communication* (Cambridge, 1987), 49.

[4] Giovan Pietro Giussano, *Vita di S. Carlo Borromeo* (Rome, 1610), 38.

This chapter examines bishops as saint-makers and as saints in their own right. A fundamental mechanism behind both roles was imitation. Copying each other or the bishop saints of the past, prelates from the end of the Council of Trent (1545–1563) through the eighteenth century looked backward and sideways to models old and new. In late antiquity, bishops had acted as electricians of the sacred in order to justify their position amid growing wealth inequality. In the early modern world, they did so with the sense that they were being watched – by each other and by their society, but also perhaps by the future, in the same way they looked back to the past. At the same time, early modern bishops also played important parts in increasingly rigorous canonization processes for new saints, and drew attention to older ones. Bishops made saints through their "rewiring" of holy figures in their communities, through their roles as arbiters in formal canonization procedures, and sometimes through their own efforts to live like the model bishop saints they admired.

REWORKING THE HOLY PAST IN ITALIAN DIOCESES AFTER THE COUNCIL OF TRENT

The past mattered in new ways as the confessional battles of the sixteenth century wore on.[5] Historical scholarship informed technical disputes as well as religious practice. As Simon Ditchfield has shown, history was integral for the celebration of the saints in post-Tridentine Italy.[6] The history of bishop saints – like St. Ambrose, as we have already seen – became newly visible as bishops and scholars turned their attention to it.[7] For the generation of bishops who lived and worked in their dioceses after the conclusion of the Council of Trent, history provided another guide for reform, and often a more detailed one

---

[5] Anthony Grafton, "Past Belief: The Fall and Rise of Ecclesiastical History in Early Modern Europe," in *Formations of Belief: Historical Approaches to Religion and the Secular*, ed. Philip Nord, Katja Guenther, and Max Weiss (Princeton, 2019), 13–40; Stefan Bauer, "The Uses of History in Religious Controversies from Erasmus to Baronio," *Renaissance Studies* 35, no. 1 (2021): 9–23; Katherine Elliot Van Liere, Simon Ditchfield, and Howard Louthan, eds., *Sacred History: Uses of the Christian Past in the Renaissance World* (Oxford, 2012); Nicholas Hardy and Dmitri Levitin, eds., *Confessionalisation and Erudition in Early Modern Europe: An Episode in the History of the Humanities* (Oxford, 2020).
[6] Simon Ditchfield, *Liturgy, Sanctity, and History in Tridentine Italy: Pietro Maria Campi and the Preservation of the Particular* (Cambridge, 1995).
[7] Francesco Costa, "Il carteggio Peretti-Borromeo per l'edizione romana delle opere di Sant'Ambrogio," *Miscellanea Francescana* 86 (1986): 821–77.

than the Tridentine decrees. In particular, bishops in Italy and elsewhere looked to late antique and early medieval bishop saints as models for what to do during times of plague, how to interact with saintly bodies, and much else.[8]

The lives and works of patristic bishop saints – the so-called fathers of the Latin and Greek churches – were powerful resources for early modern bishops. When plague struck Milan in 1576, "soon nothing was heard in the city except 'here comes the *monato* with the cart' with which to transport the sick and the dead," according to one contemporary diarist.[9] While the cart-driver collected bodies, Borromeo, in the words of his former employee and eventual hagiographer Carlo Bascapè, "zealously sought to collect the writings of the ancients" about pastors who did not desert their flock "especially during time of plague."[10] Borromeo's favorite text was the third-century letter about plague by Dionysius, bishop of Alexandria, known through the Church history of Eusebius of Caesarea.[11] Dionysius's account of the plague of Alexandria presented a holy Christian community cheerfully at work taking care of the ill and dead without fear. Bascapè mentioned briefly that Borromeo had his collection of ancient writings about plague put into a little book, but he did not point out, as Borromeo's modern biographer Danilo Zardin has, that this book was in the vernacular, and intended for an audience that included regular clergy and lay heads of households.[12] This small anthology included Dionysius's letter as the first text. In a prefatory letter to the people and clergy of Milan, Borromeo expressed hope that the pestilence would "spur them to carry out the holy deeds" recounted by the "holy Fathers."[13] Borromeo's use of the past responded to local circumstances. This patristic response to the plague, which entailed turning back to a series of exemplary ancient texts by the likes of bishop saints Cyprian, Dionysius, Basil, and Augustine, was enshrined in the legislation of Borromeo's fifth provincial council.[14]

---

[8] They of course also looked to more recent models; see Hubert Jedin, *Il tipo ideale di vescovo secondo la riforma cattolica* (Brescia, 1985).

[9] Giambattista Casale, "A Reformation City: The Diary of Giambattista Casale (1554–98)," in *Readings in Western Civilization: The Renaissance*, ed. Julius Kirschner and Eric Cochrane (Chicago, 1986), 424.

[10] Carlo Bascapè, *De vita et rebus gestis Caroli S.R.E. cardinalis, tituli S. Praxedis archiepiscopi Mediolani* (Ingolstadt, 1592), 136.

[11] Ibid. The letter in question is in Eusebius, *Historia ecclesiastica*, VII.22.

[12] Danilo Zardin, *Carlo Borromeo: Cultura, santità, governo* (Milan, 2010), 68–81.

[13] Milan, Biblioteca Braidense F.VI.428; *Raccolta di varii ragionamenti di alcuni santi, sopra la cura et aiuto de i poveri e infermi, et la fortezza nel morire* (Milan, 1577), sig. A 3r.

[14] Zardin, *Carlo Borromeo*, 69, 73.

Ambrose was an especially important figure for Borromeo, who sought to refashion the saint's image in various ways. These included putting an end to the medieval tradition of depicting Ambrose brandishing a whip on horseback, as he had allegedly appeared to intervene in a fourteenth-century battle, and also advocating for a more historically accurate depiction of the saint as clean-shaven rather than bearded.[15] These seemingly superficial changes aligned both with efforts by Borromeo's household to historicize the saint and with Borromeo's own preferences for the image and appearance of a reforming bishop. Appropriating Ambrose as a model was deeply political: The archbishop and the Spanish governor tussled over the memory of the saint who had famously excommunicated a Roman emperor. Borromeo turned Milan's cathedral into an Ambrosian space, which it had previously not been, by translating the saint's dalmatic (a liturgical vestment) there and having scenes from Ambrose's life depicted in the choir. At the same time, he separated the seats of the secular rulers, including the Spanish governor, from the choir. Both the governor and Borromeo invoked Ambrose during their ongoing jurisdictional disputes: Borromeo prayed publicly before the body of the saint in the church of Sant'Ambrogio, and the governor snapped that he would never again call Borromeo a "second Ambrose," as he had on an earlier occasion.[16]

For Borromeo, Ambrose was someone to turn to in difficult times. In personal correspondence, Guglielmo Sirleto, the Vatican librarian, told Borromeo that Ambrose had invoked "the inheritance" of his saintly predecessors in office, and that "just as that saint consoled himself with the examples of his predecessors, so too you can console and restore yourself with the example of that Saint."[17] Indeed, Ambrose was a particularly influential model for how to interact with the saints. Like so many of the broadsheets and books Borromeo issued from the time of plague on, the cover of Borromeo's anthology of patristic sources on plague featured the Ambrosian seal – a roundel with Ambrose seated between the two martyr saints whose bodies he translated, Gervasius

[15] Alessandro Rovetta, "Ambrogio in Pinacoteca Ambrosiana: Attestazioni iconografiche di età Borromaica," *Studia Ambrosiana: Annali dell'Accademia di Sant'Ambrogio* 4 (2010): 164; Annalisa Albuzzi, "La barba di Ambrogio: Iconografia, erudizione agiografica e propaganda nella Milano dei due Borromeo," in *La mémoire d'Ambroise de Milan: Usages politiques d'une autorité patristique en Italie: Ve–XVIIIe siècle*, ed. Patrick Boucheron and Stéphane Gioanni (Paris, 2015), 155–207.
[16] Marie Lezowski, "Le sceau d'Ambroise: L'exemplaire dans l'épiscopat de Charles Borromée," in Boucheron and Gioanni, eds., *La mémoire d'Ambroise de Milan*, 535–36.
[17] Milan, Biblioteca Ambrosiana [BA], P 27 inf., fol. 143v, Sirleto to Borromeo, October 11, 1567.

and Protasius. It was Ambrose as a translator of relics – as an electrician of the sacred – whom Borromeo and other Italian bishops referenced in their own dealings with the saints.

This is clear if we return to the relic translations carried out by Borromeo's contemporary and friend in Bologna, Gabriele Paleotti, who oversaw three relic translations. In 1578, he moved the bodies of Bologna's martyrs, Vitalis and Agricola, from their eponymous church into his newly built cathedral crypt. In 1582, he and Borromeo carried out a massive translation of Milanese saints, centered on the bishop saint Simpliciano, and Paleotti also joined in Borromeo's translation of another Milanese bishop saint, John the Good, around the same time. And finally, in 1586, Paleotti moved Bologna's early bishop saints, Zama and Faustiniano, from the church of San Felice into the cathedral crypt. At each of these, Paleotti was modeling himself on earlier bishop saints who had themselves translated the relics of others – going so far as to walk in their footsteps. Ambrose was a key exemplar in this respect, both in Milan and in Bologna, where he once worked with bishop Eusebius to translate Vitalis and Agricola. Paleotti also brought the relics of this early Christian past into his renovated cathedral, centralizing the sacred. Observation (in the form of pious postmortems) and ancient texts were seen to align, strengthening the connection between past and present: The pamphlet accompanying the translation of Vitalis and Agricola described how anatomists identified each relic, and the notary recorded that the globules of congealed blood corresponded to what Ambrose had written about the martyrs' "triumphal blood."[18] Paleotti had asked the scholar Carlo Sigonio to write a history of Bolognese bishops, which he later invoked in subsequent relic translations.[19] For the procession of bishop saints Zama and Faustiniano, the Bolognese cathedral featured Bologna's earliest bishops standing on stucco pillars, framed by tapestry, and all seventy-four of Paleotti's predecessors represented on gilded stucco squares, with "their inscriptions and dates conforming to the series of Sigonio's history."[20] Church history came to life during such translations.

---

[18] *Ordine et Cerimonia servatasi in Bologna nella processione della traslatione delle sacre Reliquie de' SS. Vitale, & Agricola* (1578), 9. On anatomy and the saints, see Bradford Bouley, *Pious Postmortems: Anatomy, Sanctity, and the Catholic Church in Early Modern Europe* (Philadelphia, 2017); Nancy Siraisi, "Signs and Evidence: Autopsy and Sanctity in Late-Sixteenth-Century Italy," in *Medicine and the Italian Universities, 1250–1600* (Leiden, 2001), 356–80.

[19] Carlo Sigonio, *De episcopis Bononiensibus* (Bologna, 1586).

[20] Archiginnasio 17.A.II.37, *Ordine et modo servatosi in Bologna nella ceremonia solenne della Translatione de' sacri corpi del primo Vescovo di Bologna S. Zama, & del secondo che fù S. Faustiniano* (Bologna, 1586), p. 75.

Paleotti's relic translations in Bologna and Borromeo's in Milan took place as part of episcopal administration. They served as the grand finale to synods, the legislative meetings of bishops, which saw a resurgence after the Council of Trent as a means to enact reform. Synods were also opportunities to engage with the saints – politically, devotionally, and historically. It was at synods that Borromeo decreed (and enforced) that the bishops within the Milanese archdiocese look into the history of their episcopal predecessors and have the images of the diocese's bishop saints displayed in the episcopal palace.[21] Ultimately, synods became important for the memory of early modern bishops' own sanctity. The ideal of attentive, informed governance encapsulated by the synod, and modeled on earlier councils, would be celebrated among the deeds of early modern bishop saints like Borromeo and his contemporary archbishop of Lima, Toribio de Mogrovejo (1538–1606, beat. 1679, can. 1726).[22]

The beatification and canonization of bishop saints invited new readings of their sixteenth-century synods. In 1582, for Borromeo's final provincial synod, the facade of Milan's archiepiscopal palace had been covered with labeled depictions of all 123 of the city's past bishops.[23] According to Borromeo's hagiographer Giovan Pietro Giussano, whose book came out the same year as the archbishop's canonization in 1610, the images of Borromeo's predecessors plastered to the front of his episcopal palace had prompted some to speculate "that the cardinal Carlo would be placed there one day, with the title of saint."[24] Giussano doggedly advanced the argument that Borromeo's synods and translations gave viewers an impression of the archbishop's sanctity. He reported that Paleotti would say that while he had gone to Milan to venerate the relics of dead saints, "I saw a living relic – a living saint" in the person of Borromeo.[25] Interacting with dead saints was a way for living bishops to put forward their ideas about sanctity as well as their own (and each other's) holiness.

(THE VERY MODEL OF) A MODERN BISHOP SAINT: ST. CARLO BORROMEO (1610)

At the same time that Giussano recalled the facade of Milan's past archbishops and episcopal saints at the Milan provincial synod, another

---

[21] Borromeo, *Acta ecclesiae Mediolanensis* (Milan, 1582), fols. 46v and 74v.
[22] Constanza Lamerain López, "Toribio de Mogrovejo, Roma y la creación de un esquema de gobierno diocesano en Sudamérica," *Allpanchis* 48, no. 87 (2021): 117–53.
[23] Giussano, *Vita di S. Carlo Borromeo*, 431.
[24] Ibid., 431.
[25] Ibid., 436.

Figure 1.1 Matthäus Greuter, engraving, facade for St. Peter's for the canonization of Borromeo, 1610. Rome, Biblioteca Angelica, C^.2.11, n. 1.

such facade was constructed for St. Peter's in Rome, to celebrate Borromeo's canonization in 1610 (see Figure 1.1). This temporary architecture showed Borromeo, standing in his cardinal's garb, surrounded by Milan's many bishop saints, dressed in cope and miter. The artist

Matthäus Greuter recorded this decor in an engraving that also included a numbered list as a guide to identifying the respective bishop saints. If the 1582 synod's ephemeral decoration had prompted viewers to imagine Borromeo among Milanese bishop saints, the 1610 ephemeral artwork turned that into a reality. Greuter's engraving makes clear how early modern bishop saints stood on the shoulders of their saintly forebears. At the same time, it also hints at how Borromeo the living archbishop working to reshape sanctity and Borromeo the dead and canonized saint differ: In Greuter's image, Ambrose is shown holding his whip. Some of Borromeo's reform efforts evidently died with him. Given Borromeo's significance as the first contemporary Counter-Reformation saint, the fastest to be canonized in this era and the last without formal beatification, it is worth considering how Borromeo as a saintly model was created and contested leading up to and after his canonization.[26]

Even in his lifetime, Borromeo had proved an influential model: Agostino Valier (1531–1606), the bishop of Verona, said he had Borromeo's example in mind as he "painted" the figure of an ideal bishop in *Episcopus* (1575).[27] The push for his canonization, however, began in earnest in 1601, when the first papally sanctioned celebration was held in Milan, and a diocesan synod convened by Carlo's cousin and successor Archbishop Federico Borromeo voted to send a delegation to Rome to initiate the cause. Different types of evidence were rallied for this effort. Most importantly, Milanese ecclesiastics gathered testimonies by interviewing men and women about Borromeo's life, character, accomplishments, and (mostly posthumous healing) miracles. Various Roman congregations examined these testimonies in addition to thoroughly rereading Borromeo's legislative compendium of his synods, the *Acta ecclesiae Mediolanensis*.[28] Images of the archbishop were central in many posthumous miracle stories, and the ubiquity of the prospective saint's likeness played an evidentiary role as well.[29] Hymns, madrigals, and sermons also

---

[26] On these qualities of Borromeo's sainthood, I am indebted to Jan Machielsen for pointing out the first to me, and for the others to Bouley, *Pious Postmortems*, 27; Grace Harpster, "Figino's Efficacy: Portraits, Votives, and Their Makers After Trent," *Oxford Art Journal* 44, no. 2 (2021): 234.

[27] See Elisabetta Patrizi, *Pastoralità ed educazione: L'episcopato di Agostino Valier nella Verona post-tridentina (1565–1606)*, vol. 1 (Milan, 2015), chap. 2; Agostino Valier, *Episcopus* (Verona, 1586), dedication to Carlo Borromeo.

[28] Fabrizio Pagani, "Marco Aurelio Grattarola e la Canonizzazione di Carlo Borromeo," in *Carlo Borromeo e il cattolicesimo dell'età moderna*, Studia Borromaica 25 (Milan, 2011), 73–100; Angelo Turchini, *La fabbrica di un santo: Il processo di canonizzazione di Carlo Borromeo e la Controriforma* (Casale Monferrato, 1984).

[29] Harpster, "Figino's Efficacy."

proclaimed Borromeo's sanctity.³⁰ Borromeo's, along with Ignatius of Loyola's, was the first dissection to be submitted as evidence for sanctity after the Reformation, although the evidence was not considered seriously in Rome (see also Chapter 10 of this volume).³¹ The performing surgeon drew attention to various physical aspects of the dead archbishop that seemed to indicate his ascetic and abstinent lifestyle, including the absence of stomach fat and his withered-away penis, so clearly unused.³² (Disappointingly, his heart was rather normal.) Biographers for the archbishop entered the canonization process and its attendant information into their hagiographies; a saintly life was incomplete without this documented posthumous process. The kinds of evidence assembled for Borromeo helped set a standard for later canonization cases, not only of bishops but of other figures.

Yet Borromeo's canonization and role as a saintly model were also contested. In three separate inquisition trials, in Bergamo in 1611, in Milan in 1612, and in Genoa in 1623, monks were brought to trial for challenging Borromeo's sainthood and the validity of the canonization process more broadly.³³ Borromeo was, for them, exhibit A of how the Church and the pope could err in canonization, and how the use of testimonies in the process was far from fail-safe. Several of them protested that Borromeo, scion of a noble family and cardinal nephew to Pius IV, was only a saint because of his wealth and connections. They stressed that the miracles attributed to the dead archbishop by witnesses were not of high quality. The Milanese monks, brought before the inquisition so soon after the canonization, attempted to pass their past statements off as a joke or, at most, merely an intellectual dispute. It is telling that their discussion of Borromeo was joined to a larger conversation about canonization and the validity of the saints. Borromeo, as a canonized saint whose deeds were still part of local living memory, was the perfect example with which to argue about sanctity.

Even some of Borromeo's ardent supporters, like Valier, changed their mind about his utility as a model over time. Valier, who had

---

³⁰ Christine Getz, "Canonising San Carlo: Sermonising, the Sounding Word, and Image Construction in the Music for Carlo Borromeo," *Early Music History* 34 (2015): 133–89.
³¹ Bouley, *Pious Postmortems*, 40, 50.
³² Ibid., 122; Siraisi, "Signs and Evidence."
³³ Vatican City, Archivio del Dicastero per la Dottrina della Fede, St. St. G-1-h, items 10 and 12. My thanks to Jan Machielsen for bringing these documents to my attention.

lauded Borromeo in *Episcopus* and in a 1586 biography, wrote a private manuscript in 1595 for the archbishop's cousin and successor, Federico Borromeo (1564–1631). In this text, *On the Cautious Imitation of Holy Bishops*, Carlo's life became a cautionary tale about sanctity's physical toll rather than an exemplary vita. Federico would need to proceed with caution in the emulation of his forebear – not everyone, Valier thought, should imitate saintly bishops in every way.[34] As we will see, though, the caution and occasional controversy surrounding Borromeo did not stop both writers and bishops further afield from deploying him as an exemplar.

BETWEEN THE NEW AND OLD WORLDS: BISHOPS AS SAINTLY MODELS AND SAINT-MAKERS IN THE SEVENTEENTH CENTURY

Seventeenth-century hagiographers and bishops continued to rely on the Borromean model in the making of new bishop saints, including Francis de Sales (1567–1622, beat. 1661, can. 1665) and Toribio de Mogrovejo, as well as others who were not canonized in the early modern era. As Simon Ditchfield has pointed out, promotors of Mogrovejo's canonization drew parallels between his life and Borromeo's in order to bolster his cause.[35] Antonio de Léon Pinelo's 1653 hagiography cited the life of Borromeo in the margins.[36] Michelangelo Lapi's 1656 vita noted similarities in how the two men had, as children, played at being bishops, and later founded a convent of the same order.[37] And in a later life of Mogrovejo, published just after his 1679 beatification, Anastasio Nicoselli repeatedly emphasized the similarities between the archbishops of Lima and Milan, which he traced from their birth in the same year to their celebration of synods – perhaps at that point their shared qualities buttressed each other's sanctity.[38]

---

[34] BA, MS H 206 inf; Agostino Valier, *De cauta imitatione sanctorum episcoporum*.

[35] Simon Ditchfield, "Tridentine Catholicism," in *The Ashgate Research Companion to the Counter-Reformation*, ed. Alexandra Bamji, Geert Janssen, and Mary Laven (Farnham, 2013), 22.

[36] Antonio de Léon Pinelo, *Vida del ilustrissimo i reverendissimo D. Toribio Alfonso Mogrovejo* ([Madrid?], 1653), 15.

[37] University of Texas at Austin, Benson Latin American Collection (Benson), GZ 282.092 M748L, Michelangelo Lapi, *Vita del servo di Dio D. Torivio Alfonso Mogrovejo, arcivescovo di Lima* (Rome, 1656), 6, 61.

[38] Anastasio Nicoselli, *Vita del beato Toribio Alfonso Mogrobesio arciuescouo di Lima* (Rome, 1680), 5, 28, 44, 72, 115, 151, 169, 188, 212.

Seventeenth-century bishops consciously modeled themselves on earlier early modern bishops. Gregorio Barbarigo (1625–1697, beat. 1761, can. 1960), bishop of Padua, looked to de Sales, Borromeo, and Niccolò Ormaneto (one of Borromeo's former employees and also a bishop of Padua) as spiritual and governmental models.[39] The learned bishop Juan de Palafox y Mendoza (1600–1659, beat. 2011) held up Borromeo as an exemplar in his writings. As bishop of Puebla, Mexico, he wrote *Direcciones pastorales* (1646), in which he imagined the by-then classic playbook for bishops, the anthology of Borromeo's synods (the *Acta*), as a resource for the many members of the bishop's household, whose roles he outlined in the text.[40] In fact, the food of the bishop and his household were modeled on Borromeo's, much as Borromeo had once looked to earlier early modern bishops like Reginald Pole – the last Catholic Archbishop of Canterbury – for his own eating habits.[41] Like Borromeo, Palafox turned to older bishop saints, too, including in times of plague. In 1650, he published his biography of the seventh-century patriarch of Alexandria, John the Merciful, in Spain, in part to exhort people to follow John's charitable example and stop the sins that he believed had fomented the outbreak of plague in Spain.[42] At the same time, Palafox admired John's confidence in protecting episcopal rights – he might have drawn a parallel to his own ongoing jurisdictional fights with the Jesuits in New Spain.[43]

Ultimately, despite his efforts to work with long-standing models, Palafox was a failed bishop saint. Palafox's unrealized canonization cause has long been understood as a barometer for the tempestuous cultural and intellectual conflict between Jesuits and Jansenists, from the bishop's death in 1659 until the dissolution of the Society of Jesus in 1773.[44] It is also a helpful indicator for understanding the waxing and

---

[39] Celeste McNamara, *The Bishop's Burden: Reforming the Catholic Church in Early Modern Italy* (Washington, DC, 2020), 22.

[40] Ditchfield, "Tridentine Catholicism," 23.

[41] Juan de Palafox y Mendoza, *Luz a los vivos y escarmiento en los muertos...* (Madrid, 1661), 368; Carlo Marcora, "Nicolò Ormaneto, Vicario di S. Carlo," *Memorie Storiche della Diocesi di Milano* 8 (1961): 399.

[42] Juan de Palafox y Mendoza, *Vida de S. Juan el Limosnero* (Madrid, 1650), sig. ¶¶ 7v.

[43] Ibid., 92. For a modern biography of Palafox, see Cayetana Alvarez de Toledo, *Politics and Reform in Spain and Viceregal Mexico: The Life and Thought of Juan de Palafox, 1600–1659* (Oxford, 2004).

[44] On the invocation of slightly earlier bishop saints like Borromeo and de Sales during the Jansenist quarrel, see Alison Forrestal, "Revisiting Sacred Propaganda: The Holy Bishop in the Seventeenth-Century Jansenist Quarrel," *Reformation & Renaissance Review* 6, no. 1 (2004): 7–35.

waning enthusiasm for bishop saints in the later early modern period. Palafox had strong support from his dioceses in Spain and New Spain, the Spanish Crown, and various popes. Indeed, as we will see in the next section, many eighteenth-century popes were particularly eager for bishop saints to help them renew the episcopate. Yet the case fizzled out quickly once the bishop's old enemies – the Jesuits – were defeated. As Antonio Rubial García has noted, with the dissolution of the Society, Palafox's cause became less pressing.[45] While support and opposition to Palafox's cause were multifaceted, a few aspects are worth noting here. Images of the puffy-eyed bishop proliferated: In Mexico, the Inquisition confiscated more than 6,000 devotional portraits, underscoring both Palafox's failed beatification as well as local veneration.[46] Other images showed Palafox as a saint in a more acceptable way, by linking his visage to more established saintly bishops. In both Spain and New Spain, Palafox was reimagined as an older bishop saint, with his likeness used to depict a medieval bishop saint of Osma in Spain and St. Ambrose in Puebla.[47] In 1769, the archbishop of Mexico, Francisco Antonio de Lorenzana (1722–1804), described Palafox as a combination of different great bishop saints – he was:

> in profound sweetness an Ambrose, in genius an Augustine, in eloquence a Chrysostom, in constancy an Athanasius, and in happy sanctity a Gregory the Great ... in defense of the rights of his dignity and his holy church a Thomas of Canterbury and a Stanislaus, in the prodigious abundance of his alms a Thomas of Villanova and a John the Merciful, in the foundation of seminaries and zeal of his studies a Carlo Borromeo and in his appeal and affability a Francis de Sales.[48]

Lorenzana was here paraphrasing other writers on "Saint Palafox" in his longer series of lives of Mexican bishops – a project that itself followed a Borromean injunction to record the lives of past bishops.[49] He was surely aware that the material there on Palafox would be fodder for

---

[45] Antonio Rubial García, *La santidad controvertida: Hagiografía y conciencia criolla alrededor de los venerables no canonizados de Nueva España* (Mexico City, 1999), chap. "El Obispo Reformador."
[46] Antonio Rubial García, "St. Palafox: Metaphorical Images of Disputed Sainthood," in *Colonial Saints: Discovering the Holy in the Americas, 1500–1800*, ed. Allan Greer and Jodi Bilinkoff (London, 2003), 196.
[47] Rubial García, "St. Palafox: Metaphorical Images of Disputed Sainthood."
[48] Quoted in Rubial García, *La santidad controvertida*; Francisco Antonio de Lorenzana, *Concilios provinciales primero y segundo celebrados en la ... ciudad de México* (Mexico City, 1769), 263.
[49] On this kind of project, see Ditchfield, *Liturgy, Sanctity, and History*.

the bishop's then ongoing canonization case. It is telling, then, that in support of this he registered Palafox's similarities with past episcopal saints. He also praised Palafox's efforts to respect his predecessors through including their portraits in the chapter room and through translating the remains of five past prelates.[50] Another essential element, from Lorenzana's viewpoint, was the work of multiple bishops in Mexico and in Spain to gather testimony and create dossiers for Palafox's case in Rome. Lorenzana included a detailed synopsis of the efforts thus far to secure Palafox's beatification.[51] The process of paperwork – not just the saintly life – was integral to the making of a saint.

Throughout the early modern period bishops remained essential generators of the paperwork for sainthood. They continued to construct holiness with tools like relic processions, but they played saint-maker in a more literal way once canonizations resumed. The case of the "idiot" (or unlearned) hermit Gregorio López (1542–1596) shows multiple Mexican bishops over time supporting López's (unrealized) cause for canonization.[52] Pedro Moya de Contreras (d. 1591), the archbishop of Mexico, ordered a canon to serve as secretary to López, taking down his statements and recording his vita in real time. Two of Moya's successors in the next century translated the hermit's body, and one of these, Juan Pérez de la Serna (1570–1631), was tasked with creating the formal dossier for López's canonization – which included the testimony of many bishops. Palafox supported the printing of a new biography of the would-be saint in 1642. While in many respects, as Jorge Cañizares-Esguerra points out, López was "the antithesis of the Counter Reformation saint,"[53] the fact that his case was supported by *bishops*, who assembled documentation and ritually processed his body, does make him resemble other Counter-Reformation saints. For, even if other Church officials or organizations like the Inquisition intervened in documenting and authorizing cults for emerging saints, bishops continued to play a role in preparing these dossiers and promoting or discouraging worship.[54]

---

[50] Lorenzana, *Concilios provinciales*, 262.
[51] Ibid., 264–268.
[52] Jorge Cañizares-Esguerra, "The Imperial, Global (Cosmopolitan) Dimensions of Nonelite Colonial Scribal Cultures in the Early Modern Iberian Atlantic," in *Cosmopolitanism and the Enlightenment*, ed. Joan-Pau Rubiés and Neil Safier (Cambridge, 2023), 166–70. For more on López, see Rubial García, *La santidad controvertida*, chap. "El ermitaño."
[53] Cañizares-Esguerra, "The Imperial, Global (Cosmopolitan) Dimensions," 169.
[54] Bouley, *Pious Postmortems*, 16–19, 25–26.

BISHOP SAINTS IN THE EIGHTEENTH CENTURY: A VIEW FROM ROME

The eighteenth century witnessed serious shifts in both the politics of the Church and the procedure for canonization, as the causes of various bishop saints demonstrate. The papacy played an increasingly vital role in saint-making, as local bishops appealed to Rome to commence the process, while many eighteenth-century popes opened or reopened causes on their own initiative. Scholars have framed these efforts to make canonization more streamlined, centralized, and rational – exemplified in Benedict XIV Lambertini's treatise on the topic – as part of a "Catholic Enlightenment."[55] The Catholic Enlightenment should be understood, like its secular counterpart, in a nuanced way that captures the paradoxes of the so-called age of reason. An important line of thought within this disparate, contradictory movement was what scholars have dubbed a "Tridentine revival," which started with the papacy of Innocent XI (r. 1676–89) in the previous century.[56] Essentially, various figures in eighteenth-century Catholicism, including popes, looked to the earlier age of Catholic reform as their inspiration for their own projects, including an attempt at a reformed episcopate.

Popes who encouraged a return to the ideals of post-Tridentine episcopacy had good reason, then, to look back to sixteenth- and seventeenth-century bishops and to promote their cults.[57] Pope Benedict XIII Orsini picked up the thread from his seventeenth-century predecessor Innocent XI in more than one way, making a serious attempt to reform episcopacy. In 1726 he also canonized Mogrovejo, whom Innocent had beatified in 1679. A new edition of Nicoselli's Italian life of the post-Tridentine archbishop of Lima was issued to coincide with the canonization in Rome. This edition borrowed from earlier images of Mogrovejo to show Benedict XIII kneeling before an image of the saint, much as Mogrovejo had often been shown before the image of the Madonna and child.[58] In the same year, 1726, Benedict XIII reopened the cause for Palafox.

---

[55] Christopher M. S. Johns, *The Visual Culture of Catholic Enlightenment* (University Park, PA, 2015), 61–126; Ulrich L. Lehner, "Introduction: The Many Faces of the Catholic Enlightenment," in *A Companion to the Catholic Enlightenment in Europe*, ed. Ulrich L. Lehner and Michael Printy (Leiden, 2010), 25–26.

[56] Mario Rosa, "The Catholic *Aufklärung* in Italy," in Lehner and Printy, eds., *A Companion to the Catholic Enlightenment in Europe*, 226–27.

[57] Johns, *The Visual Culture of Catholic Enlightenment*, 293–316.

[58] Benson GZ 282.285 M721BN; Nicoselli, *Vita di S. Toribio Alfonso Mogrovesio* (Rome, 1726), sig. [a 1v]. Compare this image of Benedict XIII with that of Mogrovejo in, for

No pope was more influential in changing canonization in the eighteenth century, however, than Benedict XIV Lambertini, despite his canonization of only five saints. Before becoming pope, Lambertini published *De servorum Dei beatificatione et beatorum canonizatione* (1734–38), a landmark text on the process that reserved the right to sanctify to the papacy and established guidelines for considering evidence. The work was informed by Lambertini's time as "devil's advocate" (*promotor fidei*). In this official role, Lambertini contested evidence brought forward for bishop Gregorio Barbarigo's beatification. Barbarigo had not published enough, Lambertini contended, plus he had frequently abandoned his diocese to go to Venice and died in despair in his final hour. When Barbarigo's case surfaced again during his papacy, Benedict XIV once more raised the issue of whether Barbarigo had been sufficiently resident in his diocese.[59] He shaped other ongoing cases, too – for instance, by appointing an anti-Jesuit cardinal as official proponent for Palafox's canonization.[60] While Benedict XIV did not canonize any bishop saints, he did beatify two: Alessandro Sauli (1534–1592, beat. 1741, can. 1904) and Niccolò Albergati (1373–1443, beat. 1744). The selection of Sauli, a confidant of Borromeo who did his best to confront banditry and priests' concubinage in his Corsican diocese, fit with the broader "Tridentine revival." Albergati was a more personal choice, as he was known for being an early reforming bishop in Lambertini's hometown (and own archiepiscopal see) of Bologna. Benedict XIV's commitment to Albergati was such that he even stipulated the iconography for an altarpiece celebrating the bishop's beatification.[61]

The eventual beatification of Barbarigo in 1761 was similarly personal for the overseeing pope, Benedict's immediate successor Clement XIII Rezzonico. As bishop of Padua, Rezzonico had pushed for Barbarigo's case in the 1740s, under Benedict XIV. As pope, he could at last move this project through, casting Barbarigo as an updated model bishop for changing times.[62] What's more, for Clement XIII, Barbarigo's close involvement with Jesuits was in his favor, as this pope worked to support the order before its dissolution by his successor. The opposite

---

instance, Benson GZ 282.092 M748L, Antonio de León Pinelo, *Vita del servo di Dio D. Torivio Alfonso Mogrovejo* (Rome, 1656), facing page to sig. A [1r].
[59] Celeste McNamara, "Molding the Model Bishop from Trent to Vatican II," *Church History* 88, no. 1 (2019): 70, 76.
[60] Rubial García, *La santidad controvertida*.
[61] Johns, *The Visual Culture of Catholic Enlightenment*, 113–14.
[62] McNamara, "Molding the Model Bishop," 79.

was of course at play in Palafox's canonization case, and yet Clement also rubber-stamped the Congregation of Rites' approval of Palafox's writings and allowed the cause to proceed.⁶³ Palafox later looked poised to follow Barbarigo's success in much the same way when the proponent of his cause became Clement XIV Ganganelli in 1769. After dissolving the Society of Jesus, however, Clement XIV died the next year, leaving the planned beatification in limbo. The case to some degree remained live into the 1790s, as one devil's advocate continued to list oppositions. But changing geopolitics and the disruption of the Napoleonic invasion of Italy meant that the beatification of the Pueblan bishop remained unrealized in the early modern period.⁶⁴

The eighteenth-century papacy's investment in promoting various bishop saints entailed a different kind of saintly electrical rewiring than that with which we began. Popes – the bishops of Rome, of course – as well as bishops looked to earlier holy bishops as models and devotional figures. To some degree, earlier bishops, like fifteenth-century Albergati or sixteenth-century Mogrovejo, found success more easily in eighteenth-century sanctification procedures than later seventeenth-century figures like Barbarigo or Palafox, who were embroiled in the larger Jansenist–Jesuit debates that tore the eighteenth-century Church apart. The selection and celebration of bishop saints reflected the Church's changing politics and relationship to the world.

CONCLUSION: THINKING WITH BISHOPS

While historians have disagreed on how, exactly, to interpret the "reforming bishops" whose identities, if not all their actions, were closely tied to Trent, it is clear that the image of the saintly bishop – whether Ambrose, Borromeo, Mogrovejo, de Sales, or even those who were not canonized in the early modern period – was a powerful and recognizable model.⁶⁵ It is important to acknowledge, though, that these models, whether encountered in altarpieces, printed hagiographies, or even in their own words, were fragmentary. Making these men

---

⁶³ Ricardo Fernández Gracia and Pedro Lui Echverría Goñi, "La edición ilustrada de las Opera omnia de Palafox de 1762," in *Palafox: Iglesia, Cultura y Estado en el siglo XVII*, ed. Ricardo Fernández Gracia (Pamplona, 2001), 443.
⁶⁴ Rubial García, *La santidad controvertida*.
⁶⁵ Matteo al Kalak, "I vescovi riformatori: Nuove prospettive per una categoria antica," in *Ripensare la Riforma protestante: Nuove prospettive degli studi italiani*, Biblioteca universitaria Claudiana 3 (Turin, 2015), 107–22; Joseph Bergin, "The Counter-Reformation Church and Its Bishops," *Past & Present*, no. 165 (1999): 30–73.

into saints, lifting them from an earthly plane to a divine one, erased the work of their collaborators, and ironically much of what they themselves had done.[66] The partial narratives of episcopacy that early modern bishop saints represent are telling in their own way, though, about how the office of bishop was idealized through a period of immense change. In the early decades after the Council of Trent, bishops looked to late antique models and to each other's ongoing work in order to refashion the figure of holy bishop and to honor existing saints. By the seventeenth century, there were new, easily identifiable models like Borromeo to imitate (or at least cite), and in their role in canonization procedures bishops took on paperwork as another means to make saints in their dioceses. Both canonization and efforts to reform the episcopate were taken up by the papacy in the eighteenth century, when popes advanced the causes of their favorite past holy bishops. Of course, holy episcopal models were never without criticism or controversy. In fact, bishop saints were both a way to navigate controversies and sometimes integral to them, just as Borromeo became synonymous with the problems of new canonization procedures for some disgruntled Italian monks, or Barbarigo and Palafox came to signify opposite sides of the Jansenist–Jesuit quarrel. On the whole, bishops prove "good to think with" in order to recognize broader trends in saint-making across this period.[67]

---

[66] See Madeline McMahon, *Shepherds in the Dark: Bishops and the Creation of Catholic Knowledge in Early Modern Italy* (forthcoming).

[67] Simon Ditchfield, "Thinking with Saints: Sanctity and Society in the Early Modern World," *Critical Inquiry* 35, no. 3 (2009): 553.

2 Martyrs

ALEJANDRO CAÑEQUE

While actual martyrdom had become a distant memory by the Middle Ages, Christianity remained a religion based on the idea of a savior-martyr. Works on the passion of Jesus Christ, prescriptions to suffer with patience, and the art of dying well enjoyed great prestige in late medieval Christianity. That same religious culture was also dominated by the cult of saints and their relics. Martyrs had been the original saints. Many of the most popular saints in late medieval Europe (Peter, Paul, Sebastian, Lawrence, Andrew, Lucy, Barbara) had, or so it was believed, died for the faith in antiquity. In addition to their relics, whether authentic or not, vividly imagined representations of their passions and deaths were present everywhere in Europe. The *Legenda aurea sanctorum* (Golden Legend of the Saints), a work compiled in the thirteenth century by Jacob of Voragine (1230–1298), an Italian Dominican friar, bishop of Genoa, and contemporary of Thomas Aquinas, enjoyed enormous popularity in the late Middle Ages, with hundreds of manuscripts circulating throughout Europe, in both Latin and vernacular languages. The appearance of the printing press would contribute even more to its diffusion at the end of the fifteenth century.[1] This late medieval religious culture would not only persist but would be strengthened in the course of the sixteenth century because of confessional divides.

THE REFORMATION CHALLENGE

The confrontation between Catholics and Protestants was the historical event that reactivated the ideal of martyrdom and made it vividly present in European societies. In the Low Countries, France, and England, thousands of persons were judicially executed because of their

---

[1] See Jacobus de Voragine, *The Golden Legend: Readings on the Saints*, trans. William Granger Ryan (Princeton, NJ, 2012).

religious beliefs. As their supporters paid homage to them as genuine martyrs who had died defending the true religion, and their detractors denounced them as false martyrs, they became a literal embodiment of the doctrinal disagreements that characterized sixteenth- and seventeenth-century Christianity.[2] The Protestants were the first to develop their own martyrologies, in which they narrated popish cruelties in great and gruesome detail.[3] Catholics did not take long to react, and in the last decades of the sixteenth century the medieval Christian martyrologies were republished, updated, and expanded, as a way to affirm emphatically the importance of martyrdom as a divine instrument in the fight against heresy.

In the battle against Protestantism, Catholic authorities placed special emphasis on the cult of the saints and their relics. The last session of the Council of Trent in 1563 promulgated a decree that called on bishops and other religious authorities to instruct the faithful especially that "the holy bodies of the holy martyrs" should be venerated, while condemning those who asserted that the relics of saints should not be honored.[4] The rediscovery and systematic study of the catacombs of Rome, starting in 1578 when what was thought to be the catacomb of St. Priscilla was discovered, gave a great impulse to the cult of the martyrs (see Chapter 6). The number of relics multiplied exponentially in the Catholic world, since the presumption was that in those catacombs the remains of many martyrs must have been buried. The catacombs thus became the symbol of martyrdom par excellence.

The monastery of El Escorial, built between 1563 and 1584 by order of the Spanish King Philip II (1556–1598), is another paradigmatic example of this thriving culture of martyrdom. Not only was the vast complex dedicated to St. Lawrence, a martyr of antiquity of Hispanic origin, but, in addition to being a monastery, palace, and library, El Escorial was also a gigantic reliquary. Philip II was a great collector of relics, accumulating thousands of them from all over Europe. Aside from attempting to assemble all surviving St. Lawrence's relics at his monastic palace, Philip also wanted El Escorial to house relics of all of

---

[2] Brad S. Gregory, *Salvation at Stake: Christian Martyrdom in Early Modern Europe* (Cambridge, 1999).

[3] Two of the most influential Protestant martyrologies were Jean Crespin's *Recueil de plusieurs personnes qui ont constamment enduré la mort pour le Nom de nostre Seigneur Iesus-Christ* (Geneva, 1555) and John Foxe's *Actes and monuments of these latter and perillous dayes* (London, 1563).

[4] *Canons and Decrees of the Council of Trent*, original text with English translation by Rev. H. J. Schroeder, O.P. (St. Louis, MO, 1941), session XXV, pp. 215–17.

Spain's other saints. In his eagerness to collect relics Philip II was not a unique case. In Catholic Europe, the accumulation of sacred remains was a symbol of power and prestige. The emperors of the Holy Roman Empire, the archdukes of Austria, and the dukes of Bavaria were all avid collectors of relics, and displayed an even greater urgency than Philip, since the Protestant threat in Central Europe was close at hand. Yet Philip II and his successors also saw their growing collection as a rescue mission, protecting holy remains from desecration by foreign heretics, which in turn might protect Spain. Relics, as miracle-working conduits to the divine, were seen as powerful offensive and defensive weapons in the fight against Protestantism.[5]

Like relics, the pictorial representations of martyrs took on added significance at this time. The more iconoclastic Protestants became, the more Catholics insisted on the importance of images in conveying the true Christian doctrine to the faithful. The Council of Trent solemnly declared that all Christians were obliged to honor and venerate the images of Christ, the Virgin, and the saints, not because any divinity existed in those images, but because by means of them "we adore Christ and venerate the saints whose likeness they bear."[6] Hence, a few years after the conclusion of this council, a series of treatises on sacred images appeared that developed the principles it had briefly set forth. In the case of the images that described the torments of martyrs, it was asserted that, when properly represented, they possessed such force that they moved the viewer to shed tears of sorrow and to excite their piety and devotion. This was clearly stated by Cardinal Gabriele Paleotti, archbishop of Bologna, in his treatise in defense of the use of images by Catholics, when he recounted the case of a painting of St. Euphemia's martyrdom,[7] in which the suffering of the passion of the saint and her great strength were so well represented that they moved one to tears (on Paleotti, see also Chapter 1). Paleotti maintained that when we listen to the story of a saint's martyrdom, or a virgin's zeal and constancy, or the passion of Christ himself, we are deeply moved. For Paleotti, there is therefore no doubt that our devotion will only increase and penetrate into the depths of our being when the image of a martyred saint, of a suffering virgin, or of a Christ nailed to the cross are put before our eyes.

---

[5] Guy Lazure, "Possessing the Sacred: Monarchy and Identity in Philip II's Relic Collection at the Escorial," *Renaissance Quarterly* 60, no. 1 (2007): 58–93.

[6] *Canons and Decrees of the Council of Trent*, session XXV, p. 216.

[7] According to tradition, she suffered terrible tortures and died from the wound inflicted by a wild beast in Chalcedon's arena at the beginning of the fourth century, during the persecutions of emperor Diocletian.

Whoever did not experience these feelings was undoubtedly deprived of all sensitivity.[8]

MARTYRDOM AND EMPIRE

While Catholic societies were suffused with images of martyrdom, it remained extremely unlikely that Catholics would be martyred at home, especially after the first waves of confessional violence had passed, with devotion centering on particularly extreme acts. In the Low Countries, for instance, the martyrs of Gorcum, a group of nineteen priests killed by the Protestant sea beggars in 1572, became a primary conduit for Catholic memories of the Dutch Revolt from the early seventeenth century onward. Their many relics found their way into churches and convents in the Catholic south and in private collections in the officially Protestant north.[9] The principal exception, however, was the British Isles, where the judicial killing of Catholics as traitors became a routinized occurrence, and homegrown martyrdom suffused the devotional practices of a prosecuted minority faith.[10] The situation in Catholicism's Mediterranean heartlands was very different. In Spain, religious uniformity had been achieved very early on, and the few attempts to introduce Protestantism had been swiftly and mercilessly eradicated. While the subjects of the Spanish monarchy had few opportunities to experience martyrdom in their own countries, the frontiers of their immense empire offered many opportunities for them to manifest their religious fervor.[11] The archives and libraries of the Catholic world are replete with chronicles and accounts that relate the violent deaths of many members of the religious orders in the course of their attempts to convert the "heretics," "infidels," and "pagans" of the world. Most of these deaths would be conceptualized by the religious orders as "martyrdoms."

We must therefore situate early modern martyrdom within the history of European imperialism and colonialism. This was

---

[8] Gabriele Paleotti, *Discorso intorno alle immagini sacre e profane (1582)*, ed. Stefano della Torre (Milan, 2002), 79, 81.

[9] Judith Pollmann, *Catholic Identity and the Revolt of the Netherlands, 1520–1635* (Oxford, 2011), 159–61.

[10] Michael Questier, *Catholics and Treason: Martyrology, Memory, and Politics in the Post-Reformation* (Oxford, 2022).

[11] Alejandro Cañeque, "Letting Yourself Be Skinned Alive: Jerónimo Gracián and the Globalization of Martyrdom," *Journal of Early Modern History* 24, no. 3 (2020): 197–223.

fundamentally an Iberian story, as the Spanish monarchy ruled over a very large portion of the world's Catholic peoples, especially between 1580 and 1640, when Portugal and its colonies were also part of the Habsburg empire.[12] Accounts and images of foreign martyrdom were powerful tools that, in the hands of the religious orders, served, on the one hand, to fight Protestantism in Europe and Islam in the Mediterranean, and, on the other, to attempt to consolidate and expand Spanish colonialism in Asia and the Americas. These missionaries became the most active agents of Spanish colonial penetration in the New World, doggedly trying to establish new mission frontiers. In this way, they pushed forward the frontiers of empire at the expense of native populations. As this chapter argues, in these frontier regions, martyrdom would acquire its greatest significance in the second half of the seventeenth century.

THE POLITICS AND GLOBAL FRONTIERS OF MARTYRDOM

It has been argued that in the course of the evangelization of medieval Europe, "wherever Christianity encountered a frontier, it had need of martyrs."[13] The same is true for the religious orders operating within Iberia's global empires. The notion of frontier is used here in an expansive manner; it is not only applied to specific geographic areas of the world (those contact, or friction, zones where Catholic civilization encountered other religions and other cultures), but also taken as an idea, an image of the outer world, a particular manner of relating to the non-Catholic peoples of the world. The intertwining of the missionary work of the orders with political and imperial matters created tensions and, frequently, bitter disputes, the two most remarkable examples of these being the English and Japanese missions.

Four frontiers of martyrdom can be identified, which existed at different times and inspired each other in turn. The first was established within Europe, with the persecution of Catholics in England during the reign of Elizabeth I. From the perspective of the Spanish empire, England constituted the *frontier of heresy*. Numerous accounts of

---

[12] Sanjay Subrahmanyam, "Holding the World in Balance: The Connected Histories of the Iberian Overseas Empires, 1500–1640," *American Historical Review* 112, no. 5 (2007): 1359–85.
[13] Donald Weinstein and Rudolph M. Bell, *Saints and Society: The Two Worlds of Western Christendom, 1000–1700* (Chicago, 1982), 160.

Catholic martyrdom started to circulate in Europe after the clandestine Jesuit English mission was launched in 1580, which caused an increase in the persecution of English Catholics. As part of its fight against the heretical island, the Spanish crown supported the establishment of several Jesuit colleges in Spain – St. Alban's in Valladolid and St. Gregory's in Seville – where English priests were to be trained. After concluding their studies, these seminary priests would clandestinely return to England to attempt the reconversion of their native country. But once they had arrived there, it was more than likely that they would be discovered, arrested, accused of high treason, and executed in a gruesome public ritual (many other victims came from the Jesuit English colleges at Douai and Rome). This is what happened to Henry Walpole, a professor at the Valladolid seminary and its first priest to be executed in England. He was arrested just one day after arriving in the country. He spent about three months at York Castle before being transferred to the Tower of London in February 1594. There Walpole was tortured on the rack. In the spring of 1595, he was sent back to York for trial. He was tried and convicted of high treason. According to English law, those accused of high treason were to be hanged and then drawn and quartered (although Walpole was allowed to hang until he was dead, before being disemboweled). The cruelty of this form of execution would contribute enormously to spreading the idea throughout Catholic Europe that the English "heretical" regime was committing great atrocities against the country's Catholics.[14] Catholic writers contended that the condemned were not "traitors" but "martyrs," who had died because of their religion (to be considered a martyr, it had to be clear beyond doubt that an individual had been killed because of their Catholic beliefs).[15]

For the English Jesuits exiled in Spain, any compromise with the Elizabethan regime in matters of religion was unacceptable. For them,

---

[14] In reality, the regime of Elizabeth I had not innovated at all in this respect, as this form of execution dated back to the thirteenth century. See John Bellamy, *The Tudor Law of Treason: An Introduction* (London, 1979), chap. 5. For the account of Walpole's martyrdom, see Joseph Creswell, *Historia de la vida y martyrio que padecio en Inglaterra, este año de 1595 el P. Henrique Valpolo, sacerdote de la Compañia de Iesus, que fue embiado del Colegio de los Ingleses de Valladolid y ha sido el primer martyr de los Seminarios de España* (Madrid, 1596).

[15] Anne Dillon, *The Construction of Martyrdom in the English Catholic Community, 1535–1603* (Aldershot, 2002); Peter Lake and Michael Questier, *The Trials of Margaret Clitherow: Persecution, Martyrdom and the Politics of Sanctity in Elizabethan England* (London, 2011); Thomas M. McCoog, *"And Touching Our Society": Fashioning Jesuit Identity in Elizabethan England* (Toronto, 2013).

the *conformist* attitude of many English Catholics, willing to accept the demands of the English crown, was inadmissible. It was through this militant, *recusant* attitude that the discourse of martyrdom acquired all of its meaning and force, because, for the most radical faction, there existed only two options for an English Catholic: exile or martyrdom, but never the appeasement of a corrupt regime. Thus, the English exiles, with the Jesuits in the lead, produced an extensive literature on martyrdom as part of a transnational, propagandistic campaign encouraging European Catholics to support the English cause.[16] At the same time, the exiles reached the conclusion that the only way to restore Catholicism in England was with the Spanish crown's support. This led them to the conviction that English Catholic destiny was closely linked to the fate of the Spanish monarchy. But in 1630, following the Treaty of Madrid, the umbilical cord that had united, for decades, the destiny of the exiled English Catholics to the Spanish monarchy would be definitively and officially broken when Spanish authorities decided to make a 180-degree turn in their policy toward the Catholics of that country, abandoning the patronage and support they had been giving them since the accession to the throne of Queen Elizabeth. These changes were prompted by the suggestions of English Catholics themselves (including John Norton, rector of the English college in Madrid), who concluded that it was more useful and expedient to turn to the English monarch than to the Spanish king in resolving their grievances.[17] By the 1640s, Spanish lack of interest in the fate of the English Catholics was manifest. When in 1642, 1644, and 1646 three former students of the English college of Seville were executed in England, their deaths did not have any repercussion in the city, nor did anyone take it upon themselves to write an account of their martyrdom.[18]

The English persecution is of great significance, since it was the historical event that activated the phenomenon of martyrdom in the Hispanic world. Before 1580, the circulation of martyrdom stories had been practically nonexistent, and the evangelization of the New World in the first half of the sixteenth century had produced neither martyrs

---

[16] See Paul Arblaster, *Antwerp and the World: Richard Verstegan and the International Culture of Catholic Reformation* (Leuven, 2004).

[17] The attitude of English Catholics undoubtedly had to do with the fact that Charles I was married to a Catholic princess, Henrietta Maria, sister of Louis XIII of France. See Albert J. Loomie, *Spain and the Early Stuarts, 1585–1655* (Aldershot, 1996), 1154–66.

[18] Martin Murphy, *St. Gregory's College, Seville, 1592–1767* (London, 1992), 13.

nor a martyrdom literature. The first missionaries to arrive in the New World, the Franciscans in particular, were moved by an apocalyptic desire to create an ideal Christian society. With God on their side and people to convert before the world ended, the desire for martyrdom played no significant role in their motivation to cross the Atlantic. It was a time when the Protestant Reformation was taking its first steps, and the profound religious divisions that contributed to the revival of the martyrdom ideal had not yet emerged.

A second frontier, the *frontier of infidelity*, was constituted by the Mediterranean. As a consequence of the confrontation between the Spanish and the Ottoman empires, thousands of Christian captives, from all social classes, waited in places such as Algiers, Tunis, and Morocco to be ransomed by the religious orders (Mercedarians and Trinitarians).[19] The existence of this captive population gave rise to a copious literature in which those prisoners killed by the Muslim infidels were often described as Christian martyrs. Although the captivity of Christians would persist in North Africa until the beginning of the nineteenth century, the late sixteenth and early seventeenth century saw the greatest increase in their number. Algiers, in particular, became synonymous with Christian captivity and martyrdom. Starting in the second half of the seventeenth century, and due to a variety of circumstances both internal and external, North African corsair activity decreased notably and with it the number of Christian captives.

It has been argued that the literature on North Africa's captivity and martyrdom served to keep the war against the Muslim threat present in the minds of the subjects of the Spanish empire at a time when military actions against the Turks had been drastically reduced after the armistice signed in 1581 between the Spanish and Ottoman empires. In so doing, captivity authors kept a vision of the clash between Christianity and Islam alive that was more typical of the Middle Ages than of the early modern period.[20] Yet the stories of captivity and martyrdom are not as anachronistic as they may appear to be at first sight. In the seventeenth century, faith and religion still played a very significant

---

[19] Ellen G. Friedman, *Spanish Captives in North Africa in the Early Modern Age* (Madison, 1983); Robert C. Davis, *Christian Slaves, Muslim Masters: White Slavery in the Mediterranean, the Barbary Coast, and Italy, 1500–1800* (New York, 2004); Gillian Weiss, *Captives and Corsairs: France and Slavery in the Early Modern Mediterranean* (Stanford, CA, 2011).

[20] Miguel Ángel de Bunes Ibarra, "Las crónicas de cautivos y las vidas ejemplares en el enfrentamiento hispano-musulmán en la Edad Moderna." *Hispania Sacra* 45, no. 91 (1993): 67–82.

role across the Mediterranean.[21] Although the Maghreb had been associated with martyrdom since the Middle Ages, it was not until the early 1600s that it became a locus of martyrdom. The martyrdom literature corresponded to the political and religious conditions of the late sixteenth and early seventeenth century, for which reason it cannot be considered a continuation of a medieval tradition that, in reality, never existed. This literature emerged at a time when the reenergized ideal of martyrdom was reaching its apex. It reflected the power, prestige, and influence of this ideal. The authors of stories of captive martyrdom took advantage of this religious milieu in order to confer an energizing force on their accounts.

There is no better example of all of this than the many accounts of captivity and martyrdom included in Diego de Haedo's *Topographia, e historia general de Argel*, published in 1612. Haedo's captives possess all the characteristics of traditional martyrs. They endure cruel deaths with great fortitude and Christian steadfastness. For example, Captain Martín de Vargas, who was beaten to death, died "with the greatest devotion, because having suffered infinite blows and mortal strokes without complaining nor moaning ... he never renounced the holiest and most glorious name of Jesus, and that of Mary, his Holy Mother."[22] All the ill treatment and torture that precede the captive's death are narrated according to the martyrological model established in antiquity, always following the same steps: The future martyr is denounced by a traitor within his own community, after which he is taken before the authorities, who offer to pardon him, provided he renounces his religion. However, the future martyr rejects this opportunity to save his life, frequently mocking the judges in his responses. In the course of his torture, he manifests his faith by saying prayers, which causes the executioners to treat their victim even more brutally. Miraculously, the martyr takes longer than expected to die. After his death, the body is dumped by the torturers and secretly recovered by the community of believers, who bury him in a place that becomes a site of worship.[23]

---

[21] See Molly Greene, "Beyond the Northern Invasion: The Mediterranean in the Seventeenth Century," *Past and Present* 174 (2002): 42–71.

[22] Diego de Haedo, *Topographia, e historia general de Argel* (Valladolid, 1612), fol. 154r. Many scholars today believe that the true author of the *Topographia* was a Portuguese cleric named Antonio de Sosa. See Alejandro Cañeque, *Un imperio de mártires: Religión y poder en las fronteras de la Monarquía Hispánica* (Madrid, 2020), 140–44.

[23] Enrique Fernández, "El cuerpo torturado en los testimonios de cautivos de los corsarios berberiscos, 1500–1700," *Hispanic Review* 71, no. 1 (2003): 61.

It is important to point out that the phenomenon of martyrdom in North Africa and elsewhere was, for the most part, one that developed through the printing press. It may well be argued that without the printed accounts, there would have been no martyrs in the early modern period. In that regard, martyrdom may be understood as a set of discursive practices that gave meaning to and shaped the missionary activities of the religious orders. The textual approach is even more important when we study martyrdom in a colonial and imperial setting, as the martyrs' legacy was primarily textual, inasmuch as their martyrdoms took place in remote areas and not in front of hundreds or thousands of onlookers, as was the case with martyrs in Europe. This fact made their impact depend entirely upon the written word, without which their persecutions and torments would have had little repercussion. Without the existence of written and, above all, printed accounts, the religious and political force of the martyrs would have been seriously diminished.

All of this was clearly manifested in a third frontier of martyrdom, the *frontier of civilized paganism*, which opened up at the other side of the world, in Japan, during the second half of the sixteenth century. The attitude of the Jesuits in the Japan mission was, to a large measure, the opposite of those in the English mission, as their priorities in this other great frontier of martyrdom would align more closely with the interests of the Portuguese rather than with those of the Castilian crown. After all, Francis Xavier, the founder of the mission, had arrived in Japan in 1546 under the auspices of Goa's authorities, at a time when Manila, the Spanish outpost in the Philippines, did not even exist. After some initial successes by the Jesuits (by the early 1600s, they claimed to have converted almost 300,000 Japanese), at the end of that century, the Japanese rulers decided to ban Christianity from their dominions. In 1597, they executed (by crucifixion) six Spanish Franciscan friars and twenty Japanese Christians in Nagasaki, because they believed they were spies sent by a foreign ruler. The victims became the first in a long list of "martyrs of Japan." The initial decades of the seventeenth century were characterized by the harsh persecution of Christians, both foreign and native. Many members of the religious orders, disobeying the expulsion decree, stayed clandestinely in Japan. Many of them would be executed, adding to the swelling lists of martyrs of Japan, which the orders published regularly. Japan became the site of martyrdom par excellence during the first half of the seventeenth century.[24]

---

[24] Charles R. Boxer, *The Christian Century in Japan, 1549–1650* (Berkeley, CA, 1951); Reinier H. Hesselink, *The Dream of Christian Nagasaki: World Trade and the Clash*

But when in 1640 the majority of the members of a Portuguese diplomatic mission from Macau, who had traveled to Japan to request the reestablishment of trade activities, were summarily executed for contravening the orders that prohibited the entry of foreigners, Japan would cease being a land of missionary activity. One of the great ironies of the Iberian attempt to convert Japan is the striking similarity between the situation of the persecuted Japanese Christians and the equally persecuted religious minorities of the Spanish empire. For the Iberian missionaries came from a land whose rulers were equally determined to eradicate from their dominions "pernicious" religions that, in their view, undermined the unity and identity of the monarchy.

The martyrs of Japan played a prominent role in the confrontation between Spaniards and Portuguese for access to East Asia. They were also turned into a powerful weapon in the fierce competition that existed between Jesuits, on the one hand, and Franciscans and Dominicans, on the other, for the control of the East Asian missions. This confrontation was played out in Madrid and Rome, where the religious orders made great efforts to influence the pope and the Spanish monarch. The orders quickly proceeded to publicize their own martyrs with printed accounts, while ignoring, or even denying, the existence of those from rival orders. The competition between the Portuguese and the Spanish in Japan has led some historians to argue that the conflicts between Jesuits and mendicants (Franciscans and Dominicans) were but a manifestation of Portuguese resistance to Spanish hegemony between 1580 and 1640. However, reducing these conflicts and rivalries to the dichotomy of Portuguese Jesuits versus Castilian mendicants simplifies historical realities excessively, not only because there were many Spanish and Italian Jesuits in Japan, but also because the religious orders were often driven more by corporate and institutional interests than by their undivided loyalty to a particular nation.

One factor that historians tend to ignore in these discussions is the enormous prestige that the Japanese mission enjoyed among the religious

---

of Cultures, 1560–1640 (Jefferson, NC, 2016); Hitomi Omata Rappo, *Des Indes lointaines aux scènes des collèges: Les reflets des martyrs de la mission japonaise en Europe, XVIe–XVIIIe siècle* (Münster, 2020); Rady Roldán-Figueroa, *The Martyrs of Japan: Publication History and Catholic Missions in the Spanish World (Spain, New Spain, and the Philippines, 1597–1700)* (Leiden, 2021). For the uses of printed accounts to construct powerful images of martyrdom, see Alejandro Cañeque, "In the Shadow of Francis Xavier: Martyrdom and Colonialism in the Jesuit Asian Missions," *Journal of Jesuit Studies* 9, no. 3 (2022): 438–58.

orders. This was a crucial aspect in an era of great evangelical fervor, because converting the Japanese was seen as an endeavor similar to the conversion of the inhabitants of the Roman empire by the apostles. At the same time, in the first decades of the seventeenth century, Japan became the frontier of martyrdom par excellence. It was for all of these reasons that the mendicants could not give up their attempts to reach such a prized goal, while the Jesuits, as the founders of the Japanese mission, would do their utmost to ensure that the prestige inherent to this undertaking would belong only to them.

By the mid-1600s, a fourth frontier opened up. By then England, North Africa, and Japan no longer provided inspiration to the evangelical and redeeming zeal of the religious orders. Spanish Jesuits began to concentrate their missionary efforts on the New World's remote frontier regions. In their minds, these constituted another frontier of martyrdom, the *frontier of savage paganism*. The publication in Mexico of Jesuit accounts of both England's and Japan's martyrs contributed to spreading the culture of martyrdom in the New World (news from Japan arrived in Mexico before reaching Spain). The 1627 beatification of the twenty-six martyrs of Nagasaki and the fact that the Franciscan Felipe de Jesús, one of the victims, was a native of Mexico City, greatly helped to disseminate throughout the viceroyalty of New Spain the image of Japan as the quintessential locus of martyrdom. To commemorate the 1627 beatification, the walls of the Franciscan convent in Cuernavaca were decorated with scenes of the martyrs of Nagasaki. And in 1630 Mexico City's municipal council would declare Felipe de Jesús as one of the city's patron saints.[25]

All this notwithstanding, until the mid-1600s the New World was characterized by the absence of homegrown martyrs. It was not a coincidence that several Jesuit martyrdom chronicles were published for the first time in the 1640s. These works would mark the consolidation of the first mission frontiers established by the Society of Jesus, those of Sinaloa in the northwest of Mexico, Paraguay, and Chile.[26] Jesuit missionary activity in the New World had not started sooner because China

---

[25] Cornelius Conover, "Saintly Biography and the Cult of San Felipe de Jesús in Mexico City, 1597–1697," *The Americas* 67, no. 4 (2011): 441–66.

[26] In the 1630s, French Jesuits had established a mission in New France, in Huron territory. In the 1640s the mission was destroyed by the Iroquois and eight Jesuits were killed. They are known as the Canadian or North American martyrs. They were canonized by Pope Pius XI in 1930. See Alan Greer, "Colonial Saints: Gender, Race, and Hagiography in New France," *William and Mary Quarterly* 57, no. 2 (2000): 323–48.

and, above all, Japan had kept the evangelical imagination of the religious orders busy. As long as Japan appeared as the great missionary objective, the remote and, in European eyes, desolate American frontiers remained rather unappealing. By the late seventeenth century, the Jesuits' missionary impetus in the New World had not dwindled at all, as they established new mission frontiers in the Amazon region of northern Peru (Maynas) and on the wide tropical plains east of the Andes, in present-day Bolivia (Llanos de Mojos y Chiquitos). From the northernmost regions of New Spain to the farthest reaches of Chile, by the end of the 1600s, the Jesuits dominated the frontier missions of the Spanish empire. Yet this predominance did not seem enough to them. Their boundless missionary impulse would take them even beyond the American frontiers. Sailing across the immensity of the Pacific Ocean, they established themselves in the Mariana Islands, which became the great martyrdom frontier of the late seventeenth century. The initial drive to Christianize the Mariana Islands originated not from the Society of Jesus but from one Spanish Jesuit, Diego Luis de San Vítores, often referred to as "the apostle of the Marianas." He would not relent in his efforts to establish a mission in the islands, eventually securing crucial support from the Spanish crown. Upon arriving in the islands, he promptly baptized numerous infants, urged the natives to cover their nakedness with palm leaves, and unceremoniously destroyed the skulls of the islanders' ancestors, which they considered sacred objects. These actions provoked hostility among the native population, ultimately leading to San Vítores's death at their hands in 1672. The definitive account of his martyrdom was published in Madrid in 1683. This chronicle represents a refined example of Jesuit literature on martyrdom. Narrated with dynamism and written in a terse, precise style, in it, hagiography and history are combined to perfection.[27]

The New World missions never enjoyed the prestige of the English or the Japanese missions, nor could their martyrs compete with the English and Japanese martyrs, whose deaths seemed to be so similar to those of the primitive Church. In any event, the members of the Society of Jesus made a sophisticated use of the rhetoric of martyrdom to affirm and propagate their missionary work in the New World. In this manner, the Jesuits built, little by little and with the help of the blood of martyrs,

---

[27] The chronicle was widely read, being translated into Italian in 1686. It has been recently translated into English. See Francisco García, *The Life and Martyrdom of the Venerable Father Diego Luis de San Vitores of the Society of Jesus, First Apostle of the Mariana Islands*, trans. M. M. Higgins et al., ed. J. A. McDonough (Guam, 2004).

a "mission empire" on the Spanish empire's American frontiers. In stark contrast with what had occurred in Japan, in the New World the Jesuits encountered little competition from other religious orders. By the end of the sixteenth century, Augustinians and Dominicans had entirely abandoned missionary work, while the Franciscans had reduced it to a minimum. The Society of Jesus marked the consolidation of each of its missions with the publication of a great chronicle in which the discourse of martyrdom played a significant role. The Jesuits thus became the great propagators of the ideal of martyrdom in American lands, using stories and images of martyred missionaries to affirm and spread their evangelical efforts. In the New World, martyrs always appeared in the initial stages of the creation of a mission frontier, thus reviving Tertullian's famous maxim *semen est sanguis christianorum* (the blood of Christians is seed).[28] Once the mission was consolidated, martyrs tended to disappear or to recede into the background.

GENDERING MARTYRDOM

Despite the numerous early female martyrs, the culture of martyrdom had been dominated since antiquity by men.[29] In the early modern period, outside Europe, the martyrs were always men, since male religious orders were the only ones engaged in evangelical work. Nevertheless, the women of the Spanish empire also shared in the ideal of martyrdom. In one exceptional instance, that of Luisa de Carvajal, a woman was almost able to realize her wish for martyrdom thanks to her aristocratic status, which provided her with the necessary resources and influence to travel to England with the hope of suffering martyrdom at the hands of the heretics. Luisa de Carvajal y Mendoza was a peculiar character. A member on her mother's side of one of the most powerful families in Spain at the time, Luisa decided to abandon everything to lead a life of poverty, chastity, and devotion, rejecting both marriage and entry into a convent, which were the usual options for women in her position. Possessed by an enormous desire to suffer martyrdom, and taking advantage of Spain's recent peace treaty with England, in 1605 she decided to leave for London to convert its heretical inhabitants and help persecuted Catholics. Although arrested

---

[28] Tertullian (155–220 CE) was one of the main theorists of Christian martyrdom in the early Church.
[29] See L. Stephanie Cobb, *Dying to Be Men: Gender and Language in Early Christian Martyr Texts* (New York, 2008).

twice by the English authorities, she was promptly released thanks to her connections to the Spanish embassy. During the last years of her residence in London, Luisa devoted herself to organizing night expeditions to Tyburn, where Catholic priests used to be executed, to collect relics that she would then send to her contacts on the continent. Her desire for martyrdom was never realized, and in 1613 she died of natural causes in London.[30] Upon her death, her admirers were quick to describe her as a martyr, even requesting that a process of canonization be initiated.

Luisa de Carvajal could find ample support in a world of men because her project coincided with that of an influential sector of Catholicism in the late sixteenth century. In this sense, Luisa's case is neither unique nor an anomaly caused by her life experience but can be understood instead as the feminine version of militant Catholicism. Her correspondence reveals that Luisa de Carvajal identified herself completely and absolutely with the ideological position maintained by the English exiles and the most militant Spanish Catholic faction.[31] In the war against heresy there could be no compromise solutions or half measures. For the most militant English Catholics there were only two options: exile or martyrdom. As she fully identified with this attitude, Luisa self-exiled to England in the pursue of martyrdom.

A much more common way for many female religious to fulfill their burning desire for evangelization and martyrdom was to experience mystical flights and bilocations (the fact of being or the power to be in two places at the same time). The most famous of them all was María de Jesús de Ágreda (1602–1665), a Conceptionist nun, whose bilocations between Spain and New Mexico in the 1620s made her famous and a confidant of king Philip IV. Her mystical flights made María de Jesús keenly aware of the enormous diversity of peoples who existed in the world and the great number of them who did not know the Christian religion. This perception would cause her great sorrow, leading her to express a desire for martyrdom, a willingness to suffer "a thousand deaths" if this suffering would make the conversion of so many pagan peoples possible.[32]

---

[30] Glyn Redworth, *The She-Apostle: The Extraordinary Life and Death of Luisa de Carvajal* (Oxford, 2008).
[31] See *The Letters of Luisa de Carvajal y Mendoza*, trans. David McGrath and Glyn Redworth (London, 2012).
[32] See Cañeque, *Un imperio de mártires*, 279–93.

María de Ágreda was not unique. Many other female religious claimed to have similar experiences.[33] They inhabited a world that was global in scope. In the case of María de Ágreda, this may appear as startling, since she never left her hometown. But it is less surprising if we keep in mind that she grew up in a polity, the Spanish monarchy, which was conceptualized as a universal Catholic monarchy, and that this conceptualization took place at a time when Spanish and European mental horizons and geographical knowledge of the world had experienced an enormous expansion. In this context, it comes as no surprise that María de Ágreda wished to embrace the globe in the same way as royal officials and male members of the religious orders did. As women, they were largely excluded from traveling to faraway places to help in the conversion of their pagan inhabitants and suffer martyrdom; nor did they possess the influence and wealth of Luisa de Carvajal to be able to realize their ardent desires. But thanks to their mystical experiences, many nuns of the period were able to travel around the world without ever leaving their convents and, in this way, contribute to the defense of the Catholic religion and the Spanish empire. In many ways, all of these nuns' bilocations and mystical flights were the female response to the religious effervescence at the root of the early modern culture of martyrdom.

MARTYRS AND SAINTS

Despite the religious orders' arduous efforts, none of the early modern martyrs were canonized before the nineteenth century.[34] This is the great paradox of early modern sainthood. Although martyrs were the quintessential, original saints, it seems that martyrdom and canonization in the early modern period were inversely proportional: The more people were claimed to be martyrs, the more unlikely it was that they would be canonized, to the point that the intensity of the desire for martyrdom

---

[33] See the numerous examples mentioned by Jane Tar in "Flying Through the Empire: The Visionary Journeys of Early Modern Nuns," in *Women's Voices and the Politics of the Spanish Empire: From Convent Cell to Imperial Court*, ed. Jennifer L. Eich et al. (New Orleans, 2008), 263–302. Tar contends that these bilocations were propaganda devices developed by the Franciscan order and the Habsburg monarchy. But this phenomenon is too complex to simply reduce it to a matter of propaganda.

[34] The exception that proves the rule was Fidelis of Sigmaringen (1577–1622), a German Capuchin friar killed by Calvinists in present-day Switzerland and canonized in 1746. But this happened at a time when the ideal of martyrdom among Catholics had all but disappeared.

that characterized early modern Catholic societies appears to have completely precluded the canonization of any alleged martyr. This may, in part, be explained by the canonization process, which was extremely selective and laborious (see Chapter 7) and became still more so under the pontificate of Urban VIII, introducing, among many other requirements, a waiting period of fifty years after a candidate's death.[35] The Urban reforms also required that authors of hagiographical works, such as martyrdom narratives, include a "protestation" asserting that their use of the title of saint only reflected their own private opinion. It is worth noting that the title and honor of "martyr" was never regulated in the same way as those of "blessed" and "saint," therefore making canonization perhaps a less pressing an issue for martyrs. The thorny controversies in which many alleged martyrs became embroiled, which made the process still more cumbersome, might also help explain the lack of canonizations in the early modern period. In the case of the New World, however, it may have had more to do with concerns regarding the real cause of the martyrs' deaths and with the missions' lack of apostolic prestige.

But starting in the second half of the nineteenth century, things would change in a radical way. The martyrs of Nagasaki, who had been beatified in 1627, were at last canonized in 1862 by Pope Pius IX (1846–1878). A few years later, in 1867, this pontiff beatified another 205 martyrs of Japan. That same year, Pius IX also canonized the martyrs of Gorcum, beatified in 1675. With this spate of canonizations, Pius IX broke with a centuries-old tradition that had made it extremely difficult to achieve sainthood in the Catholic Church. He introduced an abbreviated process of canonization, which shortened it to only a few years. In addition, canonizations ceased to be highly individualized events.

Pius IX's canonization impetus would reach its climax in the twentieth century, with the hundreds of canonizations carried out by Pope John Paul II (1978–2005). He alone canonized 482 people, more than the total number of saints canonized by all of his predecessors together since the sixteenth century.[36] While Edmund Campion

---

[35] The only martyrs beatified (but not canonized) in the seventeenth century were the twenty-six martyrs of Nagasaki (1627), Josaphat Kuntsevych (1643), Pedro de Arbués (1664), and the martyrs of Gorcum (1675).

[36] Ufficio delle Celebrazioni Liturgiche del Sommo Pontefice. Canonizzazioni del Santo Padre Giovanni Paolo II (www.vatican.va/news_services/liturgy/saints/ELENCO_SANTI_GPII.htm). There were 82 beatifications and 52 canonizations between 1592 and 1799, and 532 beatifications and 211 canonizations between 1846 and 2009,

(executed in 1581), Henry Walpole (executed in 1595), and another thirty-eight English martyrs had been canonized by Paul VI in 1970, in 1987 John Paul II beatified another eighty-five individuals who had been executed by the English authorities between 1584 and 1679. He also canonized the three martyrs of Paraguay, who had been waiting for almost 400 years (they were killed in 1628). This pope also proceeded to abbreviate the process of canonization still further. His successor, Benedict XVI (2005–2013), continued this sanctifying push, which reached its culmination in 2013, when he announced the canonization of a group of 812 individuals, known as the martyrs of Otranto, who had been executed by Ottomans in 1480 after they had captured this Italian city.[37]

Pius IX and John Paul II, two of the greatest promoters of this avalanche of canonizations, had in common the fact that their pontificates were the longest in the history of the Catholic Church, thirty-two and twenty-seven years, respectively. This allowed them to leave an indelible mark on the Church. They also shared an extremely conservative and reactionary vision of the Catholic Church. Pius IX saw the Church and the Catholic faith immersed in a hostile world, besieged by impious enemies. He was the author of the famous *Syllabus errorum* (Syllabus of Errors) of 1864, which unequivocally condemned all the evils of the modern world: secularism, rationalism, nationalism, freemasonry, and socialism. It was precisely in the 1860s when, in the name of nationalism, the Catholic Church was deprived of the Papal States and of its primacy over the city of Rome, which became the capital of a recently unified Italy. Rather ironically, nationalism had appropriated the figure of the martyr for its own secular goals. In trying to revive the potent figure of the martyr, Pius IX undoubtedly was hoping to utilize the martyr's energizing power of centuries past to generate a spiritual rebirth, which would be used to reassert the primacy of both the Church

---

and 80 of these canonizations alone took place during the papacy of John Paul II. See Robert J. Barro, Rachel M. McCleary, and Alexander McQuoid, "The Economics of Sainthood (A Preliminary Investigation)," in *The Oxford Handbook of the Economics of Religion*, ed. Rachel M. McCleary (Oxford, 2001), 191–216.

[37] They were, in fact, canonized by Francis, since Benedict announced their canonization on the same day that he stepped down from the papacy: Lizzy Davies, "Pope Francis Completes Contentious Canonisation of Otranto Martyrs," *Guardian*, May 12, 2013, www.theguardian.com/world/2013/may/12/pope-francis-canonise-otranto-martyrs. Pope Francis will also go down in history for having given his blessing to the swift canonization of John Paul II, which took place barely nine years after his death.

and the papacy in modern societies.³⁸ Both John Paul II and Benedict XVI saw the problems of the late twentieth and early twenty-first century and their solutions in rather similar terms.³⁹

Although it could certainly be argued that this multiplication of saints and *beati* represents a democratization of sainthood, it could just as easily and more plausibly be contended that such a proliferation constitutes instead an extraordinary banalization of the notion of sanctity. In the sixteenth and seventeenth centuries, the presumption was always that saints and martyrs were exceptional, unique individuals, endowed with heroic characteristics, which, by definition, made the existence of large numbers of them impossible during this period. What early modern and modern canonizations and beatifications do have in common is their controversial character and their politicization. But unlike contemporary martyrs and saints, most of whom are often rather inconsequential and whose names few people remember, because cults for those saints and martyrs do not really exist, in the sixteenth and seventeenth centuries, canonizations could have an enormous societal impact. The notion of martyrdom proved a great mobilizing force for the members of religious orders. Yet, as the experience of early modern Catholicism proved, the martyrs' dynamic power is only effective in a society dominated by great religious fervor. It is not the cult of martyrs that revives flagging religious fervor, as Pius IX and John Paul II seemed to believe, but rather religious fervor that endows the figure of the martyr with energizing power. In this respect, it can be argued that the effects of the prodigious, ultimately anonymizing multiplication of saints in the modern era have achieved the opposite of papal aims. By devaluing their heroic uniqueness, martyrs and saints have been deprived of their appeal.⁴⁰

---

[38] Hans de Valk, "History Canonized: The Martyrs of Gorcum between Dutch Nationalism and Roman Universalism," in *More than a Memory: The Discourse of Martyrdom and the Construction of Christian Identity in the History of Christianity*, ed. Johan Leemans (Leuven, 2005), 387–89; Eamon Duffy, *Saints and Sinners: A History of the Popes* (New Haven, CT, 2006), 286–305.

[39] Duffy, *Saints and Sinners*, 369–96.

[40] In 1989, Joseph Ratzinger, the future Benedict XVI, had already shown his concern with this proliferation of saints, *beati*, and martyrs, by wondering whether any of them might be of any relevance to the faithful. See Duffy, *Saints and Sinners*, 378. However, as pope, Ratzinger would follow in John Paul II's footsteps.

3 Female Saints

REBECA SANMARTÍN BASTIDA

Female sanctity in the Counter-Reformation is usually considered to have been inspired by the models of Catherine of Siena (1347–1380) and Teresa of Ávila (1515–82). Whereas the Italian Dominican tertiary presented a model of late medieval penitential and prophetical sanctity, the Spanish Discalced Carmelite symbolized a new paradigm imposed after the Council of Trent (1545–63), which exalted the contemplative and cloistered life for women. Indeed, Teresa of Ávila, canonized in 1622, has dominated the Counter-Reformation landscape, supposedly creating a new global model of sanctity for other women to follow. Her main works – her autobiographical *Vida* (or Life) and the spiritual treatises – were first published in 1588, shortly after her death, and went through numerous editions in Spain and beyond. As a reformer of a religious order and founder of convents, Teresa opened up routes to sanctity, particularly for enclosed nuns, which stood alongside other avenues such as charitable and educational missions.

The new Teresian model coexisted for a while with the older one set by Catherine of Siena and developed by pre-Tridentine *sante vive*, first studied by Gabriella Zarri.[1] These Italian "living saints" of the second half of the fifteenth century and the first half of the sixteenth had developed a paradigm of extreme fasting, stigmata, revelations, and prophecy, the latter often closely connected to contemporary politics.[2] While the focus in Italy has been on the evolution of this model prior to Trent, studies on Spanish female sanctity – represented by the Teresian model – usually start from Teresa's canonization to analyze her many imitators, leaving a significant temporal and geographical gap.

---

[1] Gabriella Zarri, *Le sante vive: Profezie di corte e devozione femminile tra '400 e '500* (Turin, 1990); Gabriella Zarri, "Living Saints: A Typology of Female Sanctity in the Early Sixteenth Century," in *Women and Religion in Medieval and Renaissance Italy*, ed. Daniel Bornstein and Roberto Rusconi (Chicago, 1992), 219–303.

[2] See, e.g., Tamar Herzig, *Savonarola's Women: Visions and Reform in Renaissance Italy* (Chicago, 2007).

Much recent scholarship has demonstrated that the Counter-Reformation was not a monolith. This chapter reveals the existence of an overlooked "intermediate" model, which operated after Trent and before Teresa's canonization. This model, represented by a group of Castilian visionary women between 1450 and 1550, partially corresponds to the Italian model of *sante vive*. Influenced by the Sienese saint and her Italian imitators, the Spanish living saints manifested the same supernatural gifts or charisms as the *sante vive*, though they also spoke in tongues. Like their Italian counterparts, they played a political role, maintaining a close relationship with the Spanish royal court while actively participating in religious reform. Many were initially tertiaries and initiated the enclosure of the female branch of their respective religious orders with the support of the papacy, the Spanish monarchy, and the nobility. Unlike the Italian *sante vive*, until very recently none of their Spanish counterparts had been beatified or canonized – a situation that changed only in 2024. The most famous, and about whom we are best informed, were the Hieronymite María de Ajofrín (1455?–1489); the Franciscans María de Toledo (1437–1507), Juana Rodríguez (d. 1505), and Juana de la Cruz (1481–1534); and the Dominicans María de Santo Domingo (1486?–1524) and Leonor Venegas (d. 1556). These mostly illiterate women received revelations that were recorded by their confessors or companions during or shortly after their lifetime, although only three of those works are extant.[3] Particularly significant for this chapter are María de Ajofrín and Juana de la Cruz, whose beatification process was reopened in 1986 and successfully completed on November 25, 2024.

Foregrounding the cults of these Spanish living saints sheds new light on the shifting paradigms of female sanctity, both in Teresa's homeland and beyond. The women just identified maintained a reputation as saints supported not only by popular devotions but also by publications approved by post-Tridentine civil and ecclesiastical authorities. Their *Vidas* were summarized, glossed, and adapted to fit the new religious climate; the life of Juana de la Cruz was even translated and disseminated abroad. The rewriting of these lives between 1588 (when canonization resumed after the Reformation) and 1625

---

[3] For English versions, see *Mother Juana de la Cruz, 1481–1534: Visionary Sermons*, ed. Jessica Boon and Ronald Surtz (Toronto, 2016); Mary E. Giles, *The Book of Prayer of Sor María de Santo Domingo: A Study and Translation* (Albany, 1990); Borja Gama de Cossío and María José Faedo Álvarez, *The Revelations of María de Santo Domingo: A Study and Translation* (London, 2023).

(when the first new rules against unlicensed cults were brought in) shows how conceptions of female sanctity were changing before Teresa gave the final impulse and emerged as the new paradigm.[4] In other words, this posthumous process of rewriting is hugely revealing, not of the Spanish living saints themselves but of the new model of female sanctity as it emerged after Trent.

AN INTERMEDIATE MODEL

Alonso de Villegas's multi-volume *Flos sanctorum* (1578–1602) was the first Counter-Reformation compilation of saints' lives to appear in Spanish. An instant bestseller, the work was translated into several languages.[5] The third volume, published in 1588, included some of the Castilian living saints mentioned above as part of a group of so-called extravagant saints, those who did not appear in the Roman Breviary: among them, María de Ajofrín and Juana de la Cruz.[6] While the text alludes to Maria da Visitação (b. 1551), a contemporary Portuguese woman with a reputation for sanctity, the recently deceased Teresa of Ávila was nowhere mentioned. Some years afterward, in 1596 Juan de Marieta included Juana in his history of Spanish saints, and Juan Carrillo did the same in his 1613 history of Franciscan saints.[7]

From the mid-sixteenth century onward, these visionary women also appeared in chronicles of religious orders that highlighted their cult, their incorrupt bodies, and their postmortem miracles. Such monastic chronicles proliferated after Trent, and much space was devoted to María de Ajofrín and Juana de la Cruz, as the works by Juan de la Cruz (1591), José de Sigüenza (1605), and Pedro de Salazar

---

[4] Some of the sources discussed in this chapter can be consulted in the "Catalogue of Living Saints," a collection of manuscript and printed lives of Castilian living saints. For an introduction to this tool, see Pablo Acosta-García and Rebeca Sanmartín Bastida, "Digital Visionary Women: Introducing the 'Catalogue of Living Saints,'" *Journal of Medieval Iberian Studies* 14, no. 1 (2022): 55–68. The catalogue can be accessed via http://visionarias.es/en/.

[5] Francisco Javier Burguillo López, "El éxito editorial del *Flos sanctorum* de Alonso de Villegas frente al control de la literatura hagiográfica después de Trento," in *Los agentes de la censura en la España de los siglos XVI y XVII*, ed. Mathilde Albisson (Berlin, 2022), 303–40, at 307–8.

[6] Alonso de Villegas, *Adición a la Tercera parte del Flos sanctorum* (Huesca, 1588), fols. 45v–47r (María de Ajofrín), 63r–65v (Juana de la Cruz).

[7] Juan de Marieta, *Historia eclesiástica de todos los santos de España: Tercera parte* (Cuenca, 1596), fol. 85r–v; Juan Carrillo, *Segunda parte de la Historia de los santos y personas en virtud y santidad ilustres de la Tercera Orden del glorioso Padre San Francisco* (Zaragoza, 1613), 258–325.

(1612) demonstrate.[8] In this format, these Spanish living saints reached a wider European audience: an Italian version of Villegas's hagiography of Juana appeared in a Franciscan chronicle published in 1608, which in turn was translated into French the following year.[9] Another means of hagiographic dissemination was the inclusion of these figures in local histories: María, for example, was considered one of the most famous people from Toledo.[10] Thus, just as with the Italian *sante vive*, a number of lives that had already circulated in manuscript form now reached a wider audience at the end of the sixteenth century.[11] Some living saints also received individual attention: Antonio Daza's lives of Juana (1610 and 1613) were republished and translated between 1614 and 1626 into Italian, German, French, and English.[12] *Vidas* of Juana by Daza and Pedro Navarro (which appeared in 1622) made a huge impact in the Americas.[13] María de Ajofrín and Juana de la Cruz, in particular, acted as imitative models for later nuns, and several devotional images circulated at the time.[14] Between 1604 and 1621, they were repeatedly claimed as saints by renowned poets and they were the

[8] Juan de la Cruz, *Historia de la Orden de S. Hierónimo* ... (El Escorial, MS. &.-II-19), 258v–267v; José de Sigüenza, *Tercera parte de la Historia de la Orden de San Jerónimo* (Madrid, 1605), 465–97; Pedro de Salazar, *Corónica y historia de la fundación y progreso de la Provincia de Castilla de la Orden del bienaventurado Padre San Francisco* (Madrid, 1612), 511–46.

[9] Barezzo Barezzi, *Delle croniche dell'ordine de' frati minori instituito dal serafico P. S. Francesco: Parte Quarta* (Venezia, 1608), 156–69; *Quatrième partie des Chroniques des Frères Mineurs* (Paris, 1609), 159–71.

[10] Pedro de Alcocer, *Historia, o descripción de la imperial ciudad de Toledo* (Toledo, 1554), 114v; Francisco de Pisa, *Descripción de la imperial ciudad de Toledo e Historia de sus antigüedades y grandeza y cosas memorables que en ella han acontecido* (Toledo, 1605), fols. 275r, 276v.

[11] Zarri, "Living Saints," 225.

[12] Antonio Daza, *Historia, vida y milagros, éxtasis y revelaciones de la bienaventurada virgen santa Juana de la Cruz* (Madrid, 1610), amended edition 1613. For the translations, see Isabel Ibáñez, "La historia desmemoriada: Sor Juana de la Cruz y la cruzada antiprotestante. Historia y avatares de una santidad de circunstancia," in *El hombre histórico y su puesta en discurso en el Siglo de Oro*, ed. J. Enrique Duarte and Isabel Ibáñez (New York, 2015), 65–77.

[13] Pedro Navarro, *Favores del Rey del Cielo hechos a su esposa la Santa Juana de la Cruz* (Madrid, 1622); Margarita Paz Torres, *Dos visionarias del Virreino del Perú en el siglo XVII: Edición del proceso de fe de las religiosas de Santa Clara de Trujillo* (London, 2021), 69–80.

[14] See Toledo, Monasterio de Jerónimas A.J.T ª. San Pablo, MS I-33, fols. 221–23; Alonso de Torres, *Chrónica de la santa Provincia de Granada, de la regular observancia de N. Seráfico Padre San Francisco* (Madrid, 1683), 638; Inocente García de Andrés, *El Conhorte: Sermones de una mujer. La Santa Juana (1481–1534)*, vol. 1 (Salamanca, 1999), 118–28; Jesús Gómez López, "Juana de la Cruz (1481–1534) 'La Santa Juana': Vida, obra, santidad y causa," in *La clausura femenina en España: Actas del*

subjects of devotional plays, which were attended by the monarchy and nobility.[15]

After 1625, however, the number of hagiographic accounts contracted dramatically. New Roman rules on unauthorized cults negatively impacted these devotions, from which their later, posthumous rival, the recently canonized Teresa, was exempt. Although attempts to beatify Juana de la Cruz continued, even her cult gradually diminished in size. The intermediate model thus declined and landed in a historiographical blind spot, unnoticed either by medievalists or by early modernists preoccupied by Teresa. Yet the importance of these holy women was nevertheless obvious to contemporaries, as was the connection they helped form between the earlier Italian model, presented by Catherine of Siena and the *sante vive*, and the emerging Teresian model.[16] In 1613, for instance, one of Teresa's confessors, Jerónimo Gracián, placed Juana and Teresa in a genealogy of holy female writers.[17] Years later, the two women continued to be paired as saints, even appearing together with the new Peruvian saint Rose of Lima (1586–1617, can. 1671).[18]

Before 1625, during the gradual emergence of the Teresian model, it seems that chroniclers and hagiographers made the most of the vibrant popular cults of Juana and others to convey Tridentine ideas, though suppressing their more controversial features. If in Italy Serafino of Fermo had proposed a sanctity based more on virtue than on prophecy or revelations as early as 1535, and in Spain a spiritualist heretical movement, *alumbradismo*, had begun to arouse suspicions toward visionaries from the 1520s onward, it comes as no surprise

---

Simposium (II): 1/4-IX-2004, ed. Francisco Javier Campos and Fernández de Sevilla (San Lorenzo del Escorial, 2004), 1246–47.

[15] Manuel García Martín, "Compañías y repertorios teatrales en la Salamanca áurea," in *Praestans labore Victor: Homenaje al profesor Víctor García de la Concha*, ed. Javier San José Lera (Salamanca, 2005), 141– 61, at 152; Miguel Zugasti, "Santidad bajo sospecha: La vida de Sor Juana de la Cruz (1481–1534) en florilegios de santos, crónicas y escenarios del Siglo de Oro," in *Hommage à André Gallego: La transmission de savoirs licites ou illicites dans le monde hispanique péninsulaire (XIIe au XVIIe siècles)*, ed. Luis González Fernández and Teresa Rodríguez (Toulouse, 2011), 339–67, at 356–61.

[16] For a comparison between Catherine and María de Ajofrín, see Villegas, *Adición*, fol. 46v. Between Catherine and Juana de la Cruz: Daza, *Historia* (1610), fol. 24v; (1613), fols. 13v, 14v, 15v (preliminary pages), 251; Navarro, *Favores*, 193, 524. Between Teresa and Juana: Navarro, *Favores*, 28, 43, 131, 803 (together with Catherine).

[17] See Jerónimo Gracián, "Diálogos sobre su espíritu," in Ana de San Bartolomé, *Obras completas*, ed. Julián Urkiza (Burgos, 1998), 265–323, at 317; García de Andrés, *El Conhorte*, 123.

[18] Paz Torres, *Dos visionarias*, 68–82.

that a reformulation became necessary after Trent.[19] By the 1540s, visions and apparitions gradually fell victim to official suspicion, and lay people were afraid to report them due to increasing inquisitorial scrutiny. Mistrust of miraculous phenomena progressively intensified, and the Church preferred to engage with postmortem miracles, which were easier to analyze.[20] Contributing to this distrust was a growing tendency to subject the supernatural to rational and empirical analysis.[21]

The biographers of the Spanish living saints working between 1588 and 1625 set about a common task, to keep a model of sanctity alive and within the bounds of this evolving orthodoxy, even if their project aroused some anxiety. The study of what they added and omitted from pre-Tridentine manuscript and printed sources demonstrates that the following phenomena were increasingly becoming problematic by the turn of the seventeenth century: revelations, premortem miracles, stigmata, and prophecies; independence from the clergy and non-enclosure; extreme asceticism; and classification as saints. These issues raised difficulties for these authors and stimulated arguments against new, stricter definitions of the sacred. Hagiographers struggled to combine the prestige of their religious orders and the popular devotions these cults attracted, with the new sensibilities and priorities emerging after Trent. Although each author's motivations and understanding of sanctity might vary, their shared interest was to adapt ongoing and preexisting devotions to new more stringent policies.

Some hagiographers such as Sigüenza left more room for the supernatural than others like Salazar, but the general tone is a certain ambivalence toward the miracles reported in their sources. It is significant that the crucifixion that María de Ajofrín suffered in one of her mystical experiences was crossed out in the earlier surviving manuscript copy of her life, probably by one of the authors who consulted the text but omitted this incident from their own writings. (Whether

---

[19] Zarri, "Living Saints," 251. For an overview of *alumbradismo*, see Jessica Fowler, "Assembling Alumbradismo: The Evolution of a Heretical Construct," in *After Conversion: Iberia and the Emergence of Modernity*, ed. Mercedes García-Arenal (Leiden, 2016), 251–82.

[20] William A. Christian, Jr., *Apparitions in Late Medieval and Renaissance Spain* (Princeton, NJ, 1981), 183. See also Simon Ditchfield, "Tridentine Worship and the Cult of Saints," in *The Cambridge History of Christianity: Reform and Expansion, 1500–1660*, ed. Ronald Po-chia Hsia (Cambridge, 2007), 201–24, at 209, 213. On holy bodies, see also Chapter 10 in this volume.

[21] See Fernando Vidal, "Miracles, Science, and Testimony in Post-Tridentine Saint-Making," *Science in Context* 20, no. 3 (2007): 481–508.

this was Villegas, Juan de la Cruz, or Sigüenza is impossible to say.²²) The new emphasis on the quality rather than the quantity of the miracles is exemplified by a telling comment by Bishop Francisco Sosa, a member of the Council of the Spanish Inquisition. In a preface authorizing the publication of the 1613 *Vida* of Juana de la Cruz, Sosa claimed that the multitude of miracles should not be used to calculate the extent of sanctity."²³ Hagiographers defended the sanctity of these women while diminishing the miraculous. When the supernatural does appear, it is frequently supported by documentary proof. This emphasis on "truthful" miracles further justified the deletions, as Villegas and Juan de la Cruz stated and showed. Sigüenza situated himself between the credulous and the sceptics in his life of María de Ajofrín: "although I am not one of the very incredulous or those who laugh at all these visions and revelations ... I am not one of those who believes it all and craves a miracle for any little thing."²⁴

In the case of Juana de la Cruz, a number of impressive episodes originally recorded by her fellow nuns disappeared from later accounts: Juana's exorcism of a girl (controversial, no doubt, also because it transgressed gender roles) is removed in the versions of her life by Villegas, Marieta, and Salazar; and the same happens with Juana's resurrection of a child in Salazar's account. Similarly problematic was the narrative of Juana's rosary beads, which she allegedly had received from her guardian angel and which had been blessed by God.²⁵ The fervor for these beads even extended to the highest levels of society, as Pope Clement VIII, Philip II, and Philip III and his wife all possessed some.²⁶ Here popular devotion, an eagerness for relics to obtain divine assistance, and the opinion of some inquisitors (who were called "scrupulous" in the prefatory material of many hagiographies) collided, which was a reason for the censorship of the 1610 edition of Daza's hagiography.²⁷ Salazar, who was a *calificador* (theological consultant) for the Council of the Inquisition, began his hagiography in 1612 by distancing himself from Daza. Unlike his predecessor, Salazar did not mention the beads and no longer called Juana "saint," but rather a "servant of God," the standard

---

[22] El Escorial, MS C-III-3, 198v; Villegas, *Adición*, 46r-v; Juan de la Cruz, *Historia*, 259r.
[23] Daza, *Historia* (1613), fol. 12r (preliminaries).
[24] Sigüenza, *Tercera parte*, 465.
[25] Madrid, Biblioteca Nacional de España, MS 9661, fols. 32r-v, 39v, 44r. This episode is not recorded by Villegas, Marieta, or Salazar.
[26] Carrillo, *Segunda parte*, 294.
[27] For the term "scruples" and "scrupulous," see Daza, *Historia* (1613), IV, 8r-9v, 11r, 16v (preliminaries), and Navarro, *Favores*, fols. ¶¶4v-5r.

title for a candidate for sainthood.²⁸ Daza's hagiography was also amended in 1613 and a justification of Juana's beads by Bishop Sosa was added.²⁹ In his new edition, Daza changed "santa" for "sor" in the title, reduced both the miracles related to the souls in Purgatory and the nun's priestly role, expanded the sources and testimonies to reinforce the veracity of the narrative, and made Juana a devotee of official cults. After Rome dismissed the beads' supernatural origin in 1617, Juana's next hagiographer, Navarro, inserted long theological justifications to bolster her divine revelations.³⁰

The gradual decline of the supernatural element in these published lives also affected the living saints' encounters with images, which did not come to life as often as they had done in earliest sources.³¹ A prominent example of this change is the successive treatment of the veil of Veronica in the hagiographies of Juana de la Cruz, even if the speaking veil shows that the decline of the supernatural had limits, partly for confessional reasons. In the original manuscript source, the image of Christ imprinted on the cloth came alive to speak aloud to Juana "with very sweet and loving words."³² Yet in Salazar's life the miraculous speech of the Veronica is no longer reported.³³ When the episode was rewritten by Navarro ten years later, he discussed theologically how the transfiguration of the Veronica into a miraculous speaking object could have taken place.³⁴

The treatment of stigmata is another clear sign of a gradual paradigm shift. Numerous episodes were tackled with varying degrees of suspicion. In the case of María de Ajofrín, Villegas felt forced to defend the Hieronymite's stigmata in ways previous authors had not. He cited Rome's support for the pictorial representation of Catherine of Siena's wounds, included an official affidavit testifying to the reality of María's stigmata, and pointed to the similar experience of the aforementioned Maria da Visitação.³⁵ However, after the Portuguese nun was exposed as

---

²⁸ Salazar, Corónica, 511.
²⁹ Daza, Historia (1613), fols. 15v–16v (preliminaries). There is also a justification in Carrillo, Segunda parte, 290–99; Navarro, Favores, 436–95.
³⁰ Zugasti, "Santidad," 343, 354; Navarro, Favores, 64–69.
³¹ Sigüenza, Tercera parte, 499; Rebeca Sanmartín Bastida, Staging Authority: Spanish Visionary Women and Images (1450–1550) (Alessandria, 2023).
³² El Escorial, MS K-III-13, fol. 10r.
³³ Salazar, Corónica, 517.
³⁴ Navarro, Favores, 106–7.
³⁵ Villegas, Adición, 46v–47r; Alessandra Bartolomei Romagnoli, "La controversia sulla stimmate di Caterina da Siena," in Santità e mistica femminile nel Medioevo (Spoleto, 2013), 681–721, at 715–19.

an imposter, Villegas removed this allusion in a later edition, and in several extant copies of the 1588 version the text was crossed out or covered.[36] Another example of a crossed-out allusion to the stigmata found in a manuscript of María de Santo Domingo's *Revelations* corroborates the growing distrust toward this type of charism, which had once been an essential part of Catherine of Siena's political and prophetic career.[37] In the case of Juana de la Cruz, the stigmata seemed to have been less problematic because they disappeared at her request, not to draw attention to herself – the sort of skillful act of humility for which Teresa of Ávila would later become famous.[38]

Similarly, prophecies and visions ceased to be a prominent feature in post-Tridentine narratives. Some manuscript revelations were still in circulation: We know from Salazar and Juan López that Juana Rodríguez's and Leonor Venegas's remained accessible.[39] Letters dictated by María de Ajofrín seem to have existed at some point, but they disappeared during this period, as did the revelations of María de Toledo.[40] In the case of María de Santo Domingo, a striking silence surrounds her ecstatic discourses (probably because her figure was controversial during her lifetime) despite the fact that some had been printed around 1518. Even if the continued circulation of manuscript copies of Juana de la Cruz's visionary sermons attested to her fame and reputation, later hagiographies sometimes failed to mention her *Libro de Conorte*, which had become problematic due to its detailed theological discussions in the vernacular.[41] Juana's role as preacher and theologian was thus downplayed. Instead, Salazar's chronicle and

---

[36] María del Mar Cortés Timoner, "Censuras, silencios y magisterio femenino en la *Adición* a la tercera parte del *Flos Sanctorum* de Alonso de Villegas," *Specula: Revista de Humanidades y Espiritualidad* 1 (2021): 183–210, at 200.

[37] Sevilla, Biblioteca Capitular y Colombina de Sevilla, MS 57-3-21, 246r; Alessandra Bartolomei Romagnoli, "Rappresentazioni della santità mistica prima e dopo il Concilio di Trento," in *Immagini e arte sacra nel Concilio di Trento*, ed. Lydia Salviucci Insolera (Roma, 2016), 51–70, at 69. See also Tamar Herzig, "Genuine and Fraudulent Stigmatics in the Sixteenth Century," in *Dissimulation and Deceit in Early Modern Europe*, ed. Miriam Eliav-Feldon and Tamar Herzig (London, 2015), 142–64; Carolyn Muessig, *The Stigmata in Medieval and Early Modern Europe* (Oxford, 2020), esp. 239–43.

[38] El Escorial, MS K-III-13, fols. 38v–39r.

[39] Salazar, *Corónica*, 367; Juan López, *Tercera parte de la Historia general de Santo Domingo y de su Orden de Predicadores* (Valladolid, 1613), 234–35.

[40] El Escorial, MS C-III-3, fols. 199v–200v; Tomás Tamayo de Vargas, *Vida de Doña María de Toledo, señora de Pinto, y después Sor María la Pobre* (Toledo, 1616), fols. 22v–23r.

[41] García de Andrés, *El Conhorte*, 94–100.

Marieta's and Carrillo's histories of saints all emphasized her penitential practices. Of the post-Tridentine hagiographers, Navarro gave the most prominence to Juana's visionary sermons, but even he presented himself as the authoritative theologian who interpreted a simple woman's visions.[42]

The prominent relationship between Spanish visionaries and the royal court also declined when laypeople could no longer enter convents and nuns' enclosure was more strictly enforced. Salazar and Navarro took advantage of the conversion of Juana's *beaterio* (lay religious community) into a convent to criticize the previous lack of cloistering.[43] Women with reputations for sanctity were no longer summoned to court to prophesy, nor did they fall into rapture in front of a noble audience. With their forced enclosure in convents, their role in the sacralization of the secular space disappeared. As a result, post-Tridentine biographies of living saints barely mentioned the court and downplayed the relationship with the monarchy.[44] That said, the women continued to be co-opted in the religious struggles of the present. Instead of avid supporters of the Inquisition's persecution of crypto-Jews, the living saints were refashioned into precursors to the contemporary struggles against Protestantism.[45]

The process of rewriting inevitably also diminished women's religious autonomy and removed their notable criticism of the clergy. In this sense, the Spanish case confirms the Counter-Reformation shift in female sanctity "from prophecy to discipline" identified by Gabriella Zarri.[46] The living saints were noted for their humility and obedience.[47] At the same time, the extreme rigor of their asceticism was moderated. For instance, Navarro criticized Juana for her penitential undressing before the cross and emphasized the need for submission to male authorities by adding qualifications not found in his original sources,

---

[42] See Navarro, *Favores*, 325–36.

[43] Salazar, *Corónica*, 541; Navarro, *Favores*, 42–43.

[44] For an episode of María de Ajofrín in relation with the Queen that was silenced after Trent, see El Escorial, MS C-III-3, fols. 195v–196r. For the depiction of an apolitical María de Santo Domingo, see Rebeca Sanmartín Bastida, "María de Santo Domingo, desde Aldeanueva," *Archivio Italiano per la Storia della Pietà* 33 (2020): 119–41.

[45] Salamanca, Archivo Dominicano de la Provincia de España, MS D/A/ALD/1, fol. 1v; Daza, *Historia* (1610), fols. ¶¶1v, 37v; (1613), fols. 27v, 44r. Navarro, *Favores*, 13, 20, 101, 391, 440.

[46] Gabriella Zarri, "From Prophecy to Discipline, 1450–1650," in *Women and Faith: Catholic Religious Life in Italy from Late Antiquity to the Present*, ed. Lucetta Scaraffia and Gabriella Zarri (Cambridge, MA, 1999), 83–112.

[47] See, for example, Navarro, *Favores*, 133–34, 162–63.

playing up the control of Juana's confessor over the frequency of her communion.⁴⁸

Notwithstanding these changes, these visionary women were still presented as saints with reference to the cult they generated and the incorruptible status of their bodies after death. The 1625 decrees forbidding unlicensed cults would threaten burial sites as spaces of veneration. Until then, their graves had been showered with honors. Writing on Juana in 1596, Marieta noted that the living saint's body was "placed up high in the same convent of nuns, where it is venerated."⁴⁹ Some hagiographers also persisted in calling them "saints" in the sense of those to whom virtues or marvels "proper only" to saints were attributed.⁵⁰ As late as 1622, Navarro, following Bishop Sosa's suggestion, sought a middle ground by referring to his subject not as "saint (*santa*) Juana" as before, but as "*the* saint Juana," which in his view recognized that Juana was as yet uncanonized but also that she was commonly referred by that title.⁵¹

The editing and re-editing of these women's lives therefore proves that the new model of female sanctity was a negotiated process, which navigated the twin demands of propaganda and censure. The endurance of these cults, often for a century or more after a living saint's death and for decades after the closing of the Council of Trent, shows the vibrancy of this model of visionary and charismatic holiness, which forced hagiographers to grapple with evolving norms around female sanctity. Navarro's life of Juana, seeking her beatification, appeared in the year of Teresa's canonization. In 1630, the papacy recognized the heroic nature of Juana's virtues, an important step in the process.⁵² But in spite of these attempts, and the support of religious orders and local devotion, Spanish living saints were unable to preserve their social standing and holy status in the new post-Teresa era. As we shall see, Teresa's swift canonization played an important part in this process, providing an officially sanctioned outlet for popular devotions, but so too did the new Roman rules introduced between 1625 and 1634.⁵³ When the term "saint" became more restrictive, the women studied here could no longer be presented as holy models to imitate. A complex and rich

---

⁴⁸ See ibid., 96–97, 132, 142–44, 182–93.
⁴⁹ Marieta, *Historia*, fol. 85v.
⁵⁰ Tamayo de Vargas, *Vida*, iv.
⁵¹ Daza, *Historia* (1613), fol. 9r.
⁵² García de Andrés, *El Conhorte*, 141.
⁵³ Miguel Gotor, *I beati del papa: Santità, Inquisizione, e obbedienza in età moderna* (Florence, 2002).

genealogy of would-be female saints, in Spain but also elsewhere, with the new rules became reduced to the two models of Catherine and Teresa, one fading, the other only just emerging.

Both the extent of this erasure and its implications can best be captured by a remarkable passage from Sigüenza's life of María de Ajofrín, which merits quotation:

> For a little over two hundred years, there have been some holy women with whom it seems that Our Lord has wanted ... to change his approach by making himself so available to them and of so easy communication that one can do nothing but shrug one's shoulders.... In addition to this (which also stings greatly), it seems that he has wanted to make an exception to his Apostle [Paul]'s rule, which disallows women from teaching in the Church, and he has permitted (as some say) these holy women to leave behind many letters and large books of revelations and teachings for the instruction of the faithful, something that we have never seen nor beheld among any of the most holy females who have flourished for the past thousand years and on.... We must swallow all of these reports, and proceed through everything with submission.[54]

Sigüenza's comments show the importance of the living saints as a group and as a model, but they also betray some reticence toward the fact that God had enabled women to defy Paul's prohibition and teach the faithful. This recognition of the living saints as authors of spiritual works can be read as an introduction to the model with which I will deal next. While the visions of her predecessors have perished, those of Teresa of Ávila have inspired readers for centuries.

THE TERESIAN MODEL

Between her death in 1582 and her canonization in 1622, the cult of Teresa was pushed as strategically as the intermediate model I charted above. Gracián justified devotees praying to the still uncanonized Teresa based on their private belief that she was in Heaven, just as Bishop Sosa had defended the informal use of the title "saint" for Juana de la Cruz.[55] Teresa's beatification (1614) and swift canonization heralded the public arrival of a model of sanctity that, even if it showed continuities with the earlier paradigm, represented a change: that of the

---

[54] Sigüenza, *Tercera parte*, 466.
[55] Daza, *Historia* (1613), fols. 5r–6r (preliminaries); Gracián, "Diálogos," 303.

literate mystic rather than the illiterate visionary. It is also telling that three of the five women canonized in the seventeenth century (Teresa of Ávila, Maria Maddalena de' Pazzi, and Rose of Lima) were depicted as enclosed mystical guides as well as models of monastic and ascetic life, even if Rose was not a professed nun.[56] As Clare Copeland has observed, enclosure made their brand of mysticism safe, even worthy of promotion.[57]

The new model of female mysticism was embedded within new reform movements. Teresa had been very familiar with the mystical treatises of her time and was surely influenced by the spiritual environment of her hometown, Ávila, which, along with Toledo, was the city from which most of the Spanish living saints hailed.[58] With Teresa, however, a private mysticism – emerging from practices of interior prayer and spirituality shaped by the *devotio moderna* – replaced the public performance of ecstasy.[59] Even though the woman's body became more than ever a spectacle in art and literature, female ecstatic experiences were now to be found in solitude.[60] The contents of the visions also changed. Prophecy was less significant. The emphasis on Church reform and doctrinal theology, and the help given to souls in Purgatory, diminished. Instead, cultivating inner union with the divine was the goal.

With the arrival of the Teresian model we can thus identify four principal shifts in Spain, which may well hold true more widely. First, visions were no longer publicly observed and recorded by witnesses. Second, extreme asceticism became less common. Third, visions ceased to be vehicles for comprehensive ecclesiastical reform. (While Teresa was a reformer of her religious order, she did not call for reform of the

---

[56] For the construction of Rose of Lima's sanctity, see Kathryn Ann Myers, *Neither Saints nor Sinners: Writing the Lives of Women in Spanish America* (Oxford, 2003), 23–43; and Frank Graziano, *The Wounds of Love: The Mystical Marriage of Saint Rose of Lima* (Oxford, 2004), 33–66. For Maddalena de' Pazzi, see Clare Copeland, *Maria Maddalena de' Pazzi: The Making of a Counter-Reformation Saint* (Oxford, 2016).

[57] Clare Copeland, "Sanctity," in *The Ashgate Research Companion to the Counter-Reformation*, ed. Alexandra Bamji et al. (Farnham, 2013), 225–41, at 234. For another view on female confinement, see Elizabeth Lehfeldt, *Religious Women in Golden Age Spain: The Permeable Cloister* (Aldershot, 2005).

[58] Jodi Bilinkoff, *The Avila of Saint Teresa: Religious Reform in a Sixteenth-Century City* (Ithaca, NY, 2014).

[59] For the development of Spanish mysticism starting from the living saints, see Bernard McGinn, *Mysticism in the Golden Age of Spain, 1500–1650* (New York, 2017).

[60] Bartolomei Romagnoli, "Rappresentazioni," 64–70.

Church as a whole.) Finally, there was notable decline in political activity and charisms such as stigmata.

Teresa's difficulties with the Inquisition are well known. In death, her model of sanctity faced similar obstacles. As with the living saints before her, Teresa had strategically cultivated a rhetoric of feminine weakness to counteract male surveillance.[61] But a certain gender fluidity worked in her favor: Accusations of gender usurpation were eventually useful to her cause. Hagiographic accounts emphasized her manly role as an active founder of convents, which seemed to confirm her own counsel not "to be like women but like strong men."[62] Teresa embodied the double aspect of the Counter-Reformation saint: passive in the face of her ecstatic experiences before God but active in reforming her order and founding convents, at a time when such expansion was urgently needed.[63] She swiftly became a national symbol, supported by the Spanish monarchy, which rendered one last service to the earlier model through Juana de la Cruz, when Philip IV's wife, Isabella of Bourbon, visited her convent in 1622, the year of Teresa's canonization.[64]

Teresa's triumph in that year marked a major change, even if it was already underway, as shown by the hagiography of the Italian Francesca Romana (1384–1440), whose life was amended to fit a cloistered paradigm ahead of her canonization (1608).[65] Between the twelfth and fifteenth centuries the proportion of canonized women had almost tripled, but they were mostly lay saints.[66] This changed after Trent. In fact, the itinerant Teresa was key to female enclosure: After her, most of those who reached the altars were nuns. The new model was therefore primarily intended for female religious: Even if Teresa's teachings eventually became widespread, she privileged her monastic community as her

---

[61] Alison Weber, *Teresa of Avila and the Rhetoric of Femininity* (Princeton, NJ, 1990). For a similar strategy in Juana de la Cruz, see Ronald E. Surtz, *The Guitar of God: Gender, Power, and Authority in the Visionary World of Mother Juana de la Cruz, 1481–1534* (Philadelphia, 1990), 63–64.

[62] Gillian T. W. Ahlgren, *Teresa of Avila and the Politics of Sanctity* (Ithaca, NY, 1996), 114–44, 155–59. For the quotation, see *The Collected Works of St. Teresa of Avila*, trans. Kieran Kavanaugh and Otilio Rodriguez, vol. 2 (Washington, DC, 1980), 70.

[63] McGinn, *Mysticism*, 120–229; Ángela Atienza, *Tiempos de conventos: Una historia social de las fundaciones en la España moderna* (Madrid, 2008).

[64] Navarro, *Favores*, fol. ¶¶3r; Erin Rowe, *Saint and Nation: Santiago, Teresa of Avila, and Plural Identities in Early Modern Spain* (University Park, PA, 2011).

[65] Giulia Barone, "La canonizzazione di Francesca Romana (1608): La riproposta di un modelo agiografico medievale," in *Finzione e santità tra medioevo ed età moderna*, ed. Gabriella Zarri (Turin, 1991), 264–79.

[66] Donald Weinstein and Rudolph M. Bell, *Saints and Society: The Two Worlds of Western Christendom, 1000–1700* (Chicago, 1986), 220–25.

audience rather than the whole body of the Church, and the criticism of the clergy, so common in the previous model, practically disappeared.

One could argue that the decline in female canonized saints evidences a lack of Tridentine enthusiasm for female holiness, but overall, the picture appears more varied. We have seen ample male support for the intermediate model, and the Teresian model was promoted by devoted confessors (one of whom, John of the Cross, would eventually be canonized). One trend, however, cannot be ignored, and that is the shift toward autohagiography – a stark contrast from the hagiographies of illiterate holy women with which we began. Indeed, much has been written on female sanctity inspired by Teresa focusing on nuns' hagiographies and autobiographies that proliferated at that time, as well as on the relationship between these women and the confessors who sometimes put their experiences in writing. Scholars have considered these last texts to have been of mixed composition (coauthored and collaborative), or as presenting a gendered conflict between male confessors and female mystics.[67] Whichever way we view this whole editorial phenomenon, there can be no doubt about the shift from hagiography to autohagiography, when aspiring saints became conscious writers who benefited from growing literacy. The greater prominence of the female authorial voice, however, was also matched by increased subjection to the male confessor. It must nevertheless be noted that most hagiographers of the next generation were secular priests rather than members of religious orders.

The influence of the more stringent canonization procedures is hard to miss. Many of the aspiring saints who wrote following Teresa made sophisticated distinctions between types of visions (mental, imaginative, and so on), and the Tridentine emphasis on confession influenced the verbal rhetoric of these texts.[68] This aligned with the ever more demanding canonization procedures during the seventeenth century and the growing insistence on proving the authenticity of the sources (which the cause of Juana de la Cruz, for instance, was unable to provide). By lacing their work with diaries, letters, and other sources, hagiographers increasingly presented themselves as informants for future beatification processes.[69]

---

[67] Jodi Bilinkoff, *Related Lives: Confessors and Their Female Penitents, 1450–1750* (Ithaca, NY, 2005), 46–75; Isabelle Poutrin, *Le voile et la plume: Autobiographie et sainteté féminine dans l'Espagne moderne* (Madrid, 1995), 127–34; Sonja Herpoel, *A la zaga de Santa Teresa: Autobiografías por mandato* (Amsterdam, 1999).

[68] Bilinkoff, *Related Lives*, 8, 27–31.

[69] Ibid., 6, 41–45. On canonization, see Chapter 7 of this volume.

While the living saints vanished from view, the model provided by Catherine of Siena, which once inspired them, changed. Teresa's fame, even if she did not consider the Italian as her model, was in part supported by the continued popularity of Catherine's writings.[70] In Spain, some aspiring saints such as María Vela y Cueto (1561–1617) claimed inspiration from both Catherine and Teresa in their diaries.[71] Beyond Spain, Catherine inspired saints like Maria Maddalena and Rose of Lima, neither of whom can be said to be imitators of the Teresian model. However, even in these instances, Catherine was stripped of her political role, and the prevalent exile of female sanctity from politics led to the proliferation of the image of the contemplative, reading nun in the visual arts.[72]

At a local level, the intermediate model retained some of its vitality. It no longer, however, found favor with the authorities, who became increasingly concerned with alleged cases of false sanctity. Famous cases of feigned sainthood like those of Magdalena de la Cruz (1487–1560) or Lucrecia de León (b. 1567) inspired distrust of spiritual practices that might appear heretical and fostered suspicions of demonic possession and mental disorders.[73] The increased role assigned to confessors as guarantors of female mysticism eventually led to the replacement of Catherinian spiritual motherhood with a new emphasis on clerical "spiritual fathers."[74] It was no longer encouraged to mix with secular political powers, as the *false* prophetesses had done. Even if later visionaries such as Luisa de Carrión (1565–1636) and María Jesús de Ágreda (1602–1665) achieved great fame with the court, they got into trouble with the Inquisition. Despite her prestige, the great mystic from Ágreda who admired Juana de la Cruz fell short of beatification.[75]

---

[70] Poutrin, *Le voile*, 72–73.
[71] María Vela y Cueto, *Autobiography and Letters of a Spanish Nun*, ed. Susan Laningham, trans. Jane Tar (Toronto, 2016).
[72] F. Thomas Luongo, "The Historical Reception of Catharina of Siena," in *A Companion to Catherine of Siena*, ed. Carolyn Muessig et al. (Leiden, 2012), 23–45.
[73] Richard Kagan, "Politics, Prophecy, and the Inquisition in Late Sixteenth-Century Spain," in *Cultural Encounters: The Impact of the Inquisition in Spain and the New World*, ed. Mary Elizabeth Perry and Anne J. Cruz (Berkeley, CA, 1991), 105–20.
[74] Adriano Prosperi, "Dalle 'divine madri' ai 'padri spirituali,'" in *Women and Men in Spiritual Culture, XIV–XVII Centuries: A Meeting of South and North*, ed. Elisja Schulte van Kessel (The Hague, 1986), 71–90.
[75] Patrocinio García Barriuso, *La Monja de Carrión: Sor Luisa de la Ascensión Colmenares Cabezón (Aportación documental para una biografía)* (Madrid, 1986); Anna M. Nogar, *Quill and Cross in the Borderlands: Sor María de Agreda and the Lady in Blue, 1628 to the Present* (Notre Dame, IN, 2018); García de Andrés, *El Conhorte*, 125–28.

By the middle of the eighteenth century, a final shift in models of female holiness took place, noticeably in a decrease in the number of biographies of mystic women. Although mystics were still being canonized, contemplative sanctity and intercessory prayer lost out to pragmatic intervention in the real world.[76] Female aspiring saints embraced a variety of avenues that had developed in the Catholic world over the previous century. While the desire for martyrdom, as once displayed by Luisa de Carvajal y Mendoza (1566–1614) in England, had lost much of its appeal, charitable and educational missions continued to be potentially sanctifying tasks, backed by the newly founded orders.[77] The way was led by English and especially French women: Mary Ward (1585–1645), Marie de l'Incarnation (1599–1672), Jeanne de Chantal (1572–1641), and Louise de Marillac (1591–1660). They were the founders of the Sisters of Loreto, the Ursuline Order in Canada, the Visitation Order, and the Daughters of Charity, respectively.[78] The prominence of women who combined the cloistered tradition with apostolic vocations thus increased. In part, the focus on works of charity, which favored an active apostolate rather than ecstatic contemplation, was fostered by the desire to avoid the problem of false visionaries. Even so, Teresa's shadow has continued to make its mark on female sanctity to the present day.

CONCLUSION

Our study of an intermediate model between the two great models of late medieval and early modern female sanctity – Catherine of Siena and Teresa of Ávila – yields a new understanding of Counter-Reformation Spanish female sanctity as marked by a gradual and negotiated process of change, with Teresa's canonization in 1622 marking a significant paradigm shift. In the process we have charted a movement toward a new model based on enclosed mysticism rather than on thaumaturgical power, which had developed in the wake of Catherine of Siena. Once

---

[76] Bilinkoff, *Related Lives*, 113–17.
[77] See Glyn Redworth, *The She-Apostle: The Extraordinary Life and Death of Luisa de Carvajal* (Oxford, 2008).
[78] See Laurence Lux-Sterritt, *Redefining Female Religious Life: French Ursulines and English Ladies in Seventeenth-Century Catholicism* (Burlington, VT, 2005); Wendy M. Wright, *Bond of Perfection: Jeanne de Chantal and Francois de Sales*, new enhanced ed. (Stella Niagara, NY, 2001); Susan E. Dinan, *Women and Poor Relief in Seventeenth-Century France: The Early History of the Daughters of Charity* (Aldershot, 2006).

celebrated and pushed by poets, playwrights, and painters, the intermediate model would progressively fade away. Scholars have emphasized the role of enclosure in introducing a new level of clerical scrutiny of holy women. While clearly significant, enclosure began before Trent. In fact, it is not more important for defining the Counter-Reformation female saint than many of the other aspects revealed by the reworking of the hagiographies of the Spanish living saints. Our study also illuminates similar transitions taking place outside Spain, where female sanctity moved away from court presence, religious autonomy, and public prophecy.

The intermediate model offers further insight into the increasing difficulty in authenticating and recognizing sanctity at the official level. Successful saint-making emerged out of a post-Tridentine dialogue between local cults, religious orders, state institutions, and Rome. As Simon Ditchfield has demonstrated, sanctity was not merely an imposition from Rome but the result of a dialectical relationship between universal and particular devotion.[79] This chapter further shows that the Teresian model faced competition, particularly during a first post-Tridentine phase in saint-making (1588–1625). Juana de la Cruz, in particular, was established as a powerful point of reference. Her cult briefly coexisted alongside with Teresa's, as evidenced by the papal recognition of her heroic virtues to satisfy the Franciscan order, as well as a local cult in Toledo, a national cult sponsored by the monarchy, and an international cult, attested by the translation of her hagiographies. For a time, therefore, aspiring saints tried to imitate them both. Regardless of the varied reasons why neither Juana nor any other Spanish living saint achieved canonization, her case clearly illustrates the process by which a still relatively recent pre-Tridentine model was discarded in spite of years of promotion. It was Teresa of Ávila, the confined mystic and the Tridentine founder of convents, who would define a new model of female sanctity for generations, while her predecessors were mostly forgotten.

---

[79] Simon Ditchfield, *Liturgy, Sanctity and History in Tridentine Italy* (Cambridge, 1995).

4 The Virgin Mary

CHRISTINA H. LEE

The Virgin Mary occupied a special place in the early modern Catholic world. As the Theotokos – the God-bearer or the mother of God – Mary's blessed body belonged to both heaven and earth and could efficaciously mediate between both realms for the benefit of humanity.[1] Christians of all branches believed that she had given birth to Jesus Christ through divine intervention while a virgin and had remained one throughout her life. Mary was by far the saint with the largest number of shrines dedicated to her in the Catholic chapels and churches of Western Europe in the sixteenth and seventeenth centuries.[2] The intensity of devotion to Marian imagery was spurred on by Protestant iconoclasm that led to the dismantling of sacred shrines and erasure of religious art from churches and public spaces.[3] The Catholic Reformation (or Counter-Reformation) reasserted the appropriateness of devotion to sacred icons, especially those of Mary, while at the same time establishing guidelines to distinguish between idolatrous practices and the proper reverence merited by the saints.[4] It also emphasized the notion that there was only one universal Mary, the *mediatrix* between humanity and God, whose role was solely intercessory.[5] In practice, however,

---

[1] Marina Warner, *Alone of All Her Sex* (New York, 1983), 87, 285.
[2] In Spanish-speaking countries as well as the Philippines, "saints" or *santos* refer not only to the heavenly figures themselves, but also to their depiction in statues and paintings that are the object of devotion (Christina Lee, *Saints of Resistance* [Oxford, 2021], 1). Wilhelm Gumppenberg's *Atlas Marianus* (Ingolstadt, 1657) listed over 1,000 sites where Mary appeared and/or her images were found.
[3] Miri Rubin, *Mother of God: A History of the Virgin Mary* (London, 2009), 402–3; Lawrence Cunningham, "The Virgin Mary," in *From Trent to Vatican II*, ed. Raymond F. Bulman and Frederick J. Parrella (Oxford, 2006), 179. Also, as detailed by Bridget Heal in *The Cult of the Virgin Mary in Early Modern Germany: Protestant and Catholic Piety, 1500–1648* (Cambridge, 2014), Marian piety did not disappear from Lutheran countries.
[4] Cunningham, "The Virgin Mary," 179–92, 195–218.
[5] Warner, *Alone of All Her Sex*, 285–98.

shrine images of Mary, usually associated with different Marian apparitions, were generally treated as distinct agents of miracles themselves.[6]

This growth in iconographic devotional practices coincided with European expansion overseas. Wherever Catholics traveled, they carried images of their saints with them, especially of Mary. Indeed, Christopher Columbus's flagship on his transoceanic first voyage was named *Santa María*. The explorer and his crew called on different Marian advocations – apparitions associated with a particular time and place – in times of need while at sea. In what follows, I focus on one of the advocations Columbus and the early conquistadors favored and summoned during their voyages: Our Lady of Guadalupe. I briefly trace the foundation and explosive growth of devotion to this icon in Extremadura, Spain, and then analyze the cult to her namesake in Tepeyac, Mexico. As I discuss below, the indigenous neophytes of Mexico only venerated Mary under the name of Guadalupe after her image was detached from the Spanish Guadalupe thanks to an alleged new apparition, and distinct visual depiction, at the site where a maternal deity – Tonantzin – had been venerated in pre-Hispanic times. In the last section of this chapter, I examine the failed attempt of missionaries to instill the cult of Our Lady of Guadalupe of Extremadura among the Tagalog natives of Manila. I suggest that Philippine natives passed over the devotion to this Virgin because she was seen as foreign. For a Marian icon to be recognized as a Philippine Mary, her devotees had to believe that she had transformed herself into their local advocate and become an intrinsic part of the history and identity of the community where she resided, as she had in Mexico. These three different, yet related advocations of the Virgin, taken together, show how the Virgin went "global" during the early modern period, while also revealing her cults' limitations.[7]

OUR LADY OF GUADALUPE IN SPAIN

The shrine to Our Lady of Guadalupe in Extremadura attracted a vigorous, large, and sustained devotion due to the belief that she had assisted

---

[6] William Christian, Jr., *Local Religion in Sixteenth-Century Spain* (Princeton, NJ, 1981), 103.

[7] For other examples, see Karin Vélez, *The Miraculous Flying House of Loreto* (Princeton, NJ, 2019), and Simon Ditchfield, "Romanus and Catholicus: Counter-Reformation Rome as *Caput* Mundi," in *A Companion to Early Modern Rome 1492–1692*, ed. Pamela Jones, Barbara Wisch, and Simon Ditchfield (Leiden, 2019), 131–47.

the Iberian Christian kingdoms in their fight to eject Muslim invaders from the peninsula during the pivotal battles of the last stage of the period known as the Reconquest (722–1492).[8] By the early modern period, the shrine had become the richest and most popular pilgrimage site in Castile. Its fame was such that it inspired Pedro de Medina, the early modern historian and cosmographer, to include Guadalupe among his list of the "Great and Memorable Things of Spain" (1549). In Medina's reckoning, "this house of Guadalupe ... is clearly one of the unique creations of the world, where God our Lord, through his very Blessed Mother, works so many miracles and great deeds that it is impossible to describe them in a human language."[9] There were other Iberian centers of Marian pilgrimage, such as the shrines of Our Lady of Montserrat, Our Lady of Peña de Francia, and Our Lady of Pilar in Zaragoza, but Our Lady of Guadalupe was the one that loomed the largest in the historical imaginary of Spain's – and Catholicism's – expansion worldwide.

Even before Columbus and his fellow conquistadors arrived at the shrine of Guadalupe in 1493 to give thanks to their Virgin for her protection during their first voyage, they had surely heard of the long history of Our Lady of Guadalupe's championing of the rulers of Castile against its Muslim foes.[10] This small and dark statue of the Madonna and child sculpted from cedar wood was embraced by local devotees because it placed their otherwise unremarkable location in Extremadura, still Spain's poorest region today, at the center of the history of the Reconquest. By the sixteenth century it had become impossible to speak of Guadalupe without explaining how Mary herself had chosen Guadalupe as one of the special sites where she wanted to be honored. It was also not possible to speak of Guadalupe without referring to the "invasion" of the "Moors," the perseverance and courage of the Christians, and the glorious fall of Muslim Granada to the Catholic monarchs.

According to the earliest recorded version of the legend of Mary's apparition, circa 1440, it was during the Muslim takeover of Seville (ca. 712) that a group of priests fled north with a Marian icon, a gift from Pope Gregory. When the priests arrived at the hills of Guadalupe,

---

[8] See Joseph O'Callaghan, *Reconquest and Crusade in Medieval Spain* (Philadelphia, 2004).

[9] Pedro de Medina, *Obras de Pedro de Medina* (Madrid, 1944), 185. All translations are my own, unless indicated otherwise.

[10] Carla Phillips and William Phillips, *The Worlds of Christopher Columbus* (Cambridge, 1992), 193.

they dug a hole, hid the image of Our Lady in it, and covered it with large stones, before they made their way to Old Castile. The image was allegedly rediscovered several centuries later, during the reign of King Alfonso X (r. 1252–84), who according to this legend "won from the Moors much of Castile."[11] Some of the details of her apparition will be familiar to scholars of her other advocations, including more recent ones. Just as she would later appear to a shepherdess in Lourdes and to children in Fatima, the Virgin in Guadalupe appeared to a simple herdsman who had been guarding his cows when one went missing. He found the animal lying dead near a spring and was about to slaughter it when Mary appeared to him. She told him to inform the clergy that there was a statue of her under the ground where he was standing. His first audience, his fellow herdsmen, did not believe him. Upon his return home he found his wife crying. Learning that his son had just died, the herdsman declared, "I promise him to Saint Mary of Guadalupe, who will give him back to me alive and well, and I promise him as a servant in her house."[12] According to the tale, the son revived as soon as these words had been uttered. The happy father then went to the main church of the nearest town and relayed to the clergy what had happened. The group proceeded to the site of the apparition and started digging until they encountered a tomb-like cave. In it, they found the image of Our Lady, placed on a stone with a little bell next to it.[13] The participation of a lowly herdsman and his family indicates the efforts to produce the sense that all Castilians, regardless of rank, took part in the Christian reconquest of the Peninsula. This legend, which developed variants and was embellished over time, conveyed that Our Lady of Guadalupe's emergence from her forced concealment coincided with Christianity's resurgence across the peninsula.[14] Like the Virgin, Christian Spain had triumphantly reemerged from ground that had always been theirs.

---

[11] Cited in William Christian, Jr., *Apparitions in Late Medieval and Renaissance Spain* (Princeton, NJ, 1989), 89; Sebastián García, "El Real Santuario de Santa María de Guadalupe en el primer siglo de su historia," *Revista de estudios extremeños* 57, no. 1 (2001): 359–410, 386–88.

[12] Christian, *Apparitions*, 90.

[13] Ibid., 88–92. Although other legends of findings include the motif of the statue being moved by the clergy to another site and the image returning to the site of her original apparition or finding, such an element is not present in the legend of Our Lady of Guadalupe.

[14] Amy Remensnyder, *La Conquistadora: The Virgin Mary at War and Peace on the Old and the New Worlds* (Oxford, 2014), 65.

Our Lady of Guadalupe's subsequent interventions during the last stages of the Reconquest were as important as the initial discovery. It was allegedly her advocation that, in 1340, had allowed Alfonso XI to lead the most resounding Christian victory against Nasrid Granada in the battle of Salado and set the emirate up for its eventual fall to the Catholic Monarchs in 1492. A contemporary epic, *The Poem on Alfonso XI*, describes the dramatic scene as the king and his army appealed to Mary at Salado. While the original poem invoked Mary without identifying any particular advocation, later royal chroniclers converted her into Our Lady of Guadalupe. The *Great Chronicle of Alfonso XI* (1370) explained that it was due to the aid of Holy Mary of Guadalupe that the king was able to vanquish the kings of Morocco and Granada and capture the strait of Gibraltar. The *Great Chronicle* also described the king's pilgrimage to Guadalupe to thank the Virgin for her support in vanquishing the Muslim enemies.[15]

A century later, the Catholic Monarchs – Isabel of Castile and Ferdinand of Aragon – made both figurative and literal efforts to identify Our Lady of Guadalupe as the patron saint of the Reconquest. They visited the monastery of Guadalupe to pray before her shrine during their ongoing campaigns in Granada against the Nasrids at least three times (in 1482, 1486, and 1489).[16] They utilized the monastery as their palace and received funds from the guardians of the shrine, the Hieronymite order, to finance their wars against Islam's final holdout.[17] After Granada's fall in 1492, Isabel made votive offerings to the Guadalupe shrine that would remind her devotees of Mary's intervention during the final stage of the war. Isabel donated elaborate Nasrid weapons that her army had seized during the war. These were publicly displayed at the Virgin's shrine until the end of the sixteenth century. As Amy Remensnyder has observed, it was the events of 1492 that made "the connection between the Virgin of Guadalupe and Castile's crusading rulers [seem] timeless."[18]

For the conquistadors leaving Spain, Our Lady of Guadalupe was a potent advocate for Castile's boundless expansion and the spiritual war against those who opposed Christianity. Columbus and his crew invoked her during a dangerous storm on their return trip to Spain

---

[15] Ibid., 57–62, 469.
[16] Diego de Ecija, *Libro de la invención de esta santa Imagen de Guadalupe y de la erección y fundación de este monasterio* (Cáceres, 1953), 337–38.
[17] Remensnyder, *La Conquistadora*, 83.
[18] Ibid., 90–91.

during their first voyage and vowed to visit her shrine with a five-pound candle if she protected them.[19] Columbus fulfilled his promise by going to Guadalupe prior to embarking on his second trip. There, the Hieronymite monks requested that Columbus name a territory he discovered overseas in honor of their Virgin. Columbus fulfilled their wish on November 4, 1493, when he spotted an island in the Caribbean, the mountains of which reminded him of the hills of Guadalupe. He called this island Santa María de Guadalupe.[20] Other Marian advocations – notably the Virgin of the Holy House of Loreto – would follow in due course.[21] Pilgrimage to Marian shrines became a common practice for the first generation of conquistadors upon their return from the Indies.

One reason why the shrine of Guadalupe became almost a requisite stop was that many conquistadors, including Vasco Núñez de Balboa and Francisco Pizarro, just to name a few, had been local boys from Extremadura and credited their Virgin with helping them survive life-threatening events and supporting their exploits in the New World.[22] When Hernán Cortés returned to Spain in 1528, several years after the conquest of Tenochtitlan, he visited the monastery of Guadalupe with a gift of feathers and a votive offering in gratitude for a miracle that the Virgin had granted him. Her intercession was credited with saving his life after a scorpion bite. Cortes's offerings visually demonstrated the extent of the Virgin's power. The exotic feathers conjured up her aid in subjugating Tenochtitlan (modern Mexico City), and the golden scorpion jewel, containing the actual scorpion that had presumably bitten him, was a reminder that individual devotees had the Virgin's favor if they called on her.[23]

THE VIRGIN OF GUADALUPE IN MEXICO

Given the early conquistadors' devotion to Our Lady of Guadalupe of Extremadura, it would be natural to assume, simply because of the

---

[19] Linda Hall, *Mary, Mother and Warrior: The Virgin in Spain and the Americas* (Austin, TX, 2004), 48.
[20] Ibid., 51.
[21] See Luisa Elena Alcalá, *Arte y localización de un culto global: La Virgen de Loreto en México* (Madrid, 2022).
[22] Vicente Navarro del Castillo, *La epopeya de la raza extremeña en Indias* (Granada, 1978), provides a list of 6,000 Spaniards from Extremadura who traveled to the Americas and the Philippines in the fifteenth and sixteenth centuries.
[23] Fray Gabriel de Talavera, *Historia de Nuestra Señora de Guadalupe* (Toledo, 1597), 168, 178.

shared name, that the now world-renowned Virgin of Guadalupe of Mexico is a derivative of her Spanish antecessor. The image of the Virgin of Guadalupe of Mexico, however, in no way resembles the cedar-wood statue of the black Madonna and child in the main shrine of the monastery in Extremadura. The Mexican image is a life-sized painting of the Virgin, without her child, standing in an almond-shaped mandorla on a crescent moon. Devotees believe that her image was miraculously imprinted upon the *tilma* – a type of cloak worn by indigenous inhabitants of central Mexico – of an indigenous man named Juan Diego in the hills of Tepeyac, near Mexico City, in 1531.[24] This Virgin resembles the inhabitants of central Mexico: she is of olive complexion with straight black hair and wears a headdress like that of married indigenous noble women in the sixteenth century.[25] She is modestly dressed in a blue mantle and her hands are positioned in prayer. An angel hangs from the edges of the cloak.[26]

If the Mexican icon was not modeled after the Spanish one, how did she acquire her name? This question cannot be settled with absolute certainty. While the problem of the age, origin, and composition of the current image remains the object of heated controversy, it is possible that the devotion was introduced by the soldier entrusted by Cortés to finalize the conquest of Tepeyac. This theory is bound to remain speculative. Yet in support of the possibility that this soldier, Gonzalo de Sandoval, of Medellín (Extremadura), installed an image of the Extremaduran Guadalupe, which was later replaced by the current painting, we might advance the testimony of Bernal Díaz del Castillo. In his *True History of the Conquest of New Spain* (ca. 1568), Díaz del Castillo relates that Our Lady of Guadalupe of Extremadura helped the Spaniards overcome the Aztecs in Tenochtitlan. Díaz del Castillo asked his readers to pay attention to the "holy miracles that she has performed every day" and give thanks "to God and his Holy Mother Our Lady for them, because she provided us with her grace and assistance so that we

---

[24] Juan Diego was canonized in 2002 by Pope John II and declared "the first indigenous Saint of the American Continent" (www.vatican.va/content/john-paul-ii/en/homilies/2002/documents/hf_jp-ii_hom_20020731_canonization-mexico.html).

[25] Raphaèle Preisinger, "(Re)Framing the Virgin of Guadalupe: The Concurrence of Early Modern Prints and Colonial Devotions in Creating the Virgin," in *Prints as Agents of Global Exchange: 1500–1800*, ed. Heather Madar (Amsterdam, 2021), 210.

[26] Jeanette Favrot Peterson, "Creating the Virgin of Guadalupe: The Cloth, the Artist, and Sources in Sixteenth–Century New Spain," *The Americas* 61, no. 4 (2005): 571–610.

could win these lands where there is so much Christianity."²⁷ Indeed, many of Cortes's soldiers were devotees of the Guadalupe in Extremadura, and left offerings to her shrine in their wills. For example, in 1537, Bartolomé López, who was part of Cortés's regiment in Mexico, designated that funds for the shrine in Extremadura be used for 100 Masses dedicated to the welfare of his soul. Another soldier, Juan de Iniestra, stated in his will that he wanted to donate over 100 pesos to the monastery of Guadalupe a few years later.²⁸

Although early attempts to instill devotion to the Spanish Guadalupe among newly converted indigenous residents of Mexico may not have been successful, the chapel continued to gather such remarkable financial support from Spaniards abroad that, in 1574, the Hieronymite leadership in Spain commissioned Diego de Santa María to travel to Mexico to investigate the devotion in Tepeyac. Once in Mexico, Santa María learned that overseas Spaniards had been donating alms to the chapel in Tepeyac because they believed that it was dedicated to the shrine of Our Lady of Guadalupe in Extremadura. In a letter to King Philip II, Santa María suggested that either the Mexican chapel change its name to avoid confusion, or else be taken out of the control of the Mexican archbishop and be put under the charge of the Hieronymites. Neither change was ever made. By the end of the seventeenth century, there were at least two distinct images of the Virgin in the chapel in Tepeyac.²⁹ One was the actual painting that is purportedly still housed today in the Mexican basilica of Guadalupe; the other was a statue made of silver and gilt that attracted a Spanish following. The English corsair Miles Philips found himself in Mexico after a failed expedition, and in about 1568 described that image as follows:

> [T]here is an image of Our Lady of silver and gilt, being as high and as large as a tall woman, in which Church, and before which image, there are as many lamps of silver as there be days in the year, which upon high days are all lighted. Whenever any Spaniards pass by this Church, although they be on horseback, they will alight, and come into the Church, and kneel before the image, and pray to Our Lady to defend them from all evil, so that whether he be horseman or

---

²⁷ Bernal Díaz del Castillo, *Historia verdadera de la conquista de la Nueva España* (Madrid, 1796), 524.
²⁸ See Edmundo O'Gorman, *Destierro de sombras: Luz en el origen de la imagen y culto de Nuestra Señora de Guadalupe del Tepeyac* (Mexico, 2018), 11–12.
²⁹ Stafford Poole, *Our Lady of Guadalupe: The Origins and Sources of a Mexican National Symbol, 1531–1797* (Tucson, AZ, 2017), 77–80.

footman he will not pass by, but first go into the Church, and pray as aforesaid, which if they do not, they think and believe that they shall never prosper; which image they call in the Spanish tongue, Nuestra Señora de Guadalupe.[30]

It is quite possible that Spaniards as well as their American-born counterparts ("creoles") gravitated toward this sculpture, whose iconography they associated with Extremadura, while indigenous followers were instead devotees of the native painting. Yet over time, and unlike other Marian icons, such as the image of Our Lady of Remedios – who was known to have aided Cortés and his men to triumph over the Aztecs in Tenochtitlan – the legend of the indigenous origins of the Virgin of Guadalupe effectively detached her image from legends of the conquest or its conquistadors.[31]

By the 1550s, the cult at Tepeyac had become important enough to generate a bitter rivalry between Dominicans, including the Archbishop of Mexico Alonso de Montúfar, and the powerful Franciscan order. A controversy erupted in 1556 centering on whether, as the Franciscan provincial Francisco de Bustamante alleged in a sermon, the image was not miraculous but painted recently by an indigenous artist he called Marcos, and, worse, that it encouraged the natives to continue practicing idolatry. In response, the archbishop initiated an investigation into the offending sermon; in his testimony, one witness, a Spaniard named Francisco de Salazar, testified that he knew "the foundation of this chapel was, since the beginning, named after 'The Mother of God.'"[32]

The debate continued when the Franciscan Bernardino de Sahagún, in an appendix to his manuscript *General History of the Things of New Spain* (c. 1576), disparaged the cult to Guadalupe as idolatry under the guise of Marian devotion. Sahagún turned to indigenous elders in support of his argument who recognized the mother of God as the ancient goddess Tonantzin:

> In this place they used to have a temple dedicated to the mother of the gods, whom they called Tonantzin, which means "our mother.". . . The gathering of people in those days was great and

---

[30] Adapted from ibid., 75.
[31] Remensnyder, *La Conquistadora*, 327.
[32] Alonso de Montúfar, *Información* (Madrid, 1888), 28. For a discussion of the authorship of the painting, see Manuel Ortiz Vaquero, "Notas sobre la pintura 'Traslado de la imagen de la Virgen de Guadalupe a la primera ermita y primer Milagro,'" in *Imágenes guadalupanas: Cuatro siglos* (Mexico City, 1987), 37–42.

everyone would say "let us go to the feast of Tonantzin." Now that the church of Our Lady of Guadalupe has been built there, they also call her Tonantzin.... This appears to be an invention of the devil to cover over idolatry under the ambiguity of this name Tonantzin. They now come to visit this Tonantzin from far away, as far as in former times. The devotion itself is suspect because everywhere there are many churches to Our Lady and they do not go to them. They come from distant lands to this Tonantzin, as they did in former times.[33]

Sahagún suggested here that devotion to Guadalupe allowed the indigenous communities to continue worshipping their pre-Hispanic goddess. He noted that even though there were many Marian shrines in the area, the indigenous people exclusively chose to worship at Tepeyac, since they believed that Tonantzin and the Guadalupe in Tepeyac were one and the same.[34] Sahagún himself said that "nobody knows for certain from where this association with Tonantzin came."[35]

These arguments notwithstanding, devotion to the Virgin of Guadalupe was validated by Spanish authorities in the 1640s.[36] The cult followed the pattern established by Iberian shrines: The origin legend seems to have arisen as a consequence of, or subsequent to, the growth of a local devotion.[37] The first extant version of the origin legend, *Image of the Virgin Mary* (1648) was written in Spanish by Miguel Sánchez, a creole member of the secular clergy whose objective was to legitimize and promote the devotion to an ecclesiastical and elite readership.[38] For Sánchez, the Virgin of Guadalupe was like the woman in the book of Revelation (12:1–6), in that she gave birth to the Church of Mexico. The apparition of the Virgin to the native Juan Diego at the hill of Tepeyac was, in this telling, analogous to Moses's revelation in Mount Sinai.[39] Sánchez made it clear that his role was to "make reference" to the history of the apparition of the Virgin at Tepeyac, in other

---

[33] Cited in Poole, *Our Lady of Guadalupe*, 83–84.
[34] Ibid., 84.
[35] Bernardino de Sahagún, *Historia general de las cosas de Nueva España* (Mexico City, 1955), 481.
[36] See Timothy Matovina, *Theologies of Guadalupe: From the Era of Conquest to Pope Francis* (Oxford, 2018), 27; Poole, *Our Lady of Guadalupe*, 33–49.
[37] Christian, *Apparitions*, passim.
[38] Miguel Sánchez, *Imagen de la Virgen Maria Madre de Dios de Guadalupe: Milagrosamente aparecida en la ciudad de Mexico* (Mexico City, 1648).
[39] Matovina, *Theologies of Guadalupe*, 45, 73.

words, to record a preexisting story of the founding of the shrine.[40] While scholars still debate the actual antiquity of the cult and its image, an oral tradition to this effect was already in circulation from at least 1620, when a Franciscan nun named Sor Ana de Cristo stopped by the shrine. The origin story she learned from "some lay religious women (*beatas*) who were taking care of the chapel" was that "the Virgin herself asked the Indian for his cloak made of cloth, which measured from head to toe. Her image was imprinted on it and then she gave it back to the Indian, telling him to put it in that place, where it would make many miracles."[41]

Sánchez's telling, nearly three decades later, has unmistakable echoes of other Marian apparitions, including that of her Extremaduran antecessor. Juan Diego, a newly converted native, was passing by the hills of Tepeyac in December 1531 when he heard a voice calling his name. This was the Virgin, who asked him to go to the bishop of Mexico, Don Juan de Zumárraga, and tell him that she requested that a shrine dedicated to her be built at the site of the apparition. Zumárraga did not believe the neophyte and sent him away. The Virgin, who was waiting for Juan Diego at Tepeyac, told him to implore the bishop once again, and to return to her if he was unsuccessful. The bishop told Juan Diego to return with proof, namely, a sign from the Virgin. Juan Diego had intended to return to receive the promised sign from the Virgin but was waylaid due to news that his uncle was ill and needed to get a priest to give the last sacraments to him. On his way to seek a priest, the Virgin appeared and chastised Juan Diego for not showing up to their meeting to receive her sign. When he explained that his uncle was about to die, she told him that he should not be worried, as he had already been cured. She then asked him to go to the site of their previous meetings and gather the roses he saw there. Although it was winter, Juan Diego found many roses and other flowers, which he gathered into his *tilma*, and, as per the Virgin's instructions, he brought to the bishop as a sign. Once in audience with the bishop, Juan Diego let go of the "miraculous spring" he was holding and, as the roses fell, they revealed a painted image of the Virgin on his *tilma*. According to Sánchez, this was the very image housed in the new shrine built according to the Virgin's command.[42]

---

[40] Sánchez, *Imagen de la Virgen Maria*, fol. 18v.
[41] Cited in Sarah Owens, "Crossing Mexico (1620–1621): Franciscan Nuns and Their Journey to the Philippines," *The Americas* 72, no. 4 (2015): 583–606, 597–98.
[42] Sánchez, *Imagen de la Virgen Maria*, fols. 18r–30r.

This legend was both familiar and wondrous to Sánchez's public. As with the shrine of Guadalupe in Extremadura, it told of the apparition of the Virgin to a seer of humble social status unable to carry out the Virgin's request due to the illness of a loved one, followed by the miracle of the healing of the loved one, the initial reluctance of the ecclesiastical authority to believe the seer, and, finally, a display of a tangible sign from the Virgin that convinced authorities to build a shrine in her honor. As William Christian, Jr., reminds us, "[t]he different legend items are like beads, the assembled legends like necklaces. Familiar items are rearranged in apparitions into new patterns. The repetition of individual items maintains a recognizable continuity in divine behavior."[43] A roughly similar account of the apparition legend was published in Nahuatl the following year, in Luis Laso de la Vega's *Nican mopohua* (Here Is Recounted). Given the chronological proximity of their publications, it is possible that both Sánchez and Laso de la Vega structured and polished variants of a narrative that was already widespread among the devotees of the Virgin in Tepeyac.[44] While Sánchez was writing for a Spanish-speaking readership, Laso de la Vega's primary audience was the Nahuatl-speaking congregation at the Guadalupe sanctuary, where he served as vicar.[45] Laso de la Vega's account is distinguished by is its cadence and poetic style, which drew on established Nahuatl rhetorical conventions. As would befit a text intended to be used to encourage devotion among his parishioners, perhaps through sermons, the *Nican mopohua* recreates dialogues, favors diminutives, and places greater emphasis on Juan Diego's unwavering faith. Juan Diego, for example, is called by the Virgin "Juañito, Juan Dieguito," suggesting the feeling of intimacy and endearment expected between a loving parent and her child.[46]

OUR LADY OF GUADALUPE IN THE PHILIPPINES

Explorers of the Spanish Pacific followed the example of conquistadors in the Americas by invoking the name of Our Lady of Guadalupe in times of danger at sea. In 1565, Alonso de Arellano and Lope Martín, the captain and the pilot, respectively, of one of the ships that formed part of

---

[43] Christian, *Apparitions*, 92.
[44] Matovina, *Theologies of Guadalupe*, 30; Christian, *Apparitions*, 15–16.
[45] Matovina, *Theologies of Guadalupe*, 49.
[46] Luis Laso de la Vega, *La aparición de Santa María de Guadalupe*, trans. Primo Feliciano Velázquez (Mexico City, 1931), 142–83.

the fleet of Miguel López de Legazpi, the conquistador of the Philippines, called on Our Lady of Guadalupe when their ship was on the verge of sinking in the Pacific and vowed that they would go to her shrine in Mexico if she assisted them on their return voyage.[47] The power of the name of Our Lady of Guadalupe is suggested, too, by the fact that Legazpi chose it as one of the secret code names for his subordinate ships.[48] Given that Legazpi had resided in Mexico City for decades, it is possible that, like his companions Arellano and Martín, he associated the name of Guadalupe with the shrine in Tepeyac. But even so, the image the three navigators would have had in mind was probably not the painting imprinted upon the *tilma* but rather the silver and gilt statue favored by Spaniards, which they identified as the image of Our Lady in Extremadura.

Indeed, Spaniards and creoles who crossed the Pacific from Mexico to the Philippines, that most distant portion of New Spain, continued to identify the name "Guadalupe" with the shrine in Extremadura.[49] This explains why the only devotional images under the title "Guadalupe" that were brought to the Philippines were copies of the advocation in Extremadura. The first chapel dedicated to Our Lady of Guadalupe had been initially named Our Lady of Grace. It was established in 1601 by the Augustinian Order on a hill in the area of Makati, located about two leagues to the east of the city of Manila. In 1603 the name of the adjacent monastery was changed to Guadalupe, "due to the petition of the devoted people and the friars of the city, who have requested it in memory of Our Lady of Guadalupe from Spain."[50] According to an eighteenth-century chronicler of the Augustinian Order, the name change had been advocated by Pedro Navarrete – a native of Extremadura and resident of Manila, who donated 20,000 pesos – and his wife, Agustina Morales, who gave another 6,000 pesos to the

---

[47] Alonso de Arellano, "Documento 37," in *Colección de documentos inéditos relativos al descubrimiento, conquista y organización de las antiguas posesiones españolas de ultramar*, vol. 3.2 (Madrid, 1887), 1–76; relevant portion at 71–72.

[48] Miguel López de Legazpi, "Instrucciones de Legazpi sobre la navegación en conserva: Puerto de la Navidad, 21 de noviembre, 1564," *Los primeros de Filipinas: Crónicas de la conquista del archipiélago*, ed. Hidalgo Nuchera (Madrid, 1995), 135–37.

[49] Rafael Bernal, "México en Filipinas," *Historia Mexicana* 14, no. 2 (1964): 187–205.

[50] Cited by Manuel Merino in "La Provincia Agustiniana del Santísimo Nombre de Jesús de Filipinas," *Archivo Agustiniano* 58 (1964): 153–204, at 179 n. 212. The original report may be found in the *Libro primero de gobierno* (fol. 142v) at the Archivo de la Provincia Agustiniana Santísimo Nombre de Jesús de Filipinas (APAF) in Valladolid, Spain.

renamed monastery.⁵¹ The Augustinian friar Gaspar de San Agustín (1651–1724) includes in his history *Conquistas de las Islas Filipinas* (Conquest of the Philippine Islands) (1698) the stories of a dozen miracles performed by this Guadalupe between 1617 and 1645, in an effort to champion what was clearly a dwindling devotion, but without much success. He chronicles healing miracles that Our Lady of Guadalupe provided to a range of her devotees, including natives of all ranks, and Spanish and Portuguese officials and their families. The Virgin of these narratives, however, was not associated with any specific shrine image. San Agustín simply attributed the miracles to the intersession of an amalgamated Our Lady of Guadalupe. The fact that the shrine in Makati was not mentioned at all probably means that this specific advocation of the Virgin had not been accepted by the Philippine population in Manila.

Here we have the example of a Spanish devotion that never became localized and, hence, was never adopted either by the Spanish population of the Philippines or by the local indigenous communities. Spanish cults, such as the devotion to Our Lady of the Rosary of Manila, grew in popularity, especially among Spaniards and creoles, among whom she acquired a distinct identity as an advocate of Spanish expansion in the Pacific.⁵² Even then, one shrine in Manila was sufficient to serve the resident Spaniards in the Philippines, whose number remained very low, never surpassing 2,000 in the sixteenth and seventeenth centuries.⁵³ Our Lady of the Rosary became the premier advocate of Spaniards and their allies. No other Marian shrine competed with her. Furthermore, the chapel of Guadalupe near Manila never gathered enough native devotees in the seventeenth century to become an important sanctuary for the local indigenous population, in contrast with the more successful Marian shrines of Our Lady of Caysasay in Taal, and that of Our Lady of Antipolo at the foot of the Sierra Madre range in Luzon.⁵⁴

---

⁵¹ This Pedro Navarrete should not be confused with Pedro Fernández de Navarrete, the author of *Conservación de monarquías*. Agustín María de Castro, *Misioneros agustinos en el Extremo Oriente: 1565–1780*, ed. Manuel Merino (Madrid, 1953), 484–85.

⁵² For the devotion to Our Lady of the Rosary of Manila, see Lee, *Saints of Resistance*, 73–99.

⁵³ By the end of the nineteenth century, the peninsular Spanish population only made up about 1 percent of the total population of the Philippines: Vicente Rafael, "Colonial Contractions: The Making of the Modern Philippines," in *Oxford Research Encyclopedia of Asian History*, ed. David Ludden (Oxford, 2018), 268.

⁵⁴ Our Lady of the Rosary was Dominican, Our Lady of Caysasay was Augustinian, and Our Lady of Antipolo was promoted by the Jesuits. There is no relationship between

The legends of these two cults tied Mary to the supernatural powers of a specific site in the Philippine local topography. Our Lady of Caysasay was believed to have appeared in 1603 to Tagalog women near a spring that had been considered sacred in pre-Hispanic times.[55] Our Lady of Antipolo – officially named Our Lady of Voyage and Peace – was introduced by the Jesuits and promoted by the Spanish government in Manila. The official history of this image, established by the Jesuit Pedro Murillo Velarde in *Historia de la Provincia de Philipinas* (History of the Province of the Philippines) (1749) explains that Governor Juan Niño de Tavora brought the image with him on his transpacific voyage from Acapulco to Manila in the seventeenth century.[56] According to Murillo Velarde, Our Lady of Antipolo was believed to safeguard the trade galleons on their round-trip journey from Manila to Acapulco.[57] Yet it was only after the image was permanently moved to Antipolo in 1662 that she was embraced by the local Tagalogs and Aetas, who regarded her as a benevolent mother who epitomized the natural and sacred power of the *tipolo* (*Artocarpus blancoi*) trees, which had given the area its name.[58] While the image of Our Lady of Antipolo was recognized by devotees as undeniably Catholic and the personification of the mother of God, the beliefs that espoused her popular devotion drew on pre-Hispanic beliefs that certain trees were channels of divine power.[59] In contrast, the implanted Spanish Guadalupe near Manila remained foreign, aloof, and unrelatable.

There is only one shrine with the title of Our Lady of Guadalupe that has a strong local following in the Philippines, the Guadalupe of the Cave in Langub, in the suburbs of Cebu City. According to oral tradition, this image – which also represents the Immaculate

---

the success of Marian advocations and the religious orders that promoted them in the lowlands of the Philippines (see Lee, *Saints of Resistance*).

[55] This is according to an ecclesiastical investigation conducted in 1619: Bloomington, Indiana University, Lilly Library, Philippine Manuscripts II, Lot 516, "Ynformación del gran milagro del pueblo de Casasui." See Lee, *Saints of Resistance*, 39–72.

[56] Pedro Murillo Velarde, *Historia de la Provincia de Philipinas* (Manila, 1749), fols. 209r–29r. The first mention of the image by the Jesuits appears in Luis Espinelli's report "Nueva Protección y favores de nuestra señora del buen viaje y de la paz para su pueblo y residencia de Antipolo, 1653," July 15, 1654, St. Louis, MO, Vatican Film Library at St. Louis University, Roll 165, Archivum Romanum Societatis Iesu [ARSI], Philipp. 11, fols. 281r–88v.

[57] Murillo Velarde, *Historia*, fols. 209r–29r.

[58] See the annual letter by Andrés de Ledesma, "Annua de la provincia de la Compañía de Jesus del año 1665 hasta el de 1672," Vatican Film Library at Saint Louis University, Roll 164, ARSI, Philipp. 8, 830r–889r.

[59] Lee, *Saints of Resistance*, 100–127.

Conception – dates to the first decades of the conquest. It is unknown how the image became associated with Guadalupe. In fact, there is no existing documentation on the cult prior to the nineteenth century. This little statue, measuring less than two feet tall, is of a standing Virgin without her child and with her hands in prayer. Due to the global popularity of the devotion to the Virgin in Tepeyac, many present-day international visitors assume that the statue is merely a reproduction of the Mexican image. A novena (nine-day prayer) published in 1881 identifies the shrine, however, with Our Lady of Guadalupe of Extremadura, which could mean that the cult first arose with an original image meant to be a copy of the Spanish Virgin, as had been the case in Mexico.[60]

Although the legend of the Virgin in Langub cannot be traced to premodern sources, many of its narrative features share striking parallels with the legend of Our Lady of Guadalupe of Extremadura. As the Cebuano historian Resil Mojares explains, the image is believed to have been brought to the Philippines at the key moment of the conquest and Christianization of the Philippines, which began when Legazpi, under the authority of the Audiencia of Mexico, arrived in Cebu in 1565. Some devotees believe that the image came from Spain, others from Mexico, and that it was gifted to the newly converted (and conquered) Cebuanos. As in Extremadura, some narratives maintain that the image had to be hidden in a cave for protection, whether from Moro pirates – who conducted regular raids in the decades after the Spanish conquest – or from the Spaniards who wanted to take it away during the Philippine Revolution (1896–98). Legend has it that the image was rediscovered by trapper of wild cocks – a *mangangati* – at an unspecified time during the American period (1898–1946). The trapper is said to have found the statue when he sheltered in the cave during a storm, whereupon he brought it to the priest in charge in the neighboring town of San Nicolás. The legend concludes by explaining that the image was kept for some time in the main church until devotees carried it in procession to the barrio (neighborhood) where she had originally been found, at which point the image suddenly fell from her platform and came to face the direction of the cave. The object's refusal to be moved from the site of her apparition is another feature that echoes one of the variants of the legend of Our Lady of Guadalupe of Extremadura, as well as other legends of "unmovable" sacred images in Spain and Latin

---

[60] Astrid Sala-Boza. "Counterfactuals and the Image of Our Lady," *Philippine Quarterly of Culture and Society* 34, no. 3 (2006): 202–23, at 216. See Christian, *Local Religion*, 91.

America.⁶¹ As in other comparable Marian legends, devotees interpreted this event as evidence of the Virgin's wish to permanently reside in Langub, a wish that was granted.⁶²

It is possible that the Virgin in Cebu, like Guadalupe in Mexico, flourished among the local population because she was seen as belonging to the community. As in Tepeyac, Antipolo, and Taal, devotion to the Virgin took shape in the specific context of the local physical and religious landscape.⁶³ Resil Mojares posits that this devotion was embraced by the local population because the notion that the Virgin wanted to live in a cave resonated with an indigenous belief that female deities inhabited caves.⁶⁴ In contrast, Our Lady of Guadalupe of Manila in Makati never developed a following among that city's natives because the image was housed in an Augustinian monastery located away from the indigenous pueblos or barrios. As in the case of Our Lady of the Rosary of Manila, the only natives with access to the monastery were the *principales* (indigenous elite) or those who served the friars.⁶⁵ The image of Mary in Cebu, in contrast, echoed the legends of the Guadalupe in Tepeyac, Our Lady of Antipolo, and Our Lady of Caysasay in Taal, by appearing in a site that was sacred to the local population. This was a way for the Virgin to validate devotees' beliefs in the power of the natural world. Most importantly, the devotion was believed to be one that assisted the powerless, like the herdsman of Extremadura, the indigenous Juan Diego, or the Cebuano trapper of wild roosters.

CONCLUSION

Theologians in Asia, in line with their colleagues in the Americas and in Europe, attempted to regulate proper devotion to Our Lady of Guadalupe, as they did with all other Marian devotions. But the ecclesiastical efforts to oppose idolatry and guide proper devotion to the universal Mother of God, *mediatrix* between heaven and earth, were met

---

⁶¹ For Spanish cases, see Christian, *Apparitions*, 18–20. For Mexican cases, see William B. Taylor, *Shrines and Miraculous Images: Religious Life in Mexico Before the Reforma* (Albuquerque, NM, 2010), 29.

⁶² Resil Mojares, "The Woman in the Cave: Genealogy of the Cebuano Virgin of Guadalupe," in *Bisayan Knowledge, Movement and Identity* (Quezon City, 2000), 7–30, at 8–11.

⁶³ Christian, *Local Religion*, 1–26.

⁶⁴ Mojares, "The Woman in the Cave," 11.

⁶⁵ See Lee, *Saints of Resistance*, 74–99.

with the Virgin's devotees' need to adapt her shrine images and legends to their local histories. Local populations, whether in Europe, the Americas, or Asia, required their saints to adapt to their preexisting beliefs and become embedded in their local histories. Devotion to Our Lady of Guadalupe began in Extremadura just as Spain was emerging as the European center of Christianization and expansion overseas. In the New World, the advocation to Our Lady of Guadalupe was bifurcated into two advocations: one dedicated to the image from Extremadura who fought alongside the Spaniards on behalf of the Iberian empire and the other, a Virgin who belonged to the indigenous people and the pre-Hispanic landscape. Yet in the early colonial Philippines, devotion to the imported Guadalupe was instead perceived as a foreign, unrelatable intrusion, ignored by the indigenous population. Devotees of the namesake of Guadalupe in Mexico and the Philippines made it clear that their Virgin had to shed her imperial identity, as her origin legends became embedded into the histories of the local communities and adapted to native forms of spirituality. The Virgin certainly went global in the early modern period, but she had her limits.

5 Black Saints

ERIN KATHLEEN ROWE

Through the Middle Ages and early modern period, theologians and artists understood several figures from Scripture to have been "Ethiopian" or East African, including the bride in the Song of Songs, one of Moses's wives, and the Queen of Sheba. The emergence and rapid acceleration of the transatlantic slave trade beginning in the mid-fifteenth century, along with increased diplomatic relations with the rulers of Ethiopia, brought Christianity's Black history into closer view for early modern Europeans. While the promotion of Black saints could act as part of evangelization efforts to newly baptized enslaved Africans, the meanings of Black Christianity were multifaceted, evolving along distinct trajectories. European artists and authors centered ancient Black Christians as part of political and theological meditations on universal sovereignty and imperial ambition, while missionaries deployed Black saints in an effort to create good Christians. African diasporic communities, on the other hand, crafted their own ontologies. The range of meanings shaped not only the representation of Black saints, but also images that were not "racially" Black, such as centuries-old black Madonnas and black Christs. In tracing the history of Black sanctity in medieval and early modern Europe, this chapter argues that analyzing Black saints through the lens of global Catholicism provides the richest avenue for understanding how colonial, missionary, and African diasporic communities lived among the cult of the saints in dynamic ways; by extension, the chapter further suggests new ways to center non-European embrace, transformation, even rejection of early modern Catholicism.

TRADITIONS OF BLACK SAINTS

The origin story of Ethiopia's Christianity unfolded in several versions in both the Ethiopian and the Latin traditions.[1] Late medieval rulers of

[1] Andrea Ayers Achi, ed., *Africa and Byzantium* (New York, 2023).

Ethiopia traced their lineage to King Solomon, leading to their eponymous name, Solomonic dynasty.[2] In the biblical canon, the earliest references to "Ethiopians" or "Nubians" are found in the Old Testament with Moses's wife, Zipporah (Num. 12:1–10). The tradition continued in the New Testament with Queen Candace and her eunuch, who took the name of Philip after the apostle who baptized him. Philip then returned to Candace's court and brought Christianity with him (Acts 8:27–39). Yet in the Latin Christian tradition, authors also attributed Ethiopia's conversion to the work of the apostle Matthew; their understanding of the relationship between Philip and Matthew's time at the Ethiopian court became muddled in apocryphal narratives.

Beyond legendary accounts, however, it was widely known in the early medieval Mediterranean that Ethiopia was a Christian kingdom. In the sixth century, for example, the ruler of Aksum, Kaleb, gained fame throughout the eastern Mediterranean for his war against the Jewish king of Himyar, who had committed a massacre of Christians in Yemen.[3] Even earlier, Black Christians could be found throughout North Africa, including in the desert of Egypt where hundreds of hermits and early eremitical communities gathered in the early centuries of Christianity. One of the most famous of these was St. Moses, sometimes referred to as St. Moses the Ethiopian or St. Moses the Black.[4]

The early advent of Christianity in Ethiopia bound Ethiopia to the Near East. This was particularly evident in Egypt, where the Ethiopian Church came under the umbrella of the Coptic Church. There is also

---

[2] For an overview of this period of Ethiopian history, see Samantha Kelly and Verena Krebs, eds., *Companion to Medieval Ethiopia and Eritrea* (Leiden, 2020); and Verena Krebs, *Medieval Ethiopian Kingship, Craft, and Diplomacy with Latin Europe* (Cham, 2021).

[3] G. W. Bowersock, *The Throne of Adulis: Red Sea Wars on the Eve of Islam* (Oxford, 2013). Adam Simmons provides a detailed overview of the complex history of how medieval Europeans began to understand Ethiopia as "Ethiopia": *Nubia, Ethiopia, and the Crusading World, 1095–1402* (Abingdon, 2022). There is much literature on the medieval European myth of Prester John and Ethiopia; for one example, see Andrew Kurt, "The Search for Prester John, a Projected Crusade and the Eroding Prestige of Ethiopian Kings, c. 1200–c. 1540," *Journal of Medieval History* 39, no. 3 (2013): 297–320. On Kaleb of Aksum, see Stuart Munro-Hay, "A Sixteenth Century Kebra Nagast?," *Annales d'Éthiopie* 17 (2001): 43–58; Rugare Rukini, "Religious Statecraft: Constantinianism in the Figure of Nagashi Kaleb," *Theological Studies* 76, no. 4 (2020), www.ajol.info/index.php/hts/article/view/212530.

[4] Brief accounts of Moses's life can be found in Salaminium Sozomen, *The Ecclesiastical History of Sozomen: Comprising a History of the Church from AD 324 to AD 440*, trans. Edward Walford (London, 1855); Palladius of Aspuna, *The Lausiac History*, ed. John Whortley (Collegeville, MN, 2015), 36–38.

ample evidence of Ethiopian pilgrims in Jerusalem, where they would have met and mingled with Christians from various places in the Middle East and the Latin West.[5] As recent historiography has demonstrated, the European Middle Ages were always "global," and as the centuries progressed, Ethiopians themselves developed greater and greater interest in the Latin Church, Rome, and Europe more broadly.[6] Their presence through diplomacy and pilgrimage evoked much interest from Europeans, especially along the Mediterranean coast where Ethiopian monks and diplomats were the most likely to visit.

Simultaneous to these encounters between people and the attendant transfer of knowledge and objects, the figure of the Black Christian emerged in the medieval Latin Church. One of the most striking and well-known examples was found in Central European devotion to St. Maurice, an early Christian martyr-saint who purportedly was a third-century member of the Roman legion in Thebes (Egypt). During a wave of anti-Christian persecution, the devout Maurice and his fellow soldiers refused to engage in acts of violence against their co-religionists or to worship Rome's original pagan gods. As a result, they were executed.

The origins for depicting Maurice as a Black African are obscure. North African Christians were routinely described and portrayed as what we would now refer to as white – a good example of this is St. Augustine, who came from a Romanized Berber family – as just one among a larger world of Mediterranean complexions and appearances. Medieval Europeans likely experienced a range of ethnic diversity in Egypt that made it possible to imagine an Ethiopian or Nubian man as part of its military elite. Yet Maurice's Blackness was not part of most textual accounts of his life; as a result, he was represented as white throughout most of Europe. It was only in the German city of Magdeburg (which boasted his relics) and the surrounding territory that he was depicted as a Black African.[7] Scholars have puzzled over this,

---

[5] Anthony O'Mahony, "Between Islam and Christendom: The Ethiopian Community in Jerusalem before 1517," *Medieval Encounters* 2, no. 2 (1996): 140–54.

[6] See, in particular, the work of the "inventor" of late antiquity, Peter Brown, now discussed in the historian's own intellectual autobiography: *Journeys of the Mind: A Life in History* (Princeton, 2023). See also Mark Gregory Pegg, *Beatrice's Last Smile: A New History of the Middle Ages* (Oxford, 2023).

[7] Jean Devisse, "A Sanctified Black: Maurice," in *The Image of the Black in Western Art*, vol. II, part I: "From the Demonic Threat to the Incarnation of Sainthood," ed. David Bindman and Henry Louis Gates, Jr. (Cambridge, MA, 2010), 139–205. On images of St. Maurice in the early modern period, see Paul H. D. Kaplan, "Redeploying a Saint: The Black Maurice and the Shifting Iconography of Blackness in Post-Reformation Germany and the Baltics," *Zeitschrift für Kunstgeschichte* 86, no. 3 (2023): 340–67.

though the general consensus is that Emperor Frederick II (1194–1250) deployed this iconography of St. Maurice as a way of connecting the saint to Nubia and to Frederick's claim for universal sovereignty.[8]

St. Maurice provides the first example of a widely recognized Black saint in Latin Christendom. His cult points to the fact that, in the case of Black saints, the medieval metaphor of color difference could act as a physical representation of universal sovereignty. If Ethiopians existed at the edge of the known world, their inclusion in the pantheon of the Latin Church signified its global dominion. Maurice's Blackness further represents other interlocking aspects of medieval European understandings: (1) an awareness of the presence of Black Africans in Egypt, Jerusalem, and other spaces in Europe itself, and (2) the conviction that Black Africans could be part of Christendom, even as white Europeans also held unfavorable attitudes about black or dark skin. Finally, (3) Black figures could easily transition from being subjects to objects, as their visual difference and European prejudice against Blackness transformed a person into a metaphor (which also points to the ways saints have always acted as symbols and signifiers).

The history of St. Maurice is echoed in key ways in the emergence of the iconography of the Black magus, in line with growing familiarity with Ethiopia in the later Middle Ages. The biblical account of three kings (sometimes, "wise men" in contemporary English) who followed the star to Bethlehem to venerate the Christ child at his birth included no descriptive language of their appearance other than the gifts they carried. Medieval iconography of this event – called the Adoration – crafted them into men of three ages: an old man, a man in his middle years, and a young man, which underscored the all-encompassing nature of salvation and Christ's eternity. And then, somewhere in the fourteenth century, one of the trio began to appear as a Black man. Often, he was rendered as the youngest of the three, Balthazar, though his placement in visual iconography varied. Paul Kaplan has argued that this iconographic transition coincided with the increasing presence of Ethiopian monks in Europe and their diplomatic delegations of the fourteenth and fifteenth centuries. Unlike Maurice, the figure of the Black magus proliferated throughout Europe, becoming the predominant

---

[8] Devisse, "A Sanctified Black"; Effroysyni Zacharopoulou, "The Black St. Maurice of Magdeburg and the African Christian Kingdoms in Nubia and Ethiopia in the Thirteenth Century," *South African Journal of Medieval and Renaissance Studies* 25 (2015): 77–110; Gude Suckale-Redlefsen, *Mauritius: Der Heilige Mohr* (Zurich, 1987).

iconography for the Adoration by the sixteenth century; it was near-exclusive by the early seventeenth in all Latin Catholic regions.[9]

EARLY MODERN BLACK SAINTS

The medieval background is crucial to understanding the emergence of other Black saints in the late sixteenth century because it is a reminder that Europe's engagement with Africa did not exclusively center on the trafficking of enslaved people. It also shows clearly that the rise of Black saints was facilitated by the very long precedent of recognizing Black Christianity among Europeans.[10] Yet this groundwork only facilitated the pathway for veneration of Black saints; widespread devotion gained traction as a direct result of the transatlantic slave trade. The Portuguese began slaving raids and establishing trading posts along the western coast of Africa by the middle to end of the fifteenth century. The Portuguese quickly established a monopoly on the sale of enslaved West and Central Africans, a system that accelerated rapidly by the turn of 1500, transporting thousands and then millions of people to Iberia and the Americas throughout the early modern period, reaching its zenith in the catastrophic eighteenth century.[11]

---

[9] For an in-depth, recent study, see *Balthazar: A Black African King in Medieval and Renaissance Art*, ed. Kristen Collins and Bryan C. Keene, introduction by Henry Louis Gates, Jr. (Los Angeles, 2023). See also Paul H. D. Kaplan, *The Rise of the Black Magus in Western Art* (Ann Arbor, MI, 1985); Mary Joan Winn Leith and Allyson Everinham Sheckler, "Mantegna's Black Magus and Prester John," *Notes in the History of Art* 42, no. 1 (2022): 25–35; Jonathan K. Nelson, "Ethiopian Christians on the Margins: Symbolic Blackness in Filippino Lippi's Adoration of the Magi and Miracle of St Philip," *Renaissance Studies* 35 no. 5 (2021): 857–79; Alexander Vergara and Herlinda Cabrero, eds., *Rubens: The Adoration of the Magi* (London, 2004); Joseph Leo Koerner, "The Epiphany of the Black Magus Circa 1500," in *The Image of the Black in Western Art*, vol. III: "From the 'Age of Discovery' to the Age of Abolition," part 1: "Artists of the Renaissance and Baroque" (Cambridge, MA, 2010), 7–92.

[10] For an overview of the history of the African presence in Europe, see this crucial work: Olivette Otele, *African Europeans: An Untold History* (New York, 2021).

[11] The historiography on the slave trade is vast, even if one limits it to the Luso-Spanish side. On its earliest evolution, see Herman Bennett, *African Kings and Black Slaves: Sovereignty and Dispossession in the Early Modern Atlantic* (Philadelphia, 2018); Toby Green, ed., *The Rise of the Trans-Atlantic Slave Trade in Western Africa, 1300–1589* (New York, 2012); Toby Green, "Building Slavery in the Atlantic World: Atlantic Connections and the Changing Institution of Slavery in Cabo Verde, Fifteenth–Sixteenth Centuries," *Slavery & Abolition* 32, no. 2 (2011), 227–45; Eduardo Corona Pérez, *Trata atlántica y esclavitud en Sevilla, ca. 1500-1650* (Seville, 2022); David Wheat, David Eltis, and Alex Borucki, eds., *From the Galleons to the Highlands: Slave Trade Routes in the Spanish Americas* (Albuquerque, NM, 2020).

Missionary efforts to convert and baptize Africans played a role in the justification for enslavement and Portuguese military incursions into the continent, but early modern clergy understood that their routine practice of forced and mass baptism did not result in pious Christians.[12] Baptism tended to be merely the first tactic when encountering large numbers of non-Christians in a colonial context, as seen both in this case and that of Indigenous communities in New Spain. As a result, catechesis – that is, teaching Christians essential doctrine – became a core of the missionary project in Europe and colonial spaces among already baptized enslaved people, in both Europe and the Atlantic Islands. Yet, as Miguel Valerio discusses in his contribution to this volume (Chapter 16), an especially consequential feature of the Church's plan to create "good" Christians among their enslaved populations proved to be the organization of Black Christians into pious lay communities called confraternities. Confraternities had medieval origins but persisted into the early modern period and, in the early modern Iberian world, expanded and intensified during the seventeenth century.[13]

Dominican confraternities dedicated to Our Lady of the Rosary were the first to admit enslaved and free Black Christian members. In places with large Black Christian populations, however, Rosary confraternities exclusive to Black Christians appeared, given special designators such as "Our Lady of the Rosary of the Blacks." Unsurprisingly, given Portugal's central role in the early transatlantic slave trade, Black confraternities first appeared in Lusophone territories, including Cape

[12] Giuseppe Marcocci, "Blackness and Heathenism: Color, Theology, and Race in the Portuguese World, c. 1450–1600," *Anuario colombiano de historia social y de la cultura* 43, no. 2 (2016): 33–57; Giuseppe Marcocci, "Conscience and Empire: Politics and Moral Theology in the Early Modern Portuguese World," *Journal of Early Modern History* 18, no. 5 (2014): 473–94. For detailed instructions on identifying and catechizing improperly baptized Africans, see Diego de Montoya Ruiz, *Instruccion para remediar, y assegurar, quanto con la divina gracia fuere possible, que ninguno de los negros que viene de Guinea, Angola, y otras provincias de aquella costa de Africa, carezca del sagrado Baptismo* (Seville, 1614). Keep in mind, however, that the rulers of Kongo were baptized Christians in the fifteenth century and maintained an independent (i.e., noncolonial) Catholic kingdom for centuries: Cécile Fromont, *The Art of Conversion: Christian Visual Culture in the Kingdom of Kongo* (Chapel Hill, NC, 2014); and Alan Strathern, "Catholic Missions and Local Rulers in Sub-Saharan Africa," in *A Companion to the Early Modern Catholic Global Missions*, ed. Ronnie Po-chia Hsia (Leiden, 2018), 151–79.

[13] Konrad Eisenbichler, ed., *A Companion to Medieval and Early Modern Confraternities* (Leiden, 2019); Nicholas Terpstra, *Lay Confraternities and Civic Religion in Renaissance Bologna* (Cambridge, 1995); Susan Verdi Webster, "Sacred Altars, Sacred Streets: The Sculpture of Penitential Confraternities in Early Modern Seville," *Journal of Ritual Studies* 6, no. 1 (1992), 159–77.

Verde and Lisbon before 1500, though they spread rapidly throughout the sixteenth century in all corners of the Iberian empires with enslaved populations. During this expansion, Black confraternities became increasingly organized and controlled by Black Christians themselves, rather than serving exclusively as a tool for social control, a development that continued into the sixteenth and seventeenth centuries in Spanish territories as well.[14]

Yet with the exception of the cult of St. Maurice in Magdeburg, there is little evidence of Black saints being actively venerated in the sixteenth century. This is not surprising given how canonization proceeded throughout the Middle Ages and early modern period, with a central focus on white male clergy – predominantly from Italy – and with few women and even fewer people from non-elite or lay backgrounds, let alone a nonwhite person.[15] Nevertheless, this began to change in the second half of the sixteenth century thanks to two developments that led to the spread of the first global devotion to nonwhite saints in the Latin Church.

The first shift was prompted by the Church's ongoing intellectual battle with Protestant authors over the history of early Christianity and which religious tradition followed the path of the Apostles most authentically. This attention to sacred history encompassed both works of history more directly – most evident in the multivolume *Annales ecclesiastici* – and the reworking of primary liturgical texts, such as the Martyrology and Breviary.[16] Alongside the rediscovery of many (alleged) ancient martyrs from Rome's catacombs (see Chapter 6), this surge of interest in sacred history also exposed saints from

---

[14] Erin Kathleen Rowe, *Black Saints in Early Modern Global Catholicism* (Cambridge, 2019), chap. 3; Esteban Mira Caballos, "Cofradías étnicas en la España moderna: Una aproximación al estado de la cuestión," *Hispania Sacra* 66, extra II (2014): 57–88; Iván Armenteros Martínez, "De hermandades y procesiones: La cofradía de esclavos y libertos negros de Sant Jaume de Barcelona y la asimilación de la negritud en la Europa premoderna siglos XV–XVI," *Clio: Revista de Pesquisa Histórica* 29, no. 2 (2011): 1–23; Lucilene Reginaldo, "'África em Portugal': Devoções, irmandades e escravidão no Reino de Portugal, século XVIII," *História* 28, no. 1 (2009): 239–320; Célia Maia Borges, *Escravos e libertos nas Irmandades do Rosário: Devoção e solidaredade em Minas Gerais, séculos XVIII e XIX* (Juiz de Fora, 2005); Jaque H. Hidalgo Javiera and Miguel Valerio, eds., *Indigenous and Black Confraternities in Colonial Latin America: Negotiating Status Through Religious Practices* (Amsterdam, 2022).

[15] Robert Bartlett, *Why Can the Dead Do Such Great Things? Saints and Worshippers from the Martyrs to the Reformation* (Princeton, NJ, 2013).

[16] Cesare Baronio, *Annales ecclesiastici*, 12 vols. (Rome, 1588–1607); Giuseppe Antonio Guazzelli, "Cesare Baronio and the Roman Catholic Vision of the Early Church," in *Sacred History: Uses of the Christian Past in the Renaissance World*, ed. Katherine Van Liere et al. (Oxford, 2012), 52–71.

Catholicism's textual past. One of the most important of the newly emphasized saints who emerged from these revisions of sacred history was the Ethiopian ruler Kaleb (discussed above), referred to in European sources as Elesban, whose exploits in the early medieval Mediterranean were widely documented. It appears that historical attention to early Greek sources by European authors such as Cesare Baronio brought the emperor to the attention of the Latin Church. Although, as Baronio himself noted in his historical annotations to the revised Roman Martyrology of 1586, Elesban had made his appearance as early as the tenth century in the ten-volume Greek collection of saints' lives (or menologion) by the Byzantine hagiographer Simeon Metaphrastes, the saint did not make his official liturgical debut onto the global Catholic stage until Baronio's edition of the Martyrology.[17] In spite of these appearances, however, his cult did not gain much traction in Europe until later in the seventeenth century, as he became swept up in efforts to increase the visibility of his compatriot, Efigenia.

Efigenia had an older history in the Latin liturgy, appearing as early as the Carolingian period as the daughter (sometimes named, sometimes not) of an Ethiopian or Abyssinian ruler converted to Christianity by the apostle Matthew.[18] Efigenia was central to this story, because it was through her that Matthew attained martyrdom. The young woman's conversion followed her father's, but his sudden death left her – and the apostle – in a precarious position. Her uncle, a pagan, took the throne and decided that Efigenia should be his bride in order to consolidate his reign. For her part, Efigenia, like all good Christian virgins, wished to remain unmarried and dedicated to God. Withdrawing to a convent, her rejection enraged the new king, which only intensified when Matthew spoke out in support of Efigenia's decision. The king then had Matthew executed and set Efigenia's convent on fire; the fire was miraculously extinguished and the nuns survived, while the king faced divine judgment and an immediate death.[19]

---

[17] *Martyrologium Romanum* (Rome, 1586), 486 (October 27), note e. For a vernacular edition printed in Spain, see *Martyrologio romano: Reformado conforme a la nueua razon del kalendario y verdad de la historia ecclesiastica* (Salamanca, 1586).

[18] One of the most thorough accounts of the early years of Efigenia's cult can be found in Arturo Carucci, *La vergine Ifigenia negli "Acta" di San Matteo* (Salerno, 1945); and Enrique Márquez Martínez, "Santa Efigenia/Ifigenia: Hagiografía y mito en San Mateo en Etiopía, de Felipe Godínez," *Studia Aurea* 11 (2017): 319–36.

[19] For a detailed early modern account of Efigenia's life, see José Pereira de Santana, *Os dous atlantes da Ethiopia, Santo Elesbaô Emperador XLVII da Abessina, e Santa Ifigenia Princeza de Nubia ambos Carmelitas* (Lisbon, 1735–1738), vol. 2.

Efigenia's cult remained bound up in the story of Matthew's martyrdom; she did not at that time become an object for devotion herself, as separate from Matthew.

Although the chronological origin of Efigenia's active cult is difficult to pinpoint, she was venerated in Spain by the early seventeenth century at the latest. Shortly thereafter, she began to be paired with Elesban, and both became adopted by the Carmelites, a religious order that itself has a complex origin story in the East. While the early development of Efigenia's independent cult still remains obscure, her presence in the Martyrology and Breviary provided an opportunity for clergy in need of saints for newly baptized enslaved people – the new generation of "Ethiopians."

The earliest devotion to Black saints, however, was not directed toward ancient Black saints but toward contemporary ones: Benedict of Palermo and Antonio of Caltagirone, two sixteenth-century Sicilian Franciscans. Antonio (d. 1549) lived most of his life enslaved, renowned for his extreme humility and charity. Antonio Daza's chronicle of the Franciscan Order includes a life of the Afro-Sicilian that is extensive in comparison to others in the volume. The friar recounts Antonio's birth in Libya to parents who were both Black and Muslim, as well as his captivity and enslavement in Sicily, where he had several owners who were shepherds. Described as the stereotype of the "holy fool," Antonio was praised for his simplicity, ignorance, and extreme humility. Daza portrays his relationship with his owners as one of mutual respect, as the enslaved man's holiness was apparent to all. After a mass die-off of their sheep and goats, the owners were despondent, but after the prayer of Antonio, God miraculously replaced all their animals, down to the last one. Daza explains that "they feared keeping such a friend of God enslaved," and so they manumitted Antonio, which allowed him to join the Third Order of the Franciscans. Daza ends his account with testimonies of witnesses gathered as part of an early canonization process in the Sicilian town of Noto, demonstrating that he had access to this material from the Sicilian Franciscans.[20] In addition to collecting this testimony, the Sicilians commissioned a hagiography, which remained in manuscript. It seemed as though Antonio was poised to be the first major Black saint; the cult was certainly brought to Iberia along Franciscan networks, perhaps in order to bring it to the Spanish king's notice.

---

[20] Antonio Daza, *Quarta parte de la Chronica General de Nuestro Padre San Francisco y su Apostolica Orden* (Valladolid, 1611), 155–68.

The friars also brought news of Antonio's compatriot, Benedict of Palermo, who died several decades after Antonio, in 1589, and whose cause was ultimately much more successful. Benedict was the son of an enslaved woman, became a hermit in the island's mountains, and was corralled into a Franciscan convent during the reform of the order in the middle of the century. He lived the rest of his life at the Franciscan convent of Our Lady in Palermo where he died in the odor of sanctity. No Black Franciscan was permitted to take the full orders as a friar, in a pattern that continued for most Catholics of color throughout the early modern world; instead, they lived as members of the third order. Tertiaries followed the main vows of the order, but as laymen who were sometimes not resident in a community. As such, they had a lower status. They could not become priests, for example, and had more limited leadership possibilities, though the hagiographies of Benedict in particular emphasize his esteemed status within the convent. Contemporary accounts also portrayed Benedict as a powerful personality, unafraid to pursue his spiritual calling in spite of opposition and ridicule, which was largely racist in origin.[21]

Unlike Antonio, Benedict's holiness quickly gained traction and caught the eye of the king of Spain – perhaps the Franciscans in Palermo were better organized than those supporting Antonio's cause – and his cult took off on both sides of the Spanish Atlantic, with devotion quickly spreading across Portuguese possessions as well. Eventually, Antonio (often referred to as Antonio da Noto during this period) took his place by Benedict's side as a fellow Black Franciscan, although only Benedict successfully achieved canonization (in 1807).[22]

---

[21] Printed primary sources of the early phases of Benedict's *causa* can be found in Giovanna Fiume and Marilena Modica, eds., *San Benedetto il Moro: Santità, agiografia e primi processi di canonizzazione* (Palermo, 1998); Rosalia Claudia Giordano, ed., *San Benedetto il Moro: Il Memoriale del Rubbiano e l'ordinaria inquisitio* (Palermo, 2002). Manuscript versions of the processes can be found in Vatican City, Archivio Apostolico Vaticano (hereafter AAV), Congr. Riti, vol. 2179. There are many hagiographies dedicated to St. Benedict; for a couple of examples in Spanish, see Pedro de Mataplanes, *Vida de Fray Benito de S. Fradelo* (Madrid, 1702); and Antonio Vicente de Madrid, *El Negro más prodigioso: Vida portentosa del Beato Benito de San Philadelphia, ó de Palermo* (Madrid, 1744).

[22] This had been preceded not by formal beatification but by confirmation of the cult in 1743. See *Index ac Status Causarum* (Vatican City, 1999), 559. Antonio is much less well-studied than Benedict. Italian scholars have studied his life and cult most closely: Salvatore Bono, "Due santi negri: Benedetto da San Fratello e Antonio da Noto," *Africa: Rivista trimestrale di studi e documentazione dell'Istituto italiano per l'Africa e l'Oriente* 21, no. 1 (1966): 76–79; Salvatori Guastella, *Fratello Negro: Antonio di Noto, detto l'Etiope* (Noto, 1991); Giovanna Fiume, "Il pantheon

ALTARPIECES, CONFRATERNITIES, AND SAINTS

It is important to keep in mind the complexity and polyvalence of cultic devotion in that each saint had multiple trajectories, audiences, and purposes simultaneously. The absorption of the four Black saints into the two religious orders – Franciscan and Carmelite – provided them with institutional frameworks, a path to large-scale devotion through their presence in conventual churches and liturgies, and personal and communal lay devotion that could be quite detached from institutional settings. Scholars often emphasize the institutional context of saints associated with specific religious orders, particularly the role of founders. While it is true that religious orders created strong communal identities around their saints, close attention to conventual and parish churches from this era demonstrates that altarpieces displayed a mélange of saints, with certain individuals and pairs occurring regularly, no matter whose church it was – Saints Francis, Dominic, and Teresa of Ávila in particular. Francis and Dominic were often included together in the same altarpiece, suggesting that early modern Catholics viewed them as a natural pair, despite their founding of different orders, while Teresa of Ávila is almost ubiquitous in the centuries following her canonization in 1622. In some churches, altarpieces were commissioned by wealthy laypeople and confraternities, who then had control over the iconographic program of their altars and its images. But no matter the cause, it is a good reminder not to oversimplify the relationship between saints and their religious order.

In the realm of Black saints, Benedict and Efigenia were often paired together, particularly in the early phases of their cults, despite their vastly different backgrounds and association with different orders. In seventeenth-century Cádiz, the Black Rosary confraternity, hosted by the Dominicans in their parish church, boasted an altar with their titular Rosary Virgin flanked by images of Benedict and Efigenia. Remarkably, the Franciscan and Carmelite saints stood watch over a lay confraternity in a Dominican church with a Dominican Marian cult at their center.[23] Another Black confraternity in Cádiz was dedicated to the Virgin, with additional Black saints appended onto the central devotions later: Nuestra Señora de la Salud was later joined on the

---

africano: Il caso di Antonio Etiope," in *Esclavitudes hispánicas (siglos XV al XXI): Horizontes socioculturales*, ed. Aurelia Martín Casares (Granada, 2014), 59–88. For primary sources, see Antonio Daza, *Quarta parte*, 156; "Processo di beatificazione di Antonio da Noto redatto nel 1549," Palermo, Biblioteca Comunale, MS 3Qqc36, n. 15.

[23] Hipólito Sancho de Sopranis, *Las cofradías de morenos en Cádiz* (Madrid, 1958).

altarpiece by Benedict and Efigenia.[24] When Black Catholics – enslaved and free – began to form their own confraternities, they were able to create a governing structure and constitutions, as well as secure access to altars and permission for burial rites at their churches. While they faced barriers that White confraternities did not, particularly in terms of autonomous governance, several Black confraternities became comparatively wealthy and well-known, maintaining images of the Virgin that gained local reputations for being miracle-workers. They begged for alms and participated in the civic, devotional life of processions associated with major feast days, particularly during Holy Week, alongside their white counterparts. And, crucially, they venerated Black saints whose images stood at their altars alongside their major patron saint.[25]

The existence of Black saints in the Americas had the potential to provide inspiration for Black men and women wishing to devote themselves to lives within Catholic religious houses, and some of them later went on to die in the odor of sanctity. One of these, Martín de Porres, who died in Lima around seventy years after Benedict of Palermo (1639), was celebrated as a saint after his death, and eventually attained officially saintly status (beatified in 1837, canonized in 1962). The posthumous testimony collected about Martín's life contains no references to the many Black confraternities that dotted Lima's religious landscape (including one housed at Martín's own convent), nor to any of its sculptures of Benedict of Palermo. Martin was famed for his skills at healing. His grateful patients, including powerful nobles and clergy, assumed that his ability to cure could only be a gift from God.[26] His death brought lavish celebrations and almost frantic devotion, followed

---

[24] *Defensa jurídica por la cofradia de N. Sra de la Salud, San Benedicto de Palermo, y Santa Efigenia, sita en la auxiliar Iglesia del Rosario de Cadiz, en los Autos con los curas, y mayordomos de fabricas de ella, sobre restitucion de unas Alhajas* (Seville, 1760).

[25] For Black confraternities and devotion to Benedict (including discussion of images) in the Spanish Atlantic, see Rowe, *Black Saints*; Bernard Vincent, "San Benito de Palmero en España," *Studia Historica: Historia Moderna* 38, no. 1 (2016): 23–38; Cristina Cruz González, "Visualizing Corporate Piety: The Art of Religious Brotherhoods," in *A Companion to Viceregal Mexico City, 1519–1821* (Leiden, 2021), 181–212; Rafael Castañeda García, "Santos negros, devotos de color: Las cofradías de San Benito de Palermo en Nueva España: Identidades étnicas y religiosas, siglos XVII–XVIII," in *Devoción, paisanaje e identidad: Las cofradías y congregaciones de naturales en España y en América, siglos XVI–XIX*, ed. Óscar Álvarez Gila, Alberto Angulo Morales, and Jon Ander Ramos Martínez (Bilbao, 2014), 145–64.

[26] See, e.g., *Proceso de beatificación de Fray Martín de Porres*, vol. 1 (Palencia, 1960), 91.

by hagiographies and engravings.[27] Black saints, venerated by Black confraternities, created Black circuits of devotions that fed and reinforced devotion to Black holy people, even when white authors did not make these connections explicit.

POLYSEMIC SAINTS

While Black saints remain solidly within Catholic tradition – both spiritually and historically – cults of the saints have always had a polysemous nature. It is not a surprise, therefore, to see Black saints become intertwined with new religious practices that evolved in Latin America among African-descended communities. Scholars have long debated how best to analyze the relationships between African religions and Christianity in the ritual practices of enslaved Africans. How do we define and understand how rituals came into being and what believers brought to them? The framework of early modern Christianity officially created a firm line between orthodoxy and heterodoxy, but the lived experience of Christianity existed in a liminal space – it has always been inherently porous and dynamic. The place of Catholic saints in Afro-Latinx ritual is a rich space for deep analysis of the emergence of new religious forms.

The most common analytical framework used by scholars to unpack the complex processes of religious and cultural change in the early modern world has been "syncreticsm" or "acculturation."[28] The framework of conversion remains a common paradigm but is problematic for different reasons. For example, it is not in fact how early modern missionaries viewed belief and its instantiation. Missionaries did not "convert" – they baptized; after baptism came catechesis and liturgical participation. Somewhere in there, "belief" took root. And of course, focus on either conversion or baptism ties scholars to a European

---

[27] The most complete account of Martín de Porres in English is Celia L. Cussen, *Black Saint of the Americas: The Life and Afterlife of Martín de Porres* (Cambridge, 2014).

[28] See the pathbreaking work of Melville Herskovits on religious syncretism and the African Atlantic; he viewed syncreticism through the lens of conscious acceptance and rejections of certain traditions. While nearly a century old, Herskovits's research has played a key role in the development of the field of African diasporic religions. Melville J. Herskovits, "The Negro in the New World: The Statement of a Problem," *American Anthropologist* 32, no. 1 (1930): 145–55; Robert Redfield, Ralph Linton, and Melville J. Herskovits, "Memorandum for the Study of Acculturation," *American Anthropologist* 38, no. 1 (1936): 149–52. For a critique of Herskovits, see Andrew Apter, "Herskovits's Heritage: Rethinking Syncretism in the African Diaspora," *Diaspora* 1, no. 3 (1991): 235–60.

framework, which has some utility, but which represents only a sliver of the cultural dynamics at play for African diasporic people.[29] While scholars continue to struggle over the correct terminology, older frameworks of syncretism and acculturation have been replaced with conversion and hybridity, among others, which have generated critiques of their own.[30] None of these concepts captures successfully the complexity of the emergence of new religious forms.

The newly enslaved were forcibly baptized, generally in large groups with little to no catechesis. In places like Brazil, which saw the trafficking of three million people in little over a century, enslaved and free Afro-Brazilians who had been in Brazil for a century lived beside new arrivals, reigniting cultural practice and memory, while creating space for new spiritual and ritual forms. Catholic authorities in the Spanish and Portuguese Americas required at least the sheen of Catholic devotion, though in some places they evinced little interest in policing the exact forms this took. Within the system of enslavement and colonialization, rupture and brutality, Black confraternities could be a primary site for the observation of such polysemous spiritual practices, which provided legitimacy according to the Church and privacy, independence, and even (as Miguel Valerio suggests elsewhere in this volume) resistance – away from white oversight and white interference (although again, for the most part there was always white oversight in a colonial slave society).

---

[29] There is extensive scholarship on "survivals" of African culture in enslaved communities in the Americas. In addition to those cited in this section, see Ana Lucia Araujo, *African Heritage and Memories of Slavery in Brazil and the South Atlantic World* (Amherst, NY, 2015); Paul Lovejoy, "The African Diaspora: Revisionist Interpretations of Ethnicity, Culture, and Religion Under Slavery," *Studies in the World History of Slavery, Abolition, and Emancipation* 2, no. 1 (1997): 1–23; James Sweet, *Recreating Africa: Culture, Kinship, and Religion in the African-Portuguese World, 1440–1770* (Chapel Hill, NC, 2003); Jason R. Young, *Rituals of Resistance: African Atlantic Religion in Kongo and the Lowcountry South in the Era of Slavery* (Baton Rouge, LA, 2013).

[30] A crucial architect of the notion of the Black Atlantic is Paul Gilroy: *The Black Atlantic: Modernity and Double Consciousness* (Cambridge, MA, 1993). Gilroy employs the framework of hybridity, which has been critiqued by other scholars; for one example, see Mariza Milazzo, "The Ruse of Impurity: Paul Gilroy's *The Black Atlantic* and the Politics of Hybridity," *Cultural Studies* 37, no. 2 (2023): 204–23. Sylvia A. Frey provides an important overview and analysis of twentieth-century historiography: "The Visible Church: Historiography of African American Religion since Raboteau," *Slavery & Abolition* 29, no. 1 (2008): 83–110; and see Katharine Gerbner, "Theorizing Conversion: Christianity, Colonization, and Consciousness in the Early Modern Atlantic World," *History Compass* 13, no. 3 (2015): 134–47.

Some of the most significant Catholic festivals in Latin America were and are vibrantly Afro-Latinx, the legacies of Black confraternities, which gave rise to the ritual use of specific music and dance as well as entirely new practices, such as elections of a king and queen for the confraternity who served specific offices throughout the year. As scholars such as Cécile Fromont and Marina de Mello e Souza have noted, these elections – common throughout the Spanish and Portuguese Atlantic – drew from central African practices, reenacting the royal presence of the Catholic rulers of Kongo.[31] The connection between an independent Black Christian kingdom in Africa with Black Catholic practice in the Americas was crucial to the meaning of these coronations – a celebration of sovereignty, reclamation of nobility, and consciousness of a broader diasporic community. Such elected kings and queens could hold aloft sculptures of the two Ethiopian royal saints, crowns firmly in place, the saintly echo of their devotees.

Beyond such festivals, new religious systems developed among African diasporic groups (enslaved and free) in the Americas that were acts of *creation*, of what Bettina Schmidt calls "polyphonic bricolage."[32] The most widespread of these were *vodun*, *santería*, and *candomblé*. These are distinct religions, arising in distinct geographies (*vodun* in Haiti, *santería* in Cuba, *candomblé* in Brazil) as the result of specific

---

[31] The essays in this important collection engage with this topic across geographies, context, and discipline, with a particular emphasis on Central African networks: Cécile Fromont and Michael Iyanaga, eds., *Afro-Catholic Festivals in the Americas: Performance, Representation, and the Making of Black Atlantic Tradition* (University Park, PA, 2019). See also Miguel A. Valerio, *Sovereign Joy: Afro-Mexican Kings and Queens, 1539–1640* (Cambridge, 2022); Tamara J. Walker, "The Queen of Los Congos: Slavery, Gender, and Confraternity Life in Late-Colonial Lima, Peru," *Journal of Family History* 40, no. 3 (2015): 305–22; Marina de Mello e Souza, *Reis negros no Brasil escravista: História da festa e coroação de rei Congo* (Belo Horizonte, 2006); Mariza de Carvalho Soares, *People of Faith: Slavery and African Catholics in Eighteenth-Century Rio de Janeiro* (Durham, NC, 2011); Marina de Mello e Souza, "Cultural Resistance and Afro-Catholicism in Colonial Brazil," in *Indigenous and Black Confraternities in Colonial Latin America*, ed. Miguel Valerio and Javiera Jacque Hidalgo (Amsterdam, 2022), 319–34; James Sweet, "The Hidden Histories of African Lisbon," in *The Black Urban Atlantic in the Age of the Slave Trade*, ed. Jorge Cañizares-Esguerra et al. (Philadelphia, 2013), 233–47; and Lisa Voigt, *Spectacular Wealth: The Festivals of Colonial South American Mining Towns* (Austin, TX, 2016), 121–50.

[32] Bettina E. Schmidt, "The Creation of Afro-Caribbean Religions and Their Incorporation of Christian Elements: A Critique against Syncretism," *Transformation* 23, no. 4 (2006): 236–43 (quote on 242).

historical circumstances and evolutions, although they bear some similar features, including the ability to access spirits for help or protection. Two central features of these religions are that they involve some knowledge of Catholicism, particularly in the cult of the saints, along with African elements.[33] A core component of all three religions is the relationship between Catholic saints and deities: In each tradition, saints and deities can be worshipped alongside each other or associated with each other; the majority of incorporated saints were white, although Black saints could also play a role. Some historians and anthropologists have posited that Catholic saints operated as a kind of screen for the continuous worship of orisha (supernatural entities from the Yoruba tradition), such that specific Catholic saints are seen to correspond to specific orishas.[34] Andrew Apter rejects this notion: "The Catholicism of Vodoun, Candomblé and Santería was not an ecumenical screen, hiding the worship of African deities from official persecution. It was the religion of the masters, revised, transformed, and appropriated by slaves to harness its power within their universes of discourse. In this way the slaves took possession of Catholicism and thereby repossessed themselves as active spiritual subjects."[35] Apter's language of possession is powerful here, as it points toward a dynamic view of ritual that centers the embodied experience of religion as a lived experience. The saints – both Black and white – inhabited a range of meanings for Afro-diasporic people, but remained in many cases core to their spirituality, largely because of the role saints played as intermediaries, as in between the two planes of existence.

The dynamism between West and Central African and Catholic spiritualities leads to a further question: How did various audiences "read" the blackness of the images in front of them? Black saints had African origins or descent, but some objects that garnered fierce devotion in the early modern period were so-called black Madonnas and black/brown Christs. The term *negro* referred to a person, but also – all too obviously – to a pigment, or range of pigments, used in painting wood, canvas, or sculpture. What associations did people make between

---

[33] For an overview, see Nathan Samuel Murrell, *Afro-Caribbean Religions: An Introduction to Their Historical, Cultural, and Sacred Traditions* (Philadelphia, 2010); Luis Nicolau Parés, *The Formation of Candomblé: Vodun History and Ritual in Brazil*, trans. Richard Vernon (Chapel Hill, NC, 2013); D. H. Brown, *Santería Enthroned: Art, Ritual, and Innovation in an Afro-Cuban Religion* (Chicago, 2003).
[34] Melville Herskovits, "African Gods and Catholic Saints in New World Negro Belief," *American Anthropologist* 39, no. 4 (1937): 635–43.
[35] Apter, "Herskovits's Heritage," 254.

black-the-color and Black-as-a-human-descriptor?[36] More research needs to be done on the relationship between blackness in art – particularly in the cases of black Madonnas and black Christs during the context of racialization and colonialization. Early modern missionaries spent much time engaging with lavish metaphors of light and dark, white and black, in their theological discourses. This language was grounded in Scripture and was omnipresent in Christian rhetoric almost from the outset. The sudden presence of thousands of baptized *negros*, however, provided a new rhetoric of embodied spirituality for religious authors. These authors' extravagant insistence on the shared experience of a soul, its salvific potential, and its potential for great virtue never militated against racist regimes of enslavement and discrimination. Nor, really, was it meant to, since the vast majority of Spanish and Portuguese religious participated in the enforcement of enslavement and white supremacy (in addition to frequently being enslavers themselves). Conversion had, on the surface, genuine spiritual meaning to these authors, but such sincerity lived easily alongside indifference to earthly suffering and a lack of interest in human dignity for all God's people.[37] The spread of Catholicism throughout the early modern globe – through force and persuasion – transformed Catholicism itself through the process of creation, of possession, of bricolage. These practices must be read both through and beyond normative Catholicism: While some of these practices were embraced or ignored by the Church, others were intentionally kept or placed outside the confines of formal European Christianity. Whether licit or not, Black practitioners embraced the power of the saints as intermediaries and helpers. As a result, examining the complex histories of Black saints leads us through a powerful story of dispossession and possession, destruction and recreation, beyond and through Christianity even as it reshapes our understanding of global Catholicism.

---

[36] Monique Scheer, for example, suggests that the meanings of Black Madonnas fundamentally changed during the era of the slave trade: "From Majesty to Mystery: Change in the Meanings of Black Madonnas from the Sixteenth to Nineteenth Centuries," *American Historical Review* 107, no. 5 (2002): 1412–40. On Black Christs, see Douglass Sullivan-González, *The Black Christ of Esquipulas: Religion and Identity in Guatemala* (Lincoln, NE, 2016); Mardith K. Schuetz-Miller, "Black Virgins, Black Christs, and the Cult of Esquipulas," *Journal of the Southwest* 60, no. 3 (2018): 637–77.

[37] One well-known supporter of slavery was the Jesuit Alonso de Sandoval (1576–1652), who, while defending the rational souls of all enslaved people, also endorsed the violent actions of their enslavers and the racist underpinnings of slaving regimes: Alonso de Sandoval, *Naturaleza, policia sagrada i profana, costumbres i ritos, disciplina i catechismo evangelico de todos Etiopes* (Seville, 1627).

6 Catacomb Saints

NORIA K. LITAKER

In the summer of 1675, villagers in the small Bavarian town of Gars am Inn and the monks who resided in the local Augustinian cloister waited with great anticipation to welcome a distinguished foreign visitor. Father Johann Chrysostomus Hager had labored for months planning the elaborate eight-day celebration. He had procured costumes from the royal court in Munich, designed and commissioned four triumphal arches, hired musicians and an honor guard of local soldiers, and sent invitations to all the parishes, monasteries, and noble families in the surrounding area. As the sun rose on the morning of July 7, the guest of honor finally arrived. He was welcomed into town with a large procession, which included high-ranking nobles and churchmen as well as thousands of eager onlookers from nearby towns who had come to catch a glimpse of the esteemed newcomer. Yet the man they had all come to see was not a living dignitary, but the bejeweled skeleton of an ancient Roman martyr named St. Felix (Figure 6.1).[1]

St. Felix was one of thousands of Roman "catacomb saints" whose remains were sent to all corners of the world by the Catholic Church in the early modern period. In 1578, workers mining stone outside the city accidentally discovered an entrance to an ancient catacomb on the Via Salaria. The burial ground housed thousands of graves from the second to fourth centuries CE in labyrinthine underground passages. News of the discovery caused great excitement among Catholic clergy and the Roman populace alike. The ecclesiastical historian Cesare Baronio recounted how "all Rome was filled with wonder, for it had no idea that in its neighborhood there was a hidden city, filled with tombs from the days of the persecutions of the early Christians."[2]

The Catholic belief that the catacombs were "filled with the tombs from the days of the persecutions of the Christians" was particularly

---

[1] Bernhard Ebermann, "300 Jahre St. Felix in Gars," *Das Mühlrad* 17 (1975): 73–75.
[2] Vatican City, Biblioteca Apostolica Vaticana, Avvisi Urbinati, August 2, 1578, Urb. lat. 1046, f. 302.

Figure 6.1 Christian Jorhan, Altar-tabernacle with holy body of St. Felix, 1752, Felix Chapel (Gars am Inn: Kloster Gars) (Photo: Noria Litaker)

significant. Suddenly, the Church had a new, and seemingly unending, reservoir of bodily relics from early Christian martyrs at its disposal. For Catholics the discovery seemed especially providential as it underscored the sanctity and centrality of the Eternal City in Christian history and demonstrated the vital role saints and relics had played in the faith since its earliest days.[3] Since the outbreak of the Reformation

---

[3] Cesare Baronio, *Annales Ecclesiastici*, vol. 2 (Rome, 1594), 81; translation from Simon Ditchfield, "Text Before Trowel: Antonio Bosio's Roma Sotteranea Revisted," in *The Church Retrospective: Papers Read at the 1995 Summer Meeting and the 1996 Winter*

in 1517, Protestant theologians of all denominations had vigorously attacked both Roman primacy as well as the cult of saints and the veneration of holy relics. They asserted that such beliefs and practices lacked a scriptural basis and instead reflected accumulated human error and invention over the centuries.[4]

As a result of these critiques, the related issues of saints, sanctity, and relics became pressing concerns for the institutional Church. At the Council of Trent (1545–63), Catholic theologians responded to these challenges, asserting that the veneration of saints and their relics was "a practice of the catholic and apostolic church received from the earliest times of the Christian religion." These practices, they argued, had been confirmed in the following centuries by a consensus of holy fathers and sacred councils.[5] In the decades following this 1563 pronouncement, Catholic and Protestant scholars continued to research and debate the history of the early Christian Church to prove "complete identity between their own beliefs and practice and those of their earliest ancestors."[6] In Rome, Catholic historians and archaeologists, such as Baronio and Antonio Bosio (1575–1629), led an erudite campaign of "paleo-Christian revival." Working closely with Church authorities, scholars set out to use historical and archaeological evidence to prove a central thesis: the institution of the Roman Catholic Church – including practices like relic veneration – had been "ever the same" (*semper eadem*), unchanging across the centuries.[7] The discovery of the catacombs in 1578, and the relics therein, provided proponents of this thesis with new and important material evidence to support their claims about early Church history. Scholars such as Baronio and Bosio argued that the remains in the catacombs did not belong to just any saints; they belonged to ancient Christian martyrs and came from a period of Church history that even Protestants celebrated as untainted by corruption. Consequently, venerating these saints could be considered neither unorthodox nor novel.

Meeting of the Ecclesiastical History Society, ed. R. N. Swanson (Woodbridge, 1997), 358.

[4] Robert Bartlett, *Why Can the Dead Do Such Great Things? Saints and Worshippers from the Martyrs to the Reformation* (Princeton, NJ, 2013), 85–89.

[5] *Decrees of the Ecumenical Councils: Trent to Vatican II*, ed. and trans. Norman P. Tanner (London, 1990), 2:774.

[6] Simon Ditchfield, "Thinking with Saints: Sanctity and Society in the Early Modern World," *Critical Inquiry* 35, no. 3 (2009): 555.

[7] Cesare Baronio, *Annales ecclesiastici*, vol. 1 (Antwerp, 1588), 33.

The assertion that *all* those buried in the labyrinthine passages were martyrs was especially resonant in an era of renewed religious violence and martyrdom. Catholic writers connected the persecution of early Christians with the deaths of early modern martyrs to illustrate continuity over time. From the earliest years of the Church to the present day, they argued, martyrs had been willing to sacrifice their lives to defend their Catholic beliefs against tyrants and heretics; in doing so, these early Christians became the Church's first saints.[8] The conviction that the remains of catacomb saints physically embodied "the [paleo-Christian revival's] key themes of antiquity, martyrdom and Roman provenance" made them symbolically invaluable and underpinned the Catholic Church's decision to send the relics across Europe and the wider world.[9]

LOGISTICS: EXCAVATION, AUTHENTICATION, AND EXPORT

Although exciting and confessionally useful, the discovery of the catacombs also posed two significant challenges for the Church in Rome: how to regulate the excavation of relics and how to definitively identify the graves of martyrs.[10] In the century following 1578, Church policies shifted from somewhat lax oversight to increasing administrative supervision and control. In the immediate aftermath of the underground cemetery's discovery, the cardinal vicar of Rome, as the customary executor of the pope's episcopal and pastoral duties, became responsible for the excavation, authentication, and distribution of catacomb saint relics.[11]

Yet the cardinal vicar and his staff were far from the only ones removing relics from the catacombs in the late sixteenth century. The cardinal vicar – and the pope – frequently granted private excavation licenses to members of religious orders and other high-ranking officials,

---

[8] Cesare Baronio, *Martyrologium Romanum* (Rome, 1586), i–xiv.
[9] Trevor Johnson, "Holy Fabrications: The Catacomb Saints and the Counter-Reformation in Bavaria." *Journal of Ecclesiastical History* 47, no. 2 (1996): 294.
[10] Ingo Herklotz, "Wie Jean Mabillon dem römischen Index entging: Reliquienkult und christliche Archäologie um 1700," *Römische Quartalschrift für Christliche Altertumskunde und Kirchengeschichte* 106 (2011): 201.
[11] Ingo Herklotz, "Antonio Bosio und Carlo Bascapè: Reliquiensuche und Katakombenforschung im 17. Jahrhundert," in *Festschrift für Max Kunze: Der Blick auf die antike Kunst von der Renaissance bis heute*, ed. Stephanie-Gerrit Bruer and Detlef Rößler (Mainz, 2011), 93.

which allowed them to remove relics from the catacombs licitly.[12] These individuals could then either keep the relics for personal devotion or distribute them to a third party without further permission.[13] At the same time, a thriving black market in catacomb relics also emerged, as merchants and smugglers snuck into the catacombs, removed relics, and then sold them to eager clerical and lay buyers.[14] The problem of illegally excavated remains quickly became so acute that in 1599 Pope Clement VIII (r. 1592–1605) issued the first in a long line of edicts prohibiting unauthorized persons from stealing relics from the catacombs or even visiting the passages without permission. Further edicts promulgated by the cardinal vicar repeated these prohibitions; finally, in 1614, Pope Paul IV revoked all previously issued private excavation licenses granted by previous popes and cardinal vicars in an attempt to reassert institutional control over the flow of catacomb relics out of Rome.[15] Despite this action, the excavation of holy remains outside the direct supervision of Church officials continued to grow in the decades that followed. Just seven years after the previous pope had revoked all private licenses, his successor Pope Gregory XV granted a large number during his two-year reign (r. 1621–23).

Shortly thereafter, Urban VIII (r. 1623–44) began another concerted effort to more strictly regulate and control the licit and illicit export of catacomb relics, just as he also clamped down on the cults of those not yet canonized. In the early 1630s, he assembled a special committee of scholars and officials to devise a plan to prevent the persistent illegal theft of holy remains from the catacombs by relic smugglers and merchants.[16] The pope also asked the committee to formally address the second major issue posed by the discovery of the catacombs: how to identify the graves of martyrs and differentiate them from those of ordinary Christians. Up to this point, the Church had not formally

---

[12] Massimiliano Ghilardi, "'Auertendo, che per l'osseruanza si caminarà con ogni rigore': Editti seicenteschi contro l'estrazione delle reliquie dalle catacombe romane," *Sanctorum* 2 (2005): 127.

[13] Herklotz, "Wie Jean Mabillon," 201–2.

[14] Massimiliano Ghilardi, "Quae signa erant illa, quibus putabant esse significativa Martyrii? Note sul riconoscimento ed authenticazione delle reliquie delle catacombe romane nella prima etá moderna," *MEFRIM: Mélanges de l'École française de Rome. Italie et méditerranée* 122, no. 1 (2010): 87–92; A. Katie Harris, "Gift, Sale, and Theft: Juan de Ribera and the Sacred Economy of Relics in the Early Modern Mediterranean," *Journal of Early Modern History* 18 (2014): 212–15.

[15] Ghilardi, "'Auertendo,'" 124–27; Harris, "Gift, Sale, and Theft," 219.

[16] Ghilardi, "'Auertendo,'" 127; Harris, "Gift, Sale, and Theft," 219.

defined exactly which signs, letters, words, or images indicated that a particular tomb belonged to a Christian martyr.

There was, however, a strong inclination on the part of Catholic archaeologists and antiquarians to interpret multiple signs and symbols as markers of a martyr's grave, an approach Simon Ditchfield has called "text before trowel."[17] These scholars' study of the catacombs was an act of both devotion and erudition, and their interpretive frameworks were heavily influenced by knowledge of the passion accounts of early martyrs as well as other texts that contained what Ingo Herklotz has labeled "catacomb clichés." These clichés included several oft-repeated, but historically inaccurate, ideas: (1) the Roman catacombs only contained the graves of Christians, (2) there were innumerable martyrs buried in the catacombs, and (3) martyrs' graves could be identified easily by symbols or words.[18] Given the assumptions about the number of martyrs buried in the catacombs and the ease of identifying their burial sites, a rather expansive group of inscriptions, symbols, images, and objects became accepted by excavators as signs of a Christian martyr's grave.

Upon discovering a grave in the catacombs, the first step for explorers and relic excavators was to examine the inscription on the gravestone – if one existed – to see if the text identified the deceased as a martyr. On graves lacking written inscriptions, there were two common signs believed to definitively mark a martyr's grave. The first was the carved or painted image of a palm leaf, a pre-Christian symbol of victory and long a visual attribute for Christian martyrs; it was interpreted as a sign of a martyr's victory over both death and their pagan tormentors. The second sign of a martyr's grave was the presence of a blood ampule – a container of clay or glass – which was believed to contain the blood of the fallen hero collected by fellow Christians and deposited at their gravesite.[19] Other common visual symbols and images used to identify a martyr's grave included signs of eternal life – the cross, doves, fish, anchors, fruit baskets – as well as images of the good shepherd or scenes from the Old and New Testaments.[20]

Despite the confessional inclination of Catholic archaeologists to see signs of martyrdom on many graves, over the course of the early modern period critics both within and outside the Church expressed

---

[17] Ditchfield, "Text Before Trowel," 343–60.
[18] Herklotz, "Wie Jean Mabillon," 198.
[19] Ibid., 203–4.
[20] Ghilardi, "Quae signa erant illa," 95.

skepticism about (1) how many martyrs were buried in the underground cemeteries and (2) the validity of signs used by the cardinal vicar to identify their graves. In 1598, Jesuit historian Juan de Mariana sent letters to both Pope Clement VIII and King Philip II of Spain (r. 1556–98) in which he challenged the idea that all those buried in the catacombs were martyrs and questioned the criteria used to differentiate the relics of martyrs from ordinary Christians.[21] Over the next century, other erudite churchmen, including the Augustinian friar Fortunato Schacchi (1573–1643) and later Jean Mabillon (1632–1707), published treatises that echoed Mariana's concerns. Both Schacchi and Mabillon noted that signs like the palm leaf or the Chi Rho (☧) simply meant the deceased was a Christian, not necessarily a martyr.[22] Mabillon also voiced doubts about the blood ampule, asking whether these vessels might have contained perfume rather than blood.[23]

Despite the early reservations expressed by Mariana, in the 1630s Urban VIII's committee ruled that "for the future, the norms for extraction of holy bodies already observed by our elders would be followed."[24] Without a clear directive, Church-sanctioned excavators continued to use a wide variety of symbols to identify martyrs' graves. In addition, the illicit excavation of relics also continued unabated from the 1630s to the 1660s. In 1656, the cardinal vicar issued yet another edict banning unauthorized entrance in the catacombs.

Continued theft and sale of catacomb relics, and the lack of clear identification criteria for these supposed early Christian martyrs, finally forced the papal administration to devise a coherent plan to deal with the recurrent issues around the management of the catacombs and the authentication of the relics therein. In 1669, Pope Clement IX (r. 1667–69) issued a bull that reassigned oversight over relics and indulgences – which had previously been the purview of the Congregation of

---

[21] Mariana's letters to Philip II and Clement VIII, dated December 13, 1597, are included in Georges Cirot, *Mariana, historien: Études sur l'historiographie espagnole* (Bordeaux, 1905), 417–23 (Document No. 6).

[22] Fortunato Scacchi, *De cultu et veneratione servorum Dei liber primus* (Rome, 1639); Jean Mabillon, *Eusebii Romani ad Theophilum Gallum epistola de cultu Sanctorum ignotorum* (Paris, 1698).

[23] Mabillon, *Eusebii*, 7. For an overview of the Catholic Church's response to Mabillon's *Epistola*, which he was forced to revise to prevent its placement on the Index of Prohibited Books, see Herklotz, "Wie Jean Mabillon," 207–26.

[24] Antonio Ferrua, "Il Decreto dell'anno 1668 sull'estrazione dei corpi santi dalle catacombe," in *Rendiconti: Atti della Pontificia Accademia Romana di Archeologia*, vols. 23–24 (Rome, 1950), 319; Harris, "A Known Holy Body," 254–55.

Rites – to the newly created Congregation of Indulgences and Relics. Even before its official foundation, the new Congregation issued a decree stating that the presence of an image of a palm leaf together with a "blood ampule" were the "most sure" signs of a martyr's grave. The Congregation added that a second ruling on other frequently used identification signs would appear shortly.[25] Despite this promise, a decree never materialized, and a wide variety of symbols – over the persistent objections from some Catholic scholars – continued to be used to confirm catacomb saints as early Christian martyrs throughout the late seventeenth and eighteenth centuries and beyond.[26]

Although the matter of which signs indicated a martyr's grave was never fully resolved, in 1672 Pope Clement X (r. 1670–76) issued a bull that made significant additional structural reforms to strengthen the oversight and regulation of catacomb relic distribution.[27] The bull reaffirmed the jurisdiction of the cardinal vicar over the catacombs and created the position of Custodian of Sacred Relics. Appointed by and reporting to the cardinal vicar, the custodian was responsible for monitoring the sacred cemeteries and ensuring they were not profaned or violated in any way.[28] In addition to the office of the cardinal vicar, the bull named the papal sacristan, an Augustinian monk whose duties included the maintenance of the papal chapels and relic collection, as the only other legitimate source of authenticated catacomb saint relics.[29]

After 1672, clerics, pilgrims, and other petitioners desiring relics of a saint could appeal to either of these offices for a holy body or smaller relic particles. The offices of the cardinal vicar and the papal sacristan tended to attract distinct groups of supplicants: the latter catered to people of higher rank, including guests and other distinguished

---

[25] Aloisius Prinzivalli, *Resolutiones seu decreta authentica sacrae congregationis indulgentiis sacrisque reliquiis* (Brussels, 1862), 1.

[26] In 1863, the Congregation of Rites reaffirmed the 1668 decree that asserted that the palm branch and the blood ampule were signs of a martyr's grave. In 1931, the Pontificia Commissione di Archeologia Sacra finally undertook a scientific analysis of a glass container from the catacombs; the results showed the container had held aromatic oil or another essence, not blood: Herklotz, "Wie Jean Mabillon," 227–28.

[27] "Diversae ordinationes circa extractionem reliquiarum ex coemeteriis Urbis, et locorum, circumvincinorum, illarumque custodiam, et distributionem," in *Bullarium romanum* (Rome, 1733), 161–62.

[28] For information on the Custodian of Sacred Relics, see Massimiliano Ghilardi, "Il Custode delle Reliquie e dei Cimiteri," *Studi Romani* 1, no. 1 (2019): 175–210.

[29] For more information on the role of the papal sacristan, see G. Moroni, "Sagrista del papa," in *Dizionario di erudizione storico-ecclesiastica*, vol. 60 (Venice, 1853), 171–96.

ecclesiastical visitors who had direct connections within the curia, whereas the custodian fielded requests for relics from a larger and more diverse range of petitioners, including humble lay pilgrims and other visitors to Rome.[30] Petitions (*memoriali*) to these respective offices reveal that supplicants often specified whether they wanted a "holy body" (*corpus sanctus*) or merely a box of smaller relics (*scatola*), which usually included four relic particles from four different saints.[31]

Some *memoriali* contained even more detailed information on the type of "holy body" the petitioning individual or institution might want. Some preferred a male or female saint, a saint found with grave goods, or a saint with a *nomen proper* rather than a "baptized saint." During the excavation process, quarrymen found graves of ancient Christian martyrs with and without names. Saints whose names were found on their gravestones were classified as having a *nomen proper* and stored separately from anonymous remains.[32] If a grave had been identified as that of a martyr through symbols, but no name was present, the cardinal vicar or the papal sacristan "baptized" the remains with names from a list held in each respective office. The names were usually Latin words for attributes possessed by martyrs – Felix (happy, blessed), Fortunatus (lucky, fortunate), Placidus (gentle, peaceful), Victor/Victoria (victory) – and provided the relics with an identity. The number of saints whose names were not known greatly outnumbered those found with a *nomen proper*.[33]

With either a *nomen proper* or baptized name established, the cardinal vicar or the papal sacristan enclosed the remains in a sealed wooden box and provided each set of relics with an authentication certificate. The certificate described the nature of the relics – whole-body (*corpus sancti Christi Martyris*) or fragments – and included the name of the saint(s), the date and site of their excavation, and the

---

[30] Philippe Boutry, "Les corps saints des catacombes," in *Reliques romaines: Invention et circulation des corps saints des catacombes à l'époque modern.*, ed. Stéphane Baciocchi and Christophe Duhamelle (Rome, 2016), 230; Jean-Marc Ticchi, "Mgr Sacriste et la distribution des reliques des catacombes dans l'espace Italien," in ibid., 197–98, 205–6.

[31] Rome, Archivio storico del Vicariato di Roma (ASVR), Fondo Reliquie 77, Custodia d. SS. Reliquie dell' Emo Sig Card. Vicario di N.S.Corpi, Reliquie de'SS. Martiri donate, Tom. I, 1737–1783; ASVR, Fondo Reliquie 78, Custodia delle SS. Reliquie dell'Emo Signor Cardinale Vicario di N.S. Corpi, e Reliquie de' SS. Martiri donate, Tomo II, 1783–1786; ASVR, Fondo Reliquie 79, Corpi e reliquie de'SS Martiri donate Tom. III, 1786–1800.

[32] Nicolò Antonio Cuggiò, *Della giurisdittione e prerogative del vicario di Roma*, ed. Domenico Rocciolo (Carocci, 2004), 113–14.

[33] Ibid., 117.

Figure 6.2 Authentication certificate for the holy body of St. Felix, 1671 (Gars am Inn: Archiv der Münchener Provinz der Redemptoristen) (Photo: Noria Litaker)

designated recipient's name.[34] Initially written out by hand, the scale of export quickly grew so great that by the 1660s the offices began using printed fill-in-the-blank authentication forms where these details could be quickly noted (Figure 6.2).

Though some catacomb saints' bodies traveled in a direct line from supplicant or donor to their intended destination, often their paths were a bit more circuitous. The authentication certificates that accompanied the saints allowed the relics' new owner to "keep the holy relics [for themselves], to give them to others, [or] to transfer them out of Rome to be installed and exposed for the veneration of the faithful in some public church or chapel."[35] As a result, donors or agents in Rome and beyond could obtain these holy bodies from a third party, rather than directly from Church authorities, and it was not at all unusual for the relics to pass through multiple hands before reaching their final destination.

Concern on the part of papal authorities about the difficulty in regulating the trade in catacomb relics did nothing to diminish demand

[34] Ibid., 114.
[35] Ibid.

on the part of Catholics in Europe and abroad. Catholic communities from Wil, Switzerland (St. Pankratius), to Morelia, Mexico (St. Pio), to Valkininkai, Lithuania (St. Bonifatius), clamored to acquire and display the relics of ancient Christian martyrs in their local monastic, parish, and pilgrimage churches. From 1657 to 1791, the papal sacristan sent over 35,000 individual and 2,000 whole-body relics to destinations across the globe.[36] The cardinal vicar, whose extant records cover the period from 1737 to 1791, distributed thousands more catacomb bodies and fragments to churches from Portugal to Peru.[37]

CATACOMB SAINTS LEAVE ROME

Although the significance of Roman catacomb relics in the arc of Catholic sacred history was clear to Church officials and scholars in Rome, once they left the Eternal City, it was up to local communities to decide how to welcome, honor, and display the ancient bones, as the inhabitants of Gars am Inn had done. This was especially true due to the dearth of biographical information about the saints provided by their authentication certificates and the fact that human remains have "no intrinsic status as relics." As Alexandra Walsham has observed, "[t]he symbolic and semiotic value of such objects is a reflection of the subjectivity of the society that honors and prizes them. The manner in which relics are discovered, identified, preserved, displayed, and used by particular communities is thus singularly revealing about the attitudes and assumptions that structure their outlook."[38] Therefore, the close examination of catacomb relics and their reception after leaving Rome provides a useful lens through which to explore the nature of Catholic piety and the construction of early modern sanctity between the Catholic center and its periphery.

Recent research has begun to shed light on the myriad ways in which catacomb saint relics functioned in local Catholic communities as well as the varying motivations behind their acquisition. Often scholars have interpreted the distribution and use of catacomb saint relics as part of the Counter-Reformation movement to defend the cult

---

[36] Christophe Duhamelle and Stéphane Baciocchi, "Les reliques romaines 'hors la ville en quel lieu que ce soit du monde,'" in Baciocchi and Duhamelle, eds., *Reliques romaines*, 5, 11.
[37] ASVR, Fondo Reliquie 84, Regestum Primum Corpora et Reliquia SS. M.M. quae conceduntur á Custode SS. Reliquiarum ab Anno 1737–1754.
[38] Alexandra Walsham, "Introduction: Relics and Remains," *Past & Present* 206, Supplement 5 (2010): 14–15.

of saints and relics against Protestant attacks. In certain regions of Northern Europe, including areas of the Low Countries, Northern Italy, France, and Switzerland, the relics were sometimes acquired by monastic and parochial communities for explicitly anti-Protestant reasons and clustered along confessional borders.[39] In these cases, the act of obtaining and displaying relics was inherently a defensive statement by Catholic congregations as a way to assert their continued belief in the efficacy of the saints as intercessors and in the power of their relics.

However, both the timing and geographical distribution of holy bodies across Europe point to another important dimension of the use of these relics: as an affirmative expression of Catholic identity. Most catacomb saint relics were exported from Rome *after* the end of the religious wars that had convulsed Europe for the better part of a century (from c. 1550 to the end of the Thirty Years' War in 1648), and confessional boundaries had largely stabilized. Furthermore, churches in Italy, a region that had remained Catholic after the outbreak of the Protestant Reformation, acquired over half of all exported catacomb relics.[40] These trends signal that these saints did not simply play an "external role ... as guardians of Catholic territory" but an important "internal role, binding together the faithful."[41]

CATACOMB SAINTS IN BAVARIA

The state of Bavaria provides a fruitful case study to examine how these relics functioned outside the confines of the Eternal City, both because of the sheer number of translations and the practices that surrounded them. From 1590 to 1803, Bavarians imported at least

---

[39] Hansjakob Achermann, *Die Katakombenheiligen und ihre Translationen in der schweizerischen Quart des Bistums Konstanz* (Stans, 1979), 47; Stéphane Baciocchi et al., "De Rome au royaume de France: Patronages, inscriptions spatiales et médiations sociales (XVIe–XVIIIe s.): Introduction au dossier 'France,'" in Baciocchi and Duhamelle, eds., *Reliques romaines*, 413–15; Anne Bonzon, "Autour de Montpellier: Reliques romaines et reconquête catholique aux XVIIe et XVIIIe siècles," in ibid., 459–60; Annick Delfosse, "Les reliques des catacombs de Rome aux Pays-Bas: Acteurs, réseaux, flux," in ibid., 263; Christophe Duhamelle and Stéphane Baciocchi, "Des Guardes Suisses à las frontière confessionnelle: Apothéose et banalization des corps saints des catacombs," in ibid., 390–98; Ticchi, "Mgr Sacriste," in ibid., 190.
[40] Duhamelle and Baciocchi, "Les reliques romaines," 5.
[41] Ditchfield, "Thinking with Saints," 575.

384 "holy bodies" from Rome. At the beginning of the sixteenth century, the dukes of Bavaria ruled over one of the largest and most territorially consolidated states in the Holy Roman Empire. After the onset of the Reformation, the Wittelsbach co-rulers, Wilhelm IV (r. 1508–50) and Ludwig X (r. 1516–45), became some of the earliest and most important defenders of Catholicism in the Empire, and worked to maintain Catholicism as the dominant religion in their state. They published and enforced the Edict of Worms (1521), which banned Martin Luther from German lands, prohibited the circulation of Protestant books, and outlawed evangelical preaching. Wilhelm IV's successor, Albrecht V (r. 1550–79) began to adopt even more hard-line religious policies and methods of enforcing confessional conformity after the publication of the decrees of the Council of Trent in the 1560s and 1570s. The duke set up a centralized Clerical Council (*Geistlicher Rat*) to enforce orthodoxy through parish and monastic visitation and helped the preeminent Counter-Reformation order, the Jesuits, establish its first college in the territory in Ingolstadt. Albrecht's successors – Wilhelm V (r. 1579–97) and Maximilian I (r. 1597–1651) – followed in his footsteps and cultivated a particular brand of confessional culture that scholars have called *pietas Bavarica*, which emphasized Eucharistic devotion, Marian piety, the revitalization of pilgrimage sites, and participation in confraternities. During the initial stages of the Thirty Years' War, the Bavarian state fought on the Catholic side and became the larger Electorate of Bavaria in 1628, after its annexation of the Calvinist Upper Palatinate. After taking over this territory, the Wittelsbach government and its clerical allies began the forced re-Catholicization of this area.[42]

As a result of its territorial expansion, greater Bavaria contained regions with divergent confessional histories: Upper and Lower Bavaria had remained Catholic, while the Upper Palatinate had become first Lutheran and then Calvinist. A close study of the temporal and geographical distribution of the holy bodies reveals several interesting patterns that provide insights into the "internal" rather than "external" role catacomb saints served within the territory over the course of the early modern period. First, the vast majority of catacomb saints (95%) arrived in the duchy after 1648, following the end of the Thirty Years' War and the so-called Age of Confessionalization, when the veneration

---

[42] Trevor Johnson, *Magistrates, Madonnas and Miracles: The Counter Reformation in the Upper Palatinate* (Farnham, 2009).

Figure 6.3 Early modern Bavaria (Map: Ben Pease)

of saints and relics remained at its most religiously controversial. With confessional borders stabilized after the Peace of Westphalia, the period between 1648 and 1803 saw a new flourishing of religious folk life in the region as Bavarian Catholics sought ways to actively live their faith through participation in brotherhoods, religious processions, pilgrimages, and the veneration of saints.[43]

As part of this movement of baroque piety, churches in Upper and Lower Bavaria, areas that had remained Catholic throughout the Reformation, obtained far more holy bodies than the region of the Upper Palatinate, which had been taken over by Bavarians in 1628 and forcibly re-Catholicized (Figures 6.3 and 6.4).[44] These temporal and geographic distribution patterns – as well as evidence from transfer sermons, chronicles, and devotional images – indicate that the

---

[43] Walter Pötzl, "Volksfrömmigkeit," in *Handbuch der bayerischen Kirchengeschichte*, ed. Walter Brandmüller (St. Ottilien, 1991), 871.

[44] Noria Litaker, *Bedazzled Saints: Catacomb Relics in Early Modern Bavaria* (Charlottesville, VA, 2023), 17–45.

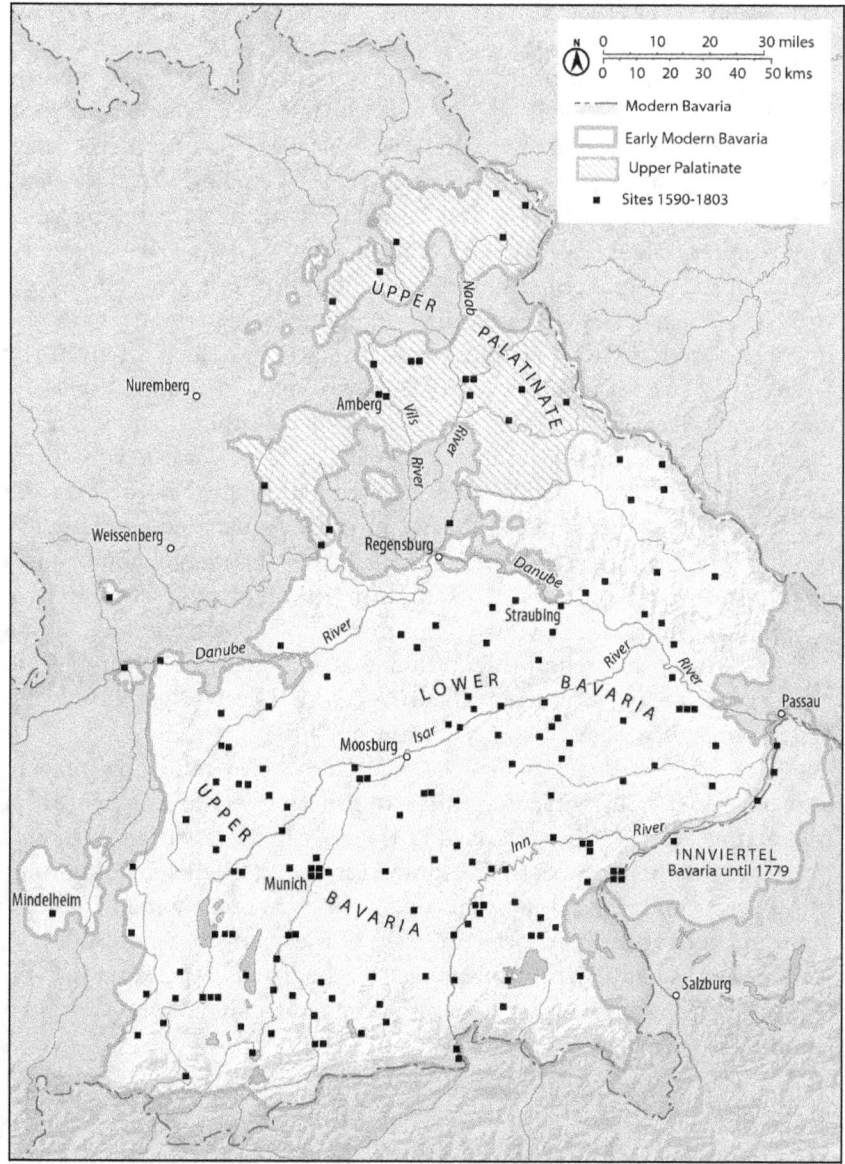

Figure 6.4 Locations with catacomb saints in early modern Bavaria, 1590–1803 (Map: Ben Pease)

acquisition of catacomb relics was not a reactionary, Counter-Reformation phenomenon linked to Wittelsbach efforts to ensure that their subjects remained – or were re-converted to – Catholicism. Rather, it was a manifestation of a broad-based baroque piety in which early modern Bavarians made active choices about how to express their Catholic faith.[45]

The determination to creatively demonstrate their Catholic confessional identity is evident in the new relic form developed by early modern Bavarians and their fellow Catholics in northern Italy, Switzerland, and Austria to display catacomb remains after 1648, and it is unique to this part of Central Europe. Instead of splitting the relics into smaller fragments – as was common during the medieval period – groups of artists, craftsmen, and relic decorators put saintly bodies *back together*. When bones were missing, carpenters created them from wood or other materials, while doctors and artists then helped arranged the bodies into sitting, standing, or lying positions. Nuns and other relic decorators then dressed the saints in lavish clothing, and carefully crafted facial features for these long-dead heroes using jewels, wire, and sometimes even wax. All these efforts culminated in the creation of shimmering "holy bodies" that communities installed permanently on church altars in glass-walled shrines. Rather than relying on dictates from government officials in Munich or the institutional Church in Rome, Bavarians, like devout communities in the surrounding Alpine region, developed a relic presentation that matched the label given to the ancient martyrs on their authentication certificates: a *corpus sancti Christi martyris* (body of a holy martyr of Christ).

This independently developed and innovative relic presentation allowed whole-body catacomb saints to function in ways distinct from fragmented relics. Using the form of the holy body, Bavarian Catholics materially demonstrated their connection to and belief in important movements and doctrines promoted by the universal Roman Catholic Church. At the same time, the presence of these holy bodies – and their human form – had a significant impact on the ritual of the saints' arrival festivities, their role as local patrons, and how they were presented within the church.

THE CASE OF ST. FELIX OF GARS AM INN

The multivalent functions served by whole-body catacomb saints in Bavaria is evident in the case of St. Felix in Gars am Inn, who arrived in the village with great pomp and circumstance in 1675. To this day, St. Felix's body sits atop an altar-tabernacle with one hand raised in

---

[45] Ibid., 1–13.

blessing and the other holding a martyr's palm (Figure 6.1). By staging his remains in this manner, the congregation at Gars made certain abstract theological doctrines visually comprehensible and concrete, namely, the sacrificial nature of the Mass and the transubstantiation of the Eucharist. Here on the altar, where Catholics believed Christ's sacrifice was performed in the liturgy, was a tangible, parallel presentation of a martyr's body, and although absent here, in many other cases the martyr held an ampule of his or her sacrificial blood. Though Christ's "own body and blood" became present in the Eucharistic elements when the priest spoke the words of institution, their external appearance remained the same.[46] By presenting catacomb saints as complete bodies, Bavarian Catholics created an immediate, embodied illustration of "high mysteries hidden in [this sacrifice]," materializing the saint's body to allude to the whole of Christ's body and blood made present during the reading of the liturgy.[47]

The Eucharistic significance of Felix's body is further underscored by the altar form in which he is housed: the altar-tabernacle. Before the sixteenth century, tabernacles – "ornamented receptacles for liturgical vessels containing consecrated bread reserved for the Communion of the sick, for communion services, and for adoration" – were separate from the main altar. This changed after Trent as the defense of the Eucharist and transubstantiation took center stage in Catholic regions.[48] Local diocesan ordinances began to require the display of the consecrated host on the main altar in tabernacles visible from all parts of the church, which made the host constantly available for veneration. As a result, tabernacles became essential to Catholic baroque high altars and often provided places to display the host or sculptures of the Crucifixion. In the altar-tabernacle at Gars, St. Felix has replaced the Eucharistic wafer or an image of Christ that would usually have been placed in the same space. The body itself has become the visual embodiment of and proxy for Christ's sacrificial body contained in the consecrated bread and wine.

While holy bodies materialized important facets of Roman Catholic Eucharistic doctrine, Bavarians also used the creative relic form of the holy body to participate in the Church-wide paleo-Christian revival. When the catacomb saints' remains arrived in Bavaria, local

---

[46] *Decrees of the Ecumenical Councils*, 2:695.
[47] Ibid., 2:734.
[48] Frederick McManus and J. B. O'Connell, "Tabernacle," in *New Catholic Encyclopedia*, 2nd ed., ed. Bernard Marthaler (Detroit, 2003).

communities were faced with the task of crafting an identity for the new patron using a box of jumbled bones and scarcely any information beyond the fact that the saint had been an ancient Roman martyr. To begin, the saints' identities were rendered legible through costume and symbolic attributes as well as grave goods placed within their shrines. Thus St. Felix, like most other catacomb saints in Bavaria, was dressed in the outfit of a Roman legionary soldier. This outfit, which conveyed the saint's antiquity and Roman provenance, usually consisted of a knee-length tunic over which waist-length body "armor" (*lorica*) was worn. The bottom of the tunic as well as the sleeves were often decorated with strips of cloth that hung over the tunic (*pteruges*). To complete the look, the soldier saints wore sandals (*caligae*) and, in some cases, a cape or helmet. In addition to their outfits, additional iconographical attributes like palm leaves, laurel crowns, blood ampules, and gravestones indicated to viewers that the saint before them was a martyr. At Gars, St. Felix holds a palm leaf in one hand and wears an elaborate crown on his head, making it visually apparent that he had sacrificed his life in the name of Christ. The form of the complete body as well as the large, transparent shrines in which they were housed proved critical in conveying these pieces of a saint's background story.

Once the saints' bodies were fully decorated in Roman garb and ready to transfer into their new homes, monks and clergymen in communities across the territory began the task of composing vitae for their ancient martyrs. Often they turned to textual sources to find background information about early Christian history and the catacombs. Using this raw material, they crafted hagiographies for these ancient Roman martyrs – of varying levels of specificity – to share at translation sermons, in printed vitae, and in devotional texts.

The monks at Gars proved particularly eager to learn more information about their new patron than his authentication certificate could provide, and used both material and written sources to construct his hagiography. According to the cloister's chronicle, St. Felix's tomb in the catacombs had included a blood ampule, and two small glass images lay near the grave when it was unearthed by excavators. One glass image showed a person in Roman clothing with a laurel wreath and palm frond in his hand labeled with the name St. Felix. The second image showed a man in priest's clothing and was labeled St. Calixtus. A piece of Calixtus's bones supposedly also lay nearby. Based on this information, the chronicler made an interpretive leap: "By leaving the glass images, the [pope] wanted to leave a clue that Felix and Calixtus both suffered a martyr's death in Rome and were buried in the same place."[49] With this information in hand – and a desire to learn more – the monks next consulted Baronio's revised *Roman Martyrology* to find a feast date that included both a St. Calixtus and a St. Felix. After some searching, they found a date that fit their criteria: "in the *Roman Martyrology*, this saint is commemorated on December 29; therefore, the feast day for St. Felix in Gars is also observed on this date."[50]

Although this bit of information was useful, the traits of another St. Felix were pressed into service to create a more well-rounded hagiography. Over the years, the saint came to be identified as one of the "Seven Brothers," who had also been martyred at a young age with a cudgel and then buried in the Calixtus catacombs. The similarities between the vitae of the two young martyrs led the Augustinians at Gars to adopt certain aspects of the "Seven Brothers" Felix for their own catacomb saint, effectively merging the lives of two separate saints with the same name into one.[51] In this particular case, the brothers at the cloister in Gars started with the objects and information given to them about St. Felix by the Church in Rome and then proceeded to use a mash-up of paleo-Christian written sources to form a more detailed vita for the saint.

With bodies built and hagiographies crafted, it was finally time for Roman catacomb saints to meet their new German neighbors. Translation festivals were critical moments in the saints' transition from foreign outsiders to local patrons and citizens. The saints' first introduction to a community typically occurred, as it did with St. Felix in Gars, with a meticulously planned procession with clerical and lay participants from the surrounding area. While communities had long celebrated the arrival of relics with *adventus* (arrival) ceremonies, Bavarians made significant modifications to these traditional ceremonies of welcome and adoption after 1648; these changes coincided directly with the shift in the presentation of catacomb relics from fragments to intact bodies. After the Thirty Years' War, festival organizers added elements from secular entry ceremonies, including triumphal arches and military escorts, to the welcome processions. Parading into town, the new saints were greeted with all the trappings of an illustrious out-of-town visitor or dignitary. The elaboration of the transfer festivities indicates the importance communities placed on greeting the new saints with great fanfare and highlights the degree to

---

[49] Ebermann, "300 Jahre St. Felix in Gars," 77.
[50] Ibid.
[51] Ibid., 78.

which they were perceived as fully present, human individuals worthy of a royal welcome.[52]

Once the whole-body saints had been successfully transferred to their new homes, their presentation as intact skeletons, in conjunction with their permanent display in glass shrines on side altars, fostered an exclusive patronage relationship between Bavarian communities and the Roman martyrs in their midst. Towns adopted the saints as patrons and held local festivals on the anniversary of their translations. Their shrines attracted local and regional pilgrims in search of saintly intercession. Devotional images, printed miracle books, and baptismal records provide further evidence of the conception and function of catacomb saints as intercessors whose reach remained limited to small areas.[53]

Many elements of the cult of St. Felix are typical of the ways in which veneration of catacomb saints became a regular part of the religious rituals and practices of individual Bavarian communities in the decades and centuries following their arrival from Rome. Just two months after St. Felix's arrival in town, a terrible fire broke out in the village. Desperate to prevent its spread, the villagers and monks paraded the saint's body through the streets along with a Eucharistic host. Miraculously, the fire was contained and Felix earned a reputation as an intercessor against deadly blazes.[54] After this incident, the martyr's reputation and veneration continued to grow among the local community. That same year, Hager, the monk who had organized the saint's translation festival, recorded in his *Tagebuch* (diary) that he had conducted a successful exorcism with the help of the saint, successfully expelling 7,000 evil spirits from a local woman named Catherina Humplin. According to Hager, the saint also miraculously helped save many villagers from a deadly fever afflicting the community in August 1675.[55]

In the years after his translation, the villagers celebrated the saint's arrival with an annual festival and continued to ask for his assistance.

---

[52] Albrecht Burkardt, "Les fêtes de translation des saints des catacombs en Bavière (XVII–XVIII siecles)," in *Les cérémonies extraordinaires du catholicisme baroque* (Clermont-Ferrand, 2009), 79–98; Trevor Johnson, "Trionfi of the Holy Dead: The Relic Festivals of Baroque Bavaria," in *Festive Culture in Germany and Europe from the Sixteenth to the Twentieth Century*, ed. Karin Friedrich (Lewiston, ME, 2000), 40–51; Litaker, *Bedazzled Saints*, 129–47.

[53] Litaker, *Bedazzled Saints*, 159–67.

[54] Munich, Universitätsbibliothek der LMU, Johann Chrysostomus Hager, *Secretum meum misi*, entry for September 3, 1675, ms 367; Ebermann, "300 Jahre St. Felix in Gars," 76.

[55] Hager, entries for July 25, 1675, and August 1676.

Figure 6.5 Anton Lichtenfurtner, fresco of St. Felix protecting the village and cloister of Gars am Inn from thunderstorms, 1754, Felix Chapel (Gars am Inn: Kloster Gars) (Photo: Noria Litaker)

In 1689 and 1690 alone, over 100 petitioners paid for the cloister's Augustinian Friars to hold votive Masses at St. Felix's altar to ask for help or to thank the Roman martyr for his intercession.[56] In the subsequent decades, veneration of the saint continued. In 1754, nearly eighty years after the saint's translation, lay brother Anton Lichtenfurtner painted three frescoes in Felix's chapel, which depict the saint protecting the Augustinian cloister and its hinterlands from fire, thunderstorms, and shipwrecks (Figure 6.5).[57] The cloister, the village of Gars,

---

[56] Ebermann, "300 Jahre St. Felix in Gars," 76.
[57] Franz Wenhardt, "Felix-Wallfahrt und Radegundis-Verehrung in Gars," in *ZeitFlussLäufe: Säkularisation der Klöster Au und Gars am Inn, 1803–2003* (Gars am Inn, 2003), 8.

Figure 6.6 Anonymous, ex-voto painting, 1675, Felix Chapel (Gars am Inn: Kloster Gars) (Photo: Noria Litaker)

as well as the surrounding fields and forests are visible in each fresco as St. Felix turns a different danger away from the town's inhabitants and their crops. The town of Gars and its surroundings also appear in several ex-voto paintings left to thank the saint for his intercession (Figure 6.6).

Both the frescoes as well as the ex-votos demonstrate a continued veneration of the saint as well as his function as a local patron who protected and helped those in and around the town of Gars with various types of difficulties common to early modern life. The local nature of the devotion to the saint was also noted in the 1754 territory-wide survey of religious festivals commissioned by the elector: "The body of the wonder-working martyr St. Felix rests in a special chapel. He is highly venerated and the entire parish of Gars as well as the surrounding neighborhood consider him a particular helper in all types of accidents. His translation festival is celebrated most solemnly each year on the Sunday after St. Ulrich's [feast day] with a large crowd of people in attendance."[58] This comment neatly illustrates how a once-foreign saint became a significant patron in a particular parish and neighborhood.

CONCLUSION

As the case of St. Felix demonstrates, the relics of catacomb saints are remarkably useful to "think with" in relation to the development and definition of early modern sanctity and its material manifestations in Catholic communities across Europe and the world.[59] Sitting at the nexus between the universal and local Catholic churches, these ostensibly ancient remains – perhaps the most widely circulated relics of the period – provide a rich opportunity to explore the negotiated nature of Catholic sanctity and its construction between the Roman center and local religious communities, not just in Bavaria, but in Catholic territories new and old around the world.[60]

---

[58] *Chur-Bayrisch geistlicher Calender auf daß Jahr MDCCLIIII: ... Rentamt München* (Munich, 1754), 451.
[59] Ditchfield, "Thinking with Saints."
[60] José Bouza Alvarez, *Religiosidad contrarreformista y cultura simbólica del barroco* (Madrid, 1990); Montserrat A. Báez Hernández, "The Corpi Santi under the Government of Pius VI, Materiality as a Sign of Identity: First Approaches to Novohispanic Cases," in *Relics @ the Lab: An Analytical Approach to the Study of Relics*, ed. Mark Van Strydonck, Jeroen Reyniers, and Fanny Van Cleven (Leuven, 2018), 21–42; Ruth Sargent Noyes, "From Rome to Myadzyel to Mosar: The Corposanto of St. Justinian and the Cult of Catacomb Relics in Belarus, 18th–21st Centuries," in *Ethno-Cultural Heritage of Belarus in the XXI Century*, ed. Irina Olunina (Minsk, 2021), 69–73.

Part II

Creating and Contesting Sanctity

7 Canonization

JAN MACHIELSEN

Spare a thought for the Franciscan friar Alonso Cueto. For years he had crisscrossed the Spanish viceroyalty of Peru. He had walked, by his own count, some 9,000 miles and interviewed some 2,000 persons, all on a holy mission: the canonization of the missionary Francisco Solano y Jiménez (1549–1610). Cueto had compiled more than 2,225 pages of testimony, recording some 900 miracles attributed to Solano. And these were not just any miracles: Solano had resurrected the dead and changed the course of rivers. When Cueto and his precious pages survived the journey from the Indies to Rome in the late 1620s, this constituted another miracle: Many other ships in his convoy had perished and thousands had drowned. The friar's safe arrival in the Eternal City with the precious evidence of Solano's sanctity intact should have been a moment of triumph. But it was not. The rules had been changed since Cueto had embarked on his holy quest. A waiting period had been introduced – the earliest the cause could now be considered was 1660, fifty years after Solano's death. Although the Church would ultimately recognize Solano's sainthood, it only beatified him in 1675 and did not canonize him until 1726, a century after Cueto's efforts.[1]

Solano's fate points to the paradox at the heart of early modern Catholicism. In the wake of the Reformation, the Catholic Church became increasingly closely identified with its cult of the saints. Where Protestants equated devotion to saints with idolatry, the Council of Trent (1545–63), during its hyperactive twenty-fifth session, defended their invocation and efficacy.[2] As this Companion shows,

---

[1] This account has been reconstructed from Vatican City, Archivio Storico de Propaganda Fide [ASPF], SOCG 182, fols. 231–89. Cueto had approached the Propaganda Fide for its intercession in 1633. The author would like to thank his coeditors, as well as Clare Copeland and Simon Ditchfield, for their comments on a draft chapter.

[2] Robert Bartlett, *Why Can the Dead Do Such Great Things? Saints and Worshippers from the Martyrs to the Reformation* (Princeton, NJ, 2013), 85–91.

sanctity was everywhere in the early modern Catholic world. And yet, at the Church's moment of crisis, while it doubled down on the saints, it also struggled in creating new ones. The last of the "medieval" canonizations in 1523 – that of the obscure Saxon bishop Benno of Meissen (c. 1040–1106) – had been encouraged by Martin Luther's opponents but became a public relations disaster. The solemn translation of Benno's relics in Meissen was parodied elsewhere in Saxony, with animal bones substituting for the saint's remains.[3] There were to be no further canonizations for another sixty-five years. Even after they resumed, the Catholic world that clamored for new saints would witness very few of them.

How can we explain this dearth of new Counter-Reformation saints? It is tempting to attribute "this failure of [papal] nerve" between 1523 and 1588 to the Reformation, as Peter Burke memorably has done, because "the very idea of a saint was under fire."[4] Burke's claim has merit, but it overlooks many of the internal factors at work within Catholicism, including the significant challenge of female mysticism (the so-called *sante vive*, or living saints).[5] The period was also not quite as fallow as commonly believed.[6] Study of the dynamics and machinery of saint-making reshapes our understanding of what new saints – the fresh faces in heaven – might tell us about the Catholic world.

Famously, Burke's study of the fifty-five "happy few" who made it through the process between 1588 and 1767 identified five principal routes to sainthood: founders of religious orders, missionaries, bishops, visionaries, and a rag-tag remnant defined by "charitable activity."[7] According to Burke, these "stereotypes of sanctity" spoke to the period, while other categories, notably theologians and martyrs, did not – absences that, Burke conceded, were "surprising."[8] Burke's analysis set to one side the ongoing

---

[3] Ronald C. Finucane, *Contested Canonizations: The Last Medieval Saints, 1482–1523* (Washington, DC, 2011), 207–40. Benno was canonized alongside Antoninus of Florence, but the Saxon bishop's cause had been approved later.

[4] Peter Burke, "How to Become a Counter-Reformation Saint," in *The Counter-Reformation: The Essential Readings*, ed. David Loebke (Oxford, 1999 [original 1984]), 129–42, at 131.

[5] Gabriella Zarri, *Le sante vive: Cultura e religiosità femminile nella prima età moderna* (Turin, 1990). Chapters 3 and 9 in this volume explore how these female mystics challenged religious authorities.

[6] Miguel Gotor, *Chiesa e santità nell'Italia moderna* (Bari, 2004), 26–27; Simon Ditchfield, "Tridentine Worship and the Cult of Saints," in *The Cambridge History of Christianity, vol. 6: Reform and Expansion, 1500–1660*, ed. Ronnie Po-chia Hsia (Cambridge, 2007), 205–6.

[7] Burke, "How to Become," 134, 138–39.

[8] Ibid., 139.

vibrant veneration of ancient martyrs and medieval saints whose holy lives continued to speak to the imagination of the faithful.[9] Yet we may also question Burke's argument on its own terms. When we consider both the input – the quality and quantity of the many canonization trials that were held across the Catholic world – and the procedures themselves, which shifted and tightened in order to cope with the deluge, a picture emerges that is very different from Burke's static survey. Such an analysis shows that not all saints were created equal, that canonizations could provoke resentment as well as delight, and that they more often succeeded when the rules were broken than followed. Exploring these wider implications requires discussion of early modern canonization procedures and the extensive changes these underwent during the seventeenth century. First, however, we must take a closer look at what canonization – and its sprightly young cousin, beatification – actually meant, as well as the role both played within the papacy's arsenal.

CANONIZATION IN CONTEXT

On January 5, 1708, a student at the Venerable English College in Rome showed up at the doors of the Holy Office. Thomas Mainwaring, a young convert to Catholicism, had entered the English seminary three years previously, but he now felt the urgent need to relieve his conscience. A week or so earlier, during the students' leisure time, the conversation had turned to the question of "whether it was dogma that the saints canonized by the pope were saved." Thomas answered no. After all, the witness testimony on which canonization depended was human rather than divine in origin, and it was human to err. Sensible though this answer might seem, the reply scandalized the other students present. It implied that the papacy and the Church could be venerating false saints.[10] The Inquisition, however, was not especially surprised and sent him away with a caution. Mainwaring was neither the first person nor even the first future cleric in early modern Italy to express such concerns, nor would he be the last.[11]

---

[9] On the continued vitality of ancient and medieval saints, see Chapter 12 in this volume.

[10] Vatican City, Archivio della Dicastero per la Dottrina della Fede [ADDF], St. St. G-1-h, doc. 9. Mainwaring apostatized upon arrival in England but returned to Catholicism late in life: Godfrey Anstruther, *The Seminary Priests: A Dictionary of the Secular Clergy of England and Wales, 1558–1850*, vol. 3: *1660–1715* (Great Wakering, 1976), 139–40.

[11] ADDF, St. St. G-1-h, doc. 7, 9, and 10, contain incidents dating to 1611, 1612, 1623, 1691, 1699, and 1753.

Such doubts about canonization raised the issue of papal infallibility, long before that became official Church dogma in 1870.[12] They did so, in part, because there was (and still is) no obvious way of acknowledging procedural mistakes. Theoretically, saints last forever – it is only their visibility in the liturgy and elsewhere that can be dialed up or down.[13] Yet infallibility also matters because saints were essential to the Catholic Church; belief in their sanctity was not an optional add-on. In 1691, an Italian friar got in trouble for declaring that it was "pious but not necessary" to believe that St. Francis of Assisi was in Paradise. (When challenged that the Church had canonized him, he sarcastically replied that "the Church knows a lot about these things."[14]) That said, canonization was *not* a form of apotheosis, a literal ascent to Heaven, as Protestants alleged.[15] While Catholic art often represented canonization in this way, formally the procedure only recognized that saints had already ascended upon dying (their merits being such that they had skipped Purgatory altogether).[16] Canonization, in other words, was only the inscription of a worthy person in the Church's catalogue of saints.[17] It was the result of a lengthy process, described in the next section, that sought to combine bureaucratic rigor with the possibility of divine inspiration and intercession – two modes of truth-making that, as Thomas Mainwaring already realized, were perceptibly different.[18]

---

[12] Donald S. Prudlo, *Certain Sainthood: Canonization and the Origins of Papal Infallibility in the Medieval Church* (Ithaca, NY, 2015), which rather understates the controversial nature of the infallibility claim.

[13] The difficulty is made apparent by the 1965 "Notification," which suppressed the cult of the (no longer Blessed) Simon of Trent, a boy supposedly killed by Jews in 1475: Magda Teter, *Blood Libel: On the Trail of an Antisemitic Myth* (Cambridge, MA, 2020), esp. 12–13. The same post–Vatican II period also saw the removal of some of the more legendary saints from the liturgical calendar, such as Saints Christopher and Catherine of Alexandria, though the latter was later reinstated. On the interplay between canonization and the liturgy, see Chapter 11 in this volume.

[14] ADDF, St. St. G-1-h, doc. 9.

[15] See, e.g., Sebastian Niemann (praeses), *Canonizatio sanctorum pontificia* (Jena, 1664), sig. A3r–A4r.

[16] Robert Bellarmine discussed the devotions permitted to "sanctos non canonizatos": Robert Bellarmine, *De controversiis Christianae fidei* (Ingolstadt, 1586), vol. 1, col. 2017.

[17] See, e.g., Angelo Rocca, *De canonizatione sanctorum commentarius*, 2nd ed. (Rome, 1610), 3; Benedict XIV (Prospero Lambertini), *De servorum Dei beatificatione et beatorum canonizatione*, ed. and trans. Vincenzo Criscuolo, 4 vols. in 8 parts (Vatican City, 2010–), vol. 1/I, 103 (bk. I, c. I).

[18] The place of divine intercession, at the very end of the process, meant that the pope ultimately acted upon inspiration from the Holy Spirit: Birgit Emich, "The Production of Truth in the Manufacture of Saints: Procedures, Credibility and Patronage in Early

The universality and finality of saint-making have profound implications for our understanding of the process in general and of the papacy's role within it. First of all, the successful conclusion of any cause can seem inevitable after the fact. Early modern Catholicism looks very different when we consider canonization as a contingent process, often delayed, frequently riven by conflict and competition. Many causes for those now considered central to the Counter-Reformation, notably those of England's martyrs, did not succeed until the twentieth century.[19] Even the traditional narrative of a "heavily authoritarian" Counter-Reformation that is centered on "great men" indirectly owes much to the cult of the saints, and yet it misses the crucial roles played by the many witnesses who testified to holy lives lived and graces received – from servants and even former slaves to cardinals and queens – and it ignores the heroic efforts of officials across the globe who worked toward these canonizations.[20]

Canonization owes its universality, at least in practice, to its status as an exclusive papal prerogative claimed by the popes during the early thirteenth century. Before then, any investigation (if there was one) would have been conducted by the local bishop, who oversaw the translation of the saint's relics to a place of honor.[21] Most ancient and medieval saints, therefore, escaped the full rigors of a lengthy canonization procedure.[22] From the 1200s onward, however, the papacy reserved saint-making to itself, which in effect offered saints worldwide recognition. Universality became especially useful during the early modern period, when the papacy was increasingly buffeted by the competing demands of Europe's leading Catholic powers. Because saints were universal, they served as powerful and prestigious diplomatic gifts, obtainable from no other source. Pope Sixtus V made no secret of the fact that his 1588 canonization of Diego of Alcalá, the first new saint since poor

---

Modern Processes of Canonization," in *Making Truth in Early Modern Catholicism*, ed. Andreea Badea et al. (Amsterdam, 2021), 165–90, at 176.

[19] A particularly helpful resource is the *Index ac status causarum* published by the Congregation for the Causes of Saints, although its most recent edition (Vatican City, 1999) is showing its age.

[20] Michael A. Mullett, *The Catholic Reformation* (London, 1999), x.

[21] The shift took place between 1200 and 1234: Bartlett, *Why Can the Dead Do Such Great Things?*, 57–58.

[22] There is no space here to discuss the papacy's recognition of local devotions through a process that became known as "equipollent" canonization. Such recognition of long-standing, mostly medieval local cults was usually the equivalent of beatification. See the "Confirmationes cultus" section of the *Index ac status causarum*.

Benno of Meissen, was a special favor to Philip II of Spain.²³ The pope foresaw that the king's Armada against England, a country ruled by "the most degenerate and depraved woman, soaked in every crime, and defiled by every heresy," could do with another celestial helper.²⁴

As a result of such obvious politicking, historians have commonly reduced saint-making to questions of geopolitical dominance. Yet as Clare Copeland has shown, scholars have been wrong to characterize the famous group canonization of 1622 of four Spaniards and one Italian as simply the result of political "triumphalism that ritually claimed Rome for the Spaniards."²⁵ Saints were more than national symbols: The two Spanish (more accurately, Navarrese or Basque) Jesuits canonized in 1622 – Ignatius of Loyola and Francis Xavier – were also global figures.²⁶ Other factors also shaped canonization decisions: Both Diego of Alcalá and the pope who canonized him were Franciscans, for example. Nor was the papacy just the plaything of major powers. Saints provided opportunities for popes to assert their influence beyond Italy; the papacy could leverage the prospect of new saints to promote compliance with other – unwelcome – rules that it could not otherwise police. When Pope Urban VIII imposed new restrictions on saint-making in the early 1630s, he did so because earlier decrees regulating the devotion to unrecognized cults had not been "observed by many in some places and in particular in Madrid."²⁷ The carrot of sainthood was dangled to encourage the observation of unpopular restrictions on devotions to candidates who might in future be worthy of the honor. If supporters wished to see their candidate canonized in St. Peter's Basilica, they would have to play by the papacy's rulebook.

---

[23] L. J. Andrew Villalon, "San Diego de Alcalá and the Politics of Saint-Making in Counter-Reformation Europe," *Catholic Historical Review* 83, no. 4 (1997), 691–715.

[24] Pietro Galesino, *Sancti Didaci Complutensis canonizatio* (Rome, 1588), 69.

[25] Thomas Dandelet, *Spanish Rome, 1500–1700* (New Haven, CT, 2001), 185; Clare Copeland, "Spanish Saints in Counter-Reformation Italy," in *The Spanish Presence in Sixteenth-Century Italy: Images of Iberia*, ed. Piers Baker-Bates and Miles Pattenden (London, 2016), 103–23. The Roman joke that the ceremony saw the canonization of four Spaniards and a saint (Philip Neri) is of uncertain but possibly seventeenth-century origin: Miguel Gotor, "'Han canonizado a cuatro españoles y un santo': La propuesta hagiográfica del oratoriano Felipe Neri entre 'el esplendor de Iberia' y 'la gloriosa memoria de Enrique IV,'" *Anuario de historia de la Iglesia* 29 (2020): 261–89.

[26] Simon Ditchfield, "Thinking with Jesuit Saints: The Canonization of Ignatius Loyola and Francis Xavier in Context," *Journal of Jesuit Studies* 9, no. 3 (2022): 327–37.

[27] ADDF, St. St. B-4-e, doc. 2, fol. 16r. The undated (1633?) letter was signed by the papal sacristan.

The apparent finality of saint-making also had a similarly profound impact on the procedure itself. Causes only ever moved in one direction – forward – but for that reason they rarely moved at all. As we shall see in the next section, the canonization process became more complex, time-consuming, and costly throughout the seventeenth century. The first manuals (just as those for the validation of relics studied in Chapter 8) emerged around 1600 to guide candidates through the maze. Over time, these works grew exponentially longer, culminating in Prospero Lambertini's exhaustive four-volume, 3,218-page *De servorum Dei beatificatione et beatorum canonizatione* (1734–38).[28] The process lengthened as well. Beatification became an obligatory intermediate step. Carlo Borromeo, canonized in 1610, was the last saint to avoid it.[29] While beatification resembled canonization in many respects, and popes (when it suited them) played up the similarity, formally the two were radically different. Whereas saints belonged to the universal Church, the blessed, or *beati*, were theoretically available only to a specified group of followers. Beatification was only "a document or indulgence conceded by the pope either through a brief or verbally" to a "certain city, religious order, province, or kingdom."[30] (In theory, then, though hardly in practice, beatification could still be revoked.[31]) Some *beati* have languished in the canonization antechamber for a very long time.[32]

The length of the journey to sanctity affects historians today: Paperwork for a given cause can remain inaccessible if the cause is still "live" and seen as likely to succeed in the future.[33] We are therefore usually granted access only to the stories of successful *beati* or

---

[28] Benedict XIV, *De servorum Dei*.
[29] On Borromeo, see Chapter 1 in this volume.
[30] Luca Castellini, *Elucidarium theologicum de certitudine gloriae sanctorum canonizatorum* (Rome, 1628), 66; Carlo Felice de Matta, *Novissimus de sanctorum canonizatione tractatus in quinque partes divisus* (Rome, 1678), 6.
[31] Benedict XIV, *De servorum Dei*, I/2, 104 (bk. 1, c. XLII) conceded that popes were not infallible where beatification was concerned. The only – modern – example I am aware of is that of Simon of Trent (see n. 13), although that cause had never been subjected to a formal beatification procedure.
[32] The longest suffering *beata*, Margherita da Città di Castello, beatified by Paul V in 1609, was canonized by Francis I in 2021.
[33] I am aware of only one canonization process – of the Spanish cardinal Francisco Jiménez de Cisneros – where the papers were deposited in the Vatican Archives because the process had been actively terminated rather than abandoned over time: Vatican City, Archivio Apostolico Vaticano [AAV], Cong. dei Riti 3180. His cause is one of many that deserves further study. The AAV, however, also holds others that appear to have been forsaken.

saints, which are transferred to the Vatican Archives.[34] The long journey also exposes strategies of papal decision-making. The growing bureaucratic complexity of saint-making offered a delaying strategy (as it had been, to a lesser extent, in the Middle Ages).[35] The position of the papacy was such that postponing a decision was often the better part of valor. Such delays proved a particularly useful test of the would-be saints because the resulting pressure exerted on the papacy – the clamor for canonization – was (perhaps perversely) itself an indicator of a candidate's holiness. Seen from this perspective, beatification looks different as well: It acts as a convenient holding pen, a bone thrown to those who have put in the effort. Where papal inaction is concerned, it is always worth assessing whether it reflected a position of weakness or strength.

New saints, then, were rare. In 1695, when the officials pushing the cause of the Carthusian martyr Fidelis of Sigmaringen (1577–1622) suffered yet another defeat in Rome, they declared the Roman lawyers who dismissed their paperwork to be "enemies of all canonization" with "hearts of stone."[36] They were not wrong. Saint-making, for the structural reasons discussed above, was meant to be difficult. At the same time, their frustration is easily enough understood because other causes *did* succeed, at times even quite rapidly. Those causes where the papacy felt forced to act, or even to set aside the normal rules, should take on a special significance in any historical analysis, which a static survey like Burke's cannot grant them. In order to understand how the process created a varied obstacle course that affected different causes differently, we need to study how it was meant to work.

A BRIEF HOW-TO GUIDE TO SAINT-MAKING

Formally, a potential saint – or Servant of God, to use the technical title – needed to possess two essential attributes. The first was a virtuous life or, more precisely, the proven, public reputation of having lived one (the so-called *fama sanctitatis*). The second were

---

[34] The *processus*, held in the Congregazione dei Riti *fondo*, can be consulted solely through the indexes 1047, 1147, 1147A, available in the Sala Indici "Leone XIII" in the Vatican Archives.
[35] André Vauchez, *Sainthood in the Later Middle Ages*, trans. Jean Birrell (Cambridge, 1997), 68.
[36] Matthias Emil Ilg, *Constantia et fortitudo: Der Kult des kapuzinischen Blutzeugen Fidelis von Sigmaringen zwischen "Pietas Austriaca" und "Ecclesia Triumphans,"* 2 vols. (Münster, 2016), 2:978.

miracles worked in death. Those worked in life, while useful, did not suffice. These requirements had not changed from the Middle Ages, although their precise definition had. Candidates were meant to possess a "heroic" level of virtue, a concept that became more common after 1602 in the wake of discussions surrounding Teresa of Ávila's beatification.[37] Like the miracles they worked, a Servant's virtues were also meant to be superhuman – apparently only achievable with divine assistance. Witnesses for the causes of the Jesuit novice Luigi Gonzaga and the Dominican tertiary Rose of Lima, for instance, described in disturbing detail the superhuman mortifications that these aspiring saints imposed on their bodies.[38] Testifying during Gonzaga's canonization process in 1609, his confessor Robert Bellarmine recalled how he had reassured the young novice in his care when the teenager, in moments of doubt, worried that "he had given scandal by doing too much penance and austerity."[39]

While the discussion of virtue could generate considerable controversy – for instance, whether saints could lie – the question of miracles posed a much greater challenge.[40] In theory, there was no limit to the form a miracle could take. The martyrs of Gorcum, killed by the Dutch Sea Beggars in 1572, allegedly obtained the death of their principal assailant, Guillaume II de La Marck, from the bite of a rabid dog. (This was considered a fitting end; a man who "lived like a dog died like a pig."[41]) Still more remarkable was a miracle attributed to Francisco Jiménez de Cisneros. The Spanish cardinal was said to have halted the passage of the sun across the sky for four hours, so as to prolong a successful battle against the Moors near Oran in which 4,000 infidels died.[42] Neither of these miracles was accepted. In fact, most miracles scrutinized were never settled – the papacy approved only the

---

[37] Vauchez, *Sainthood in the Later Middle Ages*, 519, dates the first use to Boniface VIII. For the traditional claim linking the term to Teresa's cause, see Pierluigi Giovannucci, "Genesi e significato di un concetto agiologico: La virtù eroica nell'età moderna," *Rivista di storia della chiesa in Italia* 58, no. 2 (2004): 433–78.

[38] Rose's mortifications structure the questions of the informative trial held in September 1617, less than a month after her death: AAV, Cong. dei Riti 1570, esp. fol. 6r–v.

[39] Rome, Archivum Romanum Societatis Iesu (ARSI), Archivio della Postulazione 72, fol. 74.

[40] Benedict XIV, *De servorum Dei*, I/I, 391 (bk. I, c. XVII), who tactfully does not identify the holy liar nor mention the outcome.

[41] Paris, Bibliothèque nationale de France (BnF), H-935. Prospero Bottini, *Responsio super dubio an constet de martyrio*, 15.

[42] Vatican City, AAV, Cong. dei Riti 3180, fol. 96r.

minimum required (typically two) and these would be listed on the published decree.[43]

Contemporary manuals endlessly attempted to organize the supernatural into different types or levels of miracle, and debated the number and type that sufficed for beatification or canonization.[44] The issues involved meant that the expert saint-maker, as one manual put it, had to be skilled "in all the main sciences," including "philosophy and medicine for the explanation of miracles."[45] It was especially difficult to link a miracle to a particular Servant of God; for this reason, saints' bodies (preferably incorruptible, heavenly scented) became important miracle sites.[46] Perhaps inevitably, many of the miracles put forth in canonization procedures were supernatural healings of devotees, who testified during the process. The manuals, too, focused much of their discussion on this type, many of which (not coincidentally) mirrored those Christ himself had worked in the New Testament.

The legal process that captured all this information changed dramatically over the seventeenth century, especially in its opening decades. The underlying nuts and bolts, however, remained essentially medieval.[47] The proceedings began with an "ordinary process," held by an "ordinary" – that is, a bishop – in his diocese, often, though not always, after permission had been sought from the papacy.[48] Another medieval holdover was the postulator (or procurator) whose task it was to identify potential witnesses and shepherd the cause through Rome's

---

[43] For the beatification of Pius V in 1672, delayed by the Urban regulations discussed below, Pope Clement X approved the two miracles originally put forth in 1630 (a healing miracle and a painting of Pius that escaped a severe fire), as well as two further ones (the multiplication of grain at a convent in Prato and Pius's vision of the Christian victory over the Turks at Lepanto): *Beatificationis, et canonizationis san. mem. Pii Papae V*, dated March 8, 1672.

[44] For instance, Benedict XIV, *De servorum Dei*, 4/I, 217 (bk. 4, c. VI), set the minimum number of miracles required for beatification and canonization at two, if there were eyewitnesses, but four when these were *de auditu*.

[45] Matta, *Novissimus de sanctorum canonizatione tractatus*, preface.

[46] See Chapter 10 in this volume.

[47] Ditchfield, "Tridentine Worship and the Cult of Saints," 207; Villalon, "San Diego de Alcalá," 711–13.

[48] Rocca, *De canonizatione sanctorum*, 69–70, lists the request by a prince or by "optimates" as the first step. Permission was sought from Rome for Carlo Borromeo's process in 1603: Angelo Turchini, *La fabbrica di un santo: Il processo di canonizzazione di Carlo Borromeo e la Controriforma* (Casale Monteferrato, 1984), 16, but in the case of Maria Maddalena de' Pazzi some ten years later, Pope Paul V indicated the process could begin under the Florentine archbishop's authority: Clare Copeland, *Maria Maddalena de' Pazzi: The Making of a Counter-Reformation Saint* (Oxford, 2016), 106.

obstacle course – this was the frustrating role that Cueto would perform for Francisco Solano.[49] The papacy, if it chose to open the process, would then assign it to three auditors of the Rota, the Church's highest legal tribunal, for study. Their reports in turn would be scrutinized by a group of cardinals of the pope's choosing.[50] Sixtus V's creation of the Congregation of Sacred Rites in 1588 did no more than put this traditionally ad hoc process on an institutional footing.[51]

Once the paperwork proved persuasive after close and often exhaustive examination, the secretive bureaucratic mode gave way to an entirely scripted and increasingly public "spiritual mode" wherein God's blessing was sought. Close to its conclusion, the cause was introduced to three consistories of the College of Cardinals, where the candidate's saintly credentials were celebrated. On each occasion, the pope would indicate that he was inclined toward canonization but would call for prayer and implore further divine illumination.[52] The process culminated in an elaborate canonization ceremony held at St. Peter's Basilica.[53] Where the ceremony played up the "spiritual mode" with further public prayer, the subsequent bull of canonization presents a rather different blend – the elaborate outline of correct bureaucratic procedure mingled with the equally necessary divine illumination. Close reading of these documents often reveals when and where difficulties emerged during the process.[54]

Two observations naturally follow from this description of events. First, its starting point indicates that throughout the premodern period, the papal role in saint-making was fundamentally responsive.[55] The

---

[49] Vauchez, *Sainthood in the Later Middle Ages*.
[50] On the continued significance of the Auditors, see Giovanni Papa, *Le cause di canonizzazione nel primo periodo della Congregazione dei riti, 1588–1634* (Rome, 2001), 78–95.
[51] On the Congregation of Rites, see Niccolò Del Re, *La curia romana: Lineamenti storico-giuridici*, 4th ed. (Vatican City, 1998), 332–37; Papa, *Le cause di canonizzazione*.
[52] Emich, "The Production of Truth," 173–76.
[53] Pamela M. Jones, "Celebrating New Saints in Rome and Across the Globe," in *A Companion to Early Modern Rome*, ed. Pamela M. Jones et al. (Leiden, 2019), 148–66.
[54] The beatification decree (not bull) for Pius V, discussed at n. 43, reveals that the first two miracles were approved by the Congregation of Rites on March 4, 1630, but only approved by the papacy on November 15, 1671.
[55] For the essentially "responsive" mode of papal authority, see Simon Ditchfield, "Exemplary Lives in the Making of a World Religion," in *Making Saints in a Glocal Religion: Practices of Holiness in Early Modern Catholicism*, ed. Birgit Emich et al. (Cologne, 2024), 309–32. For a nineteenth-century counterexample, see Hans de Valk, "History Canonized: The Martyrs of Gorcum Between Dutch Nationalism and

initiative came from outside the Curia, even if "outside" (as we shall see) could still be within Rome. Second, the process was obviously time- and labor-intensive, benefiting religious orders and monarchies with an established presence in the Eternal City. It was therefore costly as well: Everything, including the copying of paperwork and the scrutiny by auditors, required payment. In 1674, with the beatification of the martyrs of Gorcum assured, the postulator of their cause estimated that the process over the preceding forty years had cost some 300,000 Italian scudi and "many more" Brabant florins – and he was writing, cap in hand, for still more funds to pay for the elaborate ceremony to be held at St. Peter's Basilica.[56]

If the procedure sketched here already seems complex – writing in 1610, Angelo Rocca was able to reduce it to a "mere" twelve steps – then it grew still more so, and in three different directions, during the early 1600s. First, the number of mandatory local processes multiplied. The precise number already depended on the cult's geographic reach. For instance, the 1606 process for Ignatius of Loyola, the founder of the Society of Jesus, was held in ten locations in Spain (including Mallorca), four in Italy (including Rome), and in Brussels, where some particularly long-lived Jesuits still remembered him from their youth.[57] Second, the process was now also typically split into different parts, with separate processes investigating the Servant of God's virtues and miracles. For martyrs, the process on virtue was replaced by one investigating the circumstances of their alleged martyrdom. (Martyrdom was considered a form of baptism "by blood" and an extreme act of faith and charity, making further discussion of the Servant's other virtues moot.[58])

Third, the process also effectively doubled in length, starting with Carlo Borromeo's cause in 1605, which introduced a second "apostolic" (i.e., papal rather than episcopal) process after the earlier "ordinary"

Roman Universalism, 1864–1868," in *More than a Memory: The Discourse of Martyrdom and the Construction of Christian Identity in the History of Christianity*, ed. Johan Leemans (Leuven, 2005), 371–94. One could similarly point to Pope Francis's decision to pair the popularly desired canonization of John Paul II with the (much less heralded) cause of John XXIII in 2014.

[56] Leuven, KADOC, Persoonarchieven OFM, MS 5010, unpaginated folio. The unsigned and undated letter is addressed to the vicar general and the abbots of the Premonstratensian abbeys; the copy was likely sent to nearby Park Abbey.

[57] *Monumenta Ignatiana, ex autographis vel ex antiquioribus exemplis collecta*, vol. IV/2: Scripta de Sancto Ignatio de Loyola (Madrid, 1918), viii; a selection from these trials runs from 597 to 927.

[58] Luca Castellini, *De inquisitione miraculorum in sanctorum martyrum canonizatione* (Rome, 1629), 7, 11.

process.⁵⁹ In the apostolic process, so-called remissorial letters were sent from Rome, containing a detailed set of questions that witnesses were expected to answer. These interrogatories were based in theory on the original ordinary (or "informative") process, but in fact often seem prompted by more recently published hagiographies prepared as part of the cause.⁶⁰ Reforms introduced by Urban VIII in 1634 required one further investigation for more recently deceased Servants, a so-called process *de non cultu* meant to demonstrate that the candidate had not been the subject of public veneration. (Why these rules were introduced will become apparent in the next section.) These many steps had one small positive effect: They created minor victories on the way to sainthood that could be celebrated – the opening of the process, the confirmation of its validity, the issuing of remissorial letters, and so on. Taken together, however, they nonetheless made for an intimidatingly long road with many stumbling blocks.

The process was made still more difficult by the introduction of beatification as an intermediate step. The terms *beatus* and *beata* (blessed) had been an ancient, mostly unregulated, honorifics, equivalent to that of saint.⁶¹ The remodeling of beatification into an official procedure was slow: It first emerged in the 1590s and 1600s as a newfangled invention in search of a procedures. Rocca's manual (1601, 2nd ed. 1610), for instance, does not mention it. The first beatification *may* have taken place in 1601, but, as Simon Ditchfield has rightly observed, the uncertainty and fluidity as to what beatification actually meant makes it both impossible and pointless to identify a clear starting point.⁶² When, in 1605, Paul V "beatified" the Jesuit novices Luigi Gonzaga and Stanisław Kostka (ahead of Ignatius himself), he did so without prior investigation. It was simply a papal concession that the late young men could be called *beati* and be given a liturgy.⁶³ As late as 1613, Robert Bellarmine still argued that the right to concede a local cult to *beati* should pertain to bishops, rather than be reserved to the pope.

When the procedure outlined above was transposed onto beatification, the impact on canonization (now stage two) took time to become

---

⁵⁹ Papa, *Le cause di canonizzazione*, 130–34; Turchini, *La fabbrica di un santo*, 17.
⁶⁰ E.g., Copeland, *Maria Maddalena de' Pazzi*, 93–98.
⁶¹ Vauchez, *Sainthood in the Later Middle Ages*, 85; Copeland, *Maria Maddalena de' Pazzi*, 107
⁶² Miguel Gotor, *I beati del papa: Santità, Inquisizione e obbedienza in età moderna* (Florence, 2002), 212–13; Ditchfield, "Tridentine Worship," 211–12.
⁶³ Papa, *Le cause di canonizzazione*, 101–2.

clear. During the 1610s, canonization still required a full fresh set of trials as well as reexamination of all the paperwork generated by the original process.[64] Even Rome's bureaucrats found this excessive, and such rigor was swiftly abandoned. By Prospero Lambertini's time, over a century later, "only miracles which happened after beatification were examined," as "new signs of the divine will."[65] Beatification, then, lengthened but did not double the journey time. Its novelty, however, caused considerable uncertainty as the ground shifted, yet again, under the saint-makers' feet. Moreover, the gradual regulation of *beatus* as an official title, in turn, encouraged the use of other honorifics. By 1700, for example, the title *venerabilis* (venerable) had become a new, unofficial, lower-tier honor, customarily given to Servants of God – those potential saints with an active cause in Rome – but it was officially meaningless.[66]

Unsurprisingly, this growth in paperwork was also accompanied by increased bureaucracy. Key here was the creation, around 1630, of the position of Promoter of the Faith, more commonly known as the *advocatus diaboli*.[67] This was the role later held by Lambertini, the author of *De servorum Dei beatificatione*, and the sole person to rise from devil's advocate to Christ's vicar, as Pope Benedict XIV (r. 1740–58).[68] The promoter's task was to scrutinize trial documents, auditors' reports, and the postulators' submissions, and flag any difficulties in a report to the cardinals. This position rendered the process more explicitly adversarial. Lambertini could not find any cause since the 1630s where he or his predecessors had not raised any doubts, however minor, about the Servant's virtues, miracles, or martyrdom.[69] Starting around 1660, the promotor's formal reports and the postulator's responses were committed to print, although only for dissemination within the Congregation, not for public consumption. These documents offer a vital entry point into the underlying mass of handwritten witness

---

[64] Benedict XIV, *De servorum Dei*, I/1, 537 (bk. I, c. XXV), who notes that the causes of Philip Neri, Teresa of Ávila, and Ignatius of Loyola had all been subjected to this.

[65] Ibid., 537, 541.

[66] The adoption and spread of "venerable" requires further study; it only became regulated in 1913 when it was restricted to those Servants whose heroic virtues or martyrdom had been officially recognized: "Decretum de aliquorum locorum disciplina in initio causarum Servorum Dei emendanda, et de historicis documentis ad ipsas causas recte adhibendis," *Acta Apostolicae Sedis*, vol. 5 (1913), 436–38, dated August 26, 1913.

[67] Papa, *Le cause di canonizzazione*, 72, 205–6.

[68] See the introduction to Benedict XIV, *De servorum Dei*, I/1, 9–59.

[69] Ibid., I/1, 399.

material; they identify, for example, which miracles were deemed particularly significant or problematic.[70]

The growing complexity of canonization procedures profoundly affects how historians should understand the underlying testimony and the realities of saint-making. The need to comply with papal regulations and to align with expected models of sainthood entailed a flattening or refashioning of the candidate.[71] In addition, witness testimony, even from ordinary lay persons, was not as artless or untrained as it might first seem. Many witnesses clearly knew what was expected of them and shaped their evidence accordingly, even backing up their testimony with references to a published vita, or Life. That said, uncertainty about Rome's shifting expectations and the lack of formal training still throw up unexpected pearls. When, in 1628, seventy-nine-year-old Hildegund van Est was asked about her conversations with the martyrs of Gorcum more than half a century earlier, she primly berated the officials that "men in religious orders do not interact with worldly folk like young girls."[72] Similarly, one of the witnesses testifying in Nagasaki in 1622 to the miracles worked by the 1597 martyrs downplayed the supposed incorruptibility of their crucified bodies: "there was not much in this because, as it was winter, the bodies did not decay that quickly."[73]

The consequences of this complexity for Catholic saint-making are important. For one, the increasing burden ruled out certain causes from the start. Catholic martyrs in Reformation Britain, for instance, wholly lacked the necessary institutional and financial support.[74] The resulting dearth of saints from the British Isles was recognized at the time.

---

[70] The reports were separated from the Vatican Archives following Napoleon's conquest of the Italian Peninsula and are now held in the Bibliothèque nationale de France, obliging historians of sanctity to spend extended periods of time in both Paris and Rome. The nearly 1,400 volumes have not been properly inventoried; most are missing from the BnF's online catalog. The best available catalog, in German, is Wilhelm Schamoni, *Inventarium processuum beatificationis et canonizationis* (Hildesheim, 1983). Copies are often held in the *postulazione* archives of religious orders in Rome.

[71] See, e.g., Pierre Delooz, "Towards a Sociological Study of Canonized Sainthood," in *Saints and Their Cults: Studies in Religious Sociology, Folklore, and History*, ed. Stephen Wilson (Cambridge, 1983), 189–216, at 195.

[72] AAV, Cong. dei Riti 963, fol. 353.

[73] AAV, Cong. dei Riti 1222, fol. 42r. These trials took place far from Rome on heretical or pagan soil (and were therefore not overseen by a bishop).

[74] Alexandra Walsham, "Welsh Saints-in-Waiting: The Politics of Canonization in a Minority Catholicism," in Emich et al., eds., *Making Saints in a "Glocal" Religion*, 165–92.

In 1717, a visiting Irish mendicant friar got into trouble in Tuscany for claiming that the pope would have canonized a "dog" for money, and that Ireland was "an island of saints but there was no money to canonize them."[75] Second, even causes that did progress enjoyed varying speeds and degrees of success, because the process judged them differently. Recent candidates, as we shall see next, faced much greater challenges than their medieval counterparts, but the rules also affected the various *typologies* of saints in ways that could aid or hinder their success. While some Catholic historians have praised the rule-making process as one of "ever-increasing maturity," the reality was very different.[76] Canonization became so complex that ultimately, it rarely succeeded except when the rules were set aside. To understand how this happened, we must finally examine the candidates themselves and consider why the more recent ones proved to be so troublesome.

THE PROBLEM WITH SAINTS

The Belgian sociologist Pierre Delooz memorably observed that saints are only saints "for other people." Although Catholic sainthood was officially universal, no saint was truly for everyone.[77] Cults competed with one another for this exceptionally rare honor; one saint's early success therefore potentially upset the rest of the waiting room. This situation was made much worse by the long sixteenth-century drought in saint-making. Catholic Reform – in particular, the founding of new religious orders – had generated a reservoir of apparent holiness that grew while canonization remained blocked. Even worse, everyone knew that the papacy could act swiftly when it wanted to. Angelo Rocca's handbook, for example, included a list of rapid medieval canonizations, some of which had taken place within a year of a saint's death.[78]

The problem of the so-called *beati moderni* – the puzzle as to how and when to canonize Catholicism's most recent saints-in-waiting without wider discord or upset – could have come to a head much sooner, if Pope Sixtus V had not died when he did. In May 1587, one of Rome's local holy figures, Felice da Cantalice, passed away in the odor of sanctity. The canonization of Diego of Alcalá was already well in train, and Pope Sixtus V pushed for that of the Capuchin friar to follow

---

[75] ADDF, St. St. G-1-h, doc. 11.
[76] Papa, *Le cause di canonizzazione*, 332.
[77] Delooz, "Towards a Sociological Study," 194.
[78] Rocca, *De canonizatione*, 63–64.

swiftly – *caldo caldo*, "hotly, hotly" – opening an ordinary process less than a month after Felice's death.[79] But the ardent pope did not live to see this campaign through. If he had, such a light-speed canonization would surely have tested the patience of devotees of other *beati moderni*. Ignatius of Loyola, for instance, had passed away thirty years earlier but remained without a cause. When Felice was eventually canonized in 1712, it still prompted the Irish friar's outburst above; in the mendicant's view, the late (Catholic) King James II "had worked three miracles and lost three kingdoms," whereas Felice only "begged for bread."[80] Canonizations can cause upset as well as joy.

Faced with this problem, the Congregation's first canonizations were of uncontroversial medieval figures – Hyacinth of Poland (d. 1257, can. 1594), Raymond of Penyafort (c. 1175–1275, can. 1601), and Francesca Romana (1384–1440, can. 1608).[81] Not only had these cults waited patiently for centuries; their canonization also formalized smaller papal concessions that had been granted during the fallow years of the sixteenth century.[82] But the *beati moderni* could not be ignored. The issue came to a head with the 1595 death of Philip Neri, the "second apostle of Rome" and founder of the Roman Oratory. Oratorians set to work to promote the sanctity of their founder in every conceivable way. They distributed engravings of their *beato* complete with halos. In 1602, they translated Neri's remains to a new chapel, "the most beautiful and most rich" in Rome, in a procession resembling that of a saint's relics.[83] Cesare Baronio, the Church historian who succeeded Neri as superior of the Roman Oratory, even slipped a mention of Neri into a marginal note to the Roman Martyrology, the Church's official calendar of saints.[84] Baronio also recognized that Neri's cause and that of Ignatius ran parallel. In 1599, Baronio even publicly

---

[79] Papa, *Le cause di canonizzazione*, 23; Gotor, *I beati del papa*, 46.

[80] ADDF, St. St. G-1-h, doc. 11. On this failed canonization, see Andrew Starkie, "A Lost Cause? The Cause for the Canonization of King James II (Invited Commentary)," *Studies in Religion and the Enlightenment* 1 (2) (2019): 6–9.

[81] The canonization of Diego of Alcalá (c. 1400–1463) just predated the founding of the Congregation but also fits this pattern.

[82] E.g., Ronald C. Finucane, "Saint-Making at the End of the Sixteenth Century: How and Why Jacek of Poland (d. 1257) Became St. Hyacinth in 1594," *Hagiographica* 9 (2002): 207–58, esp. 215–17.

[83] Ruth S. Noyes, *Peter Paul Rubens and the Counter-Reformation Crisis of the Beati Moderni* (London, 2017), 176.

[84] On this inclusion and how it intersects with Baronio's own saintly aspirations, see Jan Machielsen, "An Aspiring Saint and His Work: Cesare Baronio and the Success and Failure of the Annales Ecclesiastici (1588–1607)," *Erudition and the Republic of Letters* 2, no. 3 (2017): 233–87.

approached Ignatius's tomb to install a portrait of the would-be saint.[85] (With the exception of Teresa of Ávila, the crisis of the *beati moderni* was strikingly male, unlike the challenge posed by *sante vive* earlier in the century.)

The translation of Neri's remains to a new chapel in 1602 prompted a papal backlash against unlicensed images and public devotions that brought the problem firmly into view. Papal inaction, then, became increasingly unviable. Clement VIII opted for that most bureaucratic of solutions, the creation of a learned committee to study the issue. To this new and ultimately inconclusive *Congregazione dei Beati*, the pope complained that Neri's and Ignatius's graves had been bedecked with images, candles, and votive objects: "had they been canonized they could hardly have anything more." He admitted that the *beati moderni* should be recognized, but "not without our authority."[86] Under Clement's successor Paul V, beatification emerged as a convenient compromise, offering formal recognition of a *beato*'s holiness, which extended *only* to the territory or religious order that had asked for it. In 1610, Paul presided over the canonization of the first modern saint, Carlo Borromeo (an event that, as Chapter 1 in this volume shows, also provoked anger and opposition).[87] This was followed in 1622 by Gregory XV's famous group canonization. The inclusion of four modern figures – Ignatius, Philip, Teresa of Ávila, and Francis Xavier – was an obvious attempt to sidestep issues of competition and precedence between the new saints' religious orders. Their last-minute addition caused considerable bemusement among the Spanish devotees of the fifth saint. The four *beati moderni* had effectively hijacked the canonization of the medieval Isidore the Farmer, who now had to share a stage that had originally been built for him alone.[88]

No other "modern" post-Reformation saint was canonized for another thirty-six years. Saint-making, the papacy discovered, also begat an insatiable desire for even more saints. After Carlo Borromeo's canonization in 1610, the number of causes before the Congregation of Rites exploded. The Congregation discussed more than 180 potential saints

---

[85] Simon Ditchfield, "'Coping with the Beati Moderni': Canonization Procedure in the Aftermath of the Council of Trent," in *Ite Inflammae Omnia: Selected Historical Papers from Conferences Heald at Loyola and Rome in 2006*, ed. Thomas M. McCoog (Rome, 2010), 413–39, at 433–34.

[86] Benedict XIV, *De servorum Dei*, II/1, 155–56; Ditchfield, "'Coping with the Beati Moderni,'" 424–25.

[87] On Paul's more liberal attitude, see Gotor, *I beati del papa*, 203–8.

[88] Copeland, "Spanish Saints," esp. 110.

during the first decades of its existence, most of them in the 1610s and 1620s.[89] At the same time, official anxiety about unregulated devotions only grew. Two Inquisition decrees in 1625 sought to ban all public cults that had not first received papal authorization – no portraits with halos, no lamps, no votive objects on graves, and so on.[90] The Congregation of Rites added restrictions of its own, including the introduction of a fifty-year waiting period between a person's death and the initiation of canonization proceedings – this was the rule that had thwarted Alonso Cueto upon his arrival in Rome. These rules were codified in Urban VIII's 1634 bull, *Caelestis Hierusalem cives*, which effectively created a two-track process. Unlike earlier saints, modern causes (defined as anyone deceased within the previous century, i.e., after 1534) were required to demonstrate a *lack* of public veneration, using the aforementioned process *de non cultu*.

Where public devotion had once furnished the primary proof of *fama sanctitatis*, such acts of veneration were now considered positively disqualifying. This complete and paradoxical about-turn was pointed out by the Archbishop of Florence as early as May 1625, following the Inquisition's first decrees against public cults. Alessandro Marzi de' Medici had been in the midst of an apostolic process for Ippolito Galantini. More than 130 witnesses had already testified to Galantini's virtues and miracles ("there is not a baby who does not know how to invoke the name" of the founder of the Congregation of Christian Doctrine). Remissorial letters from Rome had required the archbishop to question witnesses about votive tablets at Galantini's grave, but the new decree required him to take them away.[91] What had been asked in order to prove Galantini's holiness now established the exact opposite. To complicate matters still further, medieval (pre-1534) candidates were exempt from these new regulations, meaning that their causes were still *required* to establish the presence of a continuous public cult.[92]

Inevitably, these complex regulations set an impossibly high standard and prompted another general pause in canonizations (1629–58).

---

[89] Clare Copeland, "Sanctity," in *The Ashgate Research Companion to the Counter-Reformation*, ed. Alexandra Bamji et al. (Farnham, 2013), 232, puts the figure at 213 between 1592 and 1675; the present estimate for the total number of causes is based on the index in Archivio del Dicastero delle Cause di Santi (ADCS), MS Regestum Servorum Dei, vol. 1, 1592–1654; further quantitative analysis is necessary.
[90] Gotor, *I beati del papa*, 285–307; for images, see also Chapter 13 in this volume.
[91] ADDF, St. St. B-4-b, fol. 320r.
[92] Papa, *Le cause di canonizzazione*, 350–53.

Saint-making thereafter essentially took place only when rules were disapplied or set aside. The thirty-one saints canonized in the century after 1634 all appear to fit into one of three categories. Eleven were medieval saints, grandfathered in and excused from the later rules. Thirteen had been beatified before 1634. Because their followers had already been granted a public cult, they too were exempted from Urban VIII's regulations. Like their medieval counterparts, the causes of the Capuchin Felice da Cantalici and the Jesuit novices Luigi Gonzaga and Stanisław Kostka were still required to show evidence of a public cult. The remaining seven cases – including those of Francisco Solano and Rose of Lima – all received papal exemptions in one form or another. For one candidate, Francis de Sales, the papacy even waived the fifty-year waiting period.[93] Of course, the rules did not themselves determine the outcome, but they did make the path to canonization steeper for some candidates. Some might have succeeded only because of an exemption, whether by chance (an early beatification) or through papal intervention in the face of overwhelming pressure. These bureaucratic factors were at least as important as any geopolitical considerations. Indeed, convoluted, counterintuitive rules suited the papacy very well. Popes received praise for any exemption but could blame inaction on the rules themselves. Urban's decrees remained in force until the twentieth century, when they were gradually repealed because they were belatedly deemed "too complex" and "an obstacle" for the timely instruction of trials.[94]

HOW TO BECOME A COUNTER-REFORMATION SAINT

The early modern period was not a golden age of canonizations. The present day, however, is. The number of canonizations already began to tick up in the late nineteenth century, but it was Pope John Paul II who, in 1983, swept away most of Urban's restrictions, transforming the saint-making workshop into an assembly line. During his twenty-six-year pontificate, the Polish pope created more saints – 482 in 52 ceremonies – than all his predecessors combined.[95] Pope Francis eclipsed John Paul's number with his very first canonization ceremony, when he presided over the canonization of the 813 martyrs of Otranto (fulfilling a

---

[93] On Sales's exemption, see Papa, *Le cause di canonizzazione*, 310.
[94] Fabijan Veraja, *Le cause di canonizzazione dei santi: Commento alla legislazione e guide pratica* (Vatican City, 1992), 12.
[95] Michael J. Walsh, "Pope John Paul II and His Canonizations," *Studies in Church History* 47 (2011): 415–37, at 423.

decision originally made by his predecessor Benedict XVI). Francis's pace did not slow during the remainder of his pontificate; he approved the canonization of three saints in the month before his death.[96]

The current "banalization" of saint-making (to borrow a term used by Alejandro Cañeque elsewhere in this volume), then, offers a useful counterpoint to the early modern period. Taking the long view, we might observe that the increase in saint-making reflects the gradual weakening of the papacy, both in its position within the wider world and in its relationship toward the Catholic faithful. Nineteenth- and twentieth-century canonizations became opportunities to warn against the dangers of modernity, secularism, socialism, and even (still!) heresy. More recently they have also become pleas for the role of faith in everyday life. At the same time, canonizations also serve to give the faithful what they want.

From this perspective, the inaction of sixteenth-century popes looks rather different. Rather than the failure of nerve attributed to them in Peter Burke's canonical essay, papal stasis may have reflected a position of strength. Certainly, early modern popes were able to withstand pressures from the faithful that their modern successors cannot. The real trouble only began after saint-making resumed in the years after 1588, and the queue of candidates awaiting processing grew. The greatest threat to saint-making was not the challenge of Protestantism but the Catholic Church's own internal dynamics.

What about the Counter-Reformation saints themselves? We have noted the limitations of Burke's original attempt at categorization. His decision to include twenty medieval saints in his survey of the canonized obscures the exceptionally low success rate of the *beati moderni*. The prominence of founders of religious orders also seems almost inevitable from our study of the process: Only religious orders consistently possessed the desire, resources, and know-how to get their founders canonized. More importantly still, our survey accounts for the relative dearth of certain other types of saints: Their causes were particularly adversely affected by the new rules. The causes of theologians, for instance, suffered because a candidate's writings had to be examined, and canonizing a theologian meant canonizing their theology. In the wake of the Jansenist controversy, this factor delayed Robert

---

[96] Vatican News, "Pope Clears Path for Canonization of PNG Blessed Peter To Rot," www.vaticannews.va/en/pope/news/2025-03/pope-francis-saints-decrees-peter-to-rot-maloyan.html.

Bellarmine's sainthood for centuries.⁹⁷ Theologians were lacking among the Counter-Reformation saints, not because they were insignificant, but rather because they mattered *too much*, reflecting divisions within the Church.

Finally, attention to the procedure and its changes over time reveals an even more vital and possibly unexpected determinant for success: To become a Counter-Reformation saint, one had to be fortunate with the date of one's death. Most of the ultimately successful *beati moderni* were beatified before Urban's reforms, allowing them to avoid the full impact of these strict regulations. By contrast, Ippolito Galantini and Robert Bellarmine, who passed away in 1619 and 1621, respectively, died too late. Their causes had progressed virtually at hyper-speed during the 1620s but were suddenly knocked back under the new rules.⁹⁸ Bellarmine was canonized only in 1930. Galantini was beatified in 1825; his canonization is still pending. Whether in life or in death, patience was the virtue that aspiring Catholic saints needed most.

---

[97] See, for instance, Cardinal Decio Azzolini's lengthy *voto* against recognizing the heroicity of Bellarmine's virtues in the 1680s: Vatican City, Bibliotheca Apostolica Vaticana, Vat.lat.13654, fols. 78r–97v. The postulators of Bellarmine's cause wisely decided against the publication of an *Opera omnia* edition of his writings: ARSI, Archivio della postulazione, MS 496, unnumbered item entitled "Progetto di una nuova edizione dell'Opera del Card. Bellarmino."

[98] For Bellarmine, see Papa, *Le cause di canonizzazione*, 308–9.

8 Regulating Relics

A. KATIE HARRIS

On September 6, 1721, a special subcommittee of the Congregation of Sacred Rites gathered in the Quirinal Palace to hear arguments surrounding the bones of St. John of Matha (d. 1213). The theft of his relics in 1655 from a little church in Rome and their removal to Madrid had spawned a long-running legal case over the identity of the ill-gotten remains. Without proper documentation, such as a notary's account or testimony from credible eyewitnesses, how could the cardinals and their expert advisors be sure that the remains were truly those of the saintly founder of the Trinitarian Order? Among the proofs put before the Congregation by Trinitarian defenders of Matha's relics were details about the bones' material qualities – their color, shape, and smell – together with documentation that recorded the long-standing common opinion that the remains that had once been in Rome were the same as those now in Madrid. Such public knowledge, they noted, was not in itself sufficient proof, "but greatly contributes to the proving of the identity of relics." In support of this assertion, the Trinitarians pointed to treatises on relics by the Jesuit rhetorician and theologian Jean Ferrand (1586–1672) and the legal scholar Domenico Anfossi (fl. 1626).[1] "It is true," commented Ferrand, "that although reputation alone does not clearly and completely prove the identity of the relics of the saints, at any rate it contributes not a little to strengthening it."[2] Such arguments seem to have found favor with the assembled judges, who ruled that the stolen bones were indeed those of St. John of Matha.[3]

---

[1] *Sacra Rituum Congregatione. Eminentissimo, & Reverendissimo D. Card. Paulutio pro Eminentissimo, & Reverentissimo D. Card. Annibale Albano ponente Hispaniarum identitatis corporis S. Ioannis de Matha Fundatoris Ordinis Sanctissimae Trinitatis Redemptionis Captivorum. Positio* (Rome, 1721), 30.
[2] Jean Ferrand, *Disquisitio reliquiaria sive De suspicienda, et suspecta earumdem numero reliquiarum, quae in diversis ecclesiis servantur, multitudine* (Lyon, 1647), 283.
[3] A. Katie Harris, *The Stolen Bones of St. John of Matha: Forgery, Theft, and Sainthood in the Seventeenth Century* (University Park, PA, 2023).

The inclusion of Ferrand's and Anfossi's arguments among the proofs adduced in the case of Matha's remains points toward a small clutch of treatises on relics that emerged in the first half of the seventeenth century. This important but seldom discussed group of books on the bodies of the saints responded to trends within early modern Catholicism and external to it, as Catholic authorities sought both solutions to concrete problems associated with the administration and control of the veneration of the relics of the saints, as well as strategies to defend the cult from Protestant critics and Catholic skeptics alike. This essay examines the early modern relic manuals, using them as a lens through which to approach changes and developments in the cult of relics in the centuries that followed the ecumenical gathering known as the Council of Trent (1545–63), as Church authorities sought to encourage devotion among the faithful to the earthly remains of the saints while simultaneously regulating the cult and bringing it more firmly under clerical control.

While Catholic veneration of the saints dates from the earliest centuries of Christianity, reverence for their relics developed somewhat later.[4] By the second century, the tombs and the bodies of Christian believers executed by the Roman state were the objects of veneration within local Christian communities. Such martyrs, whose deaths bore witness to Christian truths, were understood to intercede for others before God and were venerated in remembrance of their sacrifice and of the promise of the coming resurrection of the dead. By the end of the fourth century and the legalization of Christianity, early devotion to the martyrs and their bodies had undergone a sea change that laid the groundwork for the cult of relics as it would develop in the centuries to come. As the bodies of the saints came to be seen as miracle-working objects of great power, believers set aside long-established prohibitions against touching the dead and began to disinter, dismember, and distribute the remains of the martyrs. Divided and subdivided, the physical remains of the martyrs, their relics – in Latin, *reliquiae*, or remains; in Greek, λείψανα – and their cults spread quickly throughout the expanding Christian world.[5]

As the cult of the saints flourished and grew, so too did the veneration of their bodies, around which developed a complex array of beliefs and devotional practices. The remains of particularly important or popular saints attracted pilgrims who came seeking cures or in

---

[4] Robert Wisniewski, *The Beginnings of the Cult of Relics* (Oxford, 2018).
[5] Robert Bartlett, *Why Can the Dead Do Such Great Things? Saints and Worshippers from the Martyrs to the Reformation* (Princeton, NJ, 2013), 3–56.

fulfillment of a vow. Stored in elaborate containers called reliquaries and housed in altars and shrines, relics magnified the spiritual authority and earthly wealth of cathedral churches and abbeys or advertised the power and piety of kings and princes, who gathered together great collections of holy bodies. Other pious Christians, less exalted but still devout, might wear pendants containing relics around their necks. The contents of reliquaries might be whole bodies or teeth, hair, or tiny fragments of bone; they might also be contact relics, such as clothing worn by the saint, beds in which they had slept, or other material objects and substances that had touched the saint and thus acquired some of his or her miraculous power. Contact relics could take a host of forms, from dust from a tomb or oil from the lamps that marked the site of the saint's remains. The most revered relics were those of Christ and the Virgin, whose bodies were understood not to exist on Earth but in Heaven. Items associated with Jesus's crucifixion, such as nails, thorns, blood, or pieces of the cross, were some of Christianity's most potent and sought-after sacred objects, but even humble bits of string used by devout visitors to measure Christ's burial place in Jerusalem's Holy Sepulcher could be prized contact relics.[6]

Cities and towns took comfort in the protection afforded by the remains of their patron saints, which sometimes accompanied armies into battle, and processions of relics marked festive celebrations and plaintive pleas for saintly assistance in communities both large and small. Though after the eleventh century the Gospels gradually came to replace saintly bodies as objects upon which oaths were sworn, well into the early modern period gifts of relics were common tools for cementing diplomatic alliances or family ties. Relics might also be the source of friction when pious and patriotic devotees engaged in *furta sacra*, holy theft, stealing the bodies of saints from rival communities or religious institutions for the benefit of their own hometowns. Though Church law prohibited the sale or purchase of the remains of the saints, relics could also be commodities traded on a sometimes barely concealed black market.[7]

In sum, relics were not some marginal oddity of medieval religious life but instead were an essential aspect of the cult of the saints. Their

---

[6] On measurement relics, see Caroline Walker Bynum, *Dissimilar Similitudes: Devotional Objects in Late Medieval Europe* (New York, 2020).

[7] Patrick Geary, *Furta Sacra: Thefts of Relics in the Central Middle Ages* (Princeton, NJ, 1990); A. Katie Harris, "Gift, Sale, and Theft: Juan de Ribera and the Sacred Economy of Relics in the Early Modern Mediterranean," *Journal of Early Modern History* 18 (2014): 193–226.

veneration did not go without comment, of course. Long before Luther, figures like Guibert of Nogent (d. 1124) decried the superstitious credulity of the laity and the cupidity of the shrine clergy, critiques that were later reiterated in the fourteenth century by the reforming English theologian John Wycliff. By the early sixteenth century, humanist scholars like Desiderius Erasmus and Thomas More urged that the cult be purged of its superstitious excesses but stopped short of advocating the elimination of the saints and their relics entirely. It would not be right, argued More, "that God should have left the occasion of merit and reward that good folk would, with his help, deserve by his coming, for the harm that wretches would take thereof by their own sloth and malice. Nor, in like wise, right were it none that all worship of saints, and reverence of holy relics, and honor of saints' images – by which good devout folk do much merit – we should abolish and put away because some folk do abuse it."[8] By contrast, for Protestant reformers, the veneration of the saints was not merely superstitious or corrupt but both pointless and pernicious.[9] For Luther, the saints and their relics were "a completely unnecessary and useless thing," utterly extraneous to justification through unearned divine grace.[10] For Calvin, they were far worse, an "evil" with ancient roots: "instead of discerning Jesus Christ in his Word, his Sacraments, and his Spiritual Graces, the world has, according to its custom, amused itself with his clothes, shirts, and sheets, leaving thus the principal to follow the accessory."[11] Protestant detestation for holy remains often moved from words to deeds, as reforming crowds swept churches clean of relics, images of the saints, and other traditional Christian *sacra*.

The Catholic Church's robust response to these attacks transformed the cult of relics even as it affirmed and reinforced it. Prior to the

---

[8] Thomas More, "A Dialogue of Sir Thomas More, Knight," in *The Essential Works of Thomas More*, ed. Gerard B. Wegemer and Stephen W. Smith (New Haven, CT, 2020), 630.

[9] Stéphan Boiron, *La controverse née de la querelle des reliques à l'époque du Concile de Trente (1500–1640)* (Paris, 1989); Alain Joblin, "L'attitude des protestants face aux reliques," in *Les reliques: Objets, cultes, symboles; Actes du colloque international de l'Université du Littorial-Côte d'Opale (Boulogne-sur-Mer) 4–6 septembre 1997*, ed. Edina Bozóky and Anne-Marie Helvétius (Brepols, 1999), 122–41.

[10] William R. Russell, *Luther's Theological Testament: The Schmalkald Articles* (Minneapolis, 1995), 126.

[11] John Calvin, *Treatise on Relics* (Amherst, NY, 2008), 53–54; Pierre-Antoine Fabre and Mickaël Wilmart, "Le Traité des reliques de Jean Calvin (1543): Texte et contextes," in *Reliques modernes: Cultes et usages chrétiens des corps saints des Réformes aux révolutions*, vol. 1, edited by Philipe Boutry, Pierre Antoine Fabre, and Dominique Julia (Paris, 2009), 29–68.

Council of Trent, notes Julia Smith, relics were "not core aspects of dogma to be interpreted by theologians and passed on by instruction to the faithful, but were rooted in the quotidian behavior of most Christians. Until Trent, relics were *habitus,* not creed."[12] Nor were all medieval Christians united in their understanding of just what relics were, how they were to be understood, and how they were to be treated. In its twenty-fifth session, the Council took up the question of the veneration of saints and of relics and, in so doing, set in motion a process that would clarify and codify beliefs and practices surrounding the bodies of the saints and bring them more firmly under the control of ecclesiastical authorities. The assembled prelates vigorously opposed Protestant views, affirmed the importance of the veneration of saints and their remains, and charged bishops with the task of instructing the public on how the saints intercede before God on behalf of the faithful to obtain "blessings from God through his Son our lord Jesus Christ, who is our sole redeemer and saviour." They further instructed bishops to regulate the cult and prune back the excesses of popular culture and issued special directives aimed at eliminating error or fraud. In the case of new relics – that is, newly discovered remains of established saints – bishops were to consult with "theologians and other devout men and decide as truth and devotion suggest." Especially difficult cases were to be remanded to a provincial council and the pope himself was to be consulted.[13]

Beyond these general instructions, however, Trent said little about just how bishops were to go about the disciplinary responsibilities with which they were charged. Instead, these particulars were worked out at the provincial and diocesan levels in the actions of local councils and reform-minded bishops. The decrees of the Fourth Council of Milan (1576), convoked by the future saint Cardinal-Archbishop Carlo Borromeo, were especially influential in their expansion upon Trent's laconic injunctions with a thorough exposition of the ways that relics were to be contained, handled, and displayed. Relics were not to be held in private homes nor handled by laymen, for example, but could be touched only by priests and kept only in churches, in highly visible locations but "well fenced, and adorned on all sides," locked with at

---

[12] Julia M. H. Smith, "Relics: An Evolving Tradition in Latin Christianity," in *Saints and Sacred Matter: The Cult of Relics in Byzantium and Beyond,* ed. Cynthia Hahn and Holgar A. Klein (Washington, DC, 2015), 50.

[13] Council of Trent, session 25, December 3–4, 1563, "On Invocation, Veneration and Relics of the Saints, and on Sacred Images," in *Decrees of the Ecumenical Councils,* vol. 2, ed. Norman P. Tanner (Washington, DC, 1990), 774–76.

least two different keys and properly marked with identifying inscriptions. Processions of holy bodies, public showings, and transfers, or "translations," were similarly hedged about with liturgical specifications meant to demonstrate and heighten their sacredness. The authorities in Milan also laid out the methods by which bishops were to undertake the "recognition" – that is, the investigation and identification – of the relics under their care. The process rested upon the examination of documents, inscriptions, witness testimony, and other forms of historical evidence. Bishops were enjoined to make copies of these written records and preserve them in their archives, together with a careful accounting of any relics that might be discovered or acquired in the future.[14]

The detailed decrees of the Fourth Council of Milan laid the groundwork for the treatment of relics by many other provincial councils, such as those of Aix-en-Provence (1585), Mexico City (1585), or Narbonne (1609).[15] Given the long medieval legacy of conflicting and ambivalent ideas surrounding holy bodies, however, and the related dispersal of discussions about relics throughout a more than 1,000 years' worth of theological texts, sermons, histories, hagiographies, legal commentaries, and other forms of writing, ecclesiastical authorities who sought to implement Trent's decrees on relics very likely found the assignment confusing. One cleric, tasked in 1639 with researching how to authenticate newly discovered relics, likened it to navigating a sea without a guide.[16] One response to the challenge posed by holy bodies was the emergence of a group of manuals that focused directly on relics, pulling together all of the scattered discussions into a coherent, manageable form for the use of the clergy.

---

[14] Pius XI, *Acta ecclesiae mediolanensis ab eius initiis usque ad nostram aetatem*, vol. 2 (Milan, 1890), cols. 300–302.

[15] Dominique Julia, "L'Église post-tridentine et les reliques: Tradition, controverse et critique (XVIe–XVIIe siècle)," in *Reliques modernes*, ed. Boutry, Fabre, and Julia, 69–120 (at 72); "Concilio III Provincial mexicano celebrado en México el año 1585: Aprobación del concilio confirmación del sínodo provincial de México Sixto V, Papa para futura memoria," in *Concilios provinciales mexicanos: Época colonial*, ed. María del Pilar Martínez López-Cano (Mexico City, 2004; online edition, 2014) https://historicas.unam.mx/publicaciones/publicadigital/libros/concilios/docs/3er_002.pdf, accessed April 20, 2022.

[16] Francisco de Santa María to Baltasar de Moscoso y Sandoval, December 1, 1639, in Biblioteca Nacional (BN), ms. 6184, 29r–v, cited in Katrina B. Olds, "The Ambiguities of the Holy: Authenticating Relics in Seventeenth-Century Spain," *Renaissance Quarterly* 65, no. 1 (2012): 135–84.

EARLY MODERN RELIC MANUALS

The first such treatise seems to have been Bolognese theologian Giambattista Segni's (d. 1610) *Reliquiarium, sive de reliquiis, et veneratione sanctorum in quo multa de necessitate, praestantia, usu, ac fructibus reliquiarum pertractantur* (1600; 2nd ed. 1610).[17] In this brief text, Segni compiled a wealth of information about relics of the saints from a wide range of ancient, medieval, and early modern sources to create a comprehensive manual. He was quite aware of the novelty of his work: "I have," he noted, "found no one who has prepared a complete and ordered book on this subject. Many, indeed, learnedly and elegantly prove their veneration against the heretics; others, speaking of their translations, illustrate them very well. Many carefully question them in some way. Some carefully discuss their revelation and discovery; some diligently design the rules and formulas for the manner of transferring, storing, and displaying them. But I do not know of any other book than ours to include all these things in one."[18] Segni's wide-ranging discussion centered on several key points, such as the discernment of relics (how to differentiate true relics from false; questions surrounding veneration of unauthorized versus authorized, canonized versus uncanonized saints); the discovery of relics (why and how such events occur, and problems that may be associated with them); the capacities and abilities of relics and the miracles associated with them; the proper veneration, treatment, and handling of relics; and the ways in which they may be moved from one place to another. For each topic, he gave extensive examples drawn from hagiography and sacred history, with an emphasis on Christianity's earliest centuries. His treatment was simultaneously devotional, practical, and apologetic. Drawing from a broad range of sources, Segni combined meditations on the meanings of relics and concrete guidelines for the proper use and management of the bodies of the saints with anti-Protestant talking points. The cult was not without problems, he admitted, "But let these mad and impudent criminals, who want a sacred, pious, and good thing to be taken away because of abuse, depart. Let the practice be preserved; let proven abuse be removed." His little manual was successful enough to be republished in an expanded edition, and, judging by how frequently one finds it cited

---

[17] Giovanni Fantuzzi, *Notizie degli scrittori bolognesi*, vol. 7 (Bologna, 1789), 377–78.

[18] Giambattista Segni, *Reliquiarium, sive de reliquiis, et veneratione sanctorum in quo multa de necessitate, praestantia, usu, ac fructibus reliquiarum pertractantur*, 2nd ed. (Bologna, 1610), 244.

throughout the seventeenth century, it became one of the go-to sources for practical matters related to relics.

Significantly less digestible but equally informative was jurist Domenico Anfossi's *De sacrarum reliquiarum cultu, veneratione, translatio, identitate, atque vindicatione* (1610). In this text, which reads as more a miscellany than a coherent manual, Anfossi, a naturalized citizen of Pavia, defended the saints and the sacred history of his adopted hometown.[19] Along the way, he took up a wide range of tangential topics – Emperor Justinian's jurisdiction over ecclesiastical personnel and possessions, for example, or the difference between ignorance and heresy – but also many others that directly connected to the cult of relics, such as papal inerrancy in canonization, the ways in which the bodies of the saints may be acquired and the identity of contested relics, or the conceptual logic and historical reasons behind the apparent duplication of bodies of saints in different locations. Unlike Segni, whose central interest lay in refuting Protestant critics and shoring up the sacredness of relics among Catholics, Anfossi's main concern was defending Pavia's claims to possess the remains of important saints, and his treatment of more practical questions was ancillary to concerns about the details of local history. Only its index made it usable as a guide to relics in general, but much like Segni's more accessible text, Anfossi's text seems to have become one of the standard references on the subject.

Relic manuals' apologetic discourse and practical discussions were frequently interwoven with arguments about the historical roots of relics and their veneration. Some texts focused on historical narratives that grounded the veneration of relics in Scripture and in the ancient history of the Church to rebut Protestant claims that the cult was superstitious and of human, rather than divine, origin. One representative example, Bishop Sancho Dávila y Toledo's (1546–1625) *De la veneración que se deue a los cuerpos de los sanctos y a sus reliquias y de la singular con que se a de adorar el cuerpo de Iesu Christo n[uest]ro Señor en el sanctissimo Sacramento* (1611), traced relics' history through time, from Abel to Job in "the time of natural law," through the "time of written [i.e., Mosaic] law," to the coming of Christ and the "time of the evangelical law."[20] In Dávila's reading, Scripture proved that the veneration of

---

[19] *Memorie e documenti per la storia dell'Università di Pavia, e degli uomini più illustri che v'insegnarono*, vol. 1 (Pavia, 1878), 194.

[20] A. Katie Harris, "'A Known Holy Body, with an Inscription and a Name': Bishop Sancho Dávila y Toledo and the Creation of St. Vitalis," *Archiv für Reformationsgeschichte* 104 (2013): 245–71.

relics was established by God, and the actions and decrees of the popes, doctors, councils, apostolic churches, and secular emperors and kings demonstrated that the Church and the faithful had never wavered or deviated from the divinely instituted obligation to the bodies of the saints. This *semper eadem* (always the same) argument was fundamental to Catholic historical writing of the period; its application to relics offered a potent rejection of Protestant polemics and reinforced the sacredness of holy bodies and their important place in Catholic life.[21]

Writers of relic manuals sought not only to refute critics and to enhance the sacred, but also to impose new order upon the motley array of beliefs and practices that crowded around the bodies of the saints. Perhaps the best example of this is Jean Ferrand's *Disquisitio reliquiaria sive de suspicienda, et suspecta earumdem numero reliquiarum, quae in diversis ecclesiis servantur, multitudine* (1647).[22] Like other writers on relics, Ferrand ranged widely, gathering together ancient, medieval, and modern sources, as well as pagan and Protestant authors. As its title suggests, his treatise was in part an overt apology for the multiplicity and duplication of relics decried by Calvin and others. In the first half of the text, he explained why it is that so many relics can be found in more than one place. The causes, he argued, are divine (manifestations of God's power), natural (relics' inherent divisibility), and human (faith, piety, error, cupidity, etc.). In the second half, he laid out the ways in which true holy remains could be recognized and differentiated from false ones. Three types of evidence could be brought to bear on the question of relic discernment: human, divine, and a mixed category that combined the first two. Human evidence included the physical qualities of relics, textual and other forms of documentation, witness testimony, and local tradition, while miracles associated with holy bodies were classified as divine evidence. The mixed human-divine category was more heterogeneous, including trial by fire, submersion of relics and other methods for achieving cures, and sermons, offerings, miracle books, pilgrimages, processions, and liturgical commemorations. The end result of Ferrand's list of evidence was a kind of regularization or rationalization of relics, "an imposition of order on relics' juridical definition as it had been gradually forming through customary practice over the course of the Middle Ages."[23]

---

[21] For another example of the *semper eadem* argument at work in the history of relics, see Louis-Géraud de Cordemoy, *Traité des saintes reliques* (Paris, 1715).

[22] Julia, "L'Église post-tridentine et les reliques."

[23] Ibid., 81.

Ferrand's attention to evidence and the question of how to discern true relics from false was a common feature of early modern relic manuals. Segni, for example, pointed to three "signs" by which newly discovered saints' relics could be known (an ineffable smell, angelic voices and lights, and the inward emotions of observers, who were moved not to horror but to devotion), while Anfossi stressed the key role of tradition in establishing the identity of questionable relics.[24] As we have seen, the Council of Trent affirmed the duty of bishops to investigate newly discovered bodies of established saints, and indeed, bishops and other local Church officials in early modern Europe not infrequently confronted bones or other remains said to be of ancient martyrs or medieval saints, whose provenance, status, or authenticity was uncertain (the remains of more recent saints, whose lives were closer in time and whose bodies tended to be well documented, were much less likely to present such problems). Sometimes, as in Córdoba in 1575, the questionable relics had been uncovered during building renovations; in other cases, as in Palermo in 1624, the locations of supposed saintly remains were disclosed by miracles or revelations. When neither fortuitous accidents nor divine action were forthcoming, some prelates brought would-be relics to light through planned relic-hunting excavations, as in Cagliari in 1614 or in Villanueva de la Reina (Jaén) in 1628.[25] The relative frequency of such events suggests that the guidance offered by relic manuals was not merely theoretical but instead quite practical.

For writers of relic manuals, miracles were only one of the many forms of evidence by which investigating authorities might authenticate the bodies of the saints. Traditionally, relics' potential to work miracles was a key element of their attraction and an important proof of their authenticity and of the sanctity of the holy woman or man to whom they had belonged. Despite the pope's condemnation in 1682 of

---

[24] Segni, *Reliquiarium*, 33–36; Domenico Anfossi, *De sacrarum reliquiarum cultu, veneratione, translatio, identitate, atque vindicatione* (Brescia, 1610), 167–69.

[25] Córdoba: Cécile Vincent-Cassy, "The Search for Evidence: The Relics of Martyred Saints and Their Worship in Cordoba After the Council of Trent," in *After Conversion: Iberia and the Emergence of Modernity*, ed. Mercedes García-Arenal (Leiden, 2016), 126–52; Palermo: Valero Petrarca, *Genesi di una tradizione urbana: Il culto di santa Rosalia a Palermo in età spagnola* (Palermo, 1986); Cagliari: Donatella Mureddu, Donatella Salvi, and Grete Stefani, *Sancti innumerabiles: Scavi nella Cagliari del seicento; Testimonianze e verifiche* (Oristano, 1988); Villanueva de la Reina: Manuel Rodríguez Arévalo, "Potenciana: Santa tejedora," in *Actas del III Congreso de Historia de Andalucía, Córdoba, 2001, vol. 2: Las mujeres en la historia de Andalucía* (Córdoba, 2002): 169–80.

the famous lead books of Granada, for example, supporters argued that the copious miracles that had heralded their discovery were evidence that the human remains found with the forged texts were in fact authentic saintly relics, since "not just [in] Heaven but also on earth many miracles have been seen, which act as unimpeachable witnesses."[26] Miracles were not taken at face value, however, and just as the miracles allegedly worked by candidates for canonization were subjected to careful testing and examination, so too were those said to have been brought about by relics. Not every supposed miracle passed the test. In 1580, for example, Carlo Borromeo investigated a collection of supposed saints' bones in the village of Liano (Brescia) that were alleged to issue a great quantity of water once a year. Finding nothing to definitively establish the remains' identity as holy relics, "he had the tomb and also the bones well dried, and then placed them in the care of trustworthy priests on the very night that the water customarily would flow; and [when] there appeared no sign at all of water, he discovered that [the miracle] had been done with artifice and deceit."[27] Documents, including histories, hagiographies, legal instruments, inscriptions, and other texts, as well as the labels, provenance documentation, and other kinds of paperwork known collectively as *authentica*, often provided more clear-cut evidence than miracles, though they too were subject to increasingly exacting examination. The saints and their bodies were not immune from the new trends at work reshaping the writing of history in the sixteenth and seventeenth centuries, and the critical approaches to historical sources pioneered by the Jesuit hagiographers known as the Bollandists were reflected in both in relic manuals and in the practices of ecclesiastical authorities on the ground.[28]

REGULATING THE CULT OF RELICS

The concern expressed by writers on relics for recognizing and distinguishing the true relics from the false mirrored a broader interest in distinguishing God's true saints from those whose sanctity was pretended, deluded, or even demonic. Such issues, together with the drive to regularize, centralize, and codify, were a central task of the Roman

[26] *Relación de la grande autoridad, y certeza de las reliquias del Sacro Monte* (Granada [?], 1682 [?]), fol. 1v.
[27] Giovanni Pietro Giussano, *Vita di S. Carlo Borromeo...* (Rome, 1610), 402.
[28] On the Bollandists, see Robert Godding, Bernard Joassart, Xavier Lequeux, François De Vriendt, and J. van der Straeten, *Bollandistes, saints et légendes: quatre siècles de recherche* (Brussels, 2007).

Congregation of Rites, which was established in 1588. This powerful committee is best known as the body in charge of the creation of new saints, but it also governed the liturgy and the veneration of existing holy men and women. It is not surprising, then, that relic manuals bear many similarities to and overlaps with the related genre of treatises that detailed procedures for the beatification and canonization of saints, nor that the most important of the canonization treatises, Benedict XIV's celebrated magnum opus *De servorum Dei beatificatione et beatorum canonizatione* (1734–38), would bring both genres together into a single, comprehensive treatise.[29] The Congregation frequently received questions about proper devotion to and treatment of holy bodies. Some of the questions about relics had to do with questions of discernment. One early example was that of St. Medicus of Otricoli, whose bones were discovered in 1611 alongside those of fifty-seven companions. Though the local bishop judged all the remains to be likely those of martyrs, the Congregation of Rites overruled him, arguing that the evidence was insufficient and that only the bones of St. Medicus himself could be venerated as holy relics.[30] Much more common, however, were questions about how relics could be handled, moved, or liturgically celebrated. In 1658, for example, the Congregation received a request from the chapter of the church of Sts. Peter and Paul, in the southern Italian town of Pisticci, which sought authorization to expand their liturgical celebrations of their newly installed collection of relics. The committee's response was surely disappointing to the petitioners – it responded not with the requested permission but with a blanket prohibition on any liturgical celebration at all, since none of the Pisticcian martyrs were listed in the Roman Martyrology.[31]

Other Roman institutions also intervened in the regulation of the cult of relics. For example, the Congregation of the Council, a standing committee created in 1564 to oversee the implementation of the decrees of the Council of Trent, occasionally received inquiries related to veneration of relics, and the Congregation of the Holy Office of the Inquisition also took an interest in relics, especially ones with dubious provenance or questionable status. The latter was first established in 1542 as a response to the danger of Protestant influence on Catholic

---

[29] Benedict XIV, *De servorum Dei beatificatione et beatorum canonizatione* (Bologna, 1734–38; 2nd ed., Pavia, 1743; 3rd ed., Rome, 1747–51).

[30] Giovanni Papa, *Le cause di canonizzazione nel primo periodo della Congregazione dei Riti (1588–1634)* (Vatican City, 2001), 219–20.

[31] *Analecta juris pontificii*, 7th ser. (Rome, 1864), col. 348.

believers, but by the end of the sixteenth century had expanded its area of activity into a wide array of concerns, including the veneration of the saints and their remains. In 1638, for example, the Congregation of the Inquisition intervened to suppress the veneration of questionable relics found in Assisi. In another case, in 1655, the Inquisition's agent in Naples notified the committee of a Capuchin friar who had forged authenticating documentation for a martyrial relic. In this instance, the authorities in Rome declined to take action and instead returned the case to be adjudicated by local Church officials.[32] Other authorities in Rome intervened in the cult of relics in a more specialized way. The discovery of new catacomb tomb complex in Rome in 1578 sparked a resurgence of interest in the martyrs' remains assumed to lie under the Eternal City, and the decades that followed saw a flood of catacomb relics to churches and chapels around the increasingly global Catholic territories. Efforts to control the trade came from different sectors of the papal government, from the cardinal vicar of Rome to a special committee assembled in the 1630s to solve the problem of thefts from the underground tombs. By 1669, another institution, the Congregation of Indulgences and Relics, was established to regulate relics, and in 1672, controls over catacomb remains were tightened up further under a new office within the administration of the cardinal vicar, the office of the Custodian of Holy Relics and Cemeteries.[33]

Beyond Rome, on the Iberian Peninsula and around the globe, the task of regulating relics might also fall to agents of the Spanish or Portuguese Inquisitions. In 1699, for example, the Spanish Inquisition prosecuted a man in Puebla, Mexico, who had been distributing holy relics, including pieces of the True Cross, threads from the Virgin Mary's mantle, and many others – all forged. The culprit was found guilty and sentenced to appear in an *auto de fe*, but by 1713 he was at it again, manufacturing relics from animal bones or remains stolen from tombs.[34] Most of the time, however, it was bishops and episcopal administrators who were charged with the practical implications of

---

[32] Miguel Gotor, *I beati del papa: Santità, inquisizione e obbedienza in età moderna* (Florence, 2001), 338–40; Archivio della Congregazione per la Dottrina della Fede (hereafter ACDF), S.O., St. St., B4, p. 10.

[33] See Chapter 6 in this volume on the catacombs.

[34] Carolina Yeveth Aguilar García, "Entre la verdad y la mentira: Control y censura inquisitorial en torno a las reliquias en la Nueva España," in *Inquisición y derecho: Nuevas visiones de las transgresiones inquisitoriales en el nuevo mundo: del antiguo régimen a los albores de la modernidad*, ed. Luis René Guerrero Galván (Mexico City, 2014), 103–4.

regulating the cult of relics. While the relic manuals did not explicitly say so, it was likely they who formed the primary audience for the texts. Writers on relics agreed that decisions surrounding the bodies of the saints were the purview of the clergy, especially the leadership. Segni, for example, made it clear that God preferred to reveal lost or ignored holy bodies to prelates and pious priests, and that the task of inquiring into recently recovered relics and the revelations that often accompanied them was one for trained specialists, presumably clerics: "they should be theologians, not just anyone, and able to argue with precision according to the rules of Aristotle. And they should be especially trained in theological practice and well versed in the sacred writings."[35] Writers on relics offered guidelines for religious authorities who faced nuts-and-bolts questions about ensuring proper treatment of the bodies of the saints and reinforcing the post-Tridentine push to police the boundaries between sacred and profane people, places, and things. A common topic was the difference between the veneration due to saints (*dulia*) or to the Virgin Mary (*hyperdulia*) versus that due to Christ (*latria*), and hence how to enforce those distinctions in concrete ways. In his *Lucubrationum ecclesiasticarum* (1643), for example, the jurist Antonio Ricciulli (1582–1643) pointed to these categories in noting that relics should be kept within churches in appropriate reliquaries, ideally made of gold, silver, or ivory, yet "although it may be large and spacious, the relics of the saints must not be stored in the tabernacle where the Most Holy Sacrament of the Eucharist is preserved, since *latria* is due to the Sacrament, while *dulia* is due to relics."[36] Similarly, said Ricciulli, relics should not be given the worship due to God, nor should relics be brought to the sick, presumably because this was the proper role of the Viaticum.[37]

This concern for categories was also expressed in discussions of ambiguous relics or relics that defied easy definition. According to Ricciulli, ecclesiastical authorities confronted with the task of discerning saintly remains mixed with other substances or the remains of the common dead had to take special caution. If the remains were bones or some other solid material, he said, but it was impossible to distinguish which were holy from those which were not, they should be put aside in some decent place "until the Lord deigns to reveal something." However, in the case of liquid relics, like blood, milk, or manna, that

---

[35] Segni, *Reliquiarium*, 27.
[36] Antonio Ricciulli, *Lucubrationum ecclesiasticarum libri sex* (Naples, 1643), 78.
[37] Ibid., 104–5.

were mixed with some other, worldly fluid, authorities needed to know the relative proportions of holy to mundane in order to authorize veneration.[38] The attention to classification was reflected in a concurrent systematizing redefinition of relics themselves. As we have seen, in earlier centuries, the category of relic was generous and encompassing, including everything from the bones of the saints to shreds of their garments and dust swept from their tombs. Even pebbles gathered by pilgrims to Jerusalem found their way into the collections gathered by the powerful and pious.[39] After Trent, writers on relics continued to put forward broad definitions of what could be considered to be a relic. At the same time, however, the Congregation of Rites gradually developed distinctions about which liturgical honors could be rendered to which kinds of holy remains, eventually sorting relics by size and bodily integrity into those that were "distinguished" (*insigne*) and those that were not. Such categories, which did not necessarily map onto local or individual understandings, reflected a drive toward centralization and standardization and an incremental narrowing of the range of possibilities.[40]

The practical advice offered by relic manuals reflected the concerns of local officials who sought simultaneously to foster popular devotion to the bodies of the saints and to tame its excesses. Traditional customs like dunking relics in water as ways of imploring or coercing heavenly aid in times of drought, for example, frequently came in for criticism from reforming prelates like Archbishop Pedro Manrique of Zaragoza in 1614 or Cardinal-Bishop Étienne Le Camus of Grenoble in 1687, who, while they encouraged veneration of the saints, found such practices to be superstitious.[41] Periodic inspections called pastoral visits regularly included examinations of the relics held in parish churches. Bishops or their agents inspected parish churches, reviewing all aspects of their infrastructure and contents, including altars, retables, and liturgical ornaments, objects, and vestments. As a matter of course, inspectors examined relics to verify that they were properly stored and possessed the necessary documentation that proved their authenticity. During a

---

[38] Ibid., 82–83.
[39] Renana Bartal, Neta Bodner, and Bianca Kuhnel, *Natural Materials of the Holy Land and the Visual Translation of Place, 500–1500* (London, 2017).
[40] Smith, "Relics," 46.
[41] Francisco Diego de Aynsa y de Iriarte, *Fundación, excelencias, grandezas y cosas memorables de la antiquíssima ciudad de Huesca* (Huesca, 1619), 442–43; Keith P. Luria, *Territories of Grace: Cultural Change in the Seventeenth-Century Diocese of Grenoble* (Berkeley, CA, 1991), 123.

pastoral visit to the churches of Huelva in 1700, for example, the archbishop of Seville found it necessary to order that the long-forgotten remains of an erstwhile patron saint, St. Vital, be at least placed in an altar.[42] Improper storage and handling was a serious matter since it implied a disrespectful or casual attitude toward the sacred. The outcome of the Mexican Inquisition's 1648 investigation of a man in Valladolid, Yucatán, who claimed to be in possession of several relics that he used to effect cures on local women is unknown, but the fact that the tribunal confiscated the supposed holy remains suggests that among the tribunal's concerns was the fact that the relics (if indeed they were such) were stored in a little bag rather than in a proper reliquary.[43]

Both writers on relics and ecclesiastical authorities involved in the efforts to authentic relics in situ were similarly concerned with the mobility of holy bodies, including the ways in which the remains of the saints could be exchanged and moved from place to place. Relic manuals generally agreed that in most cases, holy bodies could only be exchanged as donations or gifts, never by sale or by theft. The only real exception, noted Segni, were relics that were endangered by "pagans and other infidels," which could be appropriated "not only by stealth but also by force."[44] Even so, post-Tridentine Church officials were loath to permit even emergency evacuations of relics without appropriate controls. In 1626, for example, when the Duke of Alcalá requested permission from the Congregation of the Inquisition to rescue relics of St. Norbert and other saints from churches in Germany where they were imperiled by Protestants, the cardinals required investigations into the history of the remains – that is, their authenticity – before permission could be granted.[45] Other, more formal movements of holy bodies similarly came under increased control. After 1583, for example, papal authorization was required for relic translations.[46] Relic manuals outlined the rituals required for the elaborate, formal displays of relics known as *ostensiones*, stressing the importance of priestly control and the separation of the sacred from the mundane. In his comprehensive

---

[42] Manuel José de Lara Rodenas, "Los mundos devotos en la Huelva del antiguo régimen: Perfiles y contexto," in *Religiosidad y costumbres populares en Iberoamérica*, ed. David González Cruz (Huelva, 2000), 148.

[43] Aguilar García, "Entre la verdad y la mentira," 104–5.

[44] Segni, *Reliquiarium* (1610), 183. See also Marc'Antonio Boldetti, *Osservazioni sopra i cimiteri de' Santi Martiri, ed antichi cristiani di Roma* ... (Rome, 1720), 740–47.

[45] ACDF, S.O, St. St., B 4 c, fasc. 4.

[46] Aristede Sala, *Documenti circa la vita e le gesta di San Carlo Borromeo*, vol. 1 (Milan, 1857), 464.

1721 treatise on relic displays, Pietro Moretti, a cleric attached to the Roman church of Santa Maria in Trastevere, stressed that the bodies of the saints were absolutely not to be touched or carried by laymen, and that even kings and other luminaries who wished to do so had to be either (honorary) churchmen or granted special license to do so. Further, he said, prelates who handled reliquaries during the solemn public viewings must wear gloves in colors appropriate to the status of the relics, "in order to declare how much veneration and reverence the Church thinks worthy of sacred relics."[47]

CONCLUDING REMARKS

The characteristic emphasis on reinforcing respect for the sacred demonstrated in Moretti's text and in the other treatises on relics points us toward the significance of holy bodies for early modern Catholics. While it is certainly true that "relics became a hallmark of the new Tridentine movement, a tool to counter Protestant heresy whilst simultaneously acting as a reminder of the relationship between the Catholic Church's past and present," the remains of the saints did much more than this.[48] The ecclesiastical authorities who, with the aid of relic manuals, sought both to control the cult of relics and to foster devotion to saintly remains among the laity did so at least in part because of the broader truths that those remains embodied. Relics were emblematic of Catholic Christianity's all-encompassing understanding of the sacred; they also encapsulated the Church's understanding of the links between holiness and matter, links that were closely related to a host of hotly debated questions, like that of the resurrection of the body, of Christ's real presence in the Eucharist, even of Christ's incarnation and of salvation itself.[49] Relics were about much more than the physical remains of any particular individual, no matter how special that person may have been. In sum, the early modern cult of relics and the drive to regulate that cult are testimony to its important place in Counter-Reformation Catholicism.

---

[47] Pietro Moretti, *De ritu ostensionis sacrarum reliquiarum ... dissertatio historico-ritualis* (Rome, 1721), 90.
[48] James E. Kelly, *English Convents in Catholic Europe, c. 1600–1800* (Cambridge, 2020), 139–40.
[49] Harris, *The Stolen Bones*, 139.

9 Mysticism and the Discernment of Spirits
ELEONORA CAPPUCCILLI

Medieval theologians loved order and systems. Even mystical experiences could not escape classification. It was the Sorbonne theologian Jean Gerson (1363–1429) who provided the essential framework of discernment of spirits (or, in Latin, *discretio spirituum*) that laid out not only how mystical encounters should be scrutinized but even how they should be experienced. With this, he set in motion a dialectic of close connection and simultaneous conflict between visions and their interpretation, an uneasy relationship between mystical experiences and elite scrutiny that sustained and revitalized Christian spirituality into the early modern period.[1]

Under Gerson's influence, practices of discernment changed during the fifteenth century. Discernment was no longer presented as a spiritual gift (following the Apostle Paul), but rather as an experiential and intellectual process that could be facilitated by the study of Scripture. At the same time, especially in the post-Tridentine era, mysticism also influenced the development of new models and practices of sanctity. These provide an additional context in which mystical experiences need to be situated, as the visions of new aspiring saints dragged the discourse and practice of the discernment of spirits into controversy. To what extent should mystical encounters follow ecclesiastical rules, rites, and doctrines? Could they diverge from, or even correct them? When did a supernatural encounter indicate the presence of God, and when that of the devil? In Catholic art, the latter difficulty became associated with the tormented figure of St. Anthony of Egypt, an early desert father famous for successfully recognizing and resisting diabolical temptation.

---

[1] Wendy Love Anderson, *The Discernment of Spirits: Assessing Visions and Visionaries in the Late Middle Ages* (Tübingen, 2011); Gabriella Zarri, "Introduzione," in *Storia della direzione spirituale*, vol. 3: *L'età moderna*, ed. Giovanni Filoramo and Gabriella Zarri (Brescia, 2008), 5–53. All translations are by the author. This chapter has received funding from the European Union HORIZON-MSCA-2022-PF-01 Grant agreement No. 101107702.

Good and proper discernment, in effect, became a hallmark of sanctity; a saint should know when the devil was trying to seduce them.[2] Mysticism and mystics thus sparked a great deal of controversy and even anxiety within early modern Catholicism, because the divine and the demonic could prove hard to separate. Yet discernment also played a crucial role in defending the cult of saints against Protestant assault. Successful discernment confirmed the accuracy and divine origin of charismatic inspiration and thus undergirded the creation of new saints.[3]

Mysticism – whether as a social construct, a variegated literary genre, or as direct knowledge of God, an experience of union with God made manifest through ecstasy, visions, and raptures – has always been divisive.[4] During the Counter-Reformation, however, it became a privileged path both to sanctity *and* to the denial of sanctity. In contrast to medieval mysticism, which was devoted to the simplicity of the soul, early modern Catholic mysticism attracted particular attention and scrutiny from the Church, particularly from the Iberian and Roman Inquisitions. Inevitably, Catholic mystics were mocked, derided, and condemned by Protestants as well.

These profound changes need to be placed within a wider context of continuities. Mysticism has often been presented as an integral aspect of female piety in an almost ahistorical fashion. Female mystical practices are often characterized by their physicality. Mystical gifts, revelations, ecstasies, visions, apparitions, and erotic-affective tension are accompanied by miraculous lactation, mystical pregnancy, catatonia, and stiffening of the muscles.[5] However much it was transformed into an "attribute of the soul,"[6] the body was still often seen as its polar opposite.[7] It was women's bodies, as well as their voices, however, that confessors and ecclesiastical institutions scrutinized. Two late

---

[2] Stuart Clark, "Afterword," in *Angels of Light? Sanctity and the Discernment of Spirits in the Early Modern Period*, ed. Clare Copeland and Jan Machielsen (Leiden, 2013), 293–304.

[3] Clare Copeland and Jan Machielsen, "Introduction," in Copeland and Machielsen, eds., *Angels of Light?*, 6.

[4] Livia Kohn, "Mysticism," in *Religion Past and Present*, ed. Hans Dieter Betz (Leiden, 2008), 657.

[5] *Femmes, mysticisme et prophétisme en Europe du Moyen Âge à l'époque moderne*, ed. Helene Michon et al. (Paris, 2021); *Scrittrici mistiche italiane*, ed. Giovanni Pozzi and Claudio Leonardi (Genoa, 1998).

[6] Claudia Marsulli, *Mistica eccentrica* (Florence, 2022), 91.

[7] See Katharine Park, "Was There a Renaissance Body?," in *The Italian Renaissance in the Twentieth Century: I Tatti Studies*, vol. 19, ed. Walter Kaiser and Michael Rocke (Florence, 2002), 21–35.

medieval saints, Catherine of Siena[8] and Birgitta (or Bridget) of Sweden, became crucial reference points both as guides to successful discernment and as essential spiritual models worthy of imitation[9] – even though Jean Gerson himself had opposed Birgitta's canonization at the Council of Constance.

This chapter will survey the disagreements, proposed definitions, and discontinuities in theories of mysticism and the discernment of spirits and observe how these worked in practice using two case studies. The first is that of Teresa of Ávila (1515–1582), the celebrated Carmelite mystic, prolific author, and the first woman to be proclaimed a doctor of the Church, who has been the subject of widespread historical study. The second is the less-studied Dominican nun Caterina de' Ricci (1522–1590), who represents a transition away from the prophetic mysticism inspired by the spirituality of Girolamo Savonarola (1452–1498) – the controversial Dominican preacher burned at the stake for his radical ideas for political and religious reform – and whose delayed canonization throws light on changing Counter-Reformation norms and regulations. These case studies have been selected to restore the complexity of the phenomena in question while retaining the centrality of the female voice. They represent a landscape densely populated by mystical expressions of spirituality, which persisted even after the Council of Trent, despite increasing barriers to their official recognition by the Church and political institutions. The contrast between Teresa's rapid canonization and the century and a half that passed prior to Caterina's elevation adds further nuance to our assessment of the complex and often fraught relationship between mysticism and sainthood.

Above all, these two case studies illustrate the impossibility of imposing a single, coherent narrative on mysticism, a widespread spiritual movement that was often at odds with itself. They also lay bare the

---

[8] Amelina Correa Ramón, *Las venas de los lirios: De místicas, visionarias y santas vivas en la literatura de Granada (ss. XVI–XX)* (London, 2022), 47; Nancy Bradley Warren, *Embodied Word: Female Spiritualities, Contested Orthodoxies, and English Religious Cultures, 1350–1700* (Notre Dame, IN, 2010); Gillian T. W. Ahlgren, "Ecstasy, Prophecy, and Reform: Catherine of Siena as a Model for Holy Women of Sixteenth-Century Spain," in *The Mystical Gesture: Essays on Medieval and Early Modern Spiritual Culture in Honor of Mary E. Giles*, ed. Robert Boenig (Abingdon, 2018), 53–65.

[9] Correa Ramón, *Las venas*, 46; María Morrás, "Introduction," in *Gender and Exemplarity in Medieval and Early Modern Spain*, ed. María Morrás et al. (Boston, 2020), 5–6; Ryan D. Giles, "'Mira mis llagas': Heridas divinas en las obras de Brígida de Suecia y Teresa de Jesús," *eHumanista* 32 (2016): 34–49.

extent to which the dialectic between mysticism and the discernment of spirits remained unresolved. Post-Tridentine sanctity was driven by mystical practices that the Catholic Church sought to regulate through *discretio spirituum*, which, in turn, through spiritual manuals and writings, created a reservoir of knowledge that made mysticism replicable as a form of theoretical knowledge. These writings prescribed behavior that, at least in theory, should have prevented mystics from being suspected of diabolical inspiration and which made their mystical practices acceptable to the authorities called to assess their orthodoxy. As a result, *discretio* ceased to be the exclusive gift of those personally illuminated by the spirit and instead became a framework of rules that (male) scholars, confessors, and others could learn and apply. As we shall see, the regulation of disordered mystical expressions and their connection to new models of sanctity proved both a huge challenge to the Catholic Church and a valuable opportunity to defend the miraculous and the holy from Protestant assault.

THE QUEST FOR WORDS AND THE DISCERNMENT OF TRUTH

Mystical experiences are meant to be ineffable; they cannot be adequately put into words. The purpose of discernment of spirits is to study them and to sift truth from hidden falsehoods, bearing in mind that Satan could transform himself into "an angel of Light" (2 Cor. 11:14). More than any other theologian, it was Jean Gerson who classified and defined these concepts, though he did not clear the field of possible ambiguities and semantic confusion. In his *Mystica theologia*, Gerson recognizes in mysticism the utmost inner experience of God, while in *De distinctione verarum visionum a falsis* and *De probatione spirituum* he teaches how to "distinguish between angelic revelations and demonic illusions." On the one hand, he defines mystical theology (the source of knowledge that is "most perfect and sure" because it is founded on "experiences known with more perfect certainty") in negative terms, as a means of seeing "through negation and mental projection," "as hidden."[10] On the other, he admits the impossibility of any definitive method or infallible rule for spiritual discernment: "If this were possible, we would not have to have only faith in our prophets,

---

[10] Jean Gerson, *Oeuvres complètes*, vol. 3, ed. Mgr. Glorieu (Paris, 1960), 252.

and consequently in our religion, for we would have the certitude of what was evident."[11]

Mysticism underwent three significant changes in the late Middle Ages. It was, first of all, democratized through a growing conviction that any Christian might rejoice in the presence of God. It was also vernacularized, in the sense of its expression through the vernacular and a consequent multiplication of mystical languages. Finally, it was secularized, with both male and female mystics increasingly "being in the world," unlike the anchorites of earlier periods.[12] In the age of early modern religious reform, mysticism was further transformed as part of wider societal changes. The laicization of religion, that is, the increased contact between religious and laity, reinforced the belief that religious vocations were not a monopoly of the clerics alone. Religious renewal further placed a greater emphasis on the inner life over external practice. The influence of humanism and reform movements promoted simplicity over ceremonial pomp.[13]

Mysticism was (and is) also experiential; it cannot function without reflection on what has been experienced. Crucial in this regard is analysis of the relationship between the mystical and the imagination, which does not offer a comprehensive explanation of the mystical phenomenon but nevertheless reveals profoundly different approaches. In the case of the great upsurge of mysticism in the Iberian Peninsula, Ignatius of Loyola (1491–1556) epitomizes rigid control of the human imagination, while Teresa represents disassociation from the imagination, which is conceived as an inert faculty, and John of the Cross (1542–1591), more than any other thinker, encapsulates the denial of the imagination, the surprisingly influential idea that God can only be experienced in His absence, as expressed in the evocative formula of the "dark night of the soul."[14] While we can identify signs of so-called cataphatic (positive) mysticism in Ignatius's approach to imagination, and signs of apophatic (negative) mysticism in John of the Cross's Teresa somehow stands in between these two approaches.

---

[11] Jean Gerson, *On Distinguishing True from False Revelations*, in *Early Works*, ed. Brian Patrick McGuire (New York, 1998), 335.

[12] Bernard McGinn, "The Changing Shape of Late Medieval Mysticism," *Church History* 65, no. 2 (1996): 197–219.

[13] Edward Howells, "Early Modern Reformations," in *Cambridge Companion to Christian Mysticism*, ed. Amy Hollywood and Patricia Z. Beckman (Cambridge, 2012), 114–34.

[14] Roland Barthes, *Sade, Fourier, Loyola* (Baltimore, 1997).

From the late Middle Ages onwards, it was recognized that women were endowed with greater mystical graces and more disposed to spiritual possession.[15] As already noted, female mystical experiences have often reflected certain time-honored themes including erotic language, conflict with authority, penitential practices, and charismatic gifts such as visions and ecstasies.[16] The Counter-Reformation entailed a decisive reassessment of such experiences, which were forced above all to toe an increasingly fine line between approved and feigned mysticism.[17] Female religious were subjected to stricter control than their male counterparts, at least on a formal level. This helped ensure that their traditional mystical qualities still demonstrated respect for the virtues extolled by Tridentine reform, chief among them obedience to superiors. Nuns, who faced the forced enclosure of their convents following the Council of Trent, were navigating the difficulties of discernment in a particularly challenging context. Their attempts at articulating their experiences (their union with God and rejection of the devil) in writing as a form of discernment of spirits brought them into conflict with authorities keen to institutionalize discernment.

Like the watchful authorities, the historian does not have access to the spiritual experiences described in the sources. The (divinely or demonically) possessed woman always exists outside normative fields of discourse because the speaking subject is unrepresentable, displaced from speech.[18] Nevertheless, as charismatic subjects, visionaries claimed to speak to or for God, and divine sanction therefore needed to be established – a subject that historians can analyze. Even though mysticism and *discretio spirituum* did not exclusively concern women, any instance of female mysticism attracted greater suspicion and was susceptible to more scrupulous examination on account of the decisive connection, originally established by Gerson, between women and mental weakness.[19] Because of the structural and phenomenological

---

[15] Gabriella Zarri, "Dal consilium spirituale alla discretio spirituum: Teoria e pratica della direzione spirituale tra i secoli XIII e XV," in *Consilium: Teorie e pratiche del consigliare nella cultura medievale*, ed. Carla Casagrande et al. (Florence, 2004), 77–107.

[16] Alison Weber, "Gender," in Hollywood and Beckman, eds., *Cambridge Companion to Christian Mysticism*, 315–27.

[17] Gabriella Zarri, "Female Sanctity," in *Cambridge History of Christianity*, vol. 6: *Reform and Expansion 1500–1660*, ed. Ronnie Po-chia Hsia (Cambridge, 2008), 195.

[18] Michel de Certeau, *The Writing of History* (New York, 1988), 244–48.

[19] Dyan Elliott, *Proving Women: Female Spirituality and Inquisitional Culture in the Later Middle Ages* (Princeton, NJ, 2004); Nancy Caciola, *Discerning Spirits: Divine and Demonic Possession in the Middle Ages* (Ithaca, NY, 2003).

similarities between demonic possession, witchcraft, and mysticism, early modern discernment of spirits was closely connected with the persecution of witches and spiritual direction.[20] The association between women and discernment was nevertheless not solely a negative one. Gerson's theory, whose theological and political impact played a constant and decisive role in the reassessment of sanctity during the Counter-Reformation, was directly addressed to women and especially women mystics, influencing and often shaping their behavior.[21]

Female mystics did not meet these challenges and suspicions alone. They had allies as well as suspicious superiors. "Confessors, Inquisitors, spiritual advisers, directors of conscience, and mother superiors of spiritually inclined nuns" – indeed, all those who practiced mystical religiosity – were part of the process of discernment, which became not only a form of regulation but a collective and collaborative movement, a "redrawing of the new maps of interiority."[22] The active involvement of other nuns, abbesses, and guardians in the observation, recording, and examination of mystical phenomena, both their own and those of others, underlines the important contribution of women to processes of discernment.[23] As practitioners and objects of discernment, spiritual direction, and sometimes persecution, women offer a privileged perspective on discernment, which reveals how this discursive practice was simultaneously collegial and conflictual. The cases of Teresa of Ávila and Caterina de' Ricci are part, therefore, of a very long history of transcendent experiences, which during the Counter-Reformation witnessed an abundance of competing models and discursive practices.

---

[20] Stuart Clark, *Thinking with Demons: The Idea of Witchcraft in Early Modern Europe* (Oxford, 1997); Michela Catto, ed., *La direzione spirituale tra medioevo ed età moderna: Percorsi di ricerca e contesti specifici* (Bologna, 2004); Daniela Camillocci Solfaroli and Malena Adelisa, "La direzione spirituale delle donne in età moderna: Percorsi della ricerca contemporanea," *Annali dell'Istituto storico italo-germanico in Trento* 24 (1998): 439–60; Albano Biondi, "L'inordinata devozione' nella 'Prattica' del Cardinale Scaglia (ca. 1635)," in *Finzione e santità tra medioevo ed età moderna*, ed. Gabriella Zarri (Turin, 1991), 306–25; Fernanda Alfieri, *Veronica e il diavolo. Storia di un esorcismo a Roma* (Turin, 2021).

[21] Yelena Mazour-Matusevich, "Gerson's Legacy," in *A Companion to Jean Gerson*, ed. Brian Patrick McGuire (Leiden, 2006), 357–99; Rosalynn Voaden, *God's Words, Women's Voices: The Discernment of Spirits in the Writing of Late-Medieval Women Visionaries* (Woodbridge, 1999).

[22] Moshe Sluhovsky, *Believe not Every Spirit: Possession, Mysticism, and Discernment in Early Modern Catholicism* (Chicago, 2007), 7, 8.

[23] Anna Scattigno, "I processi di canonizzazione," in *Memoria e comunità femminili: Spagna e Italia*, ed. Gabriella Zarri and Nieves Baranda Leturio (Florence, 2011), 138–42.

COUNTER-REFORMATION DEFINITIONS AND MODELS

Even though mysticism and *discretio* intersect, they also retain their own specific characteristics. The latter, as we already noted, was possible as an intellectual – and even as an institutional – exercise without direct experience with the divine. The origin of the discernment of spirits lies in the connection of the cognitive and ethical category of *discretio* with *spirituum*, through which it assumed a meaning of discernment between true and false, good and evil, divine and diabolical inspiration, while simultaneously remaining a middle way leading to perfection. This connotation was associated with the qualities of the person endowed by God with supernatural gifts, and in mysticism corresponds with the fundamental relationship between the contemplative life and action in the world, as well as the importance of Christocentrism, which in the case of women was accompanied by forms of Marian spirituality.[24]

In the religious culture of the late Middle Ages *discretio* became the "founding element of the mystical path and the prudence that went together with it was the privileged virtue for acquiring pious behavior."[25] During the early modern period, Catholic sanctity was reformulated not only through the centralization and formalization of the canonization process, but also because of a shift in the ideal model of sainthood itself, with a new emphasis on heroic virtues over spiritual encounters with the divine.[26] Mysticism consequently attracted greater suspicion and was subjected to frequent attempts at regulation through confessional practices and spiritual treatises. Yet *discretio spirituum* never became a straightforward tool for the repression of female religiosity, which was tolerated to a greater degree where it remained private, cloistered, and out of view. Indeed, when mystical visions or experiences were robust enough to pass scrutiny, discernment helped

---

[24] María Morrás, "Introduction," in Morrás et al., eds., *Gender and Exemplarity*, 17; Rosa Vidal Doval, "Discernment of Spirits and Spiritual Authority: The Tractatus de vita spirituali and Its Afterlife," in ibid., 112–35; Jane Ackerman, "Teresa and Her Sisters," in Boenig, ed., *The Mystical Gesture*, 107–40; Eleonora Carinci, "Maria e le donne, variazioni e interpretazioni della figura della Vergine come modello femminile nella prima età moderna," in *Transitions et variations marianes du Moyen Age à aujourd'hui*, ed. Elisabetta Barale (Paris: Classiques Garnier, 2023); Unn Falkeid, "Constructing Female Authority: Birgitta of Sweden, Catherine of Siena, and the Two Marys," in *Sanctity and Female Authorship in Birgitta of Sweden and Catherine of Siena*, ed. Unn Falkeid and Maria H. Oen (New York, 2020).

[25] Zarri, "Introduzione," 6.

[26] Giuseppe Dalla Torre, "Santità ed economia processuale: L'esperienza giuridica da Urbano VIII a Benedetto XIV," in Zarri, ed., *Finzione e santità*, 231–63.

transform them into a powerful vehicle for sacrality, as demonstrations of Catholic truths against Protestant falsehoods.

Given these many different possible outcomes, from prosecution to canonization, mysticism comprised a wide range of subjects, practices, and textual forms that contradicted or were in conflict with one another – and with the discernment of spirits. Riven by internal fractures that were often provoked by practitioners themselves, mysticism and the discernment of spirits were disjointed phenomena, especially during the Counter-Reformation period. As we have already stressed, there was no single mysticism, no single *discretio spirituum*; rather, there were models and counter-models, disputes, and imitations, often unique or depicted as exceptional, with their outcomes dependent on specific social, religious, and political contexts. Together, however, they contribute to a collective story of social regulation that this chapter will illuminate using two carefully chosen case studies.

As we have seen, early modern confessional conflict provides the backdrop for the transformation of mysticism and the discernment of spirits. While the great spiritual figures of the seventeenth century "should not be seen just from the perspective of the reaction of Catholicism to the Protestant threat, but as the flowering of developments rooted in the spirituality of the late Middle Ages,"[27] Catholic reform nevertheless played a fundamental role in endowing mysticism with new meaning and reshaping its relationship to *discretio spirituum*. In promoting and institutionalizing sainthood as a pillar of renewal, the Catholic Church oscillated between attempts to regulate and police mysticism and a desire to embrace and promote it. Regulation and promotion were often at odds targeting the same person: Even Ignatius of Loyola was put on trial by the Inquisition, and his acclaimed *Spiritual Exercises* was attacked by the Dominicans. The *Exercises*, which presented a method to achieve union with God through the visualization and meditation on the scenes of the life of Christ and provided detailed instructions for discernment, significantly influenced later Counter-Reformation mysticism.

While Roman institutions were clearly pivotal in the reshaping of mysticism and discernment, the more positive role of others cannot be ignored. During the early modern period, the remarkable proliferation of mystical experiences was promoted by sovereigns searching for sacred legitimacy, by local religious authorities attempting to stir the

---

[27] Bernard McGinn, *The Persistence of Mysticism in Catholic Europe: France, Italy, and Germany, 1500–1675* (New York, 2020), 412.

emotions of the faithful, and by members of religious orders searching for an authentic relationship with God. Beginning from the late sixteenth century, Carmelite and Teresian spirituality stimulated a surge in mysticism in France, Spain, Italy, and overseas that spilled over into streets and convents, and onto the pages of religious literature. Within this problematic context, the saints selected here as case studies certainly embraced a Tridentine Catholic spirituality; yet they also challenged it internally, developed variations upon it, and enriched it through "anti-patriarchal" interpretations in order to establish, recreate, and defend their own authority and authorship.[28]

Indeed, for all that Teresa of Ávila and Caterina de' Ricci embody the post-Tridentine monastic model, they did not allow themselves to be confined inside the walls of enclosed convents.[29] Both practiced *discretio* in original ways. Their homelands, Spain and Italy, were the heartlands of Catholic Reform.[30] The posthumous fate of both women also illustrates the discussion of gender above, and the insight that female mystics "almost always emerge as the sole object of inquisitorial attention."[31] In each case the Inquisition represented a looming threat before canonization, in life and in death. The differences are important as well, however. Although Teresa was put on trial where Caterina was not, the former was swiftly canonized while the latter was forced to wait for 150 years. Both Teresa and Caterina claimed to be humble and uneducated women while addressing the problem of women's religious autonomy, thus shaping a new model of female sainthood and mysticism that, as shown in Chapter 3 in this book, displaced others. In both cases, their reflection was at once part of the Counter-Reformation and intrinsically critical of it.

TERESA OF ÁVILA: INTERIORITY, REFORM, AND AFFIRMATION OF AUTHORSHIP

Much has been written on the *Life* of Teresa of Ávila, published in 1588. A precious autobiographical source that illuminates her rhetoric of obedience to her confessor, and the process of spiritual regulation and

---

[28] Maria H. Oen and Unn Falkeid, "Introduction," in Falkeid and Oen, eds., *Sanctity and Female Authorship*, 1–13.
[29] Clare Copeland, "Sanctity," in *The Ashgate Research Companion to Counter-Reformation*, ed. Alexandra Bamji et al. (Farnham, 2013), 234.
[30] Ronnie Po-chia Hsia, *The World of Catholic Renewal* (Cambridge, 2005).
[31] Adriano Prosperi, *Tribunali della Coscienza* (Turin, 2009), 443.

discernment,[32] it is also a "manual for mass conversion," a sort of "mysticism for the masses" that describes the proper combination of reading and prayer and the right kind of spiritual direction that can lead to God.[33] The *Life* remained in the hands of her confessors for thirteen years, and the publication of all of Teresa's writings followed the same uneven path. In 1580 the inquisitorial confessor and theologian Diego de Yanguas ordered Teresa to burn her *Meditations*, and in 1589, following her death, inquisitors sought to have her works destroyed.[34]

Born in Ávila in 1515, Teresa came from a noble family of *conversos*. Her own long journey to conversion began with a "powerful rapture" experienced during a conversation with a Dominican father.[35] Her origins, passion for mental prayer, and autonomous reading of the Scriptures led her to be suspected of *alumbradismo*.[36] This Spanish mystical movement, widespread in the sixteenth century, was associated with Protestantism and was condemned by the Spanish Inquisition as heretical because it was accused of claiming that the *alumbrados* were illuminated by God and therefore free from sin. Prior to writing her *Life*, Teresa penned accounts of the supernatural phenomena she experienced, using these to describe her method of prayer. The content of these accounts is reproduced in a text written for her confessor, García de Toledo, in 1562 and expanded in 1564–65 to include the history of the foundation of the first reformed Carmelite convent. García, who was taught mental prayer by Teresa, was both her confessor and her spiritual son. As confessor, he ordered her to draw up an account of her spiritual life without neglecting to include her transgressions. As he was her spiritual son, Teresa demanded his devotion and humility in accepting her guidance: "O my son!... I beseech Your Reverence, let us all be mad, for the love of Him Who was called mad for our sakes.... You are my confessor, my father."[37] Her relationship with John of the Cross, an avid admirer of the reformist ideas she applied in founding the

---

[32] Jodi Bilinkoff, "Confessors, Penitents, and the Construction of Identities in Early Modern Avila," in *Culture and Identity in Early Modern Europe, 1500–1800: Essays in Honor of Natalie Zemon Davis*, ed. Barbara B. Diefendorf and Carla Hesse (Ann Arbor, MI, 1993), 93.

[33] Carlos Eire, *The Life of Saint Teresa of Avila* (Princeton, NJ, 2019), 7, 97.

[34] Alison Weber, *Teresa of Avila and the Rhetoric of Femininity* (Princeton, NJ, 1990), 41.

[35] Teresa of Ávila, *The Book of Her Life*, in *The Collected Works of St. Teresa of Avila, I: The Book of Her Life, Spiritual Testimonies, Soliloquies* (Washington, DC, 1976) (henceforth *Life*), chap. 34.

[36] Weber, *Teresa of Avila*, 39.

[37] Teresa of Ávila, *Life*, 16, 99.

Discalced Carmelite order, was similarly characterized by reciprocal respect and humility that made her simultaneously the mother and daughter of his soul.

Teresa was profoundly affected by the growth of the Protestant heresy. In the opening to *The Way of Perfection* (1.2), she writes that the religious wars in France made such an impression as to inspire her reform of the Carmelites. Reimagining these communities in terms of poverty and simplicity would, in God's eyes, atone for the errors of the Lutherans.[38] Despite these efforts, however, Teresa herself was beset by accusations of heresy during her lifetime and immediately following her death, albeit (as we have seen) of a different nature.[39] It was her canonization in 1622 that finally silenced these suspicions and consolidated her image as a heroine of the "European anti-Protestant offensive ... in defence of the Spanish monarchy and the Catholic religion."[40]

Teresa's spirituality, influenced by Augustine, Gerson, and Ignatius, is experimental, committed to discovering "one's inner space as acategorical perception, as aconceptual knowledge.[41] And yet her spirituality was not only experience, but also reflection on it; that is, it was also a form of discernment.[42] Her "incarnational spirituality"[43] drew together theological and political interests, notably her defense of women's autonomy and their freedom to practice mental prayer, her criticism

---

[38] Rowan Williams, "Teresa, the Eucharist and the Reformation," in *Teresa of Avila: Mystical Theology*, ed. Peter Tyler and Edward Howells (London, 2017), 67–76.

[39] Adriano Prosperi, "Diari femminili e discernimento degli spiriti: Le mistiche della prima età moderna," *Dimensioni e problemi della ricerca storica* 2 (1994): 77–103.

[40] Marina Caffiero et al., "La santa 'encantadora': Cinquecento anni dalla nascita di Teresa d'Ávila," *Dimensioni e problemi della ricerca storica* 2 (2017): 8; see also Hsia, *The World of Catholic Renewal*, 127ff.; Carlos M. N. Eire, "Ecstasy as Polemic: Mysticism and the Catholic Reformation," *Irish Theological Quarterly* 83, no. 1 (2018): 3–23.

[41] Bernard McGinn, "True Confessions: Augustine and Teresa of Avila," in Tyler and Howells, eds., *Teresa of Avila: Mystical Theology*; Peter Tyler, "Mystical Affinities: St. Teresa and Jean Gerson," in ibid., 201; Alison Weber, "Teresa di Gesù e la direzione spirituale," in Filoramo and Zarri, eds., *Storia della direzione spirituale*, 289–309; Vincenzo Lavenia, "Spiriti, apparizioni e imposture: Carisma femminile e discernimento in un testo del XVII secolo," in *Soggetti diritti poteri: Studi per Giovanna Fiume*, ed. Ida Fazio and Rita Loredana Foti (Milan, 2020), 161–73; Wietse De Boer, "Invisible Contemplation: A Paradox in the Spiritual Exercises," in *Meditatio: Refashioning the Self: Theory and Practice in Late Medieval and Early Modern Intellectual Culture*, ed. Karl A. E. Enenkel and Walter Melion (Leiden, 2010), 235–56.

[42] Adriana Valerio, *Donne e Chiesa: Una storia di genere* (Bologna, 2016), 138.

[43] Leslie K. Twomey, "Speaking of Heaven in Conventual Women's Writing (Constanza de Castilla, Teresa de Cartagena, Isabel de Villena, and Teresa de Jesús), in Morrás et al., eds., *Gender and Exemplarity*, 212–50.

of the climate of suspicion fed by the Inquisition, and her teachings on mystical visions and union with God.[44]

In her *Spiritual Relations*, Teresa writes that she was ashamed of her spiritual graces and that "it distressed her more to speak of them than if they had been sin."[45] In the same work she describes her rapture, differentiating between "inner recollection," "sleep of the powers," "union," "ravishment," "rapture," "flight of the spirit," and "impetus," all things that are "supernatural" and "hard to describe" because they "happen very quickly." There is an attempt to specifically define her "rapture" (*arrobamiento*):

> I would like, with the help of God, to be able to describe the difference between union and rapture, or elevation, or what they call flight of the spirit, or transport – which are all one. I mean that all these different names refer to the same thing, which is also called ecstasy.[46]

Teresa is aware of the differing definitions of these labels but selects one in a gesture of authority that is both theological and political. The same is true of her ecstatic practice, described in chapter 29 of her *Life*, which one scholar has characterized as an "ecstasy of transverberation – total ecstatic experience ... capable of involving the body in an orgasmic experience."[47]

In Teresa's most important works – the *Life*, *Interior Castle*, and *Way of Perfection* – the visionary experience is accompanied by the dissociation of *sight* and *vision*, since it is only in some cases that she sees an image. When she does *see*, her experience is rooted in the present, and she is confronted with a vivid image: "For if what I see is an image, it is a living image – not a dead man but the living Christ ... not as He was in the sepulcher, but as He was when He left it after rising from the dead."[48]

Teresa thus favors a form of intellectual vision, which is deeper and more acute than its corporeal equivalent, which passively gathers the forms of the imagination. As already noted earlier in passing, in this she

---

[44] Gillian T. W. Ahlgren, *Teresa of Avila and the Politics of Sanctity* (Ithaca, NY, 1996), 85.

[45] Teresa of Ávila, 'Spiritual Relations,' in *The Complete Works of St. Teresa of Jesus*, vol. 1 (London, 1957), IV.5, 321.

[46] Teresa of Ávila, *Life*, 20.1. See Bernard McGinn, "Ecstasy in Classic Christian Mysticism," *Lo Sguardo: Rivista di filosofia* 33 (2021): 208.

[47] Rosa Rossi, *Teresa d'Avila: Biografia di una scrittrice* (Rome, 1999), xxvi.

[48] Teresa of Ávila, *Life*, 28.7, 8.

differs from the descriptions and prescriptions of her fellow Carmelite John of the Cross, in whom we encounter a total absence of images, and Ignatius, where vision is regulated through the imagination of biblical scenes. Teresa, by contrast, struggles to employ the imagination in an active and ordered manner in meditative prayer.[49] Vision is experience, not initiative, and visions of Paradise look not only to future joys but offer a glimpse of present possibility.[50] Since vision concerns the current moment, Teresian mysticism, though centered on the contemplation of God, is a call to action and love of one's neighbor.[51]

The Teresian discourse and practice of discernment display original traits, especially when read against the context of late sixteenth-century Spain, where a division emerged between the Dominicans and Franciscans.[52] Particularly prominent is a fear of diabolical deception, which is described in the reports Teresa sent to her spiritual directors (referring to herself in the third person):

> [Teresa] was a very timorous person, and afraid sometimes to be alone ... as she could not avoid seeing these visions, however hard she tried, she would be most distressed by them, fearing they might be a delusion of the devil.... The more they tested her, the more experiences she had.[53]

Teresa spoke of her precarious position as a "woman, as a descendant of conversos, and as someone making claims easily associated with *alumbradismo*."[54] As a result, she is dedicated to her own and others' watchfulness against "the wiles of the devil," for it is easy to misinterpret the words of he who "counterfeits the spirit of light," and pretends to be God.[55] Experience and interpretation are inseparable: "Teresa presented

---

[49] Teresa of Ávila, *Life*, 4.7. See Rebeca Sanmartín Bastida, "Era Teresa tan amiga de las imagenes?," in *Cinco siglos de Teresa: La proyección de la vida y los escritos de Santa Teresa de Jesús*, ed. Esther Borrego and José Manuel Losada Goya (Madrid, 2016), 89–107.

[50] Leslie K. Twomey, "Seeing and Knowing God: Reinterpreting Vision in the Writing of Teresa of Ávila and Other Cloistered Women Writers," in *St. Teresa of Ávila: Her Writings and Life*, ed. Terence O' Reilly et al. (Cambridge, 2018), 193–212.

[51] Teresa of Ávila, *Interior Castle*, in *The Collected Works of St. Teresa of Avila*, vol. III, V, 3, 348ff.

[52] Álvaro Huerga, "La edición cisneriana del *Tratado de la vida espiritual* y otras ediciones del siglo XVI," *Escritos del Vedat* 10 (1980): 303 n. 15; Vidal Doval, "Discernment of Spirits," 114–16.

[53] Teresa of Ávila, *Spiritual Relations*, IV, 3, 320–21.

[54] Constance M. Furey, "Discernment as Critique in Teresa of Avila and Erasmus of Rotterdam," *Exemplaria: Medieval, Early Modern, Theory* 26, nos. 2–3 (2014): 254–72.

[55] *Interior Castle*, VI.3.16, 377; I.2.15, 295.

herself as both receptive in relation to the angel who acted upon her and active in interpreting the effects of that encounter for herself, her confessors, and other potential readers."[56]

Discernment is connected to spiritual direction, especially of nuns, and may be carried out by all regardless of their gender, position within the Church, or level of learning.[57] Teresa nevertheless displays an extreme reluctance to take responsibility for the direction of souls. Writing on the occasion of a provincial Carmelite father's death, she admits that "it seems to me a very dangerous thing to have the charge of souls."[58] Discernment is an encounter with the word of God, with superiors, readers, the text,[59] and – it might be added – one's own fears, and thus oneself. Nevertheless, Teresa is willing to commit her visions to writing, making them the object of discernment by others, not only in order to convince her confessors of the (divine) goodness of her inspiration, but also because they will become a vehicle for conversion and spiritual direction only through public exhibition. Print enabled Teresa to spread her teaching far and wide. Unlike many other female mystics of her time, Teresa succeeded in convincing her superiors (at least in some cases), and her visions became a classic of spiritual autobiography.

CATERINA DE' RICCI: A SAVONAROLAN SAINT BETWEEN RAPTURES AND COMMUNITY GOVERNANCE

Caterina de' Ricci occupied a central position within the sociopolitical landscape of Florence and Prato in the second half of the sixteenth century. The Dominican fathers Niccolò Alessi and Serafino Razzi, both of a Savonarolan tendency, wrote her first hagiographies, the *Libellus de gestis* (1552–55) and *Vita della reverenda serva di Dio Caterina dei Ricci* (1594), respectively.[60] Important details of Caterina's life emerge from her letters, the chronicles of her convent, and the *Ratti*, an account

---

[56] Furey, "Discernment as Critique," 259.
[57] Weber, *Teresa of Ávila*; Moshe Sluhovsky, "Discernment of Difference: The Introspective Subject, and the Birth of Modernity," *Journal of Medieval Studies* 36, no. 1 (2006): 185.
[58] Teresa of Ávila, *Life*, 38.26.
[59] Furey, "Discernment as Critique," 258.
[60] Miguel Gotor, *I beati del papa: Santità, inquisizione e obbedienza in età moderna* (Florence, 2002).

of her mystical ecstasies created by her fellow nuns and confessors. All these works can be accessed in the modern edition by Domenico Guglielmo di M. Agresti.

Caterina, née Alessandra, was born in 1522 into a noble family associated with the gold-beating trade in Florence and Prato. Her father Pierfrancesco de' Ricci was married twice, first to Caterina di Pier Capponi and later to Fiammetta Diacceto. He was initially strongly opposed to Caterina's entry into the Dominican order and specifically into the enclosed convent of San Vincenzo in Prato. Gabriella Zarri has described Caterina as a transitional figure between the early sixteenth-century hagiographic model of Catherine of Siena – centered on precocious mystical gifts, extreme fasting,[61] imitation of Christ's passion, and marriage and the exchange of hearts with Christ – and the model of the female religious promoted by Tridentine reform, based on heroic virtue and cloistered religiosity far from the public gaze.[62] As we shall see (and as the *Ratti* clearly demonstrates), Caterina's spiritual life was initially imbued with prophetic inspiration of a particularly Savonarolan kind, although this does not at all emerge from the published *Vitae* or her correspondence studied as part of her canonization process. Given Savonarola's grim fate, this editing likely reflected efforts to ensure a successful outcome.[63]

In 1540, a long illness that had seemed terminal was cured through the intercession of Savonarola, and Caterina's visions came to an end. She became prioress of the convent of San Vincenzo, which she administered with an assured hand and practical sense. She had frequent epistolary exchanges (gathered in no fewer than five volumes of letters) with humble men and women of God, notable Florentines and Pratesi, prominent figures at the Medici court, and even a succession of popes. Through her experience of managing the convent and her letters, it is possible to discern a figure characterized by a strong sense of "realism" in both politics – conventual, civic, and ecclesiastical – and religion. Upon her death in 1590 she was widely considered a saint. Although her process began as early as 1623, she was only canonized in 1746, after an interruption that a string of nineteenth- and twentieth-century

---

[61] Caroline Walker Bynum, *Holy Feast and Holy Fast: The Religious Significance of Food to Medieval Women* (Berkeley, 1987); Rudolph M. Bell, *Holy Anorexia* (Chicago, 1985).
[62] Gabriella Zarri, *Le sante vive* (Turin, 1990), 98.
[63] Tamar Herzig, *Savonarola's Women: Visions and Reform in Renaissance Italy* (Chicago, 2008), 186–87.

historians have attributed to her Savonarolan sympathies.⁶⁴ Her journey to sainthood was thus long and arduous when compared with that of Teresa, whose cause had also been far from simple.

The *Ratti* penned by Ricci's fellow nuns allows us to grasp the essence of her mystical experience and spiritual discernment. She constantly experienced ecstasies that would last for hours at a time: "standing on her feet motionless, or kneeling as it pleases God, or sitting ... with her eyes open and motionless and thus the whole body motionless, with an appearance that excites and pulls greatly toward God." This "concrete" representation of the ecstasies is followed by an attestation of Caterina's virtuous denial of her nocturnal raptures: "she always calls it dormition instead of rapture ... out of humility."⁶⁵ Caterina thus avoids any definition of the nature of her own experience as supernatural.⁶⁶

The same fear of being deceived by the devil that we encounter in Teresa is present in Caterina: "darkness" and "terror" beset her mind, "which comes in doubt that all things of mine are devilish." The *Ratti* pays little attention to mysticism as regulation and control, despite the impact of Ignatian spirituality on Caterina,⁶⁷ and it is action that prevails as a remedy to the diabolical threat. During one vision of Christ, the Virgin, Mary Magdalene, and St. Thomas, she made the sign of the cross and spat in the face of the celestial court:

> to obey her superior, so that if it was a diabolical illusion he would leave, having been told that the saints cannot be defiled by our spitting but cherish obedience, and all the opposite is done by the devil who does not suffer those who are not obedient, but still flees their contempt.⁶⁸

Among her spiritual gifts was the reliving of Christ's Passion, which she experienced in 1541 during a "long rapture."⁶⁹ Suffering is central to many mystical experiences, but an even more important foundation is the request (of Christ) for "knowledge of me and you," or knowledge of

---

⁶⁴ Anna Scattigno, "La santità e le sue 'riletture': Caterina de' Ricci dai dossier agiografici alla canonizzazione," in *Fra trionfi e sconfitte: La politica della santità dell'Ordine dei predicatori*, ed. Gianni Festa and Viliam Stefan Doci (Rome, 2021), 107–29.
⁶⁵ Scattigno, *Sposa di Cristo: Mistica e comunità* (Rome, 2011), 152.
⁶⁶ Ibid., 32, n. 61.
⁶⁷ Ibid., 35, n. 74.
⁶⁸ Ibid., 148.
⁶⁹ Ibid.

self.⁷⁰ Unlike Teresa, Caterina's gifts never prompted official inquisitorial investigation, although Pope Paul III dispatched Cardinal Roberto Pucci to examine her through the convent grille so that "no occasion be given to heretics and evil Christians to say it is a business."⁷¹ Nevertheless, notable Florentines and others from across Europe – among them Eleanor of Toledo, the second daughter of the viceroy of Naples and wife of Cosimo de' Medici; Bernardo Antonio de' Medici, the bishop of Forlì; and a "Spanish lord" named Don Pedro – enhanced Caterina's fame by travelling to meet her. Upon witnessing an ecstasy, Maria Salviati, the mother of Archduke Cosimo I, declared to the sisters who were present that it was neither false nor diabolical, but entirely divine.⁷²

Girolamo Savonarola's influence is evident throughout the *Ratti*. On Christmas Day 1540, for example, Caterina

> saw that holy father [Savonarola] coming from the altar ... together with the Queen of Heaven and with her little son in her arms ... Because of the great fright she fell to the ground and Father Girolamo ... helping her up said to her: "Come up my daughter."... She got up and made the sign of the cross.⁷³

The paternal figure of Savonarola is crucial in guaranteeing obedient conduct. During the so-called apparition of the three martyrs of 1540, one spoke to her, saying, "We have come to visit you although you do not deserve it." Struck by doubt, she responded, "You are tempters," which a second martyr, Savonarola, denied:

> [W]e are not tempters, but do you know who was the tempter? The one who made you disobedient.... [Y]ou consented to him by tiring your head too much, wanting to do what we never do, being in mortal flesh as you are.⁷⁴

The condemnation of excessive mortification that emerges from this visionary exchange, as well as the call to obedience to superiors, is repeated at various points in the manuscript, revealing the weakening of a mystical model associated with Catherine of Siena that was based on extreme fasting and annihilation of the body. The exhortation is often explicitly addressed to her fellow sisters. In another exchange with

---

[70] Ibid., 69.
[71] Ibid., 157.
[72] Ibid., 163.
[73] Ibid., 175.
[74] Ibid., 178.

Savonarola, Caterina voices her criticism of her fellow nuns, stating that "obedience is not given as it should be given, promptly and voluntarily, and silences are not kept as they should be kept"; the friar threateningly responds that "the nuns should be advised to repair their way of life, because the aforementioned tribulations would soon arrive."[75] Nevertheless, the discipline and obedience demanded of the nuns – in anticipation of the reform of the convents desired by Caterina, like Teresa – are not necessarily integral to the mystical experience but were needed for their good health, which dispelled the danger of false visions and diabolical temptations. In a vision, the Virgin Mary commands the nuns to take care of themselves:

> My daughters, understand me well: neither I nor your spouse [Christ] want you to suffer your needs; I want you to eat and sleep and satisfy your other needs, but I do not want you to be too delicate, and satisfy them all in my son and your spouse, which is what he wants.[76]

In this way, bodily health is reclaimed along with its intimate connection to the spirit, the two united in mystical experienced validated by autonomous *discretio*. Fragments of mysticism and discernment are scattered throughout the *Ratti*, indicating their composition was no less chaotic than Caterina's passions in her union with God.

CONCLUSION

The cases of Teresa and Caterina demonstrate in different ways the interplay between mysticism and *discretio spirituum*. The former points to the disorder of the visionary experiences, the latter to the impossibility of its codification. Placing her trust in the passive reception of interior images, Teresa structures a mystical language based on an experience that is unavailable to those whose position and power rests on theological training. She diminishes the relevance of discernment and establishes a counter-codification of the mystical, that is, an alternative form of codification in terms of freedom from control. In contrast, Caterina de' Ricci embodies the dissolution of the very mystical canon that she appropriates and models as a woman. She carries out a practical self-discernment of spirits and her varied mystical experiences are expressed through multiple definitions. Unlike Teresa,

---

[75] Ibid., 185.
[76] Ibid., 240.

Caterina did not write a first-person account of her experiences, which were instead recorded by her fellow nuns and were therefore shaped through dialogue between the mystic and her religious community. Although her canonization followed a less straightforward path than Teresa's, Caterina is still one of very few women to achieve sainthood during the early modern era. Both women developed influential discourses and practices for both mysticism and spiritual discernment, albeit in an asystematic manner, which made them central figures in the vexed attempts at theorizing the relationship between the two.

In discussing the two case studies, we have considered the significance of the attitudes of ecclesiastical institutions in debates concerning mysticism and spiritual discernment. As we have seen, post-Tridentine sanctity absorbed and simultaneously entered into conflict with the mystical. Attempts to discipline or regulate mysticism through discernment and spiritual direction created a common reservoir of knowledge that made its replication and imitation possible. The Counter-Reformation bore witness to countless attempts to impose order and structure on mysticism – a phenomenon that was intrinsically heterogenous because it was based on individual experience. Promoting mystical models of sainthood and rewriting the experience of mystics at the point of their canonization were key to such efforts. Nevertheless, the Counter-Reformation Church was forced to reckon with the vindication of mystical experiences. Rooted in encounters with the divine, their authority could not come exclusively from their ecclesiastical codification, and notions of sainthood needed to be stretched and rethought in order for them to accommodate different types of visionaries. Codification, then, was invariably insufficient and its regulation incomplete. For Catholic reformers, mysticism proved a double-edged sword: While it brought spiritual perfection within the grasp of all, it constantly risked a perpetual rewriting of the rules in an effort to attain that perfection, resulting in challenges to the Church's monopoly over the conduct of souls.

The influence of Ignatius's *Spiritual Exercises* on both Teresa and Caterina is evident from the constant dialogue between mystical spirituality and self-practiced discernment. Nevertheless, both women depict their visions in entirely non-Ignatian terms. While for Ignatius visual representation is an intellectual operation, for the two female saints it is the product of an immediate and ecstatic experience. The problem of mediation, necessary and contested, is present in both. Teresa prefers a mystical, spiritual, and thus unmediated reading of the Bible, implicitly maintaining that "access to God cannot ultimately be controlled by the institutional church."⁷⁷ Caterina's contact with God and the saints is entirely free from ecclesiastical mediation. While it takes place in the presence of her superiors and fellow nuns, as witnesses their ultimate role is only to reintroduce the necessity of human mediation of divine experience.

The interiority of the two mystics was thus, above all, a subjective and collective call to an unmediated relationship with God. In the context of the Counter-Reformation, such a demand was viewed with suspicion when it moved beyond external behavior – the only indicator that could be scrutinized by the Church – to the interior life. In response to "male" attempts to codify and systematize the mystical and reintroduce the issue of mediation – through Ignatian prayer, exercises, and regulation – the two women in different ways enacted a counter-codification that disrupted the mystical canon from within. Their experiences and practices testify to mysticism's inherent heterogeneity; despite the Church's best efforts, mysticism could never be contained by institutions – at most it could be guided by the practice of discernment. Paradoxically, however, institutional discernment was not only impossible; it was also necessary to ensure that the search for union with God did not fall into sin.

If the discernment of spirits powerfully reintroduces the dilemma of mediation, female mystics challenge the clerical monopoly through offering their own definitions of *discretio spirituum* and enacting the discursive practice upon themselves. They reappropriated mysticism, discernment, and discretion while accepting their subordination to earthly authorities in accordance with their obedience to the supreme authority of God. While offering original prescriptions for the union with God, Teresa and Caterina also willingly subscribed to the discursive mystical canon – which they then rewrote from within, declaring the impossibility of its uniformity. By revealing the hidden structure of mysticism, they invited all Christians to participate in it, while simultaneously affirming the exceptional nature of their experiences of direct union with God.

---

⁷⁷ Ahlgren, *Teresa of Avila*, 85.

10 Miracles and Holy Bodies

BRADFORD BOULEY

On June 9, 1612, the body of Isidore the Laborer, who had been dead since circa 1130, was unearthed in Madrid. In accordance with the letters from Rome that opened the apostolic phase of his canonization, the local judges ordered three physicians – Juan de Atiensa, Juan de Negrete, and the physician-surgeon Luís de Orseon – to examine the body.[1] They were charged with searching for any abnormal signs at the tomb that might either confirm or deny Isidore's sanctity. The physicians' report stated, first, that the body had not been embalmed, nor had any other attempt at preservation been made.[2] They then surveyed the corpse and found it was still totally covered with skin, with even the hair still in place. The only flaws in the prospective saint's body were some missing teeth and the caving in of his ears and nose, which they argued were signs that would have been present in even the best-preserved body. A missing finger was explained as having been taken by a relic hunter.[3] In comparing Isidore's body both with previous corpses they had seen and with what they, as trained physicians, knew about human decay and decomposition, the examiners declared that the state of preservation of the corpse was totally "beyond nature."[4] That is, they asserted that the body had staved off rot, vermin, and decay in ways that could only be attributed to a miracle.

This chapter examines the role that medical testimony played in establishing miracles and sanctity in the early modern period. The idea that the bodies of the holy dead might show some connection to the divine dates back to the earliest days of Christianity. For the Middle Ages, André Vauchez has observed that an incorrupt and sweet-smelling

---

[1] Vatican City, Archivio Apostolico Vaticano (hereafter AAV), Processi dei Riti (RP) 3192, fols. 655r–v.
[2] Ibid., fol. 657r.
[3] Ibid.
[4] Ibid., fol. 657r–v.

body was a de facto requirement for canonization, even if it was not an official one, and veneration of a holy person could stop quickly if the body was thought to emit a foul odor.[5] In the early modern period, the burden of evidence necessary for successful saint-making increased, and the process increasingly relied on medical expertise. Although there had been medical testimony for miracles in the medieval period, it now became a requirement for canonization.[6] This was true both for healing miracles, which required a physician to declare that a recovery could not be natural, and for establishing that the body of a prospective saint demonstrated signs of its holiness. The determination of when a body was starting to rot changed from being a matter of popular acclaim to one confirmed by medical expertise in the period around 1600. This was a deliberate decision made by theologians and canon lawyers involved with canonization, and nearly every saint canonized between 1588 (when modern saint-making resumed) and 1700 underwent a postmortem medical examination, frequently with a full autopsy.[7]

This new requirement was indebted to trends in both medicine and Catholicism: Medicine had grown in prestige, especially in the field of anatomy, during the very years in which the Catholic Church was seeking to redefine saint-making. The mutual development of these fields meant that the Church began using physicians and surgeons trained in anatomy to help discern miracles. They were thought to be able to best determine whether something that occurred to a human body fell within the realm of the natural. However, the boundaries of nature were not unambiguous, and negotiation between medical expertise, local expectations, and Church authority was key to defining early modern holiness. This negotiation was evident, for example, in Isidore's case, described above, in which, despite some actual signs of decay – caved-in ears and nose, a missing finger and teeth – the physicians drew on their medical expertise to argue that a miracle had still occurred. This chapter will use such negotiations to argue that medicine became

---

[5] André Vauchez, *Sainthood in the Later Middle Ages*, trans. Jean Birrell (New York, 1997), 427–28.

[6] David Gentilcore, *Healers and Healing in Early Modern Italy* (New York, 1998), 187–98; Fernando Vidal, "Miracles, Science, and Testimony in Post-Tridentine Saint-Making," *Science in Context* 20, no. 3 (2007): 481–508; Bradford Bouley, *Pious Postmortems: Anatomy, Sanctity and the Catholic Church in Early Modern Europe* (Philadelphia, 2017). See also Jacalyn Duffin, *Medical Miracles: Doctors, Saints, and Healing in the Modern World* (New York, 2009), which is a thorough survey of doctors' involvement in healing miracles through the twentieth century.

[7] Bouley, *Pious Postmortems*, appendix 1.

an essential but contested part of canonization during the early modern period. This argument will begin with a brief overview of the changes to medicine in the early modern period and how the new medical practices came to be useful for Church officials. A series of case studies will then specifically explore three distinct categories of bodily holiness that Church officials and medical experts highlighted in their reports: the incorrupt, the ascetic, and the wondrous corpse.

MEDICINE AND THE CATHOLIC CHURCH

The range of people involved in the healing arts was exceptionally broad in early modern Europe and included women and men of diverse social and economic backgrounds. Any urban area of even modest size would include within its walls licensed healers such as physicians, surgeons, barbers, apothecaries, and midwives, as well as practitioners who might exist beyond or in a liminal state within the official medical system. These might be charlatans and other hawkers of medical cures, female healers of various stripes, and specialized healers, who were sought after for the cure of a particular ailment. In Bologna, for example, there existed a group of healers called *norcini* who specialized in lithotomy (surgery to remove one or more stones from a duct or organ) and who, in addition, performed hernia surgery.[8] Even rural areas could frequently boast a handful of informal medical practitioners, including self-trained cunning folk or white witches. Official attitudes toward those active in this vibrant medical marketplace varied. While many informal healers had run-ins with religious authorities, the canon lawyers and theologians who oversaw canonization processes began to rely on the testimony of physicians, who were university-trained like them. Their reports frequently included specific anatomical details, as the study of anatomy underwent a period of renewal in the sixteenth century, which will be discussed in greater detail below.

This preference for physicians emerges in cases where the evidence was ambivalent, and determining whether a miracle had occurred required an awareness of medical theories about decay and even some theology. In the case of Giacomo della Marca (d. 1476), for example, two postmortem examinations, in 1609 and then again in 1624, yielded ambiguous evidence of incorruption, which was resolved through

---

[8] Gianna Pomata, *Contracting a Cure: Patients, Healers, and the Law in Early Modern Bologna* (Baltimore, 1998), 72.

physician testimony. Giacomo's body seemed well-preserved in some areas, but in others the skin was black and dry, the eyes had decayed, the nose had totally collapsed, and the skin on the chest had been partially eaten away by vermin – all this despite an embalming effort through which the entrails had been removed and the body filled with flax.[9] In this case, both surgeons and physicians testified about the state of Giacomo's body. However, the surgeons described just the evidence of the body, whereas the physicians used an Aristotelian explanatory framework taught to medical students to argue that the body was still wondrous despite the obvious issues presented by the cadaver.[10] In another case, discussed further below, physicians presented the unusual anatomy of Philip Neri's enlarged heart as a sign of his sanctity. The recognition of unusual, miraculous anatomy required knowledge of the latest medical discoveries.[11]

This preference for university-trained physicians had some antecedents in the medieval Church but was also based on recent innovations in the field of medical knowledge. As early as the thirteenth century, medical professionals had testified to healing miracles in canonization proceedings.[12] They were asked to take part because they could authenticate the testimonies of "simple people" that might have otherwise been dubious. Local physicians in particular were important, as they could rule out possible natural explanations for a healing.[13] Such testimony was not a requirement, however, and was based principally on the local availability of medical practitioners.[14] Medical testimony about healing miracles in late medieval canonization proceedings was therefore ad hoc and represented a supporting but almost superfluous addition to other witness testimony, rather than a replacement of it. After the Council of Trent (1545–63), verification of healing miracles in canonization proceedings changed in two significant ways. First, testimonies became more technical, with medical witnesses relying on both experience and philosophical training to rule out natural explanations for a miraculous cure. Second, medical

---

[9] AAV, RP 2012, fol. 232r–v.
[10] AAV, RP 2009, fol. 447r–v.
[11] Nancy Siraisi, "Signs and Evidence: Autopsy and Sanctity in Late Sixteenth-Century Italy," in *Medicine and the Italian Universities, 1250–1600* (Boston, 2001), 374.
[12] Joseph Ziegler, "Practitioners and Saints: Medical Men in Canonization Processes in the Thirteenth to Fifteenth Centuries," *Social History of Medicine* 12, no. 2 (1999): 210.
[13] Ibid., 220.
[14] Ibid., 219–23.

verification of a healing miracle became regular in this period and, by 1678, a specific requirement.[15]

The confirmation of healing miracles differed significantly from the study of posthumous holy bodies; it both required a different set of skills and implied a different relationship between medicine and religion. In order to confirm a healing miracle, a medical professional would be forced to admit that he was unable to explain how the healing occurred and that, to his knowledge, the recovery that had happened was impossible in nature. The success of healing miracles thus required the failure of medicine. In contrast, to judge a body holy a physician would employ experience, knowledge of modern and classical medical writers and philosophers, and surgical skill to isolate and explain unusual anatomical features.[16] Therefore, postmortems on saints were a judgment by the Church of the positive contribution that medical professionals could make in defining the boundaries of the natural, rather than, in the case of healing miracles, forcing such practitioners to admit the inadequacy of their skills. The study of holy bodies presented a more positive and more collaborative relationship between the Church and medicine than the forced admission of failure needed for the confirmation of a healing miracle.

The Catholic Church had good reason to view the medical profession, and especially anatomy, positively in the sixteenth and seventeenth centuries. By the sixteenth century, the practice of opening human bodies had long been accepted, having begun in the medieval period for a number of reasons: (1) to embalm the elite as part of burial practices, (2) to determine the cause of death, (3) to check physical signs of a saint's holiness, and (4) to investigate murders.[17] From at least the twelfth century, medical practitioners had also engaged in anatomical investigations for an additional reason: to confirm knowledge gleaned from classical sources, many of which were just then being translated into Latin. The first known use of a dissection to advance a medical

---

[15] Gentilcore, *Healers and Healing*; Vidal, "Miracles, Science, and Testimony," 481–508.

[16] Elisa Andretta, "Anatomie du Vénérable dans la Rome de la Contre-réforme: Les autopsies d'Ignace de Loyola et de Philippe Neri," in *Conflicting Duties: Science, Medicine and Religion in Rome, 1550– 1750*, ed. Maria Pia Donato and Jill Kraye (London, 2009), 258. Andretta makes the same point that autopsy to discern holiness and the medical verification of healing miracles required different sets of expertise.

[17] Katharine Park, "The Criminal and the Saintly Body: Autopsy and Dissection in Renaissance Italy," *Renaissance Quarterly* 47 (1994): 3–4; Siraisi, "Signs and Evidence."

theory dates to as early as 1316. Normally, however, dissections usually served a pedagogic rather than exploratory purpose.[18] That is, they were meant to illustrate the principles observed in the canonical treatises of Galen, Aristotle, and Hippocrates, not to challenge them. It was for this purpose that the Universities of Bologna and Padua established yearly, public anatomical dissections. The practice of public dissection was commonplace by the time it was recorded in the 1405 university statutes of Bologna and in the 1465 statutes of Padua.[19]

Therefore, when canonization officials turned to anatomy to help establish bodily miracles, they drew on long-standing autopsy practices in Europe. The initial and ostensible reason that many saintly bodies were opened was to embalm the corpse for display. However, forensic motivations also inspired the dissectors, who sought anatomical explanations of unusual ailments or behavior in prospective saints. Finally, since these medical men were testifying in a legal context, the established practice of using medical professionals as expert witnesses in criminal proceedings likely also inspired canonization officials. In short, that canonization officials turned to anatomy to help demonstrate sanctity was in some ways a logical step, since the opening of human bodies had been commonplace in a number of related legal, funerary, and medical contexts. Indeed, Katharine Park argues that a similar mix of motivations led to the opening of female saintly bodies as early as the fourteenth century.[20]

While there was, then, some precedent, new medical and anatomical practices changed both who became involved in the postmortems of prospective saints and how the evidence gathered was interpreted. In the medieval examinations of holy women, a physician generally was not present when the body was opened, whereas in the sixteenth and seventeenth centuries, the Church required specifically that physicians undertake the examination themselves.[21] This change in personnel also represents a revised understanding of a physician's duties and knowledge. Physicians were now expected both to find any unusual

---

[18] Nancy Siraisi, *Medieval and Early Renaissance Medicine: An Introduction to Knowledge and Practice* (Chicago, 1990), 81–86; Andrea Carlino, *Anatomical Ritual and Renaissance Learning*, trans. John Tedeschi and Anne C. Tedeschi (Chicago, 1999), 2; Mondino dei Liuzzi, *Anatomies de Mondino dei Luzzi et de Guido de Vigevano* (Paris, 1926).

[19] Siraisi, *Medieval and Early Renaissance Medicine*, 88; Carlino, *Anatomical Ritual*, 2.

[20] Katharine Park, *Secrets of Women: Gender, Generation, and the Origins of Human Dissection* (New York, 2006), 39–60.

[21] Ibid., 48–50.

details in the human body and to interpret them as part of a discussion of what should be natural for a specific body. That is, canonization officials expected physicians to draw on both empirical and theoretical medical knowledge to speak about human bodies in general and a specific corpse in particular.

The Church's new expectations of their physician-testators were based on changes in how knowledge was made in medicine in the early modern period. Although still rooted in classical medical authorities such as Galen and Hippocrates, medicine by the early sixteenth century was undergoing what has been termed a "Renaissance" in its understanding of the human body.[22] This revival was fueled by the increasing availability of texts by ancient Greek and Roman authors, and the circulation of some newly discovered works from the ancient world. Humanist scholarship had, for example, produced a landmark collection of Galen's works in 1525, which provided many medical practitioners with a much more comprehensive view of what ancient physicians had known about the human body.[23] During the sixteenth century, medicine increasingly emphasized firsthand experience of anatomy as a guide to understanding the human body. Direct observation as a guide to practice, traditionally considered a low form of knowledge-making relegated to non-physician practitioners, became increasingly important for the medical profession. New works, in fact, that sought to share such information circulated widely – a clear indication of its value for the profession.[24]

By the early sixteenth century, then, a few physicians, including Alessandro Benedetti, Jacopo Berengario da Carpi, and Niccolò Massa,

---

[22] Andrew Cunningham, *The Anatomical Renaissance: The Resurrection of the Anatomical Project of the Ancients* (Brookfield, VT, 1997); Mary Lindemann, *Medicine and Society in Early Modern Europe* (New York, 2010), 91–97; Siraisi, *Medieval and Early Renaissance Medicine*, 190–93. A few others have also pointed out that as early as the fifteenth century some physicians had begun to use firsthand observations and particular evidence to add to their overall knowledge of the human body. See Danielle Jacquart, "Theory, Everyday Practice, and Three Fifteenth-Century Physicians," *Osiris*, 2nd Series, vol. 6 (1990): 140–60; Katharine Park, "Natural Particulars: Medical Epistemology, Practice, and the Literature of Healing Springs," in *Natural Particulars: Nature and the Disciplines in Renaissance Europe*, ed. Anthony Grafton and Nancy G. Siraisi (Cambridge, MA, 2000), 347–68.

[23] Vivian Nutton, "The Rise of Medical Humanism: Ferrara, 1464–1555," *Renaissance Studies* 11 (1997): 2–19; Owsei Temkin, *Galenism: Rise and Decline of a Medical Philosophy* (Ithaca, NY, 1973), 125.

[24] Gianna Pomata, "Observation Rising: Birth of an Epistemic Genre, 1500–1650," in *Histories of Scientific Observation*, ed. Lorraine Daston and Elizabeth Lunbeck (Chicago, 2011), 45–80.

had conducted autopsies with their own hands as a way of uncovering new knowledge about the workings of human anatomy.[25] Real change in attitudes toward dissection is evident in the 1543 publication of Andreas Vesalius's *On the Fabric of the Human Body*. Despite his reliance on Galen in some respects, Vesalius also argued forcefully for the utility of firsthand knowledge of dissection.[26] Indeed, Vesalius's work represented a fusion of various knowledge-making techniques: He employed the empirical methods characteristic of surgeons and apothecaries alongside traditional classical texts to understand the human body.[27] Other anatomists, including Realdo Colombo and Charles Estienne, also engaged in this synthesis of empirical and learned practices and elaborated their own arguments about the structure of the human body based on these methods.[28] Publications documented for the first time the valves in human veins, the mechanisms of digestion, the structure of female reproductive anatomy, and, finally, the circulation of blood.[29] By the seventeenth century, Vesalian methods of dissection "had become the golden method for anatomical investigation."[30]

By 1600, many physicians had embraced an epistemology that fused empirical investigation with textual evidence to understand the human body. When the Church turned to physicians to conduct postmortems on holy individuals, it thus drew on existing legal, funerary, and medical

---

[25] Andrea Carlino, *Anatomical Ritual and Renaissance Learning*, trans. John Tedeschi and Anne C. Tedeschi (University of Chicago Press, 1999), 2; Roger French, *Dissection and Vivisection in the European Renaissance* (Brookfield, VT, 1999), 96.

[26] Numerous authors have written about the importance of Vesalius and debated to what extent 1543 counts as a turning point. See Carlino, *Books of the Body*, 1, 44; French, *Dissection and Vivisection*, 163–79; Lindemann, *Medicine and Society*, 92–95; Charles O'Malley, *Andreas Vesalius of Brussels, 1514–1564* (Berkeley, CA, 1964).

[27] Pamela O. Long, *Artisan/Practitioners and the Rise of the New Sciences, 1400–1600* (Corvallis, OR, 2011), 56–58.

[28] Realdo Columbo, *De re anatomica libri XV* (Venice, 1559); Charles Estienne, *De dissectione partium corporis humani libri III* (Paris, 1545).

[29] I am referring here to the publications of Fabricius of Acquapendente, who described the valves present in human veins in 1603; Gasparo Aselli of Padua (d. 1626) and Franciscus Sylvius of Leiden (d. 1672), who uncovered the workings of digestion; Gabriele Falloppio (d. 1562), who made significant contributions to the anatomy both of the ear and of female genitalia; and ultimately William Harvey, who in 1628 correctly demonstrated the circulation of blood in the human body.

[30] Roy Porter, "Medical Science," in *The Cambridge History of Medicine*, ed. Roy Porter (New York, 2006), 138. On the increasingly important role of anatomy in medical education, see Cynthia Klestinec, "Practical Experience in Anatomy," in *The Body as Object and Instrument of Knowledge: Embodied Empiricism in Early Modern Science*, ed. C. T. Wolfe and O. Gal (New York, 2010), 33–57.

precedents relating to autopsies along with new trends in how medical professionals gained knowledge about the human body. The following sections detail how this collaboration between medicine and religion developed in the specific areas of incorruption, asceticism, and anatomical irregularity.

NEGOTIATING INCORRUPTION

On March 26, 1612, the bishop of Coimbra exhumed the body of Queen Elisabeth of Portugal (1271–1336), who had been dead for 276 years. Elisabeth's corpse, witnesses noted, smelled sweet and had not rotted, despite having lain in the ground for centuries.[31] As we have seen, these were the typical attributes of holy bodies, going back to medieval times.[32] However, in accordance with the new standards of evidence that the Church was developing, the three judges called expert witnesses to examine the corpse. Two physicians and one surgeon consequently conducted a thorough survey of Elisabeth's body.[33]

In their investigation of the corpse, these medical men found that Elisabeth's face was still "covered by white flesh," her head was "full of hair," which seemed as if it had been "just washed," her "eye sockets, ears, and nose were whole," and her breasts were "similarly totally white and dry," and upon probing, "they remained solid and firm."[34] These experts deliberated the details and employed both their scholarly knowledge of the relevant literature and their long practical experience in the burgeoning art of anatomy in an attempt to explain what had happened to the corpse. The doctors concluded that the state of Elisabeth's corpse was "beyond nature."[35] That is, they declared the preservation of her body miraculous, despite some signs of decay.

Incorruption was a long-standing sign of sanctity, but theologians and canonization judges especially emphasized its importance after the Reformation for offering an unambiguous bodily connection between God, the miraculous, and the saints. Francisco Peña (1540–1612), a

[31] AAV, RP 501, fol. 43v.
[32] Vauchez, *Sainthood in the Later Middle Ages*, 24. For a broader work on bodily incorruption in popular culture, see Piero Camporesi, *The Incorruptible Flesh: Bodily Mutation and Mortification in Religion and Folklore*, trans. Tania Croft-Murray (New York, 1988).
[33] AAV, RP 501, fols. 40v–41r.
[34] Ibid., fols. 43v–44r, 596r.
[35] Ibid., fol. 596r.

Spanish canon lawyer and judge for the Tribunal of the Rota, regularly oversaw canonizations from the 1580s until his death and explicitly emphasized incorruption as a key criterion in discerning sanctity.[36] As Peña stated during the canonization proceedings for Raymond of Penyafort (canonized 1601), "the sweet odors that issue from the tombs of the dead are miraculous" and are, indeed, "the sign that within them resides the Author of life [God]."[37] Furthermore, in his vita of Francesca Romana (canonized 1608), Peña considered incorruptibility to be one of the most important signs of her holiness: a "sweet odor ... issued from her body, with which Divine Mercy well demonstrates the holiness of his servant."[38] Felice Contelori (1588–1652), a principal legal advisor to Pope Urban VIII (1623–1644), similarly stressed the importance of incorruption in his authoritative 1634 manual on canonization, *Tractatus et praxis de canonizatione*.[39] Contelori gave precedence to a corpse's incorruption and sweet odor by listing these as the first two miracles that could count for canonization.[40] He also specifically asserted that physicians and surgeons held authority as expert witnesses and claimed that they were allowed to interpret evidence – even if they had not been present when the supposed miracle occurred.[41]

Medical expertise was especially necessary in discerning incorruption because it was not a hard boundary, but one open to interpretation. If a body had been buried for 500 years, but had a small amount of decay, could it still be considered miraculous? As we have already seen, the answer could easily be yes. However, what about differences between corpses that had lain in arid, dry conditions that would have preserved them and those that had been exposed to humid conditions that might encourage rot? In determining whether the state of a body was miraculous, physicians relied on three basic categories into which phenomena could be assigned: the natural, preternatural, and supernatural, building on distinctions first codified by Thomas Aquinas

---

[36] On Peña, see Peter Godman, *The Saint as Censor: Robert Bellarmine Between Inquisition and Index* (Boston, 2000), 90, 404–5; Vincenzo Lavenia, "Peña, Francisco," in *Dizionario Storico dell'Inquisizione*, 4 vols., ed. Adriano Prosperi with Vincenzo Lavenia and John Tedeschi (Pisa, 2010), 1186–89.

[37] Francisco Peña, *Relatione summaria della vita, de' miracoli, & delli atti della canonizatione di S. Raimondo di Penafort* (Rome, 1600), 26–27.

[38] Francisco Peña, *Relatione summaria della vita, santità, miracoli et atti della canonizatione di Santa Francesca Romana* (Rome, 1608), 29.

[39] On Contelori, see Giovanni Camillo Peresio, *Vita di Monsig. Felice Contelori* (Rome, 1684).

[40] Felice Contelori, *Tractatus et praxis de canonizatione* (Lyon, 1634), 144–45.

[41] Ibid., 209.

(1225–1274). Natural occurrences were those that were brought about and could be explained by the normal workings of nature. A preternatural event was inspired by some sort of unusual occurrence but was not divine and was potentially demonic. Monstrous births were considered preternatural occurrences, as were many of the signs exhibited by those convicted of false holiness. Such events were believed to happen through some secret workings of nature, which demons could have exploited. Hence, they were still part of the natural world, but it required an expert – such as a physician – to decipher how nature brought about a preternatural phenomenon. In contrast to both of these categories, supernatural events, as the name suggests, exceeded nature and therefore constituted divinely inspired miracles.[42]

In determining whether the level of decay found in a human body was natural, preternatural, or supernatural, seventeenth-century physicians drew heavily on their new, practical experience with human anatomy. With increasing frequency, they undertook empirical testing of the corpse, sometimes including an autopsy. The physicians who examined potential saints Giacomo Della Marca and Andrea Corsini, for example, opened the chest cavity of each of the deceased to inspect the effects of previous embalming efforts on the body. In Della Marca's case, one physician even noted that he and his colleagues had checked "by hand" the interior of the holy man's corpse. This detail underlines the importance of careful, firsthand examination that medical professionals undertook in verifying the incorruption of a body.[43] A physician who examined Elizabeth of Portugal in 1612 was careful to point out that he had tested her flesh in multiple places to make sure that her bodily integrity extended throughout her frame. He stated that he "did not only look but also touched by hand from the right shoulder down the whole arm to the hand."[44] In the case of Teresa of Ávila, the medical practitioner Luis Vasquez felt her abdomen in several locations to check for rot. Finding that the skin seemed smooth and lifelike, he repeated this tactile examination on numerous occasions, returning at different times of day and in different weather conditions to see if the flesh had changed.[45] Vasquez thus relied on firsthand experience and testing of the corpse at different times and in different atmospheric

---

[42] Lorraine Daston and Katharine Park, *Wonders and the Order of Nature, 1150–1750* (New York, 1998), 120–28.
[43] AAV, RP 2009 (Giacomo della Marca), fol. 446r; ASV, RP 762 (Andrea Corsini), fol. 149
[44] AAV, RP 501, fol. 596r.
[45] AAV, RP 3156, unfoliated, estimated fol. 712.

conditions to help determine whether the preservation of Teresa's body should be considered supernatural.

Medical expertise was an important factor in determining whether or not a prospective saint's body could be considered miraculous, but it was by no means definitive or considered the only factor. Local opinion, ecclesiastical authority, political pressures, medical expertise, and theological concerns all contributed to the attempt to define the boundary of the natural when it came to a rotting human body.[46] As Aviad Kleinberg has noted for the cases of medieval saints, "the status of saint was conferred upon a person in a gradual process that involved disagreement and negotiation, as well as collaboration and even collusion."[47] Medical approval, however, altered the meaning of incorruption, turning it not just into a matter of popular opinion and acclaim but, instead, a medical fact. Thus, even if negotiation went into the creation of this "fact," the end result was the appearance of more reliable and robust evidence of holiness. Such attempts to create sure knowledge of holiness through negotiation over the body of the saint continued in discussions about asceticism and anatomical wonder.

ASCETICISM

Aspiring saints needed more than just miracles in order to achieve sainthood; they also needed to demonstrate *fama sanctitatis*, evidence of a holy virtuous life. Their posthumous bodies could furnish this type of evidence as well. Asceticism, or the willing endurance of rigorous acts of self-denial, including fasting, bodily mortification, and sleeplessness, was long considered a marker of virtue and piety for Christians. This was especially true for Church leaders, whose control over their bodily needs was equated with spiritual authority.[48] André Vauchez has argued that the figure of the outwardly impressive bishop who secretly disciplined his body at night was already a widely cited model of sanctity in the Middle Ages.[49] This model became even more prevalent in the period after the Council of Trent, when the authority of ecclesiastical office needed to be bolstered against attacks from Luther and other reformers. As shown in Chapter 1 in this volume, the bishop who

---

[46] Bouley, *Pious Postmortems*, 70–90.
[47] Aviad M. Kleinberg, *Prophets in Their Own Country* (Chicago, 1992), 4.
[48] Conrad Leyser, *Authority and Asceticism from Augustine to Gregory the Great* (Oxford, 2000), 33; Philip Rousseau, *Ascetics, Authority and the Church in the Age of Jerome and Cassian*, 2nd ed. (Notre Dame, IN, 2010), 9–11.
[49] Vauchez, *Sainthood in the Later Middle Ages*, 300–1.

seemed to be sacrificing himself for his diocese, in the model of Carlo Borromeo, provided justification for the office itself.[50]

The problem, however, was that asceticism was supposed to be kept secret if it were to count for holiness. As early modern aspiring female saints discovered to their cost, public displays of asceticism, such as surviving for years on the Eucharist alone, had fallen out of official favor, precisely because such acts imbued those who performed them with a kind of authority.[51] And what if that individual later spouted heretical ideas after performing wondrous deeds? What if they were not particularly pious, despite apparent acts of asceticism? What if they were feigning their miraculous feats altogether? Such doubts fueled a growing concern about "false" or "affected" saints in the early modern period.[52] Canon lawyer Felice Contelori echoed many when he expressed deep reservations about the ability of canonization judges to establish the holiness of an individual life. He argued that the human testimony upon which canonization judges relied was "fallible."[53]

To help wade through the difficulties of distinguishing real and pious ascetics from insincere frauds, the Catholic Church again turned to medical professionals. In multiple cases from the sixteenth and seventeenth centuries, medical evidence from autopsies promoted an image of a saintly prelate who had practiced secret asceticism. Two of the most eminent saints of the Tridentine period, Carlo Borromeo and Ignatius of Loyola, had the rigor of their spiritual lives confirmed in

---

[50] Celeste McNamara, *The Bishop's Burden: Reforming the Catholic Church in Early Modern Italy* (Washington, DC, 2020); Giuseppe Alberigo, "Carlo Borromeo come modello di vescovi nella chiesa post-tridentina," *Rivista storica italiana* 79 (1967): 1031–52; Joseph Bergin, "The Counter-Reformation Church and Its Bishops," *Past and Present* 165 (1999): 30–73; Mario Rosa, "L'immagine del vescovo nel seicento," *Ricerche di storia sociale e religiosa* 46 (1994): 49–59.

[51] Schutte, *Aspiring Saints*; Anne Jacobson Schutte, *Pretense of Holiness, Inquisition, and Gender in the Republic of Venice, 1618–1750* (Baltimore, 2001), 138–43.

[52] There has been a wealth of recent literature on this topic, but see in particular Andrew Keitt, *Inventing the Sacred: Imposture, Inquisition and the Boundaries of the Supernatural in Golden Age Spain* (Boston, 2005); Andrew Keitt, "The Miraculous Body of Evidence: Visionary Experience, Medical Discourse, and the Inquisition in Seventeenth-Century Spain," *Sixteenth Century Journal* 36, no. 1 (2005): 77–96; Adriano Prosperi, *Tribunali della coscienza: Inquistori, confessori missionari* (Turin, 1996), 431–64; Schutte, *Aspiring Saints*; Anne Jacobson Schutte, "Pretense of Holiness In Italy: Investigations and Persecutions (1581–1876)," *Rivista di storia e letteratura religiosa* 27, no. 2 (2001): 299–321; Moshe Sluhovsky, *Believe Not Every Spirit: Possession, Mysticism and Discernment in Early Modern Catholicism* (Chicago, 2007); Gabriella Zarri, ed., *Finzione e santità tra medioevo ed età moderna* (Turin, 1991).

[53] Contelori, *Tractatus et praxis de canonizatione*, cap. X, 105.

postmortem examinations.[54] The surgeon examining Borromeo saw "no sign of fat" in his body and considered this proof of his extreme asceticism. This judgment offered medical confirmation of a long-standing image of the holy prelate – the man who had deprived himself so much that he was merely skin and bones beneath his bishop's robes.[55] In this way a standard element of sanctity also became medical fact. Medicine could also add new evidence to signs that a prelate had endured an ascetic life. During the autopsy of Ignatius of Loyola (1491–1556), founder of the Society of Jesus, the presiding physician found that Ignatius had quietly suffered extensively from kidney and bladder stones.[56] Numerous early modern accounts – as well as modern ones – attest to the excruciating pain that an unpassed stone inflicts on the body. Loyola's patient suffering – so patient, in fact, that nobody knew of the stone until his autopsy – could therefore be considered a quasi-miraculous mark of asceticism. The physician who performed the autopsy, Realdo Colombo, reacted in disbelief to the number and variety of stones found in the Jesuit's bladder.

In suffering agonies without complaint, Loyola was not alone: Patience in bearing kidney or bladder stones became the most frequent sign of asceticism found in the bodies of reputedly holy individuals, likely because these could be detected only through medical evidence that was not easily refuted. An autopsy likewise revealed that Francis de Sales (1567–1622) had "many small stones of various colors and shapes" that affected him to such an extent that there was not left "a drop of humor in the gall bladder."[57] Such an ailment would have been painful and possibly life-threatening. Similarly, the Archbishop of Reggio Calabria, Annibale d'Afflitto (1560–1638), was found during his autopsy to have "a stone the size of a walnut" in his kidney.[58] All these stones suggested that these holy prelates had conquered their flesh; they provided firm evidence of holiness that could only be refuted by another expert witness. A clinical judgment was made that to bear such

---

[54] On Borromeo as a model for the early modern Catholic bishop, see Alberigo, "Carlo Borromeo come modello di vescovi nella chiesa post-tridentina."

[55] Giovanni Baptista Carcano Leone, *Exenterationis cadaveris illustrissimi Cardinalis Borrhomaei Mediolani Archiepiscopi* (Milan, 1584), 3. On Borromeo's dissection and the meaning of the fat found in his body, see Siraisi, "Signs and Evidence," 356–80.

[56] Realdo Colombo, *De re anatomica libri XV* (Venice, 1559), 266–67.

[57] *Relatio facta in consistorio secreto coram S.D.N. Alexandro P. VII ... super vita, sanctitate, actis canonizationis, et miraculis Beati Francisci de Sales Episcopi Genevensis* (Rome, 1662), 14.

[58] Giuseppe Fozi, *Vita del Venerabile Servo di Dio Annibale d'Afflitto Arcivescovo di Reggio* (Rome, 1681), 156–57.

sufferings required a heroic act – an act enabled by their faith in God and by their role in the Church hierarchy.

ANATOMICAL IRREGULARITY AND THE HOLY BODY

In contrast to incorruption and asceticism, both long-standing aspects of sanctity, the evidence provided by medical postmortem suggests growing emphasis on a new category of miraculous holiness: divinely inspired supernatural anatomy. Take the most prominent early modern example: Philip Neri (1515–1595), the founder of the Oratorian order. Neri died in Rome in the odor of sanctity on May 25, 1595. During his life he had exhibited unusual physical ailments that, combined with the belief in his sanctity, inspired the brothers of his order to request that his body be opened the night after his death. The autopsy took place in the central church of his order, Santa Maria in Vallicella, also called the Chiesa Nuova. Because they were in Rome, and given Neri's prominence, the Oratorians were able to assemble a medical team that included some of the finest physicians in Catholic Europe. Four former papal physicians – including Angelo Vittori,[59] Andrea Cesalpino,[60] Angelo Porto,[61] and Ridolfo Silvestri – as well as the surgeon Giuseppe Zerla and the barber-surgeon Marco Antonio del Bello, testified numerous times during the canonization process about the autopsy.[62] What they found in Neri's body was extremely unusual: his fourth and fifth ribs had broken, seemingly to make room for his large and extraordinary heart. The precordia, or front tissue of his heart, was strangely large and

---

[59] Vittori was the principal physician to Pope Gregory XIII and a doctor for the Oratorians from 1585. He testified four times for Neri, in 1595, 1599, 1600, and 1610. In 1613 he published a treatise on Neri's autopsy, *De palpitatione cordis et admirabili fractura costarum beati Philippi Nerii, florentini, Congregationis Oratorii Romae fundatoris*, which is contained in a briefer edition in Vittori's testimonies of 1600 and 1610.

[60] Cesalpino was the principal physician of Clement VIII. He produced a treatise on the circulation of the heart and testified three times during Neri's process, in 1595, 1597, and 1599.

[61] Porto was the principal physician of Sixtus V. He testified three times for Neri in 1595, 1597, and 1599. He was also the first doctor to produce a Latin medical treatise in which he discusses Neri's miraculous injuries. This document was dedicated to Federico Borromeo; the original is in the Biblioteca Ambrosiana. A printed version can be found in Luigi Belloni, ed., "L'aneurisma di S. Filippo Neri nella relazione di Antonio Porto," *Rendiconti dell'istituto lombardo di scienze e lettere* 83 (1950): 665–90.

[62] Silvestri was another principal physician for Gregory XIII. He testified twice for Neri, in 1595 and 1599.

muscular; the pulmonary artery was twice as large as normal; the pericardium, which surrounds the heart like a wrapper, was devoid of fluid; and, finally, there was no blood in the ventricles.[63] In interpreting this wondrous evidence, the physicians unanimously proclaimed that what they had seen in Neri's anatomy was a miracle: His heart had been supernaturally inflamed by divine love and so his heart, lungs, and ribs had all been altered to make room for the intense heat.

The conclusion that Neri's unusual anatomy reflected his holiness drew on some of the most recent anatomical knowledge available in Europe. Aristotle, and centuries of subsequent commentary in both Christian and philosophical traditions, had first established the central role of the heart in the physiology of the body and connected its functions with the movement of the soul.[64] However, prior to the early modern period, it was the liver – not the heart – which was considered the origin of blood in the body; the heart was seen as merely helping to move blood to the various muscles and organs in the body. Only in the late sixteenth century did pioneering work begin to establish an embryonic concept of circulation. Andrea Cesalpino (1524–1603) was the first to identify the pulmonary artery and its function, in a discovery that would prove crucial for William Harvey's eventual work postulating the circulation of the blood. Cesalpino was one of the physician-testators in Neri's case and drew on his new understanding of anatomy as part of his claims for the Oratorian's sanctity.[65] After all, the presence of an oversized pulmonary artery such as Neri's could not be fitted into a scheme of normal/abnormal anatomy unless the function of that part was fully understood.[66]

---

[63] Antonio Gallonio, *The Life of Saint Philip Neri*, trans. Jerome Bertram (San Francisco, 2005), 210–12. These details also appear in testimony in the canonization process, but Gallonio summarizes the findings.

[64] On the long-standing symbolism of the heart, see John Martin, "Inventing Sincerity, Refashioning Prudence: The Discovery of the Individual in Renaissance Europe," *American Historical Review* 102, no. 5 (1997): 1326–33; Catrien Santig, "*De affectibus cordis et palpitatione*: Secrets of the Heart in Counter-Reformation Italy," in *Cultural Approaches to the History of Medicine*, ed. Willem de Blécourt and Cornelie Usborne (New York, 2004), 11–35; Scott Manning Stevens, "Sacred Heart and Secular Brain," in *The Body in Parts: Fantasies of Corporeality in Early Modern Europe*, ed. David Hillman and Carla Mazzio (New York, 1997), 263–85; Heather Webb, *The Medieval Heart* (New Haven, CT, 2010).

[65] Frederick A. Willius and Thomas Dry, *A History of the Heart and Circulation* (Philadelphia, 1948), 292; Augusto de Ferrari, "Cesalpino (Caesalpinus), Andrea," in *Dizionario Biografico degli Italiani*, vol. 24 (Rome, 1980), 122–25.

[66] Siraisi, "Signs and Evidence," provides a fuller description of how the new anatomy was fundamental to a presentation of Neri's sanctity.

Neri was not the only prospective saint who was autopsied and found to have unusual changes wrought upon his heart in this period. Angelo del Pas, also dissected in Rome at the end of the sixteenth century, was discovered to have signs of Christ's lance inside his body, including a cut taken out of his heart.[67] For both of these men, the examination of their hearts seems to have been prompted both by their fame of sanctity in life and by their followers' specific contention that their hearts had been physically touched by God.[68] Despite a reputation for holiness during his lifetime, del Pas's autopsy was, atypically, carried out by a surgeon rather than a physician.[69] Perhaps this was an ominous early sign of weaker support, as the promoters of a cause had to fund the medical team themselves. Certainly, no canonization was forthcoming. While other factors would doubtlessly have been at play as well, a comparison between the two causes also suggests that canonization officials relied on the quality and currency of the medical team when they attempted to determine whether a miracle had occurred, indicating that the Church preferred physicians to other practitioners when trying to establish a body's holiness.

Wondrously abnormal hearts offered ambiguous, sometimes unverifiable evidence, and therefore featured less frequently in canonizations than did other signs of sanctity, such as bodily incorruption or extreme asceticism. Indeed, a series of late medieval potential female saints had all been found to have wondrous irregularities in their hearts, such as the instruments of the passion and stones featuring the likeness of Christ.[70] These women were not canonized. Indeed, they had, in turn, been considered holy, heretical, or even fraudulent by those who wrote about them. With such precedents, Church officials might well have been wary of this type of evidence. Detailed cardiac anatomy was also a relatively new field, less heavily supported by tradition in canonization proceedings. For all these reasons, wondrous anatomy appeared less frequently in early modern canonizations than did other bodily signs of holiness.

---

[67] AAV, RP 2811, fol. 153v; AAV, RP 2812, fol. 3r.

[68] See Giacomo Bacci, *The Life of Saint Philip Neri*, ed. Frederick Ignatius Antrobus (London, 1902), vol. 1, 24, for a description of Neri bounding into the air and shaking the room due to his unusual heart; Catrien Santig, "De affectibus cordis et palpitatione," 12, discusses the case of Angelo del Pas.

[69] Although del Pas has not (yet) been canonized, he was declared "venerable" in 1890. See AAV, RP 2812, fols. 1r–3r, for a discussion by the surgeon, Giovanni Battista Piceni, who performed the autopsy.

[70] Park, *Secrets of Women*, 47–52.

CONCLUSION

Miracles assumed new importance in early modern Catholicism, as examples of the favors with which God showered the Counter-Reformation Church. However, they also faced intense skepticism, both by Protestants who had postulated that miracles had ceased and by Catholic officials concerned with the specter of false sanctity and unlicensed devotions. These developments coincided with the flourishing study of anatomy. Elite physicians who dissected bodies with their own hands revolutionized the understanding of the human body and enhanced the prestige of medicine. Medical knowledge thus became essential for the successful discernment of the boundaries between natural, preternatural, and supernatural phenomena as they occurred within the human body. Anatomy could thereby be used to turn bodily signs of sanctity from matters of popular acclamation into matters of fact. The new anatomists investigated bodily incorruption, extreme asceticism, and anatomical wonder, and thus transformed miracles into an object of scientific inquiry. The Catholic Church used anatomy to find signs of the divine within the bodies of its saints.

Part III

Representing Saints

11 Liturgy

ANTOINE MAZUREK

On April 17, 1594, Whitsunday, Pope Clement VIII proceeded with the canonization of the Polish Dominican friar Hyacinth of Kraków (d. 1257). The pope left the Pauline Chapel located inside Rome's Apostolic Palace. Walking behind the bearer of the cross, members of the curia, auditors, bishops, archbishops, and cardinals, he processed to the choir of St. Peter's Basilica. There the canonization rite properly began: The requests by the postulators for Hyacinth's sainthood alternated three times with the singing of the litanies, hymns, and prayers until the canonization decree itself was read, stating that the Polish friar was now officially recognized as a saint, that his feast was to be celebrated every year on the anniversary of his death, and that indulgences were granted to everyone taking part in the annual commemorations. Finally, a Mass was celebrated in the new saint's honor, featuring a prayer composed specifically for him.[1]

The text and ritual of this canonization ceremony exemplify the key elements of the early modern Catholic liturgy. First and foremost, it associated Hyacinth with the Sacrifice of the Mass, a central target of Protestant attack.[2] During the Mass, the pope sought the new saint's intercession, by reciting three litanies at three moments: during the Collect, the Secret, and the Communion. Since the Middle Ages, these prayers had been included in the solemn bulls sent to the Catholic faithful worldwide after a canonization process.[3] The process of Hyacinth's canonization stretched beyond the walls of St. Peter's

---

[1] Seweryn Lubomlczyk, *De vita miraculis et actis canonizationis sancti Hyacinthi confessoris* (Rome, 1594), 399. The prayer was authored by Muzio Sforza.

[2] See the defense of the Mass "in Sanctorum honorem" by Benedict XIV, *De servorum Dei beatificatione et beatorum canonizatione*, ed. and trans. Vincenzo Criscuolo (Vatican City, 2022), vol. IV/3, 17–18.

[3] André Vauchez, *Sainthood in the Later Middle Ages*, trans. Jean Birrell (Cambridge, 1997), 56.

Basilica, however.[4] Just as the ceremony had begun with a procession that celebrated the Church's hierarchy, it was followed by another that delivered the saint's banner to the Dominican monastery of Santa Maria sopra Minerva, on the other side of the Tiber river from St. Peter's.[5] Other celebrations followed across the Catholic world, even in distant Mexico City, where an eight-day festival provided an opportunity to affirm a sense of belonging to the Church of Rome.[6]

While Hyacinth was not canonized until 1594, the medieval saint did not have to wait until this date to be worshipped. The Roman ceremony was a response to the *vox populi*, as represented by the Dominican order and by Sigismund, the king of Poland and Sweden. As the Dominican scholar Alfonso Chacón wrote the same year, "papal authority does not make saints; it proclaims and suggests their worship to the Christian people."[7] In this field of negotiation and exchange between laity and clergy, and between center and periphery, liturgy constituted the main language of legitimation and hierarchical organization. Thus, as early as 1527, Pope Clement VII (r. 1523–34) had authorized Polish Dominicans to observe an annual celebration of their medieval brother Hyacinth with an office (a set of prayers) and a Mass, before later extending this privilege to all of Poland. In this way, canonization can be seen as a simple expansion of the liturgy. Nor did Hyacinth's liturgical journey end with his sainthood. Later, under Pope Urban VIII (r. 1623–44), Hyacinth's position in the Roman Breviary – a compendium of the Church's most important liturgical prayers and readings – was upgraded to a proper office (*officium proprium*) with a prestigious double rite. His liturgical journey ended only in 1686, when he became one of the patron saints of the Kingdom of Poland and the Grand Duchy of Lithuania.[8]

---

[4] For the evolution of the definition of liturgy, see Aimé-Georges Martimort, ed., *The Church at Prayer: An Introduction to the Liturgy* (Collegeville, MN, 1986), 5–14.

[5] Lubomlczyk, *De vita miraculis et actis canonizationis sancti Hyacinthi confessoris*, 376–99.

[6] Pierre Ragon, "Les fêtes de béatification et de canonisation en Nouvelle-Espagne (XVIIe–XVIIIe siècles)," in *Les cérémonies extraordinaires du catholicisme baroque*, ed. Bernard Dompnier (Clermont-Ferrand, 2009), 563–78.

[7] Alfonso Chácon, *De martyrio ducentorum monachorum S. Petri a Cardegna ordinis S. Benedicti* (Rome, 1594), 183–84; see also Giuseppe Dalla Torre, "Santità ed economia processuale: L'esperienza giuridica da Urbano VIII a Benedetto XIV," in Gabriella Zarri, ed., *Finzione e santità tra Medioevo ed età moderna* (Turin, 1991), 231–63.

[8] Ronald C. Finucane, "Saint-Making at the End of the Sixteenth Century: How and Why Jacek of Poland (d. 1257) became St. Hyacinth in 1594," *Hagiographica* 9 (2002): 207–58.

Hyacinth thus continued to gather ever greater liturgical honors even after his canonization. We might, for instance, think of the introduction of a proper office in the Roman Breviary, particularly the additional honor of a double office – which meant that it trumped the "ferial" (or ordinary) Mass – as a kind of apotheosis. Not all saints achieved this special status; most canonization bulls provided only for a common office, which celebrated the specific saint as part of a wider category (martyr, confessor, pope, etc.) in a formulaic, pedagogical fashion.[9] By contrast, a proper office, as in Hyacinth's case, included actual biographical information regarding the saint's birth, death, and miracles, arranged in three readings for a double feast that was recited during the office at Matins, in the middle of the night. Because of their symbolic significance, these proper offices will be the focus of the pages that follow.

Hyacinth's accumulation of honors shows that Counter-Reformation liturgy was not just multifaceted – it was also alive. What a saint deserved was open to negotiation. Was he or she worthy of a common office, or a proper office complete with hymns or prayers? Should this be made mandatory or kept optional? Should it be extended geographically (to a single church, a religious order, a diocese, a country, or the entire Catholic Church) or increased in solemnity (simple, semi-double, double feast)? This liturgical flexibility, extending across time and space, encapsulates what Simon Ditchfield has memorably called the "preservation of the particular."[10] The glory of the saints in heaven depended on their merit acquired on earth, but the Church's liturgy ranked them as well, reflecting the interests and devotions of the communities that venerated them. The liturgy, then, embodied a hierarchy of sainthood, reflecting the period's overriding preoccupation with the determination and control of social status.

This chapter explores the liturgical aspects of sanctity in the early modern Catholic world. It first shows how early modern Catholic reformers confronted both the long-standing traditions on which the liturgy had been based and the authority of the Roman magisterium that claimed control over it. As the pioneering work of Simon Ditchfield has shown, the implications of this process were felt both in the

---

[9] Vauchez, *Sainthood in the Later Middle Ages*, 96; Benedict XIV, *De servorum Dei beatificatione*, 20. A common office taught the faithful the meaning and value of these categories of saints and how their imitation could aid their salvation.

[10] Simon Ditchfield, *Liturgy, Sanctity and History in Tridentine Italy: Pietro Maria Campi and the Preservation of the Particular* (Cambridge, 1995).

Catholic definition of sanctity and in the writing of sacred history and hagiography (*historia sacra*).[11] Liturgy was pivotal in shaping the veneration of the "very special dead" upon whom the communities of the early modern Catholic world projected their hopes and anxieties. Consequently, any analysis of the reform of Catholic sanctity must start with the reform of the liturgy in the wake of the Council of Trent. Liturgical works, such as breviaries and missals, had celebrated the saints long before the foundation of the Roman Congregation of Rites in 1588 and the reforms to canonization procedure by Urban VIII, studied in Chapter 7 in this volume.[12] Their reform shows the tensions that existed within Catholic Reform, and between the universal and the local – with the saints at the center of it all.

LITURGY, SANCTITY, AND REFORM

Like the Counter-Reformation as a whole, the reform of the liturgy was a lengthy process marked by tensions, doubts, and uncertainties. It reflected the contradiction inherent to all attempts to reform the Catholic Church: The traditional claim that the Church was ever the same (*semper eadem*) clashed with calls for a return to the time of the apostles or Church fathers. In this, saints were a complicating factor. They had served as witnesses (*martyres*) to Christian truths since the early Church but their number and their role in the liturgy had also grown over time. The reform of the liturgy, which provided both the medium and the evidence of sanctity, therefore had lasting consequences not only for how sanctity was understood but for how the history of the Church was written and viewed as well.

In this context, the deep continuities with the medieval past must be stressed. The famous group canonization of 1622 has often been described as a crucial Counter-Reformation moment. The canonization of Teresa of Ávila, Ignatius of Loyola, Philip Neri, and Francis Xavier in 1622 (alongside the medieval Isidore the Farmer) does indeed mark a major moment in the Church's resumption of saint-making after a hiatus that had lasted since 1588. Nevertheless, the vast majority (three-quarters) of the saints celebrated in the Roman Breviary were,

---

[11] Ibid.
[12] Unlike the canonization procedure whose reform triggered heated debates among the members of the Curia about the role to grant to bishops, the exclusive control by Rome over liturgical texts won unanimous support: see Miguel Gotor, *I beati del Papa: Santità, Inquisizione e obbedienza in età moderna* (Florence, 2002), 150.

and remained, ancient and medieval in origin, as stressed in Chapter 12 of this Companion. Nor did subsequent canonizations substantially alter this imbalance during the early modern period. The dominance of early Christian and medieval saints was not merely a matter of statistics. Despite efforts to promote the cult of recently canonized saints, the faithful typically favored long-standing intercessors who represented the immutability of the Catholic Church and who had long served their local communities well.

While many saintly devotions therefore did not change, the liturgical works in which they were embedded did. The publication of the Roman Breviary (1568) and Missal (1570) by Pope Pius V, as well as the Martyrology (1584) by Pope Gregory XIII, constituted a major change in the cult of saints.[13] The decision to reform the liturgy was made during the final session of the Council of Trent and implemented by the Holy See during the years that followed.[14] The liturgical calendar, which had seen a steady increase in the number of saints celebrated during the late Middle Ages, was refocused on the so-called *temporale*, the annual cycle of movable feasts that celebrated Christ's birth, passion, and resurrection. The number of saints' feasts was accordingly reduced. The texts used to commemorate the saints, essentially the lessons read by religious communities at Matins, were reworked into a more sober style with the elimination of apocryphal texts or unplausible stories. Revisions also placed a special emphasis on reliable sources, a more precise chronology, further detail on the location of relics, and, finally, an equal (and quite new) distribution of the readings (nine for a double office: three scriptural, three hagiographical, and three homiletic readings).[15]

The most radical changes resulted from the universal adoption of the reformed Roman Breviary and Missal themselves. For the first time, the papacy claimed the prerogative to determine liturgical celebrations, which had traditionally been controlled by bishops and religious orders. The suppression of the celebration of the mostly local saints omitted from the Breviary aroused anxiety among some bishops and cathedral

---

[13] Other official post-Tridentine liturgical books, such as the 1600 *Caeremoniale Episcoporum* and 1614 *Rituale Romanum*, mention the saints only incidentally.

[14] Michael Lang, *The Roman Mass: From Early Christian Origins to Tridentine Reform* (Oxford, 2022), 345–57.

[15] Ditchfield, *Liturgy, Sanctity and History*, 23–43. Before Trent, the nine lessons were mostly hagiographical.

chapters.[16] Even so, exceptions were made that enabled the "preservation of the particular." Concessions were made foremost to local liturgical rites older than 200 years that continued to be celebrated, with Milan as a notable example. More minor exemptions were also granted to enable churches to celebrate the feasts of their patrons or titular saints and the anniversary of their dedications, as well as those "usually celebrated with solemnity."[17] Further exceptions followed. In 1573, Spanish churches and monasteries in possession of "notable relics" were granted the right to celebrate a proper office for that saint.[18] Such rules enabled local liturgical calendars to survive, either because of the recognized antiquity of local rites or as addenda to the Roman liturgy. Inconsistencies and exceptions, therefore, persisted and these intersected with local concerns. In France, which prided itself on its "Gallican liberties," southern dioceses mostly adopted the new Roman Breviary, Missal, and Martyrology, but their northern counterparts struggled to reconcile these prayerbooks with local devotions. Northern dioceses then risked the ire of the Holy See, which consistently emphasized that the Roman books should not be altered without papal approval.[19]

The Spanish exemptions were followed by requests from churches, dioceses, and religious orders from across the Catholic world seeking approval of offices celebrating the *historia sacra* of key local figures. These included, for instance, a church's first bishop, or its most notable early martyrs and confessors. After approval, the liturgical offices for these figures were printed locally as addenda to the Roman liturgy. The

---

[16] See, for example, a letter from the bishop of León: Rome, Biblioteca Vallicelliana, G79, fol. 57r, which conveyed the disappointment of the faithful in his diocese about the disappearance of certain feasts.

[17] *Breviarium romanum: Editio princeps (Rome, 1568)*, ed. Manlio Sodi and Achille Maria Triacca (Vatican City, 1999), 23.

[18] *Acta Sanctae Sedis: Ephemerides Romanae a SSmo D.N. Pio PP. X authenticae et officiales Apostolicae Sedis actis publice evulgandis declaratae* (Rome, 1907), 40, 113–28. Cf. Antoine Mazurek, "Réforme tridentine et culte des saints en Espagne: Liturgie romaine et saints ibériques," in *The Council of Trent: Reform and Controversy in Europe and Beyond (1545–1700)*, ed. Violet Soen and Wim François (Göttingen, 2018), vol. 1, 223–47.

[19] Thomas D'Hour, "Cultes et identités en France au XVIIe siècle: Étude des calendriers et des livres liturgiques" (PhD thesis, Université de Clermont-Ferrand, 2014), 166–282; Bernard Dompnier, "Les liturgies dites néogallicanes: Retour sur une notion discutée," *Revue d'histoire de l'Église de France* 108 (2022): 263–95, esp. 274–75. In Spain, on the other hand, the Roman Missal was altered in accordance with the bull *Ad Deus nos unxit* issued by Pius V on December 17, 1570, and subsequently printed in all missals used in Spain.

number of such publications ballooned in the late sixteenth and seventeenth centuries.[20] Without altering the printed Roman Breviary or Missal, such *officia propria* nevertheless still reshaped the liturgy of a local diocese. The celebration of these additional figures could take precedence on certain feast days, trumping the celebration of other local saints or lower-ranked universal ones.

While such exemptions showed the continued regional and local diversity of Catholicism's liturgical landscape, they are at the same time also evidence of the strengthening papal control that oversaw and permitted them. The Holy See claimed the right to examine liturgy and approve any revised text, though in many parts of Catholic Europe these claims often fell on deaf ears. This was especially true in France, and to a lesser extent in Spain and the Holy Roman Empire. The task of responding to such requests originally fell to Cardinal Guglielmo Sirleto (1514–1585), the famous scholar and Vatican librarian. In 1588, the duty passed to the new Congregation of Rites, whose archives offer a valuable perspective on how the liturgy of the saints helped to articulate the dynamics between the local and the universal in the Catholic world.[21]

Roman control of the liturgy sought to ensure above all that the form of the Roman Breviary, especially the readings, was respected. In other instances, Rome's censure of local liturgies was directly linked with the cult of the saints themselves. For example, Sirleto opposed the status of patron saint given to guardian angels in several Spanish cities, notably Zaragoza and Burgos. He also demanded the abolition of certain Marian feasts celebrated in Iberia, notably the Transfixion, during which the Virgin was allegedly "transfixed" or "pierced" by the same pain Jesus experienced at the lance.[22] Censure could also address even greater theological errors. In 1659, the Congregation of Rites took issue

[20] The catalog by Robert Amiet, *Missels et bréviaires imprimés (supplement aux catalogues de Weale et Bohatta)* (Paris, 1990), 309–534, primarily focuses on France and provides a rather partial overview of this production. Between 1568 and 1800, approximately 1,500 editions were published (61 in the sixteenth century, 668 in the seventeenth, and 776 in the eighteenth), with around 1,000 specifically dedicated to dioceses and religious orders.

[21] See the list of offices approved by the Congregation of Rites drawn up by Pope Benedict XIV when he was promoter of the faith: Bologna, Biblioteca Universitaria, fondo Prospero Lambertini, MS 1135, *Officia propria sanctorum, hoc est alphabeticus elenchus sanctorum ...*, 2 vols. A quick overview of this document's index (not foliated) reveals approximately 1,300 offices for feast days, mostly for saints, granted between 1602 and 1728. These offices may include a single office for one or several saints, or a set of offices designated for a diocese or a religious order.

[22] Vatican City, Bibliotheca Apostolica Vaticana, Vat.lat 6278, fol. 163r. See Antoine Mazurek, *Une figure de la modernité religieuse: L'ange gardien* (forthcoming).

with the Office of St. John the Baptist, submitted by the archbishop of Genoa, which appeared to consider John to be an "incarnate angel."[23]

If saints sometimes raised theological concerns, the application of historical criteria to the liturgy could prove far trickier, especially when the figures concerned were local bishops and martyrs whose historicity or even existence were uncertain. This proved an almost impossible balancing act. While early modern cardinals were often unfamiliar with these figures, they nonetheless found it difficult to eliminate their feasts entirely. Such a move risked provoking outrage among the faithful or, worse, confirming Protestant criticism of the cult of saints. In 1594, when consulted about certain saints celebrated in the diocese of Burgos, a member of the Congregation of Rites asked: Should we permit the cult of any saints who have not been canonized or included in the Martyrology, and whose sanctity and cult are only proven by local documents? And, if so, what value does the papal recognition possess, especially in relation to formal canonization?[24] This issue would be dealt with, but not even then resolved, only in the following century, ultimately leading to the development of two procedures: beatification, as a precursor to canonization, and a so-called equipollent (equivalent) process whereby the papacy recognized long-standing cults without the need for a lengthy trial.[25] In many respects, the same challenges applied to the creation and subsequent revisions of the Roman Martyrology from the 1580s onward: This calendar of saints (not just martyrs) similarly had to balance its prescriptive, universal nature against the demands of geographical balance and coverage.[26]

---

[23] Bernard Dompnier, "Nuovi uffici del santorale: Finalità e metodi dei cambiamenti liturgici nel XVII e XVIII secolo," in *Barocco Padano 7: Atti del 15. Convegno internazionale sulla musica italiana nei secoli 17.–18. Milan, 14–16 luglio 2009*, ed. Alberto Colzani, Andrea Luppi, and Maurizio Padoan (Como, 2012), 53–90, at 65. St. John the Baptist was Genoa's patron saint.

[24] Vatican City, Archivio del Dicastero delle Cause dei Santi (hereafter ADCS), Positiones rescriptorum et decretorum 42, document 7. Chacón's treatise (cited above, note 7) was one of the first to consider this issue seriously. The chronological coincidence of those dossiers with the first canonization process conducted entirely by the Congregation of Rites invites further investigation of the 1590s as a crucial moment for the definition of sanctity.

[25] Fabijan Veraja, *La Beatificazione: Storia, problemi, prospettive* (Vatican City, 1983), 115–28; Benedict XIV, *De servorum Dei beatificatione*, vol. I/1, 630–59.

[26] Ditchfield, *Liturgy, Sanctity and History*, 43–44, 59–60; Giuseppe Antonio Guazzelli, "Baronio attraverso il *Martyrologium romanum*," in *Cesare Baronio fra santità e scrittura storica*, ed. Giuseppe Guazzelli et al. (Rome, 2012), 67–110. Cf. catalogs of saints not included in the Roman Martyrology, such as Filippo Ferrari's *Catalogus generalis sanctorum qui in Martyrologio romano non sunt, ex variis martyrologiis, kalendariis, tabulis, monumentisque ecclesiarum* (Venice, 1625).

Faced with so much ambiguity, it is no wonder that the examples of Roman censure mentioned above were the exception rather than the rule. Seeking to retain the appearance of overall control and authority, the Holy See in fact remained respectful of liturgical diversity in the sixteenth century. It rarely censured saints' feast days and quickly approved the saints' offices that were submitted, only warning against their proliferation. This situation changed, however, during the papacy of Urban VIII. The reform of beatification and canonization between 1625 and 1642, as described in Chapter 7 in this volume, expanded the papal reservation to every aspect of the cult of saints. The same period also saw the Congregation of Rites issue a series of decrees aimed at curbing liturgical excess: the proliferation of proper offices, a surplus of feasts, and saints' feasts being celebrated too widely or with too much solemnity (i.e., as a double or semi-double office).[27] The Congregation also reasserted its own authority over all matters pertaining to liturgy and rites. The reforms seemingly brought the dialectic between local and universal liturgy to an end: Henceforth, only freshly canonized saints were to be added to the Martyrology. Those excluded from the work could no longer be made a patron saint.[28] And yet such apparent decisiveness was a mirage. The Holy See continued to use indulgences to override its own rules and grant proper offices to long-standing local cults, as the reforming Pope Benedict XIV could not help but notice in the mid-eighteenth century.[29]

LITURGY, SANCTITY, AND THE SHAPING OF COLLECTIVE IDENTITIES

Sociology has demonstrated the relationship between sanctity and collective representations of the past and present.[30] Liturgy, likewise, makes the past present to an entire community by celebrating saints' actions, miracles, and deaths, while also providing believers with

---

[27] Between 1568 and 1741 the number of double and semi-double feasts in the Roman Breviary increased from 138 to 228. A commission assembled by Benedict XIV tried but predictably failed to expurgate the excesses: Dominique Julia, "Benoît XIV et la réforme du Bréviaire romain," in *Les cérémoniaux catholiques en France à l'époque moderne: Une littérature de codification des rites liturgiques*, ed. Cécile Davy-Rigaux et al. (Turnhout, 2009), 221–44.

[28] See Bernard Dompnier, "Les calendriers entre Pie V et Benoît XIV," *Sanctorum* 8–9 (2011–12): 13–51; Ditchfield, *Liturgy, Sanctity and History*.

[29] Benedict XIV, *De servorum Dei beatificatione*, IV/3, 70. See also note 22.

[30] Pierre Delooz, *Sociologie et canonisations* (Liège, 1969).

models worthy of admiration and imitation. As we have already seen, liturgy is a site for cooperation and contestation, where identities can be fostered and shaped. Reforms to liturgical worship, far from posing an inevitable threat to the cult of saints, also presented opportunities for communities to reshape it according to their own local agendas.

Roman reform demanded more specific links between a diocese and the saints worshipped there, whether through biography (e.g., they once lived there), physical presence (e.g., their relics were still there), or patronage (e.g., they were believed to offer special protection to the diocese). It was the bishops' task to guard their dioceses' liturgical heritage, in collaboration with their cathedral chapter. Simon Ditchfield has shown the implications of this procedure for the composition of the *historia sacra*, including the famous *Acta sanctorum* patiently compiled by the Bollandists over many centuries.[31] The choice of saints and the liturgical readings that celebrated them allowed a diocese to define its distinctive identity and trace its origins to a distant, potentially even apostolic, past. Consequently, a patron's feast day enjoyed a prominent position in the local liturgical calendar, as did any dates associated with the discovery or translation of their relics. Key patron saints were often a community's first bishop, frequently a martyr. St. Januarius in Naples, St. Julian in Cuenca, and St. Petronius in Bologna exemplify this type. Feast days to celebrate the translation (transfer from one place to another) of a saint's relics also highlighted the diocese's particular history, since the translation in question had usually brought the relics to the cathedral itself. Translation feasts increased during the seventeenth and eighteenth centuries owing to the diffusion of relics from the Roman catacombs (see Chapter 6) and the rediscovery or recovery of local saints' relics. For instance, a relic of St. Ildefonso was brought back to Toledo from Zamora in 1674, much to the satisfaction of the archdiocese. The commemoration of this Visigothic-era bishop, who had championed worship of the Virgin Mary and defeated the Arian heresy, would strengthen the diocese's claim to the primacy over all of Spain.[32] Such translations permitted local churches to celebrate a saint on a different date from the universal calendar, employing greater solemnity (including liturgical ornaments,

---

[31] Ditchfield, *Liturgy, Sanctity and History*. The *Acta sanctorum* is a mine of information for the composition of the liturgy: Nicolas Risso, *Les saints limousins dans le bréviaire de Limoges de 1783* (Geneva, 2015), 133–47.

[32] See María Tausiet, *El dedo robado: Reliquias imaginarias en la España moderna* (Madrid, 2013).

music, and candles) and using a proper office. As written, these liturgical rites detailed the steps and the actors involved in the translation, with a special emphasis on the role of the bishop, thereby rooting the cult within a specific local and sacred geography.[33]

Liturgical readings could also be rewritten to emphasize a saint's role in establishing or defending Christianity locally. In 1589, the nocturnal readings for the feast of the sixth-century St. Laureano, included in the proper offices of Seville, were reworked so as to present this semi-legendary figure as a credible precursor to the ideal Tridentine bishop. The new readings emphasized his fight against heresy and his exemplary pastoral care over any miracles he may have performed. Similarly, the writings by eminent local authors could enhance the prestige of an episcopal see.[34] In 1581 Toledo, the new Office of the Guardian Angels added excerpts from a treatise by the seventh-century archbishop Julian – whose own office was included elsewhere in Toledo's *officia propria*. This not only traced the origins of the cult to the Visigothic era but showed that the local archbishop had been among the first to provide its theological underpinnings.[35]

Meanwhile on Europe's confessional frontiers, dioceses not only firmed up long-standing liturgical traditions, but also made space for new devotions intended to enable the faithful to defend themselves from heresy. In Augsburg, the first 1597 edition of the diocesan supplement to the Roman liturgy emphasized German saints as well as local patron saints, but its 1605 edition instituted further feasts aimed specifically at countering Protestant preaching (such as feasts for the Virgin Mary, the Archangel Michael, and the Guardian Angels).[36]

This process of liturgical revision represented a general trend in Catholic Europe and can be considered a kind of liturgical competition. Dioceses assessed their relative prestige according to both the number

---

[33] Bernard Dompnier, "Les offices de translation de reliques aux XVIIe et XVIIIe siècles: Un mode cultuel de distinction," in *La mémoire des saints originels*, ed. Bernard Dompnier and Stefania Nanni (Rome, 2022), 165–89; Thomas D'Hour, "Les fêtes des reliques dans les calendriers liturgiques diocésains de la France post-tridentine (1570–1680)," in ibid., 143–63.

[34] David Berenberg, "Patrons and Petitioners: Evolution of Saint Cults and the Formation of a Local Religious Culture in Early Modern Seville" (PhD thesis, University of California, San Diego, 2005), 111–17.

[35] *Officia sanctorum ecclesiae toletanae* (Madrid, 1584), fols. 18v–19r, and *Breviarium secundum consuetudinem ecclesiae toletanae* (Lyon, 1551), fols. 337v–340v. See Mazurek, *Une figure de la modernité religieuse*.

[36] Franz A. Hoeynck, *Geschichte der Kirchlichen Liturgie des Bisthums Augsburg* (Augsburg, 1889), 304–30.

of feasts and the level of their solemnity. In the seventeenth century, French diocesan liturgies, which admittedly took some liberties with the Roman rules, had as many as fourteen feast days on average for relics, whereas the official Roman calendar had only three (relating to the cross and to St. Stephen, the proto-martyr).[37] Religious orders similarly increasingly attempted to distinguish themselves through the proliferation of feast days, but the outcome of this rivalry often, paradoxically, produced conformity rather than distinction. In the early eighteenth century, the Servite Order asked permission to honor its own saints with the highest solemnity, "in the same way many religious orders do."[38]

With the global expansion of Catholicism, the scope of liturgical reform extended beyond Europe. In Spanish Latin America, notably in New Spain, liturgical festivities were largely adopted from their Spanish counterparts, even though these churches would eventually also petition for liturgical privileges for local saints, such as Felipe de Jesús and Rose of Lima. Distinctions were also made between feast days to be observed by those of Spanish and indigenous descent.[39] In missions in Asia, where Catholics encountered other forms of Christianity, the new liturgical books and the Roman calendar served different purposes than in Europe. Here, the liturgy was deployed alongside strategies of accommodation to bring traditional forms of Christianity in line with the standards of Counter-Reformation Catholicism. In the early 1580s, Jesuit missionaries convinced Syriac Christians on the Malabar Coast to amend their liturgical books according to the Latin rite. They removed Nestorian saints such as Diodore of Tarsus, Theodore of Mopsuestia, and even Nestorius himself in favor of saints of the Roman calendar but retained the use of the Syriac language, which they valued deeply.[40] In mission areas where Christianity was newly established, the liturgy typically focused on the primary Catholic festivals

---

[37] D'Hour, "Les fêtes des reliques," 144–45.
[38] Dompnier, "Nuovi uffici del santorale," 70.
[39] Cornelius Conover, *Pious Imperialism: Spanish Rule and the Cult of Saints in Mexico City* (Albuquerque, NM, 2019), 59–83. The distinction was made by Pope Paul III and implemented by the Third Provincial Council of Mexico City in 1585. The number of feast days required of indigenous faithful were far fewer, and all of them, except for the feast of Saints Peter and Paul, focused on the life of Christ and the Virgin. See *Concilio III Provincial mexicano celebrado en Mexico el año de 1585*, ed. Mariano Galván Rivera (Mexico City, 1859), 142–43.
[40] István Perczel, "Accomodationist Strategies on the Malabar Coast: Competition or Complementarity?," in *The Rites Controversies in the Early Modern World*, ed. Pierre-Antoine Fabre and Ines G. Županov (Leiden, 2018), 191–232, esp. 212.

such as Christmas, Easter, and Ascension, while drastically limiting, or even eliminating, the number of saints' feasts, which were thought to pose the risk of idolatry. Thus, in Japan, only committed convert communities could celebrate saints, and even then, this meant only the apostles and some early martyrs, such as Stephen and Lawrence.[41]

Tridentine claims to restore the liturgy to the greater purity of the Church fathers eventually provoked a reaction in France, where a surge in historical scholarship in the second half of the seventeenth century contributed to the creation of neo-Gallican liturgical books. The production of such liturgical works should be understood primarily as an attempt to affirm the authority of local bishops in matters of ritual, rather than as a complete rejection of Rome. Concerns about the defense of French liberties against papal (ultramontane) claims to authority were typical of the period.[42] Neo-Gallican liturgists criticized French dioceses for adopting the feast days of Roman saints, arguing that their presence weakened local traditions and exposed the faithful to historically inaccurate hagiography.[43] In order to give priority to local saints, "that is, those of the diocese and the Nation, in preference to those of other countries,"[44] they chose not to include feasts of foreign popes or recently canonized foreign saints, and discarded or rewrote more historically dubious readings. Even so, such attempts at reform could not escape the very criticisms that had first prompted them: Both respect for age-old traditions and the blurred boundaries between providential and human history prevented these liturgical books from meeting new, higher standards of historicism.

These contradictions also explain the emergence of forgeries, whose authors, as Anthony Grafton noted, adopted historical methods.[45] In some dioceses, the need to "preserve the particular" led scholars not only to seek out archaeological evidence, especially relics, but also

---

[41] Jesús López-Gay, *La liturgia en la misión del Japón del siglo XVI* (Rome, 1970), 44–48.

[42] See, for example, Louis Thomassin, *Traité des festes de l'Église*, in *Traitez historiques et dogmatiques sur divers points de la discipline de l'Église et de la Morale chrestienne* (Paris, 1683), vol. 2, 136–39, cited by Dompnier, "Les calendriers entre Pie V et Benoît XIV"; Clément Meunier, "Le désir de réforme: La liturgie entre tradition et magistère (ca. 1500–ca. 1620)" (thesis, École Nationale des Chartes, 2004).

[43] Jean-Louis Quantin, *Le catholicisme classique et les Pères de l'Église: Un retour aux sources (1669–1713)* (Paris, 1999), 493–503; Xavier Bisaro, *Une nation de fidèles: L'Église et la liturgie parisienne au XVIIIe siècle* (Turnhout, 2005), 109–19.

[44] *Projet d'un breviaire a l'usage du diocese de Chartres*, Chartres, s.d. [1727], cited by Xavier Bisaro, *Une nation de fidèles*, 115.

[45] Anthony Grafton, *Forgers and Critics: Creativity and Duplicity in Western Scholarship* (Princeton, NJ, 1990).

to resort to historical forgeries promoting saints of doubtful authenticity. Such forgeries were common across Europe yet had some regional variations. While in France the phenomenon was relatively limited due to the early development of erudition, in Spain they took on unprecedented proportions with a set of "false chronicles" written by the Jesuit Román de la Higuera (d. 1611) and published after his death in several editions from 1619 to 1651.[46] Two factors enabled these Spanish chronicles: first, the lack of historical narratives documenting local martyrs from the first centuries of Christianity; second, the aforementioned 1573 exemption permitting Spanish churches to celebrate saints not already included in a venerable local liturgy, as long as they had met additional requirements such as being natives of the region or having relics held there. Andalucía, where the disappearance of such evidence was attributed to its Muslim past, was particularly affected; the years between 1620 and 1640 saw a proliferation of such "new" old saints when the archbishop of Seville and the bishop of Jaén added dozens of new proper offices to their own diocesan liturgies. Ultimately, Rome, which was theoretically able to regulate these devotions, brought these to an abrupt halt in a radical way. When the diocese of Granada requested confirmation of the 1573 privilege at the end of the seventeenth century, Rome authorized the composition of liturgical offices only for saints whose "relics [had been] transferred from Rome."[47] The process of Roman centralization, initiated under Pius V and strengthened with Urban VIII's legislation, was thus extended to the liturgical cult of relics (e.g., feasts of translation), hereafter reserved exclusively for "baptized" martyrs from the Roman Catacombs. As shown in Chapters 6 and 8 in this volume, the authentication of relics was a vexed issue, even in Rome. As the Benedictine scholar Jean Mabillon pointed out in the eighteenth century, the Holy See was taking the same liberties that it opposed elsewhere.[48]

---

[46] See Katrina B. Olds, *Forging the Past: Invented Histories in Counter-Reformation Spain*, (New Haven, CT, 2015).

[47] Rome, ADCS, not inventoried, request dated later than the decree of 1691, which confirmed the prohibition on further offices and Masses to the calendar based upon the presence of "exceptional" (*insignis*) relics. Cf. Luigi Gardellini, *Decreta authentica Congregationis sacrorum rituum* (Rome, 1824–49), vol. 3, 184–85.

[48] Jean Mabillon, *Eusebii Romani ad Theophilum Gallum Epistola de cultu sanctorum ignotorum* (Paris, 1698), 6. His book managed to evade censorship by the Index. See Dominique Julia and Stéphane Baciocchi, "Le moment Mabillon: Expérience archéologique, vérité historique et dévotion collective," in *Reliques romaines: Invention et circulation des corps saints des catacombes à l'époque modern*, ed. Christophe Duhamelle and Stéphane Baciocchi (Rome, 2019), 535–74.

If the Counter-Reformation can be understood as a dialectic between the local and the universal, the national level must not be overlooked, especially where the celebration of saints is concerned. Ever stronger political bodies, such as monarchs or national churches, increasingly intervened in ecclesiastical affairs, including the liturgy. These interventions were ultimately channeled by the Holy See through canonization processes and the election of a kingdom's patron saints.[49] While this process was far from uniform, it stimulated the creation of national saints, often presaged during the sixteenth century by the compilation of national hagiographical collections.

The methods used to establish a privileged connection between a saint and a nation were similar to those used at the diocesan level, though they were more difficult to implement in practice. The oldest and most common connection occurred when a community chooses a patron saint. While patron saints were a venerable institution, they enjoyed an unprecedented renaissance during the Counter-Reformation.[50] Just as they did at the local level, new elections of national patron saints could provoke fierce reactions, revealing various jurisdictional claims and ideological purposes, as exemplified by the co-patronage controversy in Spain.[51] While many saints chosen as patrons had been celebrated in the liturgy for a long time, such as Santiago (St. James), George, or Dennis, the early modern period saw an emergence of recently canonized saints such as Teresa of Ávila for Spain, Hyacinth for Poland in 1686, or Francis of Paola for Sicily in 1729.

Another method, not new but much more effective due to liturgical standardization, was to elevate a saint's office, giving it greater solemnity and prominence by upgrading it from a simple to a semi-double or double rank. In 1618, under sustained pressure from the French monarchy, Rome gave the feast of St. Louis universal status and assigned his feast a double office so that it could not be omitted from the calendar. This maneuver showcased the political and religious unity of the Kingdom of France and enhanced its prestige on the international stage, to the detriment of Spain, which suffered from a lack of such dynastic sacrality.[52] However, results were mixed even within France, because

---

[49] Miguel Gotor, *Santità e chiesa nell'Italia moderna* (Rome, 2004), 83–110.
[50] Diana Webb, *Patrons and Defenders: The Saints in the Italian City-States* (London, 1996).
[51] Erin Rowe, *Saint and Nation: Santiago, Teresa of Avila, and Plural Identities in Early Modern Spain* (University Park, PA, 2011).
[52] Bernard Dompnier, "La Congrégation des Rites et les sanctoraux nationaux: Édiction de la norme et contrôle des pratiques," in *Liturgie et identités nationales à l'époque*

local bishops resisted this combined royal and papal assault on their liturgies. In contrast, the Habsburgs were more successful in their own liturgical projects, imposing their own initially private devotions on all their subjects, especially those focusing on the Virgin Mary, Joseph, and the angels.[53]

The main "national" innovation of the period, however, seems to have been the composition of offices for saints on a national scale or, at the very least, on a scale larger than a single diocese. Here, Spain took the lead.[54] These feasts celebrated Spain's apostolic origins (Santiago), its Visigothic past (Isidore and Ildefonso), the Reconquista (the Exaltation of the Cross), and royal Habsburg devotions (in particular, to Mary's mother, Anne). Contemplated as early as 1568, an addendum of national feasts was first published in 1573 as a supplement to the Missal and again in 1574 as a supplement to the Breviary, undergoing continuous expansions thereafter.[55]

During the seventeenth century, similar editorial projects took place in Poland (1596), Sweden (1616), Ireland (1620), Hungary (1630), and the Holy Roman Empire.[56] Whether these initiatives originated with monarchs (e.g., Philip II, Sigismund III), national synods (e.g., Synod of Esztergom in 1630), or religious orders (e.g., Ireland), their composition shares common features.[57] These "national" liturgies often emphasized the feasts of dynastic saints (e.g., Casimir, Eric); those

---

moderne: *Les offices propres des saints nationaux*, ed. Antoine Mazurek (forthcoming).

[53] See Anna Coreth, *Pietas austriaca* (West Lafayette, IN, 2004 [1959]); Marie-Elizabeth Ducreux, "Emperors, Kingdoms, Territories: Multiple Versions of the Pietas Austriaca?," *Catholic Historical Review* 97, no. 2 (2011): 276–304.

[54] Despite Rome's refusal to extend the celebration of this series of feasts to the Kingdom of Portugal, these offices can be found in some Portuguese *Officia propria*. See, for example, *Officia sanctorum ecclesiae Olysiponensis ac totius fere Hispaniae propria* (Lisbon, 1590); cf. ADCS, Positiones rescriptorum et decretorum 952, fol. 1r.

[55] A survey of Amiet, *Missels et bréviaires imprimés*, and Alexander S. Wilkinson, *Iberian Books* (Leiden, 2010–15) comes to a total of twenty-six editions of Proper Offices for Spain and twenty-six of Proper Masses. On the genesis of the supplement, see Antoine Mazurek, "Philippe II, les saints de l'Espagne et les hiéronymites," in *The Hieronymite Musical and Liturgical Tradition within the European Context (14th – 16th c.)*, ed. Océane Boudeau et al. (forthcoming).

[56] These dates refer to the first editions in each case.

[57] *Officia SS. Patricii, Columbae, Brigidae, et aliorum quorundam Hiberniae Sanctorum* (Paris, 1620). Papal approval for these traditional Irish saints, which had been solicited by the Capuchin mission in Ireland, dates to June 1633: ADCS, Positiones rescriptorum et decretorum 9662, fol. 1r. For the broader context, see Salvador Ryan, "Steadfast Saints or Malleable Models? Seventeenth-Century Irish Hagiography Revisited," *Catholic Historical Review* 91, no. 2 (2005): 251–77.

of holy archbishops, especially those whose sees (Toledo, Gniezno, Uppsala, Esztergom) had made them primates of their respective nations; the feasts of martyrs; and historically significant feasts (such as the "Division of the Apostles," which commemorated the battle of Tannenberg in 1410). Many were presented as patron saints or were recently canonized saints. In Poland, Sweden, and especially Hungary, these offices accompanied the construction of national identities.

We cannot understand the importance of these collections of saints' liturgical offices in shaping collective identities without first examining their composition and use. For example, not all holy figures included in the proper offices for Poland were tied exclusively to Polish history. St. Wenceslas, for example, also served as a patron saint of Bohemia. Others, like Saints Francis and Jerome, had no obvious connection with Polish history at all. Nor were they celebrated with the same level of solemnity or in every part of the kingdom. Such attempts at reorganizing devotions still left space for local identities.[58] Nonetheless, it is undeniable that the prime mover behind this liturgical project, King Sigismund, had a broader political objective: The Polish king planned to retake the Swedish throne, having been deposed by the Protestant Riksdag (parliament) in 1599. His tactical publication of a Swedish *officia propria* emphasized saintly kings who predated the Reformation and who could therefore offer an interconfessional and national identity, since both Protestants and Catholics celebrated these royal figures.[59]

Publications such as these suggest that Tridentine Catholicism can also be understood as a network of national churches, all tied to Rome as the ultimate source of legitimacy and authority, yet also in competition with each other – and with Rome.[60] That is precisely how one can understand the claim by the eighteenth-century Jesuit Andrés Burriel

---

[58] Marie-Elizabeth Ducreux, "Adapter le Bréviaire romain après le concile de Trente: Jusqu'à quel point peut-on parler de propres des saints 'nationaux' dans les 'pays de l'empereur' et en Pologne-Lituanie?," in Mazurek, ed., *Liturgie et identités nationales*.

[59] *Officia propria SS. patronorum regni Sueciae ex vetustis breviariis ejusdem regni deprompta* (Antwerp, 1618); see Camille Bataille, "Une longue Réformation: La liturgie des saints en contexte suédois, v. 1530–v. 1700," in Mazurek, ed., *Liturgie et identités nationales*.

[60] Antonio Menniti Ippolito, *1664, un anno della Chiesa universale: Saggio sull'italianità del papato in età moderna* (Rome, 2011); Simon Ditchfield, "Tridentine Worship and the Cult of Saints," in *The Cambridge History of Christianity*, vol. 6: Reform and Expansion 1500–1660, ed. Ronnie Po-chia Hsia (Cambridge, 2007), 201–24.

that Spanish saints were "the greatest and strongest glory of the Nation, which Rome does not possess and which, for precisely this reason, it attacks and envies."[61] At the same time, we should never forget that saints are "for other people" and that devotions extended beyond national boundaries. Saints were therefore always more than mere national figureheads. For this reason, it is naïve to present the 1622 group canonization as the triumph of Spain simply because four of them were Spanish.[62] Study of the liturgy demonstrates that saints were known by other characteristics besides their nationality. Individual believers often felt a special devotion not only toward their name saint but also toward saints whose feasts fell on dates of personal significance. Such elements constituted a kind of common grammar for the adoption and appropriation of saints in the Counter-Reformation. Just as saints circulated through their relics, they also spread through texts and liturgy, and these, too, rendered universal figures particular and local.[63]

LITURGY OF SAINTS AND THE FAITHFUL: LAY APPROPRIATION AND ITS LIMITS

At the Basilica of Saint-Martin of Tours, the "Saint-Martin of Winter" festival continued to be celebrated into the eighteenth century. The festival began late afternoon with Vespers on the eve of November 11. The canons of Saint-Martin's and neighboring collegiate churches came in turns to sing Matins. These texts, extracted from the works of Gregory of Tours and Sulpicius Severus, described the death of the early medieval bishop and missionary Martin of Tours and even presented him as a thirteenth apostle. Masses were then recited until Prime, about nine in the morning, while eighty candles illuminated the sanctuary. The tomb of St. Martin, which had been desecrated in 1562 during the Wars of Religion, held a central place during the feast: thurifers (acolytes

---

[61] Alfonso Echánove Tuero, ed., "Apuntamientos de algunas ideas para fomentar las letras del P. Andrés Burriel," in *La preparación intelectual del P. Andrés M. Burriel*, ed. Alfonso Echánove Tuero (Madrid, 1971), 270.

[62] Clare Copeland, "Spanish Saints in Counter-Reformation Italy," in *The Spanish Presence in Sixteenth-Century Italy: Images of Iberia*, ed. Piers Baker-Bates and Miles Pattenden (London, 2015), 103–23.

[63] See the case of relics circulating with information about the date of the feast day in Nicolas Guyard, "Les reliques à l'époque moderne: Objets, pratiques et devotions," in *Les sources du sacré: Nouvelles approches du fait religieux*, ed. Nicolas Guyard and Caroline Muller (Lyon, 2019), 187–206.

bearing thuribles – vessels – of incense) came to offer incense before the tomb, while the celebrant recited the prayers nearby, with his hands folded, as in "the first centuries of the Church," as the collegiate chapter put it, asserting that St. Martin was "not inferior to the martyrs" of the Roman persecutions. While the ceremony might seem rather self-indulgent – a collegiate Church celebrating its bishop-saint – it was also directed to the faithful, who gathered in the nave and around the tomb. The bare setting and the darkness of the building contrasted starkly with the abundance of clerics (more than 100), the richness of their attire, and the illumination of the sanctuary, which highlighted the solitary presence of both the relics of St. Martin and the Gospels on the altar.[64]

Ceremonies such as this undoubtedly left a strong impression on the faithful. Indeed, the cult of saints was a synesthetic experience – part soundscape, part scent-scape, a lavish visual event grafted onto a wider sacred landscape. Accordingly, even the unlettered engaged with and to a certain extent "understood" the texts used by the liturgy of saints. Indeed, while the office, written in Latin and recited in the choir, might at first glance appear difficult to comprehend, the faithful could grasp its meaning in other ways, in the connection between words and gestures, or between words and places or proceedings. Furthermore, the regular practice of listening to, reading, and singing Latin liturgical texts rendered them familiar to the laity, especially in Romance language-speaking countries such as France, Spain, and Italy.[65] The clergy also strove in different ways to explain the liturgy to its flock. Historians have established that during the late Middle Ages and the Reformation, the laity were able to comprehend the ritual through preaching or teaching, with liturgical texts often serving as textbooks for pupils.[66]

While the Council of Trent did not officially restrict the use of vernacular by priests, the Inquisition did. In 1571, the year the

---

[64] This description is based on Christophe Maillard, "La fête de la Saint-Martin d'hiver à Saint-Martin de Tours au XVIIIe siècle: Le maintien d'une liturgie particulière dans le plus illustre chapitre collégial de France," in Dompnier, ed., *Les cérémonies extraordinaires du catholicisme baroque*, 525–44.

[65] For France, see Xavier Bisaro, *Chanter toujours: Plain-chant et religion villageoise dans la France moderne (XVIe–XIXe siècle)* (Rennes, 2010), 118; for Italy, see Alison K. Frazier, *Possible Lives: Authors and Saints in Renaissance Italy* (New York, 2005), 321–22.

[66] See, e.g., Eamon Duffy, *The Stripping of the Altars: Traditional Religion in England, 1400–1580*, 2nd ed. (New Haven, CT, 2005); Virginia Reinburg, *French Books of Hours: Making an Archive of Prayer, c. 1400–1600* (Cambridge, 2012); Nicole Bériou and Franco Morenzoni, eds, *Prédication et liturgie au Moyen Âge* (Turnhout, 2008).

Congregation of the Index was founded, Pius V issued a bull condemning the use of the vernacular in liturgical offices and restricting the permitted litanies, stating that the clergy must retain control of the liturgy. This ambition was quite specific to Italy, and even there it was soon replaced by a more realistic attitude. Across much of Catholic Europe, the composition of new litanies – prayers consisting of a series of invocations by the priest with responses by the flock – continued unabated. Few of these were ever submitted to the Congregation of Rites for approval. The sixteenth-century Jesuit Thomas Sailly collected a great many litanies, organized thematically by typology of saint (e.g., evangelists, monarchs). Despite being placed on the Index, his compendium proved a publishing sensation north of the Alps.[67]

Similarly, in seventeenth- and eighteenth-century France, the popular practice of singing the liturgy was taught to children at schools alongside reading and writing. This custom helps to explain why, although most people lacked command of Latin, they could still understand the ritual in which they participated. Such engagement mitigated the growing divide between clergy and laity and cultivated a sense of obligation among the latter for the observance and celebration of feast days. In 1741, at Suzannecourt (in the diocese of Langres, in the northeast) parishioners rang the bells for Vespers during the votive feast day of St. Anne, "without the participation and permission of the parish priest," who refused to sing the Mass for the saint.[68] Furthermore, while the canonical hours were typically sung by monks and canons in the choir of a convent, a cathedral, or a collegiate church, they could also be widely heard in simple parish churches, where they were recited and sung by remunerated priests (so-called *prêtres du chœur*). This was especially true for cities like Paris or Lille, but as Xavier Bisaro has shown, the practice also extended to the countryside.[69]

Finally, even if a significant portion of the lay faithful was unable to attend the office *in choro* and therefore participated in saints' feast days only through Mass, Vespers, and processions, the text of the liturgy itself might have been be available for private prayer.[70] An increased

---

[67] Thomas Sailly, *Thesaurus litaniarum ac orationum sacer* (Brussels, 1598).
[68] Bisaro, *Chanter toujours*, 134. See also John Bossy, "Essai de sociographie de la messe, 1200–1700," *Annales: Histoire, Sciences Sociales* 25, no. 1 (1981): 44–70.
[69] Emmanuel Phatthanasinh, "L'économie des paroisses à Paris (1580–1650)" (PhD diss., Université de Lorraine, 2023), 358; Alain Lottin, *Lille, citadelle de la Contre-Réforme? (1598–1668)* (Dunkirk, 1984), 88–90.
[70] William A. Christian, Jr., *Local Religion in Sixteenth-Century Spain* (Princeton, NJ, 1981); Anne Bonzon, *L'esprit de clocher: Prêtres et paroisses dans le diocèse de*

number of separate editions of proper offices for saints appeared in eighteenth-century France along with other liturgical texts such as litanies and so-called little offices (a kind of abbreviated liturgical office without readings) in French or in Latin; evidence shows that people of different social ranks possessed such books.[71]

The continuous evolution of the liturgy, then, was determined by the ever-changing relationship between the Catholic Church and the wider society of which it was part. Consequently, liturgy must be studied comprehensively, together with other religious practices, texts, and rituals, with full consideration of how these interacted and circulated. The calendar and liturgy, for instance, provided a framework for the composition of devotional books, with Andrés Capilla's 1572 *Libro de oración* among the earliest and most successful examples.[72] The decision to include a saint's feast in either the Roman or a local calendar frequently led to the creation or proliferation of confraternities. Conversely, local devotion to a saint, especially when encouraged by confraternities, could inspire their inclusion in the liturgy. For instance, in 1608, Spanish bishops, cathedral chapters, and Habsburg monarchs petitioned for the inclusion of the Office of the Guardian Angels in the Roman Breviary, to be celebrated *ad libitum* (i.e., voluntarily). Subsequent success led the Roman archconfraternity to request and ultimately obtain the feast's mandatory status in 1670.[73]

CONCLUSION

Liturgical reform was initially conceived of as one way to restore Church unity after the Reformation. Yet even if many bishops at Trent advocated for standardization of the liturgy, they still excluded one thing: the cult of saints. If the Mass was to be celebrated in the same manner everywhere, it could nonetheless be held in honor of a great many local saints. Attempts to regulate this abundance served as a key vehicle for asserting papal authority. Some Roman officials took a radical stance, with one consultor of the Congregation of Rites declaring

---

Beauvais (1535–1650) (Paris, 1999), 328–35; Marc Forster, *Catholic Revival in the Age of the Baroque: Religious Identity in Southwest Germany, 1550–1750* (Cambridge, 2001), 106–51.

[71] Éric Suire, *Sainteté et Lumières: Hagiographie, spiritualité et propagande religieuse dans la France du XVIIIe siècle* (Paris, 2009), 60–62.

[72] *Libro de oración en que se ponen consideraciones sobre los Evangelios de todos los domingos del año y algunas fiestas principales* (Lérida, 1572).

[73] Mazurek, *Une figure de la modernité religieuse*.

that its aim was "to do everything possible to reduce the particular [local] calendars to the uniformity of the Roman calendar."[74]

Nevertheless, many Catholics still felt a deep sense of attachment toward their local saints. Often, homegrown devotions, however strong, were not enough. Churches aspired for their own saints to achieve not merely local but global recognition through inclusion in the Roman liturgy and calendar. The Counter-Reformation was thus defined by the twin processes of particularizing the universal and universalizing the particular. Where those conflicted, Rome – its institutions, procedures, and liturgy – was consulted for answers that it all too often felt unable to provide.

---

[74] Advice from a consultor of the Congregation of Rites: "fare il possibile per ridurre i particolari calendari all'uniformità del Rito romano," cited by Dompnier, "Les calendriers entre Pie V et Benoît XIV," 50.

12 Hagiography

SIMON DITCHFIELD

Which came first: the actual life of the saint or their textual life (written, printed, or sounded out in recitation, prayer, and song)? This is not such a stupid question as might at first appear. Where the early Christian Roman martyrs are concerned, it has been acknowledged since at least the work of the Belgian hagiographer Hippolyte Delehaye (1859–1941), and more recently confirmed by the latest scholarship, that life and *Life* (or vita) are intwined. These early Christian accounts of the epic heroism (*passiones*) of Roman martyrs, composed between 500 and 700 CE (several centuries after the events they describe), instantiated and rendered the frequently fictional status of their subjects more "real" and palpable.[1] In the words of Michael Lapidge, such accounts of epic heroism "are worthless as witnesses to the actual trial and execution of Christians in earlier times."[2] Moreover, no such accounts were composed for genuine martyrs such as St. Ignatius of Antioch, executed in Rome circa 140, or Pope Fabian, also executed in Rome during the persecution of the Emperor Decius in 250.[3] But this is to miss the point of hagiography, which has traditionally aimed to transform the sites of the alleged burial of holy men and women (or parts thereof) into "storied places" and to inspire pilgrims with exemplary tales.[4] Lapidge's account of the emergence of Roman martyr stories suggests a direct link between the composition of *passiones* and the dramatic expansion of pilgrimages to martyr burial sites

---

[1] Hippolyte Delehaye, *Les légendes hagiographiques* (Brussels, 1905; English trans. of 4th ed., 1955, with new introduction by Thomas O'Loughlin, *The Legends of the Saints*, Dublin, 1998); Hippolyte Delehaye, *Les origines du culte des martyres*, 2nd ed. (Brussels, 1933).
[2] Michael Lapidge, ed. and trans., *The Roman Martyrs: Introduction, Translations and Commentary* (Oxford, 2018), 2.
[3] Lapidge, *The Roman Martyrs*, 3.
[4] Virginia Reinburg, *Storied Places: Pilgrim Shrines, Nature and History in Early Modern France* (Cambridge, 2019).

from the late fourth century CE.⁵ In other words, the written texts of these *Lives* helped to shape lived practices of saints' veneration, worship, and liturgy, as also pointed out in Chapter 11 of this book.

In his study of the Greek and Latin martyr narratives from the first four Christian centuries, Éric Rebillard makes a complementary point: "it was liturgical needs that drove the compilation of information and texts about martyrs."⁶ Even so, liturgical texts were still essentially seen as an exercise in history writing. For Rebillard, it was no less a figure than Eusebius of Caesarea (d. 339), the father of Church history, who was the first to act on the knowledge that collecting martyr narratives was essential to his task. Although his collection of lives has not come down to us, Eusebius's preface to Book Five of his *Ecclesiastical History* deliberately juxtaposed accounts of Christian martyrdom with secular counterparts to describing "victories in war, trophies against enemies, the prowess of generals, and the manly courage of soldiers who have polluted themselves with blood and myriad murders for the sake of children [and] fatherland."⁷ From the outset, then, hagiography was a form of history writing and therefore should be considered a substantially unwritten chapter in the history of historiography. Alison Frazier has reminded us, however, that the Middle Ages were also a period of deep continuities, as can be seen from the more than 200 saints' lives authored during the fifteenth century in the Italian peninsula by over 100 writers "whose 'intention to imitate ancient Latin style' identifies them as humanists."⁸ According to Frazier, the effect of the *studia humanitatis* on the field of hagiography "may be best described as an intensification and redirection of medieval concerns, not as a complete break with, or a series of challenges to, those concerns."⁹ Even so, the fact remains that in the period covered by this Companion, history in general and hagiography in particular

---

⁵ Lapidge, *The Roman Martyrs*, 3.
⁶ Éric Rebillard, ed., *Greek and Latin Narratives about the Ancient Martyrs* (Oxford, 2017), 6.
⁷ Eusebius of Caesarea, *The History of the Church: A New Translation*, trans. Jeremy M. Schott (Oakland, CA, 2019), 225.
⁸ Alison Knowles Frazier, *Possible Lives: Authors and Saints in Renaissance Italy* (New York, 2005), 9, whose definition of "humanist" is taken from Ronald G. Witt, *In the Footsteps of the Ancients: The Origins of Humanism from Lovato to Bruni* (Leiden, 2000), 22.
⁹ Frazier, *Possible Lives*, 27.

became the polemical weapon of choice not only between Catholics and Protestants, but also between Catholics themselves.[10]

THE VARIETIES OF PRINT

The dual spurs of print and polemic over the early modern period led to an unprecedented expansion of hagiographical texts in quantity, variety, and reach. Printing made possible the diffusion of accounts of saints' lives in formats as various as their purpose. At the cheaper end of the spectrum these could take the form of simple booklets of prayers and readings, which offered summaries of the life and especially miracles of the holy man or woman in question. Sometimes boasting a woodcut or engraved image, they typically accompanied celebrations of the annual feast day of a local saint.[11] Such humble publications might have been distributed to the faithful in return for a small offering, or even given away gratis to a restless, impatient crowd, meaning that far fewer survive today than do more substantial standalone single vitae, or the collections commonly known as *Flos sanctorum*, often arranged according to the calendar year, which enjoyed particular favor in the Iberian world.[12] *Flos sanctorum* was the hagiographical cousin of *florilegia*: a gathering of extracts from the writings of early Christian authors, and also sometimes of pagan philosophers, and a mainstay of medieval manuscript culture (only later did this term come to refer mainly to botanical illustrations).

At the top end of the hagiographical book market may be found reference works, clearly aimed at institutional libraries or monasteries, such as Luigi Lippomano's eight-volume *Sanctorum priscorum patrum vitae* (1551–60) or the expanded and improved edition, the seven-volume *De probatis sanctorum historiis* (1570–81), by the Carthusian

---

[10] Simon Ditchfield, *Liturgy, Sanctity and History in Tridentine Italy: Pietro Maria Campi and the Preservation of the Particular* (Cambridge, 1995); Kate van Liere, Simon Ditchfield, and Howard Louthan, eds., *Sacred History: Uses of the Christian Past in the Renaisance World* (Oxford, 2012); Tommaso Caliò, Maria Duranti, and Raimondo Michetti, eds., *Italia sacra: Le raccolte di vite dei santi e l'inventio delle regioni (secc. XV–XVIII)* (Rome, 2013).

[11] Peter Parshall and Rainer Schoch, eds., *Origins of European Printmaking: Fifteenth-Century Woodcuts and Their Publics* (New Haven, CT, 2005), cat. nos. 5, 6, 9–11, 14, 26–28, 30, 35–37, 48, 58, 83, 93–106.

[12] Jonathan Greenwood, "Floral Arrangements: Compilations of Saints' Lives in Early Modern Europe," *Journal of Early Modern History* 22 (2018): 181–203; Jonathan Greenwood, "Readable Flowers: Global Circulation and Translation of Collected Saints' Lives," *Journal of Global History* 13, no. 1 (2018): 22–45.

Lorenz Sauer (Surius), which had thematic indexes making it more suitable for polemical use by Catholic preachers.[13] This learned tradition of hagiography culminated in what eventually became the sixty-eight-folio volume *Acta sanctorum*, authored by a team of Jesuit scholars known as the Bollandists, after their founder Jean Bolland (1596–1665).[14] Organized by the Church's liturgical calendar, the *Acta sanctorum* began publication in 1643 with two lengthy volumes devoted to just the month of January. Becoming more detailed and exhaustive with every subsequent month, it still had only reached the start of December when the main series came to a close in 1940.[15]

The bulky "middle market" of hagiography, so to speak, was taken up by printed accounts of individual or smaller groups of saints (often linked by their common place of burial). These often included, by way of an appendix, the liturgical office of the saint or saints who were the subject of the volume. In all but the smallest dioceses of the Mediterranean heartlands of Christendom, the local pantheon of saints usually consisted of one or two early Christian martyr bishops, along with a selection of holy male and female members of religious orders, who had either founded or simply lived and died within the city's convents and monasteries that then enjoyed custody of their bones. In Northern and Eastern Europe including Scandinavia, the overall distribution of local holy heroes was certainly later in date, if not that much sparser. More rarely, these iron rations of the holy might be supplemented by the occasional local layperson who had died in odor of sanctity and whose resting place was usually dependent on family or confraternal affiliation. Occasionally, the landscape of holiness would be enlivened by the presence of relics of saints who enjoyed wider or even universal renown. In the early modern period, as shown in Chapter 6, the saintly menu might be rendered more exotic still by

---

[13] Serena Spanò Martinelli, "Cultura umanistica, polemica antiprotestante, erudizione sacra nel 'Probatis sanctorum historia' di Lorenzo Surio," in *Raccolte di vite di santi dal XIII al XVIII secolo: Strutture, messaggi, fruizioni*, ed. Sofia Boesch Gajano (Brindisi, 1990), 131–41.

[14] Robert Godding, Bernard Joassart, Xavier Lequeux, and François de Vriendt, eds., *De Rosweyde aux Acta Sanctorum: La recherche hagiographique des Bollandistes à travers quatre siècles* (Brussels, 2009); Jan Machielsen, "Heretical Saints and Textual Discernment: The Polemical Origins of the Acta Sanctorum (1643–1940)," in Clare Copeland and Jan Machielsen, eds., *Angels of Light? Sanctity and the Discernment of Spirits in the Early Modern Period* (Leiden, 2013), 103–41.

[15] M. David Knowles, "Presidential Address: Great Historical Enterprises I. The Bollandists," *Transactions of the Royal Historical Society*, 5th series, 8 (1958): 147–66.

the arrival of the bodies of those who were believed to be early Christian martyr saints that had been extracted from the Roman catacombs. They might also be supplemented by the appropriation of relics from elsewhere, which in some cases, as shown in Chapter 8 in this volume, might be the result of straightforward theft.

This "hagioscape" is striking for its diachronic nature: It gathered together saints from multiple periods of Christian history.[16] In a major city such as Naples, by 1600 Europe's largest with a population of some 300,000, the number and nature of printed saints' lives between 1540 and 1750 is instructive. Jean-Michel Sallmann has counted 271 hagiographical titles in 327 editions between 1501 and 1750.[17] Moreover, each volume potentially dealt with several saints within a single cover.[18] The same time period witnessed the canonization of only three saints with direct connections to the Kingdom of Naples: Cajetan/Gaetano of Thiene (1480–1547), cofounder of the Theatines; his confrere Andrea Avellino (1521–1608); and the Franciscan preacher James of the Marches (1394–1476), all of whom died in the city. What is remarkable is the relatively scarce attention these new saints received. Sallmann noted a sustained high interest in the saints of Late Antiquity (representing 77.6% of vitae between 1551 and 1600, and 42% from 1601 to 1650) as against those relating to the Counter-Reformation period (which only made up 2.6 percent in the earlier period and rose to 29.1% from 1601 to 1650). The time delay in beatification and canonization of these so-called *beati moderni* (those recently deceased with a reputation for sanctity) only partly explains the disparity.[19] More important was the role played by early Christian holy men and women as patron saints of local communities. By contrast, according to Sallmann at least, saints of the Counter-Reformation were non-local and universal in character.[20]

---

[16] For the term "hagioscape," see *Hagioscape: How Mobility and Materiality Shaped Pre-Modern Geographies of Devotion (400–1700)*, ed. Marianne Ritsema van Eck and Steffen Hope (forthcoming).

[17] Jean-Michel Sallmann, *Naples et ses saints à l'âge baroque, 1540–1750* (Paris, 1994), 24 (tableau 2).

[18] Although to put things in perspective, it should be noted that these titles represented only 5 percent of the grand total of books printed and published in the city: Sallmann, *Naples et ses saints*, 22.

[19] Simon Ditchfield, "'Coping with the Beati moderni': Canonization Procedure in the Aftermath of the Council of Trent," in *Ite Inflammate Omnia: Selected Historical Papers from Conferences Held at Loyola and Rome in 2006*, ed. Thomas M. McCoog (Rome, 2010), 413–39; Ruth Noyes, *Peter Paul Rubens and the Counter Reformation Crisis of the Beati moderni* (London, 2018).

[20] Though arguably the cults of both Philip Neri and Francesca Romana were preeminently Roman in origin and substantially remained so: Louis Ponnelle and

The election of new patron saints similarly suggests a persistent preference for Christianity's earliest saints, explaining why they dominated the hagiographical landscape. Between 1630 and 1750, over 200 towns in the Kingdom of Naples chose at least one or two new patron saints, on average, although the choices were not entirely original to each location: Of the 410 new patron saints, the vast majority came from a same roster of 130 individual saints. Regulations for the election of patron saints had been set down only in 1630 as part of Urban VIII's legal redefinition of sanctity. Only those whose names were included in the Roman Martyrology, and who therefore were officially recognised as saints, were eligible to be included.[21] Of the four types identified by Sallmann – members of the Holy Family, saints of Late Antiquity, saints of the Middle Ages, and those of the Counter-Reformation – the second category commanded a clear lead (37.5%) with the final category, those of the aforementioned *beati moderni*, taking last place (16.1%), which was significantly behind medieval saints (27.7%) and just behind those from the Holy Family (18.8%).[22]

One obvious reason for the surge in hagiographical writing was the Reformation. The cult of saints needed defending and championing as a direct consequence of Protestant polemic, which disputed the efficacy of intercessory prayers addressed to the dead for the spiritual benefit of both the dead and the living. However, the polemic was not just *inter*-confessional (Catholic versus Protestant). It was also, as noted above, *intra*-confessional (Catholic versus Catholic). Rivalry between Roman Catholic churches, villages, towns, and dioceses played out in claims and counterclaims made by the proud custodians of particular saints' bodies or relics. Catholic belief held that even possession of, say, one part of a saint's skull would confer on the owner the same spiritual benefits as the entire skull, encouraging the fragmentation of the holy in the form of body parts, mostly bones. Erasmus, Luther, Calvin, and many others mercilessly lampooned the frequently unedifying spectacle of the apparent duplication of holy body parts.[23] Rome therefore

---

Louis Bordet, *St Philip Neri and the Roman Society of his times, 1515–1595*, trans Ralph F. Kerr (London, 1932), and Alessandra Bartolomei Romagnoli and Giorgio Picasso, eds., *La Canonizzazione di Santa Francesca Romana: Santità, cultura e istituzioni a Roma tra Medioevo ed età moderna* (Florence, 2013).

[21] As shall be explained in greater detail below, the vast majority of saints publicly venerated have never received papal canonization.

[22] Sallmann, *Naples et ses saints*, 76.

[23] E.g., "Naufragium/shipwreck (1523)," in Erasmus, *Collected Works of Erasmus*, vol. 39, trans. and ed. Craig R. Thompson (Toronto, 1997), 351–67; Luther, "Against

increasingly frowned upon disputes over relics, and sought to suppress them before they became easy targets for Protestant polemicists.[24] The newly revised Roman Breviary of 1568, with its pruned saints' calendar and rewritten hagiographical readings at Matins, likewise inspired authors into busy efforts to refurbish local cults, whose practices and even legitimacy would now be examined carefully and critically not only in Wittenberg or Geneva, but also in Rome.[25] The result was a veritable renaissance of ecclesiastical erudition (c. 1550–1750) as writers sought to defend and celebrate their local cults and devotions.[26] Indeed, in the wake of the Protestant and Catholic Reformations, attitudes to the cult of saints provided perhaps the most visible boundary that marked the confessional divide. Hagiography, as sung, recited, printed, and engraved, therefore assumed renewed importance as a defining feature of Roman Catholic devotional practice.

NEW GENRES OF HAGIOGRAPHY

Accounts of saints' lives encompassed an unprecedented range of genres in the early modern period. The late sixteenth century introduced several substantially new forms, in addition to those discussed above. These included Latin epic, such as the Jesuit Francesco Benci's *Quinque martyres* (1591), a 5,600-hexameter, six-book, neo-Virgilian account of the so-called martyrs of Salsete near Goa in India, and also missionary reports, especially the Annual Letters (*litterae annue*) from members of the Society of Jesus to their Roman headquarters, which were then

---

the New Idol and Old Devil to be elevated at Meissen (1524)," in Martin Luther, *Werke*, vol. 15 (Weimar, 1899), 183–98; Jean Calvin, *Traité des reliques (1543)*, ed. Irena Backus (Geneva, 2000). See also Spencer J. Weinreich, "An Infinity of Relics: Erasmus and the Copious Rhetoric of John Calvin's Traité des Reliques," *Renaissance Quarterly* 74, no. 1 (2021): 137–80.

[24] Such rivalries might sometimes resemble the Cold War "arms race" as each side tried to "manufacture" more relics than its competitor. For the case of Cagliari versus Sassari in the 1630s, see A. Katie Harris, "'An Immense Structure of Errors': Dionisio Bonfant, Lucas Holstenius, and the Writing of Sacred History in Seventeenth-Century Sardinia," in *The Early Modern Hispanic World: Transnational and Interdisciplinary Approaches*, ed. Kimberley Lynn and Erin Rowe (Cambridge, 2017), 243–67. For the wider context see Chapter 8 in this volume.

[25] For the case study of the North Italian diocese of Piacenza located in the wider context post-Trent, see Ditchfield, *Liturgy, Sanctity and History*. For the role played by the Holy Office in policing the cult of saints, see Miguel Gotor, *I beati del Papa: Santità, Inquisizione e obbedienza in età moderna* (Florence, 2002).

[26] Ditchfield, *Liturgy, Sanctity and History*, 328–60. For the Italian peninsula as a whole, see Caliò et al., eds., *Italia sacra*.

reworked and recirculated in more polished and therefore persuasive prose.[27] Benci himself (1542–1594) worked in both genres, contributing to *litterae annue* from 1586 to 1591 before writing his Latin epic poem.[28] Ignatius of Loyola himself had specified what such letters should include. In a letter to the Flemish missionary to India, Gasper Berze, he demanded something edifying be written

> regarding the cosmography of those regions where ours [i.e., members of the Society] live. They want to know, for instance, the length of the days in summer and in winter.... Finally, if there are other things that might seem extraordinary, let them be noted, for instance, details about animals and plants that are either not known at all or not of such a size. And this news – sauce for the taste of a certain curiosity (*y esta salsa, para el gusto de alguna curiosidad*), that is not evil and is wont to be found amongst men – may come in the same letters or in other letters separately.[29]

This was precisely what Benci's fellow Jesuit Daniello Bartoli (1608–1685) did over half a century later in the *Istoria della compagnia di Gesù* (1653–73), his official vernacular history of the global missionary activity of the Society. Although it was left incomplete at the author's death, the text covered not only South and East Asia, but also Italy and England.[30] In the volume on Asia, first printed in 1653, the first four of its eight books were dedicated almost entirely to the person considered effectively the cofounder of the Society, and its first missionary saint: Francis Xavier (1506–1552). Bartoli drew extensively on both existing printed vitae of the saint and witness testimony from Xavier's

---

[27] Paul G. Gwynne, ed. and trans., *Francesco Benci's Quinque Martyres: Introduction, Translation and Commentary* (Leiden, 2018); Paul Nelles, "Jesuit Letters," in *The Oxford Handbook of Jesuits*, ed. Ines Županov (Oxford, 2019), 44–72.

[28] See Markus Friedrich, "Circulating and Compiling the *Litterae annuae*: Towards a History of the Jesuit System of Communication," *Archivum historicum societatis Iesu* 77 (2008): 3–39, at 35–36.

[29] *Monumenta Ignatiana: Epistulae et instructiones*, vol. 6 (Madrid, 1907), 357–59 (at 358). For the English translation, see John Correia-Afonso, *Jesuit Letters and Indian History: A Study of the Nature and Development of Jesuit Letters from India (1542–1773) and Their Value for Indian Historiography* (Bombay, 1955), 14.

[30] See Simon Ditchfield, "Baroque Around the Clock: Daniello Bartoli SJ (1608–1685) and the Uses of Global History," *Transactions of the Royal Historical Society*, Sixth Series, 31 (2021): 49–73. See also the excellent entry by Alberto Asor Rosa in the *Dizionario biografico degli italiani* 6 (1964).

canonization trials, as summarized in the report for the Rota, the highest court of the Roman curia.[31]

These narratives circulated not only from Roman Catholic peripheries to the centre in Rome, but also from periphery to periphery, as in the case of Pedro Morejón (c. 1562–1634), procurator of the Jesuit mission to Japan. Morejón's account of Christian martyrdom there was first published in Spanish in Mexico City in 1616, and swiftly reprinted three years later in English for the consolation of the oppressed Catholics living in the British archipelago, as its prefatory letter of dedication makes clear. The translator "W.W." writes: "I knew not to whome I might better direct it than to you the poore afflicted Catholikes of this our country."[32] This is one example of a wider phenomenon: Rady Roldán-Figueroa, for example, has identified at least 382 texts from the Spanish world that referenced Christian martyrdom in Japan (1598–1700).[33] More remarkably still, these were published in nine languages in at least eighty-eight cities in Europe, New Spain, and the Philippines. Likewise, when Pope Urban VIII beatified the twenty-six martyrs of Nagasaki in 1627, thirty years after they were crucified for their faith, this was marked a year later by publications of Japanomartyrology in five languages, twenty-two cities, and a range of genres: traditional hagiographies, but also letter collections, sermons, newsletters, and descriptions of the beatification festivities.[34]

The insatiable demand for news of missionary derring-do and spiritual heroics was so strong that they sometimes came to be invented (or at least elaborated upon with fictional detail). By the second quarter of the seventeenth century, we can identify in the Italian peninsula a fully articulated sacred counterpart to one of the

---

[31] Daniello Bartoli, *Istoria della Compagnia di Gesù. L'Asia*, ed. Umberto Grassi and Elisa Frei, 2 vols. (Turin, 2019), vol. 1, 33, 34, 146, 147, 156, 167, 252–55, 341–42, 409, 444, 461, 471–72, 475, 479, 490, 491–93, 499, 501, 527.

[32] Pedro Morejón, *Breve relación de la persecución que huvo estos años contro la iglesia de Japón* (Mexico City, 1616); Pedro Morejón, *A Briefe Relation of the Persecution Lately Made Against the Catholic Christians in the Kingdom of Japonia* ([Saint-Omer], 1619). The quotation is at sig. A3r of the English translation.

[33] Rady Roldán-Figueroa, *The Martyrs of Japan: Publication History and Catholic Missions in the Spanish World; Spain, New Spain and the Philippines, 1597–1700* (Leiden, 2021), 265–303.

[34] Ibid., 1–2. For the diffusion of the iconography of the martyrs of Japan, see Hitomi Omata Rappo, "From the Cross to the Pyre: The Representation of the Martyrs of Japan in Jesuit Prints," *Journal of Jesuit Studies* 10 (2023): 456–86; Hitomi Omata Rappo, *Des Indes lointaines aux scènes des collèges: Les reflets des martyrs de la mission japonaise en Europe (XVIe–XVIIIe siècle)* (Münster, 2020).

most popular literary genres of the day: the romance (*romanzo*).[35] Characterized by the often fantastical development of a weak plot, the genre of the "Romanzo sacro" was remarkable for three features: its popularity, its relatively short-lived nature, and its geographical limits. It flourished for scarcely more than fifty years – from Giovanni Francesco Biondi's *L'Eromena* (1624) to Girolamo Brusoni's *La Peota smarrita* (1662) – in three principal Italian cities: Genoa and Bologna, but especially Venice. So popular was this genre (a modern bibliographical survey lists some 865 editions, including reprints) – that it spawned several identifiable subgenres.[36] These included, foremost, the so-called *historia devota*, modeled on the works of Jean-Pierre Camus, the French author, preacher, and bishop of Belley (1582–1653). Camus's compositions included a life of the supposed daughter of St. Peter: *Petronille: Accident pitoyable de nos jours, cause d'un vocation religieuse* (1632). Other forms included *sacre historie*, narratives of directly biblical inspiration, such as Luigi Mazzini's *La vita di Tobia e le Battaglie d'Israele* (1637), or accounts based on the lives of individual saints, such as Anton Giulio Brignole Sale's *Maria Maddalena peccatrice convertita* (1636). Finally, there were fanciful biographies of only recently deceased holy heroes, such as that of the Scots Calvinist–turned–Capuchin missionary George Leslie (d. 1637), who took the name "Archangel" with his vows. First published in Macerata in 1644, *Il Cappuccino scozzese*, by Giovanni Battista Rinuccini, archbishop of Fermo and later papal nuncio to Ireland, enjoyed a wider circulation than other examples of the genre, since it went through seven Italian editions in two years before being translated into most of the languages of Catholic Western Europe.[37] In 1657 it was turned into a lengthy play of seventy-six scenes by the Jesuits in their college of Metz, and in 1673 an Italian stage version was made. Owing to the hostility of Scots Catholics, no full English translation of the text was ever published.[38]

---

[35] Mariella Muscariello, *La società del Romanzo: Il romanzo spirituale barocco* (Palermo, 1979).

[36] Albert N. Mancini, "Il Romanzo del '600: Saggio di bibliografia," *Studi secenteschi* 11 (1970): 205–74, and 12 (1971), 444–98.

[37] For a recent reprinting, see Clizia Carminati and Stefano Villani, eds., *Storie Inglesi: L'Inghilterra vista dall'Italia tra storia e romanzo (XVII sec.)* (Pisa, 2011), 229–96. See also the article on *il Cappucino scozzese* by Martino Capucci (ibid., 83–95).

[38] See the entry by Mark Dilworth on "Leslie, George [name in religion Archangel]" in the *ODNB*: https://doi.org/10.1093/ref:odnb/16489.

HAGIOGRAPHY AS A MULTISENSORY EXPERIENCE

Such acting out of saints' lives in the form of sacred plays (*sacre rappresentazioni*) (frequently performed in the open air as street theater, sometimes on wagons as mobile stages) was already widespread by the later Middle Ages, at least in northern and central Italy. These performances transitioned to the age of print with ease, as they were invariably promoted and illustrated extensively using cheap woodcuts.[39] Thus when the Oratorian historian and hagiographer Cesare Baronio decided in 1597 to stage the translation of the relics of the early Christian martyr saints Nereo and Achilleo from his congregation's church of Santa Maria in Vallicella in central Rome to the basilica dedicated to them in the uninhabited neighborhood of the Baths of the Caracalla, he was building on a long-established tradition. The superior of the Congregation of the Oratory, who had just been made a cardinal in 1596, had deliberately chosen the basilica as his titular church, and carefully choreographed the translation in the form of a Christian Triumph. Its route not only climbed the Capitoline Hill and traversed the Roman Forum but was also decorated with lengthy inscriptions that "baptized" the several triumphal arches it passed under (those of Septimius Severus, Titus, and Constantine).[40] This event occasioned the printing of a life of the two saints, together with those of their mistress Flavia Domitilla by Baronio's Oratorian colleague, Antonio Gallonio (1556–1605), as well as the production of a single-sheet *relazione* of the procession, complete with the texts of the psalms and spiritual songs (*laudi*) that were to be sung en route.[41] The latter reportedly derived from the liturgy of Rome's earliest persecuted Christians. The first volume of *laude* printed for the Oratory's early gatherings was the *Primo libro delle laudi spirituali* (1563), with music by the Florentine composer Giovanni Animuccia (1520–1571). This repertory

---

[39] For a pioneering treatment, see Vincenzo de Bartholomaeis, *Laudi drammatiche e rappresentazioni sacre* (Florence, 1943). Cf. Paola Ventrone, "Acting and Reading Drama: Notes on Florentine *sacre rappresentazioni* in Print," *Journal of Early Modern Studies* 8 (2019): 69–132.

[40] Richard Krautheimer, "A Christian Triumph of 1597," in *Essays in the History of Art Presented to Rudolf Wittkower*, ed. Douglas Fraser, Howard Hibbard, and Milton J. Lewine (London, 1967), 174–81.

[41] Antonio Gallonio, *Historia della vita e martirio de'gloriosi santi Flavia Domitilla vergine, Nereo et Achilleo conalcune vite brevi de'santi parenti di S. Flavia Domitilla*, (Rome, 1597); Anne Piéjus, "Entre hagiographie et prière: Chanter les premiers saints dans la Rome Tridentine," in *La mémoire des saints originels entre XVIe et XVIIIe siècle*, ed. Bernard Dompnier and Stefania Nanni (Rome, 2019), 204–28, at 210–11.

drew more directly on the Florentine heritage of the Oratory's founder, Philip Neri, specifically his attachment to the memory (and cult) of the Dominican radical firebrand Girolamo Savonarola (1452–1498).[42] Many of its texts drew on Savonarolean poets and at least one poem – *Iesu sommo conforto* – was written by Savonarola himself. The *laude* were meant to be simple, as the *Terzo libro delle laudi spirituali* (1577) says explicitly. Even so, the Oratorian *laude* were nonetheless mostly sung by professional musicians, who acted as "spokesmen of the faithful" and whose singing functioned as vocal prayer, often preceded by a sermon and followed by mental prayer.[43]

ROME AS A STORIED PLACE

As home to a quantity of saints' relics unmatched in number or antiquity anywhere in the world, from the perspective of Roman Catholics at least, Rome was arguably the most "storied place" on earth. As St. Pius V (r. 1566–72) was reported to have observed to the ambassador of the King of Poland: "It is well known to many that the soil of the Vatican [hill] was soaked in martyrs' blood."[44] Gallonio, whom we have just encountered as hagiographer of Philip Neri and champion of such early Christian virgin martyr saints as Nereo, Achilleo, and Flavia Domitilla, could be considered one of the preeminent "re-imagineers" of "Roma Sancta" in the half-century after the closing of the Council of Trent.[45] His work assisted visitors to Rome as they began to return in such numbers from the Holy Year of 1575, repopulating the city's churches and sacred places in their minds' eye with bleeding and suffering martyrs from the first Christian centuries.[46]

---

[42] Piéjus, "Artistic Revival and Conquest of the Soul in Early Modern Rome," in *Listening to Early Modern Catholicism: Perspectives from Musicology*, ed. Daniele Filippi and Michael Noone (Leiden, 2017), 149–72, at 154–63.

[43] Ibid., 163 n. 31 and 168.

[44] *Acta sanctorum*, vol. May I (Antwerp, 1680), 715E.

[45] I have derived this from the term "imagineering" used by Nicola Denzey Lewis, *The Early Modern Invention of Late Antique Rome*, (Cambridge, 2020), 3. Lewis herself borrowed it from Dennis Trout, "Theodolinda's Rome: 'Ampullae,' 'Pittacia' and the Image of the City," *Memoires of the American Academy in Rome* 50 (2005): 131–50, at 134. On Gallonio, see the entry by Simon Ditchfield, *Dizionario Biografico degli Italiani* 51 (1998), and Jetze Touber, *Law, Medicine and Engineering in the Cult of the Saints in Counter-Reformation Rome: The Hagiographical Works of Antonio Gallonio, 1556–1605* (Leiden, 2014).

[46] Simon Ditchfield, "Reading Rome as a Sacred Landscape, ca. 1586–1635," in *Sacred Space in Early Modern Europe*, ed. Will Coster and Andrew Spicer (Cambridge, 2005), 167–92.

Before being assigned to promote the cult of the founder of the Congregation of the Oratory, Philip Neri, Gallonio had been known almost exclusively for publications on the cult of female early Christian Roman virgin martyr saints (and by his Oratorian brethren for having assembled so much hagiographical material for Cesare Baronio).[47] This focus aligns with the well-known commitment of Oratorian scholars, most famously Baronio, to demonstrate the continuity of the existing Roman Catholic Church with its earliest history, *semper eadem*, and also with the particular role of Oratorian priests, such as Gallonio, as confessors to aristocratic women, counterparts to those who laid down their lives during the persecutions of successive pagan Roman emperors. Gallonio, specifically, confessed the nuns of the convent at the foot of the Capitoline Hill of Tor de Specchi, which had been founded by Francesca Romana (1384–1440), whose cult and canonization the Oratorians supported.[48]

Gallonio also attended to the spiritual needs of female aristocratic virgins who had not yet professed as nuns. One such person was Elena de' Massimi, daughter of one of the leading patrons of the Oratorians during their early years. She died of cancer at the age of thirteen and Gallonio wrote her vita, which remained in manuscript until it was published in the nineteenth century.[49] As Jodi Bilinkoff has taught us, such vitae of contemporary exemplary subjects functioned as guides for confessors in their dealings with female penitents.[50] Elena had at least six sisters who entered Tor de Specchi and four at other convents. Their names suggest the sixteenth-century popularity of first-century Christian female saints: Costanza, Caterina, Elena, Cecilia, two

---

[47] Biblioteca Vallicelliana, Rome [BVR], MSS H. 2–14, 16, and 18–20. See Simon Ditchfield, "An Early Christian School of Sanctity in Tridentine Rome," in *Christianity and Community in the West: Essays for John Bossy*, ed. Simon Ditchfield (Aldershot, 2001), 183–205, at 191 n. 29.

[48] Simon Ditchfield, "Gli Oratoriani e l'agiografia: Filippo Neri, Cesare Baronio, Antonio Gallonio," in *La canonizazzione di Santa Francesca Romana*, ed. Alessandra Bartolomei Romagnoli and Giorgio Piccaso (Florence, 2013), 195–214.

[49] The autograph manuscript, entitled *Istoria della divotissima e spiritualissima vergine di Giesu Christo Helena nobilissima Romana di Casa Massimi*, may be found at BVR, MS I. 11. The work was printed in Rome in 1857.

[50] Bilinkoff gives the example of the Jesuit Pedro de Ribadeneyra's unpublished vita of Estefania Manrique: Jodi Bilinkoff, "The Many 'Lives' of Pedro de Ribadeneyra," *Renaissance Quarterly* 52 (1999): 180–96, at 188–89, and her important monograph study: *Related Lives: Confessors and Their Female Penitents, 1450–1750* (Ithaca, NY, 2005).

Giulias, and a Domitilla.⁵¹ As we have seen, Gallonio would also publish a life of the namesake of this last sister: Flavia Domitilla, niece of one saint, the consul Flavius Clemens, and closely associated with two more, her eunuch servants Nereo and Achilleo (although they actually lived in the third century CE). All of them were believed (mistakenly) to have been martyred together by Emperor Domitian in the first century CE.⁵² Shortly after Gallonio's death, Rubens depicted them more than life-size on slate panels that still flank the High Altar of the Oratorian mother church of Santa Maria in Vallicella, across from the soldier saints Papias and Maurus (whose relics lay under the high altar), who are shown on either side of Pope Gregory the Great (who had built the original church on the site).⁵³ Gallonio's illustrated vita was an extract from a much more ambitious project he never published, but which now, thanks to the patient work of Giuseppe Finocchiaro, can be identified as nothing less than a visual counterpart to what might perhaps be considered "Baronio's Baedeker": the Roman Martyrology of 1586.⁵⁴

Such a context helps us to understand the papal enthusiasm, shared by Clement VIII, Paul V, and Urban VIII, for signaling their universal, apostolic authority by sponsoring (directly or indirectly) carefully staged translations of the bodies of Roman virgin martyr saints: Cecilia (1599), Agnese (1605), Bibiana (1624), and Martina (1634) in their respective Roman churches. In all cases sponsorship included extensive artistic remodeling of the martyrs' tombs, and in all but one case (Agnese) the writing of individual lives of each saint.⁵⁵ Cardinal Paolo Camillo Sfondrati, briefly papal nephew to Gregory XIV (December 1590 to October 1591), undertook the restoration of his titular church of Santa Cecilia (complete with Stefano Maderno's revolutionary recumbent

---

⁵¹ Giovanni Incisa della Rocchetta and Nello Vian, eds., *Il primo processo per S. Filippo Neri nel Codice Vaticano Latino 3798 e in altri esemplari dell'archivio dell'Oratorio di Roma*, 4 vols. (Vatican City, 1957–63), vol. 1, 205 n. 568.

⁵² Antonio Gallonio, *Historia della Vita e martirio de'gloriosi santi Flavia Domitilla vergine, Nereo et Achilleo et più altri con alcune vite brevi dei santi parenti di S. Flavia Domitilla et alcuni annotationi* (Rome, 1597).

⁵³ Michael Jaffé, *Rubens and Italy* (London, 1977), ad indicem under S. Maria in Vallicella.

⁵⁴ Giuseppe Finocchiaro, *Antonio Gallonio scrittore di Santi: Agiografia nella Roma di Clemente VIII* (Florence, 2019).

⁵⁵ Antonio Bosio, *Historia passionis sanctae Caeciliae* (Rome, 1600); Domenico Fedini, *La vita di S. Bibiana vergine e martire romana* (Rome, 1627); Marsilio Honorato, *Historia di santa Martina vergine, martire Romana* (Rome, 1635).

sculpture), on the alleged site where she lived, was martyred, and later reburied.[56] Sfrondati also took over restorations of Santa Agnese fuori le mura, the titular church of Gregory's successor Leo XI. When the latter died after less than a month, the next pope, Paul V, nonetheless paid to restore Santa Agnese's high altar. In the case of Saint Bibiana, whose translation coincided with the Holy Year of 1625, Pope Urban VIII (r. 1623–44) paid to restore the church where she was buried, thought to sit on the site of her family palace. This work included commissioning a sculpture of the saint by the young Gian Lorenzo Bernini, the famed sculptor and architect, with frescoes by Pietro da Cortona. The pope also wrote a new hymn in Bibiana's honour to be included in the revised Roman Breviary of 1631. Finally, for Saint Martina, Urban VIII visited her recently rediscovered body in the church of Santi Luca e Martina on the edge of the Roman forum on November 28, 1634, barely a month after its discovery on October 25, accompanied by a dozen cardinals. He proclaimed a plenary indulgence for those who visited her tomb.[57] By supporting martyr-virgin saints performatively rather than solely through print, these popes championed the particularization of the universal in the most concrete way possible, in precisely the period when saint-making took on the shape and norms that continued to be in force until 1983, when Pope John Paul II published the Apostolic constitution on the revised procedure for the canonization of saints, *Divinus perfectionis magister*.[58]

From this comprehensive hagiographical remodeling, which involved the printing of new lives with their liturgical offices, artistic reimaginings, and a central role in papal ceremonial, it was but a small and logical step for saints' lives to furnish the subject matter for the latest genre of music theater to appear in the early seventeenth century: opera. Stefano Landi (1587–1639), a Barberini client with a long career in sacred music for St. Peter's and various confraternities, composed *S. Alessio*, a *dramma musicale* devoted to the life of the fictional early Christian Roman patrician St. Alessio of Rome, with libretto by Giulio

---

[56] Tobias Kämpf, "Framing Cecilia's Sacred Body: Paolo Camillo Sfondrato and the Language of Revelation," *Sculpture Journal* 6 (2001): 10–20.
[57] Jörg Merz, "Le Sante Vergini Romane: Die Repräsentation frühchristlicher Jungfrauen und Märtyrerinnen in ihren restaurierten Titelkirchen in Rom im späten 16. und im 17. Jahrhundert," *Wiener Jahrbuch für Kunstgeschichte* 57 (2008): 133–64.
[58] John Paul II, "Apostolic Constitution: Divinus Perfectionis Magister," www.vatican.va/content/john-paul-ii/en/apost_constitutions/documents/hf_jp-ii_apc_25011983_divinus-perfectionis-magister.html (accessed June 13, 2025).

Rospigliosi (the future Pope Clement IX).⁵⁹ This early opera was possibly performed in 1631, though more likely 1632, within the Palazzo Barberini. A revised and expanded form was repeated at the Carnival of 1634, on the visit to Rome of Alexander Charles Vasa, brother of Ladislau IV King of Poland.⁶⁰

Such diverse genres helped readers and listeners from different strata of society to "see," "hear," and sound out the saints and their miraculous deeds. Indeed, throughout the period covered by this volume (and beyond) saints' lives were commonly performed or read out orally in company rather than read in private silence. We have it on Daniello Bartoli's own testimony that even his decidedly lengthy and learned life of Ignatius, which became the first volume of his *Istoria*, was read out in the refectory of his Roman residence.⁶¹ As Jenny Richards has rightly insisted, we must learn to listen to early modern texts and, as scholars and readers, become much more voice aware. The "Age of Print" did not silence the written word. Rather it "aligned eye, tongue and ear" and "allowed oral literacy to flourish" as never before.⁶²

ASYMMETRICAL SANCTITY BETWEEN CELEBRATION AND CONTROL

Much historical attention has centred on official Roman attempts to regulate sanctity and its representation. Miguel Gotor's pioneering study into the determining role of the Inquisition or the Holy Office, as opposed to the Congregation of Rites, in controlling saint-making and veneration must be given its due.⁶³ Gotor drew attention to the Inquisition's decree on March 13, 1625, forbidding any public manifestations of cult for those figures who had died with a saintly reputation, but who had not yet received official papal recognition. The ban extended to the depiction of halos or miracles, whether in paint, in

---

⁵⁹ Frederick Hammond, *Music and Spectacle in Baroque Rome: Barberini Patronage Under Urban VIII* (New Haven, CT, 1994), 201–5, 210–14. Hammond also scotches the claim that Gian Lorenzo Bernini was in any way involved in designs for the sets used to stage the opera.

⁶⁰ *Il S. Alessio dramma musicale dall'eminentissimo et reverendissimo signore Card. Barberino fatto rappresentare* (Rome, 1634).

⁶¹ See the letter from Bartoli to Giovanni Girolamo Brunelli, dated December 30, 1651, in *Lettere edite ed inedite del padre Daniello Bartoli e di uomini illustri scritte al medesimo*, ed. Giuseppe Boero (Bologna, 1865), 13.

⁶² Jennifer Richards, *Voices and Books in the English Renaissance: A New History of Reading* (Oxford, 2019), 10.

⁶³ Gotor, *I beati del Papa*. See also Chapters 7 and 13 in this volume.

engravings, or in person (by the placing of candles or other lights before an image or tomb). This blanket ban, however, was modified by a measure making significant concessions, published barely five years later on June 5, 1631.[64] This measure granted permission to authors wishing to write about such aspiring saints, so long as they printed a disclaimer at the beginning of their work declaring that any (miraculous) deeds being recounted did not claim or presuppose official, papal recognition.[65] The proviso had been made necessary as a consequence of the decree issued at the same time – *de non cultu* – which specifically required that to be considered for beatification or canonization, candidates should show no evidence of having "jumped the gun" by manifesting signs of a cult, either textual or visual as well as liturgical, before receiving official, papal approval.

This disclaimer will be familiar to scholars working in the field of early modern hagiography or just plain sacred erudition; it prefaced all such works from 1631 onward. Of course, technically speaking, such a requirement only affected lives and histories printed in areas within the Italian peninsula that recognized the authority of the Roman Inquisition (though examples of books printed elsewhere in Europe can also be found). At that time this excluded Sicily and Sardinia. In the cases of the Republic of Venice and Kingdom of Naples, such external legal interference was reluctantly tolerated and sometimes contested. However, the relevant point for this chapter is that the papacy, in the form of the Holy Office, was now seen to acknowledge publicly the distinction between those who officially enjoyed veneration, including all who had been papally canonized, and the many more men and women whose saintly reputation was merely local and unofficial.

Scholars today might wonder why the Roman Catholic Church tried so actively to control the process of bestowing official saintly status on holy men and women, yet at the same time continued to engage with unofficial saints: the ever-growing host of figures who enjoyed a local or at least non-universal reputation for sanctity. Its ongoing involvement with both groups should not be considered a

---

[64] This bid to simultaneously prohibit and yet to permit and enable distinctly echoes Gregory XIII's bull of 1573, which moderated the recent imposition of the revised Roman saints' calendar by permitting those churches and dioceses that possessed relics of a saint to celebrate their cult with a proper office. See Chapter 11 in this volume.

[65] For an indicative "Protestatio," see *Urbani VIII Pontificis Optimi Maximi Decreta servanda in Canonizatione et Beatificatione Sanctorum* (Rome, 1642), 18–19.

dissonant tension, but rather a consequence of Rome's objectives: on the one hand, to defend itself from Protestant polemic; on the other, to regularize devotion and worship. This last obligation also required it to balance a set of universal protocols with the particular needs of local churches throughout the Roman Catholic world.

The problem with unsanctioned saints was not limited to contemporary *beati moderni*; it also had a historical component, which was itself debated. Two contrasting numbers exemplify the tension within Catholicism over the quantity of medieval saints. On the one hand, there is the low-ball figure provided by Angelo Rocca (1545–1620), an Augustinian friar whom Sixtus V had called to oversee the reorganization of the Vatican Library consequent of that pope's enlargement and building of new premises. Rocca's *De canonizatione sanctorum* (1601) lists only fifty-seven official canonizations between 803 (when Charlemagne successfully petitioned Pope Leo III to canonize the Northumbrian eighth-century missionary St. Suidbert, allegedly the Bishop of Verdun) and 1601, the canonization of Raymond of Penyafort, the thirteenth-century Dominican friar and canonist.[66] Rocca's figure contrasts with modern calculations; David Herlihy, for instance, counted 3,276 saints over fifteen centuries using the *Bibliotheca hagiographica latina*.[67] Early modern Roman officials preferred saints to be much rarer than they were and the process of saint-making to be more rigorous than in the early Middle Ages. This discrepancy can perhaps be aptly described as "asymmetric sanctity," a term I have borrowed and adapted from Jonathan Greenwood. It captures the difficulties surrounding the multimedia celebration of innumerable saints and miracles attributed to holy women and men who had never had their claims vetted by papally appointed authorities, in contrast to the much more restricted number who had.[68] Many of these unvetted

---

[66] Angelo Rocca, *De canonizatione sanctorum commentarius* (Rome, 1601), 135–41. This contrasts with the seventy-one canonization proceedings that André Vauchez lists over the shorter time period of 1198–1432 in his *Sainthood in the Later Middle Ages* (Cambridge, 1997), 559–83.

[67] Robert Bartlett, *Why Can the Dead Do Such Great Things? Saints and Worshippers from the Martyrs to the Reformation* (Princeton, NJ, 2013), 138. This figure should be compared with the number of 20,000 saints listed in the *Bibliotheca sanctorum*, 12 vols. (1961–69), which remains "the most complete scholarly list of saints from all periods" (Bartlett, *Why Can the Dead*, 137). The *Bibliotheca sanctorum* has since been supplemented by three further volumes plus two dedicated specifically to saints in the Eastern Church, which number a further 2,200 entries.

[68] See Jonathan Greenwood, *Sainthood in the Early Modern Hispanic World: Ignatius Loyola, Miracles and the Transformation of Canonization* (forthcoming). Greenwood

saints appeared in the Roman liturgy and so achieved special prominence. Several hundred holy men and women populated the widely consulted registers of mostly Roman Christian martyrs, arranged sequentially by month, such as the so-called *Hieronymian Martyrology*.[69] Their presence in the prayer cycle made it impossible to avoid venerating certain saints who predated the advent of papal canonization. Several key dates have been proposed for the demarcation moment between the formally canonized – an extremely limited few – and the exponentially bigger number of the informally venerated: the publication of the Canons and Decrees of the Council of Trent in 1564, the foundation of the standing papal committee or Congregation of Rites and Ceremonies in 1588, and the publication of the papal brief *Coelestis Ierusalem cives* that brought to a close a decades-long process of gradual change in 1634. More important than all these dates, however, is 1586. This year marked the publication of the first edition of the Roman Martyrology printed with historical notes (composed by the Oratorian Cesare Baronio), which was also the first to be decreed as universally valid for all of those who celebrated the Roman rite.[70] It drew on Usuard and Ado of Vienne's ninth-century revisions of the Hieronymian Martyrology and then built on the valuable work of the fourteenth-century bishop Petrus de Natalibus before incorporating Guglielmo Sirleto's edition of Greek saints' lives: the *Menologion*.[71] It was Sirleto (1514–1585) who had commissioned Baronio to provide the Roman Martyrology with extensive historical notes for every single day of the calendar year, as well as an introductory historical treatise on the book's origins and history.[72] By asserting the historical and liturgical

---

describes the mismatch between what miraculous evidence the Sacred Congregation of Rites and that of the Holy Office regarded as admissible in support of a candidate for beatification and canonization and that which supporters of such candidates believed worthy of note, celebration, and dissemination.

[69] This volume had in fact been compiled in Italy in the mid-fifth century but owed its canonical status to the traditional but mistaken attribution to St. Jerome (c. 341–420).

[70] However, the *editio princeps* of the *Martyrologium romanum*, which Gregory XIII mandated to be of universal authority, was published in 1583.

[71] Giuseppe A. Guazzelli, "L'Immagine del *Christianus Orbis* nelle prime edizioni del Martyrologium romanum," *Sanctorum* 5 (2008): 261–84. On the range and significance of Sirleto's interests and achievements, see Benedetto Clausi and Santo Lucà, eds., *Il "Sapientissimo Calabro": Guglielmo Sirleto nel V Centenario della Nascita, 1514–2014: Problemi, ricerche, prospettive* (Rome, 2018). See also Gigliola Fragnito's entry on Sirleto in *Dizionario biografico degli italiani*, 92 (2018).

[72] Guazzelli, "Cesare Baronio e il Martryrologium romanum," in *"Nunc alia tempora, alii mores": Storia e Storici in età postridentina*, ed. Massimo Firpo (Florence, 2005), 47–89.

legitimacy of so many early Christian saints whose cults preceded papal canonization, Sirleto therefore deserves the credit for enabling this balancing act of "asymmetric sanctity," that is, the successful inclusion of not only official saints whose cults were explicitly permitted to be celebrated publicly in every Roman Catholic church and chapel but also the many unofficial holy men and women who were denied universal public veneration while still enjoying the unofficial, courtesy title of "saint" or "blessed."

Sirleto, not coincidentally, was also the energizing coordinator of the revision of the Roman Breviary (1568) and Missal (1570), related office books of the Roman liturgy, as part of a single, overarching project to bring the Roman liturgy back to "the original standard of the Fathers [of the Church]" (*ad pristina patrum norma*).[73] A central task of this project was to reduce the number of saints' feasts that interfered with the reading of the ordinary, ferial (non–feast day) liturgy and prevented the Breviary from serving as a "pocket seminary" for its clerical readers.[74] The ferial office was built on the reading of the psalms (all 150 of which were meant to be read weekly) together with other, key passages from Scripture (many of which were accompanied by brief homilies, frequently of patristic authorship). Between 1100 and 1500 at least 200 saints had been added to the calendar, the festal office marginalizing the non-festal ones. Such an unbalanced use of the Breviary had a major impact on its users, since liturgy, prayer, and the cult of saints served important didactic functions. These functions need reaffirming, since many historians have approached religious pedagogy only by questioning the effectiveness of the stipulation made in the Canons and Decrees of the Council of Trent that every diocese set up a seminary for the education and training of its secular clergy.

One further, crucial detail in what has come to be known collectively as the Tridentine reform of worship is that the papal bull, *Quod a nobis*, which prefaced the revised Roman Breviary of 1568, was careful to retain those offices of unofficial local saints whose veneration could prove uninterrupted use of at least 200 years. This concession was probably the direct result of a memorandum, early in April 1562, from Spanish bishops to the papal legates who oversaw proceedings during

---

[73] Simon Ditchfield, "Giving Tridentine Liturgy Back Its History," *Studies in Church History* 35 (1999): 199–226, at 207.

[74] For this and what immediately follows, see Simon Ditchfield, "Tridentine Worship and the Cult of Saints," in *The Cambridge History of Christianity*, vol. 6: *Reform and Expansion 1500–1660*, ed. Ronnie Po-chia Hsia (Cambridge, 2007), 201–24, at 201–2.

the final period of the meeting of the Council of Trent. The memorandum suggested that "a unified breviary and missal [be] used in all churches *with a separate proper of saints* [i.e., a supplement of saints' offices] *for each diocese*."[75]

It is thus entirely of a piece that Cardinal Sirleto, the person who had done so much to demonstrate that the reformed Roman Rite was consonant with the practices of the early Church, should also have encouraged Baronio to write a comprehensive history of that Church, which would demonstrate that it had remained "ever the same" (*semper eadem*). In this way liturgy and history were brought into line with one another in mutually reinforcing symmetry. This history became the twelve-volume *Annales ecclesiastici* (1588–1607), which established Baronio as the Eusebius of the Counter-Reformation age. It was a direct rebuttal to the Protestant *Magdeburg Centuries* (1559–74), written by a team of scholars under the direction of Matthias Flacius Illyricus (1520–1575), which had argued the contrary: that Roman Catholic practice had progressively fallen away from Apostolic purity from at least the sixth century CE.[76]

Thus, when looking at hagiography in first 150 years of the Reformation era, we cannot consider only the tightened-up criteria for canonizing new saints, as emphasized by Peter Burke, Miguel Gotor, and others. We must also recognize the historical recovery of knowledge, especially about early Christian holy heroes, which, as we have seen, should be dated from the publication of the revised Roman Martyrology with Baronio's historical annotations in 1586. Moreover, we must remember that even the refurbishment of canonization measures still took half a century to complete, with the publication of the papal brief *Caelestis Ierusalem cives* on July 5, 1634. For this reason, I have stressed the importance of hagiography and its cognate genres, both printed and performed, in helping the Roman Catholic Church and its adherents to negotiate the tensions between what was permitted and

---

[75] Uwe Michael Lang, *The Roman Mass from Early Christian Origins to Tridentine Reform* (Cambridge, 2022), 346 (emphasis added). See also the papal concession of 1573 noted above in n. 64 that all churches of the Spanish Church be permitted to celebrate the feasts of saints whose relics they possessed with their own proper office (*officium proprium*) even if they were not included in the Roman calendar of saints. See also Chapter 11 in this volume.

[76] On Baronio, for a reliable guide to the extensive literature, see Giuseppe A. Guazzelli, Raimondo Michetti, and Francesco Scorza Barcellona, eds., *Cesare Baronio tra santità e scrittura storica* (Rome, 2012), and on Flacius: Harald Bollbuck, "Searching for the True Religion: The Church History of the Magdeburg Centuries Between Critical Methods and Confessional Polemics," *Renaissance Studies* 35 (2021): 100–117.

what was to be actively promoted. Perhaps, given the increasingly global nature of early modern Catholicism, we can also suggest that hagiography, in its multisensory presentations, created in the minds, eyes, and ears of its various Roman Catholic audiences a collective "imagined community" fully two centuries before Benedict Anderson identified and located the secular counterpart of this phenomenon.[77]

---

[77] Benedict Anderson, *Imagined Communities: Reflections on the Origin and Spread of Nationalism* (London, 1983).

13 Images

CLOE CAVERO DE CARONDELET

The image of the saint in early modern Catholicism is often viewed as the visual manifestation of a tightly controlled ideological machine. As the usual narrative goes, following the radical challenge to traditional forms of Christian devotion brought about by the advent of Protestantism in the sixteenth century, the Catholic Church had to reaffirm the legitimacy of the saintly image. In response to its critics, the Church drew on ancient and medieval apologists for images, but also sought to impose new forms of control over their appearance in order to avoid doctrinal errors and superstitious practices. The image of the saint, as a central aspect of the cult of saints more generally, thus became a standard element of confessional propaganda in the hands of the Counter-Reformation Church.

It was during the twenty-fifth session of the Council of Trent, celebrated in 1563 and dedicated to the veneration of the relics and images of the saints, that the ecclesiastical elite sought to produce a general guide for the imagery of saints across the Catholic world.[1] According to the traditional historiographical narrative, this decree served as both the culmination of the debate about sacred images and its conclusion, inaugurating a period of intense aesthetic transformation.[2] But this account is incomplete for several reasons. To begin with, the status of saint's image continued to be deeply debated in the following century. This was due to a variety of reasons, chiefly the fact

---

[1] See Pierre Antoine Fabre, *Décréter l'image? La XXVe session du Concile de Trente* (Paris, 2013), and the recent discussion by Wietse de Boer, *Art in Dispute: Catholic Debates at the Time of Trent: With an Edition and Translation of Key Documents* (Leiden, 2022).

[2] Seminal studies are Werner Weisbach, *Der Barock als Kunst der Gegenreformation* (Berlin, 1921), and Emile Mâle, *L'art religieux après le Concile de Trente* (Paris, 1932). More recently, see Marcia B. Hall, *The Sacred Image in the Age of Art: Titian, Tintoretto, Barocci, El Greco, Caravaggio* (New Haven, CT, 2011).

that the statements dedicated to sacred images in the famous Tridentine decree were far from precise. The decree stated that images of saints should be venerated for the prototypes they represented, but apart from a general reference to avoiding lasciviousness and superstition it did not specify the criteria for creating such likenesses. In fact, rather than being the final word on sacred images, the 1563 decree marked the point of departure for decades of intense theological and artistic debate about how should saints look. Popes, bishops, and inquisitors issued and enforced regulations that sought to impose uniformity on images of saints in an attempt to restrain the previous license taken by artists and patrons. The authors of treatises on art did the same, publishing their recommendations on how the saints and other individuals renowned for holiness should be represented. In turn, artists attempted to meet the challenge of innovating saintly images in what was an increasingly regulated environment. But the existence of prescriptive regulations should not be taken as evidence for compliance with them. Instead, the sustained elaboration of decrees and guidelines by ecclesiastical authorities, theologians, and art theorists during this period tells a very different story, which is that images of saints continued to be a constant concern for the post-Tridentine Church, and one very difficult to resolve. It was nearly impossible to foresee all the potential problems in the artists' representation of saints, and therefore no set of instructions was able to account for all the possible norms. The difficulties in implementing such guidelines across the diverse geography of the early modern Catholic world, ranging from Manila to Lima, was another issue. The establishment of new, centralized image regulations paved the way, perhaps paradoxically, for increasing attempts to bypass official controls, and helped give rise to new forms of artistic exploration, expertise, and ingenuity. The image of the saint after Trent was not, or not only, a rigid bulwark against heresy. It was a site of deep uncertainties and imaginative creativity.

LEGISLATING THE IMAGE OF THE SAINT AFTER TRENT

Images and sainthood have had a symbiotic relationship since the medieval period. On the one hand, the Church's recognition of a man, woman, or child as a saint led to the creation of hundreds of paintings, sculptures, and prints depicting the portrait, miracles, or martyrdom of these holy individuals. On the other, portraying an individual with signs of sainthood frequently led to what has been termed "canonization by image," the unofficial bestowal of the category of saint that over time acquired an official status.³ In other words, sainthood gave rise to images, and images could likewise confer sainthood. The Protestant Reformation wrought a dramatic change in the status of the saintly image. Criticism of the veneration of images of saints led the Catholic Church to halt all canonizations, and this in turn slowed down the production of images of saints. It was not until 1588 that canonizations began again, and by then the Roman Congregation of Rites had been created as the entity responsible for regulating and processing the creation of saints.⁴ However, the vague text of the Council of Trent's 1563 decree on sacred images failed to provide guidelines for how the images of saints should look. The council had granted bishops responsibility over the control of sacred images, but without issuing any specific directives concerning how they should do so. With few exceptions, episcopal instructions, provincial councils, and diocesan synods were similarly vague when addressing sacred imagery.⁵ As a result, theologians and artists went on to propose new sets of guidelines for how sacred images should appear.⁶ Notable attempts were made by the Bishop of Bologna, Cardinal Gabriele Paleotti (1522–1597), with his *Discourse on Sacred and Profane Images* (1582), which he intended as a guide for bishops, intellectuals, and artists interested in sacred art. Later, he also sought to create a system for expurgating sacred images akin to the Inquisition's treatment of books.⁷ The failure or limited success of these and other initiatives led to the sacred image, and thereby images of saints, being relegated to a

---

[3] André Vauchez, *Sainthood in the Later Middle Ages*, trans. Jean Birrell (Cambridge, 1997), 88.

[4] Simon Ditchfield, "Tridentine Worship and the Cult of Saints," in *The Cambridge History of Christianity*, vol. 6: *Reform and Expansion, 1500–1660*, ed. Ronnie Po-chia Hsia (Cambridge, 2007), 201–24; and Giovanni Papa, *Le cause di canonizzazione nel primo periodo della Congregazione dei Riti: 1588–1634* (Rome, 2001).

[5] See Alfonso Rodríguez G. de Ceballos, "Image and Counter-Reformation in Spain and Spanish America," in *Sacred Spain: Art and Belief in the Spanish World*, ed. Ronda Kasl (Indianapolis, 2009), 14–35; and Grace Harpster, "Sacred Images in Carlo Borromeo's *Instructiones*: Between Liturgy and the Antique," in *Renaissance Religions: Modes and Meanings in History*, ed. Peter Howard, Nicholas Terpstra, and Riccardo Saccent (Turnhout, 2021), 155–74, at 163.

[6] Gabriele Paleotti, *Discourse on Sacred and Profane Images*, ed. Paolo Prodi and trans. William McCuaig (Los Angeles, 2012); Christian Hecht, *Katholische Bildertheologie der frühen Neuzeit. Studien zu Traktaten von Johannes Molanus, Gabriele Paleotti und anderen Autoren* (Berlin, 2016 [1997]); Johannes Molanus, *Traité des saintes images*, ed. François Boespflug, Olivier Christin, and Benoît Tassel (Paris, 1996); and Francisco Pacheco, *Arte de la pintura*, ed. Bonaventura Bassegoda (Madrid, 1990).

[7] See Paleotti, *Discourse on Sacred and Profane Images*; and Paolo Prodi, "Ricerche sulla teorica delle arti figurative nella riforma cattolica," *Archivio italiano per la storia della pietà* 4 (1965): 121–212.

regulatory limbo. The late sixteenth-century revival of canonizations made it clear that the Tridentine guidelines' lack of clarity posed serious risks for the Catholic Church, leading in turn to a long and meandering process during which the Church endeavored to create regulations for the images of saints.

The impossibility of visually distinguishing between saints officially canonized by the papacy and individuals merely renowned for their holiness became the focus of the post-Tridentine debates on images of saints. This was by no means a new problem. The absence of any regulation defining the category of candidates for sainthood, as well as of their cult and imagery, had posed a problem for the Church since the medieval period.[8] The seventeenth-century redefinition of beatification as an indispensable intermediary step for canonization was not accompanied by any regulation about what the images of those who attained the status of blessed (*beatus*) should look like, and this further complicated the artistic panorama. In addition to the subsequent proliferation of categories applied to those aspiring to canonization, a significant degree of uncertainty persisted concerning the image of the saint itself. Artistic practices such as the historic tradition of painting halos for individuals renowned for holiness, as well as the custom of enhancing portraits of prominent individuals with markers of sanctity, had blurred the visual language of sainthood for many centuries.[9] For the post-Tridentine Church, this lack of visual clarity posed a challenge for its ambition of controlling sainthood across the Catholic world.

The Jesuit campaign to promote the canonization of their founder Ignatius of Loyola (1491–1556, beat. 1609, can. 1622) highlighted how the lack of regulation concerning images of saints could lead to disputes over papal authority on sainthood. Among the many images produced at this time, one printed portrait of Ignatius of Loyola represented him as a saint with his head surrounded by a radiant light. The image also included depictions of his miracles, and above there was a scroll inscribed *"beatus"* (Figure 13.1). In many ways, this composition continued the medieval tradition of canonization by image, but due to the

---

[8] Vauchez, *Sainthood*, 85–88; Papa, *Le cause*, 147–214.
[9] See Ruth S. Noyes, "On the Fringes of Center: Disputed Hagiographic Imagery and the Crisis over the *Beati moderni* in Rome ca. 1600," *Renaissance Quarterly* 64, no. 3 (2011): 800–846, at 813–14; James Hall, "Simulating and Appropriating the Sacred: The Background to a Papal Ban on Saintly Portraits of Non-Saints," in *Sacred Images and Normativity: Contested Forms in Early Modern Art*, ed. Chiara Franceschini (Turnhout, 2021), 118–35; and, most recently, Adam Jasienski, *Praying to Portraits: Audience, Identity, and the Inquisition in the Early Modern Hispanic World* (University Park, PA, 2023).

Figure 13.1 Francesco Villamena, *Life and Miracles of Ignatius of Loyola*, 1600 (Vienna: Albertina Museum)

renewed interest in controlling images and the increasing anxiety regarding new saints, the image was condemned. Clement VIII (r. 1592–1605) gave orders for this print as well as other similar ones to be removed from circulation because they falsely suggested that Loyola's beatification had been granted papal approval. This conflict gave rise to intense debates on the status of candidates for sainthood, and eventually led the pope to establish the Congregation of the Blesseds (Congregazione dei Beati) in 1602, as the standing committee in charge of controlling the cult of the early modern candidates for sainthood and regulating the imagery associated with them.[10]

---

[10] Images were also at the center of debate in the coetaneous campaigns for the canonizations of the Jesuit Francis Xavier (1506–1552, beat. 1619, can. 1622) and the Oratorian founder Philip Neri (1515–1595, beat. 1615, can. 1622). Noyes, "On the

The impact of the Jesuit campaign on image regulations was exceptional, but the problem it revealed was not. Similar cases of perceived visual transgressions in the representations of candidates for sainthood were encountered across the Catholic world. Barely a decade later, for example, the Archbishop of Valencia and the Spanish Inquisition ordered the confiscation of images of the recently deceased priest, Jerónimo Simón, who was renowned for his sanctity, and it was explicitly stated that no signs of sainthood could be included in portraits of him.[11] Here again, the wide diffusion of printed portraits was both an instrument in the hands of those who wished to promote the cult and the act that caught the attention of the concerned authorities. As with other aspects of the Catholic reform, the regulation of images of saints was implemented as a response to existing problems.

The most significant post-Tridentine reform of the image of the saint occurred during the papacy of Urban VIII (r. 1623–44). One of his principal aims was to put an end to the existing ambiguity regarding the status of recently deceased individuals renowned for their sanctity, and images played a central role in this issue. However, he also issued regulations to restrict the veneration of ancient saints whose cults had never been granted papal approval. Urban's reform evolved over various phases through two decrees issued in 1625 by the Congregation of the Holy Office (i.e., the Roman Inquisition) and then a papal brief issued in 1634. The first decree (March 13, 1625) was the most severe of one of the three. It prohibited any portrayal of aspiring saints with visible signs of sanctity, such as halos, aureoles, or beams of light, unless these had been explicitly approved by the papacy. It also ruled that lamps, candles, or ex-votos could not be placed before their tombs, as these were practices that suggested these individuals had the status of a saint. Furthermore, the decree completely prohibited the production and circulation of hagiographic texts and images concerning candidates for sainthood, a ban that covered all media and locations, whether public or private. Urban VIII's decree established punishments for the patrons of such works, as well as the artists and writers who produced them.

Fringes." For the cult of the blessed, see Simon Ditchfield, "'Coping with the beati moderni': Canonization Procedure in the Aftermath of the Council of Trent," in *Ite inflammate omnia: Selected Historical Papers from Conferences Held at Loyola and Rome in 2006*, ed. Thomas M. McCoog (Rome, 2010), 413–40. On the Congregation of the Blesseds, see Miguel Gotor, *I beati del papa: Santità, inquisizione e obbedienza in età moderna* (Florence, 2002), 127–253.

[11] Miguel Falomir, "Imágenes de una santidad frustrada: El culto a Francisco Jerónimo Simón, 1612–1619," *Locus amoenus* 4 (1998–99): 171–83.

Given the far-reaching impact of this regulation across the Catholic world – at that time there were hundreds of cults that had not been granted explicit papal approval – before long a number of details were revised. In an appendix, any cults considered ancient were excluded from the decree's remit.[12] Then, just a few months later, on October 2, 1625, Urban VIII permitted the conservation of portraits and ex-votos of aspiring saints so long as they were kept in private spaces. The aim of this modification was to facilitate the opening of new beatification and canonization processes.[13] On July 15, 1634, Urban VIII extended the two inquisitorial regulations through his brief *Caelestis Hierusalem Cives*, which defined cults as ancient if they had been actively venerated since at least 1525.[14] In addition to circulating by word of mouth and in manuscript, in 1642 the two decrees and the papal brief were revised and printed in a small volume.[15] The attention with which Urban VIII regulated the representation of saints and candidates for canonization underscores the central role images played in the construction of post-Tridentine sainthood.

Although it is undeniable that Urban's reforms had a major impact on the image of the saint, a number of aspects require closer scrutiny. The papacy hoped that this new series of regulations would lead to the construction of a reliable visual language of sainthood. It sought to provide guidance for painters and patrons when creating and commissioning images of both official and aspiring saints, while also ensuring that the faithful could clearly distinguish between the two categories. Yet it is unreasonable to suppose, as traditional historiography would have it, that issuing these new regulations resolved immediately and definitively all problems concerning images of saints. As will be seen below, episodes of both conscious and involuntary visual subversion constantly occurred over the decades that followed. In short, the question of how and to what extent Urban VIII's reform actually affected the production of images of saints, whether officially recognized or those who were still only candidates, remains open for debate.

Reception of the new papal regulations differed across the diverse Catholic regions. Indeed, one of the reasons why the papacy issued the brief in 1634 was that it was apparent that in Madrid and elsewhere the

---

[12] Gotor, *I beati*, 285–87.
[13] Ibid., 295.
[14] Ibid., 308–20.
[15] Ibid., 320–25.

1625 decrees were not being observed.[16] Second, responsibility for enforcing the regulation of images of saints was undertaken by the Inquisition as part of its remit to prevent the dissemination of heresy. Already in 1551, the Spanish Index established the inquisitors' obligation to prevent derision or irreverence to the saints through images.[17] But it is crucial to remember that while the Inquisition was a centralized institution, it was overseen by different authorities (the pope for the Italian Inquisition and the Spanish crown for the Spanish Inquisition) and its more than twenty tribunals were spread across territories as diverse as Rome, Mexico, and the Canary Islands. This meant that inquisitors controlling representations of saints had to combine their adherence to general instructions with the acknowledgment of local artistic traditions, which often resulted in discordant assessments of similar images across the Catholic world.[18] It is only through a comparative study of the way in which the different inquisitions and inquisitorial tribunals applied Pope Urban's legislation that we can form an in-depth understanding of how the image of the saint functioned during the Counter-Reformation.

TRUE PORTRAITS OF NON-SAINTS

The true revolution of the image of the saint during the Counter-Reformation was brought about by the development of portraits of aspiring saints.[19] These were, in other words, individuals, alive or recently deceased, who were famed for their sanctity, but whom the Catholic Church had not officially recognized as saints. This category included individuals who were being examined for the intermediary phase of beatification. These so-called Servants of God gradually began to enjoy the then still unregulated title of Venerable during the seventeenth century. The most significant images of potential candidates for sainthood produced during this period were those that fall into the category of

---

[16] Ibid., 287–88, 307–9.

[17] Chiara Franceschini, "Arti figurative e Inquisizione. Il controllo," in *Dizionario Storico dell'Inquisizione*, ed. Adriano Prosperi (Pisa, 2010), vol. 1, 102–5.

[18] On the coexistence of different, competing norms around sacred images, see Chiara Franceschini, "Introduction: Images as Norms in Europe and Beyond: A Research Program," in *Sacred Images and Normativity: Contested Forms in Early Modern Art*, ed. Chiara Franceschini (Turnhout, 2021), 13–27, at 16–19.

[19] As pointed out in Helen Hills, "'The Face Is a Mirror of the Soul': Frontispieces and the Production of Sanctity in Post-Tridentine Naples," *Art History* 31, no. 4 (2008): 547–73, at 549.

the "true portrait." This type of portrait was characterized by an attentive and individualized representation of the subject's physiognomy, which it claimed to reproduce accurately.[20] The sacred authority of these images functioned akin to the *acheiropoietoi* (icons not made by human hands) of Christ, based on the understanding that, as faithful reproductions of a divine original, they were bestowed with sacred power. True portraits had been central to the iconography of the saints as early as the fifteenth century, and were especially important following the reactivation of canonizations after the Council of Trent. From the late sixteenth century onward, portraits of individuals renowned for their sanctity multiplied across the Catholic world. Made – or so it was said – as truthful depictions of their subjects' appearance, they were either painted while the pious individual was alive or on their deathbed, or else recourse was made to a funerary mask.[21]

Despite this aspiration to objective likeness, true portraits were, just like other images, the product of an artist's creative process. A drawing of the Archbishop of Milan, Cardinal Carlo Borromeo (1538–1584, can. 1610), made during the campaign for his canonization and attributed to Ambrogio Figino offers an insight into how they were made (Figure 13.2). The artist combined red and black chalk to animate the archbishop's features, thereby giving the spectator the impression that the artist had made the drawing following their firsthand observation of his subject. However, this process of artistic animation conceals the fact that the drawing was most probably made from a funerary mask, or else a carved bust of the archbishop, and so what we see is the product of the painter's artifice.[22] Irrespective of how they were produced, true portraits of aspiring saints were deployed as mediators for the sought-after status of saint across the Catholic world.

---

[20] Fernando Quiles, "Between Being, Seeming and Saying: The *Vera Effigies* in Spain and Hispanic America during the Baroque," in *Fiction sacrée: Spiritualité et esthétique durant la premier âge moderne*, ed. Ralph Dekoninck, Agnès Guiderdoni, and Emilie Granjon (Leuven, 2013), 181–200; Marta Cacho Casal, "The 'True Likenesses' in Pacheco's *Libro de retratos*," *Renaissance Studies* 24, no. 3 (2010): 381–406; Jasienski, *Praying to Portraits*, 53–90. See also Emily C. Floyd, "Reconstructing the Faces of the Saints, an Interview with Friar Luis Enrique Ramírez Camacho, O. P.," *MAVCOR Journal* 1, no. 1 (2017).

[21] This is discussed in Nina Niedermeier, *Die ersten Bildnisse von Heiligen in der Frühen Neuzeit: Portätähnlichkeit in nachtridentinischer Zeit* (Regensburg, 2020). For antecedents, see Urte Krass, *Nah zum Leichnam: Bilder neuer Heiliger im Quattrocento* (Munich, 2012), 87–210.

[22] Grace Harpster, "Figino's Efficacy: Portraits, Votives, and Their Makers After Trent," *Oxford Art Journal* 44, no. 2 (2021): 226–45, at 233–34.

Figure 13.2 Ambrogio Giovanni Figino, *Carlo Borromeo*, c. 1563–1608. Inscription added in 1700 by Sebastiano Resta. (London: © The Trustees of the British Museum. All rights reserved)

By prohibiting the circulation and public display of the images of candidates for sainthood, Urban's reforms affected the status of their true portraits. The great majority of these were completed prior to these individuals' canonization or beatification, and thus became objects inherently subject to inquisitorial vigilance. However, the benefits of these portraits far exceeded any risks. If the portrayed individual was eventually beatified or canonized, the true likeness became the most valuable image and principal model used for constructing their iconography as a saint. The religious orders knew this all too well, and besides investing in campaigns to promote canonizations, they took great care to produce portraits of their notable members.[23] Obtaining and conserving portraits of men and women renowned for their holiness, or who had died as martyrs, were therefore of indisputable value for promoting the formal commencement of papal inquiries into their sainthood.

The portrait of the aspiring saint was unstable in the sense that it was susceptible to being transformed into an image of a saint (and therefore into a sacred image) following the conclusion of the legal canonization process. Furthermore, it was visually ambiguous. In Counter-Reformation art, the distinction between a saint and a non-saint was very often nonexistent. A revealing passage in the influential treatise *Art of Painting* (1649), by the painter and writer Francisco Pacheco (1564–1644), indiscriminately refers to official saints and potential candidates for sainthood while discussing the importance of true portraits as a mode of representing saints.[24] The portrait that Diego Velázquez painted of Jerónima de la Fuente (1556–1630), a member of the Order of St. Clare, just before she set sail for Manila in the Philippines to found a convent, illustrates this widespread phenomenon of visual uncertainty (Figure 13.3). The painting's life-sized scale and the nun's severe features, which deny any possible idealization, suggest this portrait was based on direct observation of the nun. On the other hand, the full-length, three-quarter profile composition with the nun holding a crucifix evokes pictorial conventions for Franciscan saints that would have been familiar to the public during this period.[25] Velázquez deliberately ensured that the comprehension of the sitter's identity was not to be derived from her image; instead, it depended to a large extent on a prior knowledge of Jerónima's renown for sanctity. There is nothing in the portrait that allows us to state with any degree of certainty whether this is the portrait of a saint, a nun who has been beatified, or simply a nun deemed worthy of having her portrait painted. It is only the inscription, which was added after the portrait was completed, that provides the spectator with the relevant information. Therefore, effigies of official saints and potential candidates for sainthood were to a large extent interchangeable.

---

[23] They also obtained the most saints. See Peter Burke, "How to Be a Counter-Reformation Saint," in *The Historical Anthropology of Early Modern Italy: Essays on Perception and Communication* (Cambridge, 1987), 48–62, at 45–55.

[24] Pacheco, *Arte de la pintura*, 710.

[25] Felipe Pereda, *Crime and Illusion: The Art of Truth in the Spanish Golden Age* (Turnhout, 2018), 94–119; Tanya J. Tiffany, *Diego Velázquez's Early Paintings and the Culture of Seventeenth-Century Seville* (University Park, PA, 2012), 66–67.

Figure 13.3 Diego Velázquez, *The Nun Jerónima de la Fuente*, 1620. Madrid: Museo del Prado (History & Art Collection/Alamy Stock Photo)

The lack of any clear distinction between portraits of official saints and those of mere candidates for sainthood prompted the development of artistic practices that blurred further the vague boundaries between the two. Across both the Old and New Worlds, the Inquisition moved against those who overstepped the limits of what were considered to be acceptable conventions by removing hundreds of portraits of aspiring saints from circulation. One particular practice that regularly emerges from the inquisitorial archives is the use of existing images of official saints as the basis for portraits of other individuals renowned for their holiness. A portrait of Eugenia de la Torre, a Spanish visionary woman tried by the Inquisition in 1639, was purportedly superimposed onto an image of St. Teresa of Ávila. Deeply concerned with this portrait's potential danger, the inquisitors ordered it to be taken down from the home where it was displayed and sequestered it. This pictorial practice, which sought to exploit the authority of an official saint to promote an aspiring one, underscores the unstable nature of saints' images, and of early modern portraiture more generally.[26] By pushing the already porous limits between the figurative genres of the sacred image and the portrait, artists and the promoters of causes for canonization challenged the homogenous and centralized image of sainthood to which the post-Tridentine Church aspired.

One of the major differences between the images of aspiring and official saints was how they were displayed. Following the resumption of canonization, Church authorities often questioned the exhibition of images of candidates for sainthood. Urban VIII prohibited their public display and veneration and restricted their contemplation to private spaces, commonly the interior of a convent to which the individual had belonged. The anxiety surrounding the images of candidates for sainthood also affected the material with which they were made. Although promoters frequently commissioned portraits on canvas, such as the aforementioned image of Jerónima de la Fuente, the most broadly used medium was the printed image. Prints, being inherently multiple and portable, permitted the wide circulation of images of those aspiring to canonization. Moreover, the close association of printed images with practices of private devotion may have also appeared to some as an opportunity to sidestep the contemporary concerns over the public display of portraits of candidates to sainthood. For example, missionary orders circulated hundreds of prints of their respective martyrs, glorifying their evangelizing experience while defending their potential claims to sainthood.[27] On other occasions, the biographies of the potential saints were paired with a portrait of their subject, thus exploiting an established publishing practice to promote their holiness.[28] For

---

[26] Jasienski, *Praying to Portraits*, 81–86. Also see Doris Bieńko Peralta, "Las *verae efigies* y los retratos simulados: Representaciones de los venerables angelopolitanos, siglos XVII y XVIII," in *La función de las imágenes en el catolicismo novohispano*, ed. Gisela von Wobeser, Carolina Aguilar, and Jorge Luis Merlo (Mexico, 2018), 269–77; and Anne Jacobson Schutte, "'Questo non è il ritratto che ho fatto io': Painters, the Inquisition and the Shape of Sanctity in Seventeenth-Century Venice," in *Florence and Italy: Renaissance Studies in Honour of Nicolai Rubenstein*, ed. Peter Denley and Caroline Elam (Exeter, 1988), 419–27.

[27] Grace Harpster, "Illustrious Jesuits: The Martyrological Portrait Series *Circa* 1600," *Journal of Jesuit Studies* 9, no. 3 (2022): 379–97 (381–87); Cloe Cavero de Carondelet, "A Copperplate of the Dominican Martyrs of Japan Reused by Murillo," *Print Quarterly* 40, no. 3 (2023): 251–64.

[28] There are countless examples. See here Helen Hills, "'The Face Is a Mirror of the Soul,'" 566–70; and Helen Hills, "Demure Transgression: Portraying Female 'Saints' in Post-Tridentine Italy," *Early Modern Women: An Interdisciplinary Journal* 3 (2008): 153–207.

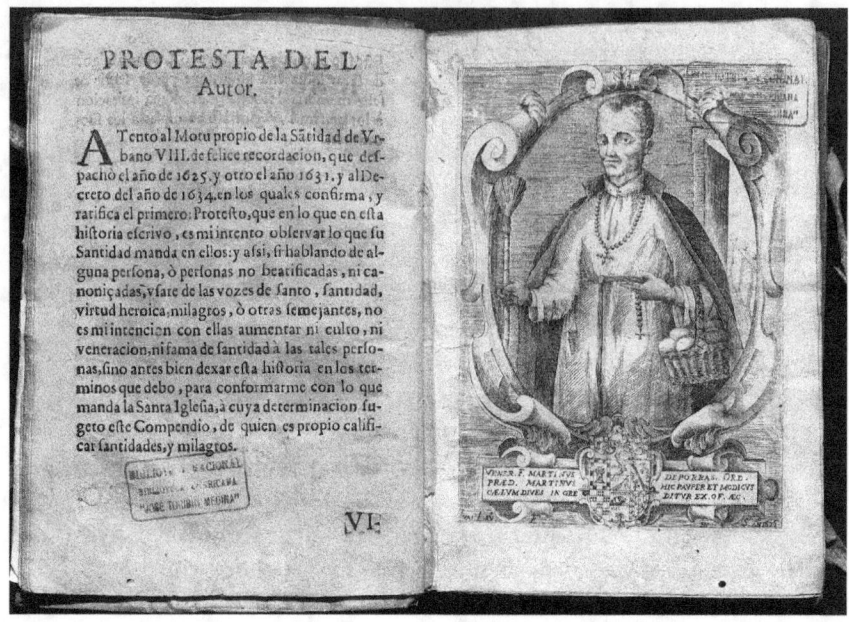

Figure 13.4 Juan de Laureano, *Fray Martín de Porres*, 1676. Included in Bernardo de Medina, *Vida prodigiosa del venerable siervo de Dios Fr. Martin de Porras* (Madrid, 1675). (Santiago de Chile: Biblioteca Nacional de Chile)

example, the earliest extant printed portrait of the Afro-Peruvian Dominican Martín de Porres (1579–1639, beat. 1837, can. 1962) was included as the frontispiece to the first biography of this friar in 1673. Such printed portraits often served as models for new images produced to further diffuse the candidates' claims for sainthood. This is the case with a rare portrait of Porres that survives stitched into the 1675 edition of his biography (Figure 13.4). The wear of the engraved plate can be discerned on this print, which signals how this portrait had been replicated on a massive scale during the first stages of the lengthy campaign for his beatification.[29] Existing beyond the limits of legality, the images of potential candidates to sainthood coexisted in different media and various formats with images of official saints.

[29] Larissa Brewer-García, "The Composite Pardo of Seventeenth-Century Lima: Blackness, Whiteness, and Creole Self-Fashioning in the Earliest Portraits of Martín de Porres," *Colonial Latin American Review* 30, no. 2 (2021): 272–304; Celia L. Cussen, *Black Saint of the Americas: The Life and Afterlife of Martín de Porres* (Cambridge, 2014), 160–63.

REDEFINING THE HALO

In an attempt to visually distinguish official saints from candidates for sainthood, Urban VIII restricted the use of halos, beams of light, and luminous radiance to those who had been canonized by the papacy. The halo is a long-established symbolic element that was and still is used in Christian visual culture to identify those figures considered to be holy.[30] The form and materiality of halos have changed over time and place; they have ranged from perfect gold ovals and beams of light to a glowing resplendence surrounding the head of the individual considered to be a saint. On occasions these variations served as a visual mechanism for distinguishing between saints and candidates for sainthood, yet they have mostly been used in a more fluid and interchangeable manner.[31] It was the combination of the indiscriminate use of the halo and its immense efficacy as a sign of sainthood for both an educated and non-educated public that led post-Tridentine theologians to place it at the center of debates on sainthood. In the early seventeenth century members of the Congregation of the Blesseds engaged in a profound debate on whether candidates for sainthood should be represented with a halo or not, and, if so, what this type of halo should look like.[32] However, it would not be until the reform undertaken by Urban VIII that the halo was irreversibly redefined as a universal sign of a sainthood regulated by the papacy and policed by the Inquisition.

Urban's reforms established that a deceased individual who was renowned for their sanctity could be represented with a halo only after their canonization. Discovery of a halo on a candidate's portrait during beatification could invalidate their cause, reinforcing the importance of adhering to this norm. However, the visual clarity that the Church sought to achieve with this reform was constrained by the limited scope of efforts of the Inquisition and the relevant ecclesiastical authorities in charge of enforcing it. Research in inquisitorial archives has revealed cases when images depicting potential candidates for sainthood with halos were withdrawn from public view, thereby giving the impression

---

[30] For a survey of the history of the halo up until the fifteenth century, see Marthe Collinet-Guérin, *Histoire du nimbe des origines aux temps modernes* (Paris, 1961).
[31] Vauchez, *Sainthood*, 85–88, 98.
[32] Noyes, "On the Fringes"; Gotor, *I beati*, 127–253.

that the Inquisition enforced Urban's norms efficaciously.[33] However, in order to fully grasp the status of the halo after Urban's reforms, inquisitorial sources must be contrasted with other visual and textual sources. These demonstrate that during this period, hundreds of portraits of aspiring saints continued to include a halo, or were otherwise displayed in ways that departed from the papal decrees.

The afterlife of a series of images of the "Martyrs of Japan" is a good example of both the scope and limitation of Urban's regulations. When the first decrees were issued in 1625, the missionary religious orders whose members had been executed in Japan were immersed in numerous beatification processes in which images played a central role. The Franciscans martyrs of Nagasaki (d. 1597, beat. 1627) were the focus of one of the most dramatic episodes of censure caused by Pope Urban's decree. In 1626, the Sacred Congregation of Rites ordered the removal of a painting of the martyrs – it is not known whether they were depicted with or without halos – from the walls of the Roman Church of Santa Maria in Aracoeli because it contravened the prohibition on the public display of images of non-beatified individuals.[34] Nevertheless, the removal of this painting coincided with the production and circulation of several prints of other non-beatified martyrs of Japan who were depicted with halos. Published shortly before or just after the issue of Urban's decree, these printed images were not subject to the same censure as the Roman painting. One of these is the frontispiece to a book published in Madrid in 1626 (Figure 13.5). It depicts the haloed effigies of two Spanish Dominicans who had recently been martyred in Japan, a visual transgression that seemingly went unpunished. The contrasting fate of these images suggests that the ecclesiastical authorities implicitly or explicitly established hierarchies of priorities when it came to applying Pope Urban's guidelines. Images exposed publicly in churches had greater potential to represent an individual's sanctity, and given that they were unique objects, it is reasonable to suppose that they were subject to greater and more efficient control than prints.

Caught in an increasingly regulated context, promoters of aspiring saints and artists experimented with different media, iconographies, and forms of display as a way to advance their agendas. The development of

---

[33] José Sánchez Castro, "La censura de la figuración artística en España (1487–1820)," *Boletín del Museo e Instituto "Camón Aznar"* 65 (1996): 37–98 (56, 58); Jasienski, *Praying to Portraits*, 152.

[34] Hitomi Omata Rappo, *Des Indes lointaines aux scènes des collèges: Les reflets des martyrs de la mission japonaise en Europe (XVIe–XVIIIe siècle)* (Münster, 2020), 353–54.

Figure 13.5 Alardo de Popma after Agustín Leonardo de Argensola, *Alonso Navarrete and Alonso de Mena, Martyrs in Japan*. Frontispiece of Pedro Fernández Navarrete, *Conservación de Monarquías* (Madrid, 1626). (Munich: Bayerische Staatsbibliothek)

alternative signs of sanctity was one of the strategies that emerged in this moment. Perhaps the most widespread practice was the representation of candidates for beatification with pseudo-halos surrounding their heads.[35] An extraordinary example of this is provided by a print of the Dominican nun Rose of Lima (1586–1617), created after her death but long before her beatification (1668) and canonization (1671) (Figure 13.6).[36] One of the arches of the intricate architectural interior

---

[35] This was first signaled by Romeo De Maio, *Pittura e Controriforma a Napoli* (Rome, 1983), 138. See especially Hall, "Simulating and Appropriating."

[36] There are at least two different versions of this print. See Ramón Mújica Pinilla, *"Rosa limensis": Mística, política e iconografía en torno a la patrona de América* (Lima, 2001), 324–27.

Figure 13.6 Jean Matheus (printmaker) and Jean Messager (publisher), *Rosa de Santa María (St. Rosa de Lima)*, c. 1619–20 (Amsterdam: Rijksmuseum)

surrounding the figure of the nun conspicuously frames her head, thereby exploiting the evocative power of the halo but without transgressing Urban's regulation.

At other times, those promoting the cause of a potential candidate for sainthood used more imaginative strategies and made recourse to other figurative elements from the repertory of signs traditionally associated with holiness. An illustrative case is that of the portraits of the Bishop of Puebla, Juan de Palafox y Mendoza (1600–1659), who became the focus of an intense phenomenon of popular devotion while still alive. Among the thousands of painted and engraved portraits of Palafox that were produced in Puebla at that time, were some in which he appeared with angelic wings. The addition of this motif was clearly intended to elevate and distinguish the bishop's allegedly extraordinary qualities from those of other people. Despite their enormous symbolic potential, the wings were not explicitly prohibited in Urban's decree and therefore their use in the portrait of a potential saint was a priori legitimate. However, the tribunal of the Inquisition of New Spain decided that the wings evoked sainthood in the same way as a halo, and prohibited their use. These illegitimate portraits of Palafox were destroyed and repainted, and it seems that none have survived.[37] The invention of new pictorial signs of holiness complicated the visual distinction between saints and non-saints that Urban VIII sought to establish, revealing that the new visual landscape of sainthood was more heterogeneous and irregular than is generally assumed.

Pope Urban's reform also redefined the status of the halo in the images of early Christian and medieval saints, which particularly affected those medieval saints whose regional cult had existed for centuries but who had never received papal approval. In these cases, Urban established a regulatory *viam cultus* to conclude their canonization. The success of this process depended on the saints' promoters being able to demonstrate that the candidate had been the object of an uninterrupted cult from at least 1525 (in other words, 100 years prior to the publication of the 1625 decree). During the subsequent process of compiling and assessing evidence, images of saints were considered convincing proof of the long-standing existence of their cult.[38] Therefore, and in contrast to what happened with early modern candidates for sainthood, the display of portraits of medieval saints with halos was not considered a point of dispute, but rather core proof of their cult, and, therefore, evidence of their de facto sanctity. By permitting the coexistence of haloed images of medieval saints both with and without

---

[37] Jasienski, *Praying to Portraits*, 91–122. On the wider controversy around Palafox's cult, see Antonio Rubial García, *La santidad controvertida: Hagiografía y conciencia criolla alrededor de los venerables no canonizados de Nueva España* (Mexico, 1999), 239–47.

[38] María Cruz de Carlos Varona, "'The Authority of Sacred Paintbrushes': Representing Medieval Sainthood in the Early Modern Period," in *Sacred Spain: Art and Belief in the Spanish World*, ed. Ronda Kasl (Indianapolis, 2009), 100–119; Simon Ditchfield, "How Not to Be a Counter-Reformation Saint: The Attempted Canonization of Pope Gregory X, 1622–45," *Papers of the British School at Rome* 60 (1992): 379–422.

papal approval, Urban's reform created a new zone of visual uncertainty about saintly status.

Given their technical expertise and knowledge, painters were often called on as expert witnesses for the process of evaluating the images of medieval saints proposed for canonization *viam cultus*.[39] A key example is that of Ferdinand III (d. 1252), King of Castile and León, who was canonized in 1671. His conquest of territories in southern Spain following the collapse of the Almohad Caliphate's control over Al-Andalus had led to this king being venerated as a Reconquest saint. In the late sixteenth century, Sixtus V (r. 1585–90) officially acknowledged his sainthood and explicitly approved representations of Ferdinand with a halo. However, Urban's new decrees obliged his promoters to submit a request for official recognition to Rome. Between 1649 and 1652, and as part of the process of compiling evidence of the uninterrupted nature of this cult, the painters Bartolomé Murillo and Francisco López Caro were commissioned to inspect extant effigies of the king. The paintings they assessed included many artworks whose iconography was based on a modern print of Ferdinand III with a halo, issued in Rome with the express permission of Urban VIII (Figure 13.7). However, the images that were most valuable as evidence in favor of the king's sanctity were clearly the oldest. Among these was a painting of Ferdinand III, haloed and surrounded by mace bearers, in the Convent of San Clemente, which Murillo and López Caro evaluated as "over one hundred years old."[40] Whether made with or without papal approval, centuries ago or more recently, in portraits of medieval saints the halo was a constant and effective sign of sainthood.

HOW TO LOOK LIKE A COUNTER-REFORMATION SAINT

The aims of papal regulations concerning the images of saints that emerged in the wake of the Council of Trent were only partially achieved. It was not long before the shortcomings of both the Church's and the Inquisition's capacity to effectively control the visual representation of saints across the vast Catholic geographic territories under their supervision became apparent. However, perhaps the most

---

[39] De Carlos Varona, "The Authority," 106–7.
[40] Fernando Quiles, "En los cimientos de la iglesia sevillana: Fernando III, rey y santo," *Boletín del Museo e Instituto "Camón Aznar"* 75–76 (1999): 203–49 (206); Amanda Wunder, "Murillo and the Canonization Case of San Fernando, 1649," *Burlington Magazine* 143, no. 1184 (2001): 670–75, at 672.

Figure 13.7 Charles Audran, *King Ferdinand III*. Frontispiece of *Hispalen. Canonizationis servi Dei, Gloriosissimi, Inuictissimi, ac Sancti Regis D. Ferdinandi III, Regis Castellae* (Rome, 1638). (Madrid: Biblioteca Nacional de España)

significant outcome of the normative redefinition of the image of the saint was the parallel development of a renewed visual ambiguity. Promoters of candidates for sainthood imitated the conventions used for the images of official saints, and likewise created new visual strategies for evoking the status of sainthood. All these factors led to an uncertain context in which the Church's concern to establish the distinction between saints approved by the papacy and those individuals who merely had a reputation for sanctity yielded results that were neither clear nor unequivocal. The image of the saint that emerged from the Counter-Reformation was not that sought after by the papacy. Instead, an alternative and far broader image emerged, the outcome of the creativity of both artists and patrons, as well as of popular devotion.

Over thirty years ago, Simon Ditchfield proposed a fruitful alternative to Peter Burke's seminal essay on sainthood during the Counter-Reformation by shifting attention away from the success to the failure of canonization processes.[41] Adopting this perspective for an analysis of images of saints can offer a range of insights that provide a deeper understanding of the visual culture of the Counter-Reformation, which illuminates the problematic issues faced by the papacy, inquisitions, and other ecclesiastical authorities.[42] Moreover, as in other fields, the history of the image of the saint has, as a rule, been written by the winners. Historians of early modern art have paid considerable attention to the immense iconographic corpus of saints who were beatified or canonized between the sixteenth and eighteenth centuries typically in triumphant and positive language.[43] Contrasting such images with depictions of individuals who were denied canonization, or those who became mired in bureaucracy for centuries, or those whose canonizations were never officially pursued would open up new and stimulating lines of inquiry for the status of the image of the saint during the Counter-Reformation.[44] Moving beyond a regional focus to take a broader, comparative perspective within the larger Catholic world would also help to complicate the supposed universality of Urban's guidelines, while also revealing differences and similarities between various territories and artistic contexts. Essentially, we must study the image of the saint not as an end product, but as part of a complex process that united individuals from a range of professions and social strata from across the world. By analyzing the ways in which artists made men, women, and children famed for their sanctity look like Counter-Reformation saints, we will be able to better understand the nature of the relationship between images and sainthood.

---

[41] Ditchfield, "How Not to Be"; Burke, "How to Be."
[42] Other productive avenues of research include interrogating the visual relationship between sanctity and place. See Helen Hills, "How to Look like a Counter-Reformation Saint," in *Exploring Cultural History: Essays in Honour of Peter Burke*, ed. Melissa Calaresu, Filippo De Vivo, and Joan-Pau Rubiés (Farnham, 2010), 207–30.
[43] A central study is Vittorio Casale, *L'arte per le canonizzazioni: L'attività artistica intorno alle canonizzazioni e alle beatificazioni del Seicento* (Turin, 2011).
[44] Raphaèle Preisinger et al., "Promoting Sanctity by the Means of Artworks: The GLOBECOSAL Project," in *Profiling Saints: Images of Modern Sanctity in a Global World*, ed. Elisa Frei and Eleonora Rai (Göttingen, 2023), 97–124.

14 Literature

SUSANNAH BRIETZ MONTA

Any writing about a saint could arguably constitute hagiographic literature. This essay necessarily narrows its focus to examine how writing about saints and sanctity affected and was impacted by early modern literary cultures. The work of early modern English authors makes a particularly good subject for the study of sanctity as that work operated against a backdrop of rapid religious change and persecution that made the construction of sanctity an immediate, urgent concern. Attacks on late medieval hagiography by reformers such as John Foxe and John Bale exposed the wondrous aspects of saints' lives as either cynical fabrications or historical evidence of demonic activity.[1] The Counter-Reformation response to Protestant criticisms such as these was to prune hagiographic excesses and to insist on the validity and spiritual usefulness of what remained.[2] Yet Protestant writers did not discard traditional saints wholesale. For instance, St. George's Day remained in the *Book of Common Prayer*, and while many English Protestants either dismissed George's famous dragon fight or turned it into light entertainment, Edmund Spenser in his *Faerie Queene* invested the dragon fight with serious spiritual meaning.[3] Nor did Catholic writers simply

---

[1] Helen Parish, *Monks, Miracles, and Magic: Reformation Representations of the Medieval Church* (London, 2005). Foxe's attitude toward medieval saints' lives was, however, more complex than his most overt statements might indicate; see Susannah Brietz Monta, *Martyrdom and Literature in Early Modern England* (Cambridge, 2005), chap. 3, and Thomas S. Freeman and Susannah Brietz Monta, "'Straunge and Prodigious Miracles'? John Foxe's Reformation of Virgin Martyr Legends," *Reformation* 24 (2019): 76–91.

[2] See, for instance, Cesar Baronio's preface to his *Martyrologum Romanum* (Rome, 1586); he writes that he has revised the calendar of saints after studying learned sources and in ways faithful to history. Sherry Reames, *The Legenda Aurea: A Reexamination of Its Paradoxical History* (Madison, WI, 1985), has shown that sixteenth-century humanists such as Juan Vives, Melchior Cano, and Georg Witzel exemplify a Catholic intellectual scorn for the excesses of the *Legenda Aurea*, already discredited before the onset of the Reformation.

[3] Monta, *Martyrdom and Literature*, chap. 4.

recycle traditional forms and approaches; they adapted imaginative retellings of saints' lives to contemporary controversies, religious changes, and political pressures.

In the case studies discussed below, taken from three broad generic categories – drama, poetry, and prose – literary work engages in substantive, contemporary dialogues between the shifting conventions of literary genres and of hagiography. This literature serves not just as a record of changing ideas about sanctity in the post-Reformation period or as an unwitting preserver of hagiographic traces, but also as a site where those changes are negotiated. In other words, these responses were *creative*. The enduring impact of hostile Protestant polemic still makes itself felt in the scholarly tendency to see writing about saints either as a relic of the medieval past or as an archaeological trace left in other forms of writing. The neglect of Catholic writers has also enabled the underestimation of the impact of ideas about sanctity on literary culture. For this reason each of the case studies below focuses on English Catholic writers, with brief comparative glances at Protestant and at continental figures. English Catholic writers addressed readers facing the legal proscription of their religion even as they remained in contact with the evolving practices of post-Tridentine Catholicism. These authors revitalized saints as intercessors and models for holiness while using ideas about sanctity to push the boundaries and conventions of their chosen genres with aims that were simultaneously religious and literary. Their writings not only worked to figure persuasive, sophisticated forms of sanctity; they were meant to sanctify literary culture as well.

HISTORY OR HAGIOGRAPHY? THE CASE OF EDMUND CAMPION'S *AMBROSIA*

During the early modern period, the generic boundaries of "hagiography" were far from set, such that hagiography overlapped significantly with other forms of writing. In the *Oxford English Dictionary*, "hagiography" is first documented for the seventeenth century in Peter Heylyn's *Historie of St. George*, which describes another work as a "Hagiographie or History of the Saints."[4] Indeed, in the early modern period history and hagiography could be subsumed, though not without complexity, under the concept of *historia sacra*, or history of the

---

[4] Peter Heylyn, *The historie of that most famous saint and souldier of Christ Jesus; St. George of Cappadocia* (London, 1631), 10.

community of the Church broadly construed.⁵ *Historia sacra* could take multiple forms, including saints' lives, ecclesiastical history, and liturgy. It was not merely a backward-looking phenomenon but was sensitive to developments in humanist historiography. Lorenzo Valla's scholarship both disproved the historicity of the Donation of Constantine and drove his hagiographical compositions.⁶ *Historia sacra* was not declining in the sixteenth century; if anything, there was a renaissance after the Council of Trent.⁷ At the same time, in the English context, saints' plays were on the wane, just as the history play gained prominence as a new genre in the later sixteenth century.

St. Edmund Campion's neo-Latin play *Ambrosia*, authored by an Englishman trained at Oxford and on the continent, offers an excellent opportunity to study the interplay between hagiography and history, a saint's life and a history play, within English and European contexts. Campion's play, written in 1578, stages episodes from the life of St. Ambrose, the fourth-century Church father and bishop of Milan. It illuminates the boundaries of the edifyingly believable in late sixteenth-century Catholic intellectual circles, as well as the inevitably politicized dimensions of early modern writing about saints. Campion was born in London in 1540 and was educated at a grammar school in the city; he entered Oxford's new St. John's College in 1558 (the college had recently been founded, with spectacularly ill timing, to preserve Catholicism in England). He received a BA in 1561 and an MA in 1564. In 1568, Campion was named a junior proctor of the University and was ordained a deacon in 1569. He then left St. John's after his conversion to Catholicism, likely sometime in 1569. He traveled to Ireland, then to Douai, where he took a degree in scholastic theology, and thence to Rome, where he entered the Jesuit order. He served his novitiate in Prague and was ordained there in 1578. In the spring of 1580, the English Jesuit Robert Persons requested Campion for a mission to

---

⁵ Simon Ditchfield has argued that the distinction between hagiography and history was made firm in continental historiography only in the nineteenth century: "'Historia Magistra Sanctitatis'? The Relationship Between Historiography and Hagiography in Italy After the Council of Trent (ca. 1564–1742)," *Studies in Medieval and Renaissance History* 18, no. 3 (2006): 159–84.

⁶ Alison Frazier, *Possible Lives: Authors and Saints in Renaissance Italy* (New York, 2005), esp. chapters 2 and 4.

⁷ See Ditchfield, "'Historia Magistra Sanctitatis'?". Influential examples include the works of Cesar Baronio, Luigi Lippomano, and Laurentius Surius. The sixteenth century also saw major editions of patristic saints' *Opera*, including the Erasmian edition of Ambrose's works (in 1538) from which Lippomano and Surius drew for their primary documents.

England. Campion was betrayed by an acquaintance in July 1581, arrested, tortured, and, alongside two other priests, executed in December 1581. Campion's literary accomplishments and his martyrdom together guaranteed posthumous international fame.[8]

It is tempting to read *Ambrosia* in light of Campion's subsequent martyrdom. One early reader did so; in an epigram that prefaces the play in its single extant manuscript, this reader argues that the play's staging of the discovery of martyrs' relics is prophetic of Campion's own fate.[9] The play is certainly interested in the conflicts between state and religion that ultimately cost Campion his life. It is just as interested, however, in defending hagiography against Protestant polemical attacks. In this latter aim, it is part of a broad effort. As shown in Chapter 12 in this volume, many Catholic reformers shared what John Cox has called a "skeptical faith," that is, a commitment to pruning hagiography of its least substantiated elements and a humanist interest in the value of the edifying – even when the edifying might not meet modern understandings of historicity.[10] Campion's play may be situated within these efforts. At least one reader understood the play's defensive aims; manuscript annotations on the play's first two acts indicate contemporary sources that corroborate and explain Campion's scenes.[11] The play's generic hybrid of saint's play and history play, in other words, resonates with developments in early modern Catholic writing about saints.

Like other Jesuit neo-Latin dramas, Campion's *Ambrosia* is a didactic play for student actors. First performed in Prague in 1578, a city divided roughly between a Catholic elite and a Protestant populace, it

---

[8] On Campion's biography, see Michael A. R. Graves, "Campion, Edmund [St. Edmund Campion] (1540–1581)," *ODNB*, and Thomas M. McCoog's introduction to *The Reckoned Expense: Edmund Campion and the Early English Jesuits* (Rochester, NY, 1996).

[9] Simons includes this epigram in his edition of the play (Campion, *Ambrosia: A Neo-Latin Drama by Edmund Campion, S.J.*, ed. Joseph Simons [Assen, 1970], 2). All citations of *Ambrosia* are to line numbers provided in this edition; I have sometimes adapted Simons's translations slightly.

[10] For instance, John Cox argues that More's and Erasmus's critiques of faked miracles manifest a "skeptical faith" in which critique of fake miracles coexisted with a desire to preserve apparently genuine marvels (*Seeming Knowledge: Shakespeare and Skeptical Faith* [Waco, TX, 2007], chap. 1).

[11] The annotations may stem from the manuscript's owner, Jakob Gretser (a recognized neo-Latinist), or may originate with Campion; source and analogue annotations are a common feature of later Jesuit dramas. The surviving manuscript is in codex 221 of the Studienbibliothek Dillingen (Dillingen Research Library, Dillengen an der Donau, Germany), fols. 135–69. See Simons's introduction, xi.

was praised in its own day.[12] *Ambrosia* contains several confrontational episodes from Ambrose's life. In 386, Ambrose forced a standoff with the emperor Valentinian and his mother Justina over a request that he surrender a basilica for Arian worship. The standoff was resolved in part by Ambrose's fortuitous discovery or "invention" of the relics of two previously unknown martyrs, Saints Gervasius and Protasius. The relics' location was revealed to Ambrose in a vision; the relics' historicity was established by a text found buried with them. The wonders these relics worked enabled Ambrose to win his struggle with the Arian imperial court. The difference between the hagiographic use of *inventio* as "finding" and the English valence of "invention" with possible pejorative connotations of fabrication points nicely to early modern controversies over the episode's veracity.[13] After treating the Gervasius and Protasius events, the play portrays Ambrose's role in the conversion of St. Augustine and then devotes its second half to Ambrose's 390 rebuke of the emperor Theodosius for colluding with a massacre at Thessalonika.

The play gives a Catholic view of the proper relationship between secular and ecclesiastical authorities.[14] Ambrose was a controversial figure in the years following the Elizabethan Settlement. Campion may have known the contours of the controversy from his years at Oxford. For example, John Jewell, stung by the Catholic Thomas Harding's accusation that English churchmen were subject to their

---

[12] The epigram in the play's single manuscript lists its performance date as October 1578 (2–3). Simons lists early modern publications that praise Campion's *Ambrosia*. These include the *Concertatio ecclesiae Catholicae in Anglia* (Trier, 1588), f. 67t (a Latin poem by Gregory Martin); Pietro Bombino, *Vita et Martyrium Edmundi Campiani Martyris Angli e Societate Jesu* (Mantua, 1620), in which Campion's teaching abilities are praised as well as his play; and Philippe Alegambe, *Mortes illustres et gesta eorum de Societate Jesu* (Rome, 1657). The 1631 Antwerp edition of Campion's *Rationes decem* prints a letter from Campion to a fellow Jesuit in which Campion states that he no longer has the *Ambrosia* manuscript and that the play should be revised by a skilled person before it is performed again. There is evidence for its performance at Munich in 1591 as well as in Prague in 1578. See Simons, ix–xi.

[13] Neil B. McLynn criticizes those who see in the episode either proto-modern skepticism on the part of Justina or cynical manipulation by Ambrose: "the fourth-century cult of the martyrs was not a pantomime staged for the vulgar but a channeling of powerful energies too intractable for the bishop to have controlled at will, and too pervasive for him to have thought to try" (*Ambrose of Milan: Church and Court in a Christian Capital* [Berkeley, CA, 1994], 215).

[14] Alison Shell, "'We Are Made a Spectacle': Campion's Dramas," in McCoog, ed., *The Reckoned Expense*, 103–18; Robert S. Miola, "Jesuit Drama in Early Modern England," in *Theatre and Religion: Lancastrian Shakespeare*, ed. Richard Dutton, Alison Findlay, and Richard Wilson (Manchester, 2003), 71–86.

prince in religious matters, responded with Ambrosian authority: "We say to the prince as St. Ambrose sometime said to the emperor Valentinian ... 'Trouble not yourself, my lord, to think that you have any princely power over those things that pertain to God.'"[15] (Jewell was careful to suggest that Ambrose was at his firmest with Arian heretics, not Christian emperors.[16]) Elizabeth's dean of St. Paul's, Alexander Nowell, saw Ambrose's example of ministerial rebuke as fitting with exhortations in Calvin's work.[17] In the Protestant martyrologist John Foxe's *Actes and Monuments*, Ambrose's authority is occasionally invoked, as by the martyr John Philpot, who quotes Ambrose: "the thinges of God are not subject to the power and authority of Princes."[18]

Yet Foxe also questions the association of Ambrose's authority with histories of "strange and unnecessarie miracles."[19] Indeed, while Gervasius and Protasius occasionally merit brief mentions in English Protestant histories of the early Church, the miracles associated with their relics, which helped Ambrose turn the tables on secular authorities, were most often adduced as examples of Catholic historical abuses.[20] By contrast, in sixteenth-century Catholic sources concerning Gervasius and Protasius, including those mentioned in the play's manuscript annotations, their miracles were defended, as in Laurentius Surius's *De probatis sanctorum historiis*.[21] Campion's *Rationes decem*, a defense of the Catholic faith written for an English Protestant audience, briefly invokes Arius as the forerunner of modern heresy and

---

[15] *Works of John Jewel*, ed. J. Ayre, vol. 4 (Cambridge, 1850), 898; cited in Patrick Collinson, "If Constantine, then also Theodosius: St. Ambrose and the Integrity of the Elizabethan *Ecclesia Anglicana*," in *Godly People: Essays on English Protestantism and Puritanism* (London, 1983), 109.

[16] Collinson, "If Constantine, then also Theodosius," 116. The relatively conservative Richard Hooker remarked that the histories of Ambrose were unusual, "strange and admirable" (ibid., 114), but with uncertain analogy to the present.

[17] Ibid., 113. As Collinson discusses, Ambrose figures in the Cartwright/Whitgift debates and appears in Bishop Thomas Bilson's anti-Jesuit treatise *The True Difference Between Christian Subjection and Unchristian Rebellion* (London, 1585); Bilson suggests that Jesuits, in particular, have misused Ambrose's story.

[18] *Acts and Monuments* (London, 1570), 1967.

[19] Ibid., 119.

[20] George Abbott, *The reasons which Doctour Hill hath brought, for the upholding of papistry, which is falsely termed the Catholicke religion* (Oxford, 1604), 248–49; Richard Baxter, *The safe religion, or, three disputations for the Reformed Catholike religion against popery* (London, 1657), 448.

[21] The reference in Surius is at 699 (*De probatis sanctorum historiis*, vol. 3 [Cologne, 1572]); the note in the play's manuscript is at 20–21. Luigi Lippomano's *Historiae ... de vitis sanctorum* is another likely source for the play.

Ambrose's celebration of Gervasius and Protasius as an example of the proper disposition toward saints.[22] Campion's play arguably goes further, defending dramatic performance as a means for asserting both the historical and didactic value of *miracula*.

The medieval cliché of the performed, fake miracle persisted in Protestant polemic, Catholic reformers' work, and Shakespeare's *Henry VI, Part 2* alike. Yet in *Ambrosia* the performance of marvels is to enhance, not demystify, faith in the wonder. The play relates the miracles connected with the relics' invention through three performative modes: liturgy, sermon, and finally the acting out of two miracles. In the play's opening Justina and her general, aptly named Furius, plot Ambrose's destruction. After two scenes of Arian raging, Ambrose enters along with a choir of clerics singing antiphonally to praise the martyrs; the Arian pursuers watch and listen.[23] Campion omits the struggle over the basilica; the conflict instead is about doctrine, and the martyrs' histories affirm Nicene orthodoxy. A cleric bearing icons indicating the instruments of the martyrs' deaths narrates their stories "lest anyone should be ignorant of their history."[24] Campion is independent of his printed sources in the presentation of liturgy, the content of the sung texts, the insertion of historical narration into liturgical celebration, and the liturgy's precedence over other narrations of the martyrs' stories. Here, dramatic liturgical performance promotes the validity of the saints whose wonders the play will go on to describe.

Campion next stages the ecclesiastical authority behind liturgical performance. In the following scene, Ambrose delivers a sermon describing his finding of the relics, guided by a vision in which the Apostle Paul tells him where to look. Much of the sermon's content is collated from the hagiographical collections of Luigi Lippomano and Laurentius Surius, though Campion makes a few changes, establishing the vision as a divinely guided source that pointed Ambrose to historical and religious truth.[25] The sermon revises content from a surviving letter

---

[22] Campion, *Rationes decem quibus fretus, certamen adversariis obtulit in causa fidei* (Henley-on-Thames, 1581), 16v.

[23] Campion recalls the antiphonal psalm-singing Ambrose encouraged during his standoff with the Arian court, noted by Augustine in Book 9, chapter 7 of his *Confessions*.

[24] Campion, *Ambrosia*, 95–96.

[25] "Certos temporum articulos tenet / Ille, ille Deus" (148–49): Divine authority is emphasized by its placement at the phrase's end and the repetition of "Ille." In Surius, there is little sense that Ambrose's vision is opposed to history, or that the imaginative would be at odds with the historical. Surius marks the story of the vision with a sidenote that reads simply "Usus imaginum tempore S. Ambrosii" – the

of Ambrose to his sister in which Ambrose records that the Arians doubted the wonders worked by the relics. In the play, that doubt is intensified: Ambrose claims that the Arians called the martyrs "fictitious demons."[26] The play thus moves the Arians' skepticism from the miracles to the martyrs themselves. Campion seems concerned to present and defeat a challenge to the martyrs, perhaps glancing at parallels between the contested invention of these martyrs and contemporary controversies over true and false martyrs. Campion, as much as John Jewell and John Foxe, thinks analogically about history, permitting the past its own reality even as parallels with the present are highlighted, a technique some have found in Reformation-era revisions of saints' plays.[27] As in the source material, Ambrose's vision is confirmed by a text found with the saints' bodies that narrates the saints' lives and martyrdoms under Nero. Ambrose's wondrous vision and the relatively sober text reinforce each other.

After the sermon, Campion presents two scenes that perform miracles attested in his sources, miracles that resemble biblical wonders: the exorcism of a madman and the healing of a blind man.[28] The historical Ambrose described these miracles in a letter to his sister.[29] In Campion's play, the blind man states that he has been blind his entire life, and that his blindness is well known. He then prays to the martyrs for restored sight. His prayer is immediately granted, and he names what he now can see: reliquaries, altars, the gathered crowd (the scene

---

use of images in the time of St. Ambrose. While the phrase marks some historical distance – invoking a specific "time" – it does not imply that images or vision undermine history (*De probatis sanctorum historiis*, vol. 3, 700).

[26] "Hos Ariani daemones fictos vocant" (174). The letter is the primary modern source for the events surrounding the invention of Gervasius and Protasius; see McLynn, *Ambrose of Milan*.

[27] See Benjamin Griffin, "The Birth of the History Play: Saint, Sacrifice, and Reformation," *SEL: Studies in English Literature* 39, no. 2 (1999): 217–37; on analogical thinking in Elizabethan and early Stuart history writing (including drama), see Paulina Kewes, "History and Its Uses: Introduction," *Huntington Library Quarterly* 68, nos. 1–2 (2005): 1–31, esp. 13–14.

[28] The healing of a blind man at Milan through the intercession of Gervasius and Protasius is also reported in *Confessions*, Book 9, chapter 7, and in *De civitate Dei* 22.8, a chapter in which Augustine departs from his usual reluctance to invoke miraculous evidence.

[29] Epistola XXII, Ambrosius Mediolanensis, *Epistolarum classis I*, Patrologia Latina, vol. 16, ed. J. P. Migne (Paris, 1845), accessed in the Patrologia Latina Database (published by Chadwyck-Healey), https://artflsrvo4.uchicago.edu/philologic4.7/PLD/navigate/367/2/27. For an English version, see Ambrose of Milan, *Letters*, trans. Mary Melchior Beyenka. *The Fathers of the Church: A New Translation*, vol. 26 (Washington, DC, 2001), 376–84.

calls for at least eight characters on stage), details of Furius's costume, and so on. We are asked to see the stage anew through the actor's description; our vision aligns with his, encouraging corporate participation in a performed miracle. After hearing of these miracles, Justina countermands her threat, though again the struggle over the basilica is elided. For Campion, more than Church property is at stake; he seeks to align hagiography with edifying history and to defend against accusations of deceptive fiction-making.

Yet Campion also seems to wonder about his auditors' ability to learn what he has to teach. If we are to find Campion in the play, we might look not only to its martyrs but to the character of a teacher who appears late in the play. Unfortunately, his words are discounted; hounded by his high-born pupil's threats, he escapes into exile.[30] Campion, an exiled scholar in the 1570s, chose to critique Elizabethan Erastianism with a play about Ambrose, that most muscular of early Church bishops, using dramatic performance to defend saintly miracles and underscore the productive permeability between history and hagiography. His experiment with the emergent genre of the history play is itself a powerful argument – unheeded of course by the Elizabethan authorities whom he would shortly encounter – for the intertwining of hagiography and history, and for the continuity of the Church for which, in his own understanding, he would give his life.

LACHRYMOSE SAINTS AND THE REFORMING OF POETRY: ST ROBERT SOUTHWELL'S VERSE

Campion's fellow English Jesuit St. Robert Southwell (1561–1595) is best known for two things: his February 1595 martyrdom and his poetry, editions of which became early modern best-sellers on the legal London print market within one month of his execution on treason charges. In recusant Catholic manuscripts and early printed collections of his poetry, Southwell's verse is prefaced by a prose epistle in which he asserts that the art of poetry has been profaned by writers of amatory verse and strayed far from the religious poetics authorized by the Bible itself. In response, he proposes to "weave a newe Webb in theire owne loome," offering devotional verse that builds emotional range and intensity in part

---

[30] Campion, *Ambrosia*, Act IV, scene iv. In 1578 the Jesuit Superior General was still resisting any mission to England for fear that such a mission would become mired in politics and present an unacceptable risk to missionaries. See Graves, "Campion, Edmund."

by redeploying the conventions of love lyric.[31] Southwell's rebuke of contemporary literary fashions produced quick results; it is not an overstatement to claim that Southwell's work undergirds the flourishing of English devotional lyric in seventeenth-century print.[32]

Several of Southwell's new poetic webs offer reconceptions of sanctity. Southwell's saints, unlike Ambrose, are biblical figures. His desire both to write for Catholic readers *and* reform English literary culture is perhaps visible here, for biblical saints could serve as models for Catholic and Protestant readers alike.[33] Also unlike Ambrose, Southwell's saints are, at least within his poetic work, emphatically untriumphant. His narrative poem *Saint Peters Complaint*, a revision and expansion of Luigi Tansillo's *Le lagrimi di San Pietro*, and his lyrics "Josephs Amazement," "Mary Magdalenes Blush," "Marie Magdalens Complaint at Christs death," "Saint Peters Remorse," "Saint Peters Complaynte," and "Saint Peters Afflicted Minde" focus on biblical saints in their most trying moments: St. Joseph in Matthew 1:18–19, after discovering his fiancée is pregnant but before an angelic vision explains the child's divine paternity; Mary Magdalene lamenting her sinful past (Southwell accepts the traditional conflation of the Magdalene with the woman of Luke 7) before experiencing forgiveness; Mary Magdalene mourning Christ at his tomb before he appears to her; and St. Peter in despair after denying Christ three times but before his post-resurrection reconciliation with Christ. In each poem, Southwell draws on contemporary poetic fashions – including Petrarchan verse and complaint poetry – and echoes poets such as Edmund Spenser and Philip Sidney to fashion his depictions of struggling saints.[34] Developed

---

[31] Southwell, [Epistle], in *St. Robert Southwell: Collected Poems*, ed. Peter Davidson and Anne Sweeney (Manchester, 2007), 2. All citations of Southwell's work are to this edition.

[32] Alison Shell, *Catholicism, Controversy, and Early Modern Literary Culture* (Cambridge, 1998), chap. 2; Susannah Brietz Monta, "Martyrdom in Print in Early Modern England: The Case of Robert Waldegrave," in *More than a Memory: The Discourse of Martyrdom and the Construction of Religious Identity in the History of Christianity*, ed. Johann Leemans and Jurgen Mettepenningen (Leuven, 2005), 271–93.

[33] On Southwell's appeal to Protestant readers, see Jillian Snyder, "Pricked Hearts and Penitent Tears: Embodying Protestant Repentance in Robert Southwell's *Saint Peter's Complaint*," *Studies in Philology* 117, no. 2 (2020): 313–36.

[34] Emily Ransom discusses Southwell's use of complaint in "Complaint as Reconciliation in the Literary Mission of Robert Southwell," in *Precarious Identities: Studies in the Work of Fulke Greville and Robert Southwell*, ed. Vassiliki Markidou and Afroditi-Maria Panaghis (Abingdon, 2020), 223–66. On Southwell in relation to Spenser, Sidney, and Petrarchism, see below.

from fragments of secular lyric, produced in dialogue with biblical precedent and Jesuit practices of meditation, and adapted to the lives of English recusant Catholics, the portraits of sanctity Southwell produces coalesce not in joyful triumph or steady piety but in heartfelt remorse and/or suffering persistence. In each case, the reenvisioning of sanctity aims to minister to his readers and reorient the English literary marketplace.

The prefatory poem to *Saint Peters Complaynt*, which appeared both in the first printed edition of Southwell's poetry (printed by John Wolfe in March 1595) and in the manuscript tradition, marks Peter's flawed sainthood as instructional for readers: "Muse not to see some mud in cleerest brooke, / They once were brittle mould that now are Saints. / Theyr weakenes is no warrant to offend, / Learne by their faults, what in thine owne to mend." Southwell forbids smug readings, and characterizes our sins, which far outweigh Peter's, as at least partly literary:

This makes my mourning Muse resolve in teares,
This theames my heavy penne to plaine in prose,
Christs Thorne is sharp, no head his Garland weares:
Still finest wits are stilling Venus Rose.
In paynim toyes the sweetest vaines are spent:
To Christian works, few have their tallents lent.

The literary expenditure of "wit" on amatory verse means that no poetic "head" wears Christ's "Garland," much as Peter's betrayal left Christ to bear his thorns alone. The poem's final stanza is part invocation, part prayer. Southwell asks that "heavenly sparks of wit" may show "native light," that his pen might find a "pheere" – a companion, a soul to move to repentance much as Peter (after nearly 800 lachrymose lines) will be.[35]

In *Saint Peters Complaynt* as in this prefatory poem, Southwell combines literary reform with spiritual remorse. Peter's agony over his betrayal of Christ (Southwell is especially inspired by Luke 22:54–62) is shaped by reoriented literary conventions. His opening stanza echoes Petrarch's *Rime Sparse* 189 with its anatomy of the grief-stricken self-in-love as a troubled ship. Peter, like the speaker of *Rime Sparse* 189, seems headed for nothing less than "Shipwracke," though in Peter's case the ship has endangered itself (there is no desirable woman to

---

[35] "The Author to the Reader," lines 3–6, 13–18, 20, 19.

blame here, as Peter, in a misogynistic rant, will later lament). The poem also borrows and recasts lines from Spenser, responding to an Elizabethan politicization of love language.[36] In Book IV of Spenser's *Faerie Queene*, Timias, functioning in this passage as a figure for Sir Walter Raleigh, voices a love lament over the virginal huntress Belphoebe, a Diana figure and one of Spenser's allegorical shadows for Queen Elizabeth I. Caught between the painful experiences of loving a woman who will never return his love and the disloyalty that an attempt to stop loving her would entail, Timias rebukes himself repeatedly: "Dye rather, dy, then ever love disloyally.... Dye rather, dye, then ever from her service swerve.... Dye rather, dye, then ever so faire love forsake."[37] Berating himself for his betrayal of Christ, Southwell's Peter echoes these lines in his complaint but places Christ in the position of the beloved and leaves himself not at a crossroads but, at least temporarily, in despair: "Die, die, disloyall wretch, thy life detest: / For saving thine, thou hast forsworne the best."[38] In case the Spenserian echo is not clear enough, two stanzas later Southwell borrows language from *The Faerie Queene*'s first canto, a study in the inevitable errancy that accompanies even a would-be saint – in Spenser's case, an eventually reformed St. George – as he quests through the world. In his poem, Southwell makes fulsome use of the language of Spenserian errancy to characterize not the nigh-inevitable wanderings of a would-be-saint in the world but the dangers of a life without Christ: "life, the maze of ... straying waies," "erring steps ... strow'd with baites."[39] While Spenser's poem seeks to fashion a gentleman through a renewed St. George figure, Southwell works to fashion repentance in his poem's titular saint, in his readers (that "pheere" he seeks in the dedicatory poem), and in literary culture, through the religious reorientation of its amatory tropes.

Echo poems were a popular subgenre in Elizabethan amatory verse. In Thomas Watson's *Hekatompathia* XXV, for instance, a forlorn lover

---

[36] The classic if controversial touchstone is Arthur F. Marotti, "'Love is not love': Elizabethan Sonnet Sequences and the Social Order," *English Literary History* 49, no. 2 (1982): 396–428.

[37] *The Faerie Queene*, ed. A.C. Hamilton et al. (London, 2001), III.v.45.9, 46.9, 47.9.

[38] Saint Peters Complaynt (hereafter SPC), lines 83-4 in *Robert Southwell: Collected Poems*, ed. Davidson and Sweeney. In Book I, canto I, of *The Faerie Queene* Spenser's Redcrosse and Una "wander" (10.5) as in a "labyrinth" (xi.4) and stumble onto the monster Errrour's cave; Errour's name puns on erring and errancy.

[39] SPC, lines 91, 92, 93. Southwell's implicit rebuke to Spenser resonates with his cousin Anthony Copley's *A Fig for Fortune*, in which Copley shows both his admiration for and desire to offer a Catholic correction to Spenser. See *A Fig for Fortune: A Catholic Reads "The Faerie Queene,"* ed. Susannah Brietz Monta (Manchester, 2016).

and Echo together bewail their "passion of love."⁴⁰ Southwell may allude to this subgenre in the most accomplished section of his poem, the extended apostrophe to Christ's eyes. As Peter gazes at Christ, Christ's eyes reflect not Peter as he is but as he *may* be, as he ought to be:

> O living mirrours, seeing whom you shew,
> Which equall shadows worths with shadowed things.
> Yea make things nobler then in native hew,
> By being shape'd in those life-gyving springs;
> Much more my image in those eyes was grac'd,
> Then in my selfe, whom sinne and shame defac'd ...
> By seeing things, you make things worth the sight,
> You seeing, salve, and being seene delight.⁴¹

Echo becomes redemptive in and through Christ's eyes, as in Southwell's interweaving of "Eccho" with an image for Christ's eyes taken from that most sensuous of biblical books, the Song of Songs:

> O Pooles of Hesebon, the bathes of grace ...
> Where saints rejoice to glasse theyr glorious face,
> Whose banks make Eccho to the Angels quires:
> An Eccho sweeter in the sole rebound,
> Then Angels musick in the fullest sound.⁴²

Philip Sidney's *Astrophil and Stella* 60 features a paradox that captures Astrophil's hopeless situation, a stasis of emotional entrapment in which he can never fully enjoy his beloved "Whose absence, presence, presence absence is"; this paradox, encapsulating the restless dissatisfaction of unrequited love, is picked up again in the first line of sonnet 106: "O absent presence, Stella is not here."⁴³ Southwell's Peter sorts this paradox out, using its application to Christ's eyes to recast its logic: "O Sunnes, all but your selves in light excelling, / Whose presence, day, whose absence causeth night."⁴⁴ No more paradox here: The amatory impasse is cleared up so long as Christ's eyes remain present.

Other poems follow similar patterns, taking their phrasing and imagistic bearings from amatory lyric but reorienting its priorities.

---

⁴⁰ Watson, *Hekatompathia* (London, 1582).
⁴¹ *SPC*, lines 367–72, 377–78.
⁴² *SPC*, lines 379, 381–84.
⁴³ *Sir Philip Sidney: The Major Works*, ed. Katherine Duncan-Jones (Oxford, 2009).
⁴⁴ *SPC*, lines 397–98.

The first eight lines of "St. Peters Afflicted Mind" could easily serve as an amatory poem about the torments of unrequited love, while in "Mary Magdalens Blush" Mary regrets her previous vulnerability to Cupid's wounds and asked heaven to lament that sensuality or "sense" "robbeth" heaven "of Sayntes."[45] The calls for both literary and spiritual reform are easily visible here. Sometimes Southwell straightforwardly appropriates language from contemporary love lyric, fitting it to the troubled situations of his suffering saints. For instance, the paradox with which Sidney ends his sequence ("in my woes for thee thou art my joy / And in my joys for thee my only annoy," *Astrophil and Stella* 108) appears in "Mary Magdalens Blush," in which she claims that her former "joy" causes her only pain and her current "annoy" is her only joy ("Whose joy annoy").[46] In "Josephs Amazement," similar language encapsulates Joseph's suspension between love and torment, an emotional stalemate familiar from secular lyric: "So dye must I cutt from my roote of joye / And throwen in darkest shades of deepe annoy."[47] The closeness of "Marie Magdalens Complaint at Christs Death" to love lyric is evident in that a selection from this poem was treated as amatory verse and set to music in the seventeenth century.[48] Yet the religious import of saintly lament is clear when the poem is read in its entirety: Southwell's Magdalene takes thinly veiled swipes at the "Paynted meate" of a false sacrament, and identifies as "dooble treason" not the Catholic practices that constituted treason under Elizabethan law but the spear that pierced Christ's side, removing, as she says, life and love together. The poem's last two lines distill one of Southwell's dominant models for sanctity – suffering persistence: "Though my life thow dravst awaye / Maugre the my love shall staye."[49] The call to a suffering but resilient Catholicism rings loudly here.

But persistent suffering is not Southwell's only model of sanctity. In "Saint Peters Remorse," Southwell offers a sanctity that lies in our very origins. Peter seeks to find some way to persuade himself that God will "Let penance ... prevayle" as he requests forgiveness for his

---

[45] "Mary Magdalens Blush," line 31.
[46] "Mary Magdalens Blush," line 3.
[47] "Josephs Amazement," lines 71–72.
[48] Davidson and Sweeney note this poem's "long life in songbooks as an apparently secular love song" and its "appearance in the *Songs and Fancies* of John Forbes of Aberdeen (editions 1662, 1666, 1682)" (Davidson and Sweeney, eds., *St Robert Southwell: Collected Poems*, 158).
[49] "Marie Magdalens Complaint at Christs Death," lines 23, 39, 41–42.

"highest Treasons." Peter uses an image taken from Southwell's own poetics to persuade himself of God's mercy. Much as Southwell set out to "weave a new Webbe" in the "loom" of secular poetry, so Peter asks whether "mercye" did "spynn the thredd / To weave in Justice Loom." In this case, however, the import is that mercy's threads are not intended for this loom; they are, artistically, independent of justice. The poem's consolation, the mercy it extends, is phrased in the terms of authorship: God is Peter's origin, the "Author of my self," such that his role as judge of sin is secondary. The ending stakes its direct address to God on this idea: "Confirme thy former deede / Reforme that is defilde. / I was I am I will remayne / Thy charge thy choise thy childe."[50] Hope for reconciliation is based in identity, not consistently virtuous actions; in the authored self, not in that self's inevitably flawed penance. This is a capacious, generous model for sanctity, an escape from the vacillations of self-loathing and self-importance so prevalent in amatory poetry. Because this sanctity is rooted in origins, it is inalienable – and inseparable from the literary images of authorship upon which it draws.

HAGIOGRAPHY AND ENGLISH CATHOLIC LIVES

Perhaps English recusant Catholics' most urgent hagiographical productions were martyrologies produced about English priests and laypeople who suffered under recusancy laws. In the wake of Campion's December 1581 death, texts such as Thomas Alfield's *A true report of the death and martyrdome of M. Campion ... M. Sherwin, & M. Brian* (1582) and William Cardinal Allen's *A briefe historie of the glorious martyrdom of twelve reverend priests* (1582), in English, and the *Concertatio ecclesiae Catholicae in Anglia* (1583, first ed.), in Latin, proclaimed that Catholics executed under treason charges died as martyrs for religion. In *A true reporte*, Alfield challenges the treason charges under which Campion died by linking his martyrdom to hagiographic precedent, reporting the few words Edmund Campion was able to speak from the scaffold: "we are made a spectacle, or a sight unto God." Campion's words come from 1 Corinthians 14:9, a verse central to Christian discourses of martyrdom, as in Origen's *Exhortation to Martyrdom*. In reporting Campion's words, Alfield hopes to place Campion firmly within martyrological history.[51]

[50] "Saint Peters Remorse," lines 5, 23, 33–34, 31, 57–60.
[51] Alfield, *True Report*, fols. B4v–C1r; Monta, *Martyrdom and Literature*, 25.

Generic flexibility also proved invaluable as writers accommodated martyrological and hagiographic traditions to the complex realities of contemporary English Catholic life. After years of defiant recusancy, on March 10, 1586, Margaret Clitherow of York, a butcher's wife, was arrested on charges of harboring priests. She refused to plead and was subjected to the penalty of *peine forte et dure* – pressing to death. John Mush, a secular priest and her confessor, wrote a biography of Clitherow that intercedes in contemporary intra-Catholic debates over whether Catholics should conform to legal requirements for monthly attendance at Church of England services or embrace strict recusancy.[52] Clitherow opted for the latter course, as Mush underscores, even at the cost of martyrdom. The last half of Mush's biography is devoted to her arrest, examinations, and execution, and makes the case for her sanctity, most dramatically in Mush's final apostrophe to her in which he requests her aid and "gratious Intercession": "sacred Martyr ... Remember mee, I beseech thee ... in tyme past thy unworthy father, & now most unworthy servant ... I was not so able to help thee, as thou art noew to procure mercie & grace for mee. For thou art now all-washed in thy sacred bloud, from all spots of frailetie, securely possessing God himself."[53] And it was her trial and martyrdom that most interested continental writers and printers: The 1594 edition of the *Concertatio ecclesia Catholicae in Anglia* includes only her execution and a description of her husband's grief; Richard Verstegan's *Theatrum crudelitatem haereticorum nostri temporis* uses a sensational illustration of her death as anti-Protestant propaganda; and a 1619 printing of Mush's *Life* contains only the portion of the narrative concerning her arrest and martyrdom.[54] What was judged appealing for continental readers, in other words, was that portion of her life that most resembled martyrdom's familiar contours. Yet in the manuscript account intended for readers in England, Mush ends the first half of his biography – concerning her daily life, holy housekeeping, pious practices, sheltering of priests, and commitment to recusancy – with a plea that readers not "curiously" seek to know about her death without recognizing that her final "victorie" depends on the "foundation" of her virtuous life. He thus urges them to "Endeavour to Imitate this her first martyrdome of a vertuous life,

---

[52] Peter Lake and Michael Questier, *The Trials of Margaret Clitherow: Persecution, Martyrdom, and the Politics of Sanctity in Early Modern England* (London, 2011).
[53] Bar Convent (York, England) MS, 143.
[54] *Concertatio ecclesiae Catholicae in Anglia*, sig. 410v; John Mush, *An abstract of the life [and martirdome] of Mistres Margaret Clitherowe* (Mackline, 1619).

wherein the Chiefest glorie in this life consisteth."⁵⁵ In the manuscript tradition, the meaning of martyrdom is stretched to include the daily practice of a defiantly recusant Catholicism. This "first martyrdome" invests English intra-Catholic debates, political and legal pressures, and recusant domesticity with ultimate martyrological meaning.

Nor do martyrological conventions stay put within martyrological narratives like Mush's. Writers adopted and adapted those conventions as they worked out other models of holy living, as with pious figures who suffered for their religion but were not executed for it. At stake are updated models of exemplarity, articulated through familiar generic habits. A seventeenth-century manuscript account of the life of St. Philip Howard, earl of Arundel, narrates the life of a politically complex figure and incorporates hagiographic conventions as the narrative proceeds. Howard was reconciled to the Catholic Church in the fall of 1584. He was arrested in April 1585 and imprisoned for attempting to flee England; after a trial in Star Chamber, he was charged 10,000 pounds and imprisoned at the queen's pleasure. On April 14, 1589, he was brought to trial and convicted of treason for, among other supposed offenses, allegedly arranging Masses for the success of the Spanish Armada. His *Life* is a significant, careful production. Elizabeth Patton has established that its anonymous author was probably the English Jesuit Provincial Richard Blount.⁵⁶ It is clear from the biographer's own statements about information he derived from the earl's widow Anne Howard that he collaborated with her to produce an account of Philip Howard's life that loosely follows an Augustinian paradigm: a profligate youth followed by a dramatic conversion and holy maturity.⁵⁷ His biographer blames the vices of Howard's early life – excessive spending, an inordinate desire for courtly preferment, and sexual promiscuity – on his Protestantism and poor influences at the Elizabethan court.⁵⁸ After his conversion, instead of Augustine's ecclesiastical success and towering theological output, the earl's biography offers a portrait of a scrupulous man with only a modest literary footprint, a man devoted to his faith and regular practices of piety.⁵⁹

---

⁵⁵ Bar Convent MS, 76.
⁵⁶ See Patton's work on authorship in *The Lives of Philip Howard, Earl of Arundel and Anne Howard, Countess of Arundel*, ed. Susannah Brietz-Monta, Earle Havens, and Elizabeth Patton (forthcoming).
⁵⁷ Arundel Castle MS BN8, 6–9.
⁵⁸ On the likely collaboration of Anne Howard with Blount, see ibid.
⁵⁹ Among the earl's productions were his 1585 "Letter to the Queen," which circulated widely in manuscript, and his poem on the "Four Last Things," sometimes erroneously attributed to Southwell. Ibid.

While the biographer cloaks himself in anonymity, he does claim an identity as a researcher. He refers to information he has read in letters Anne Howard shared with him, heard from Anne Howard and others who knew the earl (Blount almost certainly never met him), or gathered from reliable witnesses.[60] His concern to ground his life of the earl in seemingly reliable sources acknowledges that the biography swims rather upstream in its attempt to present a man convicted of treason as a lay model of faithful piety. In addition to invoking his sources, the biographer interweaves hagiographic and marytrological conventions with the realities of Elizabethan prison life and the particulars of the earl's personality. When he was seized during his April 1585 escape attempt, for instance, the biographer notes that he was not daunted but had a "joyfull & a merry countenance," much like the "joyful countenance" that Mush claimed Margaret Clitherowe displayed as she walked to her execution.[61] The biographer claims to quote a letter in which the earl wrote that he was ready to lay down as many lives as necessary for his religion – a statement resembling those made by Catholic martyrs such as the layman John Rigbie and the priest Edmund Geninges.[62] It is common for both Protestant and Catholic martyrologists to claim that persecutors do not fare well, often dying in painful or shameful ways.[63] Thus shortly after the earl's death, William Bennet, a priest who testified against the earl at his treason trial, "fell ... into a grievous disease whereof he also died miserably with great remorse and grief for what he had done."[64] In a remarkable final paragraph, the biographer turns to the Jesuit theologian Cornelius a Lapide for language to describe and elevate the life that Blount, in collaboration with Anne Howard, has carefully shaped. Unlike his spiritual advisor Robert Southwell, Philip Howard was not martyred. Yet the biographer's quotation of Lapide's assertion that the earl was "a Glorious Confessor, yea a Martyr," does not come as a total surprise: Throughout the *Life*, the biographer aligns martyrological conventions

---

[60] Ibid.
[61] Arundel Castle MS BN8, 32; Bar Convent MS, 90.
[62] Arundel Castle MS BN8, 87; Thomas Worthington, *Relation of sixtene martyrs glorified in England in twelve months* (Douai, 1601), fol. B6r; John Geninges, *The life and death of Mr. Edmund Geninges priest* (St. Omer, 1614), 85.
[63] See, for instance, the unhappy end of a Catholic bishop who preached against the Protestant martyr George Marsh (*Actes and Monuments* [London, 1563], 1122; *Actes and Monuments* [London, 1570], 1738).
[64] Arundel Castle MS BN8, 73.

with the earl's sustained suffering under political charges.⁶⁵ The *Life* implicitly argues that a reliably sourced biography can also conform to familiar hagiographic patterns.

The secular priest Richard Smith's Latin biography of Anne Howard's aunt Magdalene Browne, Viscountess Montague (first published in Rome in 1609; an English translation was published in 1627), has been discussed as an intra-Catholic political text, aimed at promoting a traditional model of Catholic piety endorsed by England's secular priests, connected to England's Catholic past, and resistant to Jesuit influences.⁶⁶ Smith makes sure to note Browne's support for secular priests, for example, and conspicuously omits English Jesuits from his tally of over 120 secular priests martyred for their faith.⁶⁷ Yet Smith does not take his bearings from the religious politics of early modern England alone, for he repeatedly connects his biography to the hagiographic past. His preface claims that he imitates Jerome, Augustine, and Gregory the Great, who each wrote of the pious women of their times, and Smith anticipates objections from those who believe that "the lives only of such persons ought to be recorded, whose worthy sanctity meriteth that they be enrolled in the catalogue of saints."⁶⁸ Smith obviously dissents, pointing out that Jerome wrote not only about Saints Paula and Marcella but also Blesilla and Fabiola, even noting that Augustine wrote about St. Monica when he thought she might still be in Purgatory. Smith draws an elaborate analogy to justify the middle ground he seeks between hagiography and biography: "as God's power doth not only shine in the composition of the sun and moon, but appeareth also in the fabric of the lesser stars, so His heavenly grace doth not only give a lustre in the perfection of famous saints, but shineth even in the worth of every pious person." Spiritual usefulness is at issue: Smith writes that it is easier to aim at "the piety of less virtuous persons" than "climb the highest mountain" of admirable but nearly inimitable saints. He thus proposes "a woman, not famous for rudeness of habit, or rigours of diet, or severity of discipline, or abnegation of the world, but one that was humble, chaste, meek, patient, and pious, neither resplendent by miracles, but abounding with virtues, so

---

⁶⁵ Arundel Castle MS BN8, 95, 96.
⁶⁶ The author thanks Peter Lake and Michael Questier for sharing their work in draft on the intra-Catholic politics of Catholic biography.
⁶⁷ A. C. Southern, ed., *An Elizabethan Recusant House, Comprising the Life of the Lady Magdalen Viscountess Montague (1538–1608)*, trans. Cuthbert Fursdon (London, 1954), 42–43.
⁶⁸ Ibid., 2.

that they who despair to imitate the admirable sanctity of Mary Magdalene may see themselves capable to attain the piety of Magdalen Viscountess Montague."[69]

As Browne's "lesser star" status makes her a more accessible model for imitation than saintly suns and moons, so the biography makes room for a few deviations from hagiographic precedent. Even as he praises her humility through a loose quotation from a hagiography written by Surius, Smith also includes a realistic physical description, noting that she was "fat and gross in body." He does not claim fasting or other asceticisms as a significant part of her devotions, as Jerome had for Paula.[70] Yet Smith's "lesser star" still sometimes shines with a luster borrowed from early Christian figures, as Smith uses language from Jerome (most often concerning Paula) and Augustine (on Monica) to suggest that aspects of Browne's life and virtues resemble theirs. Smith lightly links Browne's life with Jerome's life of Paula through some similarities in structure. Jerome begins his letter on Paula with an account of her high birth, marriage to a noble man, their love, and social success in Rome before narrating her conversion and extensive pilgrimage to and through the Christian holy lands. Smith begins with five chapters on Browne's noble birth, education, years at court under Mary Tudor, marriage to Anthony Browne, first viscount Montague, her husband's virtues, and their mutual love. After Jerome narrates St. Paula's travels, he discusses her virtues beginning with humility; humility is also the first of Browne's virtues that Smith discusses, beginning with an adaptation of words from the parallel spot in the life of Paula ("The first or chief virtue of a Christian is humility") and going on to quote Jerome again on the humility of Paula and Blesilla (Paula's daughter). Smith's next chapter concerns chastity, the next virtue Jerome discusses; from that point on, the virtues Smith selects sometimes overlap with those Jerome chooses. Both women are praised for liberality, and Jerome's praise of Paula for her docility, or willingness to be guided by religious superiors, is roughly parallel to Smith's praise of Browne's obedience of priests.

At other times, the virtues Smith highlights are adjusted for early modern English Catholic life, as in his praise for Browne's "zeal and

---

[69] Ibid., 4.
[70] Smith quotes Surius on Luigi Lippomano, but claims that the words he uses concern the humility of St. Thomas of Canterbury, thereby Anglicizing the quotation for use in his biography of Browne. See Southern, ed., *An Elizabethan Recusant House*, 84 n. 1.

constancy in supporting and professing the Catholic faith" in "turbulent" times.[71] He echoes Jerome when he writes that nobody would believe him if he included many other good things about Browne, and is so eager to use quotations ostensibly about Paula that he sometimes runs afoul of his sources. For instance, he either accidentally or deliberately misappropriates words concerning Paulina, Paula's daughter, claiming that they indicate the mother's desire to remain chaste in her widowhood much as Browne chose to do.[72] Still, Smith's touch is gentle; the point is that Browne's way of living is a modern, accessible adaptation of Paula's life. Where Jerome's life of Paula gives us an extensive description of the monastery she ran, for instance, Smith gives us an account of a recusant Catholic home in which the regular liturgies Browne hosted earned her household the nickname "Little Rome."[73]

It is instructive also to compare Smith's use of Augustine on Monica with a popular Counter-Reformation treatment of Monica. The *Flos sanctorum* renders a nearly flawless St. Monica, in contrast with the admired, pious, but very human woman Augustine portrays in his *Confessions*. For example, where the *Flos sanctorum* claims that "*S. Augustine* said boldly in a speech unto God, that his mother after she was Baptised, never spoke word against the divine commaundements," that moment in the *Confessions* is quite different: "For though she had been made alive in Christ, and ... so lived that Your name was glorified ... yet I dare not say that from the moment of her regeneration in baptism no word issued from her mouth contrary to Your command."[74] Noting that Magdalene Browne died the day before the anniversary of Monica's death, Smith closes his biography with just this passage from the *Confessions*, linking his portrait of Browne to Augustine's more realistic, balanced praise of Monica rather than to a perfected image like that in the *Flos sanctorum*. Browne is still elevated through Smith's comparisons of her with this pious but imperfect Monica, and his use of Augustine's passage brings to a fitting conclusion his efforts to depict an intermediate space (that "lesser star") for Browne to inhabit. The repeated references to early Christian saints – Paula and Monica most prominently – advocate for continuity between ancient

---

[71] Southern, ed., *An Elizabethan Recusant House*, 41.
[72] Ibid., 33, 31 (and 79 n. 6).
[73] Ibid., 43.
[74] *Flos Sanctorum*, trans. Edward and William Kinsman (Douai, 1609), 69; Augustine, *Confessions*, trans. Francis J. Sheed (Indianapolis, 2006), 183–84.

Christendom and the form of English Catholicism he preferred. These saints bring into focus an intermediate sanctity, shaped through light touches drawn from hagiographic precedent and suited to navigate the space between steadfast Catholic practice and seemingly perfect, inimitable sanctity, the space Smith hoped more English Catholics would inhabit.

CONCLUSION

As these case studies illustrate, early modern English Catholic literary treatments of saints and sanctity represent the paradoxes of a living tradition, one that seeks to maintain its connections with the past but remains in constant dialogue with the cultures of the present. These literary representations of sanctity are not mere traces persisting from earlier ages; they are not nostalgic or conservative in the sense of preserving earlier models largely unchanged. Rather, they evince a real dynamism with respect to both hagiographic precedent and literary fashion. Hagiographic literatures thus matter broadly for the period's literary cultures: for the relationship between *historia sacra* and the performance of history on stage, for the relationship between amatory and sacred verse, and for the drawing and negotiating of the boundaries between hagiography and biography that begin to emerge in the period.

Part IV

Living with Saints

15 Material Culture
ANNE MARISS

The vita of Andrea Avellino (1521–1608), a saint known and venerated for his chastity, includes a memorable anecdote about an aged lecher who carried a rosary with a medal of the saint. Although the religious medal was securely attached to the rosary, it jumped off as soon as its loose-living owner indulged in unclean thoughts.[1] This brief episode draws our attention to the importance of religious materiality in pre-modern times, to the power of religious objects, and to the agency that believers attributed to them. Sacred architecture, relics, devotional objects, and holy images were fundamental for Christian liturgy, everyday religious practices, and beliefs since the formation of the early Church and throughout the Middle Ages. During the Reformation, however, the salvific power of objects and images as well as the sanctity of holy sites and landscapes were called into question and contested.[2]

Both Protestants and Catholics could be defined by their changing approaches to materiality. While the Roman Catholic Church adhered to the belief in the power of sacred things and images, officially approving the invocation and veneration of relics and holy images during the Council of Trent (1545–63), Protestants rejected the sacrality of objects and, more specifically, their agency. Despite their overall disapproval of sacred matter, neither Lutheranism nor Calvinism can be understood exclusively on the premise of the rejection or destruction of images and

---

I would like to thank the participants of the research colloquia of Early Modern History at the Universities of Regensburg and Frankfurt for comments on earlier versions of this chapter. I am likewise grateful to Minou Schraven for the invitation to the KNIR in Rome and to the many helpful suggestions I received at the workshop on "Handling Devotional Objects" that followed in May 2023. Thanks are also due to Lena Moser for helping me polish the manuscript and to the editors of this volume for their critical revision.

[1] Johann Edlweckh, *Leben des Heiligen Andreas Avellinus*, vol. 1 (Munich, 1765), 12.
[2] Caroline Walker Bynum, *Christian Materiality: An Essay on Religion in Late Medieval Europe* (New York, 2011), 272.

objects, but each developed their own stance toward materiality. Martin Luther (1483–1546) had an indifferent attitude toward things and images, aptly captured in the contemporary term "adiaphora," which resulted in the long-term preservation of material culture in Lutheran churches.³ John Calvin (1509–1564), by contrast, radically dismissed images as "deceptive" and despised devotional objects as mere Catholic "tat."⁴ Yet whether certain religious objects or images were removed or destroyed in the course of the Reformation did not depend exclusively on religious concerns; local and sociopolitical circumstances likewise had a strong influence on iconoclastic outbursts.

As much recent research has shown, the study of religious materiality is pivotal for our understanding of early modern sanctity.⁵ Building on the interdisciplinary scholarship on early modern devotional practice and religious material culture, this chapter explores how early modern saints were venerated through the handling of devotional objects and how people used sacred items to navigate the hardships of everyday life. By following an object-centered approach, I will focus on two rosaries from the collection of the Diocesan Museum in Freising in Upper Bavaria. While both rosaries were created, owned, and used within the Holy Roman Empire, they belonged to and took part in a truly global Catholic material culture. Even though the selected rosaries and their various pendants differ greatly from each other in their materiality, form, and function, they can be assigned to the same religious context, that is, the early modern cult of saints and their veneration and invocation with the help of devotional items. Due to their material "openness" – rosaries could be rearranged or restrung, enhanced by

---

[3] Robert W. Scribner, "Incombustible Luther: The Image of the Reformer in Early Modern Germany," *Past & Present*, no. 110 (1986): 38–68; Caroline Walker Bynum, "Are Things 'Indifferent'? How Objects Change Our Understanding of Religious History," *German History* 34, no. 1 (2016): 88–112; Andrew Spicer, "*Adiaphora*, Luther and the Material Culture of Worship," *Studies in Church History* 56 (2020): 246–72.

[4] See on Calvinistic iconoclasm, for instance, Carlos M. N. Eire, *War Against the Idols: The Reformation of Worship from Erasmus to Calvin* (Cambridge, 1989); David Freedberg, *The Power of Images: Studies in the History and Theory of Response* (Chicago, 1991); Joseph Leo Koerner, *The Reformation of the Image* (Chicago, 2004).

[5] See, for instance, on Switzerland and the Netherlands the monographs by Daniel Sidler, *Heiligkeit aushandeln: Katholische Reform und lokale Glaubenspraxis in der Eidgenossenschaft (1560–1790)* (Frankfurt, 2017), esp. 236–60, and Ruben Suykerbuyk, *The Matter of Piety: Zoutleeuw's Church of Saint Leonard and Religious Material Culture in the Low Countries (c. 1450–1620)* (Leiden, 2020), esp. 146–51. See, on early modern Italy, Abigail Brundin, Deborah Howard, and Mary Laven, "Sacred Stuff," in *The Sacred Home in Renaissance Italy*, ed. Abigail Brundin, Deborah Howard, and Mary Laven (Oxford, 2018), 113–48.

pendants or amulets, often from far-flung locations – they were highly suited for the daily performance of saintly veneration. Medals with images of saints or sacred sites, reliquaries containing small particles of saints, crosses, or other religious pendants allowed for a very personal expression of belief, which could manifest itself in different material designs and compositions. They therefore make an ideal entry point to the study of Catholic material culture as well.

Small, portable, and often cheap devotional objects like rosaries were of great importance to the dissemination, circulation, and acceptance of sacred cults in early modern Catholicism. They were meant to transport sacred powers from holy sites or saints to other parts of the world, transmitting sanctity as a kind of "mobile proxy."[6] The high mobility of small things of faith was especially crucial for the global spread of Catholicism in the colonial peripheries where priests were thin on the ground. Missionaries from all four corners of the globe reported the constant desire of the indigenous population for sacramentals from Europe. In a letter from November 1717, the Jesuit missionary Joseph Bonani (1685–1752), for instance, noted that the baptized "Indians" of Baja California were fond of sacred images, rosaries, and consecrated medals.[7] Yet the situation was not entirely different back in Europe, where the consumption of devotional objects gained momentum in the wake of the Counter-Reformation. Devotional objects and images lent themselves perfectly to the global transmission of Catholic doctrines as they could transcend difficulties in cross-cultural communication and tie in with local traditions. Prayer beads, for instance, were already widespread in Buddhist culture when the first Jesuit missionaries started evangelizing in Asia in the second half of the sixteenth century. Rosary beads, it seems, were therefore highly suited for assimilating beliefs in neophyte missions. However, they were also able to carry "pagan" ideas and traditional rituals, thus confronting Catholic missionaries with the difficult decision of tolerating local practices or banning them as dangerous "syncretism."[8]

---

[6] Paul Nelles, "Devotion in Transit: Agnus Dei, Jesuit Missionaries, and Global Salvation in the Sixteenth Century," in *Connected Mobilities in the Early Modern World: The Practice and Experience of Movement*, ed. Paul Nelles and Rosa Salzberg (Amsterdam, 2023), 186.
[7] Joseph Bonani, Letter 717 to Sigismund Pusch, November 13, 1717, Hacienda de San Borja (Mexico), in *Allerhand So Lehr- als Geist-reiche Brief/ Schriften und Reis-Beschreibungen*, vol. 7, ed. Joseph Stöcklein (Augsburg, 1726), 73.
[8] Rie Arimura, "The Origins, Spread and Interfaith Connections Around the Prayer Beads: A Case Study of the Evangelization of Japan," *Anales del Instituto de Investigaciones Estéticas* 43 (119): 209–47.

Sacramentals or sacred matter such as oils, waters, candles, crosses, rosaries, medals, and scapulars received their sanctity from a superior authority such as a holy place, person, or liturgical act of consecration. In everyday religious practice, however, popular understanding of the precise source from which devotional objects derived their supernatural power was often hazy or blurred. Even when the Church explicitly endorsed sacred items as tools of spiritual and physical healing, their proper handling always posed a challenge. One illustrative example of the ambivalent attitude of the Roman Catholic Church toward devotional objects is the development of the St. Benedict medal, which enjoyed a widespread popularity in early modern Germany. The medals depict the monastic founder Benedict of Nursia (480–547) in different designs, but always with the blessing attributed to him that was said to ward off the devil and all evil. According to legend, several women accused in a witch trial in 1647 argued that they could not have harmed the Benedictine St. Michael's Abbey in the Bavarian town of Metten because the Benedictus blessing had been applied to the gates, doors, and walls there. A broadsheet from 1664 recommends placing the medal in water to cure sick animals or in the cream barrel to make the butter firm.[9] Even though the Catholic Church did not take concerted action against those medals, some episcopal decrees banning them have survived. It was only in 1741/42 that Pope Benedict XIV recognized their use and that the Congregation of Indulgences officially granted the privilege of consecration to the Benedictines.[10] The case of the St. Benedict medal demonstrates the influence believers could have on the implementation of cults that were eyed with suspicion by the curia.

Scholars researching the close connection between sanctity, devotion, and material culture have traditionally focused their attention on relics and their often extremely expensive reliquaries, their transcultural mobility, as well as their sites of veneration.[11] The role of devotional artifacts in the veneration of saints in the wake of Trent has received less attention. This scholarly lacuna probably reflects the low monetary and aesthetic value of these small, mass-produced objects,

---

[9] Johann Tomaschek, "Benediktus-Medaille, Benediktus-Kreuz und Benediktus-Segen: Frömmigkeitsgeschichtliche und theologische Bemerkungen zum 'Benediktischen Kreuzamulett'," in *Kulturtechnik Aberglaube: Zwischen Aufklärung und Spiritualität; Strategien zur Rationalisierung des Zufalls*, ed. Eva Kreissl (Bielefeld, 2013), 299–326, at 309.

[10] Prosper Guéranger, *The Medal or Cross of St. Benedict: Its Origin, Meaning, and Privileges* (London, 1880), 70.

[11] For relics, see Chapters 6 and 8 in this volume.

since, traditionally, the preferred subjects of art history were artworks like altarpieces or church frescos. Furthermore, the study of devotional objects has long been hampered by disciplinary boundaries. While numismatics, for instance, was concerned with the indexing of medals depicting saints, holy sites, or miracle-working objects, anthropological or folklore studies examined the early modern uses – often deemed "superstitious"[12] – of religious pendants like charms or talismans. Interdisciplinary scholarship on religious materiality has now started to bring together the different strands of research into history, Church history, art history, archaeology, and anthropology in order to understand the meanings and uses of devotional objects in various historical contexts.[13] The two rosaries studied in this chapter capture in miniature the importance of common but sacred objects in the devotional lives of the Catholic faithful. Both objects illustrate the development of saintly cults in material culture through the practice of attaching various kinds of pendants to rosaries. Personalizing their rosaries in this way enabled early modern believers to practice a much more intimate form of devotion than their medieval forebears.

ROSARIES AS POLYVALENT TOOLS OF SAINTLY VENERATION

Although rosaries have already received some in-depth scholarly attention, their central importance for the production of sanctity needs further study.[14] A late medieval invention, they became popular prayer

---

[12] Wolfgang Brückner, *Volkskunde als historische Kulturwissenschaft: Gesammelte Schriften; Nachträge IV* (Würzburg 2018); Christoph Kürzeder, *Als die Dinge heilig waren: Gelebte Frömmigkeit im Zeitalter des Barock* (Regensburg, 2005).

[13] See, for instance, the contributions in Suzanna Ivanič, Mary Laven, and Andrew Morrall, eds., *Religious Materiality in the Early Modern World* (Amsterdam, 2019), and in Salvador Ryan, Samantha Leanne Smith, and Laura Katrine Skinnebach, eds., *Material Cultures of Devotion in the Age of Reformation* (Leuven, 2022).

[14] On rosaries and their meaning for Catholic devout culture, see Nathan D. Mitchell, *The Mystery of the Rosary: Marian Devotion and the Reinvention of Catholicism* (New York, 2009); Irene Galandra and Mary Laven, "The Material Culture of Piety in the Italian Renaissance: Re-Touching the Rosary," in *The Routledge Handbook of Material Culture in Early Modern Europe*, ed. Catherine Richardson, Tara Hamling, and David Gaimster (London, 2017), 338–53; Erminia Ardissino, "Literary and Visual Forms of a Domestic Devotion: The Rosary in Renaissance Italy," in *Domestic Devotions in Early Modern Italy*, ed. Maya Corry , Marco Faini, and Alessia Meneghin (Leiden, 2018), 342–71. On the sensual qualities of rosaries, see Lisa Beaven, "The Early Modern Sensorium: The Rosary in Seventeenth-Century Rome," *Journal of Religious History* 44, no. 4 (2020): 443–64, and Rachel King, "The Reformation of the Rosary Bead: Protestantism and the Perpetuation of the Amber

aids for the contemplation of the life and death of Jesus and Mary from the fourteenth and fifteenth centuries onward.[15] The regular form of a rosary consists of five sets of ten beads (a decade) used for counting the repetitions of the Ave Maria (Hail Mary) and contemplating the important events in the lives of Christ and Mary, that is, the joyful, the sorrowful, or the glorious mysteries. Each of the five decades is separated by an – often larger – Paternoster bead on which the Our Father is recited. Although this form was the most widespread, there were numerous other ways of arranging the beads, including the short form of a tenner (ten Ave beads prayed on each hand of the finger, usually worn by men), psalters with fifteen decades amounting to 150 beads equaling the number of psalms, or the rosary of St. Bridget of Sweden, with sixty-three beads for each year of Mary's life.

The propagation of the rosary was primarily driven by the religious orders, especially the Dominicans. According to legend, the Virgin Mary donated the first rosary to their founder, St. Dominic (1170–1221), charging him with the task of promoting the devotional object. Rosary confraternities succeeded in encouraging its adoption among both the laity and the clergy. Not long after the closing of the Council of Trent, it received a new impetus through the military victory of the Holy League over the Ottomans at Lepanto (1571), which Pope Pius V attributed to the veneration of the rosary. The object's ability to adapt to changes within early modern Catholic reform in liturgy, representation, and devotion ensured its attraction until well into the twentieth century.[16] Its popularity was at least partly due to the considerable indulgences associated with the prayer for the benefit of the living, but also the dead suffering in Purgatory. Another factor was its flexibility, enabling the user to communicate with God, Mary, and the saints at any time of their choosing. Early modern believers could pray during Mass in church, during processions, at home, in the field, or onboard a ship; they could do so as part of a church community, by coming together as a family, or they could make their devotions alone.[17]

With their diverse medals, amulets, and crosses, rosaries fulfilled various functions in the lives of Catholics. Offering a variety of materials with different sensory qualities, they aided in prayer and offered

---

Paternoster," in *Religious Materiality in the Early Modern World*, ed. Suzanna Ivanic, Mary Laven, and Andrew Morrall (Amsterdam, 2019), 193–210.

[15] On the late medieval origins of the rosary, see Anne Winston-Allen, *Stories of the Rose: The Making of the Rosary in the Middle Ages* (University Park, PA, 1997).

[16] Mitchell, *The Mystery*, 3.

[17] Galandra and Laven, "The Material Culture," 342.

protection and help in times of personal crisis and severe illness; they functioned as a means of propaganda and evangelization in Catholic missions; they were used in catechesis and left as offerings at places of pilgrimage. Lavish designs could make them valued possessions within the domestic sphere. Moreover, the materials used for the prayer beads, such as amber, coral, or aromatic woods, were often charged with apotropaic virtues, allowing them to act as miracle-working items. Rosaries must be placed alongside other devotional objects, such as *Agni Dei*, crucifixes, pilgrimage badges, and holy images, as instruments for the propagation of the Catholic faith across the globe, but rosaries nevertheless stand out because of their adaptability and widespread popularity.

Carrying and praying a rosary was crucial to the central practices of saints' cults. Saints were models to be imitated (*imitatio*) and heavenly helpers to be invoked (*invocatio*); their bodily remains were the material substrates of religious remembrance (*veneratio*). Early modern Catholics embraced rosaries for their potential to unite all three areas of saintly veneration, imitation, and invocation, especially by attaching various religious pendants to rosaries that were believed to be imbued with sacred powers. In what follows, I first examine the bodily practices that emerged around this specific handling of rosaries by considering an ivory medallion from a Dominican context and a reliquary, both attached to our two objects of study. I then explore the plurality of religious medals depicting old and newly canonized saints as well as saints from different religious orders, analyzing the practices emerging around these medals. I conclude by considering a medal from the pilgrimage sites of Sirolo near Loreto in Italy and Mariazell in southern Austria to trace the mobilization of sacred power through the transfer of devotional objects and their meaning for the early modern veneration of saints and holy sites.

BODILY PRACTICES OF VENERATION

Rosaries were versatile devotional tools enabling the believer to worship saints using various bodily practices. The appealing material qualities of prayer beads – made of smooth red coral, amber that warmed in the hands, or even of spiky viper vertebrae – called for bodily interaction and performance. Amulets, medals, or crosses attached between the prayer beads also prompted physical actions and gestures such as kissing, rubbing, or pressing against the body. One striking example of the close connection between these bodily practices of devotion and the veneration of saints is a beautifully crafted ivory rosary, adorned with a

Figure 15.1 Ivory rosary, second half of the seventeenth century, southern Germany, Bavaria. Dommuseum Salzburg (Photo: J. Kral)

pendant made of the same material and set in gold (Figure 15.1). It consists of ivory beads arranged in five decades corresponding to the post-Tridentine style of praying the rosary, which involved contemplating the mysteries of the life of Mary and Christ by reciting the five decades followed by an Our Father. One particularly prominent pendant suggests that this rosary possibly belonged to a member of the order or to someone who was otherwise very close to the Dominicans. The large oval ivory pendant shows Mary's donation of the rosary to St. Dominic (1170–1221) (Figure 15.2). Mary, with the baby Jesus in her arms, is sitting in a cloud, handing a rosary to the saint, easily recognizable by his iconic attributes, the torch and the dog lying at his feet. The infant Jesus is imitating the gift-giving gesture of the Virgin with his right hand, suggesting the introduction of rosaries into Catholic devotion. The obverse shows the Dominican tertiary St. Rose of Lima (1586–1617) with a crown of roses and her eyes closed while holding the baby Jesus in her arms, the infant lying on a bed of roses and tenderly touching her cheek (Figure 15.3).[18] This loving, motherly portrayal of Rose, and Jesus's soft hand motion, virtually called for the owner to imitate the gentle gestures of the saint and Christ. Rosaries like this one were predestined to take on close associations with specific saints beyond the object's intrinsic identification with Christ and the Virgin Mary.

---

[18] Peter Keller, ed., *Edelsteine, Himmelsschnüre: Rosenkränze und Gebetsketten (Katalog zur 33. Sonderschau des Dommuseums zu Salzburg, 9. Mai bis 26. Oktober 2008)*, 2nd ed. (Salzburg, 2010), 274.

Figure 15.2 Obverse of medallion depicting Mary's donation of the rosary to St. Dominic, second half of the seventeenth century, southern Germany. Diözesanmuseum Freising (Photo: Anne Mariss)

Thus, the physical practice of wearing the rosary directly on the body, holding it in one's hands, caressing it in devotion, or rubbing it between the fingers during prayer can be seen as an attempt to establish a closeness to patron saints and perhaps even make them favorably disposed toward the wearer's needs.

Among the different types of materials available for the crafting of rosaries and other devotional objects, ivory was particularly sought after, lending itself perfectly to carvings and sculptures. The light color of the material evoked ideas of transcendence, purity, and imperishability. Due to its bone-like substance, ivory also summoned associations of living corporeality and the incorruptibility of sacred bodies.[19]

[19] Ruth Sargent Noyes, "'Purest Bones, Sweet Remains, and Most Sacred Relics': Re-Fashioning St. Kazimierz Jagielloczyk (1458–84) as a Medieval Saint Between Counter-Reformation Italy and Poland-Lithuania," *Religions* 12, no. 11: 1011;

Figure 15.3 Reverse of medallion depicting St. Dominic and Rose of Lima, second half of the seventeenth century, southern Germany. Diözesanmuseum Freising (Photo: Anne Mariss)

Above all, its pleasant feel and soft resilience called for bodily practices and invited emotional handling, such as touching the beads and caressing or kissing the pendant during prayer. The lavishly worked ivory rosary is exceptional due to its elaborate design and exclusive materials and thus provides a typical example of outstanding collection objects. Given the relatively few signs of abrasion, this particular rosary was probably not used on a daily basis but rather on special occasions such as feast days or processions. Since both the object and the medallion are relatively large (ca. 52 centimeters long, ca. 5 centimeters in diameter), they were most likely intended for ostentatiously staged veneration, possibly a further sign of the owner's affiliation with the Dominicans.

Alberto Saviello, "Berührungen mit Elfenbein: Körperbild, Körperkontakt, Körperersatz," in *Schrecklich schön: Elefant – Mensch – Elfenbein; Humboldt Forum*, ed. Stiftung Humboldt Forum (Munich, 2021), 60–71, 67.

Another aspect of the physical performance of rosaries and their pendants was their capability to transmit sacred powers by touching relics or holy images. Miracle reports and hagiographies commonly describe how early modern believers touched saints' relics with their rosaries.[20] Moreover, rosaries enabled the wearer to carry small relics or contact relics like pieces of cloth or other material that had come into touch with a holy person. Various surviving rosaries include small containers destined to carry relics of saints or holy substances, like the small bottles of liquid from the sarcophagus of St. Walburga in Eichstätt (Upper Bavaria).

In contrast to the sumptuous and elaborate reliquaries of churches, these simpler receptacles were portable and used by believers in their everyday religious practice. A small reliquary of that type is attached to our second example. The rosary consists of turned wooden Ave beads, while the Paternoster beads are additionally set in brass half shells (Figure 15.4). With its various pendants, this rosary can be considered an instructive example of the quotidian handling of sanctity in the early modern period. In contrast to the ivory rosary, it consists of simple materials such as wood and brass and was probably used for prayer on a regular basis. Some of the medals attached to it show traces of abrasion as a result of frequent touching and rubbing. Overall, however, the rosary and its pendants are well preserved, suggesting that it may have been one of several rosaries in the owner's possession. On the other hand, the object likely had more than one user over time. While its devotional medals were most probably struck during the first half of the eighteenth century, the crucifix from the Austrian pilgrimage site of Mariazell probably dates from the beginning of the nineteenth century. The rosary as it exists today was clearly created over an extended period, and possibly handed down within a family across several generations.

The rosary's reliquary capsule (Figure 15.5) contains tiny relics of John the Baptist and his holy parents Zachariah and Elizabeth, easily identifiable by small paper name tags. The reliquary thus unites a holy family, indirectly referring to the biblical narrative of John's wondrous birth and his role as a forerunner of Christ. The relic fragments are set into fine gold filigree work, a technique known under the term "cloister work" (*Klosterarbeit*). The name derives from the fact that this elaborate and time-consuming work was mainly practiced by nuns in

---

[20] Cynthia J. Hahn, *The Reliquary Effect: Enshrining the Sacred Object* (London, 2017), 207.

Figure 15.4 Wooden rosary with various pendants, Austria/Germany, eighteenth to nineteenth century. Dommuseum Salzburg (Photo: J. Kral)

convents for the appropriate presentation of whole saints' bodies as well as smaller relics, which were decorated with gold thread, glass beads, sequins, and tulle – materials without special value that, however, contributed to a worthy setting of the relics through being painstakingly worked and arranged.[21] Relics that, ultimately, were nothing

[21] Ibid., 197.

Figure 15.5 Reliquary capsule, eighteenth century, Diözesanmuseum Freising (Photo: Anne Mariss)

but bones needed "the mediation of the reliquary to configure their cosmological and social significance."[22] When preparing reliquaries or setting relics in precious metals, small fragments of bone always remained that were kept and later processed in religious objects such as the relic capsule of the rosary. The tiny relics were placed under crystal or glass panes, for both protection and visibility. Unlike the larger reliquaries kept in sacred spaces, the capsule was portable and allowed for a close bodily experience of sanctity. Early modern Catholics collected those small relics in the hope that the wearer would benefit from the powers of the respective saints. Worn upon the body or close to it, the reliquary attached to the rosary offered protection

---

[22] Karen Overbey, "Seeing Through Stone: Materiality and Place in a Medieval Scottish Pendant Reliquary," *Res: Anthropology and Aesthetics* 65–66 (2014–15): 242–58, 243. https://doi.org/10.1086/691037.

against any harm and evil, establishing a close connection between the saints and the owner of the rosary.[23]

Far more widespread than reliquaries or sumptuous medallions like the examples discussed above are religious medals depicting saints or sacred sites. Indulgence medals or coins depicting old and new saints played a central role in the daily lives of early modern Catholics.[24] Often mass-produced in the wake of canonizations, especially at the expense of religious orders or powerful patrons, those consecrated medals were distributed among the faithful during parish meetings, catechism lessons, missions, and pilgrimages.[25] Crucial for the widespread popularity of these medals or pennies were the indulgences that accompanied the use of consecrated rosaries, images, and medals of newly minted saints.[26] Beyond their potential to convey and increase indulgences, religious medals also possessed talismanic qualities. The ritual act of consecration imbued them with the sacred power of the respective saint(s), and they could be used in manifold ways. As good luck charms they were buried among the foundation stones of buildings; as burial gifts they accompanied the dead; and as talismans they were worn on the body.[27] This last aspect is essential for the Jesuit medals that were attached to the rosary. These display Ignatius of Loyola (1491–1556) holding the statutes of the Society of Jesus, as well as Luigi Gonzaga (1568–1591) and Stanislaus Kostka (1550–1568), depicted with halos and praying on their knees in the direction of the radiating Christogram above their heads (Figure 15.6).

---

[23] Marta Crispí, "The Use of Devotional Objects in Catalan Homes," in "Domestic Devotions in Medieval and Early Modern Europe," special issue of *Religions* 11, ed. Salvador Ryan (2020): 72–104, at 94.

[24] On the modern *beati*, see Simon Ditchfield, "Coping with the *Beati moderni*: Canonization Procedure in the Aftermath of the Council of Trent," in *Ite inflammate omnia: Selected Historical Papers from Conferences Held at Loyola and Rome in 2006*, ed. Thomas M. McCoog (Rome, 2010), 413–40.

[25] Minou Schraven, "Miracle-Working Portraits of a Cardinal Saint: Managing the Devotional Medals of San Carlo Borromeo," in *Portrait Cultures of the Early Modern Cardinal*, ed. Piers Baker-Bates and Irene Brooke (Amsterdam, 2021), 319–40, at 330.

[26] *Verzeichnuß der Abläß welche Benedictus XIII. verwilliget, nachdeme von deroselben Aloisius Gonzaga, und Stanislaus Kostka den 31. December 1726 in die Zahl deren Heiligen gesetzet worden* (Ofen, 1728). Diözesanbibliothek Würzburg, Sign.: 0006/Conciones misc. B.N. F 52 751.

[27] Minou Schraven, "Beyond the Studiolo: Ritual and Talismanic Qualities of Coins, Medals and Agni Dei in Early Modern Italy," *Numismatische Zeitschrift* 122–123 (2017): 71–83, 71.

Figure 15.6 Brass medal, reverse with the Jesuit saints Aloysius and Stanislaus, first half of the eighteenth century. Diözesanmuseum Freising (Photo: Anne Mariss)

In general, saints were supposed to provide comfort in times of crisis and were called upon for help to alleviate difficult situations and misfortune. The first and most revered Jesuit saints, Ignatius of Loyola and Francis Xavier (1506–1552), were particularly popular for their miraculous healings of serious illnesses and for alleviating difficult childbirths. As part of their efforts to promote their founder's canonization, the Jesuits spread the news of his miraculous assistance in their annual letters and biographies, thereby laying the foundation for Ignatius's veneration on a global scale.[28] Ignatius medals were believed to have curative properties and to ward off all sorts of diseases and mischief,

---

[28] Jonathan E. Greenwood, "Miracles in Writing: Obstetric Intercessions, Scribal Relics, and Jesuit News in the Early Modern Global Cult of Ignatius of Loyola," *Journal of Jesuit Studies* 9, no. 3 (2022): 338–56.

providing round-the-clock protection.²⁹ In one of his German vitae, prayers for the use of Ignatius's relics, water, oil, and medals gave instructions on how to invoke the saint in times of sickness or despair. Furthermore, believers were advised always to carry the blessed objects close to the body to ward against any harm and to worship them with devout looks and kisses.³⁰

The medals of the two teenage Jesuit saints Luigi and Stanislaus, coined on the occasion of their canonization in 1726, similarly enjoyed considerable popularity. Blessed medals of St. Aloysius were reportedly not only capable of curing the sick but also of multiplying grain and transforming bad wine into good. One German print relates the miraculous healing of a young Genoese woman named Maria Sambuceti, who suffered a serious injury to her arm after falling down the stairs. She only recovered after she had cut her cramping hand on the setting of her reliquary capsule containing relics of St. Luigi, and after her cousin Teresia had begun to treat the wound with the saint's oil. The miraculous healing was further promoted by the constant invocation of the Jesuit saint, with the help of his medal as well as persistent worship of his image at the nearby church.³¹ It was precisely this combination of different devotional practices – employing objects, worshipping images, adopting a devout, God-fearing attitude – that led to miraculous healing. The richness of Catholic material culture can never be underestimated. Religious medals were more than powerful objects through which saints could affect miraculous healings; they also exemplified the ways early modern believers could appropriate the saints. The next section considers the mutually reinforcing relationship between saints of different religious orders and between old and new saints.

THE MATERIAL PLURALITY OF SAINTS

Early modern Catholicism was defined by the perpetual interplay between universality and plurality. As Birgit Emich has argued, the main focus of the Roman curia was to promote unity, which could only be achieved by balancing its own claim of centrality with the diversity

---

²⁹ Trevor Johnson, *Magistrates, Madonnas and Miracles: The Counter Reformation in the Upper Palatinate* (Farnham, 2009), 222.
³⁰ Nikolaus Pottu, *Dreyfache Glory deß heiligen Vatters Ignatii, der Societät Jesu Stiffters* (Mainz, 1710), 344.
³¹ Hermann Goldhagen, *Vollständige Anweisung zur Andacht gegen den wunderthätigen H. Aloysius Gonzaga aus der Gesellschaft Jesu* (Munich, 1775), 24–30.

encountered in the often-remote regions where the Catholic Church was represented.[32] This ambivalent task manifested itself in the development of canonization processes in the wake of the Counter-Reformation. While officially recognized saints were venerated on a global scale, the cults of the blessed were rooted in more particular contexts.[33] (See Chapter 7.) There were consequently many saints and *beati* to choose from, from a wide range of backgrounds, allowing individual Catholics to develop their own custom-made devotional practices. Religious medals were ideally suited to convey and celebrate these two sides of the cult of the saints: their universality and their plurality.

Mostly mass-produced for supporting beatification or canonization processes, medals with saints were distributed in local religious communities or sold at sacred sites from where they transcended their locality by traveling via pilgrimage routes or as gifts in social and religious networks. Early modern Catholics made use of this material plurality of early modern saints and *beati* in order to customize their own devotional practices. By attaching various religious medals to their rosaries, the wearer could seek the protection of particular saints and seek their specialized intercession against disease and harm. Since rosaries could be personalized, they often included religious medals of saints from different religious orders, though owners usually limited themselves to no more than two orders on the same object.[34] Our second rosary demonstrates the daily handling of saintly plurality through the material coexistence of Franciscan and Jesuit saints and *beati* on one and the same object. The fact that it includes two medals associated with the Franciscans but only one Jesuit might indicate that the owner had a slight preference for the Greyfriars. The owner was apparently content to invoke Franciscan and Jesuit saints alongside each other for their spiritual and physical well-being and religious edification, despite their well-known rivalry, especially in contested mission areas like Japan. Other rosaries indicate that our owner was by no means unique. One of the "Franciscan" medals of our rosary, which depicts Clare of Assisi (1194–1253) and Michelina of Pesaro (1300–1356), can likewise be interpreted as a material example of this specific handling of

---

[32] Birgit Emich, "Uniformity and Polycentricity: The Early Modern Papacy between Promoting Unity and Handling Diversity," in *Pathways Through Early Modern Christianities*, ed. Andreea Badea, Bruno Boute, and Birgit Emich (Cologne, 2023), 45.
[33] Ibid., 45.
[34] Keller, ed., *Edelsteine, Himmelsschnüre*, 166.

Figure 15.7 Brass medal, reverse with Blessed Michelina, first half of the eighteenth century. Diözesanmuseum Freising (Photo: Anne Mariss)

saintly diversity (Figure 15.7). The medal with Blessed Michelina was coined following her beatification by Pope Clement XII in 1737 and accompanied by numerous publications about her virtuous life.[35]

Michelina's representation with the attributes of the pilgrim's staff and hat is based on the narrative of her pilgrimage to the Holy Land. Federico Barocci's painting of the Franciscan tertiary in rapture at Golgotha, or one of the numerous copper engravings made after this painting, served as a template for the medal.[36] Notably, she is depicted as a nun with a rosary on her cincture to which a medal is attached,

---

[35] See Damián Cornejo, *Wunderbahrliches Leben der Seeligen Michelinæ von Pesaro des Dritten Ordens des Heil Vatters Francisci von der Buß genannt* (Munich, 1738).
[36] An engraving after Federico Barocci's painting which is held in the Vatican Museums can be consulted at the online collection of the British Museum: www.britishmuseum.org/collection/object/P_1874-0808-1545.

probably showing the Virgin Mary or a female saint. This depiction imagines the saint herself using a rosary, even if Michelina herself would hardly have worn this type of quintessentially Baroque rosary during the fourteenth century.

Due to their specific double-faced design, religious medals reinforced the mutual relationship between the new saints and those who had already been venerated before the Counter-Reformation revival of saint-making and whose cults were firmly established within Christianity. Ancient saints were not simply replaced by new ones; rather, their veneration paved the way for the popular acceptance of newcomers to the ranks of saints. In turn, established cults also received a boost from the new arrivals. Comparisons between old and new saints can also be found in the saints' vitae or in sermons written on the occasion of their canonization. The fact that the obverse of the medal is adorned with Clare of Assisi refers to the veneration of both saints as followers of St. Francis, the former as the founder of the order of the Poor Clares, the latter as a Franciscan tertiary. The medal's joint depiction of the two female saints associates Michelina with Clare and places her in the same tradition of veneration. Although as a canonized saint Clare of Assisi occupied a higher position, the two women were both venerated for their virtuous lives, in particular for their renunciation of all earthly riches and their works of charity, pilgrimages, and ecstatic visions, thus serving as female models of sanctity. Firmly rooted in the Italian town of Pesaro, Michelina's cult was mainly propagated by the Confraternity of the Annunciation and the Malatesta family into which she had married before becoming a nun.[37] In the early modern period, local cults like the one of Michelina of Pesaro began to spread further afield through the many portable devotional objects they produced.

SANCTITY ON THE MOVE

The case of the two rosaries and their religious pendants illustrates not only the plurality of the Catholic cult of saints but also the worldwide circulation of religious objects that contributed to the formation of an early modern Catholicism oscillating between the universal and the local. As Simon Ditchfield has argued, "it was above all the portability (and tradability) of such devotional objects – in other words, its material rather than linguistic translatability – that enabled Roman Catholicism

[37] André Vauchez, *Sainthood in the Later Middle Ages*, trans. Jean Birrell (Cambridge, 1997), 241.

to become the first world religion."[38] On the one hand, the global circulation of religious objects led to the spread of Catholicism and the formation of local beliefs; on the other hand, Europe itself was a place where "pagan" objects from Asia, Africa, and the Americas challenged existing notions of sanctity. Moreover, foreign materials such as exotic aromatic woods rose in popularity for the crafting of rosary beads, while relics from missionary martyrs, and accounts and iconographic depictions of martyrdom like Mathias Tanner's Jesuit martyrology from 1675, fueled the idea of a global Catholic community whose faith was defended even on the borders of the known world.[39]

The medal depicting Francis of Assisi (1181–1226) with the stigmata and his early modern namesake Francisco Solano (1549–1610), a Spanish Franciscan friar and missionary in Peru, exemplifies the way local cults were universalized through the dissemination of prints, images, and devotional objects (Figure 15.8). The object was coined following Solano's canonization by Pope Benedict XIII in 1726. It depicts Solano's most famous miracle, the miraculous rescue from a shipwreck during a crossing from Panama to Peru. Even though Solano's popularity grew in the wake of his canonization in 1726, he primarily remained a local patron saint – in contrast to more universal saints like the Jesuit Francis Xavier. The surviving objects in various collections support this observation. While numerous medals depicting the Jesuit saint have survived, including most notably those depicting his death on the remote Chinese island of Shangchuan, Solano medals are very rare. This can be attributed to both the fact that Solano's cult did not attain a global audience and that the Franciscans did not use medals as a means of healing to the same extent as the Jesuits did.[40]

As mentioned above, rosaries were probably the most appropriate vehicles for the personalization of one's devotional practices. It is very likely that the owner of this rosary advocated for and supported the canonization of the Franciscan missionary by choosing an uncommon religious medal to personalize his or her tool of devotion. Nonetheless, the options available to an early modern believer must not be

---

[38] Simon Ditchfield, "Translating Christianity in an Age of Reformations," *Studies in Church History* 53 (2017): 164–95, at 195.

[39] Mathias Tanner, *Societas Jesu usque ad sanguinis et vitae profusionem militans* (Prague, 1675). See also José Luis Betrán, "Martyrdom and Mission in the Early-Modern Iberian World," in *The Complexity of Hispanic Religious Life in the 16th–18th Centuries*, ed. Doris Moreno (Leiden, 2020), 38–54.

[40] For a short modern biography of Solano, see Bernard L. Fontana, *A Gift of Angels: The Art of Mission San Xavier del Bac* (Tucson, AZ, 2010), 118.

Figure 15.8 Brass medal, reverse with Francisco Solano, first half of the eighteenth century. Diözesanmuseum Freising (Photo: Anne Mariss)

overestimated, since religious pendants came together with rosaries as gifts or as tools of propaganda. While the pendant of the ivory rosary certainly reflected a conscious choice or even a commissioned work, our second rosary therefore illustrates the roles chance and availability played. Even in those circumstances, however, the choice to add a pendant to a rosary belonged to the wearer. Each rosary could be fashioned into a highly individualistic devotional object.

In spite of their very different materiality, both the elaborate ivory pendant with St. Dominic and Rose of Lima (Figures 15.2 and 15.3) and the simple brass medal depicting the Franciscan saint Francisco Solano (Figure 15.8) can be interpreted as moving objects within early modern global Catholicism. Solano's cult was shaped by his activity as a missionary in Peru and strongly anchored in a local tradition. However, in the wake of his canonization, his veneration spread throughout Europe, consolidating itself by means of reports about his pious life and the images and medals associated with the miracles he performed in the

Spanish missions. The same is true of Rose of Lima, whose cult was initially anchored locally and only spread throughout Europe after her canonization in 1671. Numerous prints and thousands of images and medals picturing the Peruvian saint were "part of a most impressive Dominican promotion strategy"[41] directed toward her successful canonization. Medals of saints minted in Europe were often returned to the missions, where they were distributed to the faithful. The Jesuit Missionary Johannes Siebert counted among the fruits of his missionary work in Cochinchina (today's South Vietnam) not only the conversion of 92 adults and the baptism of 267 children, but also the distribution of 500 rosaries, 1,250 indulgence pennies, and 600 small images of the Jesuit saints Ignatius of Loyola and Francisco Javier.[42] Praying a rosary and invoking patron saints from remote regions of the world allowed for the participation in a worldwide communion of saints. Portable, cheaply produced sacramentals were thus highly important items in the process of saint-making as well as the spread and propagation of cults throughout the early modern Catholic world.

Religious pendants such as rosaries, crosses, and medals produced and sold at holy sites were also acquired as part of pilgrimages, testifying to the mobility of early modern Catholics. The religious medal depicting the coronation of Mary and the Holy Cross of Sirolo, a polychrome wooden sculpture of the *Christus triumphans* from the thirteenth century, also known under the name of the Crucifix of Numana, is an example of the close relationship between the movement of pilgrims and the consumption and circulation of devotional objects (Figure 15.9). The cross itself, which is still kept in the church of Numana near Ancona in Italy, has a fascinating object biography oscillating between legendary account and historical veracity.[43] Between the fourteenth and sixteenth centuries, the cult of the Holy Cross became well established and turned Numana into a popular pilgrimage destination on the way to or back from Loreto. In 1613, on her pilgrimage to the Marian shrine in Loreto, Archduchess Maria Maddalena of Austria (1589–1631), the Grand Duchess of Tuscany, stopped at the

---

[41] Tristan Weddigen, "Materiality and Idolatry: Roman Imaginations of Saint Rose of Lima," in *The Nomadic Object: The Challenge of World for Early Modern Religious Art*, ed. Christine Göttler and Mia M. Mochizuki (Leiden, 2018), 103–46, at 106.

[42] Johannes Siebert, "Brief Nr. 706 an Maria Theresia, Reichs-Gräfin von Fugger zu Wellenburg, August 6th, 1741, Sinoa," in *Allerhand So Lehr- als Geist-reiche Brief/ Schriften und Reis-Beschreibungen*, vol. 5, ed. Joseph Stöcklein (Vienna, 1758), 50.

[43] Fabiola Cogliandro, "Testimonianze artistiche nella chiesa del Santissimo Crocifisso di Numana," *Il capitale culturale*, no. 20 (2019): 107–47.

Figure 15.9 Brass medal with the Holy Cross of Sirolo, first half of the eighteenth century. Diözesanmuseum Freising (Photo: Anne Mariss)

church in Numana to venerate the glorious image.[44] Many others followed in her footsteps. Archaeological finds of religious medals and pilgrims' guides demonstrate that this miraculous cross was not only a local phenomenon but a well-known destination attracting devotees from far and wide.[45] Although it is not possible to determine whether the owner of the rosary visited Numana or received the medal as a gift, the object served as a material souvenir that reminded the wearer of the

---

[44] Giovanna Pirani, "Ancona, Pellegrini e Pellegrinaggi: Fonti e Testimonianze," in *Pellegrini verso Loreto: Atti del Convegno Pellegrini e Pellegrinaggi a Loreto nei secoli XV–XVIII*, ed. Floriano Grimaldi (Ancona, 2003), 301.

[45] Stefan Fassbinder, "Steckt das Bekenntnis in der Erde? Frömmigkeit und Archäologie," in *Bekennen, Bekenntnis, Bekenntnisse: Interdiziplinäre Zugänge*, ed. Thomas K. Kuhn (Leipzig, 2014), 103–44, esp. 140–41. For variations of the medal, see José Diaz Tabernero and Christian Hesse, *Müstair, Kloster St. Johann: 2: Münzen und Medaillen* (Zurich, 2004), 178.

spiritual encounter at the sacred site and accompanied him or her throughout life.[46]

The purchase of cheap religious souvenirs was a central part of early modern pilgrimages. Devotional objects acquired during a pilgrimage provided a stimulus for the remembrance of the spiritual experience and served as a material display of the arduous undertaking. The neo-baroque crucifix of the rosary cast in brass with the engraving "M. Zell" on the reverse can also be interpreted as a pious "souvenir" of the famous Austrian pilgrimage site of Mariazell. The fourteenth-century basilica houses a small wooden statue of the Virgin Mary, dressed in a splendid robe, which was (and still is) venerated by Catholics. Both objects, the medal and the cross, point to the geographical mobility of early modern Catholics who visited sacred places near and far, acquiring religious objects that subsequently played an important role in their daily devotional practices. Sacramentals bought during a pilgrimage could be used back home as an effective remedy for all kinds of ailments. Pilgrimage medals belong to the category of religious objects "whose significance and sacred power were activated through movement," as Paul Nelles has recently argued using the example of *Agni Dei*.[47] They bridged the distance between the pilgrimage site and the place of their daily use, resulting in the dissemination and acceptance of local cults across geographical and sociocultural boundaries.[48] Even if comparably few of the cheap, mass-produced items survive today – those that do are often still attached to rosaries in collections or found in proximity to them during archaeological excavations – they point to the mobility of people and things as well as their role for the practice of hagiolatry in early modern Catholicism. As material containers of sanctity, they were able to absorb, transport, and transmit sacred power across time and space.

CONCLUSION

The making of early modern saints and *beati* depended largely on their acceptance by as broad and diverse a segment of the lay population as possible. Their veneration and invocation in everyday life were

---

[46] On pilgrimages, see Chapter 17 in this volume and Elizabeth Tingle, *Sacred Journeys in the Counter-Reformation: Long-Distance Pilgrimage in Northwest Europe* (Berlin, 2020), 191.

[47] Nelles, "Devotion," 186.

[48] Sidler, *Heiligkeit aushandeln*, 261f.

supported by a material culture whose scope ranged from relics to images of saints to religious medals. Rosaries were a central part of this religious materiality and can be considered representative of the material culture of saints as a whole. Our two rosaries illustrate the complexity of veneration, imitation, and invocation of the saints across the early modern Catholic world. Almost always, all three practices are represented in the different religious pendants attached to the rosary, though one is often predominant. While the reliquary capsule, for example, falls primarily into the category of veneration, the Jesuit medal was mainly used for invocation in times of crisis and illness. Other *beati moderni*, such as Michelina of Pesaro, were probably considered more suitable for imitation. However, the boundaries between veneration, imitation, and invocation are rarely clear-cut; rather, they overlap in historical reality, pointing to rosaries' multilayered uses and functions for early modern Catholics.

As an innovative approach to understanding the significance of saints and sainthood in the past lives of the faithful, this chapter's object-centered analysis has attempted to more clearly delineate the role of material culture in early modern practices of veneration. Attaching religious pendants to rosaries was highly important for the dissemination, acceptance, and appropriation of saints and their cults as part of everyday devotional practices. Surviving objects such as the two rosaries analyzed here show that early modern sanctity had a strong material and bodily dimension manifesting itself in daily religious use and the undogmatic choice of saints for personal needs. These devotional objects point to the mobility of things, peoples, and beliefs within early modern Catholicism – as mobile containers transferring sanctity from a holy site to a place of everyday use, as vehicles promoting the worldwide spread of local cults, as bridges between old and new saints, but above all as conduits to the divine.

16 Confraternities

MIGUEL A. VALERIO

Confraternities were the main form of lay organization in the Catholic Church during the early modern period. Confraternities practiced mutual aid, assured members of a proper burial upon their deaths, sustained kinship networks, and were devoted to the Virgin and the saints. They built hospitals; cared for the sick, dying, and disabled; commissioned art; and, among other activities, staged lavish religious processions.[1] Through their pious activities, they allowed laypersons to exercise spiritual leadership over their peers. Confraternities thus empowered the laity to have a great deal of control over their Catholic practices. In this world, confraternal devotion often determined a saint's popularity.

The importance of confraternities becomes especially apparent when we study their use by subjugated or disadvantaged groups. For them, confraternities proved most instrumental: Their collective resources allowed such groups to gain access to health care and burial, become patrons of art and architecture, build lettered archives, and more. Afrodescendants began to organize as confraternities in the Iberian Peninsula in the late medieval period and started to appear in New World in the early years of European colonization. Black confraternities (*cofradías* in Spanish, *irmandades* in Portuguese) may be responsible for many of the Black saints we know today, for they were their principal devotees, venerating these holy Black individuals centuries before they were officially recognized by the Church, as well as others who were never canonized. Black confraternities commissioned statues of saints, which they carried in lavish religious processions. This chapter thus explores how Black confraternities promoted devotion to the saints and what role saints played in their confraternal activities, as an example of the role that confraternities and saints played in

---

[1] See the essays in Konrad Eisenbichler, ed., *A Companion to Medieval and Early Modern Confraternities* (Leiden, 2019).

organizing the devotional lives of the Catholic faithful in accordance with their background.

This chapter thus takes issue with the claim that confraternities constituted another means of Iberian domination.[2] Afrodescendants' confraternal practices demonstrate that subaltern subjects imbued these Catholic institutions with their own spirit and used them for purposes beyond integrating into Iberian society. Black *cofrades* and *irmãos* (confraternity members) availed themselves of confraternities to assert their humanity; showcase their social, economic, and political agency; correlate their worlds with Catholicism; and negotiate their social standing. Rather than apparatuses of domination, then, confraternities served Black believers as powerful institutions that even allowed them to resist domination.[3] Saintly devotion was a central aspect of their daily, artistic, and festive practices.

Counter-Reformation confraternities, regardless of their ethnic makeup, operated in an environment that sought to limit their activities. *Cofradías* traditionally functioned outside the confines or control of the Catholic Church.[4] After the Council of Trent, secular and ecclesiastical authorities began to restrict *cofradías*, requiring a license for their foundation, by requiring their financial transactions to be reviewed by government or ecclesiastical authorities. One victim of these tighter controls were penitential *cofradías* – those that used corporal punishment as acts of piety. The latter restriction may have especially affected Black confraternities, as they constituted a population whose religious sincerity was often questioned.[5] Black penitential *cofradías*, for example, were outlawed in Mexico City in 1575.[6]

---

[2] For a summary of this debate, see Nicole von Germeten, *Black Blood Brothers: Confraternities and Social Mobility for Afro-Mexicans* (Gainesville, FL, 2006), 4; Lisa Voigt, *Spectacular Wealth: The Festivals of Colonial South American Mining Towns* (Austin, TX, 2016), 122–23.

[3] On this latter point, see João José Reis, *Slave Rebellion in Brazil: The Muslim Uprising of 1835 in Bahia* (Baltimore, 1995); João José Reis, *Death Is a Festival: Funeral Rites and Rebellion in Nineteenth-Century Brazil* (Chapel Hill, NC, 2003).

[4] See Martín Oliver Carrión, "Surviving Conquest: From Huacas to Cofradías in 17th Century Cuzco," *MLN* 134, no. 2 (2019): 324–50.

[5] See Karen B. Graubart, "'So color de una cofradía': Catholic Confraternities and the Development of Afro-Peruvian Ethnicities in Early Colonial Peru," *Slavery and Abolition* 33, no. 1 (2012): 43–64; Miguel A. Valerio, "'That There Be No Black Brotherhood': The Failed Suppression of Afro-Mexican Confraternities, 1568–1612," *Slavery and Abolition* 42, no. 2 (2021): 293–314.

[6] "Real cédula a Martín Enríquez, virrey de la Nueva España, para que prohíba la procesión e disciplina de la cofradía de los negros de la ciudad de México, por los inconvenientes que genera," May 15, 1575, Archivo General de Indias (AGI), México

Sometimes neighbors observed confraternities with as much suspicion as the authorities. In 1699, for example, the *mayordomo* (executive officer) Isidro Peralta of Mexico City's *mulato* confraternity of St. Nicholas Tolentino, the city's oldest Black confraternity, was accused before the Inquisition of saying Mass without being a priest – a grave offense.[7] After a three-year investigation that looked at four multi-ethnic confraternities, the Inquisition cleared Isidro of the charge, but labeled his confraternal practices (especially preaching) as indiscreet (*indyscreta*).[8] These practices included processing with statues of Saints Nicholas Tolentino and Augustine on their feast day without permission from the archbishop's office. Given this watchful environment, the continued commitment of Black *cofrades* and *irmãos* to confraternities underscores how instrumental these institutions proved for their devotional lives and sense of selfhood, and as sites for self-realization and resistance. Moreover, Black confraternities' devotion to the saints, especially Black saints, testified to a distinct form of popular religiosity – a religiosity grounded in their members' cultural heritage and lived experiences.

IBERIAN BEGINNINGS

The first Afro-Iberian confraternities were founded in the main slave port cities of late medieval Iberia, namely, Seville, Lisbon, Valencia, and Barcelona. After 1500, the number of Black confraternities expanded, especially in Seville and Lisbon, where the largest number

---

1090, L. 8, fols. 42v–43r. See Valerio, "'That There Be No Black Brotherhood'"; Germeten, *Black Blood Brothers*, 25–27.

[7] "El señor fiscal del Santo Oficio contra Ysidro de Peralta, mulato, por fundar a su modo una religion de san Agustin," Mexico City, 1699, Huntington Library (HL), Mexican Inquisition Papers, Series II, Box 6, HM35168. This same confraternity had been chastised by the archdiocesan solicitor for processing on Maudy Thursday without permission a century earlier: "Contra algunos mulatos que han fundado cofradia y salido en procesion sin licencia," Mexico City, 1600, Archivo General de la Nación (AGN), Mexico, Bienes Nacionales, vol. 810, exp. 28. On confraternity governing structure, see Miguel A. Valerio, "Black Brotherhoods in the Iberian Atlantic," in *The Oxford Research Encyclopedia of Latin American History*, ed. Stephen Webre (Oxford, 2022).

[8] "Autos contra diferentes personas que formavan nueba religion de san Agustin," Mexico City, 1702, HL, HM 35169. For a close analysis of this case, see Joan C. Bristol, "Afro-Mexican Saintly Devotion in a Mexico City Alley," in *Africans to Spanish America: Expanding the Diaspora*, ed. Sherwin K. Bryant, Rachel S. O'Toole, and Ben Vinson III (Urbana, IL, 2014), 114–35; Krystle Farman Sweda, "Black Catholicism: The Formation of Local Religion in Colonial Mexico" (PhD diss., City University of New York, 2020).

of sub-Saharan Africans had been brought, first through the trans-Saharan and later the Atlantic slave trades. The first of these Black confraternities, dedicated to Our Lady of the Angels, is believed to have been founded in Seville in the 1390s when its archbishop Gonzalo Mena Roelas established a hospital for Afro-Sevillanos.[9] It is unclear if the Afro-Sevillanos ran the confraternity themselves from the start, but Seville's Black population grew exponentially in the sixteenth century, and the Black *cofrades* certainly ran the *cofradía* by 1550.[10] Two further Black confraternities soon followed: Our Lady of the Rosary and St. Ildefonso.[11] While St. Ildefonso was made up of mixed-race (*mulato*) Afro-Sevillanos, Our Lady of the Rosary was made up of Afrodescendants brought from or through Portugal. Most Black confraternities in the Portuguese world would be dedicated to Our Lady of the Rosary after Dominican friars in Lisbon began admitting Afro-Lisboetas into their Rosary brotherhoods in 1460.[12] The Black *irmãos* of this *irmandade* started their own, exclusively Black branch in 1565. In Barcelona a group of freed Afro-Barcelonenses (*christianos nigros libertate donatos*) founded a confraternity in the parish of St. Jaume (St. James) as early as 1445.[13] This is the first Black confraternity known to have been founded on Afrodescendants' own initiative. Another one, Our Lady of Mercy, was founded in Valencia in 1472, with the stated purpose of helping Afro-Valencianos obtain manumission – mirroring the role the same Marian advocation played for European Christians.[14]

---

[9] Isidoro Moreno, *La antigua hermandad de "Los Negros" de Sevilla: Etnicidad, poder y sociedad en 600 años de historia* (Seville, 1997), 23–56. On the Black population in late medieval Seville and the Iberian Peninsula, see Alfonso Franco Silva, *Regesto documental sobre la esclavitud sevillana (1453–1513)* (Seville, 1979); Alfonso Franco Silva, *La esclavitud en Sevilla y su tierra a fines de la Edad Media* (Seville, 1979); William D. Phillips, *Slavery in Medieval and Early Modern Iberia* (Philadelphia, 2014).

[10] Moreno, *La antigua hermandad*, 57–72.

[11] Félix González de León, *Historia crítica y descriptiva de las cofradías Penitencia, Sangre y Luz fundadas en la ciudad de Sevilla* (1852; reprint Seville, 1994); Ignacio Camacho Martínez, *La hermandad de los mulatos de Sevilla: Antecedentes históricos de la Hermandad del Calvario* (Seville, 2001).

[12] *Compromisso da Irmandade do Rosário dos Homens Pretos*, Lisbon, 1565, Biblioteca Nacional de Portugal, MS 150, prologo, fol. 1r. See Jorge Fonseca, *Religião e liberdade: Os negros nas irmandades e confrarias portuguesas (séculos XV a XIX)* (Lisbon, 2016).

[13] "Ordenanzas de la cofradía de los cristianos negros de Barcelona," Barcelona, March 20, 1455, Archivo General de la Corona de Aragón (AGCA), R. 3298, fol. 3.

[14] "Fundación de la cofradía de los negros libertos de la ciudad de Valencia," Valencia, November 3, 1472, AGCA, R. 5512, fols. 217–18. See Debra Blumenthal, "*La Casa dels Negres*: Black African Solidarity in Late Medieval Valencia," in *Black Africans in*

As the main purpose of Valencia's Black confraternity suggests, Afro-Iberians joined and founded confraternities to ameliorate their precarious lives. Patricia A. Mulvey has argued that Afro-Lisboetas joined the city's Rosary brotherhoods and later started their own chapters as a form of "death insurance" – as membership guaranteed a proper burial.[15] Indeed, confraternities may have particularly appealed to Afrodescendants because Christian views on mortality paralleled West African deathways.[16] At a minimum, confraternity membership guaranteed that *cofrades* and *irmãos'* bodies were not summarily disposed on the city's outskirts, which, as we can glimpse from a royal ordinance by Manuel I of Portugal (r. 1495–1521), was a problem:

> We are informed that slaves who die in this city, as well as those brought from Guinea, like others, are not buried as well as they should be in the places where their bodies are thrown, and they are thrown onto the land in such a manner that they are uncovered, or completely exposed above ground without anything covering them, so that the dogs eat them; the majority of these slaves are thrown into a dung heap ... and also in other places nearby.[17]

Across the Iberian Atlantic, providing proper burial and caring for sick members remained the principal activities of Black confraternities, as they had been for other groups since the Middle Ages. These roles are reflected in St. Jaume's charter:

> Money should be taken from the confraternity's money box for a Mass for the soul of every deceased member on the anniversary of his or her death or on the day on which the Church celebrates the mass of the dead. This Mass should be attended by all the members who can and those who are asked by the confraternity's board.... Furthermore, if any member who is known by the board to be poor should die, his burial Mass shall be paid from the confraternity's money box.[18]

Renaissance Europe, ed. Thomas F. Earle and Kate J. P. Lowe (Cambridge, 2005), 225–46.

[15] Patricia Ann Mulvey, "The Black Lay Brotherhoods of Colonial Brazil: A History" (PhD diss., City University of New York, 1976), 15.

[16] Elizabeth W. Kiddy, *Blacks of the Rosary: Memory and History in Minas Gerais, Brazil* (State College, PA, 2005), 15–38.

[17] Lisbon, 1515, Arquivo Nacional da Torre Tombo, Provimento da saude, 1, fol. 51. Unless otherwise noted, all translations are by the author.

[18] "Ordenanzas de la cofradía de los cristianos negros de Barcelona," fol. 3v.

The confraternity would also provide care in illness: "Furthermore, it shall be a statute of this confraternity that if any member falls into poverty through illness or loss of goods or any other manner, the board shall provide for their sustenance, medicine, or any other need."[19] These central tenets formed the main social benefits that confraternities provided throughout the Counter-Reformation Catholic world, and which therefore appear in the vast majority of brotherhood constitutions. Finally, as we have already seen, many Black sodalities also helped enslaved members and even outsiders obtain manumission, usually by providing loans rather than acts of charity.

BLACK CONFRATERNITIES AND THE SAINTS IN COLONIAL LATIN AMERICA

If confraternities had been crucial to Afro-Iberians' survival and integration in Europe, they would be far more instrumental in the Americas, as more than seven million Africans were enslaved into the region. The total number of Black confraternities in the Americas surpassed 200 from 1500 to 1800 (Table 1).[20] In the Americas, Black confraternities continued the activities (devotion, kinship, mutual aid, burial, manumission, etc.) they had begun in the Iberian Peninsula, but with greater social impact, given the larger Black presence. Confraternities in the New World similarly needed to provide burial for bodies that would otherwise be simply disposed of. The Seville-born Jesuit missionary Alonso de Sandoval (1576–1652), for instance, left a vivid account of corpses abandoned on the docks of Cartagena de Indias, one of the region's main slave ports.[21]

Black confraternities begin to appear in the colonial archive by the mid-sixteenth century, almost immediately upon their forced arrival in the New World. In 1549, for example, a group of Afrodescendants in Lima were accused of meeting "under the guise of a confraternity" (*so color de una cofradía*) to drink and gamble.[22] In the 1560s, in Mexico City, two Black confraternities wrote to the Spanish crown requesting

---

[19] Ibid.
[20] On Black confraternities in the region, see, e.g., von Germeten, *Black Blood Brothers*; Mulvey, "The Black Lay Brotherhoods"; Kiddy, *Blacks of the Rosary*.
[21] Alonso de Sandoval, *Treatise on Slavery*, trans. Nicole von Germeten (Indianapolis, IN, 2008), 70–71.
[22] Graubart, "'So color de una cofradía.'" A similar complaint was made in Mexico City in 1590: Valerio, "That There Be No Black Brotherhood."

Table 1 *Black brotherhoods in the Iberian world, fifteenth to nineteenth centuries*

Brazil	165
Cuba	6
Mexico	59
New Granada	12
Peru	22
Portugal	15
Portuguese Africa	4
River Plata	5
Spain	11

Sources: Mulvey, "The Black Lay Brotherhoods," 304; von Germeten, *Black Blood Brothers*, appendix; Patricia Fogelman and Marta Goldberg, "'El rey de los congos': The Clandestine Coronation of Pedro Duarte in Buenos Aires, 1787," in *Afro-Latino Voices: Narratives from the Early Modern Ibero-Atlantic World, 1550–1812*, ed. Kathryn Joy McKnight and Leo J. Garofalo (Indianapolis, IN, 2009), 155–73.

land for each to build a hospital.[23] While these Afrodescendants were attracted to confraternities for the same reasons Europeans had founded them in the first place – namely, to sustain kinship networks, provide a safety net, and serve as burial societies – Black *cofrades* and *irmãos* gave these institutions unique characteristics. Black sodalities, for example, were known for the ceremonial royal court – later reduced to just a king and queen – they elected as part of their annual feast day celebration: the first Sunday of October in the case of brotherhoods devoted to the Rosary and the feast of the Epiphany for many others.[24] It was usually the confraternity's executive officer (*mayordomo*/*majordomo*) and their spouse who were elected king and queen (Figure 16.1). On their feast day, Black confraternities processed through the streets of

---

[23] Miguel A. Valerio, "The Spanish Petition System, Hospitality, and the Formation of a Mulato Community in Sixteenth-Century Mexico," *The Americas* 78, no. 3 (2021): 415–37.

[24] See, e.g., *Compromisso da Irmandade do Rosário dos Homens Pretos* (Lisbon, 1565), fol. 9v–10r; Kiddy, *Blacks of the Rosary*; Fogelman and Goldberg, "'El rey de los congos'"; Cécile Fromont, "Dancing for the King of Congo from Early Modern Central Africa to Slavery-Era Brazil," *Colonial Latin American Review* 22, no. 2 (2013): 184–208; Miguel A. Valerio, *Sovereign Joy: Afro-Mexican Kings and Queens, 1539–1640* (Cambridge, 2022); Tamara J. Walker, "The Queen of *Los Congos*: Slavery, Gender, and Confraternity Life in Late-Colonial Lima, Peru," *Journal of Family History* 40, no. 3 (2015): 305–22.

Figure 16.1 Carlos Julião (1740–1811), Afro-Brazilian confraternal king and queen, in *Riscos iluminados de figurinhos de negros e brancos dos Uzos do Rio de Janeiro e Serro Frio*, ca. 1775, Biblioteca Nacional do Brasil, Iconografia C.I.2.8, fol. 70, watercolor on paper. (Rio de Janeiro, Brazil: Courtesy of the Biblioteca Nacional do Brasil)

their hometown "with their king and queen."[25] Moreover, Black confraternities appeared with their royal figureheads in civic and religious festivals hosted by the larger community.[26] The king and queen normally bore the greatest financial responsibility for these festivities.

Black *irmandades* were unusually large, active, and prosperous in Brazil. As home to the largest overall number of Black *irmandades*, Brazil was also one of the very few places where they were able to establish a tangible, built presence: To wit, Afro-Brazilian brotherhoods built more than fifty churches and chapels between the mid-sixteenth century and 1800.[27] Outside Brazil, the only other places in the Iberian

---

[25] Bernal Díaz del Castillo, *Historia verdadera de la conquista de la Nueva España*, (*manuscrito "Guatemala"*), ed. José Antonio Barbón Rodríguez (ca. 1575, first printed edition: Mexico City, 2005), 755.
[26] See Valerio, *Sovereign Joy*.
[27] See Miguel A. Valerio, "Architects of Their Own Humanity: Race, Devotion, and Artistic Agency in Afro-Brazilian Confraternal Churches in Eighteenth-Century

Figure 16.2 Black saints in Black Rosary Church, Ouro Preto (Photo: Miguel Valerio, 2022)

world where Black confraternities managed to build their own sanctuaries were Seville (Our Lady of the Angels) and Cuba (The Holy Spirit). Most of Brazil's surviving Black churches and chapels were built or rebuilt in the second half of the eighteenth century, when a gold rush also filled the pockets and coffers of many *irmãos* and *irmandades*. This period was also dominated by Afro-Brazilian artists, many of whom were *irmãos*.[28] Wealth aside, the underlying factor that allowed Afro-Brazilian brotherhoods to build their own churches was the expectation in the Portuguese world that *irmandades*, regardless of race, should have their own sanctuaries as a sign of status.

It is also in Brazil where we find the best evidence of Black confraternities' devotion to Black saints. While most Afro-Brazilian confraternities (52 percent, according to one count) were dedicated to Our Lady of the Rosary, some were dedicated to Black saints (Figure 16.2),

Salvador and Ouro Preto," *Colonial Latin American Review* 30, no. 2 (2021): 238–71; Miguel A. Valerio, "Expanding the Colonial Archive," *Colonial Latin American Review* 32, no. 2 (2023): 257–70.

[28] See Valerio, "Architects of Their Own Humanity"; Miguel A. Valerio, "Atlantic Masters: Three Early Modern Afro-Brazilian Artists," *Arts* 12, no. 3 (2023).

Figure 16.3 St. Benedict, frontispiece, *Statutes of Brotherhood of St. Benedict*, Salvador, Bahia, 1683. Arquivo Público do Estado da Bahia (Photo: Miguel Valerio)

either on their own or alongside the Virgin.[29] Examples include St. Ephigenia in Ouro Preto and the double patrons St. Ephigenia and St. Kaleb in Rio de Janeiro, and the church of Our Lady of the Rosary and St. Benedict, also in Rio de Janeiro. Yet regardless of their titular dedications, visual representations of four Black saints are also regularly found inside the churches of Black confraternities in Brazil. These are St. Ephigenia of Ethiopia, St. Kaleb of Axum, St. Anthony of Noto, and St. Benedict of Palermo (Figure 16.3). (On these saints, see Chapter 5 in this volume.)

Very much like their white counterparts in Europe, processions allowed Afro-Brazilian *irmandades* to publicly demonstrate their devotions and claim their place in the public sphere. Afro-Brazilian *irmãos*

---

[29] Mulvey, "The Black Lay Brotherhoods," 61.

would process with the statues of the Black saints they kept in their churches on the relevant feast days and other religious occasions. Particularly striking evidence for what such processions may have looked like comes from Ouro Preto (known as Vila Rica at the time), the main town in the mining district of Minas Gerais, which had a large Black population. From 1730 to 1733, while the town parish church (*igreja matriz*) of Our Lady of the Pillar was being built, the Eucharist was housed in the older Black Rosary brotherhood church nearby.[30] When the Pillar church was consecrated in May 1733, the town's Blessed Sacrament brotherhood sponsored a lavish festival for the Eucharistic transfer. Inevitably, the town's Black confraternities, and especially the *irmandade* of the Rosary that had accommodated the Eucharist, wished to play a major role in the festivities. The Black Rosary brotherhood paved a road connecting their church to Pillar, so that they could have a more direct route to the new church.[31] The proud *irmãos* published an account of the procession a year later, in a pamphlet with the telling title *Triunfo Eucharistico*. In the preface, they claimed to have organized the whole festival.[32] The main text, however, assigns the town's Black confraternities a smaller role: They mainly participated by processing with statues of their saints and the Virgin. The Black Rosary brotherhood that published the *Triunfo*, for example, processed with their statues of St. Anthony, St. Benedict, and the Virgin in the middle of the procession:

> Then came the *Irmandade* of Our Lady of the Rosary of the Blacks, numerous in many *irmãos*, all wearing white silk capes. In their midst were three platforms: the first for St. Anthony [of Noto], the second for St. Benedict [of Palermo], and the third for the Virgin of the Rosary. The statues were richly dressed in golden and silver

---

[30] The Black brotherhood church was rebuilt in the 1780s: see Valerio, "Architects of Their Own Humanity."

[31] "Consulta do Conselho sobre requerimento dos oficiais da Irmandade de Nossa Senhora do Rosário dos Homens Pretos, filial da Matriz de Nossa Senhora do Pilar de Vila Rica, pedindo confirmação da area concedida pela Camara daquela Vila," Vila Rica, January 21, 1769, Arquivo Histórico Ultramarino, Minas Gerais, cx. 94, doc. 6. See Voigt, *Spectacular Wealth*, 140. This road still connects the churches today. Without this road, going from one church to the other would have a required a longer, more circuitous route.

[32] Simão Ferreira Machado, *Triunfo Eucharistico, Exemplar da Christandade Lusitana na publica exaltaçaõ da Fe na solemne Trasladaçaõ do Divinissimo Sacramento da Igreja da Senhora do Rosario, para hum novo Templo do Pilar em Villa Rica, Corte da Capitania das Minas* (Lisbon, 1734). See Voigt, *Spectacular Wealth*, 121–50.

silk, and adorned with valuable pieces of gold, and diamonds, and the platforms with silk, cords, and golden tassels, and with ornamentation of various flowers of diverse materials and colors.[33]

The town's other Black confraternities also processed with their saints – which, in addition to Anthony and Benedict, also included Ephigenia and Kaleb.

Black brotherhoods' devotions to Black saints also point toward the syncretic nature of Afro-Catholic religion. Marina de Mello e Souza, for example, has proposed that Afro-Brazilians of Congolese origin, who formed a large portion of the Black population especially during the seventeenth and eighteenth centuries, identified the statues of Catholic saints with *minkisi* (singular: *nkisi*), objects used in religious rituals by the people of the Congo Basin.[34] Bantu people believe *minkisi* are inhabited by spirits; they dress them with colorful fabrics and attach to their bodies nails and packets of medicinal and spiritual significance. Although such practices seemed have gone unnoticed by Church authorities at the time, surviving *minkisi*, called *prendas* in Cuba, have been found all over the African diaspora.[35] Moreover, two statues of eighteen-century Black saints from Brazil (St. Anthony and St. Benedict), now at the Raclin Murphy Museum of Art at the University of Notre Dame, have nails on them, similar to *minkisi*. Scholarship on how Catholicism was adapted in the early modern Congo invites us to see these practices beyond the traditional orthodox/heterodox binary, as part of a distinct Black Catholicism fashioned by Black *irmãos* and *cofrades*, one that translated African practices into Catholic devotion and also was localized, adapting to the place and the believers' circumstances.[36]

Black confraternities also venerated European saints and participated in festivals celebrating these white saints. When Mexico City, for example, celebrated the beatification of Ignatius of Loyola in 1610,

---

[33] Ferreira Machado, *Triunfo Eucharistico*, 97–98.

[34] Marina de Mello e Souza, "The Construction of a Black Catholic Identity in Brazil: Saints and *Minkisi*: A Reflection of Cultural Miscegenation," in *Africa, Brazil, and the Construction of Black Atlantic identities*, ed. Livio Sansone, Elissé Soumonni, and Boubacar Barry (Trenton, NJ, 2008), 255–68.

[35] See Bárbaro Martínez-Ruiz, *Kongo Graphic Writing and Other Narratives of the Sign* (Philadelphia, 2013). For similar arguments about Marian devotion, see Kiddy, *Blacks of the Rosary*, 60; José Ramos Tinhorão, *Os negros em Portugal: Uma presença silenciosa* (Lisbon, 1988), 122–34.

[36] The best example of this phenomenon is how Catholicism was adapted in the Congo, as Cécile Fromont has shown: *The Art of Conversion: Christian Visual Culture in the Kingdom of Kongo* (Chapel Hill, NC, 2014).

the festivities featured two Black groups with a king each, eight Black dances, and a jousting competition sponsored by members of the Black community.[37] The celebrations also included, among other things, twenty-four triumphal arches offered by the Indigenous community, which likely included some of Mexico City's Indigenous brotherhoods.[38] The account of the festivities only mentions one Black confraternity, that of Holy Christ of the Expiration and Holy Burial, which was founded and met in the city's Dominican convent. (At the time, there were nine Black *cofradías* in the city.)[39] As its name suggests, this Black confraternity was founded with the aim of providing funeral services to its members and other Afro-Mexicans.[40]

In the Eucharistic procession that took the Blessed Sacrament from Mexico City's cathedral to La Profesa, the new Jesuit church, for its consecration on July 31, 1610, the confraternity of Holy Christ of the Expiration and Holy Burial was charged with transporting the Most Blessed Sacrament. The confraternity either commissioned, rented, or borrowed a castle-shaped sacramental cart for the occasion. The Eucharist was placed in the front of this cart, while a celestial sphere in the back featured two, presumably Black, children dressed as the Virgin and St. Ignatius. The cart moved on secret wheels and was pushed by Black *cofrades* dressed as African "savages." The confraternity's mayordomo-king accompanied the Most Blessed Sacrament, which was carried on a throne on the shoulder of *cofrades* likewise dressed as African savages. The mayordomo-king acted as the confraternity's spokesperson, presenting the offering on behalf of the confraternity, as recounted by the Jesuit chronicler Andrés Pérez de Rivas:

> As the procession came out of the cathedral, it was met by forty-four canons that were fired next to a beautiful seven-yard-high castle of well-feigned masonry, an invention offered by Black creoles[41] from a

---

[37] Andrés Pérez de Rivas, *Corónica y historia religiosa de la provincia de la Compañía de Jesús en Nueva España* [c. 1600–1650], vol. 1 (c. 1600–1650, first edition: Mexico City, 1896), 242–61. For a fuller analysis of these festivities, see Valerio, *Sovereign Joy*, 126–67.

[38] See, e.g., Laura Dierksmeier, *Charity for and by the Poor: Franciscan-Indigenous Confraternities in Mexico 1527–1700* (Norman, OK, 2020).

[39] See von Germeten, *Black Blood Brothers*, 71.

[40] Fernando Ojea, *Libro tercero de la historia religiosa de la Provincia de México de la Orden de Santo Domingo* (c. 1550–76; first printed ed. Mexico City, 1897), 10.

[41] "Creole" referred to Afrodescendants born and raised in the Americas: see *Creolization in the Americas*, ed. David Buisseret and Steven G. Reinhardt (College Station, TX, 2000); *Creolizing Europe: Legacies and Transformations*, ed. Encarnación Gutiérrez Rodríguez and Shirley A. Tate (Liverpool, 2015).

confraternity in the convent of the most glorious Father Saint Dominic, [who were] moved [to do so] by those fathers (who, on this occasion, labored to favor us), as well as by the devotion which the same blacks have for Our Holy Father Ignatius. This castle, which was set on four invisible wheels, was drawn by twenty-four savages dressed in long animal hides from head to toe, and wearing masks, according to their custom: in front of the castle, on a chair, with a club, and dressed like a savage, on the shoulders of four other savages dressed in animal hide, came the king, who upon being put in front of the Blessed Sacrament, touched the castle with his club and released many rockets, and a beautifully painted globe or cloud which opened up and revealed two children, one dressed as the Blessed Virgin and the other as our holy Father Ignatius.... And then the savage king, in half a dozen octets, said how being away in the forest, he heard from his hut the echoes of the fiesta that was being celebrated in honor of the saint in Mexico City, but as he was poor, having no more valuable asset, offered this castle. Then a door opened, whence exited twelve more savages very well dressed, and performed a curious dance that delighted the procession.[42]

Like Black confraternal kings and queens in Brazil, this performance took the form of what Mary Louise Pratt has dubbed autoethnography, or colonial subjects' capacity to represent themselves "in ways that engage with representations others have made of them."[43] In other words, "presentations that the so-defined others construct *in response to* or in dialogue with" how "European metropolitan subjects represent to themselves their others."[44] In this performance, Afro-Mexicans represented themselves as Europeans had depicted them, as savages. In this instance, the Afro-Mexican confraternity adapted the widespread Afro-diasporic tradition of festive Black kings and queens to Hispanic baroque religious pomp.[45] They appeared as savages escorting the Eucharist and carrying their king on their shoulders only in order to play and subvert Euro-centric notions of Africa and Blackness. But viewed from the Black actors' perspective, this performance staged the communal sovereignty that confraternities afforded Afrodescendants.[46]

---

[42] Pérez de Rivas, *Corónica y historia religiosa*, vol. 1, 250.
[43] Mary Louise Pratt, "Arts of the Contact Zone," *Profession* (1991): 33–40, at 35.
[44] Ibid.; emphasis in the original.
[45] See Valerio, *Sovereign Joy*.
[46] See ibid.

This performance also underscores how Black confraternities took advantage of an occasion to strengthen their relationships with the religious orders that protected them. This latter strategy was particularly crucial to Black confraternities' survival, as they faced hostility and scrutiny from secular and diocesan authorities, as noted earlier.[47] In Mexico City, the viceroy and city council tried to suppress Black confraternities altogether in the last decades of the sixteenth century.[48] In the face of this antagonism, missionary support was crucial to Black confraternities' continued existence. Black confraternities therefore sought to remain in their good graces, as this Mexican example demonstrates.

Another example is found in the alliance of Afro-Brazilian mixed-race (*pardo*) confraternities forged with the Franciscans. In Brazil, the children of European colonizers and Africans were alternatively known as *mulatos*, *pardos*, or *mestiços*. But mixed-race Afro-Brazilians themselves preferred the term *pardo*, because colonial discourse was disproportionately skewed against *mulatos*, who were associated with "laziness, dishonesty, slyness, arrogance, and lack of trustworthiness."[49] In the most comprehensive study of this discourse in colonial Brazil, Raimundo Agnelo Soares Pessoa notes that "none of the [colonial] references to *mulatos* allude to a single honest attitude or action by this ethnic group."[50] Pessoa adds that "with regard to *pardos* the opposite is true."[51] This was therefore the term most mixed-race Afro-Brazilian *irmãos* preferred.

Yet choosing the term *pardo* alone did not solve the problem. *Pardos'* racial mixture still gave them a liminal social status. This status was aggravated by the lack of a *pardo* saint, which constituted a significant disadvantage in a world where the socio-symbolic was overdetermined by the sacred. Black confraternities could claim sacro-social

---

[47] See, e.g., Graubart, "'So color de una cofradía'"; Valerio, "'That There Be No Black Brotherhood.'"

[48] "Real cédula a Martín Enríquez, virrey de la Nueva España, para que prohiba la procesión e disciplina de la cofradía de los negros"; "Carta del virrey Martín Enríquez," Mexico City, April 28, 1572, AGI, México 19, N. 82, fol. 2r; *Actas del cabildo de la Ciudad de México*, vol. 14, ed. Ignacio Bejarano (1521–1822, first edition: Mexico City, 1889–1911), 277. See Valerio, "'That There Be No Black Brotherhood'"; Valerio, "The Spanish Petition System."

[49] Larissa Viana, *O idioma da mestiçagem: As irmandades de pardos na América portuguesa* (Campinas, 2007), 27.

[50] Raimundo Angelo Pessoa Soares, *Gente sem sorte: A invenção dos mulatos no Brasil colonial* (Goiânia, 2013), 50.

[51] Ibid., 53.

Figure 16.4 St. Gonçalo Garcia, Livramento church, Recife (Photo: Miguel Valerio, 2022)

prestige, or respectability, in this world through saintly devotion to Black saints.

For the Afro-Brazilian *pardos*, the issue was solved by the Franciscans, who offered them a "saint of [their] same color and accident": St. Gonçalo Garcia (Figure 16.4).[52] Born in Vasai, near present-day Mumbai, around 1556, Gonçalo was the son of a Portuguese colonizer and a South Asian woman. Moving to Manila in his youth, the future

---

[52] Sóteiro da Silva Ribeiro [Manuel da Madre de Deus Bulhões], *Summa triunfal da nova e grande celebridade do Glorioso, e invicto Martyr S. Gonçalo Garcia* (Lisbon, 1753), 3. Other Franciscan writings on St. Gonçalo from Brazil include Frei José dos Santos Cosme e Damião, *Sermam de S. Gonsalo Garcia, pregado no terceiro dia do solenissimo triduo, que celebrão os homens pardos de cidade da Bahai na cathedral da mesma cidade* (Lisbon, 1747); Frei Antonio Santa Maria Jaboatão, *Discurso histórico, geográfico, genealógico, politico e encomiástico, recitado em a nova celebridade, que dedicarão os pardos de Pernambuco ao santo da sua côr, o B. Gonçalo Garcia* (Lisbon, 1751).

saint joined the Franciscans as a lay brother, the highest rank available to him as a man of mixed-race heritage. In 1596, Gonçalo and five other Franciscans boarded the *San Felipe*, a ship that unwisely set sail for the Americas during the typhoon season and was hit by two storms. At this point the captain, Matías de Landecho, decided to seek refuge in Japan. A third typhoon left the ship without sails, but the Kuroshio current took it to Japan nonetheless. It arrived at Urado on the Japanese island of Shikoku on October 19, 1596. Miraculously, no lives were lost. But once on land, they were apprehended by Japanese forces. The Franciscan missionaries were taken to Nagasaki where they were added to a group of other Christians, including missionaries, and were executed on February 5, 1596. They were subsequently displayed crucified, as a warning against Christian conversion.[53] The Franciscans lobbied to have this group canonized right away, and they were rapidly beatified in 1627 (although canonization would remain out of reach until 1862).

Initial devotion was addressed to the martyrs as a group, not as individuals.[54] It was only in eighteenth-century Brazil that Gonçalo was finally singled out for veneration, specifically among Brazil's *pardos*. In 1745, a Franciscan missionary offered the following origin story for the *pardos'* devotion to Gonçalo:

> It must be about thirty years since a *pardo* man from Pernambuco named Antônio Ferreira, having gone to Portugal, where he was told that Blessed Gonçalo Garcia was considered the saint of his own color and accident [i.e., *pardo*], brought a small statue of the saint. He kept the statue with great love and devotion for some years until

---

[53] The Japanese were also interested in the luxuries, including a large quantity of Japanese silk, that the ship was carrying to American and European markets. The main source for these events is an account written by one of the survivors, though his name is not given: "Relación de la arribada al Japón del galeón San Felipe y martirio de franciscanos," Manila, 1597, AGI, Filipinas 79, N. 28: http://pares.mcu.es/ParesBusquedas20/catalogo/show/424541?nm, accessed August 28, 2023. See a transcription in Jorge Augusto Gamboa M. and You-Jin Kim, "El incidente del galeón San Felipe y la persecución a los cristianos en Japón (1597): Una transcripción del relato de uno de los sobrevivientes," *Nuevo Mundo/Mundos Nuevos* (2022), http://journals.openedition.org/nuevomundo/86778, accessed August 28, 2023. The best study of these martyrs is Hitomi Omata Rappo, *Des Indes lointaines aux scènes des collèges: Les reflets des martyrs de la mission japonaise en Europe (XVIe–XVIIIe siècle)* (Münster, 2020). See also Larissa Viana, "Gonçalo Garcia: identidade e relações raciais na historia de um santo pardo na América portuguesa," in *Escravidão e subjetividades no Atlântico luso-brasileiro e francês (séculos XVII–XX)*, ed. Myrian Cottias and Hebe Mattos (Marseille, 2016), 43–62.

[54] See Paulo da Trindade, *Conquista espiritual do oriente*, vol. 3, ed. Félix Lopes (1630–36; Lisbon, 1967), 529–66.

he died, and when he died he gave it a to a devout matron of this land, and today it is kept in the [private] chapel of Manoel Alves Ferreira, the lawyer for the Franciscan monastery of St. Anthony in Recife.

This devout *pardo* had made some effort to persuade others of the notion he brought from Portugal that the saint was also *pardo*. But as he had no other evidence than the notion he brought from Portugal, or because the day ordained by Divine Providence for the saint's exaltation and glory and redemption of his color had not arrived, his pious efforts had no further effect than to leave in the others' memory the desire for his devotion, which, as we said, the friars encouraged in them, but dared not go public with their project, for when they consulted friars and men of letters, none agreed that the saint (being a native of India) could have that color.[55]

The fact that devotion to Gonçalo as an individual is only documented in Brazil (and only starting in 1745) makes this version of events unlikely to be entirely factual. It is more plausible that around three decades prior to the writing of this narrative, the Franciscans offered Gonçalo to the *pardos*, who were eager to have a "saint of [their] same color and accident."[56] In this manner, both the Franciscans and the *pardos* took advantage of the liminality of mixed-race status: the former to gain devotees for their saint and a flock for their mission; the latter to sanctify their vilified ethnicity. St. Gonçalo thus enabled *pardos* to claim sacro-social prestige and counter anti-*mulato* discourse through saintly devotion.

In 1745 and 1746, *pardo irmandades* staged two festivals in honor of Blessed Gonçalo: the first took place in Recife, Pernambuco; the second, in Salvador, Bahia, the capital of the colony. These are the earliest records of devotion to an individualized Gonçalo anywhere. The festival in Recife was sponsored by two *pardo* brotherhoods – Recife's Our Lady of Livramento (founded ca. 1694) and Olinda's Guadalupe (founded ca. 1632) – and took place in the public space in front of the Livramento church (Figure 16.5). The festivities featured seventeen allegorical figures on horseback symbolizing events from Blessed Gonçalo's life and five triumphal carts, four bearing statues of different Virgins and one with Blessed Gonçalo – possibly the very statue of the

---

[55] Bulhões, *Summa triunfal*, 3–4.
[56] The church of St. Gonçalo in Recife claims to have the oldest statue of the saint in Brazil, from 1695.

Figure 16.5 Livramento church, Recife, Brazil (Photo: Miguel Valerio, 2022)

saint kept in the Livramento church today and included above as Figure 16.4.[57] The festivities in Salvador, which took place in front of the cathedral, included only four triumphal carts, possibly borrowed from Recife.[58] Both festivals were preceded by novenas to Blessed Gonçalo and included sermons by each city's most prominent Franciscan friar in defense of the nobility of mulatto-ness (*mestiçagem*) and *pardo*-ness. The festivals underscore how Afrodescendant confraternities used saintly devotion to gain social

---

[57] Bulhões, *Summa triunfal*. See also Miguel Valerio, "The Pardos' Triumph: The Use of Festival Material Culture for Sociracial Promotion in Eighteenth-Century Pernambuco," *Journal of Festive Studies* 3, no. 1 (2021): 47–71.

[58] Cosme e Damião, *Serman de S. Gonsalo Garcia*. See Voigt, "*Pública Notícia*: Black Brotherhoods and Corporate Subjectivity in Eighteenth Century Brazil," in *Slave Subjectivities in the Iberian World (15th–20th Centuries)*, ed. Ângela Barreto Xavier, Cristina Nogueira da Silva, and Michel Cahen (Leiden, 2023), 117–33. Salvador's original cathedral was demolished in 1933 due to disrepair. In 1765, the church of the Jesuits, who had been expelled in 1761, was turned into a temporary cathedral while the original cathedral underwent repairs. This situation was never reversed and the old Jesuit church is still the cathedral today.

respectability, build alliances with religious orders to ensure their survival, and claim their place in the public sphere.

CONCLUSION

If not for Black confraternities, Black saints – notwithstanding their official recognition by the Church – may have faded into oblivion. While the Franciscans from St. Benedict's home friary in Sicily pushed for his canonization, most of his devotees were Black *cofrades* and *irmãos* in the Iberian Atlantic.[59] And while the Franciscans essentially abandoned St. Anthony of Noto's cause, Black *irmãos* and *cofrades* never stopped praying to him. Moreover, although modern scholars reckon that Ephigenia of Ethiopia and Kaleb of Axum are more likely medieval inventions than actual historical figures from early Church history, their images are still found in Black confraternal churches. So, too, is that of St. Martin de Porres, to whom Black *cofrades* in Lima must have prayed during the Counter-Reformation.[60] In short, Black confraternities' devotion to the saints, especially Black saints, underscores everyday popular religiosity, a religiosity the Counter-Reformation was unable to stem, despite various attempts. Black confraternities thus played an inestimable role in advancing devotion to Black saints during the Counter-Reformation.

---

[59] See Giovanna Fiume, *Il santo moro: I processi di canonizzazione di Benedetto da Palermo (1594–1807)* (Milan, 2002).

[60] On Ephigenia and Kaleb, see Erin Kathleen Rowe, *Black Saints in Early Modern Global Catholicism* (Cambridge, 2019), 26–32; José Pereira de Santa Ana, *Os dous Atlantes da Ethiopia, Santo Elesbão, emperador XLVII da Avessina, advogado dos perigos do mar, e Santa Ifigenia, princeza da Nubia, advogada dos encendios dos edificios, ambos Carmelitas, tomo primeiro* (Lisbon, 1735); *Segundo Atlante da Ethiopia, Santa Ifigenia, princeza do Reyno da Nubia, religiosa Carmelita, advogada dos encendios dos edificios, tomo segundo* (Lisbon, 1737).

17 Pilgrimage

ELIZABETH TINGLE

The *Dictionnaire universelle* of 1690 defined pilgrimage as "a journey of devotion," and a pilgrim as a person who, out of piety, traveled to a holy place.[1] In his work *The Sacred and the Profane* (1959), Mircea Eliade proposed that the sacred was defined by both space and time, because humanity's search for the holy was frequently connected to physical sites, whether a temple, shrine, or natural feature.[2] This is certainly true of Christianity; from its earliest days, one of the faith's main religious practices was pilgrimage. Devotees traveled to the places hallowed by Christ and his apostles, then by martyr and confessor saints, to experience sanctity for themselves. They immersed themselves in the holy environment and saw and touched the remains of those who were close to God; the sacred was made real and physical at the shrine of a saint. In this chapter, the experience of early modern pilgrimage will be explored for Western Europe, using examples from France, Ireland, Spain, and Italy and with occasional references to sites further afield.

Despite the challenges of the Protestant Reformation, which saw the theological denial and physical destruction of sacred objects and places, Counter-Reformation Catholics retained a site-centered understanding of sanctity, that is, a strong belief that some places were holy. As a result, pilgrimage expanded. Most early modern Catholics undertook a pilgrimage in their lifetimes, usually to a local site such as a holy well but sometimes to a far-away destination such as Rome or Santiago de Compostela. This chapter will consider three aspects of pious travel. First, an outline of its features in this period; second, an examination of the motives and the purposes of pilgrims; and third, an exploration of the experience of early modern pilgrims at the shrine. We will see that

---

[1] Antoine Furetière, *Dictionnaire universelle*, 3 vols. (Paris, 1690), vol. 3, 85.
[2] Mircea Eliade, *The Sacred and the Profane: The Nature of Religion*, trans. W. R. Trask (New York, 1959).

pilgrimage to shrines near and far grew in terms of participants, and that the main purpose of holy travel was for cures and in thanksgiving for graces received. As the Jesuit Louis Richeome counseled in *The Pilgrim of Loreto* (1629), holy travelers had three purposes: to honor God and his saints, to undertake penitence by enduring with patience the travails and inconveniences of the road, and to grow in devotion through imitating the examples shown by the saints whom they visited.[3] Pilgrimage, in other words, was a journey to the sacred.

PILGRIMAGE IN THE REFORMATION CENTURIES

Pilgrimage was a commonplace devotional activity in medieval Europe. Pilgrims ranging from King Louis IX of France to St. Francis of Assisi to the English housewife (and mystic) Margery Kempe traveled to the sacred sites of Christendom for cures, salvation, and adventure. This is reflected in contemporary literature, such as Geoffrey Chaucer's circa 1387 "Tales" of a pilgrimage to St. Thomas Becket's shrine at Canterbury. But following the Reformation, holy travel in Europe became difficult and the practice declined. The intercessory power of saints and the significance of their special places were attacked theologically by Protestants; war and destruction made journeys hazardous; and shrines were damaged by iconoclasts or destroyed in states where the Reformation succeeded, such as Norway and Scotland. There was also a tension within the Catholic Church between pilgrims' enthusiasm for relics and miracles and theologians' caution regarding the veneration of saints. At the Council of Trent, session XXV of December 1563 ruled that it was legitimate to invoke saints, who during their earthly lives had been "living members of Christ and the temple of the Holy Spirit," and to venerate their remains, but it was enjoined upon bishops to eliminate superstition and to ensure that worship at shrines was honest, decent, and orderly.[4] Yet pilgrimage continued and was revitalized after the 1570s. It was not, however, a simple revival of medieval practices. New features appeared.

First, and most obviously, these features included the increasing localization of shrines and religious life in general, based on the parish or neighboring sites. Local shrines, wells, and saints' relics had always

---

[3] Louis Richeome, *The Pilgrime of Loreto: Performing his vow made to the Glorious Virgin Mary Mother of God*, trans. E.W. (Paris [St. Omer], 1629), 44–45.

[4] *Decrees of the Ecumenical Councils*, ed. Norman Tanner, 2 vols. (London, 1990), vol. 2, 796–97.

been important to communities, and they reemerged and increased in number in the sixteenth and seventeenth centuries; William Christian, Jr., argues that almost every Castilian parish had its own site, and over forty have been documented in the small diocese of La Rochelle.[5] Bishops and clergy sought to regulate these pilgrimages more closely; in 1660, Bishop Lescot of Blois in France prohibited all processions that could not be accomplished between sunrise and sunset on a single day, to avoid the opportunities for sinful behavior occasioned by overnight stays.[6] The localization of pilgrimage was part of a long-term trend. Certain popular pilgrimage sites were "franchised" well before the Reformation, to increase access for those who could not travel and to augment revenue for the "home" institution. The Holy Sepulcher church in Jerusalem was an early example, for it was widely modeled across Europe, such as in the "round" church of the same dedication in Northampton, England, founded by a returning crusader, Simon de Senlis, around 1100. The plenary indulgence available to pilgrims who visited the Franciscan chapel of the Portiuncula outside Assisi, rebuilt by St. Francis, was gradually extended to all the churches of the order and its affiliates, including the Observantines and Recollects in 1622 and the churches of the Tertiary Order in 1643.[7] It was thus available in many towns and cities across the Catholic world. Similarly, the devotions of the Stations of Rome and the Scala Sancta – the Holy Stairs allegedly transported from Jerusalem by St. Helena in the fourth century – had a long history of being granted to provincial churches. In the seventeenth century, the Holy House of Loreto likewise acquired imitators, full-sized replicas as well as models; there were over 150 copies in Europe and the Spanish Americas by 1800.[8]

Second, new religious orders played an increasing role at shrines as part of their missionary agenda. Jesuits, Capuchins, and others were deployed to instruct pilgrims through preaching, catechism, confession, the Eucharist, and other devotions. These guardians brought post-Tridentine practices and expectations to the holy places. They sought

---

[5] William A. Christian, Jr., *Local Religion in Sixteenth-Century Spain* (Princeton, NJ, 1981); Louis Pérouas, *Le diocèse de La Rochelle de 1648 à 1724* (Paris, 1964).
[6] Eric Nelson, "The Parish in Its Landscape: Pilgrimage Processions in the Archdeaconry of Blois, 1500–1700," *French History* 24 (2010): 337.
[7] Henry Charles Lea, *A History of Auricular Confession, and Indulgences in the Latin Church*, 3 vols. (Philadelphia, 1896), vol. 3, 245.
[8] Yves-Marie Bercé, *Lorette aux XVIe et XVIIe siècles: Histoire du plus grand pèlerinage des temps modernes* (Paris, 2011), 263–66; Karin Vélez, *The Miraculous Flying House of Loreto* (Princeton, NJ, 2018).

to purify and moralize pilgrimage, ridding it of secular influences and practices. One example is St. Patrick's Purgatory of Lough Derg in Ireland. This site was originally part of an Augustinian priory. Papal nuncio Francesco Chiericati recorded in 1517 that there were three canons on the island ministering to pilgrims. There was a prior in charge and a sacristan who, among other tasks, lowered and raised pilgrims into and out of the Purgatory cave and provided them with basic refreshment while below. Two servants fulfilled tasks such as rowing pilgrims from the shore to the island.[9] The priory was dissolved later in the century amid the chaos of war, and the Augustinians dispersed. But by the 1620s the pilgrimage had revived. Archbishop O'Reilly of Armagh invited Franciscans to care for the site, and they continued to do so across the troubles of the seventeenth century.[10]

The devotional influences of the religious orders contributed to a third change in pilgrimage practice: the dedication of shrines to universal saints – principally the Virgin Mary – at the expense of older cults. In Counter-Reformation Europe, Marian shrines were refurbished and documented in "sacred topographies" that allowed for the narration of the Virgin's triumph over heresy. The Jesuits were particularly engaged in this exercise: Wilhelm Gumppenberg's *Atlas Mariana* of 1657 attempted to show the Marian topography of the whole world.[11] However, other historians have argued for a resurgence of the attractiveness of local saints. Brittany in France witnessed an upsurge in interest in its distinctive Celtic saints, while St. Patrick became enormously popular in the defense of Irish Catholicism.[12] In practice, old saints' shrines were revived, *and* new Marian ones were created. In Ireland, at Lough Derg, the traditional attribution of the Purgatory pilgrimage to St. Patrick was augmented by association with Brigid and Columba for a particularly effective cultural statement. At the same time, a less well-known Our Lady's Island remained in use in County

---

[9] Shane Leslie, ed., *St. Patrick's Purgatory: A Record from History and Literature* (London, 1932), 64.

[10] Letter of Archbishop O'Reilly, 1631, in Leslie, ed., *St. Patrick's Purgatory*, 75.

[11] Wilhelm Gumppenberg, *Marianischer Atlas: Das ist wunderthätige Mariabilder so in aller christlichen Welt mit Wunderzaichen berhuembt durch Guilielmum Gumppenberg*, 4 vols. (Ingoldstadt, 1657–59); *L'Atlas Marianus de Wilhelm Gumppenberg: Édition et traduction*, ed. Nicolas Balzamo, Olivier Christin, and Fabrice Flückiger (Neuchâtel, 2015).

[12] Alain Croix, *La Bretagne aux XVIe et XVIIe siècles: La vie, la mort, la foi*, 2 vols. (Paris, 1981); Bernadette Cunningham and Raymond Gillespie, "The Lough Derg Pilgrimage in the Age of the Counter-Reformation," *Eire-Ireland* 39 (2004): 167–79.

Wexford.[13] In Provence, most new shrines created in the seventeenth century concerned the Virgin Mary, but existing pilgrimages continued to be associated with ancient saints' cults, linked to the first evangelization of the region.[14]

Long-distance pilgrimage to the classic sites also expanded. Jerusalem, the premier destination of the Middle Ages and still visited by Ignatius of Loyola in his youth, was less frequented after 1550 because of conflict between Habsburgs and Ottomans. Instead, Rome emerged as the most important center. Its sacred sites were refurbished and granted new indulgences; for example, Sixtus V renovated the Scala Santa in 1590.[15] Records of the pilgrim hostel of the Santissima Trinità dei Pellegrini show that visitor numbers reached a peak during the Jubilees held between 1575 and 1650.[16] Rome's outpost shrine of the Holy House at Loreto also benefited from this resurgence. In 1554, the Jesuits were appointed as confessors and established a sustained program of urban development.[17] Recent work on hospitals in France, Germany, and Spain reveals the importance of longer-distance journeys in those areas. For example, in his study of the pilgrims passing through eighteenth-century Nuremberg and its hostel for poor travelers, Christophe Duhamel estimates that perhaps one in 300 inhabitants of the region undertook long-distance journeys.[18] Santiago de Compostela; Guadalupe and Montserrat in Spain; Mont-Saint-Michel in France; Cologne, Altötting, and Mariazell in the German lands; Jasna Góra in Poland; and Mátraverebély-Szentkút in Hungary are a few examples of such shrines.

Pilgrimage attracted large numbers of pilgrims until the mid-eighteenth century, when religious cultures shifted, and political attitudes to travel brought in attempts at greater control of movement; a hardening of attitudes to vagrancy and begging, combined with military security concerns, led to increasing regulation. In Spain in 1590, Philip II

---

[13] Fiona Rose McNally, "The Evolution of Pilgrimage Practice in Early Modern Ireland" (MLitt thesis, National University of Ireland Maynooth, 2012), introduction.

[14] Marie-Hélène Froeschlé-Chopard, *Espace et sacré en Provence (XVIe–XXe siècle)* (Paris, 1994), 151–52, 315.

[15] Lea, *A History of Auricular Confession*, vol. 3, 456.

[16] Dominique Julia, "Gagner son jubilé à l'époque moderne: Mesure des foules et récits de pèlerins," *Roma moderna e contemporanea* 5 (1997): 311–54.

[17] See Bercé, *Lorette aux XVIe et XVIIe siècles*.

[18] Christophe Duhamelle, "Les pèlerins de passage à l'hospice zum Heiligen Kreuz de Nuremberg au XVIIIe siècle," in *Pèlerins et pèlerinages dans l'Europe moderne*, ed. Philippe Boutry and Dominique Julia (Rome, 2000), 48.

issued a Pragmatic against false pilgrims who disguised themselves in order to rob the innocent; thenceforth, a license was necessary to journey as a pilgrim, signed by the judicial officer of the region. Foreign pilgrims traveling in Spain required a document from their local bishop, which needed to be presented to a Spanish judicial officer, who would then issue another license when the border was crossed.[19] In France, similar laws were created under Louis XIV. Pilgrims without documents could be arrested, pilloried, and sent home.[20] But numbers of holy travelers remained high. During the jubilee year of 1779, an estimated 1.51 million pilgrims took communion in the cathedral of Santiago de Compostela, without even counting those who communicated in the city's parishes.[21] Throughout the early modern period, therefore, pilgrimage remained a significant devotional act. It was a primary means by which Catholics of all social groups encountered and experienced sanctity, grounded in place and time.

MOTIVES

The reasons why individuals sought direct experience with the holy through personal contact with sacred places were influenced by age, gender, social status, and personal needs. Women might be constrained by domestic commitments and gendered expectations of behavior that limited their movements; men might not always be able leave their farms and businesses; the old, young, and disabled might not bear the physical conditions of travel; and enclosed orders of monks and nuns could not leave their convents. Thus, we find that short-distance travel was commonly undertaken by women, children, and men, while medium-length and longer journeys were the preserve of the few, mostly men. Pilgrims to the Extremadura shrine of Our Lady of Guadalupe, visited particularly by the sick and by freed captives, skewed highly masculine: Its collection of sixteenth-century miracle

---

[19] Reproduced in Luis Vázquez de Parga et al., eds., *Las peregrinaciones a Santiago de Compostela*, 3 vols. (Madrid, 1945–49), vol. 3, 115–16.

[20] René de la Coste-Messelière, "Édits et autres actes royaux contre les abus des pèlerinages à l'étranger au XVIIe et XVIIIe siècles," *Comité des travaux historiques et scientifiques: Actes de 94e congrès national des sociétés savantes* (Pau, 1969), Section d'histoire moderne et contemporaine vol. 1 (Paris, 1971), 115–28.

[21] Dominique Julia, "Pour une géographie européenne du pèlerinage à l'époque moderne et contemporaine," in *Pèlerins et pèlerinages dans l'Europe moderne*, ed. Philippe Boutry and Dominique Julia (Rome, 2000), 51.

stories concerned around 1,000 men and 200 women.[22] Women were a little more numerous in Rome. Of the pilgrims staying in Santissima Trinità of Rome, 19-22 percent were female.[23] For the pilgrimage to Compostela, the percentage of women traveling was much lower. Only 7 percent of pilgrims who stayed overnight at the hospital at Bayonne between 1724 and 1767 were female.[24] 98 percent of the pilgrims cared for in the Hospital Real de Santiago were male.[25] Typical of women pilgrims were the Dubois family of Chalon-sur-Saône – Claude, his wife Barbe, and their daughter Françoise – who journeyed to Compostela together, in 1611-12.[26] A medium-distance healing shrine would see more female pilgrims, but these were still a minority: 28 percent of pilgrims passing through the hospital Saint-Yves at Rennes in 1650-51 were female, with a similar number, 25.6 percent, at Saint-Reine across the period from 1659 to 1777.[27] Cultural assumptions about women's behavior made their free movement difficult. Women were pilgrims, but distant journeys were largely undertaken by men.

The choice of a specific pilgrimage was often linked to the status and location of a shrine: "Low status" shrines, often local sites such as wells or chapels, drew pilgrims for problem-solving and cures, while "high-status" shrines, such as Rome or Compostela, were sought for thanksgiving and spiritual improvement. The choice of destination was also linked to the efficacy of a saint, expressed through miracles. The two principal aims of travel were relief from sickness and salvation for the soul. Both were important to early modern pilgrims, and we will examine them in turn.

To guide pilgrims on where to go and why, a long tradition of clerical manuals offered advice on the utility and purpose of visiting shrines. The most persistent reason they gave for holy travel was

[22] Françoise Crémoux, "Réalité et représentation: L'image du pèlerin dans l'Espagne du XVIe siècle à travers les recueils de miracles de Guadalupe," in *L'image du pèlerin au Moyen Age et sous l'Ancien Régime*, ed. Pierre André Sigal (Gramat, 1994), 222.
[23] Julia, "Gagner son jubilé," 318.
[24] Julia, "Pour une géographie européenne," 112.
[25] George Provost, "Les pèlerins accueillis à l'hôpital real de Saint-Jacques de Compostelle dans la seconde moitié du XVIIe siècle." In Boutry and Julia, eds., *Pèlerins et pèlerinages dans l'Europe moderne*, 131.
[26] Charles Pétouraud, "Le registre de la confrérie des pèlerins de Saint-Jacques de Compostelle à Chalon-sur-Saône," *Annales de l'Académie de Macon*, 3rd series, 49 (1968-69): 15.
[27] Jean-Christophe Brilloit, "Une population pérégrine au milieu du XVIIe siècle: Les pèlerins de Saint-Méen," *Annales de Bretagne et de l'Ouest* 93 (1986), 269; Philippe Boutry and Dominique Julia, eds., *Sainte-Reine au Mont Auxois: Le culte et le pèlerinage de sainte Reine des origines à nos jours* (Paris, 1997), 130.

Imitatio Christi, to copy "most perfectly the pilgrimage of Jesus Christ and honor in a most particular manner his status as traveler in this world, which made of him a pilgrim."[28] The life of Christ was held to be an allegorical series of pilgrimages: the journey to Bethlehem, the flight into Egypt, his preaching ministry in Judea, and the road to Calvary. Pilgrims were urged to travel the same road as Christ and the saints, that is, the route of penitence, passion, tribulation, and, ultimately, salvation.

One theme that emerged after Trent was emphasis on personal and spiritual growth. The Jesuit Gaspard Loarte, in a treatise of 1575 written to encourage visitors to Rome during the Jubilee year, proposed that pilgrimage was an opportunity to grow in the three principal theological virtues: hope, faith, and charity. These were to be "lived" through religious actions, by prayers to God, and via acts of penitence through patience and humility, particularly if the pilgrim lived from alms.[29] From the early seventeenth century, the search for a reformation of life and an interior conversion to faith became prominent, linked to introspection, interiority, mental prayer, and finding God in one's inner space. The superior of Notre Dame de Bon Secours near Nancy, writing in 1630, emphasized interior conversion to a more devout life as a greater miracle to be found at the shrine than any cure.[30] The writer of the pilgrimage pamphlet for the shrine of Notre-Dame-de-Benoiste-Vaux remarked that few had accomplished the pilgrimage who did not feel some interior transformation after having received extraordinary enlightenment and knowledge from God. Most importantly, sinners were converted at the site and received the gift of the Holy Spirit.[31]

How much this advice actually influenced most travelers on pilgrimage routes in the sixteenth and seventeenth centuries is a matter for consideration. Many of the people who traveled were illiterate and did not acquire written tracts. But their clergy could read; sermons by the mendicant orders in towns and countryside were popular and

---

[28] P.D.H., *La Guide des pèlerins de Notre Dame de Verdelays contenant les saintes dispositions dans lesquelles ils doivent être; pour obtenir de Dieu ses grâces par l'intercession de la Sainte Vierge* (Bordeaux, 1700), 10.

[29] Gaspard Loarte, *Trattato delle sante peregrinationi* (Rome, 1575).

[30] Nicolas Julet, *Miracles et grâces de Notre-Dame-de-Bon-Secours, proche Nancy, avec des instructions et une pratique générale pour les personnes qui y ont dévotion* (Nancy, 1630).

[31] Anon., *Histoire et miracles de Nostre Dame de Benoiste-Vaux ensemble les exercices & devotions du pèlerin* (Verdun, 1644), 38–40.

propagated this spirituality. Increasingly, confraternities encouraged such acts of piety. Clerical advice was thus important to pilgrims in preparing and understanding the journey they were to make. But the reasons why people chose to travel were not necessarily the same as those advocated by the clergy, even if they were often expressed in clerical terms.

The most frequent motive for pilgrimage therefore remained a pragmatic one: the cure for illness. People visited the saints for relief from suffering; as proof of the efficacy of a cult, shrine guardians frequently collected and published examples of miracles to demonstrate the powers of their holy patron. At the shrine of Notre-Dame de Liesse in northeastern France, the main form of recorded miracles was recovery from illnesses ranging from plague to paralysis, followed by escaping from accidents, war-related violence, capture, and other ills.[32] Studies of miracles recorded at myriad other shrines, from Guadalupe in Spain to Tolentino in Italy, show the same concerns and interventions.[33] Many shrines offered specialty cures. For example, the shrine of Saint-Méen, near Rennes in northern France, attracted pilgrims suffering from scabies and other skin diseases of the hand, as did that of Saint-Reine near to Flavigny, which also specialized in syphilis. Saint-Hubert in the Ardennes specialized in curing rabies and animal bites, while Saint-Fiacre reputedly healed hemorrhoids. The direction of travel was determined by need.

Pilgrimage was also undertaken in thanksgiving for a grace – or cure – already received elsewhere. People in need invoked the aid of a saint and took vows that if they were cured of illness or relieved of an accident or mishap, they would visit the shrine. The relationship thus forged between saint and client was contractual; the recipients of divine aid were bound to fulfil the promise of pilgrimage and sometimes to present a gift as well. Reneging on the promise could result in punishment by the saint. If an individual could not keep a promise to visit the saint in question, they might seek alternatives such as a substitute or proxy to travel for them. Examples related to Compostela serve as illustrations. Philip III of Spain and his queen, Margaret of Austria, vowed to visit Compostela in person during its Jubilee year of 1610, in thanksgiving for the expulsion of the Moriscos from Spain in 1609. The

---

[32] Bruno Maës, *Les livrets de pèlerinage: Imprimerie et culture dans la France moderne* (Rennes, 2016), 120–22.
[33] Crémoux, "Réalité et représentation," 221–29; Mary Laven, "Recording Miracles in Renaissance Italy," *Past and Present* 230, suppl. 11 (2016): 191–212.

vow was carried out for the royal couple by their chaplain Cardinal Diego Guzmán.[34] In 1606 a notary of Auch in France recorded the will of François de Vic, seigneur de Rieux, and his miraculous escape from Ottoman slavery. In 1594 Vic was captured by Turks near Vienna and sold, first to work the land on an estate, then as an oarsman in a Mediterranean galley fleet. When he was finally released, he undertook to give thanks to St. James (Santiago) before returning home.[35] In 1654 Canon Christophe Gunzinger of Wiener Neustadt traveled to Compostela via Italy to thank the apostle for curing a fever. As a six-year-old, Gunzinger had become mortally ill but recovered after drinking water from a cockle shell, which had become the emblem of Santiago pilgrims; his mother vowed to go on the pilgrimage and Christophe traveled to fulfil the vow for them both.[36] Personal obligation in response to saintly intervention was thus a defining motive for pilgrimage for many voyagers.

A further motive was listed simply as "out of devotion," a desire to experience the sacred. The reasons varied. Difficult tasks could call for a period of preparatory meditation: in 1543 the Jesuits Melchior Carneiro and Martín de la Cruz traveled from Coimbra to Santiago before undertaking a mission to Ethiopia.[37] A desire for intimate contact with a saint was a strong motive for some pilgrims. Henri-Marie Bourdon, archdeacon of Evreux in northern France, "always had a profound respect for the holy angels and believed he should visit a temple dedicated to Our Lord, under the invocation of his first ministers."[38] He traveled to Mont-Saint-Michel in 1665 to achieve this. Monsieur de Queriolet, a devout judge at the Parlement of Rennes who later became a priest, wished to imitate what Christ did on earth and "to study the virtues of the saints and to draw upon some portion of these in the sanctuaries where their precious relics rested."[39] He therefore journeyed to

---

[34] Diego de Guzmán, *La peregrinación a Santiago de Diego de Guzmán: Diario inédito de 1610*, ed. Julio Vázquez Castro (Santiago, 2014).
[35] M. du Carsalade du Pont, "Odyssée d'un pèlerin de Saint-Jacques de Compostelle," *Revue de Gascogne* 37 (1896): 387–89.
[36] *Peregrinatio Compostellana anno 1654: Die abenteuerliche Pilgerreise des Christoph Guntzinger von Wiener Neustadt nach Santiago*, ed. Peter Lindenthal (Innsbruck, 2014), 17, 129–30, 80–82.
[37] Luciano Huidobro y Serna, *Las peregrinaciones jacobeas*, 3 vols. (Madrid, 1951), vol. 1, 376–77.
[38] Anon., *La vie de M. Henry-Marie Boudon, grand archidiacre d'Evreux* (Paris, 1753), 272.
[39] M. Collet, *La vie de Monsieur de Queriolet, prestre et conseiller au parlement de Rennes, ami du Père Bernard* (Saint-Malo, 1771), 68.

Notre-Dame de Liesse, Rome, and Compostela to these ends. To go on pilgrimage typically meant visiting a person who was physically present in their relics and spiritually present in prayer. While relics seem to have attracted less popular devotion than they had in the fifteenth century, image shrines, as they grew in popularity, fostered a sense of religion that was historic and perpetual, the saint's remains linking the distant past to the pilgrim's present.

Finally, devotion could include a penitential element. Monsieur de Queriolet walked very long distances each day, ate poor food, and was often constrained to sleep in the open air. The pilgrimage to Compostela was the only one in which he was accompanied by another priest. To ensure that they focused entirely on God, the two men walked separately and spoke to each other only when necessary.[40] The pilgrimage to St. Patrick's Purgatory was clearly penitential because of the severe level of asceticism that was required of the pilgrim, who was expected to fast for nine days and spend twenty-four hours shut up in the Purgatory. The early sixteenth-century poem *Loch Dearg aon Róimh na hEireann* (Lough Derg Is Ireland's Premier Shrine), by Tuileagna Mac Torna, proposes that such penance is the only remedy for a stony heart, a hard eye, and a deceitful mouth.[41] Fundamental to all pilgrimage is a belief in the spiritual value of temporary physical detachment from one's familiar surroundings in order to seek the holy – liminality – which "is present in higher concentrations in certain places" and is experienced at its most heightened through hardship.[42]

Pilgrims, therefore, in one way or another, benefited from their journeys. By the later Middle Ages, indulgences became the most important reason for holy travel, even more so than visiting relics.[43] After a decline in their prestige across the middle of the sixteenth century, indulgences again became a highly visible feature of shrines. Jubilee indulgences, offering plenary remission of sins and available at shrines in special years, were particularly attractive. The most important Jubilees were those of Rome, held every twenty-five years, with the year 1600 attracting millions of pilgrims. But all shrines offered pardons to pilgrims. At Mont-Saint-Michel, medieval indulgences were still on offer when pilgrimage revived after 1600. From the 1620s, the monks

---

[40] Ibid., 65–66, 81–82.
[41] McNally, "The Evolution of Pilgrimage Practice," 20–21, 24.
[42] Victor Turner and Edith Turner, *Image and Pilgrimage in Christian Culture* (New York, 1978).
[43] Diana Webb, "Pardons and Pilgrimage," in *Promissory Notes on the Treasury of Merits: Indulgences in Late Medieval Europe*, ed. R. N. Swanson (Leiden, 2006), 241.

also obtained more "modern" indulgences from Rome: pardons associated with a new confraternity and altar of the rosary, founded in a side chapel of the abbey church in 1624; a grant of a privilege for the rosary altar in 1628, where, every Monday, each Mass said would liberate a soul from Purgatory; and plenary indulgences for the main feasts of the archangel on May 8, September 29, and October 16.[44] Papal Jubilees were also celebrated at the Mont, for example. At Easter 1668, a universal Jubilee decreed by Clement IX for prayers for his pontificate was opened on March 3 with a sermon by Dom Pierre Le Duc, after which the monastic community went in procession, and with the congregation undertook prayer stations in the chapels of the church.[45] Great crowds were attracted by such pardons.

Some pilgrimages were collective affairs, meeting a range of communal needs. Broadly, there were two main traveling communities: members of parishes or towns, and spiritual communities in the form of confraternities. Cities and villages sometimes took vows to travel, to supplicate for relief, or in thanksgiving for liberation from natural disasters, plague, or war. In 1529 the municipality of Girona sent two cathedral canons to Our Lady of Montserrat and St. James at Compostela to intercede with the saints for rain during a drought and to give a donation to their shrines.[46] In the early seventeenth century the church of San Estevan in La Val d'en Bas in southern Spain sent Maurice Danbre on pilgrimage to Santiago to represent and pray for the community, "to insure the people against contagion and to protect the crops"; he was instructed to give a gold escudo in exchange for three Masses said on the altar of Santiago.[47] Many pilgrims were members of devotional confraternities that supported pilgrimage. For example, St. James confraternities were widespread in France, the Low Countries, and Italy. Part of their function was to encourage holy travel as spiritual good work. Pilgrimage also offered an institutional framing, moral legitimation, and respectable justification for a temporary escape from mundane, domestic life. At Campan in the Bigorre in France, for example, the register of a confraternity of St. James of the period 1645–1817 records

---

[44] Thomas Le Roy, *Le livre de curieuses recherches du Mont Sainct Michel: Histoire du sanctuaire normand de l'Archange, de sa fondation à l'époque moderne*, ed. Vincent Juhel (Caen, 2008), 426.

[45] Jean Huynes, *Histoire générale de l'abbaye du Mont-Saint-Michel au péril de la mer*, ed. E. de Robillard de Beaurepaire, 2 vols. (Rouen, 1873), vol. 2, 229.

[46] Vázquez de Parga et al., eds., *Las peregrinaciones*, vol. 1, 107.

[47] Antonio López Ferreiro, *Historia de la Santa A. M. Iglesia de Santiago de Compostela*, 11 vols. (Santiago, 1898–1911), vol. 9, 335.

the names of 1,000 pilgrims who traveled to Compostela, an average of six per year for a population of around 3,000.[48]

While the Campan pilgrims, especially the young men who mostly grew up in a single locality, may well have been motivated by a desire for adventure, pilgrimage as a communal endeavor could also be used to counter the Protestant heresy. Holy travel was an overt statement of Catholic orthodoxy in the face of Luther's and Calvin's criticisms of the veneration of saints and the sacrality of place. In France in the 1580s, a wave of "white processions," penitential convoys whose participants wore the white woolen fabric of shrouds, traveled to the ancient shrines of northeastern France and the Rhineland: St. Nicolas du Port in Lorraine, Rheims, Notre-Dame de Liesse, St. Fiacre in Brie, and St. Antoine de Viennois in Dauphiné. They called upon the saints to extirpate heresy.[49] In the Dutch Republic, the prohibition of public expression of Catholicism led the faithful to cross the border to visit shrines, principally Our Lady at Scherpenheuvel in Brabant and at Kevelaer in the Upper Rhine region of modern Germany. Pilgrimage to St. Patrick's Purgatory was an even greater attestation of Catholicism by the Irish faithful, whose religion was under direct attack from the English Protestant regime. In 1625 Archbishop Fleming of Dublin wrote to the papal internuncio at Brussels that "the pious and innumerable pilgrimages of the faithful this year are a pledge of great fervor; for, like bees to the beehive, there daily flock such numbers from every corner of the kingdom, for penitential purposes."[50] The renewed destruction of the site in 1632, Oliver Cromwell's invasion of 1649–53, and the outlawing of all pilgrimages in Ireland in 1704 did not prevent the practice.

The attractions of pilgrimage were therefore largely those stated by the seventeenth-century French Dominican Vincent Reboul: the greatness of the saint's relics a shrine conserves, the miracles that take place there for the sick, and the multitude of indulgences accorded to it, all available to those who visit with devotion.[51] Pilgrims expected, above all, a personal experience of sanctity, through emotion, grace, or, preferably, miracles. Their experiences at shrines will now be considered.

---

[48] Georges Provost, "Identité paysanne et 'pèlerinage au long cours' dans la France des XVII–XIX siècles," in *Rendre ses vœux: Les identités pèlerines dans l'Europe modern (XVIe–XVIIIe siècles)*, ed. P. Boutry, P.-A. Favre, and D. Julia (Paris, 2000), 385.

[49] Dominique Julia, *Le voyage aux saints: Les pèlerinages dans l'Occident moderne (XVe–XVIIIe siècles)* (Paris, 2016), 166.

[50] Archbishop Fleming's Report 1625, in Leslie, ed., *St Patrick's Purgatory*, 95.

[51] Vincent Reboul, *Histoire de la vie et de la mort de Ste Marie Magdeleine avec les miracles, invention & translation des reliques* (Aix [en Provence], 1671), preface.

THE PILGRIMAGE EXPERIENCE

Pilgrimage constituted both a journey and a visit to a shrine, the two activities being conceived as a whole. The journey could be a few hours' long, to a local site, or many weeks, to a distant place such as Rome. There is not space here to discuss the travel ways and infrastructure of physical pilgrimage, but it should be remembered that journeys frequently lasted longer than the shrine visit itself and could involve visiting many smaller holy sites along the way, as the Camino to Santiago de Compostela still does today.[52] Whatever the initial motive might have been, or the experiences along the route, it was the sanctuary itself that was the central purpose of travel, for testimonies of pilgrims show that they expected above all else a personal, physical encounter with the sacred. It was here, at a specific and special place, that sanctity was experienced at its most intense.

For those who could not go in person, the early modern period also saw the expansion of an alternative means of holy travel, spiritual pilgrimage, where journeys took place "virtually," or in the imagination.[53] For those who could not travel, such as nuns and monks of enclosed religious orders, women, the old, the infirm, and those whose work gave them little time for leisure, virtual voyages made the major shrines accessible. Catholic reformers encouraged personal prayer and individual meditation as much, if not more, than ostentatious, external gestures; the best place to find God was in one's own interior space. Pilgrimage literature was written partially, even largely, to help the spiritual traveler find this space.

The most important destination of virtual travel was Jerusalem, which grew in popularity during the sixteenth century as physical traffic to the city was greatly reduced. Marie-Christine Gomez-Géraud has counted more than eighty early modern pilgrimage accounts to Jerusalem that enabled such spiritual travel.[54] Over time, the city's reality as an actual space began to matter less. Wes Williams argues that in early modern period, "Jerusalem gradually ceases to exist as a

---

[52] For a discussion of hospitality infrastructure, see Elizabeth Tingle, *Sacred Journeys in the Counter-Reformation: Long Distance Pilgrimage in Northwest Europe* (Berlin, 2020), chap. 3.

[53] See Jennifer Hillman and Elizabeth Tingle, eds., *Soul Travel: Spiritual Journeys in Medieval and Early Modern Europe* (Oxford, 2019). This paragraph draws on the introduction to the volume.

[54] Marie-Christine Gomez-Géraud, *Le crépuscule du grand voyage: Les récits de pèlerins à Jérusalem (1458–1612)* (Paris, 1999).

primarily real place in the European imagination, a place to be seen, witnessed, and described *in situ*. It is gradually replaced by an imagined Jerusalem conjured up by description; less a place than a topic, part of a narrative or devotional sequence: a means to prayer and a prelude to the expression of desire."[55] The expansion of print allowed ever greater numbers of people to experience an imagined Jerusalem without ever traveling; many of these believed that the true pilgrimage was that undertaken in the mind.[56] Such texts survive in both Latin and vernacular languages. The English version of Jan van Paeschen's *The Spiritual Pilgrimage of Hierusalem, Containing Three Hundre[d] Sixtie Five Dayes Iourney, Wherein the Devoute Person May Meditate on Sondrie Pointes of His Redemption* (Brussels, 1604–5) was clearly intended for daily use at home.[57] The practice of harnessing the imagination to undertake spiritual journeys was central to Jesuit spirituality in particular. The Jesuit technique of constructing biblical scenes in the mind – the composition of place (or *compositio loci*) – was the cornerstone of Ignatius Loyola's (1491–1556) *Spiritual Exercises* and was adapted by many writers of devotional guides.

Spiritual journeys, to Jerusalem or elsewhere, came in three main forms. The most common was the mental pilgrimage guided by books like Van Paeschen's *Spiritual Pilgrimage*, which aimed at imagining presence in the holy city. These texts were numerous from the fifteenth century onward, in manuscript and then in printed format. The account of the Jerusalem pilgrim and Dominican friar Felix Fabri, prepared in 1492 and often known as *Sionpilger*, offered a guidebook for imagined journeys for the sisters of the convents of Medingen and Medlingen in Germany. Fabri divided the *Sionpilger* into 208 daily readings or "journeys." The rules given in the preface recommend that the virtual pilgrim consult the text before going to sleep in order to prepare for the next day's journey.[58] The eventual publication remained in print for centuries.

The second common form of "virtual" pilgrimage was through a visit to a physical place that was a facsimile landscape. One of the most

---

[55] Wes Williams, *Pilgrimage and Narrative in the French Renaissance* (Oxford, 1998), 172.
[56] Wes Williams, "A Mirrour of Mis-Haps/A Mappe of Miserie: Dangers, Strangers and Friends in Renaissance Pilgrimage," in *The "Book" of Travels: Genre, Ethnology and Pilgrimage, 1250–1700*, ed. Palmira Brummett (Leiden, 2009), 210.
[57] Ibid., 211.
[58] Kathryne Beebe, "The Jerusalem of the Mind's Eye. Imagined Pilgrimage in the Late Fifteenth Century," in *Visual Constructs of Jerusalem*, ed. Bianca Kühnel, Galit Noga-Banai, and Hanna Vorholt (Turnhout, 2015), 409, 414.

striking forms of these was imitation Jerusalems or *sacri monti* (holy mountains). The oldest such site, at Varallo in Italy, was begun in 1481, by the Franciscan Bernardo Caimi, former Custos in the Holy Land. The site was a combination of architecture (chapels), sculpted figures, and frescos linked by pathways, with scenes in each chapel representing either the Passion narrative or major topographical features of Jerusalem. Pilgrims progressed around the landscape, spiritually envisioning the scene in Jerusalem itself.[59] Another example is the Holy Mountain of San Vivaldo in Tuscany, built in 1500 and associated with the Franciscan monastery at the site. Like Varallo, it represents the holy places of Jerusalem and its environs, with chapels that contain terracotta statues and frescos depicting events from sacred history.[60] These landscapes allowed for individual and group devotion, exercised inside or outside the official liturgy, and were particularly suited to the laity. The phenomenon became even more popular in the Counter Reformation and expanded beyond representations of Jerusalem. In Italy, meditative landscapes were created at Crea in 1590, dedicated to St. Eusebius and to the Mysteries of the Rosary; at Orta in 1592, marking the posthumous miracles of St Francis; and at Varese, constructed in 1604–90, again in honor of the Mysteries of the Rosary.[61]

The third form of virtual pilgrimage, in this case specifically to Jerusalem, deployed an allegorical landscape of images to stand in for real places. The stations of the cross were the most commonly experienced of these visits. The cycle of seven stations by Adam Kraft in Nuremberg is a prominent fifteenth-century example; stations are marked by columns topped by relief representations of the respective events of the Passion. The columns are spread at equal distances (1,100 paces) throughout the city, beginning at Pilate's House, near one of the city gates, and ending at St John's Cemetery, outside the city walls.[62] In Leuven, a series of stations were set out based on the observations of a pilgrim, Pieter Sterckx, who had returned from the Holy Land in 1505.[63]

---

[59] Dominique Julia, "Identité pèlerine, identité du passage," in *Identités pèlerines: Actes du colloque de Rouen, 15–16 mai 2002*, ed. Catherine Vincent (Rouen, 2004), 243.

[60] Tsafra Siew, "Pilgrimage Experience: Bridging Size and Medium," in Kühnel et al., eds., *Visual Constructs of Jerusalem*, 86.

[61] Bianca Kühnel, "Virtual Pilgrimages to Real Places: The Holy Landscapes," in *Imagining Jerusalem in the Medieval West*, ed. Lucy Donkin and Hanna Vorholt, special edition of *Proceedings of the British Academy*, 175 (2012): 259.

[62] Ibid., 251–53.

[63] Kathryn Blair Moore, *The Architecture of the Christian Holy Land* (Cambridge, 2017), 210.

Most stations were set up inside churches, however, and were used for processional devotions, especially during Holy Week before Easter. After the Reformation, the devotion of the stations of the cross expanded. For example, in Paris a shrine of Calvary on Mont Valérien was granted letters patent by Louis XIII in 1640. To support and promote the pilgrimage, a Confraternity of the Cross was established in 1644, and its statutes confirmed in 1707. René-François du Breil de Pontbriant, in a booklet on the pilgrimage, considered Mont Valérien "a Calvary that ceaselessly calls to mind that of Jerusalem where Jesus Christ was sacrificed and died for our salvation ... one sheds tears. One enters into transports of sympathy in imagining the sufferings and triumphs of the Saviour."[64] Rome's sacred sites – especially its church-scape – were also reconstructed. For example, in 1601, to achieve the Roman Jubilee indulgence transferred to Paris, the bishop stipulated visits to the five churches of the Cathedral of Notre Dame, the chapel of the Hôtel Dieu, and the churches of the Cordeliers, the Feuillants, the Filles Pénitentes, and the Filles de l'Ave Maria.[65] But even profane spaces could be appropriated by virtual pilgrims for whom travel was not an option. In 1500, for example, Swiss theologian Johann Geiler von Kaiserberg (1445–1510) designed a pilgrimage to Rome for prisoners and calculated that convicts could mimic the journey by pacing their cells for seven miles a day, for seven weeks.[66] Finally, on an even larger scale, whole regions and kingdoms could use relics, images, and histories from the eastern Mediterranean to imagine themselves as mirrors of the Holy Land. Adam Beaver argues that Spain under Philip II, by replicating certain features of the topography and architecture of Palestine, considered itself to be a New Jerusalem.[67] Such activities expanded the numbers of pilgrims experiencing the conceptual power of pilgrimage, even if they never visited the actual locations themselves.

Despite the growth of mindful travel, physical place remained hugely significant. An understanding of the sacred nature of place is particularly

---

[64] F. Thomas Noonan, *The Road to Jerusalem: Pilgrimage and Travel in the Age of Discovery* (Philadelphia, 2007), 123.

[65] *Déclaration catholique du jubilé & des indulgences ensemble les prières que l'on pourra dire es stations & églises ordonnées a d'estre visitées pour gaigner les indulgences dudict jubilé, Par ordonnance de monseigneur l'Evêque de Paris* (Paris, 1601), 4.

[66] D. K. Smith, *The Cartographic Imagination in Early Modern England* (Farnham, 2008), 36.

[67] Adam G. Beaver, "A Holy Land for the Catholic Monarchy: Palestine in the Making of Modern Spain, 1469–1598" (PhD thesis, Harvard University, 2008).

important for studying religious practices of post-Tridentine Catholicism, for space interacted with contemporary understandings of sanctity, divinity, and their relationship with the individual believer. For the pilgrim, presence in a special place made the relationship with the saint tangible. Virginia Reinberg has argued that the landscape of a shrine consisted of not only the physical terrain but also the myths, traditions, and narratives associated with it, so that in moving through the physical geography, a pilgrim traveled and lived through a terrain of culturally constructed symbols.[68] The effectiveness of an individual's spiritual experience was given further devotional meaning through rituals associated with that specific space. The work of Alexandra Walsham has shown that even in Protestant lands such as the British Isles and Ireland, such was the power of sacred space that former pilgrimage and holy sites retained resonance in the landscape.[69] Movement around a shrine was curated and controlled, a series of stations of objects and areas visited. This effect was achieved partly by establishing gradations of sacrality within a space, for example, the chapel within the church, the altar within the chapel. Sacred art and architecture were also designed to determine the routeways taken by pilgrims around sites, and the prayers and actions they performed. In the Middle Ages, shrines containing holy bodies were frequently placed at the east end of the church, behind the high altar itself, or, more frequently, in the retrochoir; they were accessible from the ambulatory, and entry could be regulated. Such were the great shrines of St. Thomas Becket at Canterbury and those at Rheims, Beauvais, and Amiens, all of which were cathedral churches. In many shrine churches, the positioning of relics changed in the Counter-Reformation period. For example, in Angers cathedral before the eighteenth century, three reliquary caskets were located on the altar of the retrochoir. This area was subsequently demolished, and a new high altar constructed at the entrance to the choir, under which the reliquary of St. Maurille was placed while the reliquaries of Saints René and Sérène were placed in the base of transept pillars, behind wrought-iron grills. Making shrines more easily accessible and visible reduced the need for pilgrims to enter the clerical space of the church chancel.[70]

---

[68] Virginia Reinberg, *Storied Places: Pilgrim Shrines, Nature, and History in Early Modern France* (Cambridge, 2019).

[69] See Alexandra Walsham, *The Reformation of the Landscape: Religion, Identity and Memory in Early Modern Britain and Ireland* (Oxford, 2011).

[70] Mathieu Lors, "Cathédrales, reliques et pèlerinages: L'épreuve de la modernité," in *Cathédrale et pèlerinage aux époques médiévale et moderne*, ed. Catherine Vincent and Jacques Pycke (Leuven, 2010), 113, 120.

The materiality of shrines also mattered because it permitted sanctity to be experienced in physical and embodied ways. Shrines, relics, and associated objects enabled pilgrims to visualize the invisible and materialize the immaterial. Physical contact created a tangible link and an emotional response between between a pilgrim and the saint, what Alphonse Dupront calls "the sacral charge."[71] If the relic could not be touched directly, then its container, whether a tomb or reliquary, was touched. Miracles were also a vital part of the reputation of a shrine; sanctuaries did not remain popular if wonders ceased. At an important thaumaturgical shrine such as Notre-Dame de Liesse, miracles were part of the fabric of the shrine. In 1608, François de la Rue wrote that several took place every day, and 200 were recorded for the period 1582–1776.[72]

THE JOURNEY AND THE SHRINE

Contemporary accounts of pilgrimage may help us to understand pilgrims' responses. These, however, are often problematic sources and unrepresentative of the experience of most people; they were largely written by men, about long-distance travel, and they are few in number. They occasionally describe religious or emotional responses, and more often give something of the physical nature of the experience. One of the destinations most frequently depicted was the Holy See of Rome. Two accounts from the early 1580s highlight what pilgrims found valuable, which were the physical, personal experience of being in a sacred place, and the opportunity to gain indulgences. The first of these is by Gregory Martin, an English priest resident in Rome who wrote a guide to the holy sites, *Roma sancta*. The first sixteen chapters detail the important churches, relics, and indulgences to visit, along with the necessary devotions to be followed there. The first chapter covered the most popular pilgrimage, the "Five Churches," followed by a second chapter on the "Seven" and "Nine" churches, each of which contained relics and pardons.[73] The second account is by the French writer Michel de Montaigne, who traveled to Rome and Loreto in 1581. In Rome, Montaigne records in his travel journal that on Wednesday of Holy

---

[71] Alphonse Dupront, *Du sacré: Croisades et pèlerinages; Images et langages* (Paris, 1987), 441.
[72] Bruno Maës, *Notre-Dame de Liesse: Huit siècles de libération et de joie* (Paris, 1991), 117–19.
[73] Gregory Martin, *Roma Sancta (1581)*, ed. George Bruner Parks (Rome, 1969).

Week, "I did the Seven Churches with Monsieur de Foix before dinner, and we put in about five hours at it" and that in the same week he went to a display of the Veronica relic, where he witnessed prostrate and weeping crowds.[74] At Loreto, he spent four or five days at the shrine celebrating Easter at the holy house; he erected there a silver votive plaque representing himself, his wife, and his daughter kneeling before Our Lady.[75] At Viterbo, Montaigne visited the church of the Madonna della Quercia, a mile outside town, and noted that "the church is beautiful, most religious, and full of innumerable votive tablets ... built around an oak tree."[76] For all of his supposed skepticism, Montaigne was a keen observer of and participant in pilgrimages.

Several accounts of travelers to Compostela also survive from the early modern period. The most detailed is by an Italian priest from Bologna, Domenico Laffi, who visited three times in the 1660s.[77] Laffi and his companions were deeply affected by their approach to Compostela. As they entered the final day of their outward journey, they found a spring, washed themselves, and changed their clothes. They climbed a hill Laffi called Monte del Gozo, about half a league from Compostela, where, on seeing the city, they knelt and sang the *Te Deum*. Laffi records that "we had sung no more than two or three verses when we found ourselves unable to utter the words because of the copious tears which streamed from our eyes, so intense were our feelings. Our hearts were full, and our unceasing tears made us give up singing, until finally, having unburdened ourselves and spent our tears, we resumed singing."[78] Thus they entered the outskirts of Compostela. Once arrived, Laffi and his companions went immediately to the cathedral, where they knelt before the high altar (said to contain St. James's remains) and gave thanks for their safe arrival. Then, they went behind the altar, climbed some steps, and embraced the image of St. James there. Laffi noted that pilgrims hung their hats and capes on the statue while they embraced it. The following day, Laffi returned to the cathedral to say Mass and then attended high Mass in all its splendor with the archbishop and nine canons wearing full pontifical vestments. The

---

[74] Michel de Montaigne, "Travel Journal," in *The Complete Works*, trans. Donald M. Frame (New York, 2003), 1167, 1169.
[75] Ibid., 1185.
[76] Ibid., 1253.
[77] The following is from Domenico Laffi, *A Journey to the West: The Diary of a Seventeenth-Century Pilgrim from Bologna to Santiago de Compostela*, trans. James Hall (Leiden, 1997), 161–83.
[78] Ibid., 161.

pilgrims stayed for another three days, saying and attending Mass and vespers every evening. They visited further relics and objects over the duration of the visit. On his final morning in the city, Laffi visited the great reliquary chapel of St. James, which contained the staff that the saint carried on his travels. The pilgrims also received their certificates, so-called Compostelas, and then departed.

A more common experience was to visit a regional healing shrine, such as that of St. Hubert in the Ardennes in the Southern Netherlands. The monastery where the shrine was housed included a hostel for pilgrims arriving for treatment for animal bites, including rabies. The treatment was described by visiting Benedictine monks in the early eighteenth century:

> When we were at [St. Hubert] ten people who had been bitten by a mad dog arrived from ... Tongeren. After having confessed and received communion, the sacristan made a little incision in their foreheads, inserted three little fragments of St Hubert's stole into the wound, then bound it up with a piece of linen.[79]

Pilgrims then stayed for nine days, completing a *neuvaine* (nine-day) devotion. We see similar practices at other healing shrines. At Saint-Reine in Burgundy, the saint's relics were kept in the monastery church of Flavigny, but it was to a nearby spring that pilgrims flocked. Here there was a chapel, then from 1666 a hospital. Pilgrims bathed in the waters several times a day for cures to skin diseases, and again undertook a *neuvaine* devotion of daily confession and communion.[80] This formula became a common form of spiritual and physical therapy at thaumaturgic shrines.

As part of the pilgrimage rituals, pilgrims gave gifts to the saint in thanksgiving for graces received. Robert Quatremaires, monk of Mont-Saint-Michel, advised pilgrims that as the wise men brought gifts to Christ, so was it customary for the faithful to give presents to the saints whom they visited.[81] Gifts were of two main types: donations of alms in cash, and ex-votos, or votive objects. Ex-votos are sacred objects, visible, material witnesses to the experience of invisible and infinite sacred power. In the words of Mary Laven, ex-votos constituted "archives of

---

[79] Edmond Marten and Ursin Durand, *Second voyage littéraire de deux religieux bénédictins de la Congrégation de Saint-Maur* (Paris, 1724), 145–47.

[80] Philippe Boutry and Dominique Julia, eds., *Reine au Mont Auxois: Le culte et le pèlerinage de sainte Reine des origines à nos jours* (Paris-Dijon, 1997), 18–19.

[81] Robert Quatremaires, *Histoire abrégée du Mont Saint-Michel en Normandie* (Paris, 1668), 70.

miracles."[82] They ranged from representations of cured body parts modeled in wax to crutches, the chains of freed prisoners, garments, jewelry or other precious metalwork, votive panel paintings, and three-dimensional depictions of boats and cities. Shrine walls and surfaces were covered with votives. Montaigne left a description of the Holy House of Loreto and its ex-votos: "at one end ... you see high up on the wall the image of Our Lady, made, they say, of wood; all the rest is so heavily adorned with rich votive tablets from so many places and princes, that all the way to the ground there is not an inch of space empty and not covered with some place of silver or gold."[83] For his own votive, he records, "I was able to find room there only with the greatest difficulty, and as a great favor, to place a tablet on which there are four silver figures attached: that of Our Lady, my own, that of my wife, that of my daughter.... All are in a row on their knees on the tablet and Our Lady above them in the foreground."[84] Votives were both a souvenir of a past miracle or cure and a continued representation of the donor to the saint, a means of prolonging the protection given, for they remained in the sanctuary long after their presentation.

While the experiences of pilgrims remained fundamentally similar over time, the Counter-Reformation introduced important nuances. The first was the growing importance of the Eucharist to the pilgrim experience of sanctity. Medieval pilgrimage experience was, of course, framed by liturgy, whether stations, Masses, or litanies. But a heightened emphasis on personal participation in the Eucharist was novel after 1580. One form of evidence comes from pilgrims' descriptions. For example, in 1654, Pierre de Rosivignan, son of the royal governor of Caen, led a large pilgrimage to Mont-Saint-Michel. The pilgrimage commenced in the church of Saint-Pierre of Caen where *Veni creator* was sung before departure. Along the way, the pilgrims stopped for Masses in several churches: Villedieu, Avranches cathedral, and, as they crossed the bay to the Mont at low tide, they sang litanies to the Virgin and saluted St. Michael. On the day of the visit to the abbey itself, the pilgrims began with prayers, after which their chaplains celebrated a sung Mass. On the return journey, the party attended Masses at Coutances cathedral, the church of Saint-Lô, and Bayeux cathedral. Returning to Caen, the pilgrims met again a few days later

---

[82] Laven, "Recording Miracles," 194.
[83] Montaigne, "Travel Journal," 1185.
[84] Ibid., 1185.

for a Mass in the chapel of Saints Michael and Martin in the Franciscan convent.[85] The Eucharistic Mass was central to their pilgrimage.

The second innovation was the attempt to educate pilgrims at shrines, especially through the medium of popular print. Philip Soergel argues that the pilgrimage book was a new literary genre created for those participating in the Catholic resurgence. It differed from medieval miracle books in that the contents covered a wide range of issues, interweaving polemical, apologetic, and didactic content. Often in octavo format, pilgrimage books were "pocketbook guides" to shrines for literate pilgrims; they gave the history of the site, detailed some of the contemporary miracles reported there, provided lists of the church's relics and indulgences, and offered prayers, litanies, and meditations for the pilgrim to use. They took off enormously as a genre after 1600 and were important in touching a large public and encouraging personal prayer.[86] Pilgrimage books could also foster spiritual or mental pilgrimage. Even the illiterate could benefit, for these works were often illustrated with a woodcut of the saint. They were designed to be used as an aid to prayer.

BACK HOME

The return home was frequently accompanied by rituals of thanksgiving and sometimes the deposition of a votive gift in the home church. When André Landays and his companions returned from their Mont-Saint-Michel pilgrimage to Nantes in 1622, the group held a *Te Deum* and Mass in the chapel of Saint-Jean in Pirmil church, before the image of the Archangel.[87] For certain pilgrims – mostly men of the middling sort who had traveled to a prestigious site such as Rome or Compostela – the memory and significance of the pilgrimage could be perpetuated in community with other pilgrims, in a confraternity. For pilgrims of all social groups, the shrine souvenir was perhaps the most important memorial of the journey; almost every holy traveler wanted to take home some item, whether collected or purchased, as a reminder of the

---

[85] Michel de Saint-Martin, *Le voyage fait au Mont Saint-Michel par la confrérie de Saint-Pierre de Caen avec 22 ecclésiastiques et plusieurs habitants des autres paroisses* (Caen, 1654).

[86] Philip M. Soergel, *Wondrous in His Saints: Counter-Reformation and Propaganda in Bavaria* (Berkeley, CA, 1993), 168–70.

[87] André Landays, "Voyage du Mont Sainct-Michel 1622," in *Moi, Jean Martin, recteur de Plouvellec: Curés journalistes de la Renaissance à la fin du XVIIe siècle*, ed. Alain Croix (Rennes, 1993), 92.

visit to the saint. For this reason, pilgrimage towns developed good numbers of shops and artisan-produced objects for sale. The scale of production was immense: At the modest pilgrimage site of Notre-Dame de Grace at Loos, near Lille, the shrine sold 2,940 silver religious medals, 29,700 glass ones, 7,776 crosses, 4,880 "tableaux," 3,000 holy water fonts, and 1,392 rosaries in the year 1599–1600 alone.[88] Small portable items, usually made of commonplace materials such as paper, lead or bronze, fabric, wood, water, or shell, remained prized possessions, so much such so that some were buried with their owners. In March 1672 Bernard de Busquet was buried in Bruges churchyard, near Bordeaux, dressed as a pilgrim, the curé noting in the parish register that the deceased had made the pilgrimage to Compostela some years before.[89] Souvenirs provided a tangible memento of an encounter with the sacred.

CONCLUSION

The importance of pilgrimage as a popular, grassroots Catholic devotion during the early modern period cannot be overstated. The search for sanctity in the form of an intimate encounter with a saint, by the "ordinary" Catholic, drove the resurgence of shrines. The success of the Catholic Church in retaining and expanding its base of believers was due in no small part to the spiritual opportunities offered to even the humblest visitors to holy sites. First and foremost, the majority of pilgrims journeyed "out of devotion," to make personal contact with a saint of their choice, to experience something of the power of divinity that was present at the shrine. The obligation of "devotion" arose from the pilgrim's membership of a society of honor, where a vow to a saint answered with a heavenly response – a cure, rescue, escape from accident – gave an obligation of reciprocity, to visit and venerate, and perhaps give a gift as well. The pilgrim's membership in a living community, with its many obligations, was also vital. While some pilgrims traveled alone, most went with companions and an obligation to pray for family and friends; some went as formal representatives of a larger

---

[88] Cissie Fairchilds, "Marketing the Counter-Reformation: Religious Objects and Consumerism in Early Modern France," in *Visions and Revisions of Eighteenth-Century France*, ed. Christine Adams, Jack R. Censer, and Lisa Jane Graham (University Park, PA, 1997), 48.

[89] Jean Bonnecaze, *Jean-Pierre Racq: Voyage de deux pèlerins à Compostelle au XVIIIe siècle*, ed. Christian Desplatz and Adrian Blazquez (Toulouse, 1998), 36.

community, whether confraternity, parish, or city.⁹⁰ To go on pilgrimage was an individual choice, consciously made, with a religious intent, but it was also strongly rooted in communal obligation and collective benefit. This practice of vow, journey, and gift-giving had deep roots in the Middle Ages and even antiquity, which continued across the early modern period.

Pilgrimage was also a devotion that translated into the expanding Christian empires in the Americas and Asia.⁹¹ Among the first acts of missionaries was the creation of sacred sites where miracles could take place, to awe and encourage converts. The appropriation of indigenous sacred sites for Christian worship, the creation of new martyrs, the translation of European relics, and the transformation of sites into facsimile landscapes, along with the generous provision of indulgences from Rome, helped Catholic pilgrimage become a global phenomenon. The creation of the Mexican apparition shrine of Our Lady of Guadalupe in the sixteenth century, and the church of Bom Jesus in Konkani, Goa, housing the relics of St. Francis Xavier, are only two of the most obvious examples. Pilgrimage was a sufficiently malleable activity to be reinvented in all periods and places.

Pilgrimage remained a vital activity until well into the eighteenth century.⁹² Large numbers of people moved temporarily every year; pilgrimage produced a distinctive and hugely popular genre of literature and a resulting form of devotional activity – spiritual pilgrimage. Pilgrimage was the mainstay of the material economies of many towns involved in the merchandising of holy souvenirs. Along with greater sacramental observance, mental prayer, plenary pardons, and devotional reading, pilgrimage was one of the great hallmarks of Catholic reformed spirituality in Europe and beyond. Above all, early modern pilgrimage enabled the personal and communal encounter with the sacred and the divine.

---

⁹⁰ Julia, *Le voyage aux saints*, 10.
⁹¹ For an excellent bibliography on Latin American pilgrimage, see Joel Palka and Ramon Foch, "Pilgrimage in Colonial Latin America," in *Oxford Bibliographies Online: Latin American Studies* (2020).
⁹² Noonan, *The Road to Jerusalem*, 243.

Further Reading

GENERAL READING

Bartlett, Robert. *Why Can the Dead Do Such Great Things? Saints and Worshippers from the Martyrs to the Reformation*. Princeton, NJ, 2013.
Burke, Peter. "How to Become a Counter-Reformation Saint." In *The Counter-Reformation: The Essential Readings*, edited by David Luebke, 129–42. Oxford, 1999 [original version 1984].
Christian, William, Jr. *Apparitions in Late Medieval and Renaissance Spain*. Princeton, NJ, 1981.
——*Local Religion in Sixteenth Century Spain*. Princeton, NJ, 1981.
Copeland, Clare. *Maria Maddalena de' Pazzi: The Making of a Counter-Reformation Saint*. Oxford, 2016.
——"Sanctity." In *The Ashgate Research Companion to the Counter-Reformation*, edited by Alexandra Bamji et al., 225–42. Farnham, 2013.
Delooz, Pierre. "Towards a Sociological Study of Canonized Sainthood in the Catholic Church." In *Saints and Their Cults: Studies in Religious Sociology, Folklore and History*, edited by Stephen Wilson, 189–216. Cambridge, 1983.
Ditchfield, Simon. "Thinking with Saints: Sanctity and Society in the Early Modern World." *Critical Inquiry* 35, no. 3 (2009): 552–84.
——"Tridentine Worship and the Cult of Saints." In *The Cambridge History of Christianity*, vol. 6: *Reform and Expansion 1500–1660*, edited by Ronnie Po-chia Hsia, 201–24. Cambridge, 2007.
Emich, Birgit, et al., eds. *Making Saints in a Glocal Religion: Practices of Holiness in Early Modern Catholicism*. Cologne, 2024.
Gotor, Miguel. *I beati del papa: Santità, inquisizione e obbedienza in età moderna*. Florence, 2002.
Herzig, Tamar. "Saints and Mystics: Before Trent." In *Oxford Bibliographies in Renaissance and Reformation*, edited by Margaret L. King. Oxford, 2018.
Reinburg, Virginia. *Storied Places: Pilgrim Shrines, Nature and History in Early Modern France*. Cambridge, 2019.
Rowe, Erin K. *Black Saints in Early Modern Global Catholicism*. Cambridge, 2019.
——"Saints and Mystics: After Trent." In *Oxford Bibliographies in Renaissance and Reformation*, edited by Margaret L. King. Oxford, 2018.

Sallmann, Jean-Michel. *Naples et ses saints à l'âge baroque, 1540–1750*. Paris, 1994.
Taylor, William B. *Theater of a Thousand Wonders: A History of Miraculous Images and Shrines in New Spain*. Cambridge, 2016.
Vauchez, André. *Sainthood in the Later Middle Ages*. Translated by Jean Birrell. Cambridge, 1997.
Zarri, Gabriella. "Female Sanctity, 1500–1650." In *The Cambridge History of Christianity*, vol. 6: *Reform and Expansion 1500–1660*, edited by Ronnie Po-chia Hsia, 180–200. Cambridge, 2007.
——— *Le sante vive: Cultura e religiosità femminile nella prima età moderna*. Turin, 1990.

CHAPTER 1. BISHOPS

Boucheron, Patrick, and Stéphane Gioanni, eds. *La mémoire d'Ambroise de Milan: Usages politiques d'une autorité patristique en Italie: Ve–XVIIIe siècle*. Paris, 2015.
Johns, Christopher. *The Visual Culture of Catholic Enlightenment*. University Park, PA, 2015.
McNamara, Celeste. "Molding the Model Bishop from Trent to Vatican II." *Church History* 88, no. 1 (2019): 58–86.
Messbarger, Rebecca, Christopher Johns, and Philip Gavitt, eds. *Benedict XIV and the Enlightenment: Art, Science, and Spirituality*. Toronto, 2016.
Olds, Katrina B. "How to Be a Counter-Reformation Bishop: Cardinal Baltasar de Moscoso y Sandoval in the Diocese of Jaén, 1618–1646." *Sierra Mágina: Revista universitaria* 12, special issue "Entre el cielo y la tierra: Las élites eclesiásticas en la Europa Moderna" (2009): 197–213.
Prodi, Paolo. *Il cardinale Gabriele Paleotti (1522–1597)*. Rome, 1959 and 1967. Bologna, repr. 2022.
Rubial García, Antonio. *La santidad controvertida: Hagiografía y conciencia criolla alrededor de los venerables no canonizados de Nueva España*. Mexico City, 1999, repr. 2015.
Turchini, Angelo. *La fabbrica di un santo: Il processo di canonizzazione di Carlo Borromeo e la Controriforma*. Cassale Monteferrato, 1984.

CHAPTER 2. MARTYRS

Ahern, Maureen. "Visual and Verbal Sites: The Construction of Jesuit Martyrdom in Northwest New Spain in Andrés Pérez de Ribas' *Historia de los Triumphos de Nuestra Santa Fee* (1645)." *Colonial Latin American Review* 8, no. 1 (1999): 7–33.
Arblaster, Paul. *Antwerp and the World: Richard Verstegan and the International Culture of Catholic Reformation*. Leuven, 2004.
Camamis, George. *Estudios sobre el cautiverio en el Siglo de Oro*. Madrid, 1977.
Cañeque, Alejandro. *Un imperio de mártires: Religión y poder en las fronteras de la Monarquía Hispánica*. Madrid, 2020.
Coello de la Rosa, Alexandre. *Jesuits at the Margins: Missions and Missionaries in the Marianas (1668–1769)*. New York, 2016.

Dillon, Anne. *The Construction of Martyrdom in the English Catholic Community, 1535–1603*. Aldershot, 2002.
Gregory, Brad S. *Salvation at Stake: Christian Martyrdom in Early Modern Europe*. Cambridge, 1999.
Hesselink, Reinier H. *The Dream of Christian Nagasaki: World Trade and the Clash of Cultures, 1560–1640*. Jefferson, NC, 2016.
Leemans, Johan, ed. *More than a Memory: The Discourse of Martyrdom and the Construction of Christian Identity in the History of Christianity*. Leuven, 2005.
Roldán-Figueroa, Rady. *The Martyrs of Japan: Publication History and Catholic Missions in the Spanish World (Spain, New Spain, and the Philippines, 1597–1700)*. Leiden, 2021.
Sauerländer, Willibald. *The Catholic Rubens: Saints and Martyrs*. Los Angeles, 2014.

CHAPTER 3. FEMALE SAINTS

Alabrús, Rosa Mª, and Ricardo García Cárcel. *Teresa de Jesús: La construcción de la santidad femenina*. Madrid, 2015.
Diefendorf, Barbara. *From Penitence to Charity: Pious Women and the Catholic Reformation in Paris*. Oxford, 2004.
Eire, Carlos. *The Life of Saint Teresa of Avila: A Biography*. Princeton, NJ, 2019.
Haliczer, Stephen. *Between Exaltation and Infamy: Female Mystics in the Golden Age of Spain*. Oxford, 2022.
Howe, Elizabeth T. "Teresa of Ávila." In *Oxford Bibliographies in Renaissance and Reformation*, edited by Margaret King. New York, last updated July 27, 2016.
O'Reilly, Terence, et al., eds. *St. Teresa of Avila: Her Writings and Life*. Cambridge, 2018.
Surtz, Ronald E. *Writing Women in Late Medieval and Early Modern Spain: The Mothers of Saint Teresa of Ávila*. Philadelphia, 1995.
Weber, Alison, ed. *Devout Laywomen in the Early Modern World*. London, 2016.
Wilson, Christopher G., ed. *The Heirs of St. Teresa of Ávila: Defenders and Disseminators of the Founding Mother's Legacy*. Washington, DC, 2006.

CHAPTER 4. THE VIRGIN MARY

Cunningham, Lawrence. "The Virgin Mary." In *From Trent to Vatican II: Historical and Theological Investigations*, edited by Raymond F. Bulman and Frederick J. Parrella, 179–92. Oxford, 2006.
Hall, Linda B. *Mary, Mother and Warrior: The Virgin in Spain and the Americas*. Austin, TX, 2004.
Lee, Christina H. *Saints of Resistance: Devotions in the Philippines under Early Spanish Rule*. Oxford, 2021.
Matovina, Timothy. *Theologies of Guadalupe: From the Era of Conquest to Pope Francis*. Oxford, 2018.

Poole, Stafford. *Our Lady of Guadalupe: The Origins and Sources of a Mexican National Symbol, 1531–1797*. Tucson, AZ, 2017.

Remensnyder, Amy G. *La Conquistadora: The Virgin Mary at War and Peace in the Old and the New Worlds*. New York, 2014.

Rubin, Miri. *Mother of God: A History of the Virgin Mary*. London, 2009.

Vélez, Karin. *The Miraculous Flying House of Loreto: Spreading Catholicism in the Early Modern World*. Princeton, NJ, 2018.

Warner, Marina. *Alone of All Her Sex: The Myth and the Cult of the Virgin Mary*. New York, 1983.

CHAPTER 5. BLACK SAINTS

Bindman, David, and Henry Louis Gates, Jr., eds. *The Image of the Black in Western Art*, Volume II, Part 1: From the Demonic Threat to the Incarnation of Sainthood and Part 2: Africans in the Christian Ordinance of the World. Cambridge, MA, 2010.

——eds. The Image of the Black in Western Art, Volume III: From the "Age of Discovery" to the Age of Abolition, Part 1: Artists of the Renaissance and Baroque. Cambridge, MA, 2010.

Brewer-García, Larissa, and Cécile Fromont. "From Hell to Hell: Central Africans and Catholic Visual Catechesis in the Early Modern Atlantic Slave Trade." *Art History* 46 (2023): 946–77.

Cussen, Celia L., *Black Saint of the Americas: The Life and Afterlife of Martín de Porres*. Cambridge, 2014.

Frey, Sylvia. "The Visible Church: Historiography of African American Religion Since Raboteau." *Slavery and Abolition* 29, no. 1 (2008): 83–110.

Fromont, Cécile, ed. *Afro-Catholic Festivals in the Americas: Performance, Representation, and the Making of the Black Atlantic Tradition*. University Park, PA, 2019.

Germeten, Nicole von. *Black Blood Brothers: Confraternities and Social Mobility for Afro-Mexicans*. Gainesville, FL, 2006.

Krebs, Verena. *Medieval Ethiopian Kingship, Craft, and Diplomacy with Latin Europe*. Cham, 2021.

Otele, Olivette. *African Europeans: An Untold History*. New York, 2021.

Rowe, Erin Kathleen. *Black Saints in Early Modern Global Catholicism*. Cambridge, 2019.

Soares, Mariza de Carvalho. *People of Faith: Slavery and African Catholics in Eighteenth-Century Rio de Janeiro*. Durham, NC, 2011.

CHAPTER 6. CATACOMB SAINTS

Baciocchi, Stéphane, and Christophe Duhamelle, eds. *Reliques romaines: Invention et circulation des corps saints des catacombes à l'époque moderne*. Rome, 2016.

Ditchfield, Simon. "Reading Rome as a Sacred Landscape, c. 1586–1635." In *Sacred Space in Early Modern Europe*, edited by Will Coster and Andrew Spicer, 167–92. Cambridge, 2005.

———"Text Before Trowel: Antonio Bosio's *Roma Sotterranea* Revisited." In *The Church Retrospective: Papers Read at the 1995 Summer Meeting and the 1996 Winter Meeting of the Ecclesiastical History Society, Studies in Church History 33*, edited by Robert N. Swanson, 343–60. Woodbridge, 1997.

Harris, A. Katie. "Gift, Sale, and Theft: Juan de Ribera and the Sacred Economy of Relics in the Early Modern Mediterranean." *Journal of Early Modern History* 18 (2014): 193–226.

———"'A Known Holy Body, with an Inscription and a Name': Bishop Sancho Dávila y Toledo and the Creation of St. Vitalis." *Archiv für Reformationsgeschichte* 104 (2013): 245–71.

Johnson, Trevor. "Holy Fabrications: The Catacomb Saints and the Counter-Reformation in Bavaria." *Journal of Ecclesiastical History* 47, no. 2 (1996): 274–97.

Litaker, Noria. *Bedazzled Saints: Catacomb Relics in Early Modern Bavaria*. Charlottesville, VA, 2023.

———"Lost in Translation? Constructing Ancient Roman Martyrs in Baroque Bavaria." *Church History* 89, no. 4 (2020): 801–28.

CHAPTER 7. CANONIZATION

Ditchfield, Simon. "How Not to Be a Counter-Reformation Saint: The Attempted Canonization of Pope Gregory X, 1622–45." *Papers of the British School at Rome* 60 (1992): 379–422.

Finucane, Ronald C. *Contested Canonizations: The Last Medieval Saints, 1482–1523*. Washington, DC, 2011.

———"Saint-Making at the End of the Sixteenth Century: How and Why Jacek of Poland (d. 1257) became St. Hyacinth in 1594." *Hagiographica* 9 (2002): 207–58.

Jones, Pamela M. "Celebrating New Saints in Rome and Across the Globe." In *A Companion to Early Modern Rome*, edited by Pamela M. Jones et al., 148–66. Leiden, 2019.

Papa, Giovanni. *Le cause di canonizzazione nel primo periodo della Congregazione dei Riti, 1588–1634*. Rome, 2001.

CHAPTER 8. REGULATING RELICS

Boiron, Stéphan. *La controverse née de la querelle des reliques à l'époque du Concile de Trente (1500–1640)*. Paris, 1989.

Boutry, Philippe, Pierre Antoine Fabre, and Dominique Julia, eds. *Reliques modernes: Cultes et usages chrétiens des corps saints des Réformes aux révolutions*. Paris, 2009.

Bozóky, Edina, and Anne-Marie Helvétius, eds. *Les reliques: Objets, cultes, symboles: Actes du colloque international de l'Université du Littoral-Côte d'Opale (Boulogne-sur-Mer) 4–6 septembre 1997*. Turnhout, 1999.

Geary, Patrick. *Furta Sacra: Thefts of Relics in the Central Middle Ages*. Princeton, NJ, 1990.
———"Sacred Commodities: The Circulation of Medieval Relics." In *The Social Life of Things: Commodities in Cultural Perspective*, edited by Arjun Appadurai, 169–91. Cambridge, 1986.
Harris, A. Katie. *The Stolen Bones of St. John of Matha: Forgery, Theft, and Sainthood in the Seventeenth Century*. University Park, PA, 2023.
———"Gift, Sale, and Theft: Juan de Ribera and the Sacred Economy of Relics in the Early Modern Mediterranean." *Journal of Early Modern History* 18 (2014): 193–226.
Herrmann-Mascard, Nicole. *Les reliques des saints: Formation coutumière d'un droit*. Paris, 1975.
Olds, Katrina B. "The Ambiguities of the Holy: Authenticating Relics in Seventeenth-Century Spain." *Renaissance Quarterly* 65, no. 1 (2012): 135–84.
Smith, Julia M. H. "Relics: An Evolving Tradition in Latin Christianity." In *Saints and Sacred Matter: The Cult of Relics in Byzantium and Beyond*, edited by Cynthia Hahn and Holger A. Klein, 41–60. Washington, DC, 2015.
Tausiet, María. *El dedo robado: Reliquias imaginarias en la España moderna*. Madrid, 2013.
Walsham, Alexandra. "Skeletons in the Cupboard: Relics After the English Reformation." *Past and Present*, suppl. 5 (2010): 121–43.
Wisniewski, Robert. *The Beginnings of the Cult of Relics*. Oxford, 2018.

CHAPTER 9. MYSTICISM AND THE DISCERNMENT OF SPIRITS

Ahlgren, Gillian T.W. *Teresa of Avila and the Politics of Sanctity*. Ithaca, NY, 1996.
Copeland, Clare, and Jan Machielsen, eds. *Angels of Light? Sanctity and the Discernment of Spirits in the Early Modern Period*. Leiden, 2013.
De Certeau, Michel. *The Mystic Fable, Volume 1: The Sixteenth and Seventeenth Centuries*. Chicago, 1992.
Filoramo, Giovanni, and Gabriella Zarri, eds. *Storia della direzione spirituale, III: L'età moderna*. Brescia, 2008.
Gerson, Jean. *Oeuvres complètes*. Vol. 3, edited by Mgr. Glorieux. Paris, 1960.
McGinn, Bernard. *The Persistence of Mysticism in Catholic Europe: France, Italy, and Germany (1500–1675)*. New York, 2020.
Michon, Hélène, et al., eds. *Femmes, mysticisme et prophétisme en Europe du Moyen Âge à l'époque moderne*. Paris, 2021.
Scattigno, Anna. *Sposa di Cristo: Mistica e comunità*. Roma, 2011.
Sluhovsky, Moshe. *Believe Not Every Spirit: Possession, Mysticism, and Discernment in Early Modern Catholicism*. Chicago, 2007.
Teresa of Ávila. *The Collected Works of St. Teresa of Avila*. Washington, DC, 1976–1983.

Tyler, Peter, and Edward Howells, eds. *Teresa of Avila: Mystical Theology and Spirituality in the Carmelite Tradition*. London, 2016.
Weber, Alison. *Teresa of Avila and the Rhetoric of Femininity*. Princeton, NJ, 1990.
Yarrow, Simon. *Saints: A Very Short Introduction*. Oxford, 2016.

CHAPTER 10. MIRACLES AND HOLY BODIES

Bouley, Bradford. *Pious Postmortems: Anatomy, Sanctity and the Catholic Church in Early Modern Europe*. Philadelphia, 2017.
Castel-Branco, Nuno. "Material Piety: Science and Religious Culture in Seventeenth-Century Portugal." *Renaissance Quarterly* 74, no. 4 (2021): 1162–209.
Donato, Maria Pia, and Jill Kraye, eds. *Conflicting Duties: Science, Medicine and Religion in Rome, 1550–1750*. London, 2009.
Duffin, Jacalyn. *Medical Miracles: Doctors, Saints, and Healing in the Modern World*. New York, 2009.
Ehlers, Benjamin. *Between Christians and Moriscos: Juan de Ribera and Religion Reform in Valencia, 1568–1614*. Baltimore, 2006.
Hoffmann, Viktoria von. "Epistemologies of Touch in Early Modern Holy Autopsies." *Renaissance Quarterly* 75, no. 2 (2022): 542–82.
Park, Katharine. *Secrets of Women: Gender, Generation, and the Origins of Human Dissection*. New York, 2006.
Pomata, Gianna. "Malpighi and the Holy Body: Medical Experts and Miraculous Evidence in Seventeenth-Century Italy." *Renaissance Studies* 21, no. 4 (2007): 568–86.
Siraisi, Nancy. *Medicine and the Italian Universities, 1250–1600*. Boston, 2001.
Vidal, Fernando. "Miracles, Science, and Testimony in Post-Tridentine Saint-Making." *Science in Context* 20, no. 3 (2007): 481–508.
Ziegler, Joseph. "Practitioners and Saints: Medical Men in Canonization Processes in the Thirteenth to Fifteenth Centuries." *Social History of Medicine* 12, no. 2 (1999): 191–225.

CHAPTER 11. LITURGY

Conover, Cornelius. *Pious Imperialism: Spanish Rule and the Cult of Saints in Mexico City*. Albuquerque, NM, 2019.
Ditchfield, Simon. "Giving Tridentine Worship Back Its History." In *Studies in Church History* 35 (1999): 199–226.
——*Liturgy, Sanctity, and History in Tridentine Italy: Pietro Maria Campi and the Preservation of the Particular*. Cambridge, 1995.
Ducreux, Marie-Elizabeth. "How Local Was a Local Saint? How Global Was a Regional Saint? Contrasted Cases of Recognitio Cultus in a Large Central European Space in Early Modern Times." In *Making Saints in a "Glocal" Religion: Practices of Holiness in Early Modern Catholicism*, edited by Birgit Emich et al., 121–46. Cologne, 2024.

Martimort, Aimé-Georges, ed. *The Church at Prayer: An Introduction to the Liturgy*. Collegeville, 1986.

CHAPTER 12. HAGIOGRAPHY

Delehaye, Hippolyte. *The Legends of Saints*. 1901; 4th ed. Dublin, 1998.
Frazier, Alison Knowles. *Possible Lives: Authors and Saints in Renaissance Italy*. New York, 2005.
Greenwood, Jonathan. "Floral Arrangements: Compilations of Saints' Lives in Early Modern Europe." *Journal of Early Modern History* 22 (2018): 181–203.
Knowles, M. David. "Presidential Address: Great Historical Enterprises I. The Bollandists." *Transactions of the Royal Historical Society*, 5th ser., 8 (1958): 147–66.
Touber, Jetze. *Law, Medicine and Engineering in the Cult of the Saints in Counter-Reformation Rome: The Hagiographical Works of Antonio Gallonio, 1556–1605*. Leiden, 2014.
Van Liere, Kate, Simon Ditchfield, and Howard Louthan, eds. *Sacred History: Uses of the Christian Past in the Renaissance World*. Oxford, 2012.

CHAPTER 13. IMAGES

Bieñko Peralta, Doris. "Las vera efigies y los retratos simulados: Representaciones de los venerables angelopolitanos, siglos XVII y XVIII." In *La función de las imágenes en el catolicismo novohispano*, edited by Gisela von Wobeser, Carolina Aguilar García, and Jorge Luis Merlo Solorio. 255–82. Mexico City, 2018.
Carlos Varona, María Cruz de. "'The Authority of Sacred Paintbrushes': Representing Medieval Sainthood in the Early Modern Period." In *Sacred Spain: Art and Belief in the Spanish World*, edited by Ronda Kasl, 101–19. New Haven, CT, 2009.
Casale, Vittorio. *L'arte per le canonizzazioni: L'attività artistica intorno alle canonizzazioni e alle beatificazioni del Seicento*. Turin, 2011.
Cavero de Carondelet, Cloe de. "Wounds on Trial: Forensic Truth, Sanctity, and the Early Modern Visual Culture of Ritual Murder." In *Sacred Images and Normativity: Contested Forms in Early Modern Art*, edited by Chiara Franceschini, 68–85. Turnhout, 2021.
Hills, Helen. "'The Face Is a Mirror of the Soul': Frontispieces and the Production of Sanctity in Post-Tridentine Naples." *Art History* 31, no. 4 (2008): 547–73.
———"How to Look like a Counter-Reformation Saint." In *Exploring Cultural History: Essays in Honour of Peter Burke*, edited by Melissa Calaresu, Filippo De Vivo, and Joan-Pau Rubiés, 207–30. Farnham, 2010.
Jasienski, Adam. *Praying to Portraits: Audience, Identity, and the Inquisition in the Early Modern Hispanic World*. University Park, PA, 2023.
König-Nordhoff, Ursula. *Ignatius von Loyola: Studien zur Entwicklung einer neuen Heiligen-Ikonographie im Rahmen einer Kanonisationskampagne um 1600*. Berlin, 1982.
Mújica Pinilla, Ramón. *Rosa Limensis: Mística, política e iconografía en torno a la patrona de América*. Lima, 2001.

Niedermeier, Nina. *Die ersten Bildnisse von Heiligen in der Frühen Neuzeit: Porträtähnlichkeit in nachtridentinischer Zeit*. Regensburg, 2020.
Noyes, Ruth. *Peter Paul Rubens and the Counter-Reformation Crisis of the Beati Moderni*. New York, 2017.
Omata Rappo, Hitomi. *Des Indes lointaines aux scènes des collèges: Les reflets des martyrs de la mission japonaise en Europe (XVIe–XVIIIe siècle)*. Münster, 2020.
Pereda, Felipe. *Images of Discord: Poetics and Politics of the Sacred Image in Fifteenth-Century Spain*. Translated by Consuelo Lopez-Morillas. London, 2018.
Quiles, Fernando. "Between Being, Seeming and Saying: The Vera Effigies in Spain and Hispanic America During the Baroque." In *Fiction Sacrée: Spiritualité et esthétique durant la premier âge moderne*, edited by Ralph Dekoninck, Agnès Guiderdoni, and Emilie Granjon, 181–200. Leuven, 2013.
Vincent-Cassy, Cécile. *Les saintes vierges et martyres dans l'Espagne du XVIIe siècle: Culte et image*. Madrid, 2011.

CHAPTER 14. LITERATURE

Arnold, Margaret. *The Magdalene in the Reformation*. Cambridge, MA, 2018.
Badir, Patricia. *The Maudlin Impression: English Literary Images of Mary Magdalene, 1550–1700*. Notre Dame, IN, 2009.
Chapman, Alison. *Patrons and Patron Saints in Early Modern English Literature*. New York, 2012.
Dillon, Anne. *The Construction of Martyrdom in the English Catholic Community, 1535–1603*. New York, 2003.
Grindlay, Lilla. *Queen of Heaven: The Assumption and Coronation of the Virgin in Early Modern English Writing*. Notre Dame, IN, 2018.
Lake, Peter, and Michael Questier. *The Trials of Margaret Clitherow: Persecution, Martyrdom, and the Politics of Sanctity in Early Modern England*. London, 2011.
Freeman, Thomas S., Thomas Mayer, Alec Ryrie, et al., eds. *Martyrs and Martyrdom in England, c. 1400–1700*. Woodbridge, 2007.
Monta, Susannah Brietz. *Martyrdom and Literature in Early Modern England*. Cambridge, 2005.
Reames, Sherry. *The Legenda Aurea: A Reexamination of Its Paradoxical History*. Madison, WI, 1985.
White, Helen C. *Tudor Books of Saints and Martyrs*. Madison, WI, 1963.

CHAPTER 15. MATERIAL CULTURE

Bynum, Caroline Walker. *Christian Materiality: An Essay on Religion in Late Medieval Europe*. New York, 2011.
Emich, Birgit, Daniel Sidler, Samuel Weber, and Christian Windler, eds. *Pathways Through Early Modern Christianities*. Cologne, 2023.

Evangelisti, Silvia. "Material Culture." In *The Ashgate Research Companion to the Counter-Reformation*, edited by Alexandra Bamji, Geert H. Janssen, and Mary Laven, 395–416. Farnham, 2013.

Greenwood, Jonathan. "Miracles in Writing: Obstetric Intercessions, Scribal Relics, and Jesuit News in the Early Modern Global Cult of Ignatius of Loyola." *Journal of Jesuit Studies* 9, no. 3 (2022): 338–56.

Ivanič, Suzanna, Mary Laven, and Andrew Morrall, eds. *Religious Materiality in the Early Modern World*. Amsterdam, 2019.

Kürzeder, Christoph. *Als die Dinge heilig waren: Gelebte Frömmigkeit im Zeitalter des Barock*. Regensburg, 2005.

Miller, Maureen C. "Introduction: Material Culture and Catholic History." *Catholic Historical Review* 101, no. 1 (2015): 1–17.

Nelles, Paul. "Devotion in Transit: Agnus Dei, Jesuit Missionaries, and Global Salvation in the Sixteenth Century." In *Connected Mobilities in the Early Modern World: The Practice and Experience of Movement*, edited by Paul Nelles and Rosa Salzberg, 185–214. Amsterdam, 2023.

Overbey, Karen. "Seeing Through Stone: Materiality and Place in a Medieval Scottish Pendant Reliquary." *Res: Anthropology and Aesthetics* 65–66 (2014/15): 242–58.

Ryan, Salvador, Samantha Leanne Smith, and Laura Katrine Skinnebach, eds. *Material Cultures of Devotion in the Age of Reformation*. Leuven, 2022.

Sidler, Daniel. *Heiligkeit aushandeln: Katholische Reform und lokale Glaubenspraxis in der Eidgenossenschaft (1560–1790)*. Frankfurt, 2017.

Suykerbuyk, Ruben. *The Matter of Piety: Zoutleeuw's Church of Saint Leonard and Religious Material Culture in the Low Countries (c. 1450–1620)*. Leiden, 2020.

Weddigen, Tristan. "Materiality and Idolatry: Roman Imaginations of Saint Rose of Lima." In *The Nomadic Object: The Challenge of World for Early Modern Religious Art*, edited by Christine Göttler and Mia M. Mochizuki, 103–46. Leiden, 2018.

CHAPTER 16. CONFRATERNITIES

Cormack, Margaret. *Saints and Their Cults in the Atlantic World*. Columbia, SC, 2007.

Flynn, Maureen. *Sacred Charity: Confraternities and Social Welfare in Spain, 1400–1700*. London, 1989.

Germeten, Nicole von. *Black Blood Brothers: Confraternities and Social Mobility for Afro-Mexicans*. Gainesville, FL, 2006.

Kiddy, Elizabeth W. *Blacks of the Rosary: Memory and History in Minas Gerais, Brazil*. University Park, PA, 2005.

Morgan, Ronald J. *Spanish American Saints and the Rhetoric of Identity, 1600–1810*. Tucson, AZ, 2002.

Valerio, Miguel A. *Sovereign Joy: Afro-Mexican Kings and Queens, 1539–1640*. Cambridge, 2022.

Webster, Susan Verdi. *Art and Ritual in Golden-Age Spain: Sevillian Confraternities and the Processional Sculpture of Holy Week*. Princeton, NJ, 1998.

CHAPTER 17. PILGRIMAGES

Armstrong, Megan. *The Holy Land and the Early Modern Reinvention of Catholicism*. Cambridge, 2021.

Brummett, Palmira, ed. *The "Book" of Travels: Genre, Ethnology and Pilgrimage, 1250–1700*. Leiden, 2009.

Craig, Leigh Ann. *Wandering Women and Holy Matrons: Women as Pilgrims in the Later Middle Ages*. Leiden, 2009.

Cunningham, Bernadette, and Raymond Gillespie. "The Lough Derg Pilgrimage in the Age of the Counter-Reformation." *Eire-Ireland* 39 (2004): 167–79.

Ditchfield, Simon. "Reading Rome as a Sacred Landscape, c. 1585–1635." In *Sacred Space in Early Modern Europe*, edited by Will Coster and Andrew Spicer, 167–92. Cambridge, 2005.

Hillman, Jennifer, and Elizabeth Tingle, eds. *Soul Travel: Spiritual Journeys in Medieval and Early Modern Europe*. Oxford, 2019.

Laffi, Domenico. *A Journey to the West: The Diary of a Seventeenth-Century Pilgrim from Bologna to Santiago de Compostela*. Translated by James Hall. Leiden, 1997.

Maddrell, Avril, Veronica della Dora, Alessandro Scafi, and Heather Walton, eds. *Christian Pilgrimage, Landscape and Heritage: Journeying into the Sacred*. London, 2014.

Tingle, Elizabeth. *Sacred Journeys in the Counter Reformation: Long-Distance Pilgrimage in North-West Europe*. Berlin, 2020.

Index

Individual saints and blesseds appear under their first names. We use the names by which they are best known in English (*e.g.* Carlo Borromeo but Philip Neri).

Acta ecclesiae Mediolanensis, 25, 28
Acta sanctorum, 238
Actes and Monuments, 284
d'Afflitto, Annibale, 206
Afro-Iberian confraternities, 330–33
Agricola, Saint, 18, 22
Ajofrín, María de, 55, 56–60, 65
Albrecht V, Duke, 119
Alessi, Niccolò, 186
Alfield, Thomas, 293
Alfonso X, King, 75
Alfonso XI, King, 76
Aloysius Gonzaga, *see* Luigi Gonzaga, Saint
Allen, William, Cardinal, 293
Ambrose, Saint, 18, 19, 20–22, 29
Ambrosia, 280–87
Andrea Avellino, Saint, 239, 303
Andrea Corsini, Saint, 203
Anfossi, Domenico, 162
Animuccia, Giovanni, 245
Annales ecclesiastici, 96, 255
Anthony of Egypt, Saint, 172
Antonio of Caltagirone (of Noto), 98–99, 337–38
Apter, Andrew, 105
Arellano, Alonso de, 83–84
Art of Painting, 267
asceticism, 204–7
Ashgate Research Companion to the Counter-Reformation, 4
Astrophil and Stella 60, 291–92
Atiensa, Juan de, 193
Atlas Mariana, 351
Augustine, Saint, 183

Balboa, Vasco Núñez de, 77
Bale, John, 279
Barocci, Federico, 320
Baronio, Cesare, 97, 109, 149–50, 245, 247
Bartoli, Daniello, 242
Bascapè, Carlo, 20
Basilica of Saint Peter, 213–14
Bautista de Aguirre, Juan, 2
Bavaria, catacomb saints in, 118–22
St. Felix, 122–29
Beaver, Adam, 364
del Bello, Marco Antonio, 207
Benci, Francesco, 241–42
Benedetti, Alessandro, 199–200
Benedict IV, Pope, 32
Benedict of Nursia, Saint, 306
Benedict of Palermo, Saint, 8, 98–99, 100–1, 337, 338
Benedict XIII, Pope, 31, 322
Benedict XIV, Pope, 31, 32, 139, 146, 166, 306
Benedict XVI, Pope, 52–53, 153
Benno of Meissen, Saint, 134, 138
Berengario da Carpi, Jacopo, 199–200
Berze, Gasper, 242
Bibliotheca hagiographica latina, 252
Bilinkoff, Jodi, 247
Biondi, Giovanni Francesco, 244
bishops, 33–34
as electricians of the sacred, 17–19
as saintly models and saint-makers in the seventeenth century, 27–30
St. Carlo Borromeo as model bishop, 23–27

Black magus iconography, 93–94
Black saints, 90
　altarpieces, 100–2
　confraternities of, 95–96, 100–3, 331–32, 333–47
　early modern, 94–99
　polysemic, 102–6
　traditions of, 90–94
Blount, Richard, 295
Bolland, Jean, 238
Bonani, Joseph, 305
Book of Common Prayer, 279
Borromeo, Federico, 25, 27
Bosio, Antonio, 109
Bourdon, Henri-Marie, 357
Du Breil de Pontbriant, René-François, 364
Bridget of Sweden, Saint, 174, 308
Brigid, Saint, 351
A briefe historie of the glorious martyrdom of twelve reverend priests, 293
Brown, Peter, 17, 18
Browne, Magdalene, 297–99
Brusoni, Girolamo, 244
Burke, Peter, 10, 18, 134–35, 153, 255, 278
de Busquet, Bernard, 371
Bustamante, Francisco de, 79

Caelestis Hierusalem cives, 151, 255, 263
Caimi, Bernardo, 363
Calixtus, Saint and Pope, 124–25
Calvin, John, 158, 163, 240, 241n, 284, 304, 360
Le Camus, Étienne, 169
Camus, Jean-Pierre, 244
Cañeque, Alejandro, 153
canonization, 7, 8–9, 133–35
　after martyrdom, 50–53
　of Carlo Borromeo, 144, 149–50
　competition and disagreements over, 148–52
　in context, 135–40
　crisis of, 18
　in the early modern period, 152–54
　of Francis Xavier, 216
　of Hyacinth of Poland, 213–15
　of Ignatius of Loyola, 216
　of the martyrs of Gorcum, 51, 141, 144, 147
　papal infallibility and, 136

　paperwork required for, 139–40, 146
　of Philip Neri, 216
　politicking related to, 137–38
　rarity in seventeenth century, 140
　steps in process of, 140–48
　of Teresa of Ávila, 58–59, 64–65, 141, 150, 216
Il Cappucccino scozzese, 244
Carlo Borromeo, Saint, 18, 20–23, 139, 165
　canonization of, 144, 149–50
　examination of corpse of, 205–6
　as model of modern bishop saint, 23–27
　portrait of, 265
　on relics, 159
Carneiro, Melchior, 357
Carrión, Luisa de, 69
Carvajal y Mendoza, Luisa de, 48–49, 70
catacomb saints, 107–10, 129
　in Bavaria, 118–22
　leaving Rome, 117–18
　logistics of excavation, authentication, and export of, 110–17
　St. Felix of Gars am Inn, 122–29
Caterina de' Ricci, Saint, 174, 186–92
Catherine of Siena, Saint, 54, 58, 61, 65, 69, 70
　as guide to discernment, 174
Catholic Enlightenment, 31
Catholicism: confraternities in (*See* confraternities)
　defined by sanctity, 5–6
　eighteenth-century bishop saints of, 31–33
　imagery in (*See* imagery)
　imperialism and colonialism and, 38–39
　literature of (*See* literature)
　liturgy of (*See* liturgy)
　martyrs in, 35–38
　medicine and, 195–201
　papal infallibility and, 136
　pilgrimage in (*See* pilgrimage)
　saint-making by, 7, 8–9 *See also* canonization
　study of early modern, 5 *See also* sanctity
Cesalpino, Andrea, 207, 208
Chacón, Alfonso, 214
Chiericato, Francesco, 351
Christian, William, Jr., 82, 350
Clare of Assisi, Saint, 319

Clement IX, Pope, 113, 250
Clement VII, Pope, 214
Clement VIII, Pope, 60, 111, 113, 213, 248, 261
Clement X, Pope, 114
Clement XII, Pope, 320
Clement XIII, Pope, 32–33
Clement XIV, Pope, 33
collective identities and liturgy, 221–30
Colombo, Realdo, 200, 206
Columbus, Christopher, 73, 77
Concertatio ecclesiae Catholicae in Anglia, 293, 294
confraternities, 328–30, 347
  Black, 95–96, 100–3, 333–47
  Iberian beginnings of, 330–33
  Latin American, 333–47
Congregation of Indulgences and Relics, 167
Congregation of Rites, 1, 7, 33, 113–14, 151
  liturgy and, 219–21
  regulating the cult of relics, 166, 169
  on Roman calendar, 233–34
Congregation of the Council, 166
Congregation of the Holy Office of the Inquisition, 166–67
Congregation of the Index, 232
Conquistas de las Islas Filipinas, 85
Contelori, Felice, 202, 205
Contreras, Pedro Moya de, 30
Copeland, Clare, 66, 138
Coptic Church, 91–92
Cortés, Hernán, 77, 78, 79
Council of Milan, 159–60
Council of the Spanish Inquisition, 60
  Teresa de Ávila and, 67
Council of Trent, 19, 34, 133, 156
  on duty of bishops to investigate bodies of saints, 164
  on imagery, 258–64
  on martyrs, 36
  model of saints, 54, 64
  on pilgrimage, 349
  on relics, 159
  reworking history of saints after, 19–23
  on use of vernacular by priests, 231–32
  on veneration of saints and their relics, 109
  on verification of miracles, 196
Counter-Reformation, the, 4, 6

canonization of saints in, 152–54
definitions of models of mysticism in, 179–81
imagery in art of, 267, 276–78
liturgy, sanctity, and, 216–21
new paradigm for scholarship on, 7–11
reworking history of saints in, 19–23. *See also* sanctity
Cristo, Ana de, 82
Cruz, Juana de la, 55, 56–64, 67, 71
Cruz, Magdalena de la, 69
Cruz, Martin de la, 357
Cueto, Alonso, 133–34, 143, 151
Cult of the Saints, The, 17

Dávila y Toledo, Sancho, 162–63
Daza, Antonio, 57, 60–61, 98
De canonizatione sanctorum, 252
De distinctione verarum visionum a falsis, 175
De la veneración que se deue a los cuerpos de los sanctos ... en el sanctissimo Sacramento, 162–63
Delehaye, Hippolyte, 235
Delooz, Pierre, 148
De probatione spirituum, 175
De probatis sanctorum historiis, 237, 284
De sacrarum reliquiarum cultu, veneratione, translatio, identitate, atque vindicatione, 162
De servorum Dei beatificatione et canonizatione, 32, 139, 146, 166
Díaz del Castillo, Bernal, 78
Dictionnaire universelle, 348
Diego of Alcalá, Saint, 137–38, 148
Dionysius, bishop, 20
Direcciones pastorales, 28
discernment of spirits, 172–73, 179–80
  Teresa of Ávila and, 186
  truth and, 175–78
Discourse on Sacred and Profane Images, 259
Disquisitio reliquiaria sive de suspicienda, 163
Ditchfield, Simon, 4
  on the canonization process, 278
  on catacomb saints, 112
  on celebration of saints in post-Tridentine Italy, 19
  on liturgy, 215, 222
  on portability of devotional objects, 321–22
  on sanctity and cult of saints, 11, 71

on Toribio de Mogrovejo, 27
Divinus perfectionis magister, 249
Dominic, Saint, 100, 308, 310–11, 323
Duhamel, Christophe, 352
Dupront, Alphonse, 366

Ecclesiastical History, 236
Edmund Campion, Saint, 51–52, 280–87, 293
Edmund Geninges, Saint, 296
Efigenia, Saint, 97–98, 100–1
Eleanor of Toledo, 189
Eliade, Mircea, 348
Elisabeth of Portugal, Saint and Queen, 201, 203
Elizabeth I, Queen, 39, 41, 290
Emich, Birgit, 318
empire and martyrdom, 38–39
Episcopus, 25, 27
Erasmus, Desiderius, 158
L'Eromena, 244
El Escorial monastery, 36–37
Estienne, Charles, 200
Euphemia, Saint, 36
Eusebius of Caesarea, 236
Exhortation to Martyrdom, 293

Fabian, Saint and Pope, 235
Fabri, Felix, 362
Faerie Queene, 279, 290
Faustiniano, Saint, 22
Felice da Cantalice, Saint, 148–49, 152
Felipe de Jesús, Saint, 224
Felix of Gars am Inn, Saint, 107, 108, 122–29
female martyrs, 48–50, 247–48
female saints, 70–71
  hagiography of, 247–48
  intermediate model of, 56–65
  mysticism and, 66, 69, 134, 177–78
  sante vive model of, 54–55
  shifting paradigms of, Counter-Reformation, 55–56
  Teresian model of, 54, 58–59, 65–70
Ferdinand III, Saint and King, 276
Ferrand, Jean, 163–64
Fidelis of Sigmaringen, Saint, 140
Figino, Ambrogio, 265, 266
Flavia Domitilla, Saint, 245, 246, 247
Flos sanctorum, 56, 237, 299
Foxe, John, 279, 284, 286
Francesca de Ponziani, Saint,
  see Francesca Romana, Saint

Francesca Romana, Saint, 67, 149, 202, 239n, 247
Francis, Pope, 152–53
Francis of Assisi, Saint, 100, 136, 322, 349
Francis de Sales, Saint, 27, 28, 29, 33, 152, 206
Francis Xavier, Saint, 44, 138, 150, 216, 242–43, 322, 372
Francisco Solano y Jiménez, Saint, 133, 143, 152, 322, 323
Frazier, Alison, 236
Frederick II, Emperor, 93
Fromont, Cécile, 104
frontier of civilized paganism, 44–46
frontier of heresy, 39–42
frontier of infidelity, 42–44
frontier of savage paganism, 46–48
Fuente, Jerónima de la, 267, 269

Gaetano of Thiene, Saint, 239
Galen, 199
Gallonio, Antonio, 245, 246–48
Gauillaume II de la Marck, 141
General History of the Things of New Spain, 79
Gerson, Jean, 172, 174, 177–78, 183
Gervasius, Saint, 18, 21–22
Giussano, Giovan Pietro, 23
Gomez-Géraud, Marie-Christine, 361
Gonçalo Garcia, Saint, 343–46
Gorcum, martyrs of 51, 141, 144, 147
Gotor, Miguel, 250, 255
Gracián, Jerónimo, 58, 65
Grafton, Anthony, 225
Great Chronicle of Alfonso XI, The, 76
Greenwood, Jonathan, 252
Gregorio Barbarigo, Saint, 28, 32–33
Gregory the Great, Saint and Pope, 248, 297
Gregory XIII, Pope, 217, 251n
Gregory XIV, Pope, 248
Gregory XV, Pope, 111, 150
Greuter, Matthäus, 24, 25
Guibert of Nogent, 158
Gumppenberg, Wilhelm, 351
Gunzinger, Christophe, 357
Guzmán, Diego, Cardinal 357

Haedo, Diego de, 43
Hager, Johann Chrysostomus, 107
hagiography, 13, 27, 47, 57, 60–61, 68, 124, 125, 161, 235–37

hagiography (cont.)
  asymmetrical sanctity between celebration and control portrayed in, 250–56
  English Catholic lives and, 293–300
  as multisensory experience, 245–46
  new genres of, 241–44
  Rome as storied place in, 246–50
  varieties of print and, 237–41. See also literature
halos, 271–76
Harding, Thomas, 283–84
Hekatompathia XXV, 290–91
Herklotz, Ingo, 112
Herlihy, David, 252
Heylyn, Peter, 280
Hieronymian Martyrology, 253
Hippocrates, 199
Historia de la Provincia de Philipinas, 86
historia sacra, 280–81
Historie of St. George, 280
holy bodies, 193–95, 210
  anatomical irregularities and, 207–9
  asceticism and, 204–7
  Catholic Church and medical examination of, 195–201
  material culture and, 309–18
  negotiating incorruption in examination of, 201–4
Howard, Anne, 295–97
Hyacinth of Poland, Saint, 149, 213–15

Iberian confraternities, 330–33
Ignatius of Antioch, Saint, 235
  on devotional medals, 317–18
Ignatius of Loyola, Saint, 8, 9, 26, 138, 144, 149–50, 176, 241–42
  canonization of, 216
  examination of body of, 205–6
  on imagery, 260–61
  on pilgrimage, 362
  pilgrimage by, 352
  Teresa of Ávila and, 183, 185, 191, 192
  on visualization and meditation, 176, 180
Image of the Virgin Mary, 81
imagery, 257–58
  of Counter-Reformation saints, 267, 276–78
  legislation of, after Council of Trent, 258–64
  in portraits of non-saints, 264–70
  redefining the halo in, 271–76

imperialism and colonialism and martyrdom, 38–39
Iniestra, Juan de, 79
Innocent XI, Pope, 31
Inoue, Michael, 1–2
Interior Castle, 184
Ippolito Galantini, Blessed, 151, 154
Isabella of Bourbon, 67
Isidore the Laborer, Saint, 193

Jacob of Voragine, 35
James II, King, 149
James of the Marches, Saint, 239
Japan, missionaries to, 1–3, 9, 44–48
  martyrdom of, 51, 272
Jeanne de Chantal, Saint, 70
Jesuits, 28–29, 144
  in England, 40–41
  imagery and, 260–62
  in Japan, 45–48
  in the New World, 46–48
Jesús de Ágreda, María de, 49–50, 69
Jewell, John, 283, 286
Jiménez de Cisneros, Francisco, 141
John of Matha, Saint, 156
John of the Cross, Saint, 68
  on imagination, 176
  Teresa of Ávila and, 182, 185
John Paul II, Saint and Pope, 51–53, 152, 249
John the Good, Saint, 22
John the Merciful, Saint, 28
Juan Diego, Saint, 78

Kaiserberg, Johann Geiler von, 364
Kaplan, Paul, 93
Kempe, Margery, 349
Kleinberg, Aviad, 204
Kraft, Adam, 363

Ladislau IV, King of Poland, 250
Laffi, Domenico, 367–68
Le lagrimi di San Pietro, 288
Lambertini, Prospero, see Benedict XIV, Pope
Landays, Andre, 370
Landi, Stefano, 249
Lapi, Michelangelo, 27
Laso de la Vega, Luis, 82
Latin America, confraternities of, 333–47
Laven, Mary, 4–5, 368–69
Laureano, Juan de, 270
Lawrence, Saint, 36

lay appropriation of liturgy of saints, 230–33
Legenda aurea sanctorum, 35
Leo XI, Pope, 249
León, Lucrecia de, 69
Léon Pinelo, Antonio de, 27
Leslie, George, 244
Libellus de gestis, 186
Lichentfurter, Anton, 127–29
Lippomano, Luigi, 237, 285
literature, 279–80, 300
  Edmund Campion's *Ambrosia*, 280–87
  of hagiography and English Catholic lives, 293–300
  on pilgrimages, 370
  St. Robert Southwell's verse, 287–93. *See also* hagiography
liturgy, 213–16, 233–34
  hagiography and, 252–56
  lay appropriation of, 230–33
  sanctity, reform, and, 216–21
  sanctity, shaping of collective identities, and, 221–30
Loarte, Gaspard, 355
Loch Dearg aon Róimh na hEireann, 358
López, Bartolomé, 79
López, Gregorio, 30
López Caro, Francisco, 276
López de Legazpi, Miguel, 84, 87
Lorenzana, Antonio de, 29–30
Louis XIII, King, 364
Louis XIV, King, 353
Louis IX, King, 349
Louise de Marillac, Saint, 70
Ludwig X, King, 119
Luigi Gonzaga, Saint, 141, 145, 152
Luther, Martin, 119, 134, 158, 204, 304

Mabillon, Jean, 113
Mac Torna, Tuileagna, 358
Maderno, Stefano, 248–49
Magdeburg Centuries, 255
Mainwaring, Thomas, 135, 136
Manrique, Pedro, 169
Manuel I, King of Portugal, 332
della Marca, Giacomo, 195–96, 203
Margaret of Austria, 356
Margaret Clitherow, Saint, 294, 296
Maria Maddalena de' Pazzi, Saint, 66, 142n
Maria Maddalena peccatrice convertita, 244
Mariana, Juan de, 113

Marie de l'Incarnation, Saint, 70
Martin, Gregory, 366
Martín, Lope, 83–84
Martín de Porres, Saint, 101, 270
Martin of Tours, Saint, 230–31
martyrdom, 9
  empire and, 38–39
  frontier of civilized paganism and, 44–46
  frontier of heresy and, 39–42
  frontier of infidelity and, 42–44
  frontier of savage paganism and, 46–48
  gendering, 48–50
  in Japan, 51, 272
  liturgy and, 225–26
  by nuns, 247–48
  of Pedro Bautista Blázquez, 1–3
  pictorial representations of, 36–37
  in Protestantism *versus* Catholicism, 35–38
  relics of, 36, 156, 164, 166–67
  sainthood after, 50–53
Marzi de' Medici, Alessandro, 151
Massa, Niccolò, 199–200
de' Massimi, Elena, 247–48
material culture, 303–7, 326–27
  bodily practices of veneration and, 309–18
  devotional medals, 313–18
  material plurality of saints and, 318–21
  and rosaries as polyvalent tools of saintly veneration, 307–9
  sanctity on the move and, 321–26
Maurice, Saint, 92–93, 96
Maximilian I, 119
Mazzini, Luigi, 244
medicine and miracles. *See* holy bodies
Medicus, Saint, 166
Medina, Pedro de, 74
Meditations, 182
Mena Roelas, Gonzalo, 331
Menologion, 253
Metaphrastes, Simeon, 97
Michelina of Pesaro, Blessed, 319–21
miracles, 1, 6, 7, 193–95, 210
  anatomical irregularity and, 207–9
  asceticism and, 204–7
  of Black saints, 101
  of Borromeo, 25–26
  of catacomb saints, 126
  of female saints, 56, 59–61
  of Francisco Solano y Jiménez, 133
  of Ippolito Galantini, 151

miracles (cont.)
  medical verification of, 195–201
  negotiating incorruption in investigations into, 201–4
  in process of saint-making, 140–42, 144, 146–47
  related to relics, 161, 164–65
  related to Virgin Mary, 73, 74, 77, 78, 82, 83, 85
  relics and, 37
Mojares, Resil, 87
Montaigne, Michel de, 366–67, 369
Montoya, Pedro de, 2
Montúfar, Alonso de, 79
Morales, Agustina, 84–85
Morejón, Pedro, 243
Moretti, Pietro, 171
Mulvey, Patricia A., 332
Mush, John, 294–96
Muslims in Spain, 74–75
mysticism, 172–75, 190–92
  of Caterina de' Ricci, 186–92
  changes through the Middle Ages, 176
  Counter-Reformation definitions and models of, 179–81
  discernment of spirits and, 172–73
  as divisive, 173, 174–75
  as experimental, 176
  female, 66, 177–78
  physicality of, 173–74
  quest for words and discernment of truth and, 175–78
  of Teresa of Ávila, 174, 181–86, 190–92

Natalibus, Petrus de, 253
Navarrete, Pedro, 84
Navarro, Pedro, 56–57, 61, 63–64
Negrete, Juan de, 193
Nelles, Paul, 326
New World, missionaries to the, 46–48
Nican mopohua, 82
Niccolò Albergati, Saint, 32
Nicoselli, Anastasio, 27
Niño de Távora, Juan, 86
Norton, John, 41
Nowell, Alexander, 284

O'Malley, John, 4
On the Cautious Imitation of Holy Bishops, 27
On the Fabric of the Human Body, 200
Orseon, Luis de, 193
Origen, 293

Ormaneto, Niccolò, 28
ostensiones, 170
Otranto, martyrs of, 52, 152

Pacheco, Francisco, 267
Palafox y Mendoza, Juan de, 28–30, 33, 274–75
Paleotti, Gabriele, 18, 22–23, 259
  on Catholic imagery, 36
papal infallibility, 136
del Pas, Angelo, 209
Patton, Elizabeth, 295
Paul, Apostle, 7, 166, 285
Paul III, Pope, 189
Paul IV, Pope, 111
Paul V, Pope, 145, 150, 248
Paul VI, Pope, 52
Pedro Bautista Blázquez, Saint, 1–4, 8. See also Japan, missionaries to
Peña, Francisco, 201–2
La Peota smarrita, 244
Pérez de Rivas, Andrés, 340–41
Persons, Robert, 281
Pessoa, Raimundo Agnelo Soares, 342
Peter, Apostle, 166
Petronille: Accident pitoyable de nos jours, cause d'un vocation religieuse, 244
Philip II, King, 36–37, 60, 79, 113, 138, 352–53, 364
Philip III, King, 60, 356
Philip IV, King, 49, 67
Philip Howard, Saint, 295–96
Philip Neri, Saint, 5, 138n, 146n, 149–50, 196, 207–9, 216, 246–47
Philpot, John, 284
pilgrimage, 348–49, 371–72
  experience of, 361–66
  motives for, 353–60
  in the Reformation centuries, 349–53
  responses and writings of travelers on, 366–70
  return home after, 370–71
  virtual, 362–63
Pilgrim of Loreto, The, 349
Pius IV, Pope, 26
Pius IX, Pope, 51–53
Pius V, Pope, 217, 232, 246, 308
Pizarro, Francisco, 77
Poem on Alfonso XI, The, 76
poetry, 287–93
Pole, Reginald, 28
polysemic saints, 102–6

Porto, Angelo, 207
Pratt, Mary Louise, 341
Primo libro delle laudi spirituali, 245
printing, varieties of, 237–41
Priscilla, Saint, 36
Protasius, Saint, 18, 22
Protestantism, 3, 96–97
   critiques of relics and objects, 72, 109, 118, 156, 158, 163, 241, 348
   critiques of the saints, 7, 109, 220, 240, 259, 279, 282
   critiques of miracles **285**
   martyrs in, 35–38
   as threat to Catholicism, 4, 37–38, 180, 183, 213, 255, 360. *See also* Calvin, John; Luther, Martin

Quatremaires, Robert, 368
de Queriolot, Monsieur, 357–58
Quinque martyres, 241

Raleigh, Walter, 290
Rationes decem, 284–85
Raymond of Penyafort, Saint, 149, 202, 252
Razzi, Serafino, 186
Rebillad, Éric, 236
Reboul, Vincent, 360
Reinberg, Virginia, 365
relics, 36, 171
   catacomb, 110–17
   critiques of, 158
   early modern manuals on, 161–65
   growth of cult of, 156–58
   liturgy and, 225–26
   regulating the cult of, 165–71. *See also* material culture
Reliquiarium, sive de reliquiis, et veneratione sanctorum in quo multa de necessitate, praestantia, usu, ac fructibus reliquiarum pertractantur, 161–62
Revelations of María de Santo Domingo, 62
Richeome, Louis, 349
Rigbie, John, 296
Rinuccini, Giovanni Battista, 244
Robert Bellarmine, Saint, 145, 154
Robert Southwell, Saint, 287–93, 296
Rocca, Angelo, 144, 252
Rodríguez, Juana, 55
Roldán-Figueroa, Rady, 243

Roman Breviary, 56, 96, 98, 217–18, 219, 254–55
Roman Martyrology, 96–97, 98, 125, 217–18, 220, 240, 248, 253, 255
Roman Missal, 217–18, 219, 228, 254–55
rosaries, 305
   in bodily practices of veneration, 309–18
   mobility of, 322–23
   as polyvalent tools of saintly veneration, 307–9
Rose of Lima, Saint, 58, 69, 141, 152, 224
   devotional objects depicting, 310–11, 323–24
   portrait of, 273, 274
de Rosivignan, Pierre, 369
Rospigliosi, Giulio, 249–50
Rubial García, Antonio, 29
de la Rue, François, 366

Sacred and the Profane, The, 348
Sahagún, Bernardino de, 79–80
Saint Peters Complaint, 288, 289–90
saints: bishops as models and makers of, 27–30
   Black (*See* Black saints)
   canonization of (*See* canonization)
   catacomb (*See* catacomb saints)
   connections to nations, 227–28
   female (*See* female saints)
   imagery of (*See* imagery)
   reworking of history related to, in Italian dioceses after Council of Trent, 19–23
   sanctity and, 7–8
   writing about (*See* literature). *See also* hagiography
Salazar, Francisco de, 79
Salazar, Pedro de, 56–57
Sale, Anton Giulio Brignole, 244
S. Alessio, a dramma musicale, 249
Sallmann, Jean-Michel, 239–40
Sánchez, Miguel, 81–83
sanctity, 5–6
   key conflicts within Catholicism over, 9–10
   liturgy, reform and, 216–21
   liturgy, shaping of collective identities, and, 221–30
   study of, 9–10
   unseen energy of, 17–19

sanctity (cont.)
  usefulness for historians, 8. *See also* saints
Sanctorum priscorum patrum vitae, 237
San Agustín, Gaspar de, 85
Sandoval, Alonso de, 333
Sandoval, Gonzalo de, 78
Santo Domingo, María de, 55, 62
Sauer, Lorenz, 238
Sauli, Alessandro, 32
Savonarola, Girolamo, 174, 187, 189–90, 246
Schacchi, Fortunato, 113
Schmidt, Bettina, 104
Segni, Giambattista, 161–62, 164
Serafino of Fermo, Saint, 58
Serna, Juan Pérez de la, 30
Sfondrati, Paolo Camillo, 248–49
shrines. *See* pilgrimage
Sidney, Philip, 288, 291
Sigonio, Carlo, 22
Sigüenza, José de, 56–57, 59–60, 65
Silvestri, Ridolfo, 207
Simón, Jerónimo, 262
Sirleto, Guglielmo, 21, 253–54
Sixtus V, Pope, 137, 143, 148–49, 252
Smith, Julia, 159
Smith, Richard, 297–99
Society of Jesus. *See* Jesuits
Sōdai, Kobayashi, 2
Soergel, Philip, 370
Solomon, King, 91
Sosa, Francisco, 60–61, 64, 65
Souza, Marina de Mello e, 104
Spenser, Edmund, 279, 288, 290
Spiritual Exercises, 180, 191
Spiritual Pilgrimage of Hierusalem, The, 362
Spiritual Relations, 184
Stanislaw Kostka, Saint, 145, 152
Sterckx, Pieter, 363
Surius, Laurentius, 284, 285

Tansillo, Luigi, 288
Teresa of Ávila, Saint, 8, 9, 54, 70–71
  canonization of, 58–59, 64–65, 141, 150, 216, **227**
  medical examination of corpse of, 203–4
  spiritual life and mysticism of, 174, 181–86, 190–92

  controversial portrait of, 268
  Teresian model of female saints and, 54, 58–59, 65–70
  works by: *The Book of Her Life*, 54, 60, 181–82, 184
    Meditations, 182
    Mystica theologia, 175
    Spiritual Relations, 184
    The Way of Perfection, 183, 184
Theatrum crudelitatem haereticorum nostri temporis, 294
Thomas Aquinas, Saint, 35, 202–3
Thomas Becket, Saint, 349
Thomas More, Saint, 158
Toledo, García de, 182
Toledo, María de, 55
Topographia, e historia general de Argel, 43
Toribio de Mogrovejo, Saint, 23, 27
Torre, Eugenia de la **268**
Tractatus et praxis de canonizatione, 202
Treaty of Madrid, 41
True History of the Conquest of New Spain, 78
A true report of the death and martyrdome of M. Campion...M. Sherwin, & M. Brian, 293

Urban VIII, Pope, 113, 214
  canonization under, 138, 145, 151–52, 202, 221
  hagiography under, 51, 243, 248–49
  imagery regulation under, 262–64, 266, 269, 271–76
  relics regulation under, 111

Valerio, Miguel, 95
Valier, Agostino, 25, 26–27
Valla, Lorenzo, 281
van Paeschen, Jan, 362
Vargas, Martín de, 43
Vasa, Alexander Charles, 250
Vasquez, Luis, 203–4
Vauchez, André, 204
Vela y Cueto, María, 69
Velarde, Murillo, 86
Velázquez, Diego, 267, 268
Venegas, Leonor, 55
Verstegan, Richard, 294
Vesalius, Andreas, 200
de Vic, François, 357

Villegas, Alonso de, 56, 60, 62
Virgin Mary, 72–73, 88–89
  as Our Lady of Antipolo in the
    Philippines, 85
  as Our Lady of Caysasay in the
    Philippines, 85–86
  as Our Lady of Guadalupe in
    Extremadura, 73–77, 87
  as Our Lady of Guadalupe in the
    Philippines, 83–88
  relics of, 167–68
  shrines to, 351–52
  as the Virgin of Guadalupe in Mexico,
    77–83
da Visitação, Maria, 56, 61–62
*Vita della reverenda serva di Dio
  Caterina dei Ricci*, 186
La vita di Tobia e le Battaglie d'Israele,
  244

Vitalis, Saint, 18, 22, 170
Vittori, Angelo, 207

Walpole, Henry, 40, 52
Walsham, Alexandra, 117, 365
Ward, Mary, 70
Watson, Thomas, 290–91
Wilhelm IV, King, 119
Wilhelm V, King, 119
Williams, Wes, 361–62
Wycliff, John, 158

Yanguas, Diego de, 182

Zama, Saint, 22
Zardin, Danilo, 20
Zarri, Gabriella, 10, 54, 63, 187
Zerla, Giuseppe, 207
Zumárraga, Juan de, 82

CAMBRIDGE COMPANIONS TO . . . (*continued from page ii*)

CHRISTOLOGY Edited by Timothy J. Pawl and Michael L. Peterson
THE CISTERIAN ORDER Edited by Mette Birkedal Bruun
CLASSICAL ISLAMIC THEOLOGY Edited by Tim Winter
THE COUNCIL OF NICAEA Edited by Young Richard Kim
COUNTER-REFORMATION SANCTITY Edited by Jan Machielsen, Emily Michelson, and Katrina Olds
JONATHAN EDWARDS Edited by Stephen J. Stein
EVANGELICAL THEOLOGY Edited by Timothy Larsen and Daniel J. Treier
FEMINIST THEOLOGY Edited by Susan Frank Parsons
FRANCIS OF ASSISI Edited by Michael J. P. Robson
GENESIS Edited by Bill T. Arnold
THE GOSPELS Edited by Stephen C. Barton
THE GOSPELS, 2nd edition Edited by Stephen C. Barton and Todd Brewer
THE HEBREW BIBLE/OLD TESTAMENT Edited by Stephen B. Chapman and Marvin A. Sweeney
HEBREW BIBLE AND ETHICS Edited by C. L. Crouch
THE JESUITS Edited by Thomas Worcester
JESUS Edited by Markus Bockmuehl
JUDAISM AND LAW Edited by Christine Hayes
LAW IN THE HEBREW BIBLE Edited by Bruce Wells
C. S. LEWIS Edited by Robert MacSwain and Michael Ward
LIBERATION THEOLOGY Edited by Chris Rowland
MARTIN LUTHER Edited by Donald K. McKim
MEDIEVAL JEWISH PHILOSOPHY Edited by Daniel H. Frank and Oliver Leaman
MODERN JEWISH PHILOSOPHY Edited by Michael L. Morgan and Peter Eli Gordon
MUHAMMAD Edited by Jonathan E. Brockup
THE NEW CAMBRIDGE COMPANION TO BIBLICAL INTERPRETATION Edited by Ian Boxhall and Bradley C. Gregory
THE NEW CAMBRIDGE COMPANION TO CHRISTIAN DOCTRINE Edited by Michael Allen
THE NEW CAMBRIDGE COMPANION TO JESUS Edited by Markus Bockmuehl
THE NEW CAMBRIDGE COMPANION TO ST. PAUL Edited by Bruce W. Longenecker
NEW RELIGIOUS MOVEMENTS Edited by Olav Hammer and Mikael Rothstein
NEW TESTAMENT Edited by Patrick Gray
PENTECOSTALISM Edited by Cecil M. RobeckAmos Yong Jr
POSTMODERN THEOLOGY Edited by Kevin J. Vanhoozer
THE PROBLEM OF EVIL Edited by Chad Meister and Paul K. Moser
PURITANISM Edited by John Coffey and Paul C. H. Lim
QUAKERISM Edited by Stephen W. Angell and Pink Dandelion
THE QUR'AN Edited by Jane Dammen McAuliffe
KARL RAHNER Edited by Declan Marmion and Mary E. Hines
JOSEPH RATZINGER Edited by Daniel Cardó and Uwe Michael Lang
REFORMATION THEOLOGY Edited by David Bagchi and David C. Steinmetz

REFORMED THEOLOGY Edited by Paul T. Nimmo and David A. S. Fergusson
RELIGION AND ARTIFICIAL INTELLIGENCE Edited by Beth Singler and Fraser Watts
RELIGION AND TERRORISM Edited by James R. Lewis
RELIGIOUS EXPERIENCE Edited by Paul K. Moser and Chad Meister
RELIGIOUS STUDIES Edited by Robert A. Orsi
FRIEDRICH SCHLEIERMACHER Edited by Jacqueline Mariña
SCIENCE AND RELIGION Edited by Peter Harrison
ST. PAUL Edited by James D. G. Dunn
SUFISM Edited by Lloyd Ridgeon
THE *SUMMA THEOLOGIAE* Edited by Philip McCosker and Denys Turner
THE TALMUD AND RABBINIC LITERATURE Edited by Charlotte E. Fonrobert and Martin S. Jaffee
THE TRINITY Edited by Peter C. Phan
HANS URS VON BALTHASAR Edited by Edward T. Oakes and David Moss
VATICAN II Edited by Richard R. Gaillardetz
JOHN WESLEY Edited by Randy L. Maddox and Jason E. Vickers
WOMEN AND ISLAM Edited by Masooda Bano

For EU product safety concerns, contact us at Calle de José Abascal, 56–1º,
28003 Madrid, Spain or eugpsr@cambridge.org.

www.ingramcontent.com/pod-product-compliance
Lightning Source LLC
LaVergne TN
LVHW021650060526
838200LV00050B/2291